D0984935

Heath Grammar and Composition

with a Process Approach to Writing

Complete Course

Authors
Carol Ann Bergman
J. A. Senn

D.C. Heath and Company
Lexington, Massachusetts / Toronto, Ontario

Series Titles

Heath Grammar and Composition: Third Course
Heath Grammar and Composition: Fourth Course
Heath Grammar and Composition: Fifth Course
Heath Grammar and Composition: Complete Course

Supplementary Materials (for each course)

Teacher's Annotated Edition
Teacher's Resource Book
Workbook
Tests

Contributing Authors

Florence Harris
Gerald Tomlinson

Editorial Sue Martin (Managing Editor), Barbara Brien (Project Editor), Carol Clay, Lynn Duffy, Peg McNary, Mary Ellen Walters; *Freelance Assistance:* Karen Gabler, Anne Jones, Judy Keith, William Ray, Ellen Whalen
Editorial Services Marianna Frew Palmer (Manager), K. Kirschbaum Harvie
Design Sally Thompson Steele
Cover Design Dawn Ostrer Emerson
Production Maureen LaRiccia

Acknowledgments

The authors and editors have made every effort to trace the ownership of all copyrighted selections found in this book and to make full acknowledgment of their use. Grateful acknowledgment is made to the following authors, publishers, agents, and individuals for their permission to reprint copyrighted materials.

Pages 408–409. From *King Solomon's Ring,* by Konrad Z. Lorenz. Published by Thomas Y. Crowell Company, copyright © 1952. Reprinted by permission of Harper & Row, Publishers, Inc.

Pages 429–430. "Memory Mosaic," "The Distant Past," and "Packaging the Human Brain," from *You and Your Brain,* by Judith Groch, copryight © 1963 by Judith Groch. Reprinted by permission of Harper & Row, Publishers, Inc.

Pages 461–463. "Alone," by Richard E. Byrd. From *The Spirit of Adventure,* edited by Whit Burnett, copyright © 1955. Reprinted by permission of Henry Holt & Company.

Pages 466–467. "The Fosbury Flop," from *How Did They Do That?* by Caroline Sutton, copyright © 1984. Reprinted by permission of William Morrow and Company, Inc.

(Acknowledgments continue on page xvi.)

Printed in the United States of America

Published simultaneously in Canada

International Standard Book Number: 0-669-15971-9

5 6 7 8 9 0

Complete Course

Heath Grammar and Composition

with a Process Approach to Writing

Series Consultants

Henry I. Christ
Former Chairman of the English Department
Andrew Jackson High School
St. Albans, New York

Richard Marius, Ph.D.
Director of the Expository Writing Program
Harvard University
Cambridge, Massachusetts

Reviewers

Alabama

Fran West
Red Bay High School
Red Bay, Alabama

California

Dorothy Gillmann
Portola Junior High School
Tarzana, California

Florida

Sonya M. Crown
Ely High School
Pompano Beach, Florida

Elynore Schott
South Broward High School
Hollywood, Florida

Illinois

Margaret J. Blaufuss
Glenbard East High School
Lombard, Illinois

Marion P. Johnson
Andrew High School
Tinley Park, Illinois

Virginia Riedel
Willowbrook High School
Villa Park, Illinois

Sister Julia Ann Rogers
Driscoll Catholic High School
Addison, Illinois

Maine

Michael S. Weatherwax
Camden-Rockport High School
Camden, Maine

Massachusetts

Lorraine A. Plasse, Ph.D.
Springfield Public Schools
Springfield, Massachusetts

David C. Reid
Minuteman Vocational Technical High School
Lexington, Massachusetts

Shirley M. Westrate
Hamilton-Wenham Regional High School
South Hamilton, Massachusetts

Michigan

Marilyn Bright
Andover High School
Bloomfield Hills, Michigan

New York

Joseph F. Cammarano
Patchogue-Medford High School
Medford, New York

Joseph R. Teta
Baldwin High School
Baldwin, New York

Oregon

Deborah L. Sommer
Cedar Park School
Portland, Oregon

Paul Williamson
Cedar Park School
Portland, Oregon

Pennsylvania

Sandra M. Couch
Solanco High School
Quarryville, Pennsylvania

Bernadette Fenning
Cardinal O'Hara High School
Springfield, Pennsylvania

South Carolina

Francie C. Brown
Dreher High School
Columbia, South Carolina

Idris B. McElveen, Ph.D.
Spring Valley High School
Columbia, South Carolina

Zelder N. Pressley
Keenan High School
Columbia, South Carolina

Texas

Karen Hibbs
Richland Senior High School
Fort Worth, Texas

Frankye Taylor
Euless Junior High School
Euless, Texas

Virginia

Cindy K. Driskill
Clover Hill High School
Midlothian, Virginia

Washington

Cindy Mar
Liberty High School
Issaquah, Washington

Contents

UNIT 1 GRAMMAR

UNIT 2 USAGE

UNIT 3 MECHANICS

UNIT 4 VOCABULARY AND SPELLING

UNIT 5 REFERENCE SKILLS

UNIT 6 COMPOSITION

UNIT 7 TEST TAKING

APPENDIX

Acknowledgments (continued)

Pages 495–496. "The Lure of Islands," from *My Island Home,* copyright © 1952 by the estate of James Norman Hall. Reprinted by permission of Little, Brown & Company.

Pages 501–502. "The Plane and the Planet," from *Wind, Sand and Stars,* translated from the French by Lewis Galantière, text copyright © 1939 by Antoine de Saint-Exupéry, renewed 1967 by Lewis Galantière. Reprinted by permission of Harcourt Brace Jovanovich, Inc.

Pages 507–509. "Controlling Alaska's Wolves," by Jim Reardon, and "Wolves as Scapegoats," by James L. Pitts. Copyright © 1977 by the National Wildlife Federation. Reprinted from the August-September issue of *National Wildlife Magazine.*

Page 514. From "A Reporter at Large—Country Golf," by Garrison Keillor, from the July 30, 1984, issue of *The New Yorker.* Reprinted by permission of the author.

Pages 517–518. "Central Park," from *Assorted Prose,* by John Updike, copyright © 1956 by John Updike. Reprinted by permission of Alfred A. Knopf, Inc.

Pages 518–519. "Louis Armstrong," by Truman Capote, from *Observations,* copyright © 1959 by Richard Avedon and Truman Capote. Reprinted by permission of Simon & Schuster, Inc.

Pages 526–527. "A Nincompoop," from *Anton Chekhov: Selected Stories,* translated by Ann Dunnigan, copyright © 1960 by Ann Dunnigan. Reprinted by arrangement with New American Library, New York, New York.

Pages 529–531. "The Black and White," from *A Night Out, Night School, Revue Sketches* (British title: *A Slight Ache and Other Plays*), by Harold Pinter. Copyright © 1961 by Harold Pinter. Reprinted by permission of Grove Press, Inc., and Methuen & Co. Ltd.

Page 533. "The Explorer," from *The World of Gwendolyn Brooks.* Copyright © 1959 by Gwendolyn Brooks. Reprinted by permission of Harper & Row, Publishers, Inc.

Pages 533–534. "The Road Not Taken," from *The Poetry of Robert Frost,* edited by Edward Connery Lathem. Copyright © 1916, © 1969 by Holt, Rinehart and Winston. Copyright © 1944 by Robert Frost. Reprinted by permission of Holt, Rinehart and Winston, Publishers.

Pages 537–538. By F. Scott Fitzgerald, excerpted from *The Great Gatsby.* Copyright © 1925 Charles Scribner's Sons; copyright renewed 1953 Frances Scott Fitzgerald Lanahan. Reprinted with the permission of Charles Scribner's Sons.

Page 540. *Poland* by James Michener, 1983, reviewed by Harry Hurt III in the November 1983 issue of *Harper's Bazaar* Magazine. Reprinted by permission of the author.

Page 544. From " 'The Bear' and Go Down, Moses," by Melvin Backman. Reprinted by permission of the Modern Language Association of America from *PMLA,* LXXVI (December 1961), pp. 595–600. Original title: "The Wilderness and the Negro in Faulkner's 'The Bear.' " Copyright © 1961 by the Modern Language Association.

Pages 554–555. Reprinted with permission of Macmillan Publishing Company from *Charles Babbage, Father of the Computer,* by Dan Halacy. Copyright © 1970 by Dan Halacy.

Pages 559–561. From *In the Dark,* by Richard Meran Barsam. Copyright © 1977 by Richard Meran Barsam. Reprinted by permission of Viking Penguin, Inc.

Pages 564–565. From *National Parks,* by Paul Jensen, copyright © 1964 by Western Publishing Company, Inc. Reprinted by permission.

Page 566. From *Science in the World around Us,* by William C. Vergara, copyright © 1973. Reprinted by permission of the author.

Page 569. *From Smarter Than Man? Intelligence in Whales, Dolphins and Humans,* by Karl-Erik Fichtelius and Sverre Sjölander, translated by Thomas Teal. Reprinted by permission of Pantheon Books, a division of Random House, Inc.

Page 570. From *Animals in American Literature,* by Mary Allen, copyright © 1983. Reprinted by permission of the University of Illinois Press.

Pages 581–582. "Power to the Disabled," copyright © 1982 Time, Inc., all rights reserved. Reprinted by permission from *TIME.*

Page 600. "Catching the Drift," from the September issue of *SCIENCE 84.* Reprinted by permission of *SCIENCE 85* magazine, copyright © the American Association for the Advancement of Science.

To the Student

This book is about communication — the act of expressing your thoughts and ideas effectively to someone else. Think of how much of your day is spent speaking with members of your family, friends, and many others in your school and community. Speaking, however, is only one means of communication. Writing is another, and writing clearly and concisely is an essential skill. In this electronics age, more and more businesses are using computers to communicate information. The written word — whether displayed on a computer screen or printed in books — is the backbone of communication.

Although this book is divided into different units, it has one unified goal: to help you speak and write clearly and effectively. The first unit, on grammar, shows you how the structure of the English language gives you choices to improve your speaking and writing. The next unit, on usage, explains ways to speak and write with clarity and exactness of meaning. Mechanics, the third unit, emphasizes the importance of capitalization and punctuation in precisely transmitting your written message. The fourth unit, on vocabulary and spelling, points out the power of individual words within your total message. The fifth and sixth units show you how to find, organize, and communicate information, including your own ideas and insights. The last unit, on test taking, helps you communicate what you know in a test situation.

The composition unit in this book is unique. Each chapter includes all the help and information you need to understand and write a different type of composition — from a single paragraph to an essay or a report. Within chapters, you are taken step by step through the four stages in the writing process. In the *prewriting* stage, you learn how to choose and limit a subject and how to find and organize your thoughts or information. In the *writing* stage, you learn how to write a topic sentence or a thesis statement; how to write the body of a paragraph, an essay, or a report; and how to write a conclusion. In the *revising* stage, you learn how to pull your writing together — how to give it unity and coherence. Finally, in the *editing* stage, you learn how to polish your work by applying the information in the first three units.

Going through these writing stages is like having someone sit beside you as you learn to drive a car for the first time. If you are unsure of yourself, there is an abundance of help in the form of practice, models, and checklists to show you exactly what to do, how to do it, and when to do it. Following these stages in the writing process will ensure success and build your confidence in your ability to write well.

As you go through each unit in this book, remember its underlying purpose: to help you speak and write clearly and effectively. Each chapter has been written with this goal in mind, because speaking and writing are essential skills for success in today's world.

Special Helps

Your teacher will probably go through some of the chapters in this book with you. All of the chapters, however, have been written and organized so that you can refer to them and use them on your own throughout the year. You may find some of the following features of the book particularly helpful.

Keyed Rules All the rules are clearly marked with keyed blue arrows. An index at the back of the book tells you where to find each rule.

Tinted Boxes Throughout the text, important lists, summaries, and writing steps are highlighted in tinted boxes for easy reference.

Application to Writing These sections in the first three units of the book clearly show you how you can use the various grammatical concepts you have learned to improve your writing.

Diagnostic and Mastery Tests You can use the diagnostic and mastery tests to measure your progress. The diagnostic test at the beginning of a chapter will show you what you need to learn; the mastery test at the end will show you how well you learned it.

High-Interest Exercises Many of the exercises throughout the book are based on interesting topics. You will not only practice learning a particular skill, but you will also find the material in these exercises informative and interesting.

Composition Models Clearly marked models in the composition chapters provide interesting examples by professional writers.

Composition Checklists Almost all the composition chapters end with a checklist that you can follow—step by step—when you are writing a paragraph, an essay, or a report.

Standardized Tests Standardized tests, which follow five of the units, give you practice and build your confidence in taking tests.

Appendix In a clear, concise format, the appendix at the end of the book provides assistance with various study skills, communication skills, and career skills. For example, you will find helpful information about taking notes, using proofreading symbols, speaking to an audience, and writing a résumé.

Unit 1

Grammar

1 The Parts of Speech
2 The Sentence Base
3 Phrases
4 Clauses
5 Sound Sentences

1

The Parts of Speech

DIAGNOSTIC TEST

Number your paper 1 to 10. Write the underlined words in each sentence. Then beside each word, write its part of speech: *noun, pronoun, verb, adjective, adverb, preposition, conjunction,* or *interjection.*

EXAMPLE Someone called but didn't leave a message.
ANSWER someone—pronoun but—conjunction

1. Have you seen this review of the movie at the Plaza Theater?
2. No part of Maine lies as far north as England.
3. Which of the toasters is a better buy?
4. Romanoff was the family name of the last Russian czar.
5. David never told anyone the ending of the story.
6. A lost person often travels in a circle or in a spiral.
7. The earliest possible time for dinner is 5:00 P.M.
8. Where is the movie projector?
9. Yes! This is his correct telephone number.
10. The gymnast lost his balance and fell down.

Doctors need to know which bone is the tibia and which one is the femur so that they can precisely diagnose a patient's problem. As a writer you need to know which word is a noun and which word is a verb so that you can precisely diagnose problems in your writing. Does the noun that is used as a subject, for example, agree with the verb? Knowing grammatical elements can also help you in another way. If you can identify an adverb clause, for example, you will then be able to include adverb clauses in your writing. Adverb clauses add variety and a more mature style to your writing.

The grammatical elements covered in this chapter include the eight *parts of speech: noun, pronoun, verb, adjective, adverb, preposition, conjunction,* and *interjection.* The part of speech of a word can vary, depending upon how it is used in a sentence. As you review the eight parts of speech, keep in mind that they are important because they are the tools you can use to diagnose sentence problems.

NOUNS AND PRONOUNS

There are more nouns in the English language than any other part of speech. Nouns are words that name persons, places, things, and ideas. Pronouns are words that replace nouns in a sentence.

Nouns

1a A **noun** is the name of a person, place, thing, or idea.

Nouns can be classified in several ways.

Common and Proper Nouns. A *common noun* names any person, place, or thing. Always beginning with a capital letter, a *proper noun* names a particular person, place, or thing.

COMMON NOUNS quarterback, state, car
PROPER NOUNS Sam Levin, New Jersey, Chrysler

NOTE: Some proper nouns, such as *Sam Levin* and *New Jersey,* include more than one word, but they are still considered one noun. *Sam Levin* is one person, and *New Jersey* is one state.

Concrete and Abstract Nouns. A *concrete noun* names a person or an object that can actually be seen, touched, tasted, heard, or smelled. An *abstract noun* names qualities, conditions, and ideas that cannot be perceived through the senses.

CONCRETE NOUNS	table, feather, lemon, salt, bells, roses
ABSTRACT NOUNS	courage, joy, friendship, loyality, freedom

Compound and Collective Nouns. A *compound noun* is made up of more than one word. Since a compound noun can be written as one word, hyphenated, or written as two or more words, it is always best to check the dictionary for the correct form. A *collective noun* names a group of people or things.

COMPOUND NOUNS	peacemaker, falsehood [one word] sister-in-law, bird-watcher [hyphenated] life jacket, city hall [two words]
COLLECTIVE NOUNS	squadron, quartet, flock, orchestra, crew

EXERCISE 1 Finding Nouns

Number your paper 1 to 33. Then write the nouns in the following paragraphs. (A date should be considered a noun.)

The Eiffel Tower

The Eiffel Tower is perhaps the most familiar man-made landmark on Earth. It was designed for the Paris Exposition in 1889. The tower can now accommodate 10,000 visitors annually. Some people, however, go there for publicity, not for enjoyment. Once a man climbed 363 steps on stilts, and a stunt man came down on a unicycle.

The tower is repainted every seven years, requiring thousands of gallons of paint. As part of a recent cleanup, nearly 1,000 tons of rust and dirt were shaved off. This kind of effort signifies the tremendous pride the city takes in its famous structure—even if only a very small percentage of its visitors are Parisians.

Pronouns

1b A **pronoun** is a word that takes the place of one or more nouns.

The word that the pronoun replaces or refers to is called its *antecedent.* The antecedent of a pronoun can be in the same sentence or in another sentence. In the following examples, an arrow has been drawn from each pronoun to its antecedent.

> Stephen wore **his** new jacket to school today.
>
> Rob and Beth are at the library. **They** have **their** history exam tomorrow.

Sometimes the antecedent can follow the pronoun.

> "That bicycle is **mine**," Heather said.

Personal Pronouns. Personal pronouns, which are the most commonly used type of pronoun, are divided into the following three groups.

Personal Pronouns

FIRST PERSON	(The person speaking)
SINGULAR	I, me, my, mine
PLURAL	we, us, our, ours
SECOND PERSON	(The person spoken to)
SINGULAR	you, your, yours
PLURAL	you, your, yours
THIRD PERSON	(The person or thing spoken about)
SINGULAR	he, him, his, she, her, hers, it, its
PLURAL	they, them, their, theirs

FIRST PERSON	**We** want to sell **our** old car.
SECOND PERSON	Did **you** find **your** watch?
THIRD PERSON	**He** told **them** to call **him** if **they** needed help.

EXERCISE 2 Finding Personal Pronouns and Their Antecedents

Number your paper 1 to 10. Write the personal pronoun(s) in each sentence. Then beside each one, write its antecedent.

1. "Are the pictures yours?" Megan asked Robert.
2. Danny lost his seat on the subway when he got up to look at the map.

3. "Mr. Sanchez read my term paper and wrote comments on it," Michael told Harold.
4. "Did Pat tell you that she would be there?" Sue asked Bart.
5. Lorraine, where have you put your copy of *Life* magazine?
6. David told Rosa, "I will try to save a seat for you at the assembly."
7. The Morgans will be taking their dog with them.
8. "Our duet was the hit of the show!" Jan exclaimed to Pat.
9. "We should take ours with us," Zachary told Yvonne.
10. Pamela said, "When I gave Katherine her award, she thanked me."

Reflexive and Intensive Pronouns. Reflexive and intensive pronouns are both formed by adding *-self* or *-selves* to personal pronouns.

Reflexive and Intensive Pronouns

SINGULAR	myself, yourself, himself, herself, itself
PLURAL	ourselves, yourselves, themselves

A *reflexive pronoun* refers back to the noun or the pronoun that is the subject of the sentence. It is an essential part of the sentence. An *intensive pronoun* is included in a sentence to add emphasis—or intensity—to a noun or another pronoun. Because an intensive pronoun is not a necessary part of a sentence, it can be removed without affecting the meaning of the sentence.

REFLEXIVE PRONOUN Rob taught **himself** to speak French. [*Himself* cannot be removed from the sentence without changing the meaning.]

INTENSIVE PRONOUN Rob volunteered his help **himself.** [*Himself* can be removed from the sentence: Rob volunteered his help.]

Indefinite Pronouns. Indefinite pronouns often refer to unnamed persons or things and usually do not have specific antecedents.

Common Indefinite Pronouns

SINGULAR	another, anybody, anyone, anything, each, either, everybody, everyone, everything, much, neither, nobody, no one, one, somebody, someone, something
PLURAL	both, few, many, others, several
SINGULAR/PLURAL	all, any, most, none, some

Few attended the meeting.
Most of the students did **something** to help the **many** who were homeless after the flood.

Demonstrative and Interrogative Pronouns. A *demonstrative pronoun* is used to point out a specific person, place, or object in the same sentence or in another sentence. An *interrogative pronoun* is used to ask a question.

Demonstrative Pronouns
this, that, these, those

Interrogative Pronouns
what, which, who, whom, whose

DEMONSTRATIVE PRONOUNS	**This** is the perfect place for a picnic. I bought some bananas. **These** were the ripest.
INTERROGATIVE PRONOUNS	**What** is your dog's name? **Who** wrote that song?

NOTE: *Relative pronouns* are used to introduce adjective clauses. *(See pages 80–81.)*

EXERCISE 3 Finding Pronouns
Number your paper 1 to 25. Then write each pronoun.

1. Who will be riding with them in the parade?
2. She is someone I have wanted to meet for a long time.
3. Did you find yourself something to eat?
4. I will lead the orchestra myself.

5. Many of the team members will need new equipment.
6. That is the place most of us like best.
7. All of the teachers will meet with the parents of their students during the open house.
8. What do you want for your birthday?
9. Anybody can run in the Fourth of July marathon.
10. Both of the candidates seemed to know everything about the issues.
11. Each of the radios is a good buy.
12. Which is the road to her house?
13. Tomás himself selected those.
14. Everything is ready for everybody.
15. Could these be some of the files she lost?
16. Some of the spinach salad was left, but none of the blueberry dessert.
17. The mayor herself awarded the scholarships.
18. What does she think of his new job?
19. Neither of them has heard anything about it.
20. Whom has everybody chosen?
21. He didn't like either of them.
22. Nobody wanted any.
23. Neither of the boys liked this.
24. I think you should select another.
25. Others gave much of their time.

VERBS

When you write a sentence, you must include a verb. A verb is an essential part of a sentence because it tells what the subject does, is, or has.

Action Verbs

1c An **action verb** tells what action a subject is performing.

Action verbs can show several types of action.

PHYSICAL ACTION	drive, march, soar, sing, talk, paint
MENTAL ACTION	believe, think, dream, imagine, wish
OWNERSHIP	have, own, possess, keep, control

Transitive and Intransitive Verbs. An action verb can be either transitive or intransitive. An action verb is *transitive* if it has an object. You can find an object by asking the question *What?* or *Whom?* after the verb. *(See pages 34–35 for more information about objects.)* An action verb is *intransitive* if it has no object.

TRANSITIVE I **found** a dollar the other day. [*Found* what? *Dollar* is the object.]
Brian **drove** Alicia to the dentist's office. [*Drove* whom? *Alicia* is the object.]

INTRANSITIVE We **met** only yesterday. [*Met* what or whom? *Met* has no object.]
The schooner **sailed** into the inlet. [*Sailed* what or whom? *Sailed* has no object.]

Some action verbs can be transitive in one sentence and intransitive in another sentence.

TRANSITIVE He **writes** mystery stories in his spare time. [*Writes* what? *Stories* is the object.]

INTRANSITIVE He often **writes** to me. [*Writes* what or whom? *Writes* has no object in this sentence.]

EXERCISE 4 Identifying Transitive and Intransitive Verbs
Number your paper 1 to 10. Write each action verb. Then label each one *transitive* or *intransitive*.

Fishy Facts

1. Rings on the scales of some fish show the age of the fish.
2. The electric eel throws a charge of 600 volts.
3. Rays live on the ocean bottom.
4. The Nile catfish swims upside down.
5. Minnows have teeth in their throat.
6. The female marine catfish hatches her eggs in her mouth.
7. The trout belongs to the salmon family.
8. The flounder changes its color.
9. Some fish thrive in underground streams and caves.
10. Despite their reputation, sharks rarely attack humans.

Linking Verbs

1d

A **linking verb** links the subject with another word in the sentence. The other word either renames or describes the subject.

A linking verb serves as a bridge between the subject and another word in the sentence.

Football **is** my favorite sport. [*Sport* renames the subject *football.*]

This winter **has been** exceptionally warm. [*Warm* describes the subject *winter.*]

The most common linking verbs are the various forms of *be.*

Common Forms of *Be*

be	shall be	have been
being	will be	has been
is	can be	had been
am	could be	could have been
are	should be	should have been
was	would be	would have been
were	may be	might have been
	might be	must have been
	must be	

Diane **may be** my new neighbor.

These mushrooms **will be** delicious in the salad.

NOTE: The forms of *be* are not always linking verbs. Only a verb that links the subject with another word in the sentence that renames or describes the subject can be a linking verb. In the following examples, the verbs simply make a statement.

Her coat **is** here. She **was** in Memphis on Tuesday.

Forms of *be* are not the only linking verbs. The following verbs can also be used as linking verbs.

Additional Linking Verbs

appear	grow	seem	stay
become	look	smell	taste
feel	remain	sound	turn

Jonathan **became** my best friend last year. [*Friend* renames the subject *Jonathan*.]

The barbecued chicken **looks** very tasty. [*Tasty* describes the subject *chicken*.]

Most of the additional linking verbs, listed in the preceding box, can be linking verbs in some sentences and action verbs in other sentences.

LINKING VERB That plan **sounded** perfect. [*Perfect* describes the subject *plan*.]

ACTION VERB The woman quickly **sounded** the alarm.

EXERCISE 5 Finding Linking Verbs

Number your paper 1 to 10. Then write each linking verb. If a sentence does not have a linking verb, write *none* after the number.

1. George III was the king of England during the American Revolution.
2. The hardest natural substance in the world is a diamond.
3. You looked much older with short hair.
4. He could have been the best runner in the history of our school.
5. I felt a hole in my pocket.
6. Indira Gandhi became the prime minister of India in 1966.
7. Luella will become a secretary after graduation.
8. For an hour we looked for the extra set of keys.
9. In 1900, many automobiles were electric cars, with battery-operated engines.
10. For about a month after my operation, I felt quite weak.

Verb Phrases

When one or more *helping verbs,* or auxiliary verbs, are added to an action verb or a linking verb, a *verb phrase* is formed.

1e A **verb phrase** is a main verb plus one or more helping verbs.

Common Helping Verbs	
be	am, is, are, was, were, be, being, been
have	has, have, had
do	do, does, did
others	may, might, must, can, could, shall, should, will, would

In the following examples, the helping verbs are in heavy type.

verb phrase

Jeff **has been** throwing our newspaper into the bushes.

verb phrase

You **should have been** notified of the change.

A verb phrase is often interrupted by other words.

Marvin **will** soon **apply** for that job.
She **has** always **taken** the bus to work.
I **do**n't **want** any dessert.

NOTE: Throughout the rest of this book, the term *verb* will refer to the whole verb phrase.

EXERCISE 6 **Finding Verb Phrases**

Write the verb in each sentence. Include all helping verbs.

1. At dinnertime Sheila was still practicing her scales.
2. The committee has held several meetings.
3. The group will not return for several hours.
4. The number of galaxies in the universe has been estimated at over a billion.
5. New basketball courts are being installed in the gym.
6. With his new job, George must always work on Saturdays.
7. I should never have eaten a second helping!
8. The runners have now reached the midpoint of the race.
9. The earth is traveling through space at the rate of 66,600 miles per hour.
10. Rebecca isn't working at Franklin Market anymore.

EXERCISE 7 **Time-out for Review**

Write the verb in each sentence. Then label each one *action* or *linking*. Be sure to include all helping verbs.

1. That antique jar can hold three gallons of water.
2. Leslie should be proud of her performance.
3. Stone walls and fences are favorite spots for poison ivy.
4. A redwood tree can often grow to a height of 275 feet.
5. Both Bach and Beethoven were German.
6. All the leaves on our oak tree have already fallen.
7. I have grown too tall for these jeans.
8. Picnics have always been part of summer vacations.
9. A lightning bolt does not move at the speed of light.
10. Lee exercises, at one sport or another, about an hour each afternoon.

ADJECTIVES AND ADVERBS

An adjective and an adverb have similar functions in a sentence. They both modify or describe other parts of speech. Adjectives and adverbs improve the style of sentences by adding vividness and exactness.

Adjectives

1f An adjective is a word that modifies a noun or a pronoun.

An adjective answers one of the following questions about a noun or a pronoun.

WHAT KIND?	**fresh** muffins	**plaid** shirt
WHICH ONE(S)?	**red** pencil	**those** few
HOW MANY?	**six** potatoes	**many** pages
HOW MUCH?	**extensive** damage	**much** publicity

An adjective can come in one of three places.

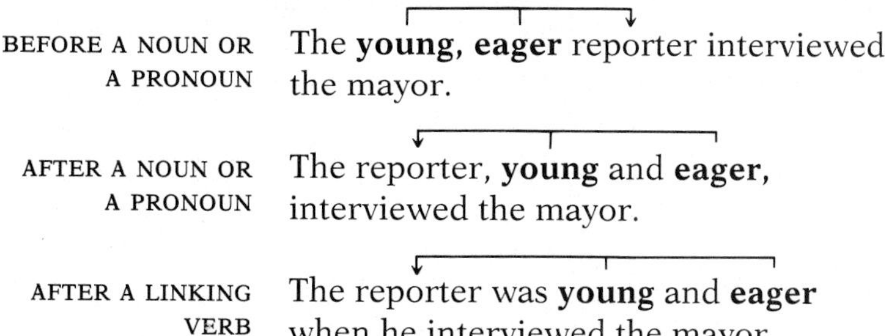

Proper and Compound Adjectives. Because a *proper adjective* is formed from a proper noun, it begins with a capital letter. A *compound adjective* is made up of more than one word. Since a compound adjective can be written as one word or hyphenated, it is always best to check the dictionary for the correct form.

PROPER ADJECTIVES	**Roman** emperor	**Hawaiian** island
	French cuisine	**Shakespearian** play
COMPOUND ADJECTIVES	**seaworthy** vessel	**long-term** loan
	spellbound child	**two-piece** outfit

NOTE: The words *a, an,* and *the* form a special group of adjectives called *articles. A* comes before words that begin with a consonant sound, and *an* comes before words that begin with a vowel sound. You will not be asked to list articles in the exercises in this book.

Other Parts of Speech Used as Adjectives. Sometimes a word can be a noun in one sentence and an adjective in another sentence.

NOUNS	flower, glass, refrigerator
ADJECTIVES	**flower** garden, **glass** vase, **refrigerator** door

A word can also be a pronoun in one sentence and an adjective in another sentence. The following words are adjectives when they come in front of a noun or a pronoun and modify that noun or pronoun. They are pronouns when they stand alone.

Words Used as Pronouns or Adjectives

Demonstrative	Interrogative	Indefinite	
that	what	all	many
these	which	another	more
this		any	most
those		both	neither
		each	other
		either	several
		few	some

ADJECTIVE	**These** records must be yours.
PRONOUN	**These** must be yours.
ADJECTIVE	**Each** player was given a new uniform before the first game of the season.
PRONOUN	**Each** of the players was given a new uniform before the first game of the season.

NOTE: The possessive pronouns *my, your, his, her, its, our,* and *their* are sometimes called *pronominal adjectives* because they answer the adjective question *Which one(s)?* Throughout this book, however, these words will be considered pronouns.

EXERCISE 8 Finding Adjectives

Number your paper 1 to 25. Then write the adjectives in the following paragraph.

The Eyes Have It

According to the ancient Greeks, eyes could reveal the personality of a person. They compared the eyes of people to the eyes of various animals. Then they attributed the personality traits of those animals to people. Lion eyes, for example, are almondlike. In a person they signified a sense of fairness, a sense of justice, and leadership skills. Monkey eyes are small in relation to the face, but they have large irises. The Greeks thought that people with these eyes were unpredictable and shy. Elephant eyes are long and narrow with several folds of skin on the upper and lower eyelids. People with elephant eyes, it was believed, could handle difficult problems and solve them in a thoughtful, methodical manner. This unusual list of eye types also included the eyes of sheep, horses, wolves, hogs, snakes, and fish.

EXERCISE 9 Writing Sentences

Number your paper 1 to 5. Skip a line after each number. Then write sentences that follow the directions below.

1. Use *green* as a noun and an adjective.
2. Use *this* as a pronoun and an adjective.
3. Use *apple* as a noun and an adjective.
4. Use *many* as a pronoun and an adjective.
5. Use *plant* as a noun, an adjective, and a verb.

Adverbs

1g An **adverb** is a word that modifies a verb, an adjective, or another adverb.

An adverb answers the question *Where? When? How?* or *To what extent?*

MODIFYING A VERB stayed **there** [Where?]

seldom speaks [When?]

answered **quickly** [How?]

MODIFYING AN ADJECTIVE **too** loose [To what extent?]

MODIFYING AN ADVERB **very** quickly [To what extent?]

NOTE: Adverbs that describe verbs modify all parts of a verb phrase.

Occasionally we have met **here.**

Although many adverbs end in *-ly,* the following common adverbs do not end in *-ly: almost, also, always, just, never, not (n't), quite, rather, so, then, too, very,* and *yet.* The words *when, where,* and *how* are also adverbs.

NOTE: Do not confuse an adverb that ends in *-ly* with an adjective that ends in *-ly.*

ADVERB We meet **weekly** with her. [When?]

ADJECTIVE That **weekly** magazine is available at the newsstand. [What kind?]

Nouns Used as Adverbs. The same word can be used as a noun in one sentence and an adverb in another sentence.

NOUN **Tomorrow** is the day my braces are removed.

ADVERB I will see the dentist **tomorrow.** [When?]

NOUN **Uptown** is a good location for the new restaurant.

ADVERB We will build the restaurant **uptown.** [Where?]

EXERCISE 10 Finding Adverbs

Number your paper 1 to 10. Write the adverbs in the following sentences. Then beside each one, write the word or words it modifies.

1. The playful porpoises will not swim away.
2. Where and when did you meet him?
3. The winner had run fast and steadily.
4. I always drive very carefully.
5. The zinnias have bloomed unusually early.
6. That friendly dog is constantly wagging its tail.
7. Don't make any plans today.
8. Here I could live happily.
9. I had an early appointment yesterday.
10. Some very important discoveries in science were made quite accidentally.

EXERCISE 11 Time-out for Review

Number your paper 1 to 10. Make two columns on your paper. Label the first column *adjectives* and the second column *adverbs*. Then under the proper column, write each adjective and each adverb.

The Sand Swimmer

1. Southwest deserts appear totally empty of life.
2. Many animals, birds, and insects survive very well in this barren land.
3. An unusual inhabitant of these bleak areas is one type of lizard.
4. This lizard can swiftly skim along the sandy surface and can easily burrow into the sand.
5. You have probably watched swimmers at the ocean or a lake on a hot summer day.
6. These bathers often run quickly to the water, dive in, and then disappear beneath the surface.
7. In the same way, this lizard runs very fast, dives into the sand, and disappears without a trace.
8. During this swift run, the lizard may actually fly for a few seconds.
9. The body of the lizard is perfectly suited for this incredible stunt.
10. During the dive a group of scales cleverly protects the eyes of the lizard.

OTHER PARTS OF SPEECH

Prepositions, conjunctions, and interjections are the three remaining parts of speech. A *preposition* shows a relationship between words, a *conjunction* connects words or groups of words, and an *interjection* shows strong feeling or emotion.

Prepositions

1h A **preposition** is a word that shows the relationship between a noun or a pronoun and another word in the sentence.

In the following example, the words in heavy type are prepositions. Notice how the different prepositions change the relationship between the plant and the table.

The plant {**on** / **beside** / **near**} the table is a geranium.

Following is a list of common prepositions. Prepositions of two or more words are called *compound prepositions.*

Common Prepositions

about	below	in front of	outside
above	beneath	in place of	over
according to	beside	inside	past
across	besides	in spite of	prior to
after	between	instead of	through
against	beyond	into	throughout
ahead of	by	in view of	to
along with	despite	like	toward
among	down	near	under
apart from	during	next to	underneath
around	except	of	until
aside from	for	off	up
at	from	on	upon
because of	in	on account of	with
before	in addition to	opposite	within
behind	in back of	out, out of	without

A preposition is always part of a group of words called a *prepositional phrase.* A prepositional phrase begins with a preposition and ends with a noun or a pronoun called the *object of a preposition.* One or more modifiers may come between the preposition and its object. The prepositional phrases in the following examples are in heavy type.

During English class we watched a film **about Shakespeare.**

On account of the snowstorm, traffic was snarled **throughout the city.**

Preposition or Adverb? The same word can be a preposition in one sentence and an adverb in another sentence. A word is a preposition if it is part of a prepositional phrase. The same word is an adverb if it stands alone.

PREPOSITION	I saw the cat ***outside*** *the house.*
ADVERB	I saw the cat **outside.**
PREPOSITION	Greg speaks well ***before*** *an audience.*
ADVERB	Have you heard this story **before?**

EXERCISE 12 Finding Prepositional Phrases
Number your paper 1 to 20. Then write the prepositional phrases in the following paragraph.

The First Airmail Service

In a sense, the French were the originators of airmail service. During the siege of Paris in the Franco-Prussian War of the 1870s, mail was sent out of the capital by balloon, along with hundreds of homing pigeons. Return letters were photoreduced on thin film, which held an average of 2,500 letters. Then pigeons delivered the letters to the capital. Approximately 300 pigeons carrying the mail were dispatched. Some of these got past the Prussian pigeon snipers. In Paris the messages were enlarged on a projection screen, copied by clerks, and delivered to addresses within the city.

Conjunctions

1i A **conjunction** connects words or groups of words.

Coordinating conjunctions are single connecting words, and *correlative conjunctions* are pairs of connecting words.

Conjunctions

Coordinating			Correlative	
and	nor	yet	both/and	not only/but also
but	or		either/or	whether/or
for	so		neither/nor	

The table is missing a *knife* **and** a *fork*. [connects nouns]

Either *write* her a note **or** *call* her. [connect verbs]

That evergreen is *tall* **but** *full.* [connects adjectives]

I can't wait any longer, **for** *I have an appointment.* [connects sentences]

NOTE: *Subordinating conjunctions* are used to introduce adverb clauses. *(See pages 77–78.)*

Interjections

1j An **interjection** is a word that expresses strong feeling or emotion.

Fear, anger, surprise, and happiness are just some of the emotions expressed by interjections. A comma or an exclamation point always separates an interjection from the rest of the sentence.

Ouch! Don't touch my sunburn.
Oh, I didn't hear you come in.
Whew! This is spicy.
Yes, I agree with you.

EXERCISE 13 **Finding Conjunctions and Interjections**
Number your paper 1 to 10. Then write the coordinating and correlative conjunctions and the interjections in the following sentences.

1. Anyone can swim or float more easily in salt water than in fresh water.
2. Whew! I just finished a short but difficult exam.
3. Oliver Wendell Holmes was both an author and an associate justice of the Supreme Court.

4. Gosh! I just ate an hour ago, yet I'm hungry now.
5. Slowly and carefully she began to open the box.
6. You'll find a pen either on the desk or in the top drawer.
7. Gertrude Stein encouraged not only young authors like Ernest Hemingway but also young painters like Picasso.
8. The beautiful cape was handwoven and made entirely of alpaca wool.
9. Mom rises early every morning, for she has to take the bus to work.
10. Neither your clock nor my watch was correct.

EXERCISE 14 Writing Sentences
Write five sentences that follow the directions below.

1. Use *either/or* to connect two nouns.
2. Use *or* to connect two verbs.
3. Use *but* to connect two adjectives.
4. Use *both/and* to connect two adverbs.
5. Use *for* to connect two sentences. (Put a comma before *for*.)

EXERCISE 15 Time-out for Review
Number your paper 1 to 25. Write the numbered, underlined words in the following paragraphs. Then beside each one, write its part of speech: *noun, pronoun, verb, adjective, adverb, preposition, conjunction,* or *interjection*.

More for Your Money

(1)Anyone who visits the Bureau of Engraving and Printing in (2)Washington can buy one hundred fifty dollars' worth of (3)United States currency (4)for seventy-five cents. (5)Oh, there (6)is a catch. The money is (7)real, (8)but it has been shredded. Every day the bureau shreds (9)tons (10)of new, misprinted (11)currency, stamps, (12)and (13)other items that are not fit for (14)circulation. (15)At the bureau's visitors center, machines (16)automatically dispense seventy-five-cent packets of shredded currency.

(17)Each of the 12 Federal Reserve district banks is also authorized to dispose of old, worn, (18)or soiled currency as (19)it sees fit. For the sum of (20)eighty-three dollars, the (21)Los Angeles branch will deliver an entire day's output—up to 5,550 pounds—to your door if (22)you live closer than the nearest dump. (23)Some of this currency (24)later (25)appears in novelty stores.

PARTS OF SPEECH REVIEW

Most creatures are born a certain color and remain that color throughout their entire lives. A chameleon, on the other hand, can instantly change its color to blend with its surroundings. Many words in English are like chameleons. They can become different parts of speech, depending upon how they are used in a sentence. The word *last,* for example, can be used as four different parts of speech.

NOUN The **last** of the guests has finally gone.
VERB The heat spell will **last** two more days.
ADJECTIVE The **last** bus to Chicago just left.
ADVERB Our relay team finished **last.**

The following summary of the eight parts of speech will help you determine how a word is used in a sentence.

NOUN Is the word naming a person, place, thing, or idea?

The **friendship** between **Ramón** and my **brother** has lasted for 15 **years.**

PRONOUN Is the word taking the place of a noun?

Everything they said to **you** is true.

VERB Is the word showing action, or does it link the subject with another word in the sentence?

I **read** the book. It **was** fascinating.

ADJECTIVE Is the word modifying a noun or a pronoun? Does it answer the question *What kind? Which one(s)? How many?* or *How much?*

That soft, comfortable chair is very **old.**

ADVERB Is the word modifying a verb, an adjective, or another adverb? Does it answer the question *How? When? Where?* or *To what extent?*

The leaves from that **rather** large oak tree are falling **very fast.**

PREPOSITION Is the word showing a relationship between a noun or a pronoun and another word in the sentence? Is it part of a phrase?

***In spite of** the rain,* we walked ***until** dark.*

CONJUNCTION Is the word connecting words or groups of words?

See **either** Ben **or** Jason, **for** they are in charge of the refreshment committee.

INTERJECTION Is the word expressing strong feeling?

Hurrah! We won.

EXERCISE 16 Determining Parts of Speech
Write the underlined word in each sentence. Then beside each one, write its part of speech: *noun, pronoun, verb, adjective, adverb, preposition, conjunction,* or *interjection.*

1. Where is the stop sign?
2. Both men saw the accident.
3. Come over this afternoon.
4. Well, that's a surprise.
5. Turn off that loud music!
6. What answer did you give?
7. Read the rest of the book.
8. Did he stop at the blinking light?
9. Oh! I forgot my lunch.
10. Don't drink the well water.
11. What is that?
12. You should rest.
13. Don't sing too loud.
14. This is your color.
15. Both are here.
16. Your ring is lovely.
17. Do you like this hat?
18. Can you jump over the fence?
19. He swims so well.
20. Did the phone ring?

Application to Writing

Anyone who reads the sports page knows that teams never *win.* They might *crush, stomp, trounce,* or *outclass*—but they never just *win.* Sportswriters use different words to avoid repetition. Follow the example of these writers and look for fresh, lively alternatives for general, overused words.

	GENERAL	FRESH, LIVELY
NOUN	accident	casualty, mishap, catastrophe
VERB	fall	sink, plummet, plunge, topple
ADJECTIVE	small	piddling, trivial, minute, tiny

EXERCISE 17 Substituting Fresh Nouns, Verbs, and Adjectives

Write at least two fresh alternatives for each of the following words. Then write sentences that use two of the fresh words from each column. Use a thesaurus or the dictionary.

NOUNS	VERBS	ADJECTIVES
1. boss	1. run	1. lively
2. friend	2. smell	2. slow
3. meal	3. rush	3. brave
4. ditch	4. demand	4. eager
5. top	5. give	5. fancy

EXERCISE 18 Writing Sentences

A heavy mist settles over you for a moment and then passes. Suddenly you begin to shrink. In approximately 10 to 15 sentences, write what happens next. Include as many fresh, lively nouns, verbs, and adjectives as possible.

CHAPTER REVIEW

A. Number your paper 1 to 20. Then write the underlined word in each sentence. Beside each word, label its part of speech, using the following abbreviations.

noun = *n.*	adjective = *adj.*	conjunction = *conj.*
pronoun = *pron.*	adverb = *adv.*	interjection = *interj.*
verb = *v.*	preposition = *prep.*	

1. It was very cold <u>outside</u> last night.
2. Did she buy a new <u>iron</u>?
3. <u>Oh</u>! We ran out of tape.
4. Look on the <u>top</u> shelf.
5. The picture fell <u>down</u>.
6. They're in <u>that</u> box.
7. That's a new <u>stop</u> sign.
8. The <u>top</u> of the mountain was covered with snow.
9. <u>Those</u> tomatoes are ripe.
10. Don't run <u>down</u> the hill.
11. He owns the <u>fish</u> market on May Road.
12. What is <u>that</u>?
13. He is <u>in</u> the store.
14. Come <u>in</u>.
15. I usually <u>fish</u> there.
16. Did you <u>iron</u> it?
17. I caught three <u>fish</u>.
18. It was cold <u>outside</u> the house.
19. <u>Those</u> are mine.
20. I can't <u>stop</u> this.

B. Copy the following sentences, skipping a line after each one. Then above each word, label its part of speech, using the abbreviations in Part A. Remember that articles are adjectives.

EXAMPLE A soccer match usually lasts for ninety minutes.

adj. n. adv. v. prep. adj. n.
ANSWER Soccer matches usually last for ninety minutes.

1. Houston is one of the largest cities in Texas.
2. My uncle will visit us today.
3. Have you ever been to Gettysburg?
4. Eighteen holes are played in a round of golf.
5. The history test was rather long and difficult.
6. Rome was originally built on seven hills.
7. Anyone can attend the meeting, but the room holds only 60 people.
8. The diameter of a basketball hoop is 18 inches.
9. Wow! Did you see that long, high drive down the field?
10. The third Sunday in June is Father's Day.

MASTERY TEST

Number your paper 1 to 10. Write the underlined words in each sentence. Then beside each one, write its part of speech: *noun, pronoun, verb, adjective, adverb, preposition, conjunction,* or *interjection.*

1. The mudskipper, an African fish, can actually skip on the ground.
2. Many people have asked for reservations on the first commercial flight into space.
3. The excitement of the crowd was contagious.
4. The pan on the stove is very hot.
5. When do wisdom teeth usually appear?
6. I couldn't do without my old but comfortable shoes.
7. We need a space divider between the two offices.
8. Oh! You just dropped something on the stairs.
9. Don't give me that many!
10. What are you going to do with all these coins?

2

The Sentence Base

DIAGNOSTIC TEST

Number your paper 1 to 10. Write the subject, the verb, and the underlined complement in each sentence. (A subject or a verb may be compound.) Then label each complement, using the following abbreviations.

direct object = *d.o.*
indirect object = *i.o.*
objective complement = *o.c.*
predicate nominative = *p.n.*
predicate adjective = *p.a.*

EXAMPLE Nelson threw a 60-yard pass for a touchdown.
ANSWER Nelson, threw pass — d.o.

1. *Newsweek* has become my favorite magazine.
2. The wind rattled the window and swirled leaves along the streets.
3. Several test scores were very high.
4. Jamie built me a cabinet for my records.
5. We will paint the walls in this room light yellow.
6. A house in the city is quite safe from lightning.
7. Marcy sent us an announcement of her graduation.
8. Canada and the United States share the longest unguarded border in the world.
9. Is Jonathan the one in the middle?
10. The band invited a guest conductor for the occasion.

A well-constructed house has a foundation, which basically holds all the other parts of the house together. Like a house, a sentence must also have a foundation. The foundation, or *sentence base,* of a sentence is composed of a subject, a verb, and sometimes a complement. It is to this foundation that all other words in the sentence are added.

2a A **sentence** is a group of words that expresses a complete thought.

A group of words that does not express a complete thought is called a *fragment.* In many cases a group of words is a fragment because it does not have a subject or a predicate. *(See pages 97–100 for more information about fragments.)*

FRAGMENT	SENTENCE
My friend Joan.	My friend Joan **is a senior.**
Under the mat.	**The house key is** under the mat.
To get a job.	**I want** to get a job.

SUBJECTS AND PREDICATES

2b A sentence has two main parts: a **subject** and a **predicate.** A *subject* names the person, place, thing, or idea the sentence is about. The *predicate* tells something about the subject.

COMPLETE SUBJECT	COMPLETE PREDICATE
My aunt from Alabama	is living in Alaska now.
The museum near us	has a new exhibition.
The box on the counter	contains coupons for the store.
Hailstones	fell for ten minutes today.

Simple Subjects and Predicates

Each complete subject and predicate can usually be narrowed down to a single word or phrase.

2c A **simple subject** is the main word in the complete subject.

2d A **simple predicate,** or **verb,** is the main word or phrase in the complete predicate.

In the following examples, the simple subjects and the verbs are in heavy type.

complete subject — complete predicate
The narrow dirt **road took** a sudden turn into a clearing.

complete subject — complete predicate
Two valuable **reporters** recently **resigned** from the *Chronicle*.

complete subject — complete predicate
Memorial Hospital in Acton **is raising** money for a new wing.

In the last example, *Memorial Hospital* is a single proper noun; therefore, both words make up the simple subject. Notice also that the verb phrase *is raising* is considered the verb of the sentence. *(See pages 11–12 for more information about verb phrases.)*

NOTE: Throughout the rest of this book, the term *subject* will refer to a simple subject, and the term *verb* will refer to a simple predicate, which may be a single verb or a verb phrase.

Finding Subjects and Verbs. To find the subject of an action verb, ask yourself *Who?* or *What?* before the verb. The answer to either question will be the subject. In the following examples, each subject is underlined once, and each verb is underlined twice.

> Mandy has taken French for two years. [The action verb is *has taken*. Who has taken? The subject is *Mandy*.]
>
> His temperature is rising rapidly. [The action verb is *is rising*. What is rising? The subject is *temperature*.]

To find the subject of a linking verb, ask yourself, *About whom or what is some statement being made?* The answer to that question will be the subject. *(See page 10 for lists of linking verbs.)*

> My brother is a freshman at Colorado College. [The linking verb is *is*. About whom is some statement being made? The subject is *brother*.]
>
> The velvet jacket feels exceptionally soft. [The linking verb is *feels*. About what is some statement being made? The subject is *jacket*.]

NOTE: When you look for a subject and a verb, it is often helpful to eliminate all modifiers and prepositional phrases from the sentence. *A subject is never part of a prepositional phrase.*

> ~~Numerous~~ masterpieces ~~of Michelangelo~~ are located ~~throughout Florence.~~ [*Masterpieces* is the subject; *are located* is the verb.]

Compound Subjects and Verbs. A sentence can have more than one subject and more than one verb.

2e A **compound subject** is two or more subjects in one sentence that have the same verb and are joined by a conjunction.

Use the method in the previous section to find a compound subject.

> The hamburgers and corn tasted delicious.
>
> Maria, Barry, and Martin attended the meeting.

2f A **compound verb** is two or more verbs that have the same subject and are joined by a conjunction.

> You can join the swim team or sing in the glee club.
>
> A diamond will cut all other substances and will resist even the strongest acids.

A sentence can have both a compound subject and a compound verb.

> Paul and his sister bought a hoop and played basketball.

EXERCISE 1 Finding Subjects and Verbs
Number your paper 1 to 20. Then write the subjects and the verbs in the following sentences.

Hunting for Buried Treasure

1. For centuries the *Atocha,* with tons of gold and silver, lay on the bottom of the sea and tempted treasure hunters.
2. In 1622, the ship was bound (for Spain) but during a hurricane sank (in the waters) (off the Florida coast.)
3. Because of a second hurricane, other vessels could not rescue the *Atocha*'s treasure.

4. The position of the ship either was never recorded or was finally forgotten.
5. Eventually ocean currents covered the ship with sand.
6. The legend of the *Atocha* and the promise of great wealth brought many treasure hunters to Florida.
7. Mel Fisher and his family joined the others and became full-time treasure hunters.
8. Mel had once run a chicken farm and then had operated a diving shop.
9. He had some original ideas about the possible location of the ship and used clever techniques in the search.
10. Mel and members of his family continued their search in the face of many hardships and much scorn.
11. Critics constantly laughed at their efforts.
12. Then in June 1975, Fisher's crew found a cannon from the *Atocha* and silenced the critics.
13. The joy of the Fisher party was intense but ended because of a tragedy.
14. On the night of July 18, 1975, Fisher's son, his daughter-in-law, and another diver drowned.
15. Mel and his wife did not stop their work.
16. The tragedies would then be meaningless.
17. They continued and salvaged more and more objects.
18. They could not keep all the treasure.
19. The state of Florida claimed a portion of the treasure and held much of it for a long period of time.
20. Perhaps some day you will see some of the *Atocha*'s treasures in a museum.

Position of Subjects

When a sentence is in its natural order, the subject comes before the verb. For various reasons a sentence can also be written in *inverted order,* with the verb or part of the verb phrase coming before the subject. Subjects in inverted order are sometimes more difficult to find.

Questions. Questions are often phrased in inverted order. To find the subject and the verb in a question, turn the question around to make a statement.

QUESTION Have you seen Luis tonight?
STATEMENT You have seen Luis tonight.

***There* and *Here*.** A sentence beginning with *there* or *here* is always in inverted order. To find the subject and the verb, place the sentence in its natural order. Sometimes the word *there* or *here* must be dropped before the sentence can be put in its natural order.

INVERTED ORDER Here is an extra sock.
NATURAL ORDER An extra sock is here.

INVERTED ORDER There will be a test given on Friday.
NATURAL ORDER A test will be given on Friday. [Drop *there*.]

Emphasis or Variety. To create emphasis or variety, you may sometimes deliberately write a sentence in inverted order. To find the subject and the verb, put the sentence into its natural order.

INVERTED ORDER Across the snow lay the black shadows of tree trunks.
NATURAL ORDER The black shadows of tree trunks lay across the snow.

Understood *You*. The subject of most commands and requests is *you*. Although *you* seldom appears in the sentence, it is still understood to be there. In the following examples, *you* is the understood subject of each sentence.

Set the alarm for six. [*You* is the understood subject.]

Ella, call Bart now. [*You* is the understood subject—even though the person receiving the command is named.]

EXERCISE 2 Finding Subjects and Verbs in Inverted Sentences

Number your paper 1 to 10. Then write the subject and the verb in each sentence. If the subject is an understood *you*, write it in parentheses.

1. There are no snakes in New Zealand.
2. Look at this advertisement for free records!
3. What equipment does a scuba diver need?

4. Over the heads of the crowd soared the Blue Angels in perfect formation.
5. Here are the names of the five finalists.
6. Have you ever angled for brook trout?
7. Wanda, hand me that pot holder on the counter.
8. Around medieval castles there was usually a moat for defense purposes.
9. When will the county fair open this year?
10. Across Virginia, from the northeast to the southwest, stretch the beautiful Blue Ridge Mountains.

EXERCISE 3 Time-out for Review

Number your paper 1 to 20. Then write the subjects and the verbs in the following sentences.

Bits about the Body

1. The average three-pound human brain is very complex.
2. During the first six months of a baby's life, the brain doubles in size.
3. Each second the brain receives and translates 100 million nerve messages from your body.
4. With increased age men and women hear fewer high-pitched sounds.
5. The human eye can discriminate between several million gradations of color.
6. At sea level there are 2,000 pounds of air pressure on each square foot of your body.
7. The nose, the windpipe, and the lungs form the respiratory system.
8. The respiratory system provides the body with oxygen and rids the body of carbon dioxide.
9. The nose cleans, warms, and humidifies over 500 cubic feet of air every day.
10. In the lungs there are millions of tiny air sacs.
11. During a lifetime an average person could consume about 60,000 pounds of food, a weight equivalent to that of six elephants.
12. Nerve signals may travel through nerve or muscle fibers at speeds up to 200 miles per hour.
13. Eighty percent of all body heat escapes through the head.
14. There are 9,000 taste buds on a person's tongue.
15. Through your circulatory system flow 680,000 gallons of blood a year.

16. In an average adult, there are approximately six quarts of blood.
17. There are approximately five million red blood cells in a cubic millimeter of human blood.
18. A baby and an adult do not have the same number of bones.
19. Ligaments and tendons connect bones to bones and muscles to bones.
20. The largest bone in the body is the thigh bone.

Application to Writing

Combining sentences that have the same subject but different verbs or the same verb but different subjects is one way to avoid unnecessary repetition in your writing.

TWO SENTENCES	Before the Constitution each state coined money. Some private individuals also coined money.
ONE SENTENCE WITH A COMPOUND SUBJECT	Before the Constitution each state and some private individuals coined money.
TWO SENTENCES	The government now coins money. The government also regulates its value.
ONE SENTENCE WITH A COMPOUND VERB	The government now coins money and regulates its value.

EXERCISE 4 Combining Sentences

Combine each pair of sentences into one sentence with a compound subject or a compound verb. Use the conjunction *and* or *but.*

The Minting of Coins

1. From 1703 to 1890, regularly issued United States coins did not show a person's portrait. They usually pictured, instead, Liberty or the American eagle.
2. The Lincoln penny broke with tradition. It became one of the first coins honoring famous people.
3. Afterward Jefferson was similarly honored. Other presidents were also honored.
4. Buffalo nickels honored the American Indian. Indian-head pennies also honored the American Indian.

5. In 1965, the government replaced silver dimes and quarters with nickel and copper coins. The government also changed the amount of silver in half-dollars.
6. Many coins are minted each year. They are then put into circulation.
7. From time to time, certain coins are needed in a hurry. They are produced under an emergency schedule.
8. A new sales tax may create a sudden demand for a particular coin. A change in subway fares may also create a demand.
9. Pennies are always in demand. Dimes are also very popular.
10. Quarters represent a relatively small percentage of the total production of coins. So do half-dollars.

COMPLEMENTS

Very often a sentence has a completer, or *complement,* which completes the meaning of the sentence. Neither of the following sentences, for example, would be complete without its complement.

Todd made **breakfast.** Michelle is **smart.**

There are five kinds of complements. *Direct objects, indirect objects,* and *objective complements* complete the meaning of action verbs. *Predicate nominatives* and *predicate adjectives,* called *subject complements,* complete the meaning of linking verbs.

Direct Objects and Indirect Objects

2g A **direct object** is a noun or a pronoun that receives the action of the verb.

To find a direct object, ask *What?* or *Whom?* after an action verb. Notice in the third example that a direct object can be compound.

d.o.
Louis removed the **lint** from his suit. [Louis removed what? *Lint* is the direct object.]

d.o.
I drove **Heather** to school. [I drove whom? *Heather* is the direct object.]

d.o. d.o.
Earl makes leather **belts** and **wallets.** [Earl makes what? *Belts* and *wallets* make up the compound direct object.]

Each part of a compound action verb can have its own direct object.

d.o. d.o.
Lance focused his **camera** and snapped the **picture.** [*Camera* is the direct object of *focused,* and *picture* is the direct object of *snapped.*]

If a sentence has a direct object, it can also have an indirect object.

2h An **indirect object** answers the question *To or for whom?* or *To or for what?* after an action verb.

To find an indirect object, first find the direct object. Then ask, *To or for whom?* or *To or for what?* after the direct object. An indirect object always comes before a direct object in a sentence. Notice in the third example that an indirect object can be compound.

i.o. d.o.
I bought **Paul** a new catcher's mitt. [*Mitt* is the direct object. I bought a mitt for whom? *Paul* is the indirect object. Notice that it comes before the direct object.]

i.o. d.o.
The coach gave the **team** a pep talk. [*Pep talk* is the direct object. The coach gave a pep talk to whom? *Team* is the indirect object. Notice that it comes before the direct object.]

i.o. i.o. d.o.
Pedro is teaching **Lee** and **Kelly** Spanish. [*Spanish* is the direct object. Pedro is teaching Spanish to whom? *Lee* and *Kelly* make up the compound indirect object.]

NOTE: Neither a direct object nor an indirect object is ever part of a prepositional phrase. *(See pages 18 and 19 for more information about prepositional phrases.)*

i.o. d.o.
We gave **Roger** an album for his birthday. [*Roger* is the indirect object. It comes before the direct object *album* and is not part of a prepositional phrase.]

d.o.
We gave an album to Roger for his birthday. [*Roger* is *not* the indirect object, because it follows the direct object *album* and is the object of the preposition *to*.]

EXERCISE 5 Finding Indirect Objects and Direct Objects
Number your paper 1 to 20. Write the indirect objects and the direct objects in the following sentences. Then label each one *indirect object* or *direct object.*

1. Lloyd sent my cousin a record of Portuguese folk songs.
2. The hyena has powerful jaws and long forelegs.
3. Mr. Roland showed Bart and me the difference between wheat and oats.
4. Some centipedes have 31 to 180 pairs of legs.
5. Yesterday Jessie gave the dogs a bath.
6. Show Angie and Peter your pictures from the dance.
7. Give that book to Howard this afternoon.
8. Robert Louis Stevenson first dreamed the plot of *Dr. Jekyll and Mr. Hyde* and then wrote it.
9. Our new neighbors brought my family a spaghetti dinner and an apple pie.
10. The pianist acknowledged the applause but did not give the audience an encore.
11. Which computer do you recommend for me?
12. Mr. Tanner sprayed our fruit trees from his Piper Cub.
13. Will you give the desk a second coat of paint?
14. Tell Craig the joke about the elephant.
15. In 1883, Buffalo Bill organized his famous Wild West Show.
16. Did you set the alarm for six o'clock?
17. During homeroom Amy will show us the yearbook.
18. A hummingbird usually lays only two eggs during the nesting period.

19. Did you buy Mittens some catnip?
20. Nervous or emotional strain may cause an increase in blood pressure.

Objective Complements

2i

An **objective complement** is a noun or an adjective that renames or describes the direct object.

To find an objective complement, first find the direct object. Then ask the question *What?* after the direct object. An objective complement will always follow the direct object. Notice the compound objective complement in the third example.

The team voted Calvin **captain.** [*Calvin* is the direct object. The team voted Calvin what? *Captain* is the objective complement. It follows the direct object and renames it.]

We consider our parakeet the perfect **pet** for a family. [*Parakeet* is the direct object. We consider our parakeet what? *Pet* is the objective complement. It follows the direct object and renames it.]

The award made Flora **happy** and **proud.** [*Flora* is the direct object. The award made Flora what? *Happy* and *proud* make up the compound objective complement. These words follow the direct object and describe it.]

EXERCISE 6 Finding Complements
Number your paper 1 to 10. Write each complement in the following sentences. Then label each one *direct object, indirect object,* or *objective complement.*

1. Chlorophyll makes grass green.
2. Wish me luck in the swim meet.
3. Have you fed the dog and the cat their dinner?
4. Nancy did a favor for Mrs. Ellis.
5. In most areas buses have made trolleys obsolete.
6. Did Leroy show you his new watch?

7. Dad built the bookcase tall and narrow.
8. Some people once raised spiders and sold the silk.
9. The lack of trail markers made me unsure of the way out of the woods.
10. The judges declared Sebastian the winner.

Subject Complements

Two kinds of complements, called *subject complements,* complete the meaning of linking verbs. *(See page 10 for lists of linking verbs.)*

2j A **predicate nominative** is a noun or a pronoun that follows a linking verb and identifies, renames, or explains the subject.

To find a predicate nominative, first find the subject and the linking verb. Then find the noun or the pronoun that follows the verb and identifies, renames, or explains the subject. Notice in the second example that a predicate nominative can be compound.

p.n.
Bart will become a **mechanic.** [mechanic = Bart]

p.n. p.n.
The winners of the scholarships are **Bryan** and **Julie.** [Bryan and Julie = winners]

Like the other complements, a predicate nominative is never part of a prepositional phrase.

p.n.
Pamela is **one** of the tellers at the First National Bank. [*One* is the predicate nominative. *Tellers* is the object of the preposition *of.*]

The other subject complement is a predicate adjective.

2k A **predicate adjective** is an adjective that follows a linking verb and modifies the subject.

To find a predicate adjective, first find the subject and the linking verb. Then find an adjective that follows the verb and modifies the subject. Notice in the second example that a predicate adjective can be compound.

p.a.
That movie was **scary.** [*Scary* modifies the subject.]

p.a. p.a.
The clothes smelled **clean** and **fresh.** [*Clean* and *fresh* modify the subject.]

NOTE: Remember that a predicate adjective follows a linking verb and modifies the subject. Do not confuse a predicate adjective with a regular adjective.

PREDICATE ADJECTIVE Carlos is **brilliant.**

REGULAR ADJECTIVE Carlos is a **brilliant** student.

EXERCISE 7 Finding Subject Complements
Number your paper 1 to 20. Write each subject complement in the following sentences. Then label each one *predicate nominative* or *predicate adjective.*

1. Benjamin Franklin was the inventor of bifocals.
2. The sting of the Portuguese man-of-war is always serious and sometimes fatal.
3. That's he with the blue baseball cap.
4. Nitrogen is the main component of air.
5. Hot apple cider tastes good on a cold afternoon.
6. Some of the products of the peanut are margarine, soap, and cosmetics.
7. Was Davy Crockett one of the defenders of the Alamo?
8. The chili tastes particularly spicy.
9. Mrs. Hanover is a tireless and unselfish person.
10. My favorite colors have always been blue and purple.
11. Air masses from Canada are often cold and dry.
12. The shore of Crater Lake in Oregon is the rim of an extinct volcano.
13. With a yearly average of less than 20 inches of rainfall, Australia is the world's driest continent.
14. The winners of the door prize were she and Lisa.
15. Heather is scared but optimistic about the test.
16. After graduation my sister became a newspaper writer.
17. The mushroom is actually a type of fungus.
18. At the end of our hike, we were tired and hungry.
19. Hydrogen is the most abundant element in the universe.
20. Maria was tired after jogging three miles.

EXERCISE 8 Time-out for Review

Number your paper 1 to 20. Write each complement. Then label each one, using the following abbreviations.

direct object = *d.o.* predicate nominative = *p.n.*
indirect object = *i.o.* predicate adjective = *p.a.*
objective complement = *o.c.*

1. The drama club hung their posters in every hallway of the school.
2. Before 8:30 A.M., the lounge in the east wing is open to all students.
3. George Washington appointed John Jay Chief Justice of the United States.
4. Lloyd became enthusiastic about speaking in the debate.
5. Ms. Williams gave the class a list of research topics.
6. Leslie can swim 50 laps in 20 minutes.
7. Birds' feathers are actually a kind of scale, like the scales of reptiles.
8. The students voted Melissa president of the class with more than 86 percent of the vote.
9. The typical American black bear can be black, white, brown, or gray-blue.
10. On February 20, 1962, John Glenn orbited the earth in the spacecraft *Friendship 7*.
11. Advertising agencies have given the English language many new words, such as *glamorize* and *personalize*.
12. The original color of that old colonial house was red.
13. Last night I reread my journal.
14. Some nutritionists consider vitamin C an effective cold preventive.
15. Our apartment is very close to public transportation.
16. In his junior year, Tomás became captain of the lacrosse team.
17. Henry Perkey of Denver, Colorado, and William Ford of Watertown, New York, gave consumers their first breakfast cereal in 1893.
18. Some icebergs appear blue or green in the sun.
19. For her birthday we gave Marcy a box of stationery and an album for her photographs.
20. The two longest rivers on the earth are the Amazon and the Nile.

EXERCISE 9 Writing Sentences
Write five sentences, using each of the five kinds of complements at least once. Then label each complement.

DIAGRAMING THE SENTENCE BASE

A *diagram* is a picture of words. By placing the words of a sentence in a diagram, you can often see the relationship between the parts of a sentence more clearly.

Subjects and Verbs

All diagrams begin with a baseline. The subject and the verb go on the baseline but are separated by a vertical line. Capital letters are included in a diagram, but not punctuation. Notice in the second and third examples that compound subjects and verbs are placed on parallel lines. The conjunction joining them is placed on a broken line between them.

He is working.

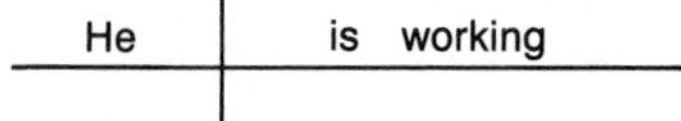

Mom, Dad, and Linda have finished.

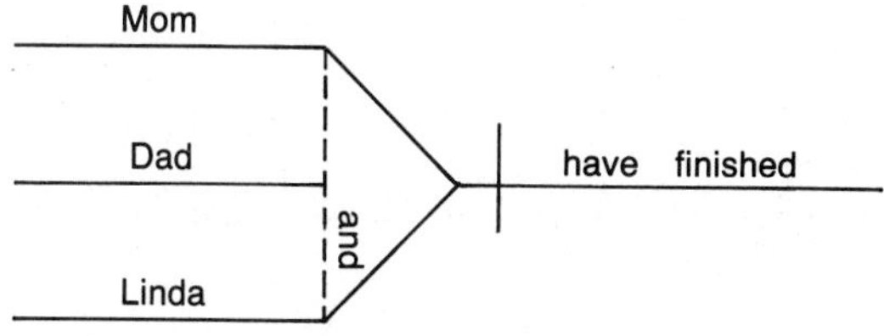

Lupe both sang and danced.

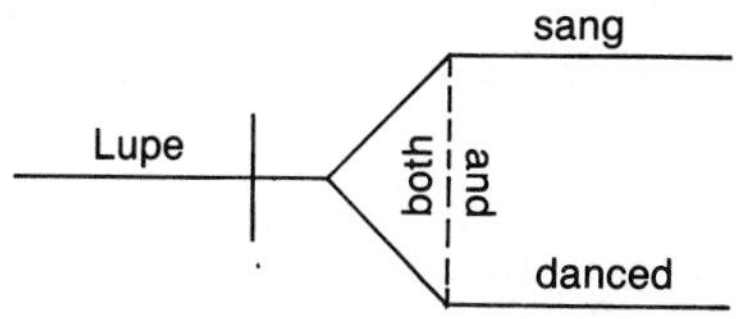

Inverted Order. An inverted sentence is diagramed like a sentence in natural order.

Have you eaten?

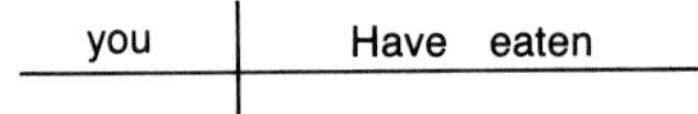

Understood Subjects. The understood subject *you* is diagramed in the subject position with parentheses around it.

Listen!

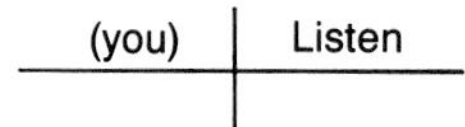

Adjectives and Adverbs

Adjectives and adverbs are connected by a slanted line to the words they modify. Notice in the second example that a conjunction joining two modifiers is placed on a broken line between them.

Her two cats ran away.

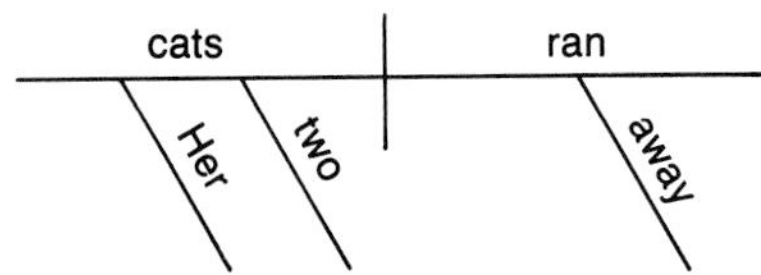

The small but valuable diamond sparkles brilliantly.

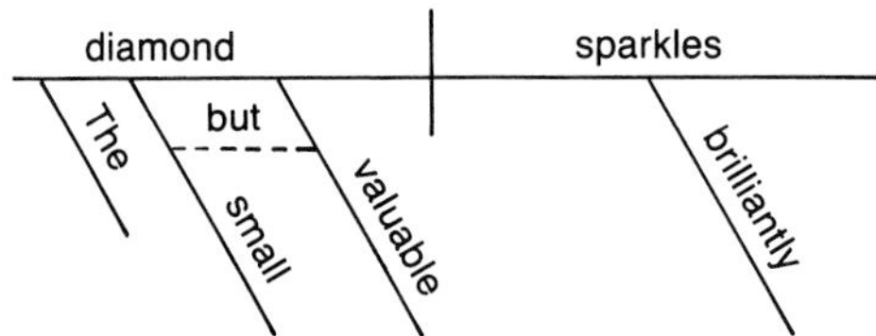

NOTE: Possessive pronouns, such as *her* in the first example, are diagramed like adjectives.

An Adverb That Modifies an Adjective or Another Adverb. This adverb is connected to the word it modifies. It is written on a line parallel to the word it modifies.

The rather stout man was walking very vigorously.

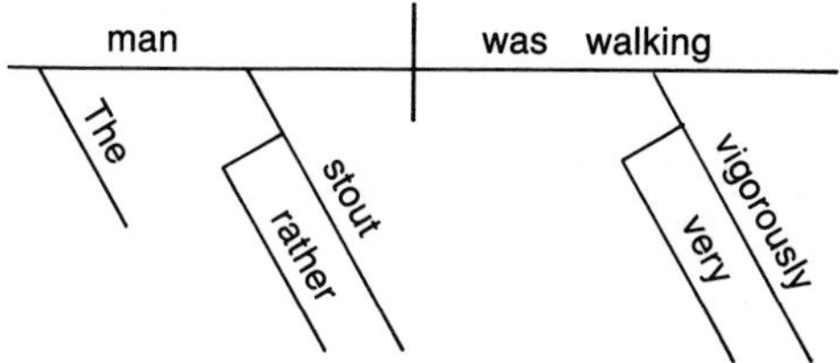

Complements

All complements except the indirect object are diagramed on the baseline with the subject and the verb.

Direct Objects. A short vertical line separates a direct object from the verb. Notice in the second example that the parts of a compound direct object are placed on parallel lines. The conjunction is placed on a broken line between them.

I have already seen that movie.

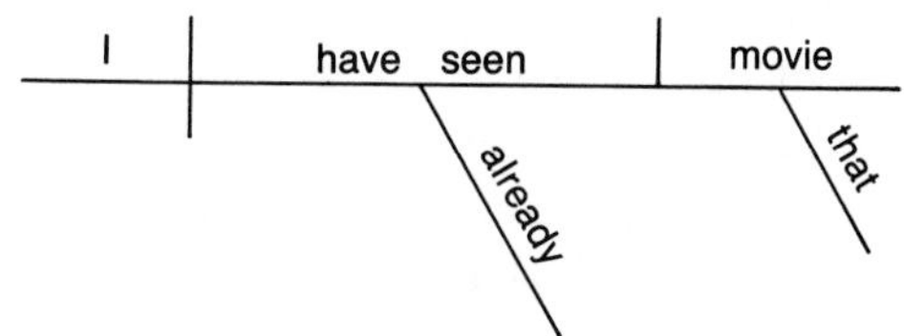

Buy four oranges and six bananas.

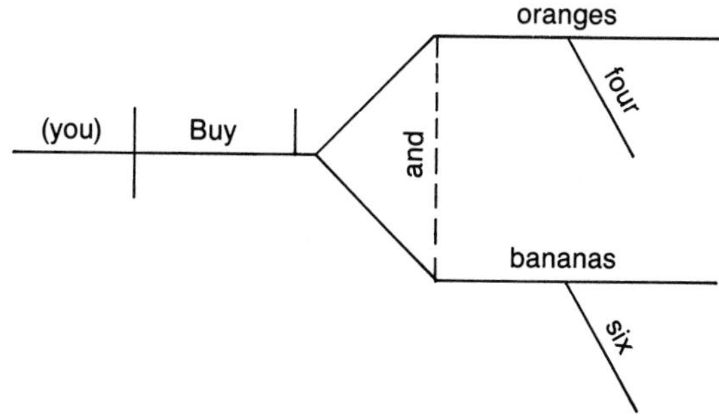

Indirect Objects. An indirect object is diagramed on a horizontal line that is connected to the verb by a slanted line. Notice in the second example that the parts of a compound indirect object are diagramed on horizontal parallel lines. The conjunction is placed on a broken line between them.

Send them an invitation.

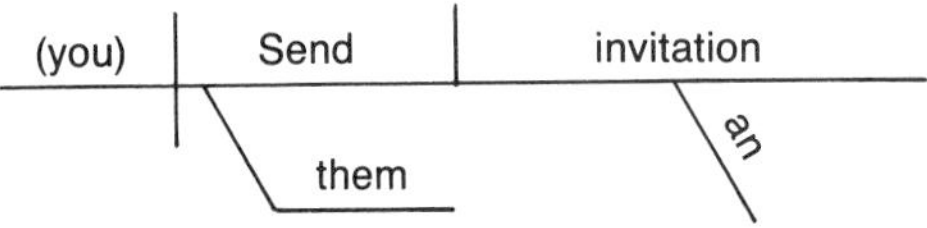

Aunt May bought David and me identical sweaters.

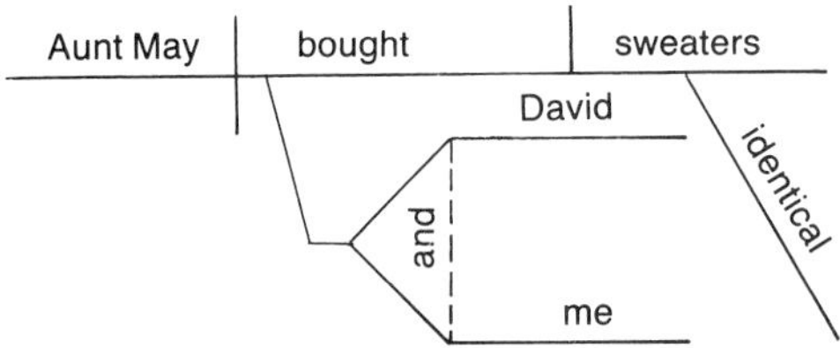

Objective Complements. Since an objective complement renames or describes the direct object, it is placed to the right of the direct object on the baseline. A slanted line that points toward the direct object separates the two complements. Notice in the second example that a compound objective complement is placed on horizontal parallel lines. The conjunction is placed on a broken line between them.

We named our dog King.

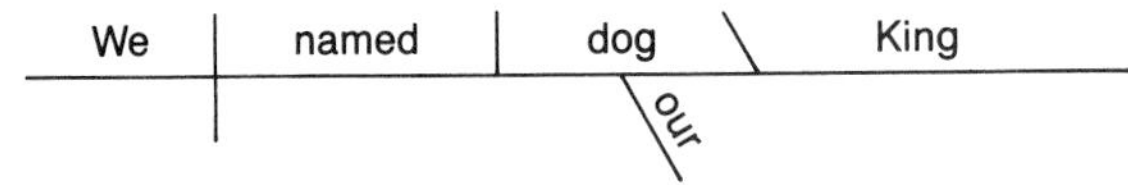

Mom will paint the kitchen yellow or green.

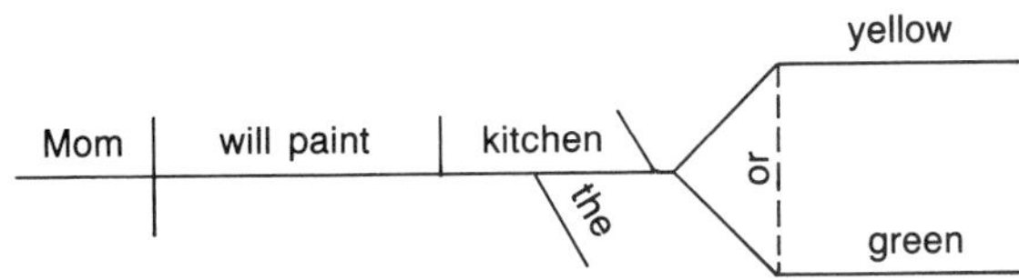

Subject Complements. A predicate nominative and a predicate adjective are diagramed in exactly the same way. They are placed on the baseline after the verb. A slanted line that points back toward the subject separates a subject complement from the verb. Notice in the third example that a compound subject complement is placed on horizontal parallel lines. The conjunction is placed on a broken line between them.

This camera was a birthday present.

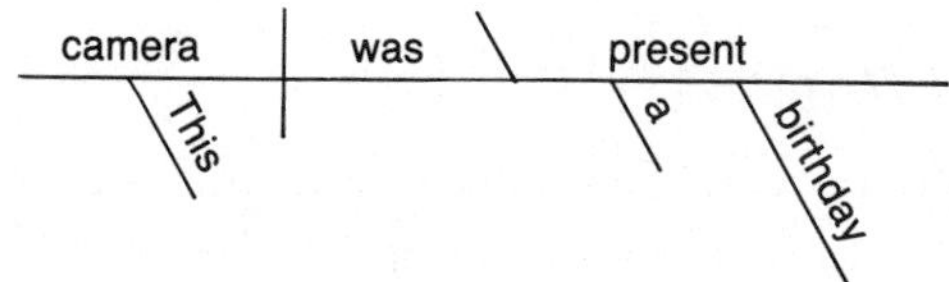

Your chili is quite tasty.

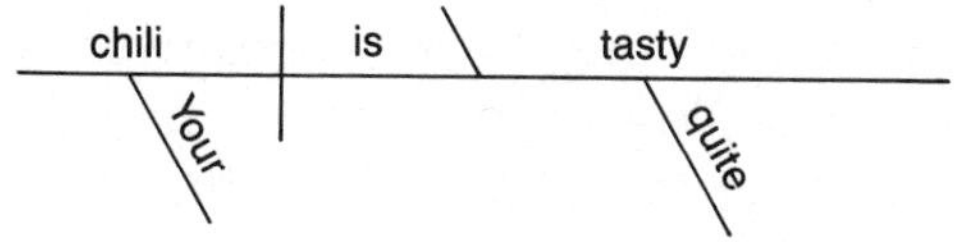

This lecture was not only interesting but also informative.

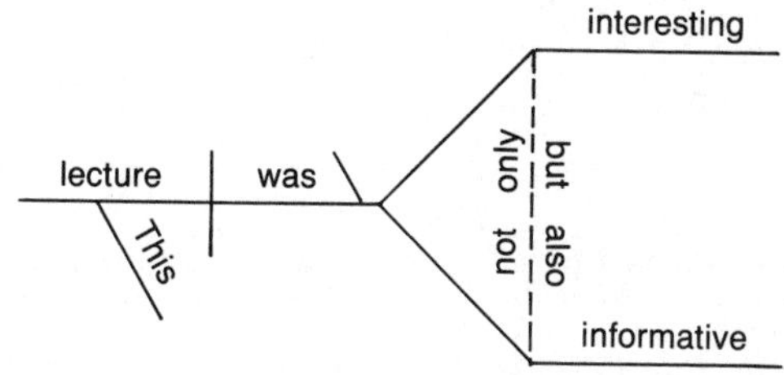

EXERCISE 10 Diagraming Sentences

Diagram the following sentences or copy them. If you copy them, draw one line under each subject and two lines under each verb. Then label each complement, using the following abbreviations.

direct object = *d.o.*
indirect object = *i.o.*
objective complement = *o.c.*
predicate nominative = *p.n.*
predicate adjective = *p.a.*

1. Our newspaper subscription should have been canceled.
2. Did you find your coat and his scarf?

3. Michael gave the officer his name.
4. Charlene became a new member yesterday.
5. The weather has been cold and dreary.
6. Read this interesting but funny article.
7. The club voted Paul chairman.
8. Very quietly the snake slithered away.
9. The lonely guard walked back and forth.
10. Stacy and Rico swam and floated.

Application to Writing

Each sentence you write seems unique—like the patterns and shapes of snowflakes. Looking more closely at the sentences you write, however, you will see that they all fall into one of six basic sentence patterns. You can vary your writing style by expanding these basic sentence patterns. They can be expanded by adding modifiers, appositives, prepositional phrases, and verbal phrases. Any of these patterns can also be expanded by making the subject, the verb, or any of the complements compound. In this way you create many variations within a particular pattern itself.

PATTERN 1: S-V (subject-verb)

S V
Cattle graze.

S V
Cattle belonging to Matt always graze in the far pasture.

PATTERN 2: S-V-O (subject-verb-direct object)

S V O
Girls swam laps.

S V O
The girls on the swim team effortlessly swam many laps.

PATTERN 3: S-V-I-O (subject-verb-indirect object-direct object)

S V I O
Todd sent me tickets.

S V I O
Todd unexpectedly sent me tickets to the Ice Capades.

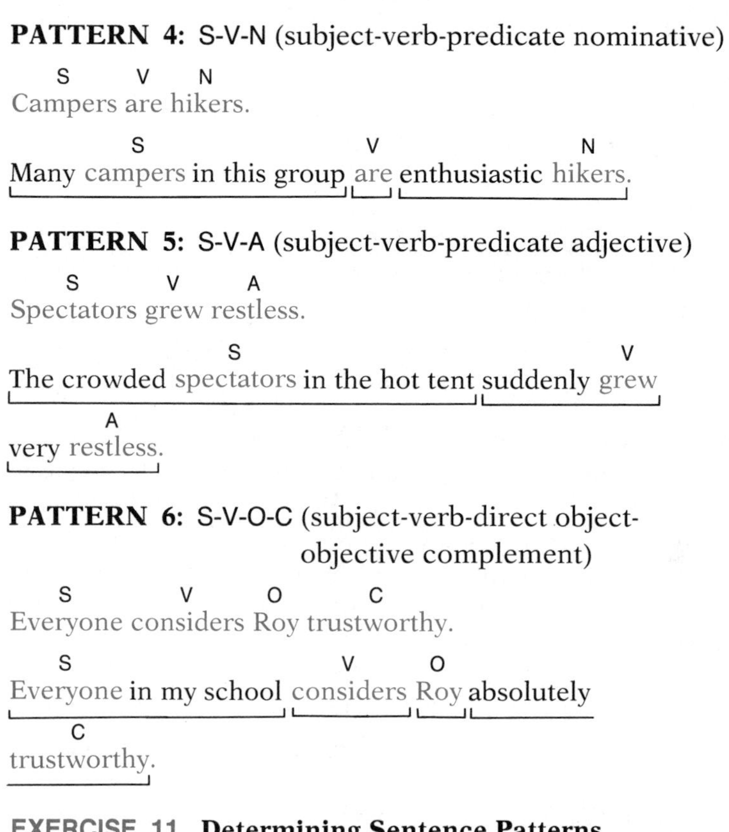

EXERCISE 11 Determining Sentence Patterns

Write the sentence pattern that each sentence follows.

1. Freshly cut hay always smells clean and sweet.
2. Many historians consider Harriet Tubman a major personality in United States history.
3. The coach of the field hockey team gave each member a certificate of achievement.
4. Fallen meteors have been discovered by scientists in various parts of the world.
5. The correct answer to the question is the last one.
6. The surprise birthday party made Melissa very happy.
7. The players on the basketball court anxiously awaited the referee's decision.
8. The sunsets along the prairie are unusually colorful.
9. The young tour guide gave us a detailed map of the area.
10. The sheet of paper in the typewriter is the last page of Kate's research paper.

EXERCISE 12 Writing Sentences

Write two sentences that follow each sentence pattern. Add prepositional phrases and other modifiers. Then after each sentence, identify the pattern.

CHAPTER REVIEW

A. Number your paper 1 to 10. Write the subjects and the verbs in the following sentences. If the subject is an understood *you,* write it in parentheses.

1. There are over 200 albums in the cabinet.
2. In Spain every large city and nearly every large town has a bull ring.
3. Did you contact the Better Business Bureau?
4. Most people remember Paul Revere's patriotism but forget his work as a silversmith and engraver.
5. Over the horizon that August day sailed the ships of Columbus's small fleet.
6. Revise your report carefully.
7. There are hundreds of inlets and bays along the coast of Nova Scotia.
8. The giant tortoise of the Galápagos Islands may weigh as much as 500 pounds and may live up to 150 years.
9. Have you seen the new computers on sale at Murphy's Hi-Tech?
10. Brad, take these shirts back to the store for a refund.

B. Number your paper 1 to 10. Write each complement. Then label each one, using the following abbreviations.

direct object = *d.o.* predicate nominative = *p.n.*
indirect object = *i.o.* predicate adjective = *p.a.*
objective complement = *o.c.*

1. Michelle showed Mom a copy of the yearbook.
2. At first the old trunk in the basement appeared empty.
3. The Puritans considered buttons a sign of vanity.
4. Many early settlers often found the Indians friendly and cooperative.
5. In Williamsburg, Virginia, we visited several shops and explored the old jail.

6. Their grandfather clock is quite old and very valuable.
7. James Monroe was the fourth president from Virginia.
8. Tell Alma and James that funny story about your uncle.
9. From the top of Mount Irazu in Costa Rica, a person can see the Atlantic Ocean and the Pacific Ocean.
10. Centuries ago a collection of books was a sign of wealth.

MASTERY TEST

Number your paper 1 to 10. Write the subject, the verb, and the underlined complement in each sentence. (A subject or a verb may be compound.) Then label each complement, using the following abbreviations.

direct object = *d.o.*
indirect object = *i.o.*
objective complement = *o.c.*
predicate nominative = *p.n.*
predicate adjective = *p.a.*

1. The state flower of Kentucky is the goldenrod.
2. This cereal has a low-sugar content.
3. Tell Marcy the score of last night's game.
4. There are many apartments in the complex still vacant.
5. I dyed the sweater maroon.
6. Kim grabbed an apple and raced to the bus stop.
7. Food and oxygen sweep in with the ocean tides and nourish the organisms on the rocks along the shore.
8. Is this his business number?
9. Our lawn and shrubs never looked greener.
10. The obedience trainer gave the dog's leash a quick snap.

3

Phrases

DIAGNOSTIC TEST

Number your paper 1 to 10. Write the phrases in the following sentences. Then label each one *prepositional, appositive, participial, gerund,* or *infinitive.*

EXAMPLE Raising beef cattle is a scientific process.
ANSWER Raising beef cattle — gerund

1. On our doorstep stood a forlorn dog without a collar.
2. George Washington, a great politician, was also a Virginia farmer.
3. Finding one's way through the new high school is not easy.
4. At parties Leslie is always asked to play her guitar.
5. Climbing the foremast, the sailor sighted dangerous coral reefs in the distance.
6. Before tomorrow morning I have to find a ride to school.
7. The bagpipe, Scotland's national instrument, can be traced back to ancient Mesopotamia.
8. My brother doesn't like waiting more than ten minutes for anyone.
9. We finally found Christopher studying in the library.
10. Delaware was the first state to ratify the Constitution.

The subject, the verb, and sometimes a complement are the foundation of a sentence. Once you are familiar with the basic structure of a sentence, you can build onto it. In a way, you become an architect. Instead of adding rooms, however, you are adding grammatical elements such as phrases. Various rooms have specific purposes, and their different shapes and sizes make a house interesting and unique. Similarly, different kinds of phrases have different purposes. Some are used to expand or qualify an idea, while others are used to show relationships between ideas. Using different kinds of phrases will also make your writing more varied and interesting.

3a A **phrase** is a group of related words that function as a single part of speech. A phrase does not have a subject or a verb.

This chapter will review prepositional phrases and appositive phrases. It will also review the three kinds of verbal phrases: *participial, gerund,* and *infinitive.*

PREPOSITIONAL PHRASES

A prepositional phrase is a group of words that begins with a preposition and ends with a noun or pronoun. That noun or pronoun is called the *object of the preposition.* *(See page 18 for a list of common prepositions.)* The prepositional phrases in the following sentences are in heavy type.

Before midnight the candidate **from Canton** conceded the election **to his opponent.**

In spite of the forecast, she is proceeding **with her plans for the barbecue.**

Prepositional phrases are used like single adjectives and adverbs to modify other words in a sentence.

Adjective Phrases

3b An **adjective phrase** is a prepositional phrase that is used to modify a noun or a pronoun.

An adjective phrase works exactly like a single adjective.

SINGLE ADJECTIVE Did you read **this** letter? [*This* tells which letter.]

ADJECTIVE PHRASE Did you read the letter **on the table?** [*On the table* also tells which letter.]

A single adjective and an adjective phrase answer the same questions: *Which one(s)?* and *What kind?*

WHICH ONE(S)? The horse **in the first stall** is a Morgan.

WHAT KIND? I like broccoli **with cheese sauce.**

An adjective phrase usually follows the word it modifies. That word could be the object of a preposition of another prepositional phrase.

Millions ***of* acres *of* the earth's surface** are still unexplored.

Two adjective phrases occasionally will modify the same noun or pronoun.

Put away the bag ***of* groceries *on* the counter.**

Adverb Phrases

3c An **adverb phrase** is a prepositional phrase that is used to modify a verb, an adjective, or an adverb.

An adverb phrase works exactly like a single adverb. Notice in the following examples that an adverb phrase, like a single adverb, modifies the whole verb phrase.

SINGLE ADVERB The senior choir will perform **soon.** [*Soon* tells when the choir will perform.]

ADVERB PHRASE The senior choir will perform **on Friday.** [*On Friday* also tells when the choir will perform.]

A single adverb and an adverb phrase answer the same question: *Where? When? How? To what extent?* or *To what degree?* Adverb phrases also answer the question *Why?*

WHERE? I left my sneakers **in my locker.**

WHEN? The rehearsal lasted **until ten o'clock.**

HOW? I planted the shrubs **according to his instructions.**

WHY? **Because of the heavy traffic,** we missed the plane.

Two or more adverb phrases can modify one verb.

For three days all the flags were flying **at half-mast.**

Over the weekend I put my records **into the cabinet.**

Although most adverb phrases modify a verb, some modify adjectives and adverbs.

MODIFYING AN ADJECTIVE Margo is kind **to everyone.**

MODIFYING AN ADVERB We arrived late **in the afternoon.**

Punctuation with Adverb Phrases

Do not place a comma after a short introductory adverb phrase—unless it is needed for clarity. You should, however, place a comma after an adverb phrase of four or more words or after several introductory phrases.

NO COMMA **From the tree** I can see the lake.
COMMA **From the tree on the hill,** I can see the lake.

EXERCISE 1 Recognizing Prepositional Phrases as Modifiers

Number your paper 1 to 10. Write the prepositional phrases in the following sentences. Then beside each phrase, write the word it modifies.

The First Modern Olympic Champion

1. The first champion of the modern Olympic Games was James Brendan Connolly.
2. In 1896, when he was a 27-year-old undergraduate at Harvard, he read about the revival of the ancient Greek games.
3. At that time Connolly was the triple-jump champion of the United States.

4. Connolly left school and went to Athens in March.
5. Ten American athletes and one trainer spent 16½ days on a ship to Naples and another day on a train to Athens.
6. On the following day, the Olympics began with the triple jump.
7. Before his turn Connolly surveyed the mark of the leader on the ground and threw his cap beyond it.
8. He then jumped beyond his cap and became the first champion of the modern Olympics.
9. He later became a journalist and the author of 25 novels.
10. Connolly died in 1957 at age 88.

EXERCISE 2 Identifying Prepositional Phrases

Number your paper 1 to 10. Write the prepositional phrases in the following sentences. Then beside each phrase, label it *adjective* or *adverb*.

A Future Space Station

1. In 1992, a United States space station may be orbiting around the earth.
2. One plan of the scientists foresees a modular station with canisterlike components.
3. These components would be ferried to the station by a space shuttle and assembled in orbit.
4. One of the many components would provide living quarters for eight crew members.
5. Electric power would be generated by huge solar panels.
6. The size of the station would totally eclipse present facilities in space.
7. The initial cost of this huge undertaking would be eight billion dollars.
8. Over the following eight years, another twelve billion dollars would be needed for additional modules.
9. The space station might perform experiments like those of a space shuttle.
10. The space station should be ready by the 500th anniversary of Columbus's discovery of the New World.

EXERCISE 3 Writing Sentences

In five to ten sentences, describe a rainstorm. Then underline each prepositional phrase.

APPOSITIVES AND APPOSITIVE PHRASES

3d An **appositive** is a noun or a pronoun that identifies or explains another noun or pronoun in the sentence.

An appositive usually follows the word or words it identifies or explains.

My friend **Bart** is moving to Kansas.

I enjoyed my favorite meal, **spaghetti.**

Most often an appositive is used with modifiers to form an *appositive phrase.* Notice in the second example that one or more prepositional phrases can be part of an appositive phrase.

New Bedford, **once the world's largest whaling port,** is located on Buzzards Bay in Massachusetts.

I just bought *Modern Poetry,* a **collection of poems by American authors.**

Punctuation with Appositives and Appositive Phrases

If an appositive contains information essential to the meaning of a sentence, no punctuation is needed. Information is essential if it identifies a person, place, or thing. If an appositive or an appositive phrase contains nonessential information, a comma or commas should be used to separate it from the rest of the sentence. Information is nonessential if it can be removed from the sentence without changing the basic meaning. An appositive that follows a proper noun is usually nonessential.

ESSENTIAL The famous artist **Manet** was born in 1832. [No commas are used because *Manet* is needed to identify which artist.]

NONESSENTIAL Manet**, a famous French artist,** was born in 1832. [Commas are used because the appositive can be removed from the sentence: Manet was born in 1832.]

EXERCISE 4 Finding Appositives and Appositive Phrases
Write the following sentences and underline each appositive or appositive phrase. Then add a comma or commas where needed.

1. Rover my golden retriever swims at the nearby pond whenever it is warm.
2. At the picnic Dad used Grandmother's chicken recipe a family secret.
3. Stainless steel a valuable alloy of iron is noted for its ability to resist rust and tarnish.
4. Georgia O'Keeffe the American abstract painter is famous for her paintings of the desert region of the Southwest.
5. Naomi Uemura a Japanese explorer was the first person to reach the North Pole alone by dogsled.
6. *Romeo and Juliet* a beautiful ballet was performed last evening.
7. The painting *Sunflowers* is one of Van Gogh's most recognized masterpieces.
8. March the first month of the Roman year was named for Mars the Roman god of war.
9. Did you check the thesaurus a good source of antonyms as well as synonyms?
10. Cheese a food rich in protein is also an excellent source of vitamins and minerals.

EXERCISE 5 Time-out for Review
Number your paper 1 to 10. Write the prepositional phrases and the appositive phrases in the following sentences. Then label each one *adjective, adverb,* or *appositive.*

Facts about Sports

1. In 1936, Jesse Owens, a famous track star, beat a horse in the hundred-yard race.
2. During the following year, Forest Towns, an Olympic hurdler, beat a horse in the hundred-yard hurdles.
3. Micki King, a gold-medal winner in the 1972 Olympics, became a diving coach at the U.S. Air Force Academy.
4. O. J. Simpson once had a severe case of rickets and wore leg braces.
5. Later Simpson set ground-gaining records in the National Football League.

6. Cathy Rigby, the first American winner in women's international gymnastics, had a lung ailment during her youth.
7. For six years Hugh Daily played baseball for several major-league teams.
8. As a pitcher he held a long-standing record of 19 strikeouts in a single game.
9. Hugh Daily was a man with only one arm.
10. Fourteen-year-old Nadia Comaneci had seven perfect scores in gymnastics at the Montreal Olympics.

VERBALS AND VERBAL PHRASES

Verbals are part of your everyday speech. If you have ever apologized for your *unmade* bed or told someone that you would be ready *to leave* at six o'clock, you have used verbals. A *verbal* is a verb form that is used not as a verb, but as a noun, an adjective, or an adverb. Because verbals are verb forms, they are usually lively words that add action and vitality to your writing. The three kinds of verbals are *participles, gerunds,* and *infinitives.*

Participles and Participial Phrases

3e A **participle** is a verb form that is used as an adjective.

Used like an adjective, a participle modifies a noun or a pronoun and answers the adjective question *Which one(s)?* or *What kind?* The participles in the examples are in heavy type. An arrow points to the word each participle modifies.

The **rising** sun was reflected on the **frozen** pond.

Broken tree branches lay across the **winding** road.

There are two kinds of participles: a present participle and a past participle. A *present participle* ends in *-ing,* while a *past participle* has a regular ending of *-ed* or an irregular ending of *-n, -t,* or *-en.*

PRESENT PARTICIPLES spinning, shrinking, ringing, winning
PAST PARTICIPLES buried, defeated, worn, bent, stolen

NOTE: Do not confuse a participle, which is used as an adjective, with the main verb of a sentence. A participle will have one or more helping verbs if it is used as a verb.

PARTICIPLE	Our **reserved** seats are in the sixth row.
VERB	We **have reserved** a room in the hotel.
PARTICIPLE	The **broken** clock on the mantel in the living room belonged to my grandfather.
VERB	During the lab period in chemistry, a glass beaker **was broken.**

Participial Phrases. Because a participle is a verb form, it can have modifiers and complements. Together these words form a *participial phrase.*

3f A **participial phrase** is a participle with its modifiers and complements—all working together as an adjective.

The following examples show three variations of the participial phrase. As you can see, a participle can be followed by an adverb, a prepositional phrase, or a complement.

PARTICIPLE WITH AN ADVERB	**Bought early,** her presents had to be hidden until her birthday.
PARTICIPLE WITH A PREPOSITIONAL PHRASE	Our dog, **barking at the back door,** wants to come in.
PARTICIPLE WITH A COMPLEMENT	Who is that young man **raising his hand?**

The present participle *having* is sometimes followed by a past participle.

Having seen *the flashing lights ahead,* we slowed down.

NOTE: Sometimes an adverb that modifies a participle can come before the participle. The adverb is part of the participial phrase.

A hurricane is a tropical cyclone **usually accompanied by heavy rains.**

Punctuation with Participial Phrases

Always place a comma after an introductory participial phrase.

Charging up the center, he streaked for a touchdown.

Participial phrases that come in the middle or at the end of a sentence may or may not need commas. If the information in a phrase is essential to identify the noun or the pronoun it describes, no commas are needed. If the information is nonessential, commas are needed to separate it from the rest of the sentence. A phrase is nonessential if it contains information that can be removed from the sentence without changing the basic meaning. A phrase that follows a proper noun is usually nonessential.

ESSENTIAL	The player **pitching for the Hornets** is Jason Sands. [No commas are used because the phrase is needed to identify which player.]
NONESSENTIAL	Jason Sands, **pitching for the Hornets,** has ten wins to his credit. [Commas are used because the phrase can be removed: Jason Sands has ten wins to his credit.]

EXERCISE 6 Finding Participial Phrases

Write the participial phrase in each sentence. Then beside each one, write the word or words it modifies.

Women Mayors

1. Winning the confidence of many voters, women have become the mayors of several large cities in the United States.
2. One report identifies some of the women elected in recent years.
3. Jane Byrne of Chicago captured the office held by Mayor Richard Daly for 21 years until his death.
4. Isabelle Cannon, having won the support of young people, became the mayor of Raleigh in a major upset.
5. Having complained unsuccessfully about a dangerous intersection, Janet Gray Hayes ran for mayor of San Jose.
6. Gaining prominence in a nonpartisan campaign, she went on to win the election.

7. Demonstrating her leadership abilities, Mayor Margaret Hance of Phoenix won a second term.
8. Mayor Carole McClellan of Austin, gathering 79 percent of the vote, also won a second term.
9. Effectively governing San Francisco, Dianne Feinstein became nationally prominent.
10. All of these outstanding women led the way for other women entering politics.

EXERCISE 7 Identifying and Punctuating Participial Phrases

Number your paper 1 to 10. Write the following sentences and underline each participial phrase. Then add a comma or commas where needed.

1. A device used as a crude steam engine about 2,000 years ago is today's lawn sprinkler.
2. Having been sewn by my great-great grandmother the patchwork quilt was a treasure.
3. Homing pigeons used as messengers fly at an average speed of 45 miles per hour.
4. The Hawthorne High School Athletic Club formed in 1980 has raised thousands of dollars for new equipment.
5. The boys rowing steadily appeared around the bend of the river.
6. Seeing the warblers in the tree Stanley stood perfectly still with his camera.
7. The light shining from the streetlight kept me awake nearly all night.
8. We found a record of our family history written in an old Bible.
9. Winding down the steep mountain road Ted drove very slowly.
10. Indians living high in the Andes have larger lungs than almost everyone else.

EXERCISE 8 Distinguishing between Verbs and Participles

Write two sentences for each of the following words. The first sentence should use the word as a verb. The second sentence should use the word as a participle in a participial phrase. Use punctuation where needed.

EXAMPLE	cracked
POSSIBLE ANSWER	Her voice cracked on the high notes. Cracked in three places, the vase couldn't be used.

1. barking
2. built
3. written
4. dashing
5. lost
6. dating
7. found
8. chiming
9. riding
10. confused

Gerunds and Gerund Phrases

3g A **gerund** is a verb form that is used as a noun.

Because a gerund ends in *-ing,* it looks like a present participle. A gerund, however, is used as a noun. The gerunds in the following examples are in heavy type.

Reading does not strain your eyes. [subject]
I thoroughly enjoy **painting.** [direct object]

Gerund Phrases. Like other verbals, a gerund can be combined with modifiers and complements to form a phrase.

3h A **gerund phrase** is a gerund with its modifiers and complements—all working together as a noun.

A gerund or a gerund phrase can be used in all the ways a noun can be used. As you can see from the following examples, a gerund phrase can take several forms. A gerund can be followed by an adverb, a prepositional phrase, or a complement.

SUBJECT	**Walking vigorously** is excellent exercise.
DIRECT OBJECT	I like **riding on roller coasters.**
INDIRECT OBJECT	My dad gave **cleaning the garage** his full attention last Saturday.
OBJECT OF A PREPOSITION	We drove to Philadelphia from Richmond without **making a single stop.**
PREDICATE NOMINATIVE	His greatest achievement was **making the Olympic team.**
APPOSITIVE	Heather's dream, **getting the lead in the play,** came true last November.

NOTE: The possessive form of a noun or a pronoun comes before a gerund and is considered part of the gerund phrase.

What do you think of **Eric's winning the high jump?**
Her finding that contact lens was fortunate.

EXERCISE 9 Finding Gerund Phrases
Write the gerund phrases in the following sentences. Then underline each gerund.

1. You can get a good seat by arriving early.
2. I couldn't understand her refusing the award.
3. Throwing a Frisbee competitively began in 1971.
4. The average grasshopper is capable of jumping a distance up to 20 times its body length.
5. My major fault is leaving everything until the last minute.
6. Abner Doubleday is generally credited with originating the game of baseball.
7. After jogging early in the morning, Leroy studied for his math exam.
8. Writing in her journal every day is a practice Jan started this year.
9. Joel's parents were delighted with his winning the art contest.
10. Doubling the diameter of a pipe increases fourfold its capacity for transmitting liquids.

EXERCISE 10 Determining the Uses of Gerund Phrases
Number your paper 1 to 10. Write each gerund phrase. Then label the use of each one, using the following abbreviations.

subject = *subj.*	object of a preposition = *o.p.*
direct object = *d.o.*	predicate nominative = *p.n.*
indirect object = *i.o.*	appositive = *appos.*

1. Collecting tiny china dogs is Julie's hobby.
2. My exercise schedule includes doing 50 push-ups each morning.
3. In 1874, Thomas Edison improved the typewriter by substituting metal parts for wooden ones.
4. For a change, give baking bread a try.
5. One distinction of Franklin Pierce's administration was his retaining the same cabinet for four years.

6. Several students from my high school succeeded in finishing the marathon.
7. Julia has an unusual job, taking three dogs for their morning walk.
8. Sarah's plans for riding her new bicycle were delayed by the storm.
9. Being a good athlete involves training the mind as well as the body.
10. The highlight of my day was seeing my article in the school newspaper.

EXERCISE 11 Distinguishing between Gerunds and Participles

Write two sentences for each of the following words. The first sentence should use the word as a gerund. The second sentence should use the word as a participle. Use punctuation where needed.

EXAMPLE taking

POSSIBLE ANSWER Karen was nervous about taking the math test.
The students taking the math test in room 401 should not be disturbed.

1. holding 2. collecting 3. finding 4. thawing 5. studying

Infinitives and Infinitive Phrases

3i An **infinitive** is a verb form that usually begins with *to*. It is used as a noun, an adjective, or an adverb.

Infinitives do not look like the other verbals because they usually begin with the word *to*. An infinitive has several forms. The infinitives of *change,* for example, are *to change, to be changing, to have changed, to be changed,* and *to have been changed.* The infinitives in the following examples are in heavy type.

I hope **to be invited.** [noun—direct object]
During the interview Pat couldn't think of anything **to say.** [adjective]
That unexpected compliment was nice **to hear.** [adverb]

NOTE: Do not confuse a prepositional phrase that begins with *to* with an infinitive. A prepositional phrase ends with a noun or a pronoun; an infinitive ends with a verb form.

PREPOSITIONAL PHRASE	I'll drive you **to school.**
INFINITIVE	When is it time **to eat?**

Infinitive Phrases. An infinitive can be combined with modifiers and complements to form an *infinitive phrase.*

3j An **infinitive phrase** is an infinitive with its modifiers and complements—all working together as a noun, an adjective, or an adverb.

The following examples show how an infinitive phrase can be used as a noun, an adjective, or an adverb. Notice that, like other verbals, an infinitive phrase can also take several forms. An infinitive, for example, can be followed by an adverb, a complement, or a prepositional phrase.

NOUN	**To sew well** requires patience. [subject]
	I tried **to get two tickets.** [direct object]
ADJECTIVE	These are the letters **to be mailed by tomorrow.**
ADVERB	We printed the story **to create public awareness.**

NOTE: *To* is occasionally omitted when an infinitive follows such verbs as *dare, feel, help, make, let, need, see,* or *watch.* It is, nevertheless, understood to be there.

We helped **collect litter from the park.** [to collect]

EXERCISE 12 Finding Infinitive Phrases

Write the infinitive phrases in the following sentences. Then underline each infinitive.

1. Jason was the first freshman to play on the varsity team.
2. To be brave from a distance is easy.—AESOP
3. Joshua helped serve the refreshments.
4. Paul was the first person to see the fire.
5. Dad wanted to raise vegetables in containers on the roof.
6. Grandfather is happy to have found an apartment.
7. Flora's plan was to jog daily.

8. Approximately 46,000 pounds of earth must be mined and sifted to produce a half-carat diamond.
9. The mechanic promised to service the car today.
10. It is about ten times easier to shoot a hole in one in golf than it is to roll a perfect 300 game in bowling.

EXERCISE 13 Determining the Uses of Infinitive Phrases
Number your paper 1 to 10. Write the infinitive phrases in the following sentences. Then label how each one is used—*noun, adjective,* or *adverb.*

1. Balboa was the first explorer to see the Pacific Ocean.
2. The early years of your life are the best time to learn a foreign language.
3. Beth hopes to enter the Air Force Academy in September.
4. The students hurried to reach their classrooms on time.
5. To become a veterinarian is my sister's chief ambition.
6. Charlene was eager to start her new job.
7. Dad suggested books to use as references for our term papers.
8. My grandmother attends the local night school to improve her Spanish.
9. Have you tried to find a summer job?
10. Jeffrey's hope is to study fashion design after high school.

EXERCISE 14 Writing Sentences
Write sentences that follow the directions below.

1. Use an infinitive phrase as a subject.
2. Use an infinitive phrase as a direct object.
3. Use an infinitive phrase as an adjective.
4. Use an infinitive phrase as an adverb.
5. Use two infinitive phrases.

EXERCISE 15 Time-out for Review
Number your paper 1 to 20. Write the verbal phrases in the following sentences. Then label each one *participial, gerund,* or *infinitive.*

Firsts for Women

1. Born in New York in 1856, Louise Blanchard Bethune is considered the first woman architect.
2. After designing many buildings, she became the first woman to gain membership in the American Institute of Architects.

3. The first woman canoeist to make a solo trip down the Mississippi River was Rebecca Johnson.
4. Starting in Minnesota, Johnson finally arrived in New Orleans 96 days later.
5. Making her first ascent in 1880, Mary H. Myers became the first woman balloon pilot.
6. She is credited with developing better balloon fabrics and designing portable hydrogen generators.
7. In 1886, Myers ascended to an altitude of four miles in a balloon filled with natural gas.
8. Making such an ascent was remarkable because the aircraft was not equipped with oxygen.
9. The first American woman to receive the Nobel Peace Prize was Jane Addams.
10. In 1931, she was recognized for establishing a center for social reform in Chicago.
11. Changing her name to Dale, Dalia Messick submitted her comic strip "Brenda Star" to the *Chicago Tribune* in 1940.
12. "Brenda Star," read by 7.5 million people today, was also the first comic strip to feature a woman.
13. The first woman to be pictured on a United States coin in circulation was suffragist Susan B. Anthony.
14. Treasury officials had first considered picturing only a representative female figure such as Miss Liberty.
15. Feminists, however, lobbied for honoring a real individual.
16. Anthony, appearing later on a one-dollar coin, was selected over Jane Addams and Eleanor Roosevelt.
17. Long before Sarah Walker became the first black woman millionaire, she supported herself by taking in laundry.
18. In 1905, after 18 years as a laundress, she decided to create a line of hair products especially for black women.
19. Working at home, she formulated shampoos and oils.
20. Concerned for other black women, Walker created many college scholarships.

MISPLACED AND DANGLING MODIFIERS

The meaning of a sentence sometimes gets confused because a modifier is placed too far away from the word it describes. When that happens, the modifier appears to describe some other word. Such modifiers are called *misplaced modifiers.* Since all the phrases, except gerund phrases, can be used as modifiers, remember to place them as close as possible to the word or words they describe.

MISPLACED Rob will answer this ad for a typist **in the *Globe.***
CORRECT Rob will answer this ad **in the *Globe*** for a typist.

MISPLACED I found my keys looking through my jacket.
CORRECT **Looking through my jacket,** I found my keys.

Another problem sometimes rises when a phrase that is being used as a modifier does not have a word to describe. This kind of phrase is called a *dangling modifier.*

DANGLING **To be a good quarterback,** calm under pressure is needed. [*Calm* cannot be a good quarterback.]
CORRECT **To be a good quarterback,** you need to be calm under pressure.

EXERCISE 16 Correcting Misplaced and Dangling Modifiers
Write the following sentences, correcting the error in each one. To do this, follow one of two steps: (1) Place a phrase closer to the word it modifies, or (2) Add words and change the sentence around so that the phrase has a noun or a pronoun to modify. Use punctuation where needed.

1. Rummaging through the trash can, we saw the raccoon.
2. I followed Lisa as she ran around the pond on my bike.
3. Rumbling and booming in the distance, I was awakened by the thunder.
4. To win a medal in the Olympics, dedication as well as training is essential.
5. I could see Mr. Blake mowing his lawn through the upstairs window.
6. Walking through the mall, Kate's eyes fell on a red coat.
7. As the plane descended, we no longer could see the sun blazing brightly in the sky through the dark clouds.
8. Rowing steadily, the boat was brought to the dock.
9. To pass the SAT's, a solid foundation in English and math is necessary.
10. Roaring loudly, Juan took a picture of the lion.

DIAGRAMING PHRASES

The way a phrase is used in a sentence determines how and where the phrase is diagramed.

Prepositional Phrases. An adjective phrase or an adverb phrase is connected to the word it modifies. The preposition is placed on a connecting slanted line. The object of a preposition is placed on a horizontal line that is attached to the slanted line. The following example includes two adjective phrases and one adverb phrase. Notice that an adjective phrase can modify the object of the preposition of another adjective phrase.

The assignment for Mr. Roger's class in English literature must be completed by tomorrow.

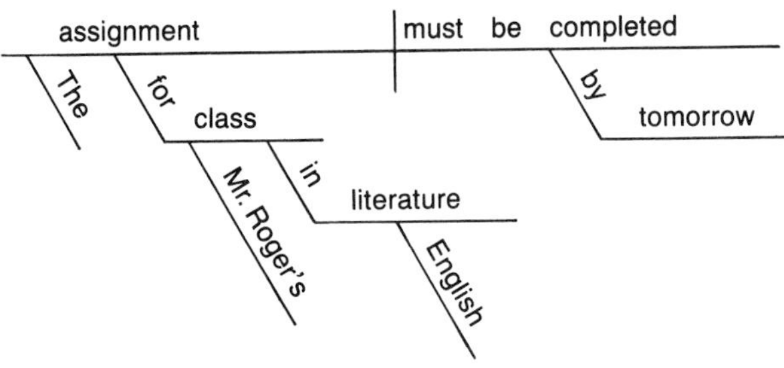

An adverb phrase that modifies an adjective or an adverb needs an additional horizontal line that is connected to the word modified.

The two trophies stood close to each other on the mantel.

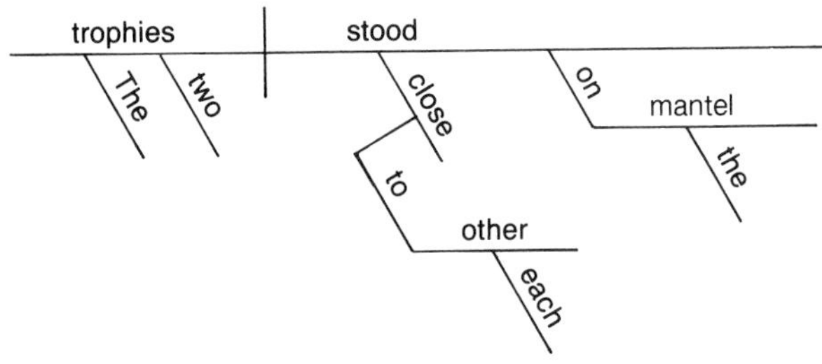

Appositives and Appositive Phrases. An appositive is diagramed in parentheses next to the word it identifies or explains. Its modifiers are placed directly underneath it.

The appetizer, egg rolls with hot mustard, was delicious.

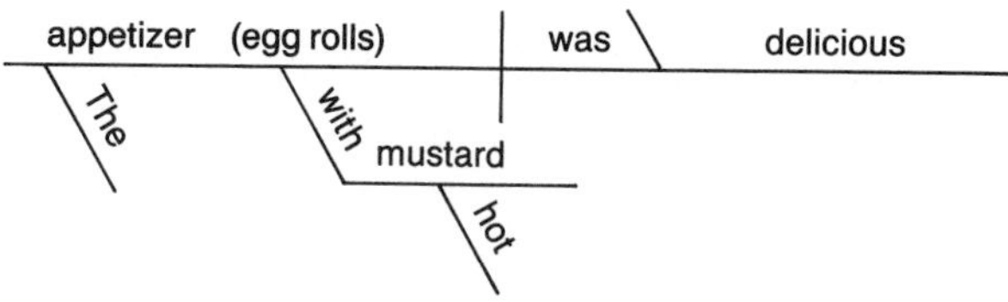

Participial Phrases. Like an adjective, a participle is always diagramed under the word it modifies. The participle, however, is written in a curve. In the following example, the participial phrase includes a complement.

Seeing the time, Marcy rushed out the door.

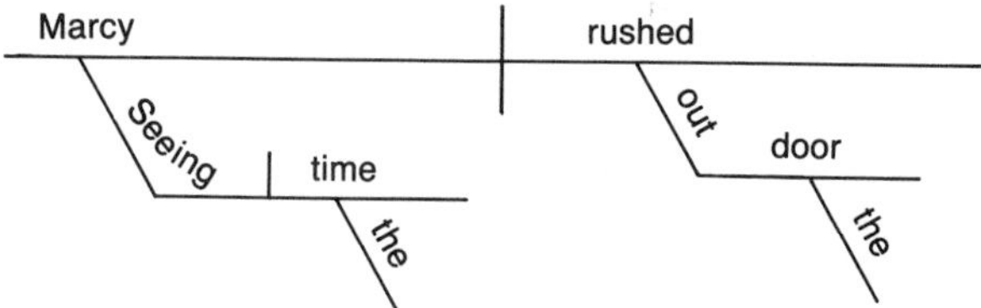

Gerund Phrases. A gerund phrase is diagramed in all the places a noun is diagramed. In the following example, a gerund phrase is used as a direct object. A prepositional phrase and an adverb are part of the gerund phrase.

I thoroughly enjoy sitting quietly by the lake.

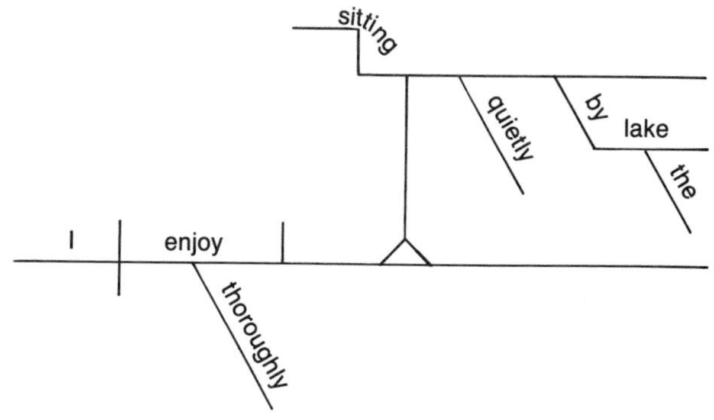

Infinitive Phrases. Because an infinitive phrase may be used as a noun, an adjective, or an adverb, it is diagramed in several ways. The following example shows one infinitive phrase used as an adjective and one used as a predicate nominative. Both infinitive phrases have complements.

The only way to have a friend is to be one.—EMERSON

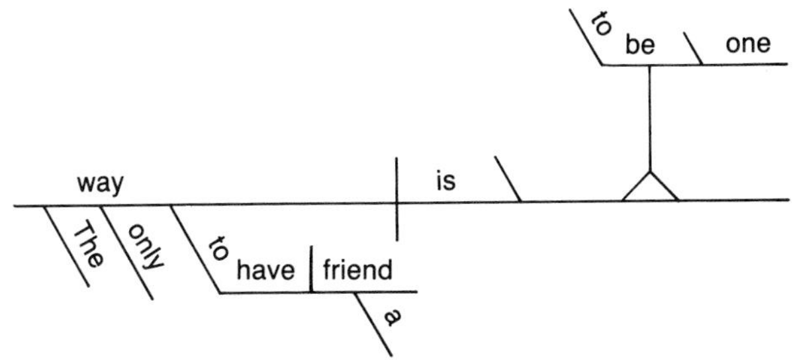

If the *to* of an infinitive is omitted from the sentence, it is diagramed in parentheses. The infinitive phrase in the following example is used as a direct object.

Do you dare interview the mayor?

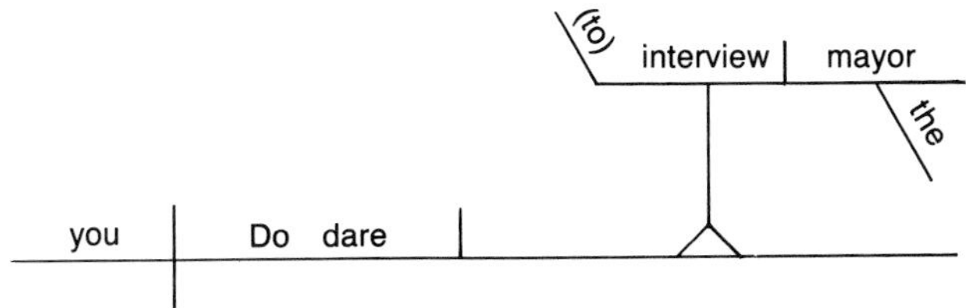

EXERCISE 17 Diagraming Phrases

Diagram the following sentences or copy them. If you copy them, draw one line under each subject and two lines under each verb. Put parentheses around each phrase. Then label each phrase *prepositional, appositive, participial, gerund,* or *infinitive.*

1. The costume from the wardrobe collection is perfect.
2. We arrived later in the evening.
3. Riding a surfboard requires skill.
4. At the fair we saw Theresa riding a unicycle.
5. My neighbors own Fix It Yourself, the hardware store on Tyler Road.

6. Michael hopes to finish his report soon.
7. Kim, the captain of the gymnastics team, won a medal.
8. Finding her notebook, Sandy sighed with relief.
9. I enjoy studying in the library.
10. Joshua did not dare contradict the referee.

Application to Writing

An old cliché states, "Variety is the spice of life." Using phrases—particularly verbal phrases—will add variety and spice to your writing. One way to include phrases in your writing is to use them to combine two sentences.

TWO SENTENCES	The Manx is an extremely rare breed of cat. It has no tail.
ONE SENTENCE	The Manx is an extremely rare breed of cat **with no tail.** [prepositional phrase]
TWO SENTENCES	Yesterday in English we read "Jabberwocky." It is a poem by Lewis Carroll.
ONE SENTENCE	Yesterday in English we read "Jabberwocky," **a poem by Lewis Carroll.** [appositive phrase]
TWO SENTENCES	We heard something outside the tent. We became alarmed.
ONE SENTENCE	**Hearing something outside the tent,** we became alarmed. [participial phrase]
TWO SENTENCES	Gary walked the first two batters. Then he struck out three in a row.
ONE SENTENCE	After **walking the first two batters,** Gary struck out three in a row. [gerund phrase]
TWO SENTENCES	We hung a dozen Japanese lanterns outside. They lighted the patio.
ONE SENTENCE	We hung a dozen Japanese lanterns outside **to light the patio.** [infinitive phrase]

EXERCISE 18 Combining Sentences with Phrases
Combine each pair of sentences by using phrases. Use punctuation where needed.

1. Henry Thoreau lived in a cabin. It was by Walden Pond.
2. Dad made a fruit salad. He planned to take it to the picnic.

3. Black labradors have webbed feet. They are skilled at retrieving objects from the water.
4. We climbed to the top of the Statue of Liberty. It was an exhausting experience.
5. The Nobel Peace Prize was first awarded in 1901. It is one of the world's greatest honors.
6. Todd lay awake most of the night. He was worried about his final exams the next day.
7. David Scott was the first person to drive a vehicle on the moon. He is an American.
8. Last night there was an informative debate. The debate was between the two Democratic candidates.
9. The desert Arabs wrap thick layers of wool around their heads. This keeps out the heat.
10. Patty Berg is a member of the World Golf Hall of Fame. She works tirelessly to help people with cerebral palsy.

CHAPTER REVIEW

Number your paper 1 to 20. Write the phrases in the following sentences. Then label each one *prepositional, appositive, participial, gerund,* or *infinitive.*

1. Scoring five runs in the first inning, the Red Sox took command of the game.
2. At the end of February, Jonathan decided to apply to the Institute of Electronics near Denver.
3. Carrying pollen back to the hive keeps bees busy.
4. Meteors, known as shooting stars, may be seen on almost any clear night.
5. Cervantes and Shakespeare, two of the foremost writers in history, both died on April 23, 1616.
6. Seaweed sometimes grows to 200 feet in length.
7. I enjoy swimming laps every morning.
8. An old game, played since ancient times, is marbles.
9. Do you want to frame your diploma?
10. Running the bases clockwise was the custom during the early days of baseball.
11. Joan, my aunt from Tulsa, was an Olympic swimmer.
12. The secretary handed me her notes, written in shorthand.

13. Dan's father enjoys restoring antique cars.
14. The President, planning a new appointment to the cabinet, studied the list of qualified candidates.
15. In some places in the world, geese are trained to tend sheep.
16. Dad and Mom stopped to admire the laurel, the state flower of Connecticut.
17. Jimmy Carter was the first president of the United States to have been born in a hospital.
18. The sun, containing 99.8 percent of the total mass of the solar system, is truly colossal in size.
19. On Career Day Susan plans to attend the dental lecture.
20. At the recital Marilyn's triumph was playing the entire sonata from memory.

MASTERY TEST

Number your paper 1 to 10. Write the phrases in the following sentences. Then label each one *prepositional, appositive, participial, gerund,* or *infinitive.*

1. Banging the gavel for order, the moderator began the meeting.
2. It is very difficult to play the French horn correctly.
3. West Point, the United States Military Academy in New York, was established in 1802.
4. Photographing old buildings is my sister's hobby.
5. Working tirelessly for three days, Dennis wallpapered the bedroom.
6. The coach doesn't like your missing Saturday's practice.
7. Every person must swim 25 laps to qualify for the swim team.
8. Mrs. Grayson, my history teacher, is president of the Historical Society.
9. One of Pepe's goals is making the varsity football team.
10. Travelers driving from Los Angeles to Reno, Nevada, will have to travel northwest.

4

Clauses

DIAGNOSTIC TEST

Number your paper 1 to 10. Then label each sentence *simple, compound, complex,* or *compound-complex.*

EXAMPLE We found the piece of the puzzle that was missing.
ANSWER complex

1. The average number of solar eclipses in a year is two.
2. Either the electricity is off, or we blew a fuse.
3. Ann explained why she chose Fisher Junior College.
4. Although whales usually bear only one offspring, baby twin whales have been reported.
5. Grove Street and Kendall Avenue will be repaved next week.
6. Bentley High, which you predicted would win, lost by 36 points.
7. I heard the alarm clock but couldn't get out of bed.
8. My first choice was the Mexican restaurant that had just opened down the road, but Elizabeth wanted Chinese food.
9. As we entered the room, we immediately noticed that the meeting had already started.
10. I wrote to the mayor, but he has not answered my letter yet.

You could paint a landscape with just one color, but it would be a dull, unrealistic picture when you finished. You could also write all simple sentences. People would certainly understand what you wrote. Like the picture painted all in one color, however, your written work would be a dull, unrealistic representation of ordinary speech.

You can add color and interest to your writing by varying the structure of your sentences. One way to do this is to include various combinations of clauses within your sentences.

4a A **clause** is a group of words that has a subject and a verb.

This chapter will cover independent and subordinate clauses and show you how a subordinate clause can be used as an adverb, an adjective, or a noun. This chapter will also show you how clauses form different kinds of sentences.

INDEPENDENT AND SUBORDINATE CLAUSES

The two kinds of clauses are *independent clauses* and *subordinate clauses.*

4b An **independent (or main) clause** can usually stand alone as a sentence because it expresses a complete thought.

When an independent clause stands alone, it is called a *sentence*. When it appears in a sentence with another clause, it is called a *clause*. In the following examples, each subject is underlined once, and each verb is underlined twice. Notice that each independent clause can stand alone as a separate sentence.

[independent clause: Greg waited a long time,] but [independent clause: his mail order never arrived.]

[sentence: Greg waited a long time.] [sentence: His mail order never arrived.]

4c A **subordinate (or dependent) clause** cannot stand alone as a sentence, because it does not express a complete thought.

A subordinate clause has a subject and a verb; nevertheless, it does not express a complete thought. It can never stand alone as a sentence. A subordinate clause is dependent upon an independent clause to complete its meaning.

subordinate clause — independent clause
When we saw the game, we sat in the bleachers.

independent clause — subordinate clause
We found some blue paint that matches the wallpaper.

EXERCISE 1 Distinguishing between Independent and Subordinate Clauses

Label each underlined clause *independent* or *subordinate*.

Charles Dickens

1. Dickens's early life gave little indication that he would become one of England's greatest writers.
2. When his father was sent to debtors' prison, Dickens, at the age of 12, was forced to work in a factory.
3. This experience was so horrible that Dickens could hardly speak of it in later life.
4. He did, however, refer to this humiliation when he wrote his autobiographical novel *David Copperfield*.
5. After Dickens was freed from the factory, his parents sent him to school.
6. While he worked as a reporter for parliamentary debates, he began to write.
7. After much early success, Dickens was asked to write comic pieces that were accompanied by illustrations.
8. Later these were turned into the famous *Pickwick Papers*, which were an enormous hit with the public.
9. When Dickens died in 1870, the whole world mourned.
10. England bestowed upon Dickens its highest honor, which was burial in the Poets' Corner of Westminster Abbey.

USES OF SUBORDINATE CLAUSES

Like a phrase, a subordinate clause can be used in a sentence as an adverb, an adjective, or a noun. Keep in mind, however, the basic difference between a clause and a phrase. A clause has a subject and a verb; a phrase does not.

Adverb Clauses

4d

An **adverb clause** is a subordinate clause that is used as an adverb to modify a verb, an adjective, or an adverb.

An adverb clause is used just like a single adverb or an adverb phrase. In the following examples, the single adverb, the adverb phrase, and the adverb clause all modify the verb *arrived.*

SINGLE ADVERB	The train arrived **late.**
ADVERB PHRASE	The train arrived **at five o'clock.**
ADVERB CLAUSE	The train arrived **while we were parking.**

In addition to the questions *How? When? Where? How much?* and *To what extent?* adverb clauses also answer *Under what condition?* and *Why?* Although most adverb clauses modify verbs, some modify adjectives and adverbs.

MODIFYING A VERB	**After Rusty had eaten,** I took him for a walk. [answers *When?*]
MODIFYING AN ADJECTIVE	Your chili tastes spicier **than mine does.** [answers *How much?*]
MODIFYING AN ADVERB	I worked harder **than I had ever worked before.** [answers *To what extent?*]

Subordinating Conjunctions. An adverb clause usually begins with a *subordinating conjunction.* Notice in the following list such words as *after, before, since,* and *until,* which can also be used as prepositions.

Common Subordinating Conjunctions

after	as soon as	in order that	until
although	as though	since	when
as	because	so that	whenever
as far as	before	than	where
as if	even though	though	wherever
as long as	if	unless	while

An adverb clause that describes a verb modifies the whole verb phrase.

You can watch the photo session **as long as you are quiet.**

As soon as you hear from the college, you must call us.

Punctuation with Adverb Clauses

Place a comma after an introductory adverb clause.

Since Jay was sick, I took his place.

If an adverb clause interrupts an independent clause, place a comma before it and after it.

The guests, **after they had eaten,** applauded the cook.

EXERCISE 2 Finding Adverb Clauses
Number your paper 1 to 10. Write each adverb clause. Then write the word or words each clause modifies.

1. When a thunderstorm strikes on a hot day, hail may occur.
2. As soon as you finish your homework, call me.
3. We went to the dance so that we could hear the band.
4. We waited for them longer than we should have.
5. After the snowstorm ended, we shoveled the walk.
6. We ate dinner later than we had originally planned.
7. We can fill all these orders if we get more help.
8. Before William Butler Yeats wrote plays for the Abbey Theater, he had written many poems celebrating Ireland.
9. Complete the application after you read the directions.
10. Because tuna need a flow of water across their gills in order to breathe, they would suffocate if they ever stopped swimming.

EXERCISE 3 Identifying and Punctuating Adverb Clauses
Write the following sentences and underline each adverb clause. Then add a comma or commas where needed.

1. When the rain occurred we ran for shelter.
2. All day we acted as though we had forgotten his birthday.
3. Because Judy studied she did well on the French test.
4. Magnesium when it is ignited burns with a white light.

5. Even though we were cold we played hockey for an hour.
6. The circumference of the earth is about 42 miles greater around the equator than it is around the poles.
7. The mayor left after he had completed his speech.
8. A blue whale gains about 200 pounds a day until it is fully grown.
9. Since Niagara Falls formed 10,000 years ago they have moved seven miles upstream.
10. If our basketball team wins we will celebrate.

Elliptical Clauses. Words in an adverb clause are sometimes omitted to streamline a sentence and to prevent unnecessary repetition. Although the words are omitted, they are still understood to be there. An adverb clause in which words are missing is called an *elliptical clause.* Notice in the following examples that the elliptical clauses begin with *than* or *as* and are missing only the verb. *(See pages 153–154 for information about pronouns used in elliptical clauses.)*

Alvin understands the rules better **than I.** [The completed elliptical clause reads *than I do.*]

A hippopotamus may weigh as much **as a medium-sized truck.** [The completed elliptical clause reads *as a medium-sized truck weighs.*]

Sometimes the subject and the verb, or just part of the verb phrase, may be omitted in an elliptical clause.

I sold more tickets this weekend **than last weekend.** [The completed elliptical clause reads *than I sold last weekend.*]

When sighted, the plane had already lost one engine. [The completed elliptical clause reads *When it was sighted.*]

EXERCISE 4 Recognizing Elliptical Clauses
Write the completed version of each elliptical clause.

1. Water has more uses than any other single substance.
2. My old coat is warmer than my new one.
3. My father is as fine a cook as my mother.
4. When told about the project, Charlene volunteered.
5. Helium weighs about one seventh as much as air.
6. That kind of boot is better for hiking than this kind.

7. *David Copperfield,* though not a biography, includes many details of Dickens's life.
8. On July 8, 1835, the Liberty Bell cracked while tolling the death of Chief Justice John Marshall.
9. Christopher and Michael did more push-ups and sit-ups today than yesterday.
10. I like football more than baseball.

Adjective Clauses

4e An **adjective clause** is a subordinate clause that is used like an adjective to modify a noun or a pronoun.

An adjective clause is used like a single adjective or an adjective phrase. In the examples, the single adjective, the adjective phrase, and the adjective clause all modify *fire.*

SINGLE ADJECTIVE	The **intense** fire destroyed the building.
ADJECTIVE PHRASE	The fire **with billowing flames and thick smoke** destroyed the building.
ADJECTIVE CLAUSE	The fire, **which raged out of control,** destroyed the building.

Like a single adjective, an adjective clause answers the question *Which one(s)?* or *What kind?*

WHICH ONE(S)?	The teachers **who chaperoned the dance last night** enjoyed themselves.
WHAT KIND?	He bought himself running shoes **that have extra support for his arches.**

Relative Pronouns. A *relative pronoun* almost always begins an adjective clause. A relative pronoun relates an adjective clause to its antecedent—the noun or pronoun the clause modifies. The word *where* or *when* is also occasionally used to introduce an adjective clause.

Relative Pronouns				
who	whom	whose	which	that

Lakeview's football team, **which won the state championship last year,** hasn't won a single game so far this year.

The Dalys have just moved here from Miami, **where they had lived all their lives.**

NOTE: The relative pronoun *that* will occasionally be omitted from an adjective clause. It is still understood to be there.

Poison ivy is something **everyone should avoid.** [*That everyone should avoid* is the complete adjective clause.]

EXERCISE 5 Finding Adjective Clauses

Number your paper 1 to 10. Write the adjective clause in each sentence. Then beside each one, write the word it modifies.

The History of Cats

1. Domestic cats, which are valued both for their beauty and ability to destroy rats and mice, have a long and colorful history.
2. The Egyptians, who are credited with domesticating cats around 3500 B.C., put cats to work protecting their grain.
3. The cat, which was revered by the Egyptians, was also used as a retriever by hunters.
4. The Egyptians, who shaved off their eyebrows to mourn the death of a cat, often made dead cats into mummies.
5. In the sixth century B.C., Aesop, whose fables sometimes included cats, suggested cats' popularity at that time.
6. Cats were also connected with astrology in China, where the cat first appeared around 1100 B.C.
7. In ancient Rome, where cats were a symbol of liberty, the people regarded these pets as guardians of their homes.
8. Domestic cats that traveled with their owners came to the New World during the 1600s.
9. The first cat show, which was held in London in 1871, started the trend toward breeding pedigreed cats.
10. Today the cat-care business, which includes everything from food to clothing, is a multimillion-dollar industry.

Function of a Relative Pronoun. A relative pronoun functions in several ways in a sentence. It usually introduces an adjective clause and refers back to another noun or pronoun in the sentence. A relative pronoun also has a function within the adjective clause itself. It can be used as a subject, a direct object, or an object of a preposition. A relative pronoun can also show possession.

SUBJECT	Amy Berger, **who lives next door,** is now a vice-president at the bank. [*Who* is the subject of *lives.*]
DIRECT OBJECT	The photographs **you saw** were taken by Rob. [The understood relative pronoun *that* is the direct object of *saw*. You saw *that.*]
OBJECT OF A PREPOSITION	The article **from which you took this material** must be quite old. [*Which* is the object of the preposition *from.* Notice that *from* is part of the clause.]
POSSESSION	Jan is the person **whose broad-jump record was broken at last night's meet.** [*Whose* shows possession of *record.*]

Punctuation with Adjective Clauses

No punctuation is used with an adjective clause that contains information essential to the identification of a person, place, or thing in the sentence. The relative pronoun *that* always begins an essential clause. A comma or commas, however, should set off an adjective clause that is nonessential. A clause is nonessential if it can be removed from the sentence without changing the basic meaning of the sentence. A clause is usually nonessential if it modifies a proper noun.

ESSENTIAL	The person **who became the first woman Supreme Court justice** was Sandra Day O'Connor. [No commas are used because the clause is needed to identify which woman.]
NONESSENTIAL	Sandra Day O'Connor, **who became the first woman Supreme Court justice,** had served as majority leader in the Arizona state senate. [Commas are used because the clause can be removed from the sentence.]

EXERCISE 6 Identifying and Punctuating Adjective Clauses
Write the following sentences and underline each adjective clause. Then add a comma or commas where needed.

1. Judo which was first included in the Olympic Games in 1964 is now an international sport.
2. The only state that borders only one other state is Maine.
3. Panama is a country where one can see the sun rise over the Pacific Ocean and set over the Atlantic Ocean.
4. The McGee Company which makes engine parts is hiring.
5. Helen Keller whose sight and hearing were destroyed by an early illness eventually conquered her handicaps.
6. I enjoyed reading the novel Mrs. Johnson assigned me.
7. In Paris the Louvre which houses one of the world's largest art collections has eight miles of galleries.
8. Did you meet my Uncle Harry who is an overseas pilot?
9. The penguin has an apparatus above its eyes that enables it to get rid of excess salt.
10. Yesterday was a day when everything seemed to go well.

EXERCISE 7 Determining the Function of a Relative Pronoun
Number your paper 1 to 10. Write the adjective clause in each sentence. Then label the use of each relative pronoun, using the following abbreviations. If an adjective clause begins with an understood *that,* write *understood* after the number and then write the use of *that.*

subject = *subj.*	object of a preposition = *o.p.*
direct object = *d.o.*	possession = *poss.*

1. Our dog, which is frisky and intelligent, is a poodle.
2. The camera that you want is on sale at Hailey's.
3. The person to whom this package is addressed has left.
4. Aerobic dancing is an exercise many people enjoy.
5. Robert Frost, whose poetry was awarded the Pulitzer Prize, first published his poems at age 38.
6. My sister, who is an accountant, has just been promoted.
7. The deli, which my neighbor owns, has good food.
8. He is the man from whom I bought the plants.
9. Janet Guthrie, who was once an aerospace physicist, has driven in the Indianapolis 500.
10. The person whose wallet you found is in the office now.

Misplaced Modifiers

To avoid confusion, place an adjective clause as near as possible to the word it describes. Like a phrase, a clause placed too far away from the word it modifies is called a *misplaced modifier.*

MISPLACED	Timothy discovered an old coin near his house that was worth about five dollars.
CORRECT	Near his house Timothy discovered an old coin **that was worth about five dollars.**
MISPLACED	Dennis ran to take the meat off the grill, which was burned to a crisp.
CORRECT	Dennis ran to take the meat, **which was burned to a crisp,** off the grill.

EXERCISE 8 Correcting Misplaced Modifiers
Write the following sentences, correcting each misplaced modifier. Use a comma or commas where needed.

1. Nancy had to mail a package at the post office that was being sent to Michigan.
2. This Ponderosa tomato was grown by my father that weighs nearly a pound.
3. A car stood in the driveway that had a flat tire.
4. In *Poor Richard's Almanac* Benjamin Franklin described the construction of a lightning rod which was published for 25 years.
5. I showed the yellow-striped sweater to my sister that you gave me.
6. O. Henry's story "The Gift of the Magi" has a surprise ending which is included in many short-story anthologies.
7. Angelo left his goggles by the pool that he had received for his birthday.
8. The bicycle belongs to my neighbor that has the new white rims.
9. The teddy bear was created by Morris Michton which was named after President Theodore Roosevelt.
10. Plants lent a bright touch to the room which filled the window.

Noun Clauses

4f A **noun clause** is a subordinate clause that is used like a noun.

A noun clause is used in all the ways a single noun can be used. The examples show some of the uses of a noun clause.

SUBJECT	**What Jenny suggested** makes sense.
DIRECT OBJECT	Julian knows **that he was wrong.**
INDIRECT OBJECT	Give **whoever volunteers** this manual.
OBJECT OF A PREPOSITION	People are often influenced by **what they see on commercials.**
PREDICATE NOMINATIVE	A good hot meal is **what I could use now** after shoveling all that snow.

The list below contains words that often introduce a noun clause. *Who, whom, whose, which,* and *that* can also be used as relative pronouns to introduce adjective clauses. Do not rely on the introductory words themselves to identify a clause. Instead, determine how a clause is used in a sentence.

Common Introductory Words for Noun Clauses

how	what	where	who	whomever
if	whatever	whether	whoever	whose
that	when	which	whom	why

EXERCISE 9 Finding Noun Clauses
Write the noun clause in each sentence.

1. Mexican food is what I like best.
2. That our pitcher was tiring was obvious to everyone.
3. The Plaza will give a half-price ticket to whoever wins.
4. I just learned that Charles Dickens first published most of his books in installments in magazines.
5. No one knows who actually made the first American flag.
6. That Jody was the best candidate was apparent.
7. Give whomever you wish an invitation to our party.
8. How people live in other countries interests me.
9. His reason was that his alarm didn't go off.
10. I read that the cost of vegetables will increase.

EXERCISE 10 Determining the Uses of Noun Clauses
Number your paper 1 to 10. Write each noun clause. Then label the use of each one, using the following abbreviations.

subject = *subj.*	object of a preposition = *o.p.*
direct object = *d.o.*	predicate nominative = *p.n.*
indirect object = *i.o.*	

1. That she works late on Saturday is common knowledge.
2. Did you know that certain species of trees have been in existence for 60 million years?
3. One explanation is that someone forgot to lock the door.
4. Send whoever answers the ad this brochure.
5. Be ready to take responsibility for what you do.
6. The coach gave whoever practiced daily his attention.
7. His reason for being late was that he took the wrong bus.
8. Where the new gym will be built is the latest news.
9. Do you know why plants need light?
10. A prize will be given to whoever raises the most money.

EXERCISE 11 Time-out for Review
Number your paper 1 to 20. Write the subordinate clauses in the following sentences. (There may be more than one subordinate clause in a sentence.) Then label the use of each one—*adverb, adjective,* or *noun.*

1. When the earth, moon, and sun are in line, an eclipse occurs.
2. What distinguished the Spartan soldiers of ancient Greece was their almost inhuman discipline.
3. The coach predicted that the game would be canceled.
4. The four-ton *Stegosaurus* dinosaur that lived 150 million years ago was about 20 feet long and 8 feet tall.
5. As a baby bird hatches, it uses a toothlike structure that enables it to break out of the egg.
6. I belong to a bowling league that meets every Friday.
7. Although the sun shone brightly, the weather forecasters maintained that the weekend would be rainy.
8. Community gardens, which are numerous in our city, offer people in urban areas the chance to be self-sufficient.
9. Honey is one of the few foods that do not spoil.
10. The sets that were used in the play were designed by a student who built and painted them as well.

11. The tomatoes grew faster than I could pick them.
12. They told me what you won at the fair.
13. Since no candidate received 50 percent of the vote, a runoff election will be held.
14. The area that developers turned into an apartment complex was first offered to the college, which refused it.
15. I read that the first railroad in the United States had wooden tracks.
16. If a car is moving at 55 miles per hour, it will travel 56 feet before the driver can shift his or her foot from the accelerator to the brake.
17. Fishing is what I often do on the weekends.
18. Granite conducts sound faster than air.
19. The Smiths, whose house we just bought, are moving to Atlanta.
20. We arrived at South Dakota's Black Hills as the sun was sinking below the horizon.

KINDS OF SENTENCE STRUCTURE

All sentences fit into one of four classifications. These classifications are determined by the number and the kind of clauses within a sentence. A sentence can be *simple, compound, complex,* or *compound-complex.*

4g A **simple sentence** consists of one independent clause.

Certain lizards can climb trees.

A simple sentence can have a compound subject, a compound verb, or both.

The old house and its barn were carefully transported and placed on new foundations in another town.

4h A **compound sentence** consists of two or more independent clauses.

A compound sentence should be composed of only closely related independent clauses joined by a coordinating conjunction such as *and, but, for, nor, or, so,* or *yet.*

independent clause — independent clause
We went to a movie last night, but it was rather boring.

independent clause — independent clause
The stew is in the oven, the salad is on the counter, and

independent clause
the dessert is in the freezer.

NOTE: See pages 251–252 and 272–273 for the punctuation of a compound sentence.

4i A **complex sentence** consists of one independent clause and one or more subordinate clauses.

independent clause — subordinate clause
We bought him a wallet that has his initials on it.

independent clause — subordinate clause
We took Ann to the hospital because we were worried

subordinate clause
that her injury might be serious.

NOTE: See pages 253 and 260 for the punctuation of a complex sentence.

4j A **compound-complex sentence** consists of two or more independent clauses and one or more subordinate clauses.

independent clause — independent clause
I have tried to lose ten pounds, but up to now I have failed

subordinate clause
because fattening foods taste too good to me.

NOTE: When punctuating a compound-complex sentence, follow the rules for both compound and complex sentences.

EXERCISE 12 Classifying Sentences

Label each of the following sentences *simple, compound, complex,* or *compound-complex.*

Eating in Space

1. In 1984, Byron Lichtenberg, who is a biomedical engineer, became a member of a space-shuttle crew.
2. Lichtenberg discovered that dealing with zero gravity was difficult.
3. The other two astronauts were able to control their movements, but at first Lichtenberg kept bouncing off the walls.
4. Lichtenberg found that eating wasn't easy either.

5. He ate with only a spoon because he had to hold on to his food with his other hand.
6. Once he tried to make a sandwich, but this task was much harder than he had expected.
7. The beef and cheese floated about, but then he clamped them together with the bread.
8. Peanuts were the most "fun" to eat.
9. When Lichtenberg tried to pour them down his throat, they escaped and floated around the cabin.
10. Eventually he chased them down like Pac Man.

EXERCISE 13 Writing Sentences
Number your paper 1 to 8. Then write two simple sentences, two compound sentences, two complex sentences, and two compound-complex sentences. Use proper punctuation.

DIAGRAMING SENTENCES

Each clause—whether independent or subordinate—is diagramed on a separate baseline like a simple sentence.

Compound Sentences. Each independent clause is diagramed like a simple sentence. The clauses are joined at the verbs with a broken line on which the conjunction is written.

The cafeteria food is good, but I still take my lunch.

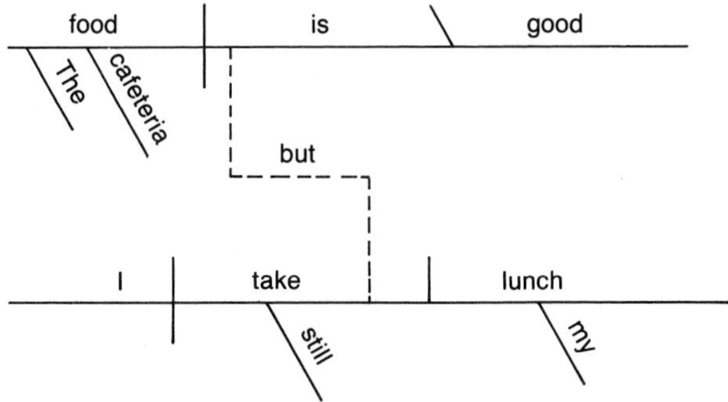

Complex Sentences. An adverb or an adjective clause in a complex sentence is diagramed beneath the independent clause it modifies. The following diagram contains an adverb clause. The subordinating conjunction goes on a broken line that connects the verb in the adverb clause to the modified verb, adjective, or adverb in the independent clause.

Before I begin my report, I must do more research.

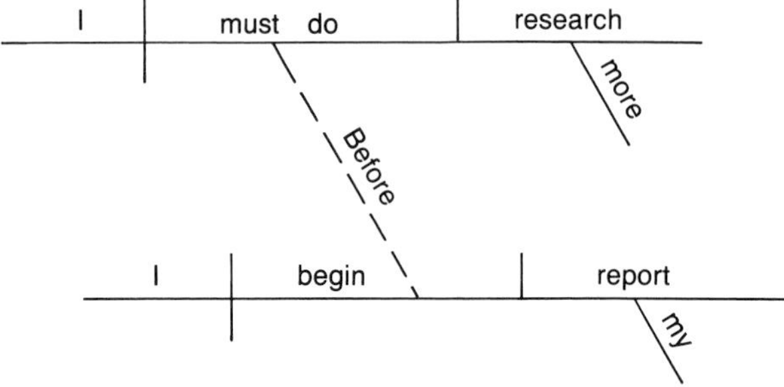

The relative pronoun in an adjective clause is connected by a broken line to the noun or the pronoun the clause modifies.

We recently bought a clock that chimes on the hour.

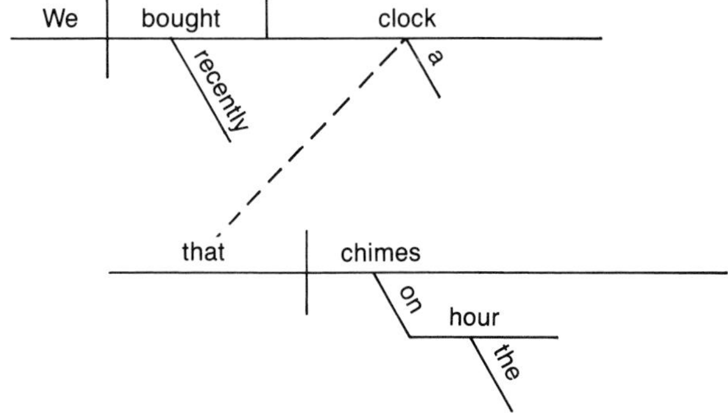

A noun clause is diagramed on a pedestal in the same position as a single noun with the same function. In the following diagram, the noun clause is used as a direct object.

Tell us what you want for your birthday.

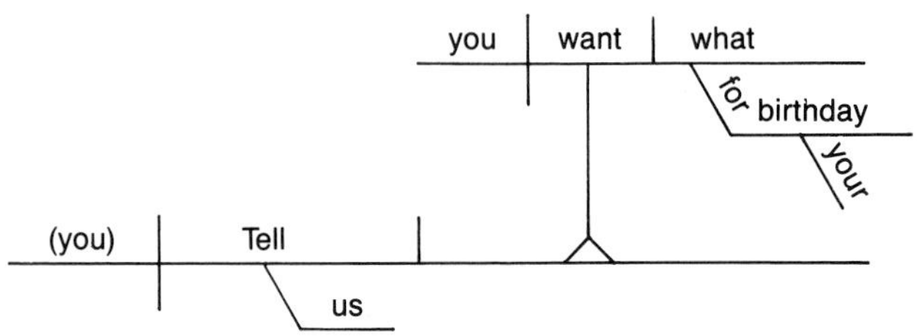

Compound-complex Sentences. To diagram these sentences, apply what you just learned about diagraming compound and complex sentences. In the following diagram, the subordinate clause is an adverb clause.

I am working tonight, but Peter isn't working because he must attend a meeting at school.

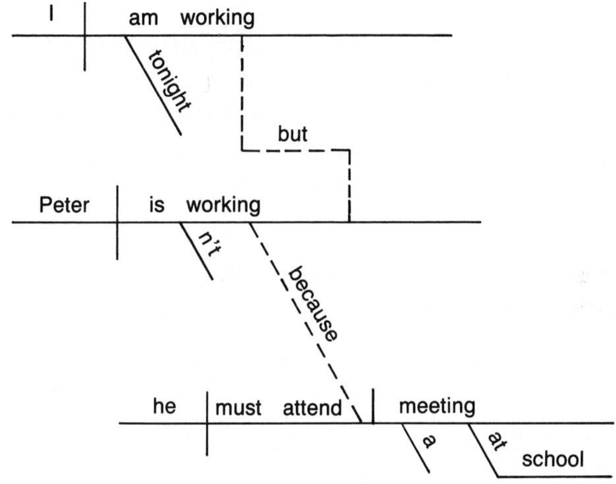

EXERCISE 14 Diagraming Sentences

Diagram the following sentences or copy them. If you copy them, draw one line under each subject and two lines under each verb. Then put parentheses around each subordinate clause and label each one *adverb, adjective,* or *noun.*

1. The gorilla may look fierce, but it is a gentle animal.
2. When the key broke in the door, we climbed through the kitchen window.
3. Many roads that the Romans built are still used.
4. You should tell the reporter whatever you saw.
5. Melodies are produced by notes in succession, but harmonies are created by notes in combination.
6. If diamonds are heated sufficiently, they will burn.
7. She turned the key, but the car wouldn't start because the battery was dead.
8. What you said to her was very helpful.
9. Do you know if Jay has arrived?
10. The bat is the only mammal that can fly.

Application to Writing

A paragraph with all simple sentences eventually becomes dull and monotonous to read. On the other hand, a paragraph with all complex or compound-complex sentences can become difficult and confusing. A paragraph that includes a combination of different kinds of sentences is by far the most interesting.

As part of your editing, analyze the structure of your sentences. If most of your sentences run two, three, and four lines long, divide some of them into shorter, simple sentences. If most of your sentences are simple sentences, combine some of them into compound or complex sentences.

TWO SIMPLE SENTENCES	The mayor favored the proposal. She could not attend the meeting.
A COMPOUND SENTENCE	The mayor favored the proposal, but she could not attend the meeting.
TWO SIMPLE SENTENCES	The hummingbird hovers in the air. Its weak feet cannot support it on a flat surface.
A COMPLEX SENTENCE	The hummingbird hovers in the air **because its weak feet cannot support it on a flat surface.** [adverb clause]
TWO SIMPLE SENTENCES	The high-wheeler bicycle had an enormous front wheel. The wheel was almost six feet high.
A COMPLEX SENTENCE	The high-wheeler bicycle had an enormous front wheel **that was almost six feet high.** [adjective clause]
TWO SIMPLE SENTENCES	A sheep dog does the work of three or four men. All ranchers agree on this.
A COMPLEX SENTENCE	All ranchers agree **that a sheep dog does the work of three or four men.** [noun clause]

EXERCISE 15 Combining Sentences
Combine each pair of sentences into a compound sentence. Use punctuation where needed.

1. A human being continually sheds skin. An entire new outer layer of skin is replaced once every 28 to 38 days.
2. Last summer I worked at the supermarket. This summer I have a job on a farm.

3. A solar eclipse can be seen in a narrow band across the earth. A lunar eclipse can be seen over very large areas.
4. Oysters are an expensive delicacy today. In medieval England they were among the cheapest foods available.
5. Carl enjoys working with wood. He is not as interested in working with metal.
6. A sunspot appears as a dark patch on the surface of the sun. Each sunspot actually has a diameter of about 20,000 miles.
7. The heavy thundercloud obscured the sun. One rim of the cloud was edged with gold.
8. I rarely take the bus to school. Today was an exception.
9. The candidate will appear at City Hall. She is unable to speak at the senior class assembly.
10. Roberto has never learned to cook. He plans to take a course in cooking this spring.

EXERCISE 16 Combining Sentences

Combine each pair of sentences into a complex sentence. Use punctuation where needed.

1. Amateur astronomers can tell a star from a planet. Only stars twinkle.
2. The first wristwatch appeared as early as 1571. It was made by Royal Clockmaker Bartholomew Newsam for Queen Elizabeth of England.
3. Rehearsal has been canceled this afternoon. Susan told me that.
4. The longest reign of an English monarch was that of Queen Victoria. She ruled over 63 years.
5. Absenteeism is far less in air-conditioned offices and factories. Studies have shown this.
6. Earl took typing for six months. He can type 75 words per minute.
7. Tomorrow will be hazy and overcast. We will not go to the beach.
8. Sandra will not pass the history quiz. She memorizes all the important dates.
9. E. E. Cummings does not use capital letters in his poetry. Our teacher told us this.
10. The rays of the setting sun pass through miles of dense lower air. This air absorbs all colors except red and green.

CHAPTER REVIEW

Number your paper 1 to 25. Write the subordinate clauses in the following sentences. (There may be more than one subordinate clause in a sentence.) Then label the use of each one—*adverb, adjective,* or *noun.*

1. Although many tornadoes occur throughout the United States, they are quite rare west of the Rockies.
2. Several champion ice-hockey teams have come from Canada, where ice-skating is a very popular sport.
3. I heard that trucks can no longer travel on Grove Street.
4. Wrap that meat in foil before you put it into the freezer.
5. Because I wanted to do better in Spanish, I decided that I would go to the language lab for help.
6. The microphone that he used had a cord attached to it.
7. If you take a trip to Mount Vernon, you will be taken back two centuries into the past.
8. Parachutists often fall a considerable distance before they pull the cord that opens the parachute.
9. Someone once said that an egotist is a person who is me-deep in conversation.
10. My mother, who seemed happy and relieved, reported that she had found a new apartment for us.
11. Don ran when he saw a huge bull approaching him.
12. Whoever is qualified for the job will have an interview.
13. Early schoolhouses were always red because red paint was the cheapest paint available.
14. The oldest fossils date back to a time when seas covered large areas that have long since become dry land.
15. Since I wasn't there, I don't know what happened.
16. Margaret Mead, who was an anthropologist, was famous for her studies of the influence of culture on personality.
17. Leroy and I cleaned out our lockers before we went to football practice.
18. Melissa was pleased with what she had accomplished.
19. The person whose ring you found is offering a reward.
20. When the power was out for two days, we learned that life without electricity is extremely inconvenient.
21. Sebastian picks strawberries faster than Matthew.
22. The painting that hangs in the cafeteria is a gift from the senior class.

23. What he told you actually happened.
24. Christina claimed that this summer she read every book on the reading list.
25. If all the blood vessels in a single human body were stretched end to end, they would form a rope that is 60,000 miles long.

MASTERY TEST

Number your paper 1 to 10. Then label each sentence *simple, compound, complex,* or *compound-complex.*

1. Look at a drop of water under a microscope, and you will see a very busy world.
2. The mule deer's coat, which is rusty red in summer, changes to grayish brown in winter.
3. The newspaper reported that most citizens of our town support the bill for a new library.
4. We wallpapered the living room but painted the kitchen.
5. Any volunteer who gives an oral report will receive extra credit.
6. Deck tennis is a game similar to tennis, but it requires rope or rubber rings instead of rackets and balls.
7. Although the dandelion is considered chiefly a pest, it is cultivated for both food and medicine.
8. We fished all day but didn't catch anything.
9. I took some pictures at the dance; and after they were developed, two of them were printed in the school paper.
10. Grass clippings that are allowed to remain on the ground soon decompose and return valuable nutrients to the soil.

5

Sound Sentences

DIAGNOSTIC TEST

Number your paper 1 to 10. Then label each group of words *sentence, fragment,* or *run-on.*

EXAMPLE Two skaters racing and circling the rink.
ANSWER fragment

1. When Barry was offered the job, he accepted it.
2. The Abyssinian cat, a breed thought to come from the jungle cat of India or Africa.
3. The seed of a cacao tree looks somewhat like an almond, it has a bitter taste.
4. From an airplane one can see the huge underwater portions of icebergs.
5. When some people answer the telephone.
6. The picture hanging above the fireplace.
7. The federal government has classified the wolf as an endangered species in every state except Alaska and Minnesota.
8. Dolphins make a wide variety of noises, their sound effects include whistling, chirping, and squeaking.
9. The streams froze snow covered everything in sight.
10. To make the best possible use of your time.

In recent years several books have been written about how to create the right impression when you apply for a job. These books include everything from how to dress appropriately to how to shake hands after an interview. Employers, teachers, college entrance boards, and admissions officers also form impressions of people by their written work. Negative impressions are often formed of students who submit written work filled with incomplete sentences and sentences that run together. This chapter will show you how to recognize and correct these two kinds of sentence errors.

SENTENCE FRAGMENTS AND RUN-ON SENTENCES

A *sentence fragment* is not a sentence at all. It is an incomplete thought that usually leaves a reader asking for more information. A *run-on sentence* is the exact opposite of a sentence fragment. It is two or more sentences that run together with only a comma to separate them or no punctuation at all. A run-on sentence gives a reader too much information too fast.

Sentence Fragments

5a A **sentence fragment** is a group of words that does not express a complete thought.

You can correct a fragment in one of two ways. You can add words to it to make a complete sentence, or you can attach it to the sentence next to it. Sometimes when you attach a fragment to a sentence, you may have to add or drop words.

There are several kinds of sentence fragments. All sentence fragments, however, have one thing in common. They all are missing one or more of the elements needed to make them sentences.

Phrase Fragments. Since a phrase is a group of words that does not have a subject and a verb, it can never express a complete thought. The fragments in the following examples are in heavy type.

PREPOSITIONAL PHRASE FRAGMENT	After 1945, many new words and expressions came into our language. **Like *baby-sit, cutback, rat race,* and *soap opera.***
CORRECTED	After 1945 many new words and expressions, like *baby-sit, cutback, rat race,* and *soap opera,* came into our language.
PARTICIPIAL PHRASE FRAGMENT	The Navahos are the most populous Indian tribe in the United States. **Numbering over 130,000.**
CORRECTED	The Navahos, numbering over 130,000, are the most populous Indian tribe in the United States.
INFINITIVE PHRASE FRAGMENT	**To provide healthful living and working conditions.** This is one aim of medical researchers.
CORRECTED	To provide healthful living and working conditions is one aim of medical researchers.
APPOSITIVE PHRASE FRAGMENT	The first woman veterinarian was Dr. Elinor McGrath. **A 1910 graduate of the Chicago Veterinary College.**
CORRECTED	The first woman veterinarian was Dr. Elinor McGrath, a 1910 graduate of the Chicago Veterinary College.

Clause Fragments. Even though a subordinate clause has a subject and a verb, it does not express a complete thought. *(See pages 75–76.)*

ADVERB CLAUSE FRAGMENT	**If it were straightened out.** The Nile River would stretch farther than the distance between New York and Los Angeles.
CORRECTED	If it were straightened out, the Nile River would stretch farther than the distance between New York and Los Angeles.
ADJECTIVE CLAUSE FRAGMENT	At the career workshop, she visited the booths. **That featured journalism.**
CORRECTED	At the career workshop, she visited the booths that featured journalism.

Other Fragments. There are other common fragments besides phrase and clause fragments.

PART OF A COMPOUND VERB	Walter Hunt patented the safety pin in 1849. **And gave the world a very useful product.**
CORRECTED	Walter Hunt patented the safety pin in 1849 and gave the world a very useful product.
NO VERB	Venus **shining brightly in the sky.**
CORRECTED	Venus was shining brightly in the sky.
CORRECTED	The astronomer could see Venus shining brightly in the sky.
ITEMS IN A SERIES	Many flowers grow from bulbs. **Daffodils, tulips, and irises.**
CORRECTED	Many flowers, such as daffodils, tulips, and irises, grow from bulbs.

EXERCISE 1 Correcting Sentence Fragments

Number your paper 1 to 10. Then correct each sentence fragment. Add capital letters and punctuation where needed. If both groups of words in an item are sentences, write *C* after the number.

1. The pouter pigeon puffs out its chest. When anyone pays attention to it.
2. Sheepskin is a spongy leather. And is often used for gloves and other light garments.
3. The warm morning sunshine shone brightly. Into the small dreary hotel room.
4. Sequoya was a Cherokee Indian. The giant sequoia tree is named after him.
5. On the hike we carried all the supplies we needed. Food, water, tents, rain gear, and sleeping bags.
6. In the Sonoran Desert is found the saguaro cactus. Which grows to a height of 15 feet before producing its first branches.
7. Reacting against the treatment of women in the nineteenth century. Charlotte Brontë wrote the novel *Jane Eyre*.
8. The calliope was first used on a riverboat. Now it can be heard under the big top.

9. Yesterday I had a flat tire. At the corner of Meriden Road.
10. To be an astronaut. This is Andrea's ambition.

Run-on Sentences

5b

A **run-on sentence** is two or more sentences that are written as one sentence and are separated by a comma or no mark of punctuation at all.

Run-on sentences result either from writing too fast or from the mistaken idea that very long sentences sound more scholarly. A run-on sentence is usually written in one of two ways.

WITH A COMMA	Buoys are the guideposts of the sea, they mark out channels.
WITH NO PUNCTUATION	In the winter some animals migrate others hibernate.

A run-on sentence can be corrected in several ways: (1) It can be written as two separate sentences, (2) It can be written as a compound sentence with a comma and a conjunction or with a semicolon, and (3) It can be written as a complex sentence by changing one part of the run-on sentence into a subordinate clause.

RUN-ON SENTENCE	The continent of Europe covers over four million square miles, it is the second smallest continent.
SEPARATE SENTENCES	The continent of Europe covers over four million square miles. It is the second smallest continent.
COMPOUND SENTENCE	The continent of Europe covers over four million square miles, and it is the second smallest continent. [with a comma and a conjunction]
	The continent of Europe covers over four million square miles; it is the second smallest continent. [with a semicolon]
COMPLEX SENTENCE	The continent of Europe, which covers over four million square miles, is the second smallest continent. [adjective clause]
	Although the continent of Europe covers over four million square miles, it is the second smallest continent. [adverb clause]

EXERCISE 2 Correcting Run-on Sentences
Number your paper 1 to 10. Then correct each run-on sentence. If a group of words is not a run-on sentence, write *C* after the number. Add capital letters and punctuation.

1. I used the word processor it made editing my report fun.
2. In professional football the quarterback is the key player on the offense, the linebacker is the pivot of the defense.
3. Surely you remember David he was the assistant coach.
4. The finch belongs to the largest family of birds and is considered the most highly developed of all birds.
5. May is my favorite month, January is my least favorite.
6. Previously I had not realized the problems of assembling a bicycle now I know.
7. Across Florida Bay lies Cape Sable, here giant turtles nest each summer.
8. A skunk will not bite and throw its scent simultaneously.
9. Handel wrote many musical compositions, perhaps his best-known work is the *Messiah.*
10. Justin reads the daily newspaper he always turns to the editorial page first.

EXERCISE 3 Time-out for Review
Correct each sentence fragment or run-on sentence. Add capital letters and punctuation where needed.

When the Martians Invaded

1. Once people believed that life existed on Mars, many authors encouraged this belief through their books.
2. One such book was a novel by H. G. Wells. Called *The War of the Worlds.*
3. In this book Martians invade Earth humans seem defenseless against them.
4. When the world appears doomed. It is discovered that the Martians have a hidden weakness.
5. They die of a human ailment. The common cold.
6. Their bodies unable to fight off the attacks of Earth's bacteria.
7. A radio program presented a dramatization of *The War of the Worlds.* On October 30, 1938.
8. Aired less than a year before the start of World War II.
9. At that time people were on edge, news bulletins were not uncommon.

10. The scene of the program was set in the United States, the Martians landed in New Jersey.
11. The program started with an ordinary weather report. To provide realism.
12. Then came a special bulletin. About a huge metal cylinder that landed in a farmer's field.
13. Some people only half listened. And missed the fact that the program was about a make-believe invasion.
14. Most people believed the invasion was real, they became hysterical.
15. People rushing out into the streets and making frantic telephone calls.
16. People's imaginations played tricks on them, some saw a fire in the distance, others smelled poisonous gas.
17. A local power failure finally persuaded listeners. That all was hopeless.
18. People got into their cars and headed west. To try to escape the Martians.
19. Calm was eventually restored. When people realized that the invasion was just a radio program.
20. No one forgot *The War of the Worlds*. For a long time.

Application to Writing

Most first drafts of compositions or reports contain sentence fragments and run-on sentences because writers are primarily thinking about subject matter, not accuracy or style. After you write your first draft, however, you should always edit your work for sentence errors. One way to do this is to read your written work aloud. The inflection of your voice will often find many of your errors for you.

EXERCISE 4 Editing for Sentence Errors
Rewrite the following paragraphs, correcting all sentence fragments and run-on sentences. Correct the errors in a variety of ways; otherwise, you will have all short, choppy sentences. Add capital letters and punctuation where needed.

Mark Twain, the Inventor

While it is true that Mark Twain was a great writer. He was also an inventor. Twain hoped to make millions on his ideas, he lost a fortune. And had to earn a living by writing.

Twain had numerous ideas for inventions. Long before they came into being. Twain predicted such innovations as microfilm, data storage and retrieval, and television. He had great ideas, he was not a good businessman. He lost $300,000, for example, on an automatic typesetting machine. Because it had 18,000 moving parts and seldom worked. Twain did make a small profit on one of his ventures. Which he called "a great humanizing and civilizing invention." It was called Mark Twain's Self-pasting Scrapbook.

CHAPTER REVIEW

Correct each sentence fragment or run-on sentence. Add capital letters and punctuation where needed.

1. Captain James Cook named the Sandwich Islands after an English noble. The fourth Earl of Sandwich.
2. Riding down the rapids of the Colorado River was exciting, twice the raft nearly capsized.
3. Ultrasound employs sound waves of high frequency, doctors use it to see within a person's body.
4. Oliver High's football team won the championship, now the baseball team is making a strong showing.
5. The tiny glass prism slowly turned on the string. And created beautiful rainbows on the wall.
6. Our subway stop is being repaired, we had to walk six blocks to the next one.
7. Victoria Park is the perfect place. To hold the Senior Class Picnic in June.
8. During the early part of the game. Predictions were that South High would win by ten points.
9. The last of the Florida Keys disappeared from sight, we headed for the open sea.
10. Eskimos sometimes buy refrigerators. To keep their food from freezing in the cold arctic temperatures.
11. There are many community merchants. Who might want to advertise in the school newspaper.
12. We watched the campfire. Growing dimmer and dimmer in the darkness.
13. The Siamese is one of the most popular breeds of cats, most experts believe that it originated in Thailand.

14. Our halfback dodged to the left. To avoid the Tigers' swift backfield.
15. Storm clouds lay over the Allegheny Mountains to the west of us occasionally we could see flashes of lightning.
16. Sarah read one novel a week. During the first two months of the school year.
17. Edward swung, the ball bounced past the third baseman for a double.
18. Water makes up about three fifths of your body weight, even your bones are made up of about one-quarter water.
19. Horses were originally transported to North America by the Spaniards. Who first brought them into Mexico.
20. Patrick raced down the muddy field. Clutching the slippery football.

MASTERY TEST

Number your paper 1 to 10. Then label each group of words *sentence, fragment,* or *run-on.*

1. The rain stopped, sunlight fell across the wet leaves.
2. To put the roast in the oven and to set the timer.
3. I hit the cold dark water feet first and plunged down to the bottom of the lake.
4. The distinguished man wearing the blue pin-striped suit.
5. Illinois is a great producer of corn Kansas is a great producer of wheat.
6. The moon is an airless and waterless world that has extremes of temperatures.
7. Waiting for the light to change at the intersection of Evergreen Avenue and Highland Road.
8. As graduation draws near, I've noticed that attendance at class meetings has increased.
9. Although the grocery store is only two blocks away.
10. The French horn is a brass instrument, the English horn is a woodwind instrument.

STANDARDIZED TEST

GRAMMAR

Directions: Look carefully at the structure of each sentence. In the appropriate row on your answer sheet, fill in circle

- **A** if the sentence is a simple sentence.
- **B** if the sentence is a compound sentence.
- **C** if the sentence is a complex sentence.
- **D** if the sentence is a compound-complex sentence.

SAMPLE Emily slept until nine o'clock this morning.

ANSWER Ⓐ Ⓑ Ⓒ Ⓓ

1. After four days in orbit, the capsule was headed home.
2. After the rooster crowed, the cow awoke and mooed.
3. Proteins repair cells, build tissues, and perform other jobs.
4. People who do not get enough protein can become gravely ill.
5. Shall we sleep late, or shall we get up to see the sun rise?
6. The sky was gloomy when we awoke, but then the sun appeared.
7. The horses grew tired, and the caravan halted before dark.
8. We waited until dawn before leaving, for the roads were icy.
9. Can you stay until the party ends, or must you leave now?
10. Was it really John who won the award, or did Ann imagine it?
11. If these records are correct, Roy walked when he was two.
12. Because of the jury's decision, Alma wept but Don cheered.
13. Everyone is curious, but no one knows what really happened.
14. *Poultry* refers to any fowl raised to yield meat and eggs.
15. The boat rolled and rocked in the storm but remained afloat.
16. If I go, I will be tired; but if I stay, I will be bored.
17. The shoes that she liked and that fit well were very cheap.
18. The mosquito knew I was there and came to get me.
19. The butler knew when to speak and when to remain silent.
20. Finding a job is easy for Kim, but keeping one is difficult.

Directions: Decide which sentence best combines each pair of sentences. In the appropriate row on your answer sheet, fill in the circle containing the same letter as your answer.

SAMPLE The pony jumped the fence. He galloped out of sight.

A The pony jumped the fence and out of sight.
B The pony jumped the fence and galloped out of sight.
C The pony galloped out of sight and jumped the fence.

ANSWER Ⓐ Ⓑ Ⓒ

21. A goatee is a kind of beard. It comes to a point.

A A goatee is a kind of beard and comes to a point.
B A goatee is a kind of beard that comes to a point.
C Coming to a point, a goatee is a kind of beard.

22. Claude was flying low over the field. He spotted a wolf.

A Claude spotted a wolf flying low over the field.
B Claude was flying low over the field spotting a wolf.
C Claude, flying low over the field, spotted a wolf.

23. A hedgehog feels threatened. Then it rolls up into a ball.

A Rolling up into a ball, a hedgehog feels threatened.
B Although a hedgehog feels threatened, it rolls up into a ball.
C When a hedgehog feels threatened, it rolls up into a ball.

24. The next meeting of the Stargazers' Society will be held on Friday. Mr. Farnsworth told me that.

A Mr. Farnsworth told me that the next meeting of the Stargazers' Society will be held on Friday.
B The next meeting of the Stargazers' Society will be held on Friday, Mr. Farnsworth told me that.
C Having Mr. Farnsworth tell me, the next meeting of the Stargazers' Society will be held on Friday.

25. *Tulip* comes from a Turkish word. It means "turban."

A *Tulip* comes from a Turkish word, that means "turban."
B *Tulip* comes from a Turkish word that means "turban."
C *Tulip* that comes from a Turkish word means "turban."

Unit 2

Usage

6

Using Verbs

DIAGNOSTIC TEST

Number your paper 1 to 10. Then write the past or the past participle of each verb in parentheses.

EXAMPLE Yesterday I (swim) the length of the pool six times.

ANSWER swam

1. Many early explorers reported that they had (see) mermaids.
2. Has the bell (ring) for third period yet?
3. Five minutes after the downpour, the sun (come) out.
4. By the time Brad arrived, Flora had already (go).
5. Wendy (break) the school's high-jump record last week.
6. The art class (make) posters for the school play.
7. No one (know) what animal had made the strange tracks.
8. Before I could stop her, Mittens had (eat) most of the hamburger.
9. Joshua has (choose) that small mare to ride today.
10. The drum major (lead) the band onto the field during halftime.

This is the first chapter in a unit on usage. The next three chapters will show you how to use pronouns correctly, how to make a verb agree with its subject, and how to determine which form of a modifier to use. These chapters on using the grammar you have learned are extremely important. Knowing grammar without knowing proper usage is like buying a new car and leaving it parked in the driveway—because you never learned to drive!

This first chapter covers verbs. Why should you know what a verb is? If you know which word in a sentence is a verb, you can consciously substitute a specific, colorful verb for a dull, general one. Once you have chosen a particular verb, however, you must know which form of that verb to use. In this chapter you will learn to use the correct forms of verbs.

PRINCIPAL PARTS

The four basic forms of a verb are called its *principal parts*. The six tenses of a verb are formed from these principal parts.

6a The **principal parts** of a verb are the *present*, the *present participle*, the *past*, and the *past participle*.

In each of the following examples, one of the four principal parts of *eat* is used as the main verb of the sentence. Notice that helping verbs are needed with the present participle and the past participle.

PRESENT	I usually **eat** lunch at noon.
PRESENT PARTICIPLE	I am **eating** lunch earlier this week.
PAST	I **ate** lunch an hour ago.
PAST PARTICIPLE	I have already **eaten** lunch.

Regular and Irregular Verbs

How a verb forms its past and past participle will determine whether it is classified as a *regular verb* or an *irregular verb*.

Regular Verbs. Most verbs are classified as regular verbs because they form their past and past participle in the same way.

6b A **regular verb** forms its past and past participle by adding *-ed* or *-d* to the present.

Because a spelling change sometimes occurs when certain endings are added to the present, you should always check a dictionary if there is any doubt in your mind.

NOTE: *Have* is not part of the past participle. It has been added to all the following examples, however, to help you remember that form. A past participle must have a *helping verb* when it is used as a verb.

PRESENT	PRESENT PARTICIPLE	PAST	PAST PARTICIPLE
talk	talking	talked	(have) talked
cook	cooking	cooked	(have) cooked
equip	equipping	equipped	(have) equipped
commit	committing	committed	(have) committed

NOTE: Occasionally the *-ed* or *-d* is incorrectly dropped from such verb forms as *asked, helped, looked, seemed, supposed, talked, used,* and *walked.*

INCORRECT Every spring we **use** to plant a vegetable garden.
CORRECT Every spring we **used** to plant a vegetable garden.

EXERCISE 1 Determining the Principal Parts of Regular Verbs

Make four columns on your paper. Label them *present, present participle, past,* and *past participle.* Then write the four principal parts of the following verbs.

1. wish
2. drop
3. turn
4. dine
5. use
6. offer
7. wave
8. stop
9. seem
10. occur

Irregular Verbs. Some common verbs are classified as irregular because they form their past and past participle in different ways.

6c An **irregular verb** does not form its past and past participle by adding *-ed* or *-d* to the present.

The following irregular verbs have been divided into groups according to the way they form their past and past participle.

Group 1

These irregular verbs have the same form for the present, the past, and the past participle.

PRESENT	PRESENT PARTICIPLE	PAST	PAST PARTICIPLE
burst	bursting	burst	(have) burst
cost	costing	cost	(have) cost
hit	hitting	hit	(have) hit
hurt	hurting	hurt	(have) hurt
let	letting	let	(have) let
put	putting	put	(have) put
set	setting	set	(have) set

Group 2

These irregular verbs have the same form for the past and the past participle.

PRESENT	PRESENT PARTICIPLE	PAST	PAST PARTICIPLE
bring	bringing	brought	(have) brought
buy	buying	bought	(have) bought
catch	catching	caught	(have) caught
feel	feeling	felt	(have) felt
find	finding	found	(have) found
get	getting	got	(have) got or gotten
hold	holding	held	(have) held
keep	keeping	kept	(have) kept
lay	laying	laid	(have) laid
lead	leading	led	(have) led
leave	leaving	left	(have) left
lose	losing	lost	(have) lost
make	making	made	(have) made
say	saying	said	(have) said
sell	selling	sold	(have) sold
send	sending	sent	(have) sent
sit	sitting	sat	(have) sat
teach	teaching	taught	(have) taught
tell	telling	told	(have) told
win	winning	won	(have) won

EXERCISE 2 Using the Correct Verb Form

Write the past or the past participle of each verb in parentheses. Then read each sentence aloud to check your answer.

1. The note (say) that Sean was staying after school for football practice.
2. Under the pressure of the water, the levee (burst).
3. I think I (leave) my raincoat in homeroom.
4. Marjorie (lay) the mat on the porch.
5. After several hours Martin finally (catch) a striped bass.
6. I should have (send) this coat to the cleaners.
7. Have you (find) the answer to the last math problem?
8. Where have you (put) the paper towels?
9. At the bake sale, the Drama Club (make) ninety dollars.
10. We should have (win) the state championship in soccer.
11. I just (sell) my old bicycle.
12. So far this year, Miguel has (hit) two home runs.
13. I haven't (feel) well all day.
14. Yesterday Gary (get) a letter telling him when the hockey season would begin.
15. How long have you (sit) here?
16. The park ranger (tell) us that the trails were open.
17. Has the table been (set) for dinner?
18. While I was shopping, I (buy) a poster for my brother.
19. I (hold) onto the bar of the roller coaster so tightly that my knuckles turned white.
20. Cindy (teach) me how to use the computer at school.
21. How long have you (keep) this scrapbook?
22. Have you (lose) your contact lens again?
23. You should have (bring) your records to the party.
24. Has anyone (let) the dog outside?
25. Two police officers on motorcycles (lead) the motorcade.

EXERCISE 3 Determining the Principal Parts of Irregular Verbs

Make four columns on your paper. Label them *present, present participle, past,* and *past participle.* Then write the four principal parts of the following verbs.

1. lose	3. sit	5. let	7. feel	9. teach
2. keep	4. put	6. find	8. cost	10. leave

Group 3

These irregular verbs form the past participle by adding *-n* to the past.

PRESENT	PRESENT PARTICIPLE	PAST	PAST PARTICIPLE
break	breaking	broke	(have) broken
choose	choosing	chose	(have) chosen
freeze	freezing	froze	(have) frozen
speak	speaking	spoke	(have) spoken
steal	stealing	stole	(have) stolen

Group 4

These irregular verbs form the past participle by adding *-n* to the present.

PRESENT	PRESENT PARTICIPLE	PAST	PAST PARTICIPLE
blow	blowing	blew	(have) blown
draw	drawing	drew	(have) drawn
drive	driving	drove	(have) driven
give	giving	gave	(have) given
grow	growing	grew	(have) grown
know	knowing	knew	(have) known
rise	rising	rose	(have) risen
see	seeing	saw	(have) seen
take	taking	took	(have) taken
throw	throwing	threw	(have) thrown

EXERCISE 4 Using the Correct Verb Form

Number your paper 1 to 20. Write the past or the past participle of each verb in parentheses. Then read each sentence aloud to check your answer.

1. Stanley has (throw) three balls through the hoop.
2. Brian (steal) three bases during the sixth inning.
3. The musician stood and (blow) a few notes on the clarinet.
4. Every day at the camp, we (draw) water from a well.
5. Because the heater in our car was (break), we were almost (freeze) by the time we reached home.
6. Last night we (see) the school's production of *Camelot.*
7. We have (grow) corn for the first time this year.
8. Alice had never (speak) before such a large group.

9. The flag slowly (rise) on the flagpole.
10. Chris hoped that she would be (choose) captain.
11. We (speak) to her before she (drive) to California.
12. The pitcher (throw) three strikes in a row.
13. We (take) Tara the irises that Grandfather had (give) us.
14. So far I haven't (draw) any money out of the bank.
15. That is the first two-dollar bill I have ever (see).
16. The sun had just (rise) as I awoke.
17. I (choose) the black-and-white puppy.
18. Before he had (drive) far, Tim (know) he had car trouble.
19. I (grow) these tomatoes myself.
20. The day after I (give) her the necklace, it (break).

EXERCISE 5 Supplying the Correct Verb Form

Number your paper 1 to 10. Then complete each pair of sentences by supplying the past or the past participle of the verb in parentheses at the beginning of the sentence.

EXAMPLE (speak) Have you ____ to him? Yes, I ____ to him an hour ago.

ANSWER spoken—spoke

1. (draw) Yesterday I ____ a picture of my mother. I have ____ several other sketches of her.
2. (know) How long have you ____ about the party? I ____ about it last week.
3. (see) Jessie ____ the Grand Canyon last summer. I have never ____ it.
4. (choose) Have you ____ the author you will read for your English project? Yes, I ____ Jane Austen.
5. (give) He ____ me some advice. He should have ____ it to me sooner.
6. (take) I have ____ the course in conversational French. I ____ it because I hope to go to Paris some day.
7. (break) Otis ____ another school track record. He has ____ three records during his high school years.
8. (rise) The dough ____ a quarter of an inch in the last ten minutes. It has ____ a total of an inch so far.
9. (drive) Have you ever ____ to Montana? I ____ there several years ago.
10. (speak) I have ____ to Peter about the rehearsal. He ____ to Charlene about it.

EXERCISE 6 Determining the Correct Verb Form

Number your paper 1 to 20. Then write the correct form of each underlined verb. If the verb is correct, write *C* after the number. (This exercise includes verbs from the first four groups.)

1. Have you took any pictures with your new camera?
2. Ever since she went to obedience school, Princess has brung in the newspaper each morning.
3. I seen her on the school bus this morning.
4. Has everyone already left for the game?
5. Ann and Paul have drove to the beach with them.
6. Hank Cooper, who throwed a perfect game, was applauded by the crowd.
7. Dad has chose a watch for Barry's graduation present.
8. You should have known about the new regulations.
9. So far I haven't catched the flu that's going around.
10. Alison has often spoke about her plans for the future.
11. For an hour the winds have blew steadily with gale force.
12. Mom has growed the biggest geraniums you have ever seen.
13. Without your help we would never have made it this far.
14. I should have sended the package by express mail.
15. We losed the basketball game by only two points.
16. Have you put the microscope in a safe place?
17. Oh, no! I have just broke the meat platter.
18. We should have froze those extra strawberries.
19. Why have you given your new jacket to Tracy?
20. I have keeped every receipt from our purchases.

Group 5

These irregular verbs form the past and the past participle by changing a vowel.

PRESENT	PRESENT PARTICIPLE	PAST	PAST PARTICIPLE
begin	beginning	began	(have) begun
drink	drinking	drank	(have) drunk
ring	ringing	rang	(have) rung
shrink	shrinking	shrank	(have) shrunk
sing	singing	sang	(have) sung
sink	sinking	sank	(have) sunk
swim	swimming	swam	(have) swum

Group 6

These irregular verbs form the past and the past participle in other ways.

PRESENT	PRESENT PARTICIPLE	PAST	PAST PARTICIPLE
come	coming	came	(have) come
do	doing	did	(have) done
eat	eating	ate	(have) eaten
fall	falling	fell	(have) fallen
go	going	went	(have) gone
lie	lying	lay	(have) lain
ride	riding	rode	(have) ridden
run	running	ran	(have) run
tear	tearing	tore	(have) torn
wear	wearing	wore	(have) worn
write	writing	wrote	(have) written

EXERCISE 7 Using the Correct Verb Form

Number your paper 1 to 20. Write the past or the past participle of each verb in parentheses. Then read each sentence aloud to check your answer.

1. Before anyone knew what had happened, Edward had (run) 20 yards for a touchdown.
2. Andy (shrink) back into the doorway to surprise his friend.
3. Some critics feel that William Wordsworth had (write) his best poetry by the time he was 30.
4. I have already (ring) the doorbell twice.
5. The tenor (sing) the aria magnificently.
6. Have you ever (tear) a shirt the first day you (wear) it?
7. I (ride) in a train for the first time last week.
8. I (lie) down after dinner, but I couldn't fall asleep.
9. As the canoe (sink), we (swim) to shore.
10. The dinner was delicious, but we should have (eat) before eight o'clock.
11. Felicia (run) a mile to try out her new running shoes.
12. I have (do) the dishes and have (come) to see if you want me to do anything else.
13. In colonial days, a shoe could be (wear) on either foot.
14. After Bart (eat) breakfast, he (begin) to paint the porch.
15. Have you ever (ride) on a subway?

16. I should have (go) to the meeting, but I (fall) asleep.
17. That group must have (sing) that song at least a hundred times by now.
18. Jeff (come) into the kitchen and (drink) half the pitcher of orange juice.
19. I (do) my laundry, but I (tear) a hole in my shirt.
20. We (write) to the manufacturer after the boat had (sink) for the second time.

EXERCISE 8 Supplying the Correct Verb Form

Number your paper 1 to 10. Then complete each pair of sentences by supplying the past or the past participle of the verb in parentheses at the beginning of the sentence.

1. (begin) The play ____ 15 minutes ago. It should have ____ a half hour ago.
2. (do) Have you ____ your homework? I ____ mine at school.
3. (run) Matthew ____ for Student Council president last year. He should have ____ again this year.
4. (drink) We ____ some ice water after running the marathon. We should never have ____ it so fast.
5. (go) Have you ____ to the supermarket yet? Yes, I ____ this afternoon.
6. (lie) After dinner Connie ____ down because she wasn't feeling well. She has ____ on the couch for two hours.
7. (write) I ____ the first draft of my essay last night. Have you ____ yours?
8. (swim) Kelly ____ from the dock to the pier. I have ____ that distance many times.
9. (sing) Have you ever ____ in public before? Once I ____ a solo in a chorus concert.
10. (eat) I just ____ an artichoke for the first time. Have you ever ____ one?

EXERCISE 9 Determining the Correct Verb Form

Number your paper 1 to 20. Then write the correct form of each underlined verb. If a verb is correct, write *C* after the number. (This exercise includes verbs from all six groups.)

1. Just recently I <u>begun</u> to think about going to college.
2. Sparky <u>come</u> home yesterday with burrs all over him.

3. At the concert last night, Tad singed a solo.
4. Keith got a seed catalog for the garden.
5. Have you wrote for the rebate yet?
6. Victoria already had ate lunch by the time I arrived.
7. Early locomotives ran on wooden tracks.
8. Before last summer I had never rode on a train.
9. In the basketball game, Otis done well, scoring 14 points.
10. Sales at the mall have been hurt by the cold weather.
11. The boat has sank in 20 feet of water.
12. Have you gave Lee the grocery list?
13. Nina had just drove away when you called.
14. I break my watch yesterday.
15. You should have worn a heavier jacket to the game.
16. Kathy has went to her grandparents' farm this weekend.
17. You must have drank milk that was sour.
18. I have sold ten tickets to the benefit concert.
19. The telephone had rang twice before he heard it.
20. Could your wallet have fell under the cushions of the sofa?

EXERCISE 10 **Using the Correct Verb Form**

Write the past or the past participle of each verb in parentheses. Then read each sentence aloud to check your answer. (This exercise includes verbs from all six groups.)

1. Diane (make) two loaves of bread for the picnic.
2. As the wheels (begin) to turn, the riverboat moved away.
3. Chester (write) his essay on a word processor.
4. Uncle Barney has (drive) a truck for 30 years now.
5. Last week the mayor (lay) the cornerstone for the museum.
6. Melba carefully (set) the vase of flowers on the table.
7. The bells in the church steeple (ring) after the wedding.
8. Many of the world's lemons are (grow) in California.
9. Who (win) first place in the poetry contest?
10. Last summer we (eat) fresh fruit every day.
11. I have not (wear) my new jacket yet.
12. At 1:32 A.M., we (see) the comet streak across the horizon.
13. I haven't (do) all the research for my report yet.
14. In 1962, in his first year as a pro, Jack Nicklaus (win) the U.S. Open in a playoff against Arnold Palmer.
15. The puma leaped from the branch and (run) swiftly.
16. You should have (give) your car a good waxing.

17. Last night Mario (go) to see a play at the outdoor theater.
18. The coach (speak) to the team about sportsmanship.
19. Rita was unanimously (choose) to be the editor.
20. Somehow the dog (lose) its identification tag.
21. Have you (tell) David which class ring you want?
22. After I (break) the dish, I tried to glue it back together.
23. The pond in the park has not (freeze) yet.
24. Shooting the movie (take) six months.
25. On Career Day, seniors (get) a chance to hear about jobs.

EXERCISE 11 Time-out for Review

Number your paper 1 to 15. Then write the past or the past participle of each verb in parentheses. (This exercise includes regular and irregular verbs.)

The Harlem Globetrotters

1. For over six decades, the Harlem Globetrotters have (bring) an unusual dimension to basketball.
2. They have (draw) some of the largest crowds in the history of the game.
3. In 1926, the Globetrotters (begin) as a serious team.
4. They (play) their first games in the Savoy Ballroom in Chicago.
5. When the dance hall (fall) on hard times, the team (go) on the road.
6. Since that time the team has never (leave) the touring circuit.
7. Abe Saperstein, who (form) the first team, always (choose) the best players he could find.
8. As a result his team eventually (get) so good that no one (want) to play them.
9. That's when Saperstein (make) an important decision.
10. He (break) from tradition and (add) comedy routines.
11. The fans had never (see) anything like it before.
12. Saperstein (expand) the clowning, and the popularity of the Globetrotters (grow).
13. Eventually the comedy routines (become) a permanent part of the team's show.
14. In 1940, the "Trotters" (get) a big boost when they (win) a world professional basketball tournament in Chicago.
15. Since then they have (give) the world a unique and wonderful game of basketball.

VERB TENSE

All the tenses of a verb are formed from the principal parts. Different verb forms express the *tense,* or time, of a verb. The six tenses are *present, past, future, present perfect, past perfect, and future perfect.* Notice in the following examples how the six tenses of the verb *drive* express action at different times.

PRESENT	Bart **drives** Tad to school.
PAST	Bart **drove** Tad to school yesterday.
FUTURE	Bart **will drive** Tad to school tomorrow.
PRESENT PERFECT	Bart **has driven** Tad to school all month.
PAST PERFECT	Bart **had** never **driven** Tad to school before March.
FUTURE PERFECT	By June Bart **will have driven** Tad to school for four months.

Conjugation of a Verb

A *conjugation* lists all the singular and plural forms of a verb in its various tenses. Following is a conjugation of the irregular verb *eat.*

Conjugation of *Eat*

PRINCIPAL PARTS

PRESENT	PRESENT PARTICIPLE	PAST	PAST PARTICIPLE
eat	eating	ate	eaten

Present

This tense expresses action that is going on now.

SINGULAR	PLURAL
I eat	we eat
you eat	you eat
he, she, it eats	they eat

Past

This tense expresses action that took place in the past.

SINGULAR	PLURAL
I ate	we ate
you ate	you ate
he, she, it ate	they ate

Future

This tense expresses action that will take place in the future. It is formed by adding *shall* or *will* to the present.

SINGULAR	PLURAL
I shall/will eat	we shall/will eat
you will eat	you will eat
he, she, it will eat	they will eat

Present Perfect

This tense expresses action that was completed at some indefinite time in the past or action that started in the past and is still going on. It is formed by adding *has* or *have* to the past participle.

SINGULAR	PLURAL
I have eaten	we have eaten
you have eaten	you have eaten
he, she, it has eaten	they have eaten

Past Perfect

This tense expresses action that took place before some other past action. It is formed by adding *had* to the past participle.

SINGULAR	PLURAL
I had eaten	we had eaten
you had eaten	you had eaten
he, she, it had eaten	they had eaten

Future Perfect

This tense expresses action that will be completed by some given time in the future. It is formed by adding *shall have* or *will have* to the past participle.

SINGULAR	PLURAL
I shall/will have eaten	we shall/will have eaten
you will have eaten	you will have eaten
he, she, it will have eaten	they will have eaten

EXERCISE 12 Conjugating a Verb

Using the conjugation of *eat* as a model, write the conjugation of the following verbs.

1. give, giving, gave, given
2. go, going, went, gone

Progressive Forms. Each tense has an additional form called the *progressive form.* It is used to express continuing action. It is formed by adding a form of the verb *be* to the present participle. Following are the progressive forms of the verb *eat.*

PRESENT PROGRESSIVE	am, is, are eating
PAST PROGRESSIVE	was, were eating
FUTURE PROGRESSIVE	shall/will be eating
PRESENT PERFECT PROGRESSIVE	has, have been eating
PAST PERFECT PROGRESSIVE	had been eating
FUTURE PERFECT PROGRESSIVE	shall/will have been eating

Emphatic Forms. The present and past tenses of a verb have an additional form called the *emphatic form,* which can be used to show emphasis. The emphatic forms are also used in questions and with *not.* They are formed by adding *do, does,* or *did* to the present. Following are the emphatic forms of the verb *eat.*

PRESENT EMPHATIC	do, does eat
PAST EMPHATIC	did eat

EXERCISE 13 Forming the Progressive and the Emphatic
Using the two preceding models of *eat,* write the progressive and emphatic forms of the verb *give.*

Conjugation of the Irregular Verb *Be*. The principal parts of the verb *be* are highly irregular. As a result, the conjugation of that verb is very different from that of other irregular verbs.

Conjugation of *Be*

PRINCIPAL PARTS

PRESENT	PRESENT PARTICIPLE	PAST	PAST PARTICIPLE
am	being	was	been

Present

SINGULAR	PLURAL
I am	we are
you are	you are
he, she, it is	they are

Past

SINGULAR	PLURAL
I was	we were
you were	you were
he, she, it was	they were

Future

SINGULAR	PLURAL
I shall/will be	we shall/will be
you will be	you will be
he, she, it will be	they will be

Present Perfect

SINGULAR	PLURAL
I have been	we have been
you have been	you have been
he, she, it has been	they have been

Past Perfect

SINGULAR	PLURAL
I had been	we had been
you had been	you had been
he, she, it had been	they had been

Future Perfect

SINGULAR	PLURAL
I shall/will have been	we shall/will have been
you will have been	you will have been
he, she, it will have been	they will have been

EXERCISE 14 Identifying Verb Tenses

Write the tense of each underlined verb.

EXAMPLE I <u>have taken</u> Spanish for three years.
ANSWER present perfect

1. At dinner tonight we <u>ate</u> fresh corn from our garden.
2. Brenda <u>will be attending</u> the press conference.
3. A male fox <u>will mate</u> for life.
4. We <u>have been</u> here for over an hour.
5. I <u>drink</u> tomato juice every day.
6. <u>Have</u> you <u>been practicing</u> your scales lately?

7. I had never tasted swordfish before last night.
8. A prairie dog is a rodent, not a dog.
9. I was taking a nap when you called.
10. There was neither cranberry sauce nor pumpkin pie at the first Thanksgiving.
11. Greg is waiting for you at the library.
12. Too much rain and too little sunshine have caused the tomato plants to fail.
13. Will you be ready at seven o'clock?
14. Joe DiMaggio's batting average fell below .300 only twice in his career.
15. Our senator will have visited 16 cities by the time he returns.
16. I did not put my books on the kitchen table.
17. Before today she had been my choice for class president.
18. Andrew has written several songs, and they're great!
19. Before Kevin joined the Raiders, he had been singing with another group.
20. Did you answer his letter?

Uses of the Tenses

Each of the six tenses and their various forms have a particular use. Clearly communicating your ideas will sometimes depend upon knowing the distinctions between these tenses.

The Present Tense. This tense mainly expresses action (or state of being) that is taking place at the present time. The present tense is also used to express customary or habitual action and general truths.

PRESENT ACTION	This small car **rides** smoothly.
HABITUAL ACTION	I **jog** a mile each day.
A GENERAL TRUTH	Haste **makes** waste.

The present progressive form expresses a present, on-going action, and the present emphatic form emphasizes a present action.

PRESENT PROGRESSIVE	Hannah **is working** at Lamont's Market.
PRESENT EMPHATIC	**Does** he **own** a bicycle?

The *historical present* is used to express past action when you want to give a certain historical event even greater impact or make it seem more immediate.

HISTORICAL PRESENT	Paul Revere **sees** the two lights in the church belfry, **jumps** onto his horse, and **heads** toward Lexington and Concord.

The Past Tense. This tense expresses action (or state of being) that occurred at a definite time in the past. Words such as *yesterday, a week ago,* and *last winter* often indicate that the action took place at a definite time. The past progressive expresses a continuous action that was completed in the past, and the emphatic past emphasizes action that occurred in the past.

PAST	Last week I **made** an important decision.
PAST PROGRESSIVE	Yesterday Danny **was watching** the children.
PAST EMPHATIC	Your package **did** not **arrive.**

The Future Tense. This tense expresses action (or state of being) that will take place in the future. The future progressive expresses a continuous action that will take place in the future.

FUTURE	I **will call** Betsy tonight.
FUTURE PROGRESSIVE	He **will be thinking** about that all summer.

NOTE: Sometimes the present or the present progressive is used to express future action as well.

Janice **goes** to the lake on Saturday.
Janice **is going** to the lake on Saturday.

The Present Perfect Tense. This tense expresses action (or state of being) that was completed at some indefinite time in the past. It also expresses action that started in the past and is still going on. All the progressive forms of the perfect tenses show continuing action.

PRESENT PERFECT — Sheila **has written** two prizewinning poems. [She wrote them at some indefinite time in the past.]

The Rosens **have been** our neighbors for six years. [The Rosens became our neighbors six years ago and are still our neighbors.]

PRESENT PERFECT PROGRESSIVE — Recently I **have been taking** swimming lessons at the YMCA.

The Past Perfect Tense. This tense expresses action (or state of being) that took place before some other event in the past.

PAST PERFECT — The *Herald* sent its best reporter to interview the senators who **had toured** China. [The touring occurred before the *Herald* sent its reporter.]

The young child was found several hours after he **had been reported** missing. [The reporting came before the child was found.]

One day after Peggy **had applied** for the job at the bakery, she started working. [The applying came before she started to work.]

PAST PERFECT PROGRESSIVE — Sheila **had been studying** for two hours before she made dinner.

The Future Perfect Tense. This tense expresses action (or state of being) that will be completed at some future time before some other future event.

FUTURE PERFECT — The plane **will have landed** by the time we get to the airport.

FUTURE PERFECT PROGRESSIVE — By April 10 we **will have been living** here for five years.

EXERCISE 15 Choosing the Correct Tense

Write the correct form of the verb in parentheses. Identify the tense you chose and tell why that tense is correct.

1. Dennis (applied, has applied) for that job yesterday.
2. I realized too late that I (left, had left) my keys at home.
3. For a month now, Carol (waited, has been waiting) for the first snowfall.
4. So far this week, King (chewed, has chewed) three socks, a pair of slippers, and my science book.
5. After Roberta (read, had read) the best-seller, she gave the book to me.
6. Before taking off for our first parachute jump, we carefully (checked, have checked) our equipment.
7. Ever since 1914, the Panama Canal (is, has been) a short-cut between New York and California.
8. Before he retired in June, Coach Randolph (was, had been) coaching football for 15 years.
9. Last Thursday we (make, made) Mexican food for dinner.
10. My mother (is, has been) working at the same company for eight years.
11. Tanya (needs, needed) to use the phone now.
12. Halfway to the lake, we remembered that we (forgot, had forgotten) to bring the picnic basket.
13. Lance (met, had met) us at the stadium.
14. Ever since 1791, the Bill of Rights (was, has been) the safeguard of our civil liberties.
15. When the waiter brought the check, Dan realized that he (left, had left) his wallet at home.
16. Many relatives and friends (come, came) to our Fourth of July party last summer.
17. Two hours after Muffin (ran, had run) away, we found her.
18. Lionel (received, has received) two letters for varsity track and basketball at the awards banquet last night.
19. At the reception tomorrow, we finally (meet, will meet) Senator Abrams.
20. I (called, have called) their apartment every half hour since noon.

Problems with Tenses

Knowing the tenses of verbs and their uses will eliminate most of the verb errors you might have been making. There are, however, a few special problems you should keep in mind when you edit your writing.

Shifts in Tense. When you write, avoid shifting from one tense to another. Use the same tense for a compound verb in a single sentence and for all verbs in compound and complex sentences *when the actions occur at the same time.* Most often an incorrect shift is made between the present and past tenses.

6d Avoid shifting tenses when relating events that occur at the same time.

INCORRECT The small plane **developed** (past) engine trouble, and **returns** (present) immediately to the field.

CORRECT The small plane **developed** (past) engine trouble, and **returned** (past) immediately to the field.

INCORRECT I **wrote** (past) the invitations, and Marcy **prepares** (present) the refreshments.

CORRECT I **wrote** (past) the invitations, and Marcy **prepared** (past) the refreshments.

INCORRECT When I **practice** (present) the piano every morning, I always **repeated** (past) the scales.

CORRECT When I **practice** (present) the piano every morning, I always **repeat** (present) the scales.

EXERCISE 16 Correcting Shifts in Tense

Number your paper 1 to 10. If the second verb in a sentence incorrectly shifts in tense, write it correctly. If a sentence is correct, write *C* after the number.

1. The fire fighters left the station and arrive at the burning house five minutes later.
2. The forest rangers found the lost hiker and call his parents.
3. Sarah walked to the library, but Nathan rides his bicycle.
4. I reached the station just as the train left.
5. Carl wrapped the presents while I decorate the dining room.

6. The movie ended, but the audience remains quietly in their seats.
7. Donna bought the album for Jody and gives it to her on her birthday.
8. The ballerina bowed and accepts a bouquet of flowers.
9. When the quarterback streaked down the field, the crowd roared.
10. Dad stripped the old varnish from the chair and sands it.

Sequence of Tenses. In complex sentences some changes in tense are correct. They are deliberately made to show precisely when the actions occur in a sequence of events. For example, if the action in the independent clause occurs in the present, use the past tense to express the dependent clause's earlier action—if that action was completed at a definite time in the past.

> present — past
>
> I **believe** that she **went** to the game with Harold. yesterday. [*Believe* is present because it is occurring now. *Went* is past because it was completed at a definite time in the past.]

If two events occur at different times in the past, use the past perfect tense to express the event that occurred first.

> past perfect — past
>
> After Mandy **had completed** the requirements for her lifesaving certificate, she **applied** for a job as a lifeguard. [*Had completed* is past perfect and *applied* is past to show that the completing came before the applying.]

NOTE: When you want to emphasize the closeness in the time of two events, use the past tense for both events.

> When the whistle **blew,** the workers **stopped** for lunch.

EXERCISE 17 Selecting Verbs in a Sequence
Write the correct verb form in parentheses.

1. The guests congratulated the cook who (prepared, had prepared) the delicious dinner.
2. After Christopher (heard, had heard) the joke, he laughed uproariously.

3. Isabel is relaxed because she (swam, has swum) 20 laps this afternoon.
4. When Mr. Glynn climbed the stairs, he (tripped, had tripped).
5. The coach canceled the game because most of the team (caught, had caught) the flu.
6. I know that Ralph (scored, had scored) 26 points in last night's basketball game.
7. There was an office building where our house (was, had been).
8. Dad thinks that Joseph already (picked, has picked) some corn for dinner.
9. When Chuck Murdock (fell, had fallen) into Horn Pond, Marie Montey rescued him.
10. She is the sophomore who (wrote, has written) the editorial about longer gym classes.

Tenses of Participles and Infinitives. Participles and infinitives have present and perfect tenses to express specific time.

	PARTICIPLE	INFINITIVE
PRESENT	talking	to talk
PERFECT	having talked	to have talked

NOTE: Add *having* to the past participle to form the perfect participle, and add *to* plus *have* to the past participle to form the perfect infinitive.

Always use the present participle or the present infinitive to express an action that happens at the same time as the main verb.

Talking intensely, the couple walked through the park.
Gail started **to talk** just as the bell rang.

Remember to use the perfect participle or the perfect infinitive to express an action that happened before the time of the main verb.

Having talked to his father about the plans for the evening, Mark left with his friends.

Julie was relieved **to have talked** to her doctor just before the operation.

EXERCISE 18 Using the Correct Participle or Infinitive
Write the correct verbal form in parentheses.

1. Mavis expected (to see, to have seen) you at the track meet on Saturday.
2. (Speaking, Having spoken) before the PTA, Claudia was extremely nervous.
3. (Buying, Having bought) a map, we set out to explore San Francisco.
4. I intended (to go, to have gone) to the exhibit at the museum last week.
5. Amy was thought (to be, to have been) the likely winner months before the election.
6. (Hearing, Having heard) the principal's welcoming remarks, we waited for the senator to address us.
7. (To help, To have helped) with the picking, David joined his brothers in the orchard.
8. (Watching, Having watched) the news on TV, Pearl recognized her history teacher.
9. Lynn hoped (to finish, to have finished) her report by now.
10. I'm proud (to participate, to have participated) in the conference in Washington, D.C., last month.

ACTIVE AND PASSIVE VOICE

All verbs have tense, but some action verbs also have voice. Transitive verbs can be in the *active voice* or the *passive voice.* *(See page 9 for an explanation of transitive verbs.)*

6e The **active voice** indicates that the subject is performing the action.

6f The **passive voice** indicates that the action of the verb is being performed upon the subject.

In the following examples, the verb in the active voice has a direct object, but the verb in the passive voice has no direct object.

ACTIVE VOICE	The referee **called** a strike. (d.o.: strike)
PASSIVE VOICE	A strike **was called** by the referee. [no direct object]

d.o.

ACTIVE VOICE Marie **sent** the letter by express mail.
PASSIVE VOICE The letter **was sent** by express mail. [no direct object]

Notice in the preceding examples that when the active voice is changed to the passive voice, the direct object becomes the subject. Notice also that both verbs in the passive voice consist of some form of the verb *be* plus the past participle—*was called* and *was sent.*

EXERCISE 19 Recognizing Active and Passive Voice
Number your paper 1 to 10. Write the verb in each sentence. Then label each one *active* or *passive.*

Money Matters

1. The early colonists used monies from many countries.
2. America once issued a five-cent bill.
3. The first Continental coin was designed by Benjamin Franklin.
4. The dies for that coin were engraved by Abel Buell.
5. Tobacco, in great demand, was used as money in Virginia and Maryland.
6. Martha Washington may have donated some of her silver forks and spoons for the minting of a series of half dimes.
7. The buffalo nickel was designed by James Earle Fraser, a famous sculptor.
8. Fraser's model was borrowed from the Bronx Zoo.
9. Nickels contain mostly copper.
10. The average United States dollar bill has a life span of less than one year.

Use of Voice

Because verbs in the active voice are more forceful and have greater impact than verbs in the passive voice, you should use the active voice as much as possible. There are two situations, however, in which the passive voice should be used: (1) when the doer of the action is unknown or unimportant and (2) when you want to emphasize the receiver of the action or when you want to emphasize the results.

Two extra innings **were played** in yesterday's game. [doer unknown or unimportant]

The first iron tools **were** probably **made** by the Hittites. [emphasis on the results]

EXERCISE 20 Using the Active and Passive Voices
Number your paper 1 to 10. Then write each sentence, changing the passive voice to the active voice if appropriate. If a sentence is better in the passive voice, write *C* after the number.

1. The earth was circled by the first satellite about once every 95 minutes.
2. This year corn was planted in the far field.
3. The new pitcher was given his instructions by Coach McKee.
4. I was sent my favorite album by my aunt.
5. The Acropolis in Athens was originally built as a group of temples.
6. During yesterday's terrible storm, our maple tree was struck by lightning.
7. The report on solar heating will be completed by Tim on Thursday.
8. In 1980, President Jimmy Carter was defeated in his bid for a second term in office.
9. The banks of the river are being cleaned of litter by some high school students.
10. Tropical fruits are often flown to northern cities by jet.

MOOD

The *mood* of a verb is the way in which the verb expresses an idea. The three moods in English are the indicative, the imperative, and the subjunctive. Because the *indicative mood* is used to state a fact or to ask a question, it is used most often. The *imperative mood* is used to give a command or to make a request.

INDICATIVE The sky **looks** very blue today.
What **makes** the sky blue?
IMPERATIVE **Look** at this article in the newspaper.

The *subjunctive mood* has two main uses.

6g The **subjunctive** mood is used to express (1) a condition contrary to fact, which begins with words like *if, as if,* and *although* or (2) a wish.

CONTRARY TO FACT If I **were** you, I'd enter the art contest. [I am not you.]

Benny and Eric look as if they **were** brothers. [They are not brothers.]

A WISH I wish I **were** a rich and famous athlete.

To form the subjunctive mood in conditions contrary to fact and in wishes, change *was,* the past indicative, to *were.*

If Patsy ~~was~~ **were** here, she could fix the television.
I wish I ~~was~~ **were** a few inches taller.

EXERCISE 21 Using the Subjunctive Mood
Number your paper 1 to 10. Write each verb that should be in the subjunctive mood. Then write it correctly.

1. I wish I was brave enough to ski the steep slopes.
2. Tom talks as if he was the athletic director.
3. I wish Earl was here.
4. If I was you, I'd learn to type.
5. You make me feel as if I was the Queen of England.
6. Lisa wished she was at the beach right now.
7. If Marnie was smaller, she could play the part of Peter Pan.
8. Our baseball team played the exhibition game as though it was a league contest.
9. If I was you, I'd order my class ring now.
10. He wishes he was as good a batter as you.

EXERCISE 22 Writing Sentences
Write sentences that follow the directions below.

1. Include an indicative-mood verb that makes a statement.
2. Include an indicative-mood verb that asks a question.
3. Include a verb in the imperative mood.
4. Include a subjunctive-mood verb that is used to express an idea contrary to fact.
5. Include a subjunctive-mood verb that is used to express a wish.

EXERCISE 23 Time-out for Review
Write the correct verb form or verbal in parentheses.

1. Ben ran into the house and (heads, headed) for the phone.
2. I'm sorry (to cause, to have caused) all of you so much worry yesterday.
3. I wish I (was, were) president of a big corporation.
4. Since noon Matthew (is, has been) at the pool.
5. Stephanie just remembered that she (promised, had promised) to pick up Claire.
6. You act as though I (was, were) the only person who voted.
7. Cora (goes, will go) to her music lesson this afternoon.
8. (Losing, Having lost) a leg in an encounter with Moby Dick, Captain Ahab vowed revenge.
9. Ted wondered if he (earned, had earned) a pay increase.
10. If James (was, were) playing, we'd have a chance to win.
11. Last night Lynn intended (to make, to have made) a scarf.
12. I (started, have started) working yesterday.
13. My grandmother paints landscapes, and my grandfather (makes, made) the frames for them.
14. (Running, Having run) the electric mixer, Donna blocked out the sound of the doorbell.
15. Leslie went to the library and (looks, looked) for some reference books for her report.
16. If Courtney (was, were) here, she'd know how to fix the copy machine.
17. Leroy is very relieved that he (found, has found) his notebook before class.
18. Ever since my freshman year, Ms. Rivera (was, has been) my guidance counselor.
19. Charlene was happy (to hear, to have heard) the good news yesterday.
20. I think that Joyce (wrote, has written) her essay last night.

Application to Writing

When editing your written work, carefully check for any errors in verb usage. Check, for example, for the correct use of the tenses of verbs and verbals and for any shifts in tense. Look also for weak passive verbs. By reading your work aloud, you also should be able to find most incorrect verb forms.

EXERCISE 24 Editing for Verb Errors

Write any incorrect verb form. Then write it correctly. If a sentence is incorrectly written in the passive voice, write the sentence in the active voice.

Now Hear This!

In 1956, several professional football teams try something new. From the sidelines, a coach speaked through a microphone. Then through a wireless receiver in his helmet, the coach's instructions could be heard by the quarterback on the field. The Cleveland Browns first use this idea in a game against the Detroit Lions. Even though the quarterback heard all the coach's plays, the Browns losed 31–14.

Having believed the system would work, Coach Paul Brown took to the airwaves again the following week. This time the radio dies mid-game. The Browns, nevertheless, winned by ten points. In a game between the Browns and the New York Giants, the Browns' radio signals were intercepted by a Giants' reserve end with a receiver of his own. The Browns once again lost 21–9. On October 18, 1956, the National Football League's commissioner come to a decision: All radio helmets were banned.

CHAPTER REVIEW

A. Write the correct verb form or verbal in parentheses.

1. Since my youth, I (was, have been) afraid of bees.
2. When the game was almost over, the quarterback (throws, threw) a pass into the end zone for a touchdown.
3. If that dog (was, were) mine, I'd train him to heel.
4. Michael suddenly realized that he (left, had left) his books in Leroy's car.
5. Pamela wants (to work, to have worked) on the senator's reelection campaign.
6. Ever since 1787, the bald eagle (was, has been) this country's national bird.
7. (Sleeping, Having slept) late, Karen missed the bus.
8. I wish I (was, were) already through college.
9. Roy realized where he (saw, had seen) the sloop before.
10. Dad knows that I (worked, have worked) at the garage this afternoon.

B. Number your paper 1 to 10. Label the verb in each sentence *active* or *passive*. Then rewrite any sentence in the passive voice that should be in the active voice.

1. Because of the storm, school was closed for the day.
2. In 1863, Abraham Lincoln made Thanksgiving a national holiday.
3. An interesting experiment was performed by Margaret in chemistry.
4. The mayor began his speech with a joke.
5. The first copy of the Declaration of Independence with the signers' names was printed by Mary Katherine Goddard.
6. The initial flight of Alan Shepard, the first United States astronaut, lasted only 15 minutes and 22 seconds.
7. A diamond can be shattered by a sharp blow.
8. During the past two decades, great interest in outer space has been shown by the United States.
9. My brother Mark pitched a no-hitter today.
10. The SAT's were taken by many seniors on Saturday.

MASTERY TEST

Number your paper 1 to 10. Then write the past or the past participle of each verb in parentheses.

1. Sue (do) a great job finding costumes for the senior play.
2. I have never (ride) on a Ferris wheel before.
3. Last winter many of the orange trees in Florida (freeze).
4. Tomatoes are (grow) in desert sand at the Epcot Center.
5. I have (write) for six college catalogs.
6. Yesterday my youngest brother (throw) a football 40 yards.
7. Our dog has (lie) in front of the heater all day.
8. Daniel never (go) to the meeting last night.
9. Who (teach) world history last year?
10. Have you (begin) to think about what you'll do after graduation?

7

Using Pronouns

DIAGNOSTIC TEST

Number your paper 1 to 10. Then write the correct form of the pronoun in parentheses.

EXAMPLE Kate and (I, me) have joined the yearbook staff.
ANSWER I

1. Are Joel and (he, him) trying out for the football team?
2. For answering questions about history, there's no one like Ramón or (she, her).
3. (We, Us) club officers should discuss the agenda.
4. With (who, whom) are you sharing a locker?
5. Let's keep the fact of (me, my) passing the driving test a surprise.
6. The two people sitting in the front row are Betsy and (he, him).
7. The seniors (who, whom) won the special scholarships are Gary and Flora.
8. Within the past year, my younger brother has become as tall as (I, me).
9. Have you seen (their, they're) new Irish setter?
10. Some of the girls haven't taken (her, their) swimming tests yet.

The colors of traffic lights are signals to motorists and pedestrians. Even before you were able to read, you learned that green means "go," red means "stop," and yellow means "caution." Without realizing it, you also learned another set of signals when you were a child. You learned, for example, that you should use the pronoun *he* in one situation, but *him* and *his* in other situations.

He, him, and *his* send out different signals because they indicate the *case* of a pronoun. A pronoun has a different form and a different function for each case. When you use a particular form of a pronoun, therefore, you are signaling to a reader or a listener how that pronoun is being used in a sentence.

NOTE: Nouns also have case, but they have only two forms. The nominative and objective *girl* becomes *girl's* in the possessive case.

7a **Case** is the form of a noun or a pronoun that indicates its use in a sentence.

THE CASES OF PERSONAL PRONOUNS

The three cases of personal pronouns are the *nominative case,* the *objective case,* and the *possessive case.*

Nominative Case

Used for subjects, predicate nominatives, and appositives

	SINGULAR	PLURAL
FIRST PERSON	I	we
SECOND PERSON	you	you
THIRD PERSON	he, she, it	they

Objective Case

Used for direct objects, indirect objects, and objects of prepositions

	SINGULAR	PLURAL
FIRST PERSON	me	us
SECOND PERSON	you	you
THIRD PERSON	him, her, it	them

Possessive Case

Used to show ownership or possession

	SINGULAR	PLURAL
FIRST PERSON	my, mine	our, ours
SECOND PERSON	your, yours	your, yours
THIRD PERSON	his, her, hers, its	their, theirs

NOTE: *You* and *it* are the same in both the nominative and the objective cases.

The Nominative Case

I, you, he, she, it, we, and *they* are the personal pronouns in the nominative case.

7b The **nominative case** is used for subjects and predicate nominatives.

Pronouns as Subjects. A pronoun can be used as a subject of an independent clause or a dependent clause.

INDEPENDENT CLAUSE	**We** enjoyed the play.
DEPENDENT CLAUSE	As soon as **he** had washed the car, the rain started.

The case of a pronoun that is part of a compound subject is sometimes not as obvious as a single-subject pronoun. That is why it is important to double check any pronoun in a compound subject to make sure that it is in the nominative case. To do this, say the nominative and the objective pronouns separately—to find out which one is correct.

Jason and (he, him) entered the art contest.
He entered the art contest.
Him entered the art contest.

The nominative case *he* is the correct form to use.

Jason and **he** entered the art contest.

This method of checking for the correct case also works if both subjects are pronouns.

(He, Him) and (I, me) waited in the cafeteria.
He waited in the cafeteria.
Him waited in the cafeteria.
I waited in the cafeteria.
Me waited in the cafeteria.
He and **I** waited in the cafeteria.

Pronouns as Predicate Nominatives. A predicate nominative follows a linking verb and identifies, renames, or explains the subject. *(See page 10 for lists of common linking verbs.)*

That was **I** who answered the telephone.

The preceding example probably sounds extremely formal—or even incorrect—to you. However, while *That was me* or *It's me* is common usage in conversation, it should be avoided in written work.

It was **she.** That is **he.** The winners are **they.**

To check to see if the pronoun in a compound predicate nominative is in the correct case, turn the sentence around to make the predicate nominative the subject. Then say the nominative and the objective pronouns separately to find out which one is correct.

The two nominees for treasurer are Ben and (she, her).
Ben and (she, her) are the two nominees for treasurer.
She is a nominee. **Her** is a nominee.
The two nominees for treasurer are Ben and **she.**

NOTE: Sometimes the wording of a sentence becomes awkward when pronouns are used as predicate nominatives. Such awkwardness can be avoided by turning the sentence around.

AWKWARD The leads in the school play are Bart and **she.**
TURNED AROUND Bart and **she** are the leads in the school play.

Appositives with *We*. An appositive is a noun or a pronoun that renames or identifies another noun or pronoun in the sentence. Occasionally when *we* is used as a subject or a predicate nominative, a noun or a pronoun is in apposition with *we*. The noun appositive that follows *we* never affects the case of *we*. The best way to check to see if you have used the correct pronoun is to drop the appositive mentally from the sentence.

> **We** *cross-country skiers* thoroughly enjoy winter. [We thoroughly enjoy winter.]
>
> The most relaxed people in the group were **we** *joggers*. [The most relaxed people in the group were we.]

Nominative Case Pronouns as Appositives. An appositive is in the same case as the noun or pronoun to which it refers. Occasionally a pronoun itself will be part of an appositive to a subject or a predicate nominative. Then the pronoun should be in the nominative case.

> The exchange students, *Yuri and* ***he***, spoke at the meeting.

Yuri and *he* are appositives to the subject *students*. Since a subject is in the nominative case, an appositive to the subject is also in the nominative case.

EXERCISE 1 Using Pronouns in the Nominative Case
Number your paper 1 to 10. Then write the correct form of the pronoun in parentheses.

1. Paula and (she, her) haven't received their invitations.
2. (He, Him) and (she, her) plan to try out for the play.
3. The officers in charge were (they, them).
4. The captain of the team is either Patrick or (he, him).
5. Ruth knew that Jay or (she, her) would be at the game.
6. The persons most concerned are (we, us) average citizens.
7. It wasn't (I, me) who answered the telephone.
8. The cocaptains, Sarah and (she, her), graduate this year.
9. (We, Us) survivors of the flood will rebuild our homes.
10. Neither Lucy nor (I, me) have a part-time job.

EXERCISE 2 Finding Errors in the Nominative Case
Number your paper 1 to 10. If an underlined pronoun is in the wrong case, write it correctly. If it is in the correct case, write *C* after the number.

1. Mom said that Monica and him would be home in an hour.
2. The witnesses to the accident were Charles and her.

3. We guides directed the European visitors through the high school.
4. During practice today Miguel and him threw passes for a total of 106 yards.
5. When Gloria and Michael left, we left also.
6. The ones most surprised by the writing awards were Ann and me.
7. Their children and them are camping this weekend.
8. The finalists in the state competition are us Central High students.
9. Two former quarterbacks, Joe Namath and him, appeared on a talk show on TV.
10. The two babies in the photograph are him and me.

EXERCISE 3 Writing Sentences
Write a sentence for each of the following groups of words. Use one group as a compound subject, one as a compound predicate nominative, and one as a compound appositive. Then label how each one is used.

1. you and I 2. he and she 3. Julio and they

The Objective Case

Me, you, him, her, it, us, and *them* are the personal pronouns in the objective case.

7c The **objective case** is used for direct objects, indirect objects, objects of prepositions, and objects of verbals.

Pronouns as Direct and Indirect Objects. A pronoun that is used as a direct object will follow an action verb and answer the question *Whom?* A pronoun that is used as an indirect object will answer the question *To whom?* or *For whom?* after the direct object.

DIRECT OBJECTS Dad will drive **us** to school.
The mayor will see **her** now.

INDIRECT OBJECTS The usher gave **me** a program. (d.o.: program)
Tell **him** that joke. (d.o.: joke)

You can check for the correct case of a compound direct object by saying the nominative and the objective pronouns separately.

Jason saw the Dyers and (they, them) at the horse show.
Jason saw **they** at the horse show.
Jason saw **them** at the horse show.

The objective case *them* is the correct form to use.

Jason saw the Dyers and **them** at the horse show.

Compound indirect objects can be checked in the same way.

Fred made Beth and (I, me) a leather wallet.
Fred made **I** a leather wallet.
Fred made **me** a leather wallet.

The objective case *me* is the correct form to use.

Fred made Beth and **me** a leather wallet.

EXERCISE 4 Using Pronouns as Direct and Indirect Objects Number your paper 1 to 10. Write the correct form of the pronoun in parentheses. Then write how each one is used—*direct object* or *indirect object.*

1. The coach chose Tim and (he, him) for the team.
2. Dad called Leroy and (I, me) for dinner.
3. Give the principal and (we, us) a copy of your speech.
4. You should ask Juan or (she, her) about the assignment.
5. Mr. Samuelson will pay (they, them) or (we, us) ten dollars to rake the leaves on his property.
6. Mr. Randolph gave Alma and (I, me) extra tickets to the graduation ceremonies.
7. The board will notify Andrea or (she, her) of its decision.
8. Neil showed (he, him) and (I, me) the new outboard skiffs.
9. Daniel will meet Scott and (we, us) at the stadium.
10. Please bring Mom and (she, her) their sweaters.

Pronouns as Objects of Prepositions. A prepositional phrase begins with a preposition and ends with a noun or a pronoun called the *object of a preposition.* A pronoun that is used as an object of a preposition is in the objective case. *(See page 18 for a list of common prepositions.)*

You can ride with **us.** [*With us* is the prepositional phrase.]

Is this note for **me?** [*For me* is the prepositional phrase.]

You can check to see that a pronoun in a compound object of a preposition is in the objective case by saying the nominative and objective pronouns separately.

Rachel left a message for David or (she, her).
Rachel left a message for **she.**
Rachel left a message for **her.**

The objective case *her* is the correct form to use.

Rachel left a message for David or **her.**

EXERCISE 5 Using Pronouns as Objects of Prepositions
Write the correct form of the pronoun in parentheses.

1. Nobody showed up except Bernie and (he, him).
2. Roy waited for the Ryans and (they, them) for an hour.
3. Would you like to go to the rodeo with Tom and (we, us)?
4. You should talk to Rebecca and (he, him) soon.
5. Why did you disagree with Clarence and (she, her)?
6. You will be seated near the Kents and (they, them).
7. Between you and (I, me), I plan to join the math team.
8. That present is from David and (we, us).
9. Like you and (I, me), Bart is also looking for a job.
10. Leave your keys with Heather or (she, her).

Pronouns as Objects of Verbals. Because participles, gerunds, and infinitives are verb forms, they can take objects. The direct object of a verbal is in the objective case. *(See pages 57–64 for an explanation of verbals.)*

PARTICIPIAL PHRASE	Seeing **her** in the restaurant, Jeff asked the movie star for her autograph. [The phrase is *seeing her in the restaurant. Her* is the object of the participle *seeing.*]
GERUND PHRASE	I don't recall meeting **him** at school. [The phrase is *meeting him at school. Him* is the object of the gerund *meeting.*]
INFINITIVE PHRASE	I want to visit **them** soon, but I am very busy. [The phrase is *to visit them soon. Them* is the object of the infinitive *to visit.*]

A pronoun in a compound object of a verbal can be checked by saying the nominative and objective pronouns separately.

I hope to see Philip and (she, her) at the game.
I hope to see **she** at the game.
I hope to see **her** at the game.
I hope to see Philip and **her** at the game.

Appositives with *Us*. An appositive of *us* does not affect the case of *us*. To check to see if you have used the correct pronoun, mentally drop the appositive from the sentence.

Take **us** *taco lovers* to the Mexican restaurant. [*Us* is used as a direct object. Take us to the Mexican restaurant.]

Objective Case Pronouns as Appositives. Occasionally a pronoun itself is part of an appositive to a direct object, an indirect object, or an object of a preposition. Then the pronoun should be in the objective case.

We found two volunteers, *Gladys and **him***, to work at the refreshment stand.

Gladys and *him* are the appositives to the direct object *volunteers*. Since a direct object is in the objective case, an appositive to the direct object is also in the objective case.

EXERCISE 6 Using Pronouns in the Objective Case
Write the correct form of the pronoun in parentheses.

1. Making (he, him) the shortstop was a wise decision.
2. The principal asked (we, us) computer buffs for a demonstration of the new hardware.
3. Finding (he, him) in the old shack, the police officers took the lost boy home.
4. Be sure to tell Carrie and (she, her) about the meeting after school.
5. At the awards ceremony, the coach gave special recognition to two athletes, Bret and (he, him).
6. It was a great disappointment to (we, us) fans when Mason struck out.
7. Alex tried in vain to find Sarah and (he, him) in the crowd.

8. I don't recall seeing Nat and (they, them) at the game.
9. They interviewed two of our neighbors, Mrs. Sousa and (she, her), for the evening newscast.
10. Watching Liz and (they, them) on stage, Mom and Dad were very proud.

EXERCISE 7 Finding Errors in the Objective Case

Number your paper 1 to 20. If an underlined pronoun is in the wrong case, write it correctly. If it is in the correct case, write *C* after the number.

1. Please save seats for Sue and him.
2. Will you show Marcia and I your canoe over the weekend?
3. Dad had warned you and she about that thin ice!
4. The engineer explained the procedure to we architects.
5. Will Roger be able to drive us home after the game?
6. We heard the speeches of the two finalists, Pat and he.
7. He should never have taken him along.
8. We saw Dad watching them on the balance beams.
9. Mom sent Harold and I to the store for some milk.
10. Be sure to call us when you get home.
11. Dad saved some turkey for Leslie and I.
12. Timing her during the race is my job.
13. Mrs. Wallace gave we workers some lunch.
14. I wanted to invite them to the party.
15. Mr. Vernon took Valerie and he through the factory.
16. Telling them the sad news was quite difficult.
17. The judges awarded Theresa and we honorable mention.
18. People like they help preserve our wildlife.
19. We should give the chefs of this great meal, Otis and she, a round of applause.
20. Mr. Dobson assigned Jeff and her the leading roles.

EXERCISE 8 Writing Sentences

Write five sentences that follow the directions below.

1. Use *the Jacksons* and *them* as a compound direct object.
2. Use *Paul* and *him* as a compound indirect object.
3. Use *Linda* and *me* as a compound object of a preposition.
4. Use *Janice* and *her* as a compound appositive.
5. Use *them* as an object of a verbal.

The Possessive Case

My, mine, your, yours, his, her, hers, its, our, ours, their, and *theirs* are the personal pronouns in the possessive case.

7d The **possessive case** is used to show ownership or possession.

Possessive case pronouns are used before a noun, before a gerund, or by themselves.

BEFORE A NOUN	This is **my** notebook.
BEFORE A GERUND	We were surprised at **his** entering the race. ["We were surprised at *him* entering the race" is *not* correct.]
BY THEMSELVES	These are **mine,** but which are **his?**

NOTE: Do not confuse certain possessive pronouns with contractions. A personal pronoun in the possessive case never includes an apostrophe. *Its, your, their,* and *theirs* are possessive pronouns. However, *it's, you're, they're,* and *there's* are contractions.

EXERCISE 9 Using Pronouns in the Possessive Case
Write the correct word in parentheses.

1. Is there any chance of (you, your) winning an athletic scholarship?
2. (Theirs, There's) is the two-door navy sedan.
3. We were surprised at (them, their) setting out to cross the bay in the heavy fog.
4. (Him, His) completing that forward pass to the ten-yard line was a lucky break for Windsor High.
5. That portable radio must be (ours, our's).
6. Coach Morgan was surprised at (me, my) losing so much weight over the summer.
7. I hadn't heard about (him, his) getting chosen for the varsity team.
8. The car and (its, it's) owner were taken to the nearest garage.
9. Dad appreciated (you, your) explaining the insurance benefits to him.
10. My parents were pleased at (me, my) doing so well on the math exam.

EXERCISE 10 Supplying Pronouns

Number your paper 1 to 10. Then complete each sentence by writing appropriate pronouns. (Do not use *you* or *it*.)

1. ____ sat with Janet and ____.
2. ____ showed Brad ____ old tent.
3. ____ will follow Inés and ____ in the truck.
4. ____ has been trying to call ____ all evening.
5. When did ____ learn that ____ house had been sold?
6. ____ is going to the game with Otis and ____.
7. ____ team members prepared a surprise party for ____.
8. The muffins were intended for Nancy, but ____ ate ____.
9. Sarah put ____ luggage in ____ car.
10. ____ doesn't recall meeting ____ at the party.

EXERCISE 11 Time-out for Review

Number your paper 1 to 20. Find and write each pronoun that is in the wrong case. Then write it correctly. If a sentence is correct, write *C* after the number.

1. They showed Alicia and me the programs for the musical.
2. Leave some of the strawberries for Leon and she.
3. Them must have been difficult for Paulo to make.
4. During the storm him and me were in a rowboat.
5. Notifying them of the change in plans will take time.
6. The sets for the play were painted by two people, Carmen and I.
7. In the car, dressed and ready to go, were Nelson and her.
8. Everyone was glad to hear of me joining the track team.
9. We want to give her luggage for graduation.
10. Us climbers started up Mount Crisco at 5:00 A.M.
11. Ask the librarians, Mr. Shelby and she, about a job.
12. The best students in the class are Beverly and him.
13. Eva was in the bus with John and they.
14. Taking him by the hand, she led the crying child home.
15. This spring vacation will give we boys a chance to work on restoring Oliver's 1934 Buick.
16. Jim and him have soccer practice every afternoon.
17. Give your dues to a class officer—Ted, Betsy, or she.
18. Scott's mother doesn't like him playing football.
19. Please find us something to eat.
20. Us girls are forming a softball team.

PRONOUN PROBLEMS

Has anyone on the other end of the telephone ever said to you, "Whom may I say is calling"? The next time you hear that expression, you will know that the speaker has just made a pronoun error. This section will cover the cases of the pronouns *who* and *whoever* as well as the correct use of pronouns in elliptical clauses.

Who and *Whom*

Like personal pronouns, the pronouns *who* and *whoever* change their forms—depending upon how they are used within a sentence.

NOMINATIVE CASE	who, whoever
OBJECTIVE CASE	whom, whomever
POSSESSIVE CASE	whose

Who and *whoever* and their related pronouns are used in questions and in subordinate clauses.

7e The correct case of *who* is determined by how the pronoun is used in a question or a clause.

In Questions. Frequently *who* and *whoever* or one of their related pronouns are used in questions. The case you should use depends upon how the pronoun is used.

NOMINATIVE CASE	**Who** found her contact lens? [subject]
OBJECTIVE CASE	**Whom** did you invite? [direct object]
	To **whom** did you speak? [object of the preposition *to*]

When deciding which case to use, turn a question around to its natural order.

QUESTION	**Whom** did you invite?
NATURAL ORDER	You did invite **whom.**

NOTE: In casual conversation you might hear people say, *Who did you invite?* This informal use of *who,* however, should be avoided in formal, written work.

In Clauses. *Who* and *whoever* or one of their related pronouns are also used to introduce adjective and noun clauses. The case you use once again depends upon how the pronoun is used in a clause. The following examples show how forms of *who* are used in adjective clauses.

NOMINATIVE CASE Heather is one of those people **who excel in any sport.** [*Who* is the subject of *excel.*]

OBJECTIVE CASE Mr. Jenkins is the man **whom the theater group consulted about the spring musical.** [*Whom* is the direct object of *consulted.* The theater group *consulted* whom.]

Peg is the person **from whom I bought this tape recorder.** [*Whom* is the object of the preposition *from. From* is part of the clause.]

The following examples show how forms of *who* and *whoever* are used in noun clauses.

NOMINATIVE CASE **Whoever sells 50 magazine subscriptions** will receive a portable radio. [*Whoever* is the subject of *sells.*]

In the dark hallways, Jerry couldn't tell **who the girl was.** [*Who* is a predicate nominative. The girl was who.]

OBJECTIVE CASE Invite **whomever you want.** [*Whomever* is the direct object of *want.* You want whomever.]

Ray persuaded **whomever he talked to.** [*Whomever* is the object of the preposition *to.* He talked to whomever.]

In the next example, notice that the case of *who* or *whoever* is not affected by any word outside the clause.

The diving course is open to **whoever is interested.** [*Whoever* is the subject of *is.* The noun clause, not the pronoun, is the object of the preposition *to.*]

NOTE: An interrupting expression such as *I believe, we know, do you suppose,* and *I hope* sometimes appears in a question or a clause. Before you decide the case of a pronoun, mentally drop this expression to avoid any confusion.

> **Who** *do you suppose* will win the track meet? [Who will win the track meet? *Who* is the subject of *will win.*]
>
> Otis, **who** *I think* is the best player on the team, is now a senior. [Otis, who is the best player on the team, is now a senior. *Who* is the subject of *is.*]

EXERCISE 12 Using *Who* and Its Related Pronouns
Number your paper 1 to 25. Write the correct form of the pronoun in parentheses. Then, using the following abbreviations, write how each pronoun is used in the question or the clause.

subject = *subj.*	direct object = *d.o.*
predicate nominative = *p.n.*	object of a preposition = *o.p.*

1. (Who, Whom) will pitch against Kenneth on Saturday?
2. On Friday I met a woman (who, whom) is an engineer.
3. Did they say (who, whom) the finalists are?
4. Tell (whoever, whomever) you see about the meeting.
5. With (who, whom) did you sit at the concert?
6. (Who, Whom) did you nominate?
7. Do you know (who, whom) the bearded man is?
8. The school board will give one hundred dollars to (whoever, whomever) writes the best school song.
9. With (who, whom) did you study for the test?
10. Mr. Davis is the teacher (who, whom) everyone respects.
11. Gregory usually likes (whoever, whomever) he works for.
12. From (who, whom) should we lease a trailer?
13. It was John Marshall (who, whom) historians agree did the most to establish the authority of the Supreme Court.
14. (Who, Whom) noticed where I put the car keys?
15. Do you know (who, whom) the trainer of the horse is?
16. (Who, Whom) do you imagine could play that role?
17. Give this message to (whoever, whomever) telephones.
18. Has anyone heard (who, whom) the new principal will be?
19. (Who, Whom) did he think should play the lead in the play?
20. Get (whoever, whomever) you need for the crew.
21. Gail is the girl with (who, whom) I always jog.

22. (Who, Whom) do you suppose will replace Ms. Bennett?
23. Jennifer asked (who, whom) the man in the blue suit was.
24. Gretchen is one person (who, whom) I think will succeed.
25. (Who, Whom) did you see at the track meet?

EXERCISE 13 Writing Sentences
Write five sentences that follow the directions below.

1. Begin a question with *who.*
2. Begin a question with *whom* used as a direct object.
3. Include *who* as the subject of a subordinate clause.
4. Include *whom* as the direct object in a subordinate clause.
5. Include *whom* as the object of a preposition in a subordinate clause.

Elliptical Clauses

An adverb clause that is only partially expressed is called an *elliptical clause.* Although words are missing from a clause, they are understood to be there by both the writer and the reader. An elliptical clause often begins with *than* or *as.*

Mr. Lee coached Eric more **than I.**
Mr. Lee coached Eric more **than me.**

Depending upon what is intended, both of the preceding examples are correct.

Mr. Lee coached Eric more **than I coached Eric.** [*I* is correct because it is the subject of *coached.*]

Mr. Lee coached Eric more **than he coached me.** [*Me* is correct because it is the direct object of *coached.*]

7f In an **elliptical clause,** use the form of the pronoun you would use if the clause were completed.

To decide which pronoun to use in an elliptical clause, mentally complete the clause. Then choose the form of the pronoun that expresses the meaning you want. An elliptical clause, however, can sometimes express only one meaning.

Do you think David is as tall as (I, me)?
Do you think David is as tall **as I am?**

EXERCISE 14 Using Pronouns in Elliptical Clauses
Complete and write each elliptical clause. Then underline the pronoun you chose.

EXAMPLE Sally is twice as energetic as (he, him).
ANSWER as he is

1. Amy made a better score on the test than (I, me).
2. In the tryouts I think Marcia did better than (she, her).
3. When working with children, Barry has more patience than (he, him).
4. Andrea is as experienced an actress as (I, me).
5. Martha likes Shirley more than (we, us).
6. At the fair Anna earned more money than (I, me).
7. Mr. Ferguson trained him better than (she, her).
8. Ben is not as tall as (she, her), but he is much heavier.
9. My sister was always better in sports than (I, me).
10. Mary praised Melissa more than (he, him).

EXERCISE 15 Time-out for Review
Number your paper 1 to 10. Find and write each pronoun that is used incorrectly. Then write it correctly. If a sentence is correct, write *C* after the number.

1. With whom is Anita dancing?
2. A reward was promised to whomever found the necklace.
3. Maria and I have belonged to the club longer than him.
4. She is the teacher whom I believe should be hired.
5. Wayne, who everyone had chosen, declined the offer.
6. They're as fast on their skates as we.
7. Do you think Joe pitches better than me?
8. Whom do you think will win the writing contest?
9. Is the governor as concerned about acid rain as them?
10. Did he tell you who the nominees are?

PRONOUNS AND THEIR ANTECEDENTS

A pronoun's *antecedent* is the word that the pronoun refers to, or replaces. A pronoun and its antecedent must agree in number and gender, since they both are referring to the same person, place, or thing.

Number is the term used to indicate whether a noun or a pronoun is singular or plural. *Singular* indicates one; *plural* indicates more than one. *Gender* is the term used to indicate whether a noun or a pronoun is *masculine, feminine,* or *neuter.*

Masculine	**Feminine**	**Neuter**
he, him, his	she, her, hers	it, its

7g A **pronoun** must agree in number and gender with its antecedent.

To make a pronoun agree with its antecedent, first find the antecedent. Then determine its number and gender. Making a pronoun agree with a single-word antecedent usually is not a problem.

Nancy must take **her** final exams early. [*Nancy* is singular and feminine; therefore, *her* is correct because it also is singular and feminine.]

Members of the prom committee presented **their** ideas to the seniors at a special meeting. [*Members* is plural; therefore, *their* is plural.]

If the antecedent of a pronoun is more than one word, you need to remember two rules.

7h If two or more singular antecedents are joined by *or, nor, either/or,* or *neither/nor,* use a singular pronoun to refer to them.

All the conjunctions listed in the previous rule indicate a choice—one *or* the other. In the following example, Harold *or* Cliff signed his name—not both of them. As a result, the pronoun must be singular.

Either Harold or Cliff signed **his** name to the petition.

NOTE: When one antecedent is singular and the other is plural, the pronoun agrees with the closer antecedent.

Neither Sue nor the other two actors brought **their** costumes to rehearsal.

7i If two or more singular antecedents are joined by *and* or *both/and,* use a plural pronoun to refer to them.

And and *both/and* indicate more than one. In the following example, both Greta and Mavis—two people—turned in term papers early. As a result, the pronoun is plural.

Both Greta and Mavis turned in **their** term papers early.

The gender of most antecedents is obvious. *Harold* and *Cliff* are masculine; *Greta* and *Mavis* are feminine. The gender of some antecedents, however, is not so obvious. Standard English solves the agreement problem in such cases by using *his* or *his or her* to refer to antecedents of unknown gender.

Each senior should rent **his** cap and gown.

Each senior should rent **his or her** cap and gown.

You can avoid this awkward wording by rewriting such sentences, using the plural form.

All seniors should rent **their** caps and gowns.

EXERCISE 16 Making Pronouns and Antecedents Agree
Number your page 1 to 20. Then write the pronoun that correctly completes each sentence.

1. Each boy on the soccer team must have ____ picture taken for the yearbook.
2. The tourists leaving the bus carried ____ own luggage.
3. Sheila and Marcia had a hard time finding ____ jackets on the crowded coat rack.
4. All cats in the pet store have had ____ shots.
5. Neither King Arthur nor ____ knights suspected ____ enemy's plan.
6. The workers at the plant must show ____ identification badges before entering.
7. Each member of the League of Women Voters contributed ____ time to the debate.
8. Whenever Larry catches a good-sized flounder or striped bass, ____ gives ____ away.

9. Both Andrew and Mark need new tires on ____ bicycles.
10. Neither Clara nor Sally remembered to bring ____ ticket.
11. Mom and Dad wanted to attend the concert, but ____ were too busy.
12. Either Juan or Don left ____ glasses in the cafeteria.
13. The baseball team and the softball team held ____ annual banquet at the Regis Hotel.
14. Neither Paula nor ____ sister has received ____ invitation to the party yet.
15. Both Devon and Maria said that ____ would join us after the game.
16. Either Uncle Elroy or the Greysons will lend you ____ power saw.
17. Baby birds digest ____ food very rapidly.
18. Neither Andrea nor ____ brothers will have ____ vacations in August this year.
19. Marshall is taking ____ parents out to dinner for ____ anniversary.
20. If you have a rubber band or some paper clips, please give ____ to me for my index cards.

Indefinite Pronouns As Antecedents

Like personal pronouns, indefinite pronouns also have number. The following chart groups the most common indefinite pronouns by number.

Common Indefinite Pronouns

SINGULAR	anybody, anyone, each, either, everybody, everyone, neither, nobody, no one, one, somebody, someone
PLURAL	both, few, many, several
SINGULAR/PLURAL	all, any, most, none, some

A personal pronoun must be singular if its antecedent is one of the singular indefinite pronouns.

Each of the girls is hiking during **her** vacation.

A personal pronoun must be plural if its antecedent is one of the plural indefinite pronouns.

Both of the men donated **their** time to the paper drive.

If the antecedent of a personal pronoun is one of the singular/plural indefinite pronouns, the personal pronoun agrees in number and gender with the object of the preposition that follows the indefinite pronoun.

Some of the dirt has mulch mixed into **it.** [singular]

Some of the teachers have graded **their** exams. [plural]

NOTE: The gender of a singular indefinite pronoun sometimes is not indicated by other words in the sentence. Standard English solves this problem by using *his* or *his or her* or by rewriting the sentence, using the plural form.

Each of the members must pay **his** dues by Monday.

Each of the members must pay **his or her** dues by Monday.

All of the members must pay **their** dues by Monday.

EXERCISE 17 Making Pronouns Agree

Number your paper 1 to 10. Then write the pronoun that correctly completes each sentence.

1. Neither of the parakeets has had ____ dinner.
2. All of the applicants had to put ____ names on a roster.
3. Both of my grandmothers recently attended ____ high school reunions.
4. Most of the sheets had a flaw in ____.
5. Each of the men in the glider class got ____ license within a few weeks.
6. If any of your shirts need buttons on ____, don't throw ____ into the laundry.
7. Several of my friends have lost the keys to ____ lockers.
8. One of the boys said that ____ would see if there were any openings at the supermarket.
9. Most of the front page of the paper had mud smeared across ____.
10. Either of the women should submit ____ résumé.

Application to Writing

Whenever you edit your written work, check to see if the pronouns you have used are in the right case and if they agree with their antecedents in number and gender. There are four other common errors that you should look for as well: pronoun shifts, vague antecedents, missing antecedents, and the unclear use of *it, you,* or *they.*

Avoid shifting person between a pronoun and its antecedent.

PRONOUN SHIFT	**I** like running because **you** feel invigorated. [There is a shift from the first person *I* to the second person *you.*]
CORRECT	**I** like running because **I** feel invigorated.

Avoid using a pronoun that could refer to two antecedents.

VAGUE ANTECEDENT	Mom bought two puppies for my sisters when **they** were only six weeks old. [Does *they* refer to the *puppies* or the *sisters?*]
CORRECT	Mom bought two puppies for my sisters when the **puppies** were only six weeks old.
CORRECT	Mom bought two six-week-old puppies for my sisters.

Avoid using a pronoun that does not have an antecedent.

MISSING ANTECEDENT	Mr. Case is a successful lawyer, but none of his sons chose **it** as a career. [*It* has no antecedent.]
CORRECT	Mr. Case is a successful lawyer, but none of his sons chose **law** as a career.

Avoid using a pronoun without a *clear* antecedent.

UNCLEAR PRONOUNS	**It** asks for three references on the application. [The antecedent of *it* is not clearly stated.]
CORRECT	The application asks for three references.

EXERCISE 18 Eliminating Pronoun Errors
Rewrite each sentence to make its meaning clear.

1. I bought ice skates because it is so much fun.
2. Rick is intelligent, but he doesn't always use it.

3. In the Carlsbad Caverns in New Mexico, they have one huge cave that covers 14 acres.
4. In Acadia National Park, they have some of the wildest and rockiest coastline in America.
5. I like to edit my work on the word processor because you can do it so quickly.
6. Tom wanted Mark to sing because he has such a fine voice.
7. In the movie they seem to take you instantly into outer space.
8. My sister is studying to be a nurse, and she likes it very much.
9. I opened the package cautiously because you never can tell when you'll get one of Uncle Frank's practical jokes.
10. After the art students had made several sketches, Mr.Botts evaluated them.
11. Andrew invited David to Virginia Beach, but they didn't take any rides in his new boat.
12. In the spring they're beginning lifesaving courses at the YMCA.
13. Ants attacked our sandwiches before we had a chance to eat them.
14. Theresa buys fast film because you can take pictures with it in poor light.
15. I like working at the hotel because you get big tips.
16. In the almanac it lists celebrities' dates and places of birth.
17. Andrea decided to become a photographer after she took a course in it.
18. When you put sunflower seeds out for the birds, put them in a feeder.
19. I like a story that keeps you in suspense until the end.
20. In this picture it shows Rembrandt's unique use of light.

CHAPTER REVIEW

A. Write the correct form of the pronoun in parentheses.

1. Mom told Kate that the hats were for Ben and (she, her).
2. (Who, Whom) do you think will win the award?
3. Roy knows more about folk music than (she, her).
4. Was it Kevin or (she, her) who saved that man's life?

5. Daniel, (who, whom) the coach promoted from junior varsity, has become one of Reading's best players.
6. The mayor promised three seniors—Carla, Chester, and (he, him)—summer jobs at City Hall.
7. Is Spencer older than (she, her)?
8. Show your pass to (whoever, whomever) is at the gate.
9. Three of (we, us) boys volunteered to load the truck.
10. Dad was surprised at (me, my) offering to clean the garage.

B. Write the pronoun that correctly completes each sentence.

1. All of the girls on the team have packed ____ gear.
2. Every duck in the pond had a piece of bread in ____ beak.
3. Neither Jerry nor Tad submitted ____ report on time.
4. One of the girls must have sold ____ bicycle.
5. Dogs perspire through ____ paw pads.
6. Both Anna and Jean have had ____ eye examinations.
7. A few of the seniors haven't ordered ____ yearbooks.
8. Each of the ballerinas knew ____ steps perfectly.
9. Either Tim or Scott bought ____ track shoes at the mall.
10. All of the food had mold on ____.

MASTERY TEST

Number your paper 1 to 10. Then write the correct form of the pronoun in parentheses.

1. (Who, Whom) did you visit in Albany?
2. Neither the blue jay nor the sparrow abandoned (its, their) nest during the storm.
3. The only ones in the store were Kim and (he, him).
4. Both Lynn and Donna brought (her, their) umbrellas.
5. When am I going to ride in (your, you're) new car?
6. The yearbook photographers—Carlotta, Lionel, and (she, her)—should be at the gym tonight.
7. Did the shop teacher approve of (him, his) project?
8. The person (who, whom) I thought was the senator turned out to be a television newscaster.
9. Is Lee's brother as blond as (she, her)?
10. Between you and (I, me), I can't wait until summer.

8

Subject and Verb Agreement

DIAGNOSTIC TEST

Number your paper 1 to 10. Write the subject in each sentence. Then next to each one, write the form of the verb in parentheses that agrees with the subject.

EXAMPLE The last two pages of the book (is, are) missing.
ANSWER pages—are

1. Neither the shortstop nor the second baseman (was, were) able to catch the grounder.
2. (Doesn't, Don't) those fresh strawberries look absolutely delicious?
3. Only two thirds of the lawn (has, have) been mowed.
4. There (is, are) two letters on the table for you.
5. The song currently at the top of the charts (has, have) been there for six weeks.
6. One of my neighbors (is, are) a helicopter pilot.
7. (Wasn't, Weren't) you notified of the change?
8. The hammer and nails (is, are) in the toolbox.
9. A person riding a bicycle on the sidewalk (is, are) a hazard to pedestrians.
10. Both of my brothers (has, have) weekend jobs.

How many times have you seen the "perfect" pair of jeans, tried them on, and then discovered that they were either too loose or too short? "Perfect" as they are, you cannot wear them because they do not fit. In a way, subjects and verbs are like jeans and people. Some fit together; others do not. When words do fit together, they are said to have *agreement*. This chapter will review the different types of subjects and verbs. Then it will show you which ones agree and which ones do not.

AGREEMENT OF SUBJECTS AND VERBS

A subject and a verb agree when they have the same number. *Number* determines whether a word is singular or plural. *Singular* indicates one, and *plural* indicates more than one.

8a A verb must agree with its subject in number.

In order to understand agreement, you must know the singular and plural forms of nouns, pronouns, and verbs. The plural of most nouns is formed by adding *-s* or *-es* to the singular form. Some nouns, however, form their plurals irregularly. For example, *children* is the plural of *child*. Certain pronouns form their plural by changing form.

NOUNS		PRONOUNS	
SINGULAR	PLURAL	SINGULAR	PLURAL
light	lights	I	we
dress	dresses	he, she, it	they
goose	geese		

Verbs also have singular and plural forms, but only present tense verbs change endings. The third person singular of present tense verbs ends in *-s* or *-es*. However, most plural forms of present tense verbs do *not* end in *-s* or *-es*.

THIRD PERSON SINGULAR he, she, it **sits**
OTHERS I, you, we, they **sit**

Notice that *I* and *you* take the plural form of the verb.

In the following box are the singular and plural forms of the irregular verbs *be, have,* and *do* in the present tense. Notice that *be* also has irregular forms for both the singular and plural in the past tense.

Present Tense

SINGULAR	PLURAL
I **am, have, do**	we **are, have, do**
you **are, have, do**	you **are, have, do**
he, she, it **is, has, does**	they **are, have, do**

Past Tense

SINGULAR	PLURAL
I **was**	we **were**
you **were**	you **were**
he, she, it **was**	they **were**

Since a subject and a verb both have number, they must agree in a sentence—except in the case of the personal pronouns *I* and *you.*

8b A singular subject takes a singular verb.

8c A plural subject takes a plural verb.

The **light shines.**	The **lights shine.**
The **dress wrinkles.**	The **dresses wrinkle.**
The **goose flies.**	The **geese fly.**
He is my brother.	**They are** my brothers.

Be, have, and *do* are often used as helping verbs. When they are, they must agree in number with the subject.

8d The helping verb must agree in number with its subject.

The **rakes were** found in the cellar.
The **birds have** flown away.
Mark **does** know the answer to the question on the application.

Interrupting Words

Often a subject and a verb are side by side in a sentence. When they are, agreement between them is usually easy to recognize. Many times, however, a phrase or a clause modifies a subject and separates it from the verb. In such sentences a mistake in agreement sometimes occurs. The tendency is to make the verb agree with the word that is closest to it—rather than with its subject. To avoid making this mistake, find the subject and make the verb agree with it.

8e The agreement of a verb with its subject is not changed by any interrupting words.

Notice that each subject and verb in the following examples agrees in number—regardless of the interrupting words.

The **posters** on the wall **were** bought at the art museum. [The plural helping verb *were* agrees with the plural subject *posters,* even though the singular noun *wall* is closer to the verb.]

The **couch,** covered with throw pillows, **was** very attractive. [*Was* agrees with *couch,* not *pillows.*]

Students who finish the test early **are** allowed to leave. [*Are* agrees with *students,* not *test.*]

NOTE: Make the verb agree with the positive subject, not with an interrupting negative subject.

A good **band,** not fancy decorations, **makes** a prom a success. [*Makes* agrees with the positive subject *band,* not with the negative subject *decorations.*]

Occasionally a parenthetical expression, beginning with a word (or words) such as *like, as well as, in addition to, including,* or *together with* will interrupt a subject and a verb. Be careful that you make the verb agree with the subject, not with a word in the parenthetical expression.

Gail, together with her sisters, **is** running an errand service. [*Is* agrees with *Gail,* not *sisters.*]
The **boys,** as well as my uncle, **are** going to the barbecue. [*Are* agrees with *boys,* not *uncle.*]

EXERCISE 1 Making Interrupted Subjects and Verbs Agree
Number your paper 1 to 20. Write the subject in each sentence. Beside each one write the form of the verb in parentheses that agrees with the subject.

1. Several students at graduation (was, were) honored for academic achievement.
2. The whale, unlike most sea creatures, (needs, need) to surface in order to live.
3. The costumes that we wore in the play (was, were) rented.
4. The square-bottomed brown paper bag, so essential to supermarkets, (was, were) invented in 1872.
5. The loaf of bread, not the rolls, (is, are) for the bake sale.
6. The average age of the signers of the Declaration of Independence (was, were) 45.
7. The beaver, as well as other small animals, (is, are) quite common in Grand Teton National Park.
8. The horns of a bighorn sheep often (weighs, weigh) up to 30 pounds.
9. Water, as well as sunlight, (is, are) needed for the growth of plants.
10. The last page of the yearbook, totally filled with photographs, (has, have) brought back many memories.
11. Louisa May Alcott, author of *Little Women,* (was, were) a nurse during the Civil War.
12. The return of the red-winged blackbirds (is, are) a sure sign of spring.
13. The people standing by the door (is, are) members of the town council.
14. The flowers that were in Karen's corsage (was, were) miniature orchids.
15. A list of lost-and-found articles (has, have) been posted on the main bulletin board.
16. The week that we spent in the Catskill Mountains (was, were) the best time I have ever had.
17. The topics for the upcoming student meeting (was, were) chosen.
18. The coffee table in the den, not the end tables, (needs, need) polishing.
19. The balloons released at the fair (was, were) either red or blue.
20. At least two spark plugs in my car (is, are) defective.

Compound Subjects

When you make two or more subjects agree with a verb, you should remember two rules.

8f When subjects are joined by *or, nor, either/or,* or *neither/nor,* the verb agrees with the closer subject.

Either Joe or Lola **writes** the sports column each week. [*Writes* agrees with the closer subject, *Lola*.]

A pencil or a pen **is** fine for the test. [*Is* agrees with the closer subject, *pen*.]

This rule also applies when one subject is singular and the other subject is plural.

Neither the umbrella nor our raincoats **were** enough to keep us dry. [*Were* agrees with the closer subject, *raincoats*—even though *umbrella* is singular.]

When compound subjects are joined by other conjunctions, however, a different rule applies.

8g When subjects are joined by *and* or *both/and,* the verb is plural.

These conjunctions always indicate more than one. Since more than one is plural, the verb must be plural also. This rule applies whether the individual subjects are singular, plural, or a combination of singular and plural.

The stapler and the glue **are** in the top drawer. [Two things—the stapler and the glue—are in the top drawer. The verb must be plural to agree with both of them.]

Both those magazines and that book **were** left in study hall. [Even though *book* is singular, the verb is still plural because the book and the magazines—together—were left.]

The second rule has two exceptions. Two subjects joined by *and* occasionally refer to only one person or thing. In such a case, the verb must be singular.

Fruit and cheese **is** my mom's favorite dessert. [*Fruit and cheese* is considered *one* dessert.]

The second exception involves the words *every* and *each*. If one of these words comes before a compound subject that is joined by *and*, each subject is being considered separately. As a result, the verb must be singular to agree with a singular subject.

Every athlete and coach **attends** the athletic banquet at the end of the school year.

Each chair and table **looks** freshly painted.

EXERCISE 2 Making Verbs Agree with Compound Subjects
Write the correct form of the verb in parentheses.

1. Neither Bolivia nor Paraguay (has, have) a seacoast.
2. Each car and truck in the lot (was, were) towed.
3. Paint and crayon (blends, blend) well in the painting.
4. Either the mountains or the seashore (is, are) enjoyable.
5. In a democracy every man, woman, and child (is, are) guaranteed certain rights.
6. Neither rain nor snow (is, are) supposed to prevent mail from being delivered.
7. Wheat and corn (grows, grow) on my uncle's farm.
8. Spaghetti and meatballs (is, are) an easy meal to make.
9. Neither the gym nor the cafeteria at our school (is, are) large enough for the graduation ceremonies.
10. Every door and window in the cottage (was, were) bolted.
11. Both Kansas and Missouri (has, have) a Kansas City.
12. Neither the saxophone, the tuba, nor the cornet (was, were) in existence before 1800.
13. Pancakes and sausage (is, are) my favorite breakfast.
14. Every mountain, hill, and trail (was, were) familiar.
15. Hornets and yellow jackets (is, are) two of the most familiar kinds of wasps.
16. Either a cucumber or cherry tomatoes (is, are) a nice addition to a lettuce salad.
17. The soccer coach and athletic director of Henderson High (is, are) Mr. Robertson.
18. Neither the daddy longlegs nor the spider (is, are) classified as an insect.
19. Cheese and crackers (is, are) a good snack after school.
20. Both Tennessee and Missouri (touches, touch) eight other states.

EXERCISE 3 Time-out for Review

Number your paper 1 to 20. Find and write the verbs that do not agree with their subjects. Then write them correctly. If a sentence is correct, write *C* after the number.

EXAMPLE Every mosquito and gnat seem to be out tonight.
ANSWER seem—seems

1. The location of the volcanic islands are not marked on this map of Italy.
2. Ivy and geraniums covers most of the area around the school's courtyard.
3. Either Steve or Maggie have decided to become a doctor.
4. The beautiful curtains in Katherine's room is handmade.
5. Neither *Othello* nor *Richard III* were presented at the Shakespeare Festival this year.
6. Six members of the swim team were able to compete in the medley relay.
7. Cheese, lettuce, and tomato are my favorite sandwich.
8. Mandarin, the tongue of millions of Chinese, top the list of the ten most widely spoken languages.
9. Every girl and boy in the athletic program has promised to help with the fund-raising drive.
10. Lake Superior, with an area of 31,700 squares miles, is the largest freshwater lake in the world.
11. The Grand Canyon and Sunset Crater is located in Arizona.
12. The daffodils that the Garden Club planted around the library are in full bloom.
13. Bread and butter were served with the meal.
14. Either the dictionary or the thesaurus are a good place to look for colorful verbs.
15. The smallest antelope in the world, weighing about five pounds, are found in Africa.
16. Flies and other small insects are the preferred food of most chameleons.
17. The secretary and treasurer of the photography club are Marvin Goldenberg.
18. Neither the Harris brothers nor David are playing in the game this afternoon.
19. Every toaster and electric mixer were on sale at the hardware store.
20. These old cans of paint is a fire hazard.

EXERCISE 4 Writing Sentences
Write a sentence for each of the following items. In each sentence include the verb *is* or *are, has* or *have,* or *was* or *were*—either as the main verb or as a helping verb.

1. either Mom or Dad
2. the pears in the bag
3. Stacy and Todd
4. each knife and fork
5. neither Ann nor her sisters

Special Agreement Problems

There are several other situations in which agreement between a subject and a verb may present a problem.

Indefinite Pronouns as Subjects. When an indefinite pronoun is used as a subject, the verb must agree with the number of that particular indefinite pronoun.

8h A verb must agree in number with an indefinite pronoun used as a subject.

The indefinite pronouns in the following chart have been grouped according to number.

Common Indefinite Pronouns

SINGULAR	anybody, anyone, each, either, everybody, everyone, neither, no one, one, somebody, someone
PLURAL	both, few, many, several
SINGULAR/PLURAL	all, any, most, none, some

A singular verb agrees with a singular indefinite pronoun, and a plural verb agrees with a plural indefinite pronoun.

SINGULAR **One** of my tapes **is** broken.

PLURAL **Many** of my tapes **are** broken.

The number of an indefinite pronoun in the singular/plural group is determined by the object of the preposition that follows it.

SINGULAR OR PLURAL **Some** of the paint **is** on sale.
Some of the tires **are** on sale.

EXERCISE 5 Making Verbs Agree with Indefinite Pronoun Subjects

Number your paper 1 to 20. Write the subject in each sentence. Next to each one, write the form of the verb in parentheses that agrees with the subject.

1. All of the players (has, have) received their letters.
2. Both of the books (includes, include) illustrations.
3. Neither of those buses (stops, stop) at the mall.
4. Some of the people (has, have) arrived.
5. All of the book (is, are) very interesting.
6. Everyone, including the musicians, (was, were) lined up for the final curtain call.
7. Several of the books (was, were) damaged.
8. All of the actress's jewelry (was, were) imitation.
9. Each of those lamps (needs, need) a new bulb.
10. None of the washing machines (is, are) on sale.
11. All of the bread in this bakery (contains, contain) bran.
12. Some of the streams (is, are) about to overflow their banks.
13. Many of those shirts (is, are) priced too high.
14. One of my sisters (has, have) just visited Gettysburg.
15. Most of the world's diamonds (comes, come) from Africa.
16. None of my homemade applesauce (is, are) left.
17. Few of those suntan lotions (gives, give) much protection.
18. Most of the voters in our town (has, have) rejected the new property tax.
19. Some of the detergent (was, were) spilled on the floor.
20. Most of the photos in the magazine (is, are) in full color.

Subjects in Inverted Order. A sentence is said to be in *inverted order* when the verb or part of the verb phrase comes before the subject. Even though a verb may precede a subject, it still must agree with the subject in number.

8i The subject and the verb of an inverted sentence must agree in number.

There are several types of inverted sentences. *(See pages 30–31.)* When you are looking for the subject in an inverted sentence, turn the sentence around to its natural order. To make sense, you must occasionally drop *here* or *there* when putting the sentence into its natural order.

INVERTED ORDER	In the hall closet **were** two unfinished model **ships.** [Two unfinished model *ships were* in the hall closet.]
QUESTIONS	**Have** the **finalists** been announced? [The *finalists have* been announced.]
SENTENCES BEGINNING WITH *HERE* OR *THERE*	Here **are** the attendance **records.** [The attendance *records are* here.]
	There **are** only two **mistakes** in your report. [Drop *there*. Only two *mistakes are* in your report.]

EXERCISE 6 Making Verbs Agree with Subjects in Inverted Order

Number your paper 1 to 10. Write the subject in each sentence. Next to each one, write the form of the verb in parentheses that agrees with the subject.

1. There (is, are) over one million species of animals on Earth.
2. Deep in the waters of the Spanish Main (lies, lie) the treasure chests of several pirate ships.
3. There (is, are) seven poodles in the show.
4. (Has, Have) they gone downtown?
5. Throughout the West (is, are) the ruins of once prosperous mining towns.
6. There (is, are) about ten million bricks in the Empire State Building.
7. Beside the walls of the little adobe farmhouse (hang, hangs) chains of scarlet chili.
8. Here (is, are) the tickets for the Rose Bowl game.
9. Which (was, were) the last state to join the Union?
10. There (is, are) no lefties on our baseball team.

Collective Nouns. A *collective noun* such as *choir, family, herd, jury, orchestra, series, majority,* and *team* names a group of people or things. Depending on how a collective noun is used in a sentence, it may be either singular or plural.

8j Use a singular verb with a collective-noun subject that is thought of as a unit. Use a plural verb with a collective-noun subject that is thought of as individuals.

The **class is** presently holding elections. [The class is working together as a whole unit in this sentence. As a result, the verb is singular.]

The **class are** casting their ballots today. [The members of the class are acting independently—each one casting his or her own ballot. As a result, the verb is plural.]

Words Expressing an Amount. Words that express amounts, measurements, or weights usually have a plural form but are often considered to be a singular unit.

8k A subject that expresses an amount, a measurement, or a weight is usually considered singular and takes a singular verb.

Five dollars is the membership fee. [*Five dollars* is one amount of money.]

Six months is needed to complete the project. [*Six months* is one period of time.]

If an amount, measurement, or weight is being thought of in its individual parts, then the verb must be plural.

Five dollars were tucked under the vase. [The five dollars are being thought of as five individual dollars.]

Six months have passed since school began. [The six months are being thought of as six individual months.]

When the subject is a fraction or a percent, the verb agrees with the object of the preposition that follows the subject.

Three fourths of my salary **goes** to the bank.

Three fourths of the seniors **are** going to the prom.

The Number of, A Number of. Although these expressions are very similar, one takes a singular verb and one takes a plural verb.

8l Use a singular verb with *the number of* and a plural verb with *a number of.*

The number of students considering college **increases** each year. [singular]

A number of these students **intend** to go on to vocational schools. [plural]

Singular Nouns That Have a Plural Form. Even though a word ends in *-s*, it may not take a plural verb. Some nouns are plural in form but singular in meaning because they name single things—one area of knowledge or one type of disease, for example.

USUALLY SINGULAR	civics, economics, gymnastics, mathematics, measles, molasses, mumps, news, physics, social studies, the United States

8m Use a singular verb with certain subjects that are plural in form but singular in meaning.

Measles is a very contagious disease.
The local **news is** on from six to seven o'clock in the evening.

A second group of similar nouns are usually plural as their form indicates. Still, a third group can be either singular or plural—depending on how they are used in a sentence. Since it is impossible to tell what number verb these words take by looking at them, it is always best to check the dictionary.

USUALLY PLURAL	barracks, data, eyeglasses, media, pliers, scissors, shears, slacks, thanks, trousers
SINGULAR/PLURAL	acoustics, athletics, headquarters, ethics, politics, tactics

Your **eyeglasses were** found in the cafeteria. [plural]

The **headquarters** for the United Nations **is** located in New York City. [singular—an administrative center]

The **headquarters were** located on the outskirts of the town. [plural—a group of buildings]

NOTE: If the word *pair* precedes a word that is usually plural, the verb is singular because the verb then agrees with the singular noun *pair*.

PLURAL Those **scissors are** dull.
SINGULAR That **pair** of scissors **is** dull.

EXERCISE 7 Making Subjects and Verbs Agree
Write the correct form of the verb in parentheses.

1. A large number of the books (is, are) bound in suede.
2. Gymnastics (takes, take) up most of my sister's spare time.
3. Two thirds of the people in the world (does, do) not get enough to eat.
4. A number of the trees (was, were) struck in the storm.
5. Ten minutes after the end of the opera, the audience (was, were) still applauding.
6. Sixty percent of the student body (has, have) never missed a single day of school this year.
7. Three miles (is, are) the distance from here to Glen Cove.
8. The jury (was, were) in complete disagreement throughout the deliberations.
9. Almost three fourths of the apples (was, were) bruised.
10. Mumps (is, are) preventable with a vaccine.
11. A number of students in the creative-writing class (has, have) entered a national writing contest.
12. Approximately four cents (was, were) paid for each acre of land in the Louisiana Territory.
13. At the end of the first quarter, the Jefferson High team (was, were) leading by six points.
14. The number of candidates for the Student Council (is, are) surprisingly large.
15. The jury (was, were) arguing about the value of the circumstantial evidence.
16. Two gallons of gasoline (is, are) enough to get us home.

17. That pair of pliers (belongs, belong) to my uncle.
18. Economics (is, are) Kevin's major in college.
19. Forty-one percent of the moon (is, are) not visible from the earth at any time.
20. The number of students attending the soccer matches (has, have) increased this year.

***Doesn't* and *Don't*.** *Doesn't* and *don't* are contractions. When checking for agreement with a subject, say the two words of a contraction separately. Also keep in mind which contractions are singular and which are plural.

SINGULAR **does**n't, **has**n't, **is**n't, **was**n't
PLURAL **do**n't, **have**n't, **are**n't, **were**n't

8n The verb part of a contraction must agree in number with the subject.

This cool **weather does**n't remind me of summer at all.
These **directions do**n't make sense.

Subjects with Linking Verbs. A predicate nominative follows a linking verb and identifies, renames, or explains the subject. *(See page 10 for lists of linking verbs.)* Occasionally, however, a subject and its predicate nominative will not have the same number. The verb, nevertheless, agrees with the subject.

8o A verb agrees with the subject of a sentence, not with the predicate nominative.

An important **crop** in Florida **is** oranges. [The singular verb *is* agrees with the singular subject *crop*—even though the predicate nominative *oranges* is plural.]

Oranges are an important crop in Florida. [In this sentence *are* agrees with the plural subject *oranges*—not with the singular predicate nominative *crop*.]

NOTE: For better sentences, avoid writing those in which the subject and the predicate nominative do not agree in number.

The orange crop in Florida is an important one.

Titles. Some titles may seem plural because they are composed of several words, some of which may even be plural in form. A title, nevertheless, is the name of only one book, poem, play, work of art, or the like. As a result, a title is singular and takes a singular verb. Most multiword names of businesses and organizations are also considered singular.

8p A title is singular and takes a singular verb.

"The Planters" is a poem by Margaret Atwood.
Barrett's Dry Goods is having a sale on fabric.

EXERCISE 8 Making Subjects and Verbs Agree
Write the correct form of the verb in parentheses.

1. Active volcanoes (is, are) a great attraction at Hawaii Volcanoes National Park.
2. This (doesn't, don't) seem to be the right road to the apple orchard.
3. *Great Expectations* (was, were) written in 1861 by Charles Dickens.
4. The only result of my gardening efforts (was, were) bigger and better weeds.
5. (Doesn't, Don't) the buses run on the hour?
6. *Romeo and Juliet* (was, were) recently performed on public television.
7. The committee (isn't, aren't) meeting tonight.
8. A snake's fangs (is, are) a special kind of teeth.
9. Murphy's Fruits and Vegetables (is, are) my favorite market.
10. (Doesn't, Don't) daylight saving time start tonight?

***Who, Which,* and *That*.** *Who, which,* and *that* are often used as relative pronouns to begin an adjective clause. When one of these words is the subject of the clause, the number of its verb will depend upon the number of the pronoun's antecedent.

8q In an adjective clause with the relative pronoun *who, which,* or *that* used as the subject, make the verb agree with the antecedent of the relative pronoun.

Bart caught a **trout** that **was** 18 inches long. [The antecedent of *that* is *trout*. Since *trout* is singular, *was* is also singular.]

Find the titles of three **books** that **deal** with space exploration. [The antecedent of *that* is *books*. Since *books* is plural, *deal* is also plural.]

If an adjective clause is preceded by the expression *one of*, then the verb in the clause is usually plural.

Soapstone was *one of* the **rocks** that **were** highly prized by the Indians. [The antecedent of *that* is *rocks*, not *one*.]

EXERCISE 9 Making Verbs Agree with Relative Pronouns
Write the correct form of the verb in parentheses.

1. Did you throw out the stack of magazines that (was, were) sitting by the kitchen door?
2. This morning's *Times* quoted one of the people who (is, are) homeless after the flood.
3. One of the fliers who (was, were) honored yesterday has flown over a hundred test flights for the Air Force.
4. Jamie copied the list of books that (is, are) required.
5. Pat is one of those people who (seems, seem) artistic.
6. *Christina's World* is one of the paintings that (has, have) been selected for the Andrew Wyeth exhibition.
7. Have you seen the collection of old records that (is, are) on display in the music room?
8. The bobwhite is one of the songbirds that (lives, live) in the same part of the country all year.
9. Helen Keller is one of the many persons who (has, have) triumphed over physical handicaps.
10. Is it Amy or Doreen who (wants, want) to go to Italy?

EXERCISE 10 Time-out for Review
Number your paper from 1 to 20. Find and write the verbs that do not agree with their subjects. Then write them correctly. If a sentence is correct, write *C* after the number.

1. The magazines on the shelf has good reference material.
2. Almost one third of these bulbs come from Holland.

3. One of the most extensive coral reefs, which extends for over a thousand miles, is off the coast of Australia.
4. Many of the fine old houses in our town dates back to colonial days.
5. *The Adventures of Tom Sawyer* were the first novel ever to be written on a typewriter.
6. Doesn't the sound of the roosters crowing in the morning wake you up?
7. There are approximately 200 geysers and 10,000 hot springs in Yellowstone National Park.
8. All continents, with the exception of Antarctica and Australia, is wider in the north than in the south.
9. The pillow, as well as the comforter, are filled with down.
10. *Stars and Bars* was the name of the first Confederate flag.
11. New England scenery and the change in seasons has greatly influenced my parents' decision to live in Maine.
12. Seventy-five percent of the nation's blueberries are grown in Michigan, New Jersey, and North Carolina.
13. Was any nineteenth-century stamps printed in two colors?
14. There is one hamburger and one ear of corn left.
15. There are sand dunes in Colorado that is over 500 feet high.
16. At the fair fifty cents were charged for each ride.
17. About one fourth of the land in the state of Alaska is part of the National Park system.
18. Only one of our first 36 presidents were left-handed—James Garfield.
19. The red cedar is one of the few conifers that doesn't have needles.
20. Several samples of yarn were available at the craft show.

EXERCISE 11 Writing Sentences

Write a sentence for each of the following items. In each sentence include the verb *is* or *are, has* or *have,* or *was* or *were*—either as the main verb or as a helping verb.

1. a number of extra chairs
2. one third of the price
3. a crowd of spectators
4. the number of students
5. the United Nations
6. measles
7. some of the space
8. ten months
9. everyone in town
10. *Gulliver's Travels*

Application to Writing

Always check for subject and verb agreement when revising any written work.

EXERCISE 12 Editing for Subject and Verb Agreement
In the following paragraphs, find and write the verbs that do not agree with their subjects. Then write them correctly.

Forever Green

Why does the needles on a pine tree stay green all year? To understand the answer to that question, you need to know that needles actually are leaves. You also need to know something about leaves themselves. The leaves on a tree has several functions. One of these functions are to make food for the tree. Carbon dioxide from the air is taken in by the leaves. Water and minerals from the soil is taken in by the root system. The chlorophyll in leaves also absorb energy from the sun. The chlorophyll then change the carbon dioxide and water into glucose. The glucose made in leaves are a tree's basic food.

Leaves also give off enormous quantities of water. Some of the water that flows from the roots to the leaves are used to make food. Most of the rest of the water in leaves evaporate through millions of tiny holes on the surface of the leaves.

In much of North America, the water supply of all trees are cut off in winter. After the ground freezes, trees need more water than they can get from the ground. To prevent water loss, many trees "lock up" by shedding their leaves. In this way evaporation through the leaves don't occur.

Certain trees, however, has different kinds of leaves. Pine, fir, and hemlock has narrow needlelike leaves with a thick, waxy outer covering. The covering on these leaves prevent the evaporation of water. As leaves, or needles, falls off, new ones grow in at the same time. Because the branches never look bare, these trees are called evergreens.

CHAPTER REVIEW

Write the correct form of the verb in parentheses.

1. New Orleans—with its ornate grillwork, marvelous food, and fascinating history—(attracts, attract) many tourists.
2. One of my presents (was, were) a box of stationery.

3. (Was, Were) many world records broken in the 1984 Olympics in Los Angeles?
4. Both the hockey team and the baseball team (has, have) won the state championship this year.
5. Mathematics (is, are) a special kind of language.
6. (Is, Are) two dollars too much for that book?
7. My uncle, not my cousins, (was, were) visiting.
8. A grouping of millions of stars (is, are) called a galaxy.
9. Ham and eggs (makes, make) a hearty breakfast.
10. In the basket (was, were) two apples, a pear, and a bunch of grapes.
11. There (is, are) some traffic signs that are understood in all countries.
12. (Doesn't, Don't) Richard play on the basketball team?
13. The number of honor students (is, are) growing.
14. Neither my brother nor his friends (wants, want) to dance.
15. Amy is one of the people who (supports, support) me.
16. (Has, Have) most of the audience been seated?
17. There (is, are) more than 19 species of buzzards.
18. Neither the center nor the guard (knows, know) the play.
19. A gift and a card (was, were) on the table.
20. All of today's newspaper (is, are) wet.

MASTERY TEST

Number your paper 1 to 10. Write the subject in each sentence. Then next to each one, write the form of the verb in parentheses that agrees with the subject.

1. Either a bookcase or some shelves (is, are) needed.
2. Two thirds of the students (has, have) voted.
3. (Has, Have) the number of applicants increased?
4. This week there (has, have) been several warm days.
5. (Doesn't, Don't) the movie start at 5:30?
6. Neither of these reports (has, have) any footnotes.
7. Barry's voice and acting ability (is, are) exceptional.
8. The number of boys who have jobs (is, are) growing.
9. Most of those cantaloupes (is, are) too soft.
10. Sam, along with members of his family, (is, are) here.

9

Using Adjectives and Adverbs

DIAGNOSTIC TEST

Number your paper 1 to 10. Then write the correct form of the modifier in parentheses.

1. Through Carlos's small telescope, you can see the rings of Saturn almost (perfect, perfectly).
2. Monday is my (less, least) favorite day of the week.
3. Alaska is larger by far than (any, any other) state.
4. Though the quarterback tried both line plunges and pass plays, there wasn't (nothing, anything) that worked.
5. Which grows (taller, tallest), the redwood or the sequoia?
6. Karla is the (older, oldest) of the two Smith sisters.
7. Richard's car runs (good, well) since he overhauled the motor.
8. Julie is the (smartest, most smartest) person I know.
9. Which is (fresher, freshest), the bread or the rolls?
10. Of the three skaters, Tina has the (more, most) original routine.

Everyone has preferences. You might feel, for example, that meat loaf tastes *good* and spaghetti tastes *better;* but a thick, juicy steak tastes the *best* of all. Adjectives and adverbs have more than one form to express such preferences. This chapter will review the different forms of comparison, as well as some problems with comparisons.

COMPARISON OF ADJECTIVES AND ADVERBS

The three forms that most adjectives and adverbs take to show the degrees of comparison are the *positive,* the *comparative,* and the *superlative.*

9a Most modifiers show the degrees of comparison by changing form.

The basic form of an adjective or an adverb is the *positive* form. It is used when no comparison is being made.

ADJECTIVE This route to school is **quick.**
ADVERB Brad can run **fast.**

When two people, things, or actions are being compared, the *comparative* degree is used. Notice that *-er* has been added to *quick* and *fast.*

ADJECTIVE Of the two routes to school, this one is **quicker.**
ADVERB Of the two runners, Brad can run **faster.**

When more than two people, things, or actions are being compared, the *superlative* degree is used. Notice that *-est* has been added to *quick* and *fast.*

ADJECTIVE Of the three routes to school, this one is the **quickest.**
ADVERB Of all the runners in the race, Brad can run the **fastest.**

Regular and Irregular Comparison

Most adjectives and adverbs form their comparative and superlative in the same way. A few modifiers, however, form their comparative and superlative degrees irregularly.

Regular Comparison. The comparative and superlative forms of most adjectives and adverbs are determined by the number of syllables in them.

9b Add *-er* to form the comparative degree and *-est* to form the superlative degree of one-syllable modifiers.

POSITIVE	COMPARATIVE	SUPERLATIVE
young	younger	youngest
hot	hotter	hottest
soon	sooner	soonest
green	greener	greenest

NOTE: A spelling change sometimes occurs when an ending is added to a modifier. If you are not sure how to form the comparative or superlative of a modifier, check the dictionary.

Most two-syllable words form their comparative degree by adding *-er* and their superlative degree by adding *-est*. Some of these words, however, use *more* and *most* because they would sound awkward or would be impossible to pronounce if *-er* or *-est* was added. You would never say, for example, "carefuler" or "famouser." *More* and *most* are also always used with adverbs that end in *-ly*.

9c Use *-er* or *more* to form the comparative degree and *-est* or *most* to form the superlative degree of two-syllable modifiers.

POSITIVE	COMPARATIVE	SUPERLATIVE
quiet	quieter	quietest
graceful	more graceful	most graceful
early	earlier	earliest
slowly	more slowly	most slowly

NOTE: If you are unsure how to spell the comparative and superlative of a two-syllable modifier, check the dictionary.

Modifiers with three or more syllables always form their comparative and superlative degrees by using *more* and *most*.

9d Use *more* to form the comparative degree and *most* to form the superlative degree of modifiers with three or more syllables.

POSITIVE	COMPARATIVE	SUPERLATIVE
dangerous	more dangerous	most dangerous
rapidly	more rapidly	most rapidly

Less and *least* are used to form the negative comparisons of all modifiers.

POSITIVE	COMPARATIVE	SUPERLATIVE
tasty	less tasty	least tasty
steadily	less steadily	least steadily

Irregular Comparison. A few adjectives and adverbs change form completely for the comparative and superlative degrees.

POSITIVE	COMPARATIVE	SUPERLATIVE
bad/badly/ill	worse	worst
good/well	better	best
little	less	least
many/much	more	most

NOTE: The endings *-er* and *-est* should never be added to the comparative and superlative forms of these irregular modifiers. For example, you should never use "worser" as the comparative form of *bad.*

EXERCISE 1 Forming the Comparison of Modifiers
Number your paper 1 to 15. Then copy each modifier and write its comparative and superlative forms.

1. weak
2. hurriedly
3. good
4. horrible
5. busy
6. light
7. different
8. bad
9. great
10. unsafe
11. little
12. quickly
13. clever
14. many
15. swift

EXERCISE 2 Using the Correct Form of Comparison
Number your paper 1 to 20. Then write the correct form of the modifier in parentheses.

1. Of the three boys, Mark wrote the (better, best) essay.
2. Rita's, not Betsy's, kite flew (higher, highest).

3. Ellen swam to the dock (more, most) rapidly than Juan.
4. Which subject do you like (better, best)—English, history, or math?
5. Which has the (more, most) beautiful song, the nightingale or the hermit thrush?
6. Of your two friends, which one is (more, most) sincere?
7. Which city has the (larger, largest) population—Chicago, Detroit, or Miami?
8. Since there are two acceptable candidates for the job, the manager has to choose the (better, best) one.
9. I don't know which I like (less, least), washing the dishes or drying them.
10. Alan is the (shyer, shyest) of all my friends.
11. Which is (longer, longest), a yard or a meter?
12. Which one—Washington, Jefferson, or Kennedy—do you think was the (better, best) president?
13. There were three math problems on the test, and I did the (easier, easiest) one first.
14. Leroy's essay was (more, most) informative than Maria's.
15. Who do you think was the (better, best) poet, Tennyson or Shelley?
16. This shirt comes in small, medium, and large, but I think the medium one would fit you (better, best).
17. Which is (taller, tallest)—the Chrysler Building, the Empire State Building, or the World Trade Center?
18. I find Amy the (more, most) able writer on the staff.
19. Which costs (less, least), the record or the tape?
20. Of the several rivers in Virginia that wind to the sea, which one is the (longer, longest)?

Problems with Modifiers

The following special problems sometimes arise when writing comparisons.

Double Comparisons. Use only *one* method of forming the comparative and superlative degrees at the same time. Using both methods simultaneously results in a *double comparison.*

9e Do not use both *-er* and *more* to form the comparative degree, or both *-est* and *most* to form the superlative degree.

DOUBLE COMPARISON	That book is **more longer** than this one.
CORRECT	That book is **longer** than this one.
DOUBLE COMPARISON	This is the **most nicest** picture of you.
CORRECT	This is the **nicest** picture of you.

***Other* and *Else* in Comparisons.** Very often one or more people or things will be compared with other people or things in the same group. When you make such a comparison, however, be sure that you do not compare a person or a thing with itself.

9f Add *other* or *else* when comparing a member of a group with the rest of the group.

INCORRECT	Dyer Road has more potholes than any road in town. [Since Dyer Road is a road in the town, it is being compared with itself.]
CORRECT	Dyer Road has more potholes than any **other** road in town. [By adding the word *other,* Dyer Road is now being compared *only* with the other roads in town.]
INCORRECT	Mandy can sing higher than anyone in the choir. [Since Mandy is a member of the choir, she is being compared with herself.]
CORRECT	Mandy can sing higher than anyone **else** in the choir. [By adding the word *else,* Mandy is now being compared *only* with the other members of the choir.]

EXERCISE 3 Correcting Mistakes in Comparisons
Number your paper 1 to 20. Then write the following sentences, correcting each mistake.

1. Alvin jumps higher and farther than any member of the track team.
2. A loosely packed campfire will burn more quicker than a tightly packed one.
3. Nathan has more wins than anyone on the wrestling team.
4. Though not the highest waterfalls in the world, the falls of the Niagara River are perhaps more famous than any waterfalls.

5. I think a rabbit's fur is more softer than even a cat's.
6. The force of gravity is more greater near the poles than at the equator.
7. Andrew worked harder than any person on the work crew.
8. The African elephant probably has larger eyes than any animal in the world.
9. This party was the most wonderfulest surprise of my life!
10. John plays more sports than anyone in his family.
11. Yellow and green can be seen more readily by the human eye than any colors.
12. Is the humidity more higher today than it was yesterday?
13. Except for Pluto the outer planets are more larger than the inner planets, including Earth.
14. Kim plays the flute better than anyone in music class.
15. That test was more harder than any test this year.
16. There are more lawyers in Washington, D.C., than in any community in the United States.
17. I think Lee is smarter than anyone I know.
18. These redwoods are the most tallest trees I have ever seen.
19. This pup is friendlier than any dog in the pet shop.
20. The cheetah can run more faster than any four-legged animal.

Illogical Comparisons. When you write a comparison, be sure you compare two or more similar things. When you compare different things, the comparison becomes illogical.

9g Compare only items of a similar kind.

ILLOGICAL COMPARISON	A dachshund's **legs** are shorter than other **dogs.** [*Legs* are being compared with *dogs.*]
LOGICAL COMPARISON	A dachshund's **legs** are shorter than other dogs' **legs.** [*Legs* are being compared with *legs.*]
LOGICAL COMPARISON	A dachshund's **legs** are shorter than other **dogs'.** [With the possessive *dogs', legs* is understood; therefore, *legs* are being compared with *legs.*]
LOGICAL COMPARISON	A dachsund's **legs** are shorter than **those** of other dogs. [The demonstrative pronoun *those* takes the place of *legs;* therefore, *legs* are being compared with *legs.*]

ILLOGICAL COMPARISON	Pam's **bread** looked quite different from the **picture.** [*Bread* is being compared with a *picture.*]
LOGICAL COMPARISON	Pam's **bread** looked quite different from the **bread** in the picture. [Now *bread* is being compared with *bread* in a picture.]

NOTE: See page 267 for information about the use of an apostrophe with possessives.

Double Negatives. Some words are considered *negatives.* In most sentences two negatives, called a *double negative,* should not be used together.

9h Avoid using a double negative.

Common Negatives

but (meaning "only")	none
barely	no one
hardly	not (and its contraction *n't*)
neither	nothing
never	only
no	scarcely

DOUBLE NEGATIVE	Sue does**n't** have **no** choice in this matter.
CORRECT	Sue does**n't** have any choice in this matter.
DOUBLE NEGATIVE	There is**n't** **hardly** any reason to meet.
CORRECT	There is**n't** any reason to meet.
CORRECT	There is **hardly** any reason to meet.

EXERCISE 4 Correcting Mistakes in Comparisons
Number your paper 1 to 20. Then write the following sentences, correcting each mistake.

1. There isn't hardly any part of the world that is entirely free of mosquitoes.
2. Tuitions in private colleges are higher than state colleges.
3. When Buzz throws a fastball, a batter has hardly no chance of getting a hit.

4. We hadn't gone barely a mile when we ran out of gas.
5. Our apartment has less space than the Jacksons.
6. Because of Don's confusing directions, we couldn't hardly find his house.
7. When the fuse blew, we hadn't but one candle in the house.
8. I think William Butler Yeats's poetry is more difficult to understand than Robert Frost.
9. The ladies' sweat shirts are more expensive than the men.
10. Two ocelots don't never have the same markings.
11. A dog's affection often seems more obvious than a cat.
12. Her schedule is busier than her husband.
13. The first practical submarine wasn't nothing but a leather-covered rowboat that could submerge for about 10 to 15 hours.
14. We don't have no portable television sets in stock.
15. Gloria's opinions are quite different from her sister.
16. The brain of an ant isn't scarcely as big as the head of a pin.
17. Are a hare's ears longer than any other animal?
18. The fog is so thick that I can't hardly see the road.
19. This movie isn't nothing like what I expected.
20. Monday's crowd at the baseball game was much larger than Thursday.

Adjective or Adverb? An adjective modifies a noun or a pronoun. Sometimes an adjective follows a linking verb. An adverb modifies a verb, an adjective, or another adverb.

ADJECTIVE That test was **easy.** [*Easy* is a predicate adjective that follows a form of the linking verb *be* and modifies the noun *test.*]

ADVERB Tad runs five miles **easily.** [*Easily* is an adverb that modifies the verb *runs.*]

The verbs *appear, feel, look, remain, smell, sound, stay, taste,* and *turn* are other linking verbs. These same verbs, however, can also be action verbs. An adjective follows a linking verb, but an adverb follows an action verb.

If you are not sure whether one of the verbs listed above is being used as a linking verb or as an action verb, substitute the verb *is.* If the sentence makes sense, the verb is a linking verb. If it does not make sense, the verb is an action verb.

ADJECTIVE He looked **handsome** in his tuxedo. [*He is handsome* makes sense. *Looked* is used as a linking verb; therefore, *handsome* is a predicate adjective.]

ADVERB He looked **carefully** through the files for the missing report. [*He is carefully through the files* does not make sense. *Looked* is used as an action verb; therefore, *carefully* is an adverb.]

ADJECTIVE In the crowd the small child appeared **nervous.** [*In the crowd the small child is nervous* makes sense. *Appeared* is used as a linking verb; therefore, *nervous* is a predicate adjective.]

ADVERB The bear appeared **suddenly.** [*The bear is suddenly* does not make sense. *Appeared* is used as an action verb; therefore, *suddenly* is an adverb.]

Good is always an adjective. *Well* is usually used as an adverb. *Well* is used as an adjective, however, when it means "in good health," "attractive," or "satisfactory."

ADJECTIVE Sally is a **good** writer.
ADVERB Sally writes **well.**
ADJECTIVE Sally doesn't feel **well** today. [in good health]

EXERCISE 5 Choosing an Adjective or an Adverb
Write the correct form of the modifier in parentheses.

1. Everyone did (good, well) on the final exam.
2. Jeff looked (hungry, hungrily) at the leftover drumstick.
3. That perfume smells rather (strong, strongly).
4. Adrienne can (easy, easily) beat Tim at racquetball.
5. You presented your ideas (good, well) at the meeting.
6. Don't you think Peter looks exceptionally (good, well) after his operation?
7. If you say your lines too (rapid, rapidly), no one will understand you.
8. I did rather (good, well) in the marathon yesterday.
9. That orange tastes very (bitter, bitterly).
10. Christopher felt (good, well) after getting an extra hour's sleep.
11. At the party all the guests appeared (happy, happily).

12. Raymond stopped (abrupt, abruptly) and walked off the stage.
13. Laurie Beckerman's homemade bread tastes (delicious, deliciously).
14. The floodwaters receded (gradual, gradually) after the severe storm.
15. After her argument with Michael, Marsha felt (bad, badly).
16. The contestant thought (careful, carefully) before giving her answer to the question.
17. Standing in the front of the room, Katherine appeared (calm, calmly).
18. Everyone hopes our Olympic team will do as (good, well) in competition as it did in the tryouts.
19. The youngster waited (cautious, cautiously) before crossing the street.
20. Silver maples grow (rapid, rapidly).

EXERCISE 6 Time-out for Review

Number your paper 1 to 20. Rewrite the following sentences, correcting each mistake. If a sentence is correct, write *C* after the number.

1. Of all the cities in the United States, I think New York City would be the more exciting place to live.
2. Is the value of gold greater than any metal?
3. Of the two teams, I think the Braves have the best chance of winning the World Series this year.
4. Prepare your speech carefully before you present it at the class meeting.
5. This year's senior play was better than last year.
6. Paula thinks that history is more interesting than her other subjects.
7. Are beagles more friendlier than basset hounds?
8. The band performed that difficult number perfect.
9. Isn't there no one you can talk to?
10. Scott likes soccer better than any sport.
11. I think the dogwood is the more beautiful of the two trees in your yard.
12. Terry's graduation ring looks different from Janice.
13. The lilies of the valley in that vase smell sweetly.
14. That was the most scariest movie I have ever seen!

15. That cocker spaniel has won more ribbons than any dog in the show.
16. I don't know which is worst, taking a test or waiting to hear the grade.
17. I think Army will beat Navy easily this year.
18. There wasn't no reason given for his resignation.
19. Those were the most tastiest strawberries I have ever eaten.
20. This clam chowder tastes particularly well.

Application to Writing

When you write a comparison, always check to see that you have used the correct form of comparison and that you have avoided the problems with comparisons.

EXERCISE 7 Editing for the Correct Use of Modifiers
Find and write each error in comparison in the following paragraphs. Then correct each error.

Earth's Twin

Venus has been called Earth's twin. Second in distance from the sun, Venus comes more nearer to Earth than any planet. Venus's diameter, density, mass, and gravity are all close to Earth. Venus's year is about three fifths as long as Earth. Venus's rotation, however, is quite different. Venus rotates from east to west; Earth and most other planets rotate from west to east.

Venus is completely masked by dense pale yellow clouds. Astronomers knew hardly nothing about Venus's atmosphere and surface until radar and unpiloted spacecraft penetrated the clouds. Despite Venus's thick clouds, its surface gets much more hotter than Earth. The temperature on Venus sometimes reaches 460°C.

Because Venus is more closer to the sun than Earth is, you can see it in the sky only when you face in the general direction of the sun. During most of the daytime, the sun shines too vivid to allow you to see Venus. When Venus is east of the sun, however, the sun sets before it. Then Venus can be seen clear in the evening twilight of the western sky. It is then called the evening star.

CHAPTER REVIEW

Number your paper 1 to 20. Then write the following sentences, correcting each mistake. If a sentence is correct, write *C* after the number.

1. We couldn't go swimming this morning because there wasn't no lifeguard on duty.
2. Who finished the crossword puzzle fastest, Theresa or Miguel?
3. On the rooftop two robins sang cheerfully.
4. Do you know that Jupiter is larger than any planet in the solar system?
5. I hope my picture of the Clydesdale horses will do good in the photography contest.
6. Before I got my new glasses, I couldn't hardly see the front board.
7. The eldest of the two Thornton children is going to Illinois State in the fall.
8. That kind of ice skate is more better for hockey than for figure skating.
9. Which of the two performances of *Romeo and Juliet* did you like better?
10. Some beetles can run very rapidly when searching for food.
11. How was China's early civilization different from Egypt?
12. An ordinary tennis racket is more larger than a paddle-tennis racket.
13. Christina plays the harpsichord better than anyone I know.
14. During your speech speak distinct and try to pause once in a while.
15. Women's fashions seem to change oftener than men.
16. Venus is more brighter than any celestial body except the sun and the moon.
17. Did Manuel do well in the finals of the swimming meet?
18. The fog was so thick I couldn't see nothing.
19. The cheetah is different from members of the cat family because it cannot hide its claws.
20. That shirt comes in blue, green, or yellow; but I think the blue looks better on you.

MASTERY TEST

Number your paper 1 to 10. Then write the correct form of the modifier in parentheses.

1. The heart performs (good, well) for the average person, beating 2½ billion times during a lifetime.
2. Which is (taller, tallest), the cypress or the elm?
3. A kangaroo's head is small and resembles a (deer, deer's).
4. Ever since Marie took lessons, she has danced (beautiful, beautifully).
5. Basketball is more popular than (any, any other) sport at our school.
6. The temperature today is (cooler, more cooler) than it was yesterday.
7. Who has the (more, most) beautiful voice, Carl or Raymond?
8. I (have, haven't) never seen the ocean.
9. Of the two routes, this one seems (less, least) hilly.
10. Which of the following cities has the (better, best) climate—Tallahassee, San Francisco, or Boulder?

Glossary of Usage

Part of the growing process is learning that some behavior is appropriate and some is not. Everyone quickly learns as a child, for example, that throwing food on the floor is definitely *not* acceptable or appropriate behavior.

As children grow older, learning becomes more complicated. No longer is everything good or bad, right or wrong. Some behavior is appropriate in some situations, but inappropriate in others. Using your fingers, for example, to eat fried chicken may be appropriate behavior at home, but it may become inappropriate at a fancy restaurant.

Different expressions of the English language are somewhat like certain types of behavior; they may be appropriate in one situation, but not in another. Using contractions in your conversations, for example, is standard and acceptable, but using contractions in a research paper may not be appropriate.

LEVELS OF LANGUAGE

Professor Higgins in *My Fair Lady* prided himself in his ability to name the town where people were born by analyzing their dialects. *Dialect* is a regional variety of language that includes grammar, vocabulary, and pronunciation. Like the English, Americans speak with different dialects. The accents and expressions of people from parts of Texas, for example, are quite different from the accents and expressions of people from parts of Massachusetts. In spite of these variations in dialect, though, people from Texas and people from Massachusetts can easily understand one another.

The place of your birth, however, is not the only influence that affects the way you speak. Your ethnic and educational background, as well as other factors, also contribute to the particular way you speak. All of these combined factors add a richness and a vibrant diversity to the English language. These factors have also created the need for different levels of expression in the English language. Traditionally these levels are recognized as *standard* and *nonstandard.*

Standard English

Almost all professional people—such as writers, television and radio personalities, government officials, and other public figures—use what is known as *standard English* in public. Standard English uses all the rules and conventions of usage that are accepted most widely by English-speaking people throughout the world. (They are the same rules and conventions that are taught in this text.) The use of standard English varies, nevertheless, in formal and informal situations.

Formal English. Formal English, which follows the conventional rules of grammar, usage, and mechanics, is the standard for all written work. It is used mainly in such written work as formal reports, essays, scholarly writings, research papers, and business letters. Formal English may include some words that are not normally used in everyday conversation and frequently may employ long sentences with complex structures. To maintain a formal tone of writing, most writers also avoid contractions, colloquialisms, and common verbal expressions. The following example of formal English is the last paragraph of Samuel Johnson's essay "On Spring."

> He that enlarges his curiosity after the works of nature multiplies the inlets to happiness. Therefore, the younger part of my readers, to whom I dedicate this speculation, must excuse me for calling upon them to make use at once of the spring of the year and the spring of life—to acquire, while their minds may be yet impressed with new images, a love of innocent pleasures and an ardor for useful knowledge. A blighted spring makes a barren year, and the vernal flowers, however beautiful, are only intended by nature as preparation to autumnal fruits.
>
> —SAMUEL JOHNSON, "ON SPRING"

Informal English. *Informal English* does *not* mean "inferior English." Just like formal English, informal English follows the rules and the conventions of standard English, but it is less rigid. It includes some words and expressions, such as contractions, that would sound out of place in formal writing. English-speaking people around the world generally use informal English in their everyday conversation. It is also used in magazines, newspapers, advertising, and much of the fiction that is written today. The following example of informal English is a diary entry that was written by Admiral Byrd during one of his expeditions to Antarctica.

> Something—I don't know what—is getting me down. I've been strangely irritable all day, and since supper I have been depressed . . . This would not seem important if I could only put my finger on the trouble, but I can't find any single thing to account for the mood. Yet, it has been there; and tonight, for the first time, I must admit that the problem of keeping my mind on an even keel is a serious one.
>
> —RICHARD BYRD, *ALONE*

Nonstandard English

The many variations produced by regional dialects, slang, and colloquial expressions are incorporated into *nonstandard English.* Since nonstandard English lacks uniformity from one section of the country to the next and from year to year, you should always use standard English when you write. Some authors use nonstandard English, however, to re-create the conversation of people from a particular locale. This, for example, was O. Henry's purpose when he wrote the following passage from the short story "The Ransom of Red Chief."

> "I was rode," says Bill, "the ninety miles to the stockade, not barring an inch. Then, when the settlers was rescued, I was given oats. Sand ain't a palatable substitute. And then, for an hour I had to try and explain to him why there was nothin' in holes, how a road can run both ways, and what makes the grass green. I tell you, Sam, a human can only stand so much. So I takes him by the neck of his clothes and drags him down the mountain . . . "
>
> —O. HENRY, "THE RANSOM OF RED CHIEF"

GLOSSARY OF USAGE

Some of the 90 entries in the following Glossary of Usage make reference to standard and nonstandard English, the terms discussed in the previous section. The glossary has been arranged alphabetically so you can use it easily.

a, an. Use *a* before a word beginning with a consonant sound and *an* before a word beginning with a vowel sound. Always keep in mind that this rule applies to sounds, not letters. For example, *an hour ago* is correct because the *h* is silent.

> **A** house on our street has just been sold.
> He asked for **an** honest evaluation of his work.

accept, except. *Accept* is a verb that means "to receive with consent." *Except* is usually a preposition that means "but" or "other than." *Acceptance* and *exception* are the noun forms.

> All the football players will **accept** all the new regulations **except** one.

adapt, adopt. Both of these words are verbs. *Adapt* means "to adjust." *Adopt* means "to take as your own." *Adaption, adaptation,* and *adoption* are the noun forms.

> If we **adopt** the dress code suggested by the report, we'll have to **adapt** it to the locale of our school.

advice, advise. *Advice* is a noun that means "a recommendation." *Advise* is a verb that means"to recommend."

> What **advice** would you give to a freshman?
> I **advise** everyone to wear sturdy boots for the hike.

affect, effect. *Affect* is a verb that means "to influence" or "to act upon." *Effect* is usually a noun that means "a result" or "an influence." As a verb *effect* means "to accomplish" or "to produce."

> Eastern Kansas was seriously **affected** by the storm.
> The **effects** of the storm cost the state millions of dollars.
> The fear of mud slides **effected** a change in the hikers' plans.

ain't. This contraction is nonstandard and should be avoided in your writing.

NONSTANDARD This **ain't** my first choice.
STANDARD This **isn't** my first choice.

all ready, already. *All ready* means "completely ready." *Already* means "previously."

Is everyone **all ready** to go?
We have **already** eaten dinner.

all together, altogether. *All together* means "in a group." *Altogether* means "wholly" or "thoroughly."

The members of our team were **all together** at the game.
The concert was **altogether** enjoyable.

allusion, illusion. Both of these words are nouns. An *allusion* is "an implied or indirect reference; a hint." An *illusion* is "something that deceives or misleads."

Many literary **allusions** can be traced to the Bible, Shakespeare, or mythology.

You can see motion in motion pictures only because of an optical **illusion.**

a lot. These words are often written as one word. There is no such word as "alot." *A lot* should be avoided in formal writing. (Do not confuse *a lot* with *allot,* which is a verb that means "to distribute by shares.")

INFORMAL Do you miss them **a lot?**
FORMAL Do you miss them very much?
The rations should be **allotted** evenly.

among, between. Both of these words are prepositions. *Among* is used when referring to three or more people or things. *Between* is usually used when referring to two people or things.

Shaking hands, the senator moved **among** the people.
Mario planted flowers **between** the shrubs and the walk.

amount, number. *Amount* refers to a quantity. *Number* refers to things that can be counted.

A small **number** of students raised a large **amount** of money for the athletic program.

any more, anymore. Do not use *any more* for *anymore. Any more* refers to quantity. The adverb *anymore* means "from now on" or "at present."

Is there **any more** lettuce in the garden?
No, I don't raise lettuce **anymore.**

anywhere, everywhere, nowhere, somewhere. Do not add *s* to any of these words.

NONSTANDARD I lost my wallet **somewheres.**
STANDARD I lost my wallet **somewhere.**

as far as. This expression is sometimes confused with "all the farther," which is nonstandard.

NONSTANDARD This is **all the farther** I can drive.
STANDARD This is **as far as** I can drive.

at. Do not use *at* after *where.*

NONSTANDARD Ask the attendant **where** we're **at.**
STANDARD Ask the attendant **where** we are.

a while, awhile. *A while* is an expression made up of an article and a noun. It must be used after the prepositions *for* and *in. Awhile* is an adverb and is not used after a preposition.

You won't get your test results for **a while.**
I think you should wait **awhile** before calling again.

bad, badly. *Bad* is an adjective and often follows a linking verb. *Badly* is used as an adverb and often follows an action verb. In the first two examples, *felt* is a linking verb.

NONSTANDARD Bart has felt **badly** all day.
STANDARD Bart has felt **bad** all day.
STANDARD He was so anxious that he did the job **badly.**

EXERCISE 1 Determining the Correct Word

Number your paper 1 to 25. Then write the word or group of words in parentheses that correctly completes each sentence.

1. The train station is (all the farther, as far as) I can take you.
2. Do you have to take (any more, anymore) final exams before graduation?
3. When Muffin disappeared, we looked (everywhere, everywheres) for her.
4. The lawn mower works so (bad, badly) that I refuse to use it anymore.
5. Can you stay for (awhile, a while) longer?
6. In her report Jill made interesting (allusions, illusions) to some of Shakespeare's plays.
7. The medicine seemed to have little (affect, effect) on my cold.
8. If I had to choose (among, between) swimming and jogging, I'd choose swimming.
9. A large (amount, number) of squawking chickens got out of the coop.
10. I don't take modern dance (any more, anymore).
11. I'm sure the doctor will (advice, advise) you to get some rest.
12. I don't think that hat looks (bad, badly) on you.
13. Do you think that the new entrance requirements at the college will (affect, effect) your acceptance?
14. Because of an optical (allusion, illusion), a horizontal straight line looks shorter than a straight vertical line of equal length placed directly beneath it.
15. A large (amount, number) of sunlight is needed to keep that plant healthy.
16. After (a, an) hour's rest, I'll feel fine.
17. The doctors had to divide the serum (among, between) their many patients.
18. How does (a, an) honeybee (adapt, adopt) to cold weather?
19. Everyone was (all ready, already) to go, but Dad couldn't find the tickets (anywhere, anywheres).
20. This (ain't, isn't) the best time for us to be (altogether, all together).
21. (Accept, Except) all parcels from the mail carrier—(accept, except) any that are damaged.

22. I think you should wait for (a while, awhile) before you (adapt, adopt) another dog.
23. The choir feels (all together, altogether) pleased with the (amount, number) of people who attended the concert.
24. (Between, Among) the six of us, I was the only one who had (all ready, already) eaten.
25. (Accept, Except) for one point, I thought Joyce's (advice, advise) made good sense.

because. Do not use *because* after *the reason.* Use one or the other.

NONSTANDARD The **reason** he joined the exercise class was **because** he wanted to feel more energetic.
STANDARD He joined the exercise class **because** he wanted to feel more energetic.
STANDARD The **reason** he joined the exercise class was **that** he wanted to feel more energetic.

being as, being that. These expressions should be replaced with *because* or *since.*

NONSTANDARD **Being as** it rained on Saturday, I didn't have to mow the lawn.
STANDARD **Since** it rained on Saturday, I didn't have to mow the lawn.

beside, besides. *Beside* is always a preposition that means "by the side of." As a preposition, *besides* means "in addition to." As an adverb, *besides* means "also" or "moreover."

Sit **beside** me in homeroom. [by the side of]

Besides the theater tickets, we also won a free dinner for four. [in addition to]

The school has a swimming pool, tennis courts, and an indoor track **besides.** [also]

both. Never use *the* before *both.*

NONSTANDARD We saw **the both** of you at the mall.
STANDARD We saw **both** of you at the mall.

both, each. *Both* refers to two persons or objects together, but *each* refers to an individual person or object.

Although **both** office buildings were designed by the same architect, **each** one is quite different.

bring, take. *Bring* indicates motion toward the speaker. *Take* indicates motion away from the speaker.

Bring me the stamps, and then you can **take** this letter to the mailbox.

can, may. *Can* expresses ability. *May* expresses possibility or permission.

Can you see the third line of the eye chart?
May I have the next dance?

can't help but. In this expression use a gerund instead of *but.* *(See pages 61–62 for more information about gerunds.)*

NONSTANDARD	I **can't help but notice** your attractive, new haircut.
STANDARD	I **can't help noticing** your attractive, new haircut.

capital, capitol. A *capital* is the chief city of a state. Also, names are written with *capital* letters, people invest *capital,* and a person can suffer *capital* punishment. A *capitol* is the building in which the legislature meets.

The **capitol** in Tallahassee, the **capital** of Florida, has a mural painted on the outside.

coarse, course. *Coarse* is an adjective that means "loose or rough in texture" or "crude and unrefined." *Course* is a noun that means "a way of acting or proceeding" or "a path, road, or route." Also, people play golf on a *course,* an appetizer is one *course* of a meal, and students take *courses* in school. *Course* is also the word used in the parenthetical expression *of course.*

Many people objected to his **coarse** remarks.
What **course** of action do you recommend?

continual, continuous. Both of these words are adjectives. *Continual* means "frequently repeated." *Continuous* means "uninterrupted."

Because of the **continual** ringing of the phone, I didn't get much done.
The rain was **continuous** for over 10 hours.

different from. Use this form instead of *different than. Different than,* however, can be used informally when it is followed by a clause.

INFORMAL	My sweater is **different than** the one Gram knitted for Maureen.
FORMAL	My sweater is **different from** the one Gram knitted for Maureen.
	His jacket is **different from** mine.

discover, invent. Both of these words are verbs. *Discover* means "to find or get knowledge for the first time." *Invent* means "to create or produce for the first time." Something that is discovered has always existed, but was unknown. Something that is invented has never existed before. *Discovery* and *invention* are the noun forms.

Who first **discovered** oil in Alaska?
Who **invented** the first computer?

doesn't, don't. *Doesn't* is singular and should be used only with singular nouns and the personal pronouns *he, she,* and *it. Don't* is plural and should be used only with plural nouns and the personal pronouns *I, you, we,* and *they.*

NONSTANDARD	He **don't** need any help.
STANDARD	He **doesn't** need any help.
NONSTANDARD	An apple a day **don't** keep the doctor away.
STANDARD	An apple a day **doesn't** keep the doctor away.

done. *Done* is the past participle of the verb *do*. When *done* is used as a verb, it must have one or more helping verbs.

NONSTANDARD	I **done** what I thought was right.
STANDARD	I **have done** what I thought was right.

double negative. Words such as *hardly, never, no, not,* and *nobody* are considered negatives. Do not use two negatives to express one negative meaning. *(See page 189 for a complete list of negative words.)*

NONSTANDARD I do**n't hardly** have any spare time.
STANDARD I do**n't** have any spare time.
STANDARD I **never** have any spare time.

emigrate, immigrate. Both of these words are verbs. *Emigrate* means "to leave a country to settle elsewhere." *Immigrate* means "to enter a foreign country to live there." A person emigrates *from* a country and immigrates *to* another country. *Emigrant* and *immigrant* are the noun forms.

Kin Fujii **emigrated** from Japan ten years ago.
He **immigrated** to the United States.

etc. *Etc.* is an abbreviation for a Latin phrase that means "and other things." Never use *and* with *etc.* If you do, what you are really saying is "*and and* other things." It is best, however, not to use this abbreviation at all in formal writing.

NONSTANDARD For the salad we need a pineapple, grapes, **etc.**
STANDARD For the salad we need a pineapple, grapes, **and other fruits.**

EXERCISE 2 Determining the Correct Word
Number your paper 1 to 25. Then write the word or group of words in parentheses that correctly completes each sentence.

1. I hope Jerry (doesn't, don't) try to dive from the high board.
2. A proper diet recommends grapefruit and oranges because (both, the both) are rich in vitamin C.
3. We should wear long pants and long-sleeved shirts and take mosquito repellent (beside, besides).
4. How is an orange different (from, than) a tangerine?
5. Please tie up the papers and (bring, take) them down to me in the basement.
6. (Because, Being that) the Canadian lynx has unusually large, broad feet, it can move easily over the snow.
7. My bicycle is the one (beside, besides) the fence.

8. That (coarse, course) material caused a rash on my arms.
9. Thomas Edison (discovered, invented) the Dictaphone.
10. (Don't, Doesn't) he know the name of that building?
11. My grandparents (emigrated, immigrated) from India in 1891.
12. (Both, The both) of us attended the concert.
13. What is the (capital, capitol) of Oregon?
14. (Because, Being as) we got a late start, we arrived at the game after Tech had already scored a touchdown.
15. (Beside, Besides) three inches of much-needed rain, the storm brought a welcome drop in temperature.
16. There is hardly (any, no) reason for his resignation.
17. I (done, have done) only half of the math assignment.
18. (Can, May) Hannah run the mile faster than Susan?
19. I don't know (any, no) reason why I can't go to the game with you.
20. (Can, May) I (bring, take) the attendance report to the office?
21. We must (discover, invent) a way to stop the (continual, continuous) showers of acid rain.
22. When my family (emigrated, immigrated) to the United States, they settled in the (capital, capitol) of Kentucky.
23. My brother (can, may) usually finish the 18 holes of a golf (coarse, course) under par.
24. How is the (capital, capitol) in Albany different (from, than) the one in Harrisburg?
25. (Beside, Besides) the (continual, continuous) honking of horns, I've been distracted by the hammering next door.

fewer, less. *Fewer* is plural and refers to things that can be counted. *Less* is singular and refers to quantities and qualities that cannot be counted.

I received **fewer** birthday cards this year than last year.
You should have put **less** water in the stew.

former, latter. *Former* is the first of two people or things. *Latter* is the second of two people or things. (Use *first* and *last* when referring to three or more.)

For the main course, we had a choice of roast beef or pork chops. I chose the **former;** Ben chose the **latter.**

good, well. *Good* is an adjective and often follows a linking verb. *Well* is an adverb and often follows an action verb. However, when *well* means "in good health," "attractive," or "satisfactory," it is used as an adjective.

The flannel shirt feels **good.** [adjective]
I work **well** in the morning. [adverb]
Pat doesn't feel **well.** [adjective—"in good health"]

had of. Do not use *of* after *had.*

NONSTANDARD If I **had of** listened to the weather forecast, I would have taken my umbrella.
STANDARD If I **had** listened to the weather forecast, I would have taken my umbrella.

have, of. Never substitute *of* for the verb *have.* When speaking, many people make a contraction of *have.* For example, someone might say, "You should've called first." Because *-ve* sounds like *of, of* is often incorrectly substituted for *have* when written.

NONSTANDARD You should **of** roasted the potatoes.
STANDARD You should **have** roasted the potatoes.

hear, here. *Hear* is a verb that means "to perceive by listening." *Here* is an adverb that means "in this place."

Stand over **here** so you can **hear** the speech.

hole, whole. A *hole* is an opening. *Whole* means "complete" or "entire."

The **whole** time I watched the **hole,** no animal went in or came out of it.

imply, infer. Both of these words are verbs. *Imply* means "to suggest" or "to hint." *Infer* means "to draw a conclusion by reasoning or evidence." A speaker implies; a hearer infers. *Implication* and *inference* are the noun forms.

Grandmother **implied** that she might be visiting soon. We **inferred** from what she said that she wouldn't be staying very long.

in, into. Use *into* when you want to express motion from one place to another.

The mixture **in** the bowl should be put **into** the blender.

irregardless. Do not substitute this word for *regardless.*

NONSTANDARD **Irregardless** of anything you say, I still think he was telling the truth.
STANDARD **Regardless** of anything you say, I still think he was telling the truth.

its, it's. *Its* is a possessive pronoun. *It's* is a contraction for *it is.*

The committee will announce **its** findings on Friday.
It's going to be a controversial report.

kind, sort, type. These words are singular and should be preceded by *this* and *that. Kinds, sorts,* and *types* are plural and should be preceded by *these* and *those.*

This kind of computer is very expensive.
These kinds of computers are very expensive.

kind of, sort of. Never substitute these expressions for *rather* or *somewhat.*

NONSTANDARD Those financial statements are **kind of** hard to understand.
STANDARD Those financial statements are **rather** hard to understand.

knew, new. *Knew,* the past tense of the verb *know,* means "was acquainted with." *New* is an adjective that means "recently made" or "just found."

We **knew** all along that a **new** gym would be built.

learn, teach. Both of these words are verbs. *Learn* means "to acquire knowledge." *Teach* means "to instruct."

NONSTANDARD Pamela **learned** me how to water-ski.
STANDARD Pamela **taught** me how to water-ski.
STANDARD I **learned** how to water-ski last summer.

leave, let. Both of these words are verbs. *Leave* means "to depart." *Let* means "to allow" or "to permit."

NONSTANDARD **Leave** me get you a glass of water.
STANDARD **Let** me get you a glass of water.
STANDARD Did the train **leave** on time?

lie, lay. *Lie* means "to rest or recline." *Lie* is never followed by a direct object. Its principal parts are *lie, lying, lay,* and *lain. Lay* means "to put or set (something) down." *Lay* is usually followed by a direct object. Its principal parts are *lay, laying, laid,* and *laid.*

LIE If you feel faint, **lie** down.
She was **lying** in the hammock when we arrived.
I **lay** awake all last night, worrying about final exams.
Mopsy has **lain** by the fire all evening.

LAY **Lay** only the living-room carpet.
Why are you **laying** your coat over the chair?
As soon as David **laid** the book down, he fell asleep.
The workers have already **laid** the foundation.

EXERCISE 3 Determining the Correct Word
Number your paper 1 to 25. Then write the word or words in parentheses that correctly complete each sentence.

1. We might (have, of) gone to the camp if the weather had improved.
2. (Leave, Let) me answer that question.
3. In her letter did Michelle (imply, infer) that she might enter her self-portrait in the art contest?
4. Did you (hear, here) the echo?
5. That article was (kind of, rather) funny.
6. How did that baby bird fall from (its, it's) nest?
7. You should (have, of) mentioned that sooner.
8. Is the dog (lying, laying) on the sofa again?
9. I just noticed that I have a huge (hole, whole) in the sleeve of my jacket!
10. The lifeguard jumped (in, into) the pool to cool off.
11. Mr. Barnes (learned, taught) me everything I know about car engines.

12. I don't wish to (imply, infer) that I am running for a second term.
13. The vacuum works (good, well) since Mom fixed it.
14. Nancy gently (lain, laid) the blanket over the sleeping baby.
15. These (kind, kinds) of potatoes are good for baking.
16. From her remarks we (implied, inferred) that she might be moving soon.
17. (Fewer, Less) people are using the park during these cold winter months.
18. (Irregardless, Regardless) of the weather, we must continue until we reach the cabin.
19. If everything turns out (good, well), we should be able to get a (knew, new) television set.
20. Did you (hear, here) that Mr. Sherman will be (learning, teaching) us fencing after school?
21. We (implied, inferred) from her silence that she didn't do (good, well) in the tryouts.
22. (Irregardless, Regardless) of what the clerk said, (its, it's) the wrong color.
23. (Its, It's) impossible to know whether Coach Murphy will (leave, let) Vincent play shortstop.
24. The (hole, whole) time we were there, I (knew, new) something was wrong.
25. You could (have, of) stopped (hear, here) on your way to the library.

EXERCISE 4 Using *Lie* and *Lay* Correctly

Number your paper 1 to 20. Then complete each sentence by writing the correct form of *lie* or *lay.*

1. Sandy ____ her mittens on a pile of snow beside the car.
2. The spare tire was ____ on the floor of the garage.
3. For a month after his gallbladder operation, Dad ____ down each afternoon.
4. For about an hour, I was just ____ on the grass, staring up at the stars.
5. Two thirds of Alaska ____ below the Arctic Circle.
6. ____ the pieces of the puzzle right side up.
7. Her ring must have ____ on the counter unnoticed for over a week.

8. In Yorktown on October 19, 1781, the British ____ down their arms and surrendered to George Washington.
9. The fleet is ____ at anchor in the bay.
10. For what seemed like hours, the snake had ____ coiled on the driveway.
11. Your sweater will dry better if you ____ it flat.
12. When we peeked in, the baby was ____ contentedly in his crib.
13. The broken tree limb had ____ across the path for two days before it was removed.
14. Why don't you ____ down and rest for a while?
15. I ____ the clean laundry at the foot of the bed.
16. For months an old ship ____ in the harbor with a great hole in her hull.
17. Sometimes our cat ____ on the sofa all afternoon.
18. When we found Martin, he was ____ under the maple tree.
19. Don't ____ down now; dinner is almost ready.
20. Who ____ the newspaper on top of the flowers?

like, as. *Like* can be used as a preposition to introduce a prepositional phrase. *As* is usually a subordinating conjunction that introduces an adverb clause. Although *like* is sometimes used informally as a conjunction, it should be avoided in formal situations.

INFORMAL I think the room is perfect just **like** it is. [clause]
FORMAL I think the room is perfect just **as** it is.
FORMAL Gloria's cat is gray-striped **like** mine. [prepositional phrase]

loose, lose. *Loose* is usually an adjective that means "not tight." *Lose* is a verb that means "to misplace" or "not to have any longer."

I will sew on those **loose** buttons.
If I leave, I'll **lose** my turn at bat.

may be, maybe. *May be* is a form of the verb *be*. *Maybe* is an adverb that means "perhaps."

This **may be** the chance of a lifetime.
Maybe he didn't see you.

most. *Most* is a noun, a pronoun, or an adjective that modifies a noun or a pronoun. *Almost,* which means "nearly," is an adverb. Do not substitute *most* for *almost.*

NONSTANDARD I finished **most** all of my term paper last night.
STANDARD I finished **almost** all my term paper last night.
STANDARD I keep busy **most** of the time.

nor, or. Use *neither* with *nor* and *either* with *or.*

Neither Fred **nor** Jane is coming to the party.
I will take **either** the red one **or** the blue one.

of. Prepositions such as *inside, outside,* and *off* should not be followed by *of.*

NONSTANDARD The ball rolled **off of** the lawn into the gutter.
STANDARD The ball rolled **off** the lawn into the gutter.

ought. Never use *have* or *had* with *ought.*

NONSTANDARD You **had**n't **ought** to arrive so late.
STANDARD You **ought** not to arrive so late.

passed, past. *Passed* is the past tense of the verb *pass.* As a noun *past* means "a time gone by." As an adjective *past* means "just gone" or "elapsed." As a preposition *past* means "beyond."

In the **past** she always **passed** her courses with *A*'s. [*past* as a noun]

For the **past** several mornings, I have walked **past** the park on my way to school. [*past* as an adjective and then a preposition]

precede, proceed. Both of these words are verbs. *Precede* means "to be, go, or come ahead of something else." *Proceed* means "to move along a course; to advance" or "to continue after a pause or an interruption."

These instructions **precede** the ones from yesterday.
Proceed down the mountain with great caution.

principal, principle. As an adjective *principal* means "main" or "chief." As a noun *principal* means "the head of a school" or "leader." *Principle* is a noun that is synonymous with *law, truth, doctrine,* or *code of conduct.*

The **principal** part in the drama was played by Mr. Rogers, the **principal** of Canton High School.

Clarence lives by a strict set of **principles.**

respectfully, respectively. *Respectfully* is related to the noun *respect,* which means "high regard or esteem." *Respectively* means "in the order given."

Everyone spoke **respectfully** to the elderly man.
Jan and Bob are from Detroit and Cleveland, **respectively.**

rise, raise. *Rise* means "to move upward" or "to get up." *Rise* is never followed by a direct object. Its principal parts are *rise, rising, rose,* and *risen. Raise* means "to lift up," "to increase," or "to grow something." *Raise* is usually followed by a direct object. Its principal parts are *raise, raising, raised,* and *raised.*

The sun **rises** an hour later now that daylight saving time has begun.
When should we **raise** the flag?

says. Do not use *says,* the present tense of the verb *say,* when you should use the past tense *said.*

NONSTANDARD Then she **says,** "I want to go with you."
STANDARD Then she **said,** "I want to go with you."

-self, -selves. A reflexive or an intensive pronoun that ends in *-self* or *-selves* should not be used as a subject. (Never use *hisself* or *theirselves.*)

NONSTANDARD Ken and **myself** were chosen.
STANDARD Ken and **I** were chosen.
NONSTANDARD They made **theirselves** sandwiches.
STANDARD They made **themselves** sandwiches.

shall, will. Formal English uses *shall* with first person pronouns and *will* with second person pronouns and third person pronouns. Today, however, *shall* and *will* are used interchangeably with *I* and *we*—except that *shall* is still used with first person pronouns for questions.

Shall I meet you at the mall?
Will you meet me at the mall?

sit, set. *Sit* means "to rest in an upright position." *Sit* is never followed by a direct object. Its principal parts are *sit, sitting, sat,* and *sat. Set* means "to put or place (something)." *Set* is usually followed by a direct object. Its principal parts are *set, setting, set,* and *set.*

Sit down and rest for a while.
Set the dishes on the shelf.

so. *So* should not be used to begin a sentence.

NONSTANDARD	**So** when are you leaving on your vacation?
STANDARD	The plane lands in five minutes, **so** we must hurry! [coordinating conjunction]
STANDARD	The dance was **so** wonderful! [adverb]

some, somewhat. *Some* is either a pronoun or an adjective that modifies a noun or a pronoun. *Somewhat* is an adverb.

NONSTANDARD	School enrollment has declined **some.**
STANDARD	School enrollment has declined **somewhat.**

EXERCISE 5 Determining the Correct Word
Number your paper 1 to 25. Then write the word or group of words in parentheses that correctly completes each sentence.

1. Barry caught that sailfish (himself, hisself).
2. The rain is (some, somewhat) heavier now.
3. Do (as, like) I say, and you'll make a good impression.
4. Tim will (precede, proceed) with his plans for the party.
5. Who took my music (off, off of) the piano?
6. The doorknob is (loose, lose) again.
7. It is easier to state (principals, principles) than to live up to them.
8. Denver, Boise, and Helena are the capitals of Colorado, Idaho, and Montana, (respectfully, respectively).

9. Mom and Dad enjoyed (theirselves, themselves) in Tampa.
10. Your sweater is blue (as, like) mine.
11. This will, dated 1978, (precedes, proceeds) the other one.
12. Today (may be, maybe) my lucky day!
13. We pulled (off, off of) the road to let the ambulance pass.
14. In the (passed, past), life was less complicated.
15. (Almost, Most) everyone at the picnic had a good time.
16. Charlie and (I, myself) are going to work the spotlights.
17. How did the dog get (loose, lose)?
18. Do (as, like) I say, not (as, like) I do.
19. The (principal, principle) (respectfully, respectively) requested the governor's presence at graduation.
20. (Almost, Most) all of the arrivals from the Midwest (may be, maybe) slightly delayed because of a storm.
21. Two weeks (passed, past) before I felt (some, somewhat) better.
22. (Shall, Will) we (precede, proceed) to the dining room?
23. Jay (says, said), "I haven't had time to swim for the (passed, past) several days."
24. (May be, Maybe) you will (loose, lose) the nomination.
25. The (principal, principle) issue that (shall, will) be discussed at the meeting is safer streets.

EXERCISE 6 Using *Rise/Raise* and *Sit/Set* Correctly
Number your paper 1 to 20. Complete each sentence by writing the correct form of *rise/raise* or *sit/set*.

1. Gail ____ to question the speaker.
2. Please ____ in that large, comfortable chair.
3. Where were you ____ in the auditorium?
4. The price of clothing is constantly ____.
5. I ____ in the dentist's office for 45 minutes.
6. ____ the flag slowly.
7. Yesterday he ____ there all day in the warm sun.
8. Have you been ____ there long?
9. Tracy ____ the box on the counter.
10. In about ten minutes, the bread will have ____ enough.
11. Should I be ____ the napkins to the right of the plates?
12. Aunt Meg always ____ her dripping umbrella in the sink.
13. The elevator started to ____ before I pushed the button for my floor.

14. If you ____ before seven, you'll have plenty of time to walk to school.
15. I have ____ in the back row all year long.
16. Who ____ the blinds?
17. Keith was ____ the checkers on the board when the telephone rang.
18. The cat has been ____ on the new sofa again!
19. The temperature has been ____ steadily for the past several days.
20. Our dog ____ his head alertly as the mail carrier approached our house.

than, then. *Than* is usually a subordinating conjunction and is used for comparisons. *Then* is an adverb that means "at that time" or "next."

I have lived in Salt Lake City longer **than** you.
Finish your homework and **then** call me.

that, which, who. These words are often used as relative pronouns to introduce adjective clauses. *That* refers to people, animals, or things and always begins an essential clause. *Which* refers to animals and things. *Who* refers to people.

The movie **that** was on TV last night is my favorite.
Gone with the Wind, **which** was shown on TV last night, is my favorite movie.

Anyone **who** responds to the ad should fill out an application.

their, there, they're. *Their* is a possessive pronoun. *There* is usually an adverb, and sometimes it can also begin an inverted sentence. *They're* is a contraction for *they are.*

Their car is parked over **there.**
They're moving to Mobile in September.

theirs, there's. *Theirs* is a possessive pronoun. *There's* is a contraction for *there is.*

The car over **there** is **theirs.**

them, those. Never use *them* as a subject or a modifier.

NONSTANDARD **Them** are from my garden. [subject]
STANDARD **Those** are from my garden.

NONSTANDARD **Them** tomatoes are from my garden. [adjective]
STANDARD **Those** tomatoes are from my garden.

this, that, these, those. *This* and *that* are singular and modify singular nouns. *These* and *those* are plural and modify plural nouns.

NONSTANDARD Does the Sport Shop sell **those** kind of bats?
STANDARD Does the Sport Shop sell **that** kind of bat?
STANDARD The Sport Shop sells **those** bats.

this here, that there. Avoid using *here* or *there* in addition to *this* or *that.*

NONSTANDARD **That there** dog looks ferocious!
STANDARD **That** dog looks ferocious!

threw, through. *Threw* is the past tense of the verb *throw. Through* is a preposition that means "in one side and out the other."

Who **threw** Sunday's newspaper away?
We turned our lights on when we drove **through** the tunnel.

to, too, two. *To* is a preposition. *To* also begins an infinitive. *Too* is an adverb that modifies an adjective or another adverb. *Two* is a number.

Two more people are **too** many **to** take in our car.

try to. Use *try to* instead of *try and,* which is nonstandard.

NONSTANDARD I will **try and** be there on time.
STANDARD I will **try to** be there on time.

unique. *Unique* is an adjective that means "the only one of its kind." Because of its meaning, *unique* should not be written in the comparative or superlative degree.

NONSTANDARD That horse has the **most unique** markings.
STANDARD That horse has **unique** markings.

way, ways. Do not substitute *ways* for *way* when referring to a distance.

NONSTANDARD We have a long **ways** to go yet.
STANDARD We have a long **way** to go yet.

weak, week. *Weak* is an adjective that means "not strong" or "likely to break." *Week* is a noun that means "a period of seven days."

For the first **week** after your operation, you'll feel quite **weak.**

what. Do not substitute *what* for *that.*

NONSTANDARD The car **what** I want is very expensive.
STANDARD The car **that** I want is very expensive.

when, where. Do not use *when* or *where* directly after a linking verb in a definition.

NONSTANDARD In the North October is **when** you should plant tulip bulbs.
STANDARD In the North October is the month when you should plant tulip bulbs.
In the North you should plant tulip bulbs in October.

NONSTANDARD The Hall of Mirrors is **where** the Treaty of Versailles was signed.
STANDARD The Hall of Mirrors is the room in which the Treaty of Versailles was signed.
The Treaty of Versailles was signed in the Hall of Mirors.

where. Do not substitute *where* for *that.*

NONSTANDARD I read **where** bowling is the number one participant sport in the United States.
STANDARD I read **that** bowling is the number one participant sport in the United States.

who, whom. *Who,* a pronoun in the nominative case, is used as a subject or a predicate nominative. *Whom,* a pronoun in the objective case, is mainly used as a direct object, an indirect object, or an object of a preposition. *(See page 150.)*

Who is coming to our party? [subject]
Howard is someone **whom** I have known all my life. [direct object of the verb in the adjective clause]

whose, who's. *Whose* is a possessive pronoun. *Who's* is a contraction for *who is.*

Whose is that suitcase?
Who's going with you?

your, you're. *Your* is a possessive pronoun. *You're* is a contraction for *you are.*

You're sure you put **your** baseball glove in the car?

EXERCISE 7 Determining the Correct Word
Number your paper 1 to 25. Then write the word or group of words in parentheses that correctly completes each sentence.

1. (Them, Those) watches are extremely accurate.
2. You should try (and, to) get a good night's sleep.
3. The praying mantis is an insect (that, who) is entirely beneficial to people.
4. Which dealer in town sells (that, these) kind of paint?
5. The basketball game (that, what) I saw was extremely exciting.
6. Mom got Sally (them, those) earrings for her birthday.
7. I couldn't sell (this here, this) old radio for any price!
8. Tree-ripened fruit is usually sweeter (than, then) fruit picked green.
9. I read (that, where) the U.S. Postal Service processes approximately 50 percent of the world's mail.
10. Ever since she sprained her ankle, it has been (weak, week).
11. Who (threw, through) the clean clothes into the hamper?
12. (Who, Whom) is sitting with Jason?
13. I want a bike (that, what) is very lightweight.
14. Earl is taller (than, then) most boys in his class.

15. (Theirs, There's) is the house with the green shutters.
16. In a magazine I read (that, where) Anne Murray earned her college degree as a physical-education teacher.
17. (Whose, Who's) taking care of (your, you're) dog?
18. (Theirs, There's) an easy way (to, too) open that jar.
19. (This, These) kind of key ring costs about (to, too, two) dollars.
20. In the Brontë family, (their, there) were six children, three of (which, whom) became famous novelists.
21. They went (threw, through) (their, they're) files, but they couldn't find the birth certificates.
22. Don't try (to, and) stay awake because we have a long (way, ways) to go yet.
23. (Your, You're) the one they want (to, too) nominate.
24. (Their, There) are streets in Quebec that are (to, too) narrow for large cars to pass each other easily.
25. I can't forget (this, these) kind of scary movie for at least a (weak, week).

GLOSSARY REVIEW

Number your paper 1 to 25. Then write the word or group of words in parentheses that correctly completes each sentence. (This exercise uses words from the entire glossary.)

1. (Whose, Who's) is that (advice, advise) you followed?
2. I have (all ready, already) gone (all the farther, as far as) I can go without help.
3. (Can, May) I (bring, take) you a glass of water?
4. Can you (accept, except) the fact that he is a better swimmer (than, then) you?
5. (Irregardless, Regardless) of the condition of the mountain trail, I can (adapt, adopt) to it.
6. In her conversation she (implied, inferred) that her salary was greater (than, then) mine.
7. The (hole, whole) community is worried about flooding and mud slides (beside, besides).
8. (Almost, Most) of the building materials (may be, maybe) donated by local merchants.
9. Try (and, to) (precede, proceed) as cautiously as possible.

10. I read (that, where) clothing is needed (bad, badly) for the people (who, whom) lost their homes in the tornado.
11. I looked (everywhere, everywheres), but I couldn't find (their, there) umbrella.
12. (Doesn't, Don't) you think we should distribute the extra refreshments (between, among) the cast members?
13. My uncle (learned, taught) me how to create the (allusion, illusion) of pulling a scarf out of midair.
14. Everyone in my history class (accept, except) Sue has the flu and is not feeling (good, well).
15. As I was (laying, lying) in bed, I could (hear, here) the foghorns in the harbor.
16. (Your, You're) really going to buy (that, that there) ten-year-old car?
17. There aren't (any more, anymore) patterns for (that, those) kind of handmade sweater.
18. We couldn't see (any, no) way to get (passed, past) the boulder blocking our way.
19. The (amount, number) of women in law is very different (from, than) what it was 50 years ago.
20. The (capital, capitol) looks (good, well) since its main chambers were redecorated.
21. Last summer (their, there) weren't (to, too) many part-time jobs available to teenagers.
22. (Them, Those) (to, two) boys have played right and left tackle (respectfully, respectively) in every game.
23. (Being as, Since) Jamie has a cold, Coach Henderson won't (leave, let) him play in Saturday's game.
24. Michael and (I, myself) didn't find (anything, nothing) of value at the yard sale.
25. Do you think (its, it's) (some, somewhat) cooler today (than, then) yesterday?

STANDARDIZED TEST

USAGE

Directions: Each sentence may contain an underlined part that is unacceptable. On your answer sheet, fill in the circle containing the letter of the unacceptable part. If there is no underlined part requiring change, fill in *E*.

SAMPLE Your (A) dad taught (B) Rita and he (C) how to swim (D). No error (E)

ANSWER Ⓐ Ⓑ ● Ⓓ Ⓔ

1. Both Ken and her (A) have (B) already (C) bought (D) their tickets. No error (E)
2. Don't (A) the moon seem unusually (B) bright (C) to you and him (D)? No error (E)
3. His (A) working doesn't (B) hardly leave (C) him time to practice (D). No error (E)
4. Every student and teacher is (A) looking carefully (B) for the earrings that (C) Jennifer lost (D). No error (E)
5. Besides (A) Edwina and I (B), whom (C) have (D) you invited? No error (E)
6. Everyone except (A) Paul and us (B) have (C) chosen (D) a topic. No error (E)
7. Neither Carlos nor Ben really wishes (A) that he (B) were (C) taller (D) than Homer. No error (E)
8. The song began (A) softly but then (B) gradually grows (C) louder (D). No error (E)
9. Some of us (A) tourists have (B) never seen (C) the capitol (D) city. No error (E)
10. Of the two boys there (A), who (B) do you think looks (C) oldest (D)? No error (E)

Directions: Each sentence is followed by four ways to write the underlined part of the sentence. Choose the best one. If the original way is best, choose *A*. Fill in the circle containing the letter of your answer.

SAMPLE Both Carol and he has felt badly all day.

A he has felt badly **C** he have felt bad
B him have felt bad **D** he have felt badly

ANSWER Ⓐ Ⓑ Ⓒ Ⓓ

11. No one hasn't taken the garbage out yet.

A No one hasn't taken
B No one has taken
C No one hasn't took
D No one has took

12. Is the pitcher more important than anyone on the team?

A more important than anyone on the team
B the most important than anyone on the team
C more important than anyone else on the team
D importanter than anyone else on the team

13. Who's dog or cat has been lying in the petunia patch?

A Who's dog or cat has been lying
B Who's dog or cat have been lying
C Whose dog or cat has been laying
D Whose dog or cat has been lying

14. When he sat on the bench, a huge number of pigeons greet him.

A a huge number of pigeons greet him
B a huge amount of pigeons greet him
C a huge number of pigeons greeted him
D a huge amount of pigeons greets him

15. Neither Laura nor her sisters have broken their promise.

A have broken their promise
B has broken her promise
C has broken their promise
D has broked her promise

Unit 3

Mechanics

10

Capital Letters

DIAGNOSTIC TEST

Number your paper 1 to 10. Then write each word that should begin with a capital letter.

EXAMPLE last summer we visited niagara falls.
ANSWER Last, Niagara, Falls

1. as we drove to memphis, we saw the mississippi river to our left.
2. did judge gershen speak at the rally on the fourth of july?
3. linda attended a school in pennsylvania before entering wildwood high school this year.
4. while searching for a northeastern route around north america, henry hudson discovered hudson bay.
5. until this year i had never read john keats's poem "ode to a grecian urn."
6. during christmas vacation we traveled from seattle to portland on mountain railroad to visit my grandparents.
7. to get to victoria park, go south on route 74.
8. during my junior year, my favorite courses were american history and art.
9. we saw the play *two gentlemen of verona* at the shubert theater on forty-fourth street.
10. georgia's family is moving to the southwest next month.

Until the advent of printing in the fifteenth century, words were written in all capital letters. In addition, no punctuation was used, which made reading even more difficult. When scribes wrote, they ran words TOGETHERLIKETHIS.

Fortunately, along with the printing press came specific uses for capital letters and the introduction of punctuation. As a result, not only could people read faster, but they could also understand more easily what they read. The correct use of capital letters and punctuation will add clarity to your writing and will prevent misunderstanding.

RULES FOR CAPITAL LETTERS

When lowercase letters were first introduced, capital letters were used only in special situations. Today, however, a capital letter marks the beginning of certain constructions and emphasizes the importance of certain words. This chapter will review the uses of capital letters.

First Words

Capital letters draw a reader's attention to the beginning of a new sentence or a new line of poetry.

10a Capitalize the first word in a sentence or in a line of poetry.

SENTENCE **T**eenagers in our community have become increasingly involved in political campaigns.

POETRY **D**oes the road wind uphill all the way?
Yes, to the very end. —CHRISTINA ROSSETTI

Capitalize the first word of a direct quotation. *(See page 281.)*

Marvin asked, "**W**ill you call me when you get home?"

Capitalize the first word of each heading in an outline. *(See page 588.)*

I. **A**rguments for a new gym
 A. **A**dditional space

Capitalize the first word in a formal resolution.

Resolved, **T**hat this school should permit seniors to leave school assemblies before other students.

Capitalize the first word of a formal statement that follows a colon.

The question was this: **C**ould a runner break the four-minute-mile record?

I and *O*

Always capitalize these single-letter words.

10b Capitalize the pronoun *I*, both alone and in contractions. Also capitalize the interjection *O*.

I **I**'m sure **I** saw her at the game.
O **O** hark, **O** hear! how thin and clear,
And thinner, clearer, farther going!

—ALFRED, LORD TENNYSON

NOTE: *Oh* is not capitalized unless it comes at the beginning of a sentence.

Proper Nouns

Beginning a noun with a capital letter can tell a reader that the noun is a proper noun—that it names a particular person, place, or thing.

10c Capitalize proper nouns and their abbreviations.

Since there are so many proper nouns, they have been divided into the following groups to help you remember them easily.

Names of Persons and Animals. Capitalize the names of particular persons and animals.

PERSONS **J**ames, **J**ocelyn **W**eiss, **A**llison **R.** **F**errara
ANIMALS **R**ex, **F**elix, **M**orris, **D**ancer, **T**hunderbolt

Surnames that begin with *De, Mc, Mac, O',* or *St.* usually contain two capital letters. However, since such names do vary, it is always best to ask individual people how their names are spelled and capitalized.

De**J**on, **M**c**G**uire, **M**ac**I**nnis, **O**'**H**ara, **S**t. **J**ames

Capitalize a descriptive name, title, or nickname that is used as a proper noun or as part of a proper noun.

Calamity **J**ane, **H**onest **A**be, the **C**ornhusker **S**tate

Capitalize abbreviations that follow a person's name.

Stephanie Wong, **M.D.**, will be tonight's guest speaker.

Capitalize common nouns that are clearly personified.

O **M**emory! thou fond deceiver. —OLIVER GOLDSMITH

Geographical Names. Capitalize the names of particular places, bodies of water, and celestial bodies.

STREETS, HIGHWAYS	**T**remont **S**treet, **M**eridan **T**urnpike, **R**oute 77, **T**hirty-second **S**treet [The second part of a hyphenated numbered street is not capitalized.]
CITIES, STATES	**R**apid **C**ity, **S**outh **D**akota; **T**erre **H**aute, **I**ndiana; **W**ashington, **D.C.**
TOWNSHIPS, COUNTIES	**P**ottsville **T**ownship, **B**roward **C**ounty
COUNTRIES	**S**audi **A**rabia, **T**hailand, the **S**oviet **U**nion, **I**reland, **C**anada
SECTIONS OF A COUNTRY	the **N**orthwest, **N**ew **E**ngland, the **S**outh [Words that are used as sections of the country are often preceded by *the*. Compass directions do not begin with a capital letter: *Go east on Route 23.*]
CONTINENTS	**S**outh **A**merica, **A**frica, **A**ustralia
ISLANDS	**L**ong **I**sland, the **P**hilippine **I**slands
MOUNTAINS	**M**ount **H**ood, the **A**llegheny **M**ountains, the **W**hite **M**ountains
PARKS	**B**ryce **C**anyon **N**ational **P**ark

BODIES OF WATER	**P**acific **O**cean, **S**outh **C**hina **S**ea, **P**ersian **G**ulf, **N**iagara **F**alls, **M**errimack **R**iver, **C**edar **L**ake
STARS	**S**irius, **N**ova **H**ercules, **N**orth **S**tar
CONSTELLATIONS	**B**ig **D**ipper, **U**rsa **M**inor, **O**rion
PLANETS	**V**enus, **N**eptune, **S**aturn, **E**arth [Do not capitalize *sun* or *moon*. Also, do not capitalize *earth* if it is preceded by *the*.]

NOTE: Capitalize words such as *street, mountain,* or *island* only when they are part of a proper noun.

Which **l**ake is larger, **L**ake **S**uperior or **L**ake **M**ichigan?

EXERCISE 1 Using Capital Letters
Number your paper 1 to 20. Then write the following items, using capital letters only where needed.

1. the columbia river
2. jackson park
3. the milky way
4. fifty-third street
5. a trip to the southwest
6. the city of louisville
7. the earth and mars
8. north on hayes highway
9. his horse dusty
10. alfred moses, jr.
11. the state of ohio
12. lake victoria
13. the new york turnpike
14. the indian ocean
15. mountains in the east
16. the gulf of suez
17. madrid, in spain
18. newport news, virginia
19. a country in africa
20. the bluegrass state

EXERCISE 2 Using Capital Letters
Number your paper 1 to 10. Then write each word that should begin with a capital letter.

1. woodrow wilson had a pet ram named old ike.
2. sparrows are not native to north america.
3. if you look east, i will show you the little dipper.
4. before they were known as the rocky mountains, they were called the stony mountains.
5. the first woman to swim the english channel in both directions was florence chadwick of california.
6. paul revere's family name originally was de rivoire.

7. the gasoline station at morgan avenue and twenty-first street has the lowest prices in town.
8. the capital of texas was changed 15 times before austin was finally chosen.
9. address the letter to rachel r. bliss, d.d.s., 8 highland road, birmingham, england.
10. the time is out of joint; o cursed spite, that ever i was born to set it right! —WILLIAM SHAKESPEARE

Names of Groups and Businesses. Capitalize the names of organizations, businesses, institutions, government bodies, and political parties.

ORGANIZATIONS	the **A**merican **R**ed **C**ross, the **B**oy **S**couts of **A**merica, the **N**ational **G**uard
BUSINESSES	**E**astern **A**irlines, **P**olaroid **C**orporation, **G. F**ox and **C**ompany, **J**acobs and **A**ssociates, **A**rborway **N**atural **F**oods
INSTITUTIONS	**H**awthorne **H**igh **S**chool, **L**akeview **H**ospital, the **U**niversity of **P**ennsylvania [Words such as *school, hospital,* and *university* are not capitalized unless they are part of a proper noun.]
GOVERNMENT BODIES	the **U**nited **S**tates **S**upreme **C**ourt, **C**ongress, the **S**enate, the **V**eterans **A**dministration, the **H**ouse of **C**ommons, **P**arliament
POLITICAL PARTIES	the **D**emocratic **P**arty, a **R**epublican

Specific Time Periods, Events, and Documents. Capitalize days of the week, months of the year, civil and religious holidays, and special events. Also capitalize the names of historical events, periods, and documents.

DAYS, MONTHS	**T**uesday, **W**ednesday, **F**ebruary, **M**arch [Do not capitalize the seasons of the year.]
HOLIDAYS	**M**emorial **D**ay, **T**hanksgiving, **H**anukkah
SPECIAL EVENTS	the **O**range **B**owl **P**arade, the **O**lympic **G**ames, the **B**oston **M**arathon
HISTORICAL EVENTS	the **T**rojan **W**ar, the **B**oston **T**ea **P**arty, the **L**ouisiana **P**urchase, **D**-**D**ay

PERIODS	the **M**iddle **A**ges, the **A**ge of **R**eason, the **G**reat **D**epression, **R**econstruction
DOCUMENTS	the **T**ruman **D**octrine, the **T**reaty of **P**aris, the **F**irst **A**mendment, the **C**ivil **R**ights **A**ct, the **V**oting **R**ights **A**ct

NOTE: Prepositions are not capitalized.

Nationalities, Races, Languages, and Religions. Capitalize the names of nationalities, races, languages, religions, and religious references.

NATIONALITIES	**C**hinese, the **M**exicans, a **S**candinavian
RACES	**C**aucasian, **O**riental, **M**ongoloid
LANGUAGES	**S**panish, **G**reek, **R**ussian, **E**nglish, **F**rench
RELIGIONS	**R**oman **C**atholic, **J**udaism, **L**utheran
RELIGIOUS REFERENCES	the **B**ible, the **O**ld **T**estament, the **T**orah, the **K**oran, **G**od [Capitalize pronouns referring to the Deity: *They prayed to God for **H**is direction.* Do not capitalize *god* when it refers to a mythological god.]

Other Proper Nouns. Capitalize other nouns that name specific places and things.

VEHICLES	***E**xplorer I, **L**usitania, **C**alifornia **Z**ephyr* [Names of vehicles are also italicized.]
AWARDS	the **N**obel **P**rize, the **D**avis **C**up
BRAND NAMES	**A**pple computer, **D**ove soap, **F**ord sedan [The product itself is not capitalized.]
MONUMENTS, MEMORIALS	**W**ashington **M**onument, **V**ietnam **M**emorial, **M**ount **R**ushmore
BUILDINGS	**M**etropolitan **O**pera **H**ouse, **S**ears **T**ower, **E**iffel **T**ower
PARTS OF A BOOK	**C**hapter II, **V**ol. V, **N**o. 4, **P**art IV
SPECIFIC COURSE NAMES	**C**hemistry II, **D**rafting I, **E**nglish

NOTE: Unnumbered courses such as *history, science,* and *art* are not capitalized. Also, do not capitalize class names such as *freshman* or *senior* unless they are part of a proper noun, such as ***S**enior **C**lass **P**icnic*.

EXERCISE 3 Using Capital Letters
Number your paper 1 to 20. Then write the following items, using capital letters only where needed.

1. math and spanish
2. the eiffel tower in paris
3. turkey on thanksgiving
4. spring and summer
5. the federal communications commission
6. the battle of saratoga
7. the stone age
8. baseball at dodger stadium
9. the new testament
10. the astor motor inn
11. nabisco crackers
12. the supreme court
13. the god zeus
14. the university of tennessee
15. an amendment to the constitution
16. a democrat from idaho
17. a hardware store in town
18. the bill of rights
19. a college in the midwest
20. the senior prom

EXERCISE 4 Using Capital Letters
Number your paper 1 to 20. Then write each word that should begin with a capital letter.

1. the cease-fire on palm sunday, april 9, 1865, ended the civil war.
2. during several months last winter, we were able to skate on the lake near our home.
3. dolley madison was voted a seat in the house of representatives on january 9, 1844.
4. john adams was a member of the federalist party.
5. chili con carne originated among mexicans living in what is now texas.
6. last year, when i was a junior, i enjoyed french, creative writing, art II, and mechanical drawing.
7. when my sister graduated from purdue university, she got a job in a computer company.
8. the fourth amendment to the constitution protects citizens from unreasonable search.
9. my first job was assembly-line work at the costello and morand company of portland, delaware.
10. the *mayflower* first touched land at the tip of cape cod on november 11, 1620.
11. since i learned to speak italian, i often speak to my grandfather in his native language.

12. in 1945, 50 nations were represented at the first meeting of the united nations.
13. have you ever visited mount vernon, george washington's home?
14. the industrial revolution started in england and spread to europe and america.
15. the store didn't have any pillsbury flour, so i bought some gold medal flour instead.
16. robert mills, designer of the washington monument, was the first native-born architect in the united states.
17. ty cobb of the detroit tigers made 4,191 base hits during his career.
18. the high school band will march in the annual parade on thanksgiving.
19. the lutheran minister read a passage from genesis at the dedication ceremony.
20. edith wharton won a pulitzer prize for her fiction.

EXERCISE 5 Writing Sentences

Write six to ten sentences that describe a city that you have lived in, are presently living in, or would like to live in. Mention its geographical location, historical background, points of interest, and notable citizens. Be sure to capitalize all proper nouns.

EXERCISE 6 Time-out for Review

Number your paper 1 to 20. Then write each word that should begin with a capital letter.

1. in an average year, santa fe, new mexico, receives 17 more inches of snow than fairbanks, alaska.
2. the first college for women, which opened in 1834, was wheaton college in norton, massachusetts.
3. andrew jackson fought in the revolutionary war when he was only 13 years old.
4. the largest natural history museum in the world is the american museum of natural history in new york.
5. because we didn't take the highway, we were able to stop at many charming towns throughout the midwest.
6. john glenn's space capsule, *friendship 7,* was picked up by the recovery ship *noah.*

7. a delegate from the soviet union will be attending the luncheon in the white house today.
8. which children's book won the newbery medal this year?
9. the people of philadelphia first celebrated the fourth of july a year after the declaration of independence had been adopted by the continental congress.
10. most of the people attending the convention are staying at the ashford motel, which faces the atlantic ocean.
11. the closest planet to the sun, mercury, is about one third the size of the earth.
12. the first woman lyricist elected to the songwriters' hall of fame was dorothy fields.
13. the tournament of roses was initiated by the valley hunt club of pasadena, california, in 1886.
14. the kodak camera was invented in 1888 in new york by george eastman.
15. if the great salt lake is an inland lake, where does the salt come from?
16. the oldest street in london, england, is watling street.
17. the mississippi river was first seen by europeans in 1541.
18. the philadelphia eagles started playing in the national football league in 1933.
19. the constitution does not mention god.
20. the last state to join the union before alaska and hawaii was arizona, admitted on valentine's day in 1912.

Proper Adjectives

Because proper adjectives are formed from proper nouns, they should be capitalized—as proper nouns are.

10d Capitalize most proper adjectives.

PROPER NOUNS	**S**pain, **I**daho, the **W**est
PROPER ADJECTIVES	**S**panish rice, **I**daho potatoes, **W**estern coastline

NOTE: When adjectives are formed from the words that refer to the compass directions such as *east,* no capital letters are used.

The wind was blowing from an **e**asterly direction.

Some proper adjectives derived from proper nouns are so common that they are no longer capitalized.

china plates, **p**asteurized milk, **q**uixotic vision

When a proper adjective is part of a hyphenated adjective, capitalize only the part that is a proper adjective.

all-**A**merican team   trans-**A**tlantic crossing

Sometimes both parts of a hyphenated adjective will be proper adjectives.

Indo-**E**uropean languages   **A**fro-**A**merican literature

EXERCISE 7 Using Capital Letters
Number your paper 1 to 10. Then write each word that should begin with a capital letter.

1. several of our neighbors fly the american flag outside their houses on state and national holidays.
2. the artifacts on exhibit at our local museum are believed to be pre-columbian.
3. a majority of the republican senators have voted for the appropriations.
4. the first non-indian visitor to arizona arrived in 1539.
5. my father has driven his american-made car for 15 years.
6. is *X* the roman numeral for ten?
7. the verrazano-narrows bridge in new york city was designed by othmar a. ammans, a swiss-american engineer.
8. many of the french-speaking people in canada live in quebec.
9. the friday afternoon traffic is quite heavy.
10. the sinking of the *maine* in havana harbor touched off the spanish-american war.

Titles

Capital letters signal the importance of titles of people and works of art.

10e Capitalize the titles of people and works of art.

Titles Used with Names of People. Capitalize a title showing office, rank, or profession when it comes before a person's name.

BEFORE A NAME	Is **J**udge **G**oodell in his chambers?
USED ALONE	Who was the **j**udge at the trial?
BEFORE A NAME	I worked on **S**enator **A**mes's reelection campaign.
USED ALONE	The **s**enator from our district is running for reelection.

NOTE: Do not capitalize the prefix *ex-* or the suffix *-elect* when either is connected to a title.

ex-**P**resident Ford   **G**overnor-elect Baray

Titles Used Alone. Capitalize a title that is used alone when it is being substituted for a person's name in direct address or when it is being used as a name. The titles for the United States *President, Vice-President,* and *Chief Justice* and for the *Queen of England* are always capitalized when they are being substituted for the person's name.

USED AS A NAME	How is the patient, **D**octor?
NOT USED AS A NAME	The **d**octor will speak to you soon.
HIGH GOVERNMENT OFFICIAL	The **P**resident and the **V**ice-**P**resident will attend the summit meeting.

NOTE: *President* and *vice-president* are capitalized when they stand alone only if they refer to the current president and vice-president.

Was John F. Kennedy the youngest **p**resident?

Titles Showing Family Relationships. Capitalize a title showing family relationship when it comes before a person's name, when it is used as a name, or when it is substituted for a person's name.

BEFORE A NAME	When did **U**ncle Ron and **A**unt Mary leave?
USED AS A NAME	Please tell **M**om that she has a telephone call.
DIRECT ADDRESS	I'll help you paint the porch, **D**ad.

Titles showing family relationships should not be capitalized when they are preceded by a possessive noun or pronoun—unless they are considered part of a person's name.

NO CAPITAL My **a**unt lives in California.
Aaron is taking Phil's **s**ister to the prom.

CAPITAL When does your **U**ncle Ralph get home from work? [*Uncle* is part of Ralph's name.]

Titles of Works of Art. Capitalize the first word, the last word, and all important words in the titles of books, newspapers, periodicals, stories, poems, movies, plays, musical compositions, and other works of art. Do not capitalize a preposition, a coordinating conjunction, or an article—unless it is the first or last word in a title.

Our assignment was to read Samuel Taylor Coleridge's poem "**T**he **R**ime of the **A**ncient **M**ariner" in our textbook ***O**ur **L**iterary **H**eritage.*

An article about Claude Monet in the ***R**eader's **D**igest* included a picture of his painting ***W**ater **L**ilies.*

The following headline appeared in the ***N**ew **Y**ork **D**aily **N**ews* about the launching of the space shuttle: "**A** **S**ight for **S**oar **E**yes." [The word *the* before the title of a newspaper or a periodical is usually not capitalized.]

EXERCISE 8 Capitalizing Titles
Number your paper 1 to 10. Then write each word that should begin with a capital letter.

1. appointed by president john f. kennedy in 1961, dr. janet g. travell served as white house physician.
2. did dad remember to buy milk and eggs, or will your brother pick them up after work?
3. napoleon I was the emperor of france's first republic.
4. i'm very glad to meet you, sir.
5. one of the stars of *the barretts of wimpole street,* a hit play of 1931, was a spaniel named flush.
6. is ex-mayor myers planning to run for office again, or will he continue to run his own business?
7. when is your grandmother moving to kansas?

8. ernest hemingway helped supply films of fishermen for the film version of his book *the old man and the sea.*
9. in the summer of 1981, prince charles of england married lady diana spencer.
10. "the successes of the space shuttle" was an article in the *earlville herald* last week.

Letters

The beginning and the end of a friendly letter and a business letter include capital letters.

10f Capitalize the first word and all proper nouns in the salutation and the first word in the closing of a letter.

SALUTATIONS	**M**y dear brother **T**om,	**D**ear **M**s. **M**ichaels:
CLOSINGS	**Y**our loving sister,	**S**incerely yours,

NOTE: Place a comma after the salutation in a friendly letter and a colon after the salutation in a business letter. Place a comma after the closing in all letters.

EXERCISE 9 Writing a Letter
Write a letter of complaint to a company. Describe a defective product that you bought and request that the item be repaired or replaced. Capitalize the correct words in the salutation and the closing of the letter, as well as any other words that should begin with a capital letter. *(See pages 608–611 for the form of a letter.)*

EXERCISE 10 Time-out for Review
Number your paper 1 to 20. Then write each word that should begin with a capital letter.

Do You Know?

1. was alan b. shepard, jr., or john glenn the first american to orbit the earth?
2. was it the pilgrims or the puritans who landed at plymouth rock in 1620?
3. what is the most westerly state in the united states, alaska or hawaii?

4. who is the author of *great expectations,* a novel written during victoria's reign in England?
5. do muslims face mecca or izmir when they pray?
6. in what country were the first olympic games held?
7. was william mckinley or franklin roosevelt the first president elected in the twentieth century?
8. what was the name of dorothy's dog in *the wizard of oz?*
9. is the geyser old faithful in wyoming or nevada?
10. "i want to hold your hand" was the first american number one single of what british group?
11. did world war II end in 1942 or 1945?
12. is the cy young award given to a baseball player or a football player?
13. is sacramento or los angeles the capital of california?
14. general lee surrendered to general grant at appomattox court house. in what state did this occur?
15. did clark kent work for the *metropolis journal* or the *daily planet?*
16. what is the russian equivalent of the central intelligence agency in the united states?
17. is the lincoln memorial or the washington monument the tallest structure in washington, d.c.?
18. the parliament of england consists of the house of commons and what other governmental body?
19. is the astrodome in chicago or houston?
20. the united kingdom consists of england, scotland, northern ireland, and what other country?

Application to Writing

An important part of editing your own writing is searching for errors in the use of capital letters. By checking the dictionary, you can find out whether a word should or should not be capitalized.

EXERCISE 11 Editing for Capital Letters
Number your paper 1 to 50. Then write all the words in the following paragraphs that should begin with a capital letter. Do not include any words that are already capitalized.

A Winged Victory

On april 25, 1979, at harper dry lake, california, young bryan allen piloted the longest human-powered flight that had ever been made—1 hour, 9 minutes, and 3 seconds. The pilot supplied muscle power for the *gossamer albatross,* a tiny craft invented and designed by dr. paul d. maccready, jr.

The next challenge for the american flight team was a european journey across the english channel. Pilot allen accomplished the mission by pedaling the aircraft *gossamer albatross II* from manston, kent, england, to a french beach. Although the flight had been far behind schedule when the craft was halfway across, the total flying time was 2 hours and 49 minutes.

On july 7, 1981, the program's 210-pound plane successfully flew 165 miles, between england and france. This unique aircraft, which was called the *solar challenger,* used no fuel except sunlight.

The story of dr. maccready's accomplishments is highlighted in *the flight of the "gossamer condor,"* a film that won an academy award in 1979. The unusual flight program is the subject of the book *gossamer odyssey,* of allen's article "winged victory of *gossamer albatross*" in *national geographic magazine,* and of numerous other publications.

CHAPTER REVIEW

A. Number your paper 1 to 20. Then write the following items, using capital letters only where needed.

1. the renaissance
2. a danish official
3. my sister ella
4. the salvation army
5. peter the great
6. pro-american
7. mobil oil company
8. bic pens
9. very truly yours,
10. my mom and dad
11. the strawberry festival
12. copley square hotel
13. a southerly breeze
14. part III, chapter X
15. physics and latin
16. eighty-sixth street
17. *the return of the native*
18. michael christos, d.d.s.
19. a company in the south
20. a famous italian opera

B. Number your paper 1 to 20. Then write each word that should begin with a capital letter.

1. dalia's new address is 432 thirty-third street, indianapolis, indiana.
2. school usually starts on the wednesday after labor day.
3. the mediterranean is one of the most polluted seas on earth.
4. mount desert island, off the coast of maine, was discovered in 1604 by champlain, a french explorer.
5. have you received your tickets for the chicago white sox game?
6. when i was a junior, my favorite course was biology, but this year i like my english course best.
7. the oscar weighs 7 pounds and is 10 inches high.
8. minnesota is called the land of 10,000 lakes, but it actually contains more than 11,000 lakes.
9. there really was a molly pitcher, but her real name was mary hayes mccauley.
10. during the battle of monmouth, she carried water in a pitcher to thirsty american soldiers.
11. when my parents went to canada last summer, they visited the small nova scotian town where mother was born.
12. have you ever read elizabeth jennings' poem "in memory of anyone unknown to me"?
13. last month the vice-president represented the president on a tour of the far east.
14. the *andrea doria* collided with a swedish ship off the coast of nantucket in 1956.
15. if you sail through the panama canal from the atlantic to the pacific, you will actually be going from northwest to southeast, not east to west.
16. i enjoy watching the television series *masterpiece theatre*.
17. we asked nurse jahan when the doctor would be able to see grandmother.
18. i saw the ballet *romeo and juliet,* which is based on shakespeare's play.
19. during the middle ages, few people, including kings, could read or write.
20. the first american novel, *the power of sympathy,* was published in boston in 1789.

MASTERY TEST

Number your paper 1 to 10. Then write each word that should begin with a capital letter.

1. the statue of liberty stands in new york harbor.
2. zachary taylor's horse, old whitey, was allowed to graze on the white house lawn.
3. did mom say that uncle ricardo will visit us this winter?
4. hot springs, new mexico, was one of the stops on our journey.
5. john steinbeck's novel *the grapes of wrath* takes place during the great depression.
6. graham mcnamee did the first play-by-play broadcast of a world series game in 1921.
7. jean transferred from central high school in kalamazoo, michigan.
8. joan payson, owner of the new york mets, wanted to call her team the meadowlarks.
9. who was the 16th president?
10. in 1931, emperor haile selassie began to rule ethiopia.

11

End Marks and Commas

DIAGNOSTIC TEST

Number your paper 1 to 10. Write each sentence, adding a comma or commas where needed. Then add an appropriate end mark.

EXAMPLE No Howard I haven't seen Susan all day
ANSWER No, Howard, I haven't seen Susan all day.

1. Send your donations to the American Red Cross 107 Spencer Highway New Haven Connecticut 06520
2. Well I'm glad you made that suggestion
3. Two-dollar bills are seldom seen for they have never been printed in great quantities
4. Wouldn't you like to live in a warm dry climate
5. Janice Flemming the captain of our debate team has won a college scholarship
6. Do you want to go to the dance to an amusement park or to the movies
7. At three o'clock in the morning the telephone rang
8. Facing the jury the lawyer gave his closing arguments
9. Gerty Cori who won a Nobel Prize in 1947 was both a physician and biochemist
10. Following Mary Ann cleared the pole at 12 feet

Long before you knew the difference between a period and a question mark or had ever seen a comma, you were learning about them. As you learned to string words together into sentences, you were also learning to pause at certain places within sentences and between sentences. When you were pausing, you were learning about commas and end marks.

Although your voice inflections indicate the use of some punctuation, such speech patterns are not totally reliable. You may, for example, be omitting some commas or adding some that are unnecessary. You can use this chapter on end marks and commas to review all the rules—those that come naturally to you and those that do not.

KINDS OF SENTENCES AND END MARKS

A sentence has one of four different functions. It can make a statement, give a command, ask a question, or express strong feeling. Depending on its function, a sentence is either *declarative, imperative, interrogative,* or *exclamatory.* The end mark you use with a particular sentence is determined by the function of that sentence.

11a A **declarative sentence** makes a statement or expresses an opinion and ends with a period.

The following examples are both declarative sentences, even though the second sentence contains an indirect question.

Hail is usually produced during the passing of a cold front.

I don't remember where the receipt is. [The direct question would be *Where is the receipt?*]

11b An **imperative sentence** gives a direction, makes a request, or gives a command. It ends with either a period or an exclamation point.

The subject of most imperative sentences is an understood *you.*

Turn left. [*You* turn left.]

Please answer the doorbell. [*You* please answer the doorbell.]

An imperative sentence ends with a period if it is said in a normal voice. It ends with an exclamation point if it expresses strong feeling.

Follow the signs to the fairgrounds. [normal voice]

Don't leave without me! [emotional voice]

An imperative sentence is sometimes stated as a question, but no reply is expected. This kind of sentence is usually followed by a period or an exclamation point, since the purpose of the sentence remains the same—to make a request.

Will you please open the window a little wider.

11c An **interrogative sentence** asks a question and ends with a question mark.

Whether a question is completely or incompletely stated, a question mark follows it.

Have you ever visited San Francisco?

Where? I don't see any empty seats.

11d An **exclamatory sentence** expresses strong feeling or emotion and ends with an exclamation point.

What a busy day this has been!

How suspenseful that short story was!

NOTE: An interjection, such as *wow* or *oh,* may also be followed by an exclamation point.

Ouch! Don't touch my sunburn.

By changing an end mark, you can vary the meaning of a sentence, the way a speaker does by a change in tone or emphasis. Notice how the end mark changes the meaning of each of the following sentences.

The concert has begun. [declarative]
The concert has begun? [interrogative]
The concert has begun! [exclamatory]

Use end marks carefully to convey your exact meaning to the reader.

EXERCISE 1 Classifying Sentences
Number your paper 1 to 10. Write an appropriate end mark for each sentence. Then label each one *declarative, imperative, interrogative,* or *exclamatory.*

1. The human brain reaches its full weight by the seventh year of life
2. Read the next chapter in your textbook for homework
3. Where did you find that stationery
4. What an exciting show that was
5. A hot drink will make you feel cooler than an ice-cold one
6. Will you hold all my telephone calls
7. What is the distance between the wingtips of a Boeing 747
8. Help The basement floor is covered with a foot of water
9. I didn't understand what you said
10. Because of the braking effect of the moon, the rotation of the earth slows down

EXERCISE 2 Writing Sentences
Choose two of the following topics. Then write a declarative sentence, an imperative sentence, an interrogative sentence, and an exclamatory sentence about each topic.

1. final exams 2. part-time jobs 3. a school dance
4. school sports 5. your plans after graduation

Periods and Abbreviations

Using abbreviations is a good way to write faster when you are taking notes, but they should usually be avoided in formal writing, such as compositions and research papers.

11e Use a period after most abbreviations.

The following list contains some abbreviations that are acceptable in formal writing. Use the dictionary to check the spelling and punctuation of other abbreviations.

TITLES WITH NAMES	Mr.	Ms.	Mrs.	Rev.	Dr.	Sr.
TIMES WITH NUMBERS	A.M.	P.M.	B.C.	A.D.		

We should meet at 7:00 P.M.

Is the pastor of that church Rev. David Moyers, Jr.?

Notice in the first sentence of the previous examples that only one period is used for both the abbreviation and the end mark of the sentence. In the second sentence, both the period for the abbreviation and the question mark are used.

NOTE: A few abbreviations are written without periods. *(See page 612 for a complete list of state abbreviations.)*

ABC CIA IRS RCA TWA GA mph km

EXERCISE 3 Writing Abbreviations
Write the abbreviations that stand for the following items, including periods where needed. If you are unsure of the spelling or the punctuation of a particular abbreviation, look it up in the dictionary.

1. Senior
2. New Jersey
3. Master of Arts
4. September
5. Captain
6. Avenue
7. et cetera
8. millimeter
9. pound
10. cash on delivery

COMMAS

Although there may seem to be many comma rules, commas have basically only two purposes: to separate items and to enclose items.

Commas That Separate

If commas did not separate certain items from each other, all writing would be subject to constant misunderstanding. There is a difference, for example, between *pineapple juice and cheese* and *pineapple, juice, and cheese*. Following are specific situations in which commas should be used to separate items.

Items in a Series. A series is three or more similar items listed in consecutive order. Words, phrases, clauses, or short sentences that are written as a series are separated by commas.

11f Use commas to separate items in a series.

WORDS	January, February, and March are the best months for working on indoor hobbies. [words]
	We swept, scrubbed, and polished the floor before our company arrived. [verbs]
PHRASES	We searched for his keys throughout the house, along the driveway, and in the car.
CLAUSES	We don't know who should march in first, where we should sit, or how the diplomas will be handed out.
SHORT SENTENCES	The curtain fell, a brief silence followed, and then there was wild applause.

When a conjunction connects the last two items in a series, a comma is optional. It is always best, however, to include the comma before the conjunction to eliminate any possible confusion or misunderstanding.

CONFUSING	I like pea, chicken, tomato and onion soup. [Do you like three or four kinds?]
CLEAR	I like pea, chicken, tomato, and onion soup. [The additional comma makes it clear that it is four kinds, not three.]

If conjunctions connect all the items in a series, no commas are needed unless they make the sentence clearer.

Their new apartment is large **and** roomy **and** bright.

NOTE: Some expressions, such as *needle and thread,* are thought of as a single item. If one of these pairs of words appears in a series, it should be considered one item.

For breakfast we had our choice of yogurt, ham and eggs, or hot cereal.

Adjectives before a Noun. When a conjunction does not connect two adjectives before a noun, a comma is sometimes used.

Driving across the long, narrow bridge was frightening.

11g Use a comma sometimes to separate two adjectives that directly precede a noun and that are not joined by a conjunction.

There is a test you can use to decide whether a comma should be placed between two such adjectives. Read the sentence with *and* between the adjectives. If the sentence sounds natural, a comma is needed.

COMMA NEEDED	I enjoyed eating that fresh, crisp salad. [*Fresh and crisp* sounds natural.]
COMMA NOT NEEDED	I enjoyed eating that fresh tossed salad. [*Fresh and tossed* does not sound natural.]
COMMA NEEDED	The fierce, shrieking wind rattled the windows. [*Fierce and shrieking* sounds natural.]
COMMA NOT NEEDED	The fierce northerly wind rattled the windows. [*Fierce and northerly* does not sound natural.]

EXERCISE 4 Using Commas to Separate

Number your paper 1 to 20. Then write each series or each pair of adjectives, adding a comma or commas where needed. If a sentence does not need any commas, write *C* after the number.

EXAMPLE We ate dinner did the dishes and went to a movie.
ANSWER ate dinner, did the dishes, and went to a movie

1. Alaska Texas and California together make up more than a quarter of the total United States acreage.
2. An alligator has thick scaly skin.
3. I might have put your scarf in the closet on your bed or in the top drawer of your dresser.
4. The ocelot and the cheetah and the jaguar belong to the cat family.
5. Dr. Salk's discovery of the polio vaccine was a brilliant scientific achievement.
6. I don't know where they went what they are doing or when they'll be back.
7. The rabbit stopped at the clearing looked around and hopped across.
8. The tall dark-haired swimmer walked to the end of the diving board and dove in a graceful arc.
9. We visited several historic places in Philadelphia.
10. The three best sandwiches in this restaurant are tuna fish ham and cheese and roast beef.

11. Four of the highest mountains in New Hampshire are Mount Washington Mount Adams Mount Jefferson and Mount Clay.
12. We became hopelessly confused after turning right and left and right again.
13. Whistles blew horns blared and the traffic halted.
14. The wagon train reached California after a long difficult trip.
15. That delicious French bread was baked just an hour ago.
16. I don't know when she will be in whether she will have time to see you or whether you should wait.
17. Sardines are actually any of a number of small thin-boned fish.
18. The trail led across a stream over some boulders and beneath a waterfall.
19. Would you like spaghetti and meatballs franks and beans or meatloaf?
20. Venice Rome Moscow Cairo Dublin Berlin Toronto Amsterdam and Vienna are all names of towns in Ohio.

Compound Sentences. The independent clauses in a compound sentence can be combined in several ways. One way is to join them with a comma and one of the coordinating conjunctions—*and, but, or, nor, for,* or *yet.* (A semicolon or a semicolon and a transitional word can also be used between independent clauses that are not separated by a conjunction. *See pages 272–273.)*

11h Use a comma to separate the independent clauses of a compound sentence if the clauses are joined by a coordinating conjunction.

My sister has caught two fish, but I haven't caught any.
Friday night is the prom, and Sunday is graduation.
She wants to leave, yet it is too early.

No comma is needed in a very short compound sentence—unless the conjunction *yet* or *for* separates the independent clauses.

NO COMMA We invited them and they came.
COMMA I lost, yet I still felt happy.

NOTE: Do not confuse a sentence that has one subject and a compound verb with a compound sentence that has two sets of subjects and verbs. A comma is not placed between the parts of a compound verb when there is only one subject.

COMPOUND SENTENCE I worked last night**,** and John attended the meeting. [comma]

COMPOUND VERB I worked last night and couldn't attend the meeting. [no comma]

EXERCISE 5 Using Commas with Compound Sentences Number your paper 1 to 10. Then write each sentence, adding a comma where needed. If a sentence does not need a comma, write *C* after the number.

1. Cod can lay up to five million eggs at one time but very few of the eggs hatch and mature.
2. You should hurry or we'll be late.
3. The giant panda is a relative of the raccoon but can weigh up to 300 pounds.
4. People have been very generous yet the hospital fund needs another three thousand dollars for new equipment.
5. At first glance the desert may seem to lack life but it actually is alive with many different plants and animals.
6. He'll meet us at six for he must talk to you.
7. The spinal cord relays information between the brain and the rest of the body and controls the reflexes.
8. Sue and I can come tonight and can help you move the books into the library.
9. Not many people came yet I had a very good time.
10. Wild pigs will eat almost anything but they won't overeat.

Introductory Elements. A comma is needed to separate certain introductory words, phrases, and clauses from the rest of the sentence.

11i Use a comma after certain introductory elements.

WORD **Yes,** those were my exact words. [*No, now, oh, well,* and *why* are other introductory words that take commas—unless the words are part of a sentence: *"Yes" was his answer.*]

PREPOSITIONAL PHRASE	**Throughout the entire baseball game,** Jessie pitched only one inning. [A comma comes after a prepositional phrase of four or more words. Do not place a comma after an introductory phrase that is directly followed by a verb: *Through the fog shone a dim light.*]
PARTICIPIAL PHRASE	**Hunting for my old jacket,** I found a long-lost pair of gloves.
INFINITIVE PHRASE USED AS AN ADVERB	**To surprise Ellen,** we all hid in the kitchen. [A comma does not follow an infinitive phrase that is used as the subject of a sentence: *To forgive him was a wise decision.*]
ADVERB CLAUSE	**Before they came in,** they removed their boots.
OTHER	**In June 1986,** 320 seniors graduated. **Far above,** a flock of geese flew by. [Commas are used in these sentences to avoid confusion.]

EXERCISE 6 Using Commas with Introductory Elements
Number your paper 1 to 20. Then write the introductory elements that should be followed by a comma, adding a comma after each one. If a sentence does not need a comma, write *C* after the number.

1. In the fifteenth century Chinese scholars compiled a 22,937-volume encyclopedia.
2. If you start hiking at 8 A.M. you should reach the summit by noon.
3. Standing on a scaffold on the tenth floor two men were washing the windows of the large office building.
4. No we will not be attending the open house.
5. To give her family security Louisa May Alcott turned to writing.
6. After tomorrow I will be a high school graduate.
7. While the band tuned up the audience gathered.
8. Walled by lava cliffs Crater Lake can be reached only by footpaths.
9. According to a recent poll taken in our school 42 percent of the seniors have already been hired for summer jobs.

10. To find the best route to Atlanta Steve checked the map.
11. After Barry Paul will take his turn.
12. Knocking down every tackle in his path Seth plowed forward for a touchdown.
13. Well that was a surprise!
14. Of the six papers to be typed three have been completed.
15. To report on the game is my assignment.
16. Why are you dressed in that costume?
17. To the top of the tree scampered the squirrel.
18. When he was less than 13 years old Alfred Tennyson wrote a 6,000-line epic poem.
19. After cooking Roger took a short nap.
20. To answer your question I will have to do some research.

Commonly Used Commas. Commas are probably used most often to separate the items in a date or an address.

11j Use commas to separate the elements in dates and addresses.

Notice in the following examples that a comma is also used to separate the last item in a date or the last item in an address from the rest of the sentence.

On Monday**,** October 3**,** 1980**,** my younger brother was born.

Send your résumé to Ms. Faye Buscone**,** Hoffman Company**,** 520 Johnson Street**,** Madison**,** Wisconsin 53703**,** before June 30. [No comma is placed between the state and the ZIP code.]

If items in an address are joined by a preposition, no comma is needed to separate them.

The company moved its headquarters to 45 Jackson Boulevard **in** Tacoma, Washington.

NOTE: No comma is needed when just the month and the year are given.

Neil Armstrong walked on the moon in July 1969.

11k Use a comma after the salutation of a friendly letter and after the closing of all letters.

SALUTATIONS	Dear David,	Dear Grandmother,
CLOSINGS	Sincerely yours,	Love,

EXERCISE 7 Using Commas Correctly
Number your paper 1 to 10. Then write each sentence, adding a comma or commas where needed.

1. On March 30 1937 President Franklin Roosevelt established the Okefenokee Swamp as a national wildlife refuge.
2. How long had you lived in Springfield Illinois before you moved to Portland?
3. If you are interested in applying for the job you should talk to the personnel director.
4. You can write to me at the University of Missouri Box 1254 Columbia Missouri 65201 after September 1.
5. Tacoma Washington lies between the Olympic Mountains and the Cascade Range.
6. Write to Writer's Supplies 843 Woodcove Avenue Pittsburgh Pennsylvania 15216 for free samples.
7. In the process of cleaning out the closet I found a long-lost sweater.
8. On Friday September 5 1985 my sister celebrated her 28th birthday.
9. Students working as stagehands for the play should be at the meeting but those trying out for acting parts need not attend.
10. On June 19 1846 the first baseball game with organized rules was played at Elysian Fields in Hoboken New Jersey.

EXERCISE 8 Writing Sentences
Write sentences that follow the directions below. Use commas where needed.

1. Include a series of verbs that describe someone hiking along a mountainous trail.
2. Include two adjectives that are separated by a comma.
3. Include two independent clauses that are joined by the conjunction *but.*
4. Include an adverb clause at the beginning of the sentence.
5. Include today's date and your address.

EXERCISE 9 Time-out for Review

Number your paper 1 to 20. Then write each sentence, adding a comma or commas where needed. If a sentence is correct, write *C* after the number.

Inventors and Inventions

1. Among the inventions of Thomas Edison are the light switch an electric pen and the microphone.
2. The parking meter was invented in Oklahoma City and was the brainstorm of Carlton Magee.
3. To pay off a debt Walter Hunt invented the safety pin.
4. Margaret E. Knight patented an improved paper machine and invented a machine for cutting out shoes.
5. James Watt was not the inventor of the first steam engine but he improved the steam engine in 1769.
6. After Humphrey O'Sullivan walked all day on the hot hard pavements of Boston he invented the rubber heel.
7. A spaghetti-spinning fork was patented in 1950.
8. Amanda Theodosia Jones invented the vacuum process of preserving food and tried to establish a factory that would use her process.
9. To improve methods of farming Englishman Thomas Coke invented a new method of crop rotation during the 1700s.
10. Leonardo da Vinci designed a flying machine and Benjamin Franklin invented bifocals.
11. On June 22 1882 the U.S. Patent Office granted a patent for a propeller-driven rocking chair.
12. Until the envelope appeared in 1839 people folded their letters and sealed them with wax.
13. According to U.S. Patent Office records Chester Greenwood held patents on earmuffs and many other items.
14. Fixing a tricycle John Dunlop invented an inflatable tire.
15. Patented by George B. Hansburg the pogo stick became an American rage during the 1920s.
16. When Sybilla Masters invented a machine that reduced corn into meal, food preparation methods were improved.
17. King Camp Gillette started his Gillette Safety Razor Company in 1901 and patented the safety razor in 1904.
18. Before the birth of Christ the Chinese made porcelain.
19. Whitcomb L. Judson a Chicago inventor patented an early form of the zipper in 1893.
20. Lee De Forest invented a vacuum tube in 1907 and this device helped develop electronic equipment.

Commas That Enclose

Some sentences contain expressions that interrupt the flow of a sentence. These expressions usually supply additional information that is not needed to understand the main idea of a sentence. If one of these interrupting expressions comes in the middle of a sentence, use two commas to enclose the expression—to set it off from the rest of the sentence. If an interrupting expression comes at the beginning or at the end of a sentence, use only one comma.

Direct Address. Any name, title, or other word that is used to address someone directly is set off by commas. These interrupting expressions are called nouns of *direct address.*

11l Use commas to set off nouns of direct address.

Kenneth, what did you do with the sports page?
Hurry**, Matt,** or we'll be late.
What time is it**, Maria?**

Parenthetical Expressions. These expressions add meaning but are only incidental to the main idea of the sentence.

11m Use commas to set off parenthetical expressions.

Following is a list of common parenthetical expressions.

Common Parenthetical Expressions

after all	however	nevertheless
at any rate	I believe (guess,	of course
by the way	hope, know, think)	on the contrary
consequently	in fact	on the other hand
for example	in my opinion	therefore
for instance	moreover	to tell the truth

By the way, did you notice Tony's new haircut?
Your advice**, of course,** was helpful.
We will proceed as planned**, nevertheless.**

NOTE: Commas are used to set off the expressions in the preceding box *only* if the expressions interrupt the flow of a sentence.

COMMAS **On the other hand,** we enjoyed the dancing.
NO COMMAS Wear that glove **on the other hand.** [In this sentence *on the other hand* is a prepositional phrase.]

Expressions other than those listed in the preceding box can also be parenthetical if they interrupt the flow of the sentence.

Irises**, like tulips,** grow from bulbs.

Contrasting expressions, which begin with *not, but, but not,* or *though not* are also considered parenthetical expressions.

Peggy**, not Angelina,** will sing a solo at the concert.
The actor**, though not well-known,** will star in the play.

Occasionally an adverb clause will also interrupt a sentence.

The temperature**, if it hits 93,** will set a record today.

Appositives. An appositive with its modifiers renames, identifies, or explains a noun or a pronoun in the sentence. *(See pages 55–57.)*

11n Use commas to set off most appositives and their modifiers.

Mr. James**, my English teacher,** attended Ohio State.

I would like the first entrée**, roast turkey with stuffing.**

An appositive is occasionally preceded by the word *or, particularly, notably,* or *especially.* Some appositives that are introduced by *such as* are also set off by commas.

Many insects**, especially honeybees,** are essential for cross-pollinating fruits.

Take warm clothing**, such as sweaters and wool socks.**

An appositive is not set off by commas if it identifies a person or a thing by telling which one or ones. Often these appositives are names and have no modifiers.

The verb ***eat*** is an irregular verb. [Which verb?]
My cousin **Lucy** is a dental assistant. [Which cousin?]

When adjectives, titles, and degrees are in the appositive position, they are also set off by commas.

ADJECTIVES The lake water**, clear and cold,** felt refreshing.
TITLES Franklin R. Moore**, Sr.,** is our chief of police.
DEGREES Alicia Ray**, M.D.,** has an office on Broad Road.

EXERCISE 10 Using Commas with Interrupters
Number your paper 1 to 20. Then write each sentence, adding a comma or commas where needed. If a sentence does not need any commas, write *C* after the number.

1. The sea otter's existence has been threatened by its two great enemies killer whales and humans.
2. Lydia have you met Mr. Robert Kahn Jr.?
3. The St. Lawrence Seaway I believe makes over eight thousand miles of coast accessible to large ocean vessels.
4. Did you know Eugene that there was a phone call for you?
5. The Greens not the Goldsteins are moving to Atlanta.
6. The hikers cold and hungry huddled around the campfire.
7. Babe Ruth's pitching skill if we are to believe the sports writers of his time was excellent.
8. The great playwright Lillian Hellman was born in New Orleans in 1905.
9. Several teachers especially Mr. Herman and Ms. Costa were particularly helpful.
10. A frog takes in water through its skin not its mouth.
11. Fagin the sinister villain in Charles Dickens' *Oliver Twist* was the focus of my English composition.
12. Hannah like Lucia manages a vegetable stand.
13. William Carlos Williams M.D. was also a noted poet.
14. The great soprano Beverly Sills became the director of the New York City Opera Company in 1979.
15. A tarantula's bite though not usually fatal is quite painful.
16. Texas the second largest state produces many kinds of livestock such as cattle and sheep.
17. Did you turn in your research paper on time Greg?
18. The swimmers wet and shivering ran for their towels.
19. The common rat not the fierce lion or tiger is the animal probably most dangerous to people.
20. Sarah Bernhardt the famous French actress was also an accomplished sculptor and painter.

Nonessential Elements. Like other interrupters you have just reviewed, some participial phrases and clauses are not needed to make the meaning of a sentence clear or complete. When a phrase or a clause is not needed to complete the meaning of a sentence, commas are used to enclose it.

11o Use commas to set off a nonessential participial phrase or a nonessential adjective clause.

A participial phrase or an adjective clause is nonessential (nonrestrictive) if it supplies extra, unnecessary information. To decide whether a phrase or a clause is nonessential, read the sentence without it. If the phrase or the clause could be removed without changing the basic meaning of the sentence, it is nonessential. A phrase or a clause that modifies a proper noun is almost always nonessential.

NONESSENTIAL PARTICIPIAL PHRASE — Cellophane**, made from wood pulp,** was invented in 1900. [Cellophane was invented in 1900.]

NONESSENTIAL ADJECTIVE CLAUSE — The Tower of London**, which is actually a group of buildings,** is located on the Thames River. [The Tower of London is located on the Thames River.]

An essential (restrictive) phrase or clause identifies a person or thing by answering the question *Which one?* Therefore, no commas are used. If an essential phrase or clause is removed from a sentence, the basic meaning of the sentence will be unclear or incomplete.

NOTE: An adjective clause that begins with *that* is essential.

ESSENTIAL PARTICIPIAL PHRASE — A lizard **called the gecko** can drop its tail and grow a new one. [*A lizard can drop its tail and grow a new one.* The phrase is needed to identify which lizard; otherwise, the sentence would mean that *all* lizards can drop their tails and grow new ones.]

ESSENTIAL ADJECTIVE CLAUSE — The book **that you wanted** was checked out of the library. [*The book was checked out of the library.* The clause is needed to identify which book was checked out of the library.]

EXERCISE 11 Using Commas with Nonessential Elements
Number your paper 1 to 20. Then write each sentence, adding a comma or commas where needed. If a sentence does not need any commas, write *C* after the number.

1. The exoskeleton of an insect is made of chitin which is lighter and far more flexible than bone.
2. The first public pay telephone installed in Connecticut in 1889 charged ten cents for a call.
3. Ralph Winters fishing in Beaver Brook caught a ten-inch trout.
4. Scientists who examine and classify insects are called entomologists.
5. We watched the geese flying south.
6. The senior playing right tackle is my cousin.
7. Did you speak to Ms. Robinson who organized the county track meet?
8. Amelia Earhart who was the first woman to fly across the Atlantic alone won the Distinguished Flying Cross.
9. In the Bay of Fundy located between New Brunswick and Nova Scotia the tide sometimes rises ten feet in one hour.
10. My Uncle Russ who recently became a licensed pilot is coming to visit us next month.
11. The Pillars featuring French food is a well-known restaurant in town.
12. The flag that inspired Francis Scott Key to write our national anthem had only 15 stars.
13. I can hardly keep up with the students who type 40 words per minute.
14. The astronomer who first made practical use of the telescope was Galileo.
15. We'll leave early to avoid the traffic which usually gets heavy around five o'clock.
16. The jet having received permission from the control tower prepared to land.
17. The shelf that I'm building is nearly finished.
18. Our neighbor's car which averages 40 miles to a gallon is much more fuel-efficient than his last car.
19. We were relieved when we found the lost tickets lying on the sidewalk.
20. The first artificial heart which was implanted in a patient in 1969 was made of dacron and plastic.

EXERCISE 12 Time-out for Review

Number your paper 1 to 20. Then write each sentence, adding a comma or commas where needed. If a sentence does not need any commas, write *C* after the number.

1. The smallest dinosaurs were about 2½ feet long and the largest were about 90 feet long.
2. Porpoises and dolphins and whales will drown if they stay underwater too long.
3. This basket was woven by Dudley Frasure whose work is the subject of a documentary film on basketry.
4. During a severe windstorm or high gale a skyscraper may sway up to six inches on either side.
5. When the glass broke the pieces scattered all over the counter.
6. To photograph this event you must set the camera at a thousandth of a second.
7. The holiday is celebrated on the 8th not the 12th.
8. An air temperature of 134°F was recorded on July 10 1913 in Death Valley California.
9. Redwood trees produce bark that is up to 10 inches thick.
10. Coyotes highly adaptable animals are known to travel up to 35 miles per hour when pursuing prey.
11. Mozart wrote his last and many think his greatest symphony in fewer than 16 days.
12. The famous ocean scientist Jacques Cousteau appeared in the documentary series about marine exploration.
13. The song that became the official national anthem of the United States in 1931 was "The Star-Spangled Banner."
14. The Fourth of July or Independence Day has been celebrated as a national holiday ever since Revolutionary times.
15. In the average human body four to five quarts of blood are circulated every minute.
16. Virginia Dare born on August 18 1587 was the first child born of English parents in the New World.
17. Garter snakes though reptiles do not lay eggs.
18. We packed a picnic lunch and left for the beach at nine o'clock.
19. The evening was cool breezy and delightful.
20. Geoffrey Chaucer the author of *The Canterbury Tales* was probably the most important writer in medieval England.

Application to Writing

When you edit your written work, always check for misused or missing commas.

EXERCISE 13 Editing for Commas
Write the following paragraphs, adding commas where needed. There are 20 commas.

Against the Odds

Elizabeth Blackwell was the first woman to earn a medical degree but she had to travel a long hard road to get that degree. Even though 29 medical schools had refused to admit her she persisted. After 3 years of private study Blackwell was finally accepted to the Medical Institute of Geneva New York. The director doubtful and concerned first passed her application on to the students for their approval. Thinking it was a joke everyone agreed that she should be admitted. When Blackwell arrived however she was greeted with shock and anger. She was ridiculed ignored refused lodging and barred from some classroom activities.

Graduating at the head of her class on January 23 1849 Blackwell continued her studies in London and Paris. She finally returned to New York City and there she opened a hospital in 1853. Called the New York Infirmary for Women and Children it was staffed entirely by women. With the help of Emily her younger sister Blackwell added a medical college for women in 1868. After a few more years in New York she returned to England and helped found the London School of Medicine for Women.

CHAPTER REVIEW

A. Number your paper 1 to 10. Write an appropriate end mark for each sentence. Then label each one *declarative, imperative, interrogative,* or *exclamatory.*

1. Tofu is a good source of protein
2. Call Michael when you get home
3. Did you see the exam schedule
4. I didn't receive the test results

5. The British word for *elevator* is *lift*
6. How happy I was to hear from you
7. Isn't she the captain of the volleyball team
8. Congratulations You've passed your driver's test
9. How invigorating an early-morning swim can be
10. Will you close the screen door when you leave

B. Number your paper 1 to 20. Then write each sentence, adding a comma or commas where needed. If a sentence does not need any commas, write *C* after the number.

1. Between now and next week you should learn the music for the first two numbers.
2. The terrain hilly and rocky made travel by car or truck impossible.
3. The little island was a great place for a rest for it was sparsely populated.
4. Medical research though expensive often pays for itself in life-saving discoveries.
5. A person who enjoys traveling on rough waters should take the ferry to Nova Scotia.
6. Sally Tompkins a captain in the Confederate army ran a hospital at her own expense in Richmond Virginia.
7. Winter sports such as sledding and skating are popular in the North.
8. You need quarters not dimes for the washing machine.
9. The pony express which has lived in legend for more than a century existed for less than two years.
10. Having eaten the dog romped off into the backyard.
11. Which of those large German clocks do you like best?
12. A potato contrary to popular belief has about as many calories as an apple.
13. Lamb not pork was the main course.
14. Edgar Allan Poe wrote poetry edited literary magazines and created the modern detective story.
15. Nancy Dickerson the first woman TV correspondent at CBS was voted Woman of the Year in 1964.
16. Well do you agree with him Sandy?
17. Although approximately 70 percent of the earth is covered with water only 1 percent the experts agree is drinkable.
18. On May 9 1936 the *Hindenburg* landed at Lakehurst New Jersey after its first successful trans-Atlantic flight.

19. During summer rainstorms are often accompanied by lightning.
20. The bicyclists lining up to start this race have come from all over the United States.

MASTERY TEST

Number your paper 1 to 10. Write each sentence, adding a comma or commas where needed. Then add an appropriate end mark.

1. In a large pond goldfish can add more than a foot to their length
2. I bought a wrench but the store was out of the paint I needed
3. Many species of butterflies like birds fly south for the winter
4. Mary Goddard who was a United States postmaster was the printer of the Declaration of Independence
5. Before sky divers open their parachutes they travel through the air as fast as 200 miles an hour
6. That old creaky chair in the dining room broke when I sat on it yesterday
7. Have you returned the toaster oven to Mendrall Products 305 Forty-first Street Sidney New York 13838
8. Thomas Edison Charles Dickens and the Irish playwright Sean O'Casey never graduated from grade school
9. Hearing the wild applause the actors waited a moment before they took their bows
10. In 1955 55 cities in the world had a million people or more

12

Other Punctuation

DIAGNOSTIC TEST

Number your paper 1 to 10. Then write each sentence, adding apostrophes, semicolons, colons, hyphens, quotation marks, and all the punctuation marks needed with direct quotations. Only a sentence with a speaker tag *(he said, she asked)* should be considered a direct quotation.

EXAMPLE Wendy asked Do you want to ride with us?
ANSWER Wendy asked, "Do you want to ride with us?"

1. Which class do you have next Sheila asked.
2. The names of the seven continents are spelled with the same first and last letters Antarctica, Europe, Asia, Australia, Africa, and America (North and South).
3. Some seniors voted for an afternoon graduation however, most voted to hold it in the evening.
4. Watch out for that pothole Jeffrey called.
5. Hay fever is not caused by hay it is an allergy caused by various kinds of pollen.
6. Everyone will need the following items a pencil, an eraser, and some scrap paper.
7. Thirty two students havent signed up Andrew stated.
8. You should try ice skating Kate suggested Its fun.
9. The party at the Smiths house will begin at 7 00 P.M.
10. Only 12 drawings have been submitted to the contest for the magazine cover the rest are graphic designs.

Although end marks and commas are the punctuation marks most commonly used, all marks of punctuation are important. This chapter will cover all the punctuation marks besides end marks and commas.

APOSTROPHES

You probably use apostrophes with contractions every time you write, but an apostrophe has another important use. It is used with nouns and some pronouns to show possession.

Apostrophes to Show Possession

By using an apostrophe, you can indicate that nouns and some pronouns are showing possession.

The Possessive Forms of Nouns. The possessive of a singular noun is formed differently from the possessive of a plural noun.

12a Add *'s* to form the possessive of a singular noun.

To form the possessive of a singular noun, write the noun without adding or omitting any letters. Then add *'s* at the end.

friend + **'s** = friend**'s**	This is my friend**'s** house.
road + **'s** = road**'s**	The road**'s** surface needs repaving.
quarter + **'s** = quarter**'s**	I need a quarter**'s** worth of nickels.

Singular compound nouns and the names of most businesses and organizations form their possessive the way other singular nouns do.

Her mother-in-law**'s** birthday is tomorrow.
I think Maher**'s** Hardware Store carries the nails you need.

To form the possessive of a plural noun, write the plural form of the word without making any changes. Then look at the ending of the plural noun. It will determine the way you will form the possessive.

12b Add only an apostrophe to form the possessive of a plural noun that ends in *s*.

If the plural noun ends in *s*, add only an apostrophe.

girls + ' = girls'	The girls' softball team has won!
Nelsons + ' = Nelsons'	The Nelsons' dog is a setter.
weeks + ' = weeks'	She took a two-weeks' course.

If a plural noun does not end in *s*, add *'s* to form the possessive —just as you would for a singular noun that does not end in *s*.

men + **'s** = men**'s**	Where is the men**'s** locker room?
oxen + **'s** = oxen**'s**	The oxen**'s** barn was cleaned.

NOTE: Do not confuse a plural possessive with the simple plural form of a noun.

POSSESSIVE	Mrs. Grayson is the twins' teacher.
PLURAL	Mrs. Grayson teaches the twins.

EXERCISE 1 Forming the Possessive of Nouns
Write the possessive form of each noun. Then use five of the forms in sentences of your own.

1. mother	6. day	11. Tuesday	16. city
2. cover	7. women	12. officers	17. penny
3. Karen	8. year	13. birch	18. David
4. Palmers	9. geese	14. men	19. doctor
5. Cheyenne	10. world	15. babies	20. bears

EXERCISE 2 Using the Possessive of Nouns
Write each word in the following sentences that needs an apostrophe or an apostrophe and an *s*.

1. A tiger stripes often serve as camouflage.
2. Who has Sunday paper?
3. All the books jackets are in good condition.
4. How long will your sister-in-law visit last?
5. We enjoyed the children art exhibit.
6. Thompson Market needs some part-time help.
7. Mr. Murphy is taking a year leave of absence.
8. Is that young woman Theresa sister?
9. Please buy a dollar worth of green beans.
10. The Wongs business is flourishing.

The Possessive Forms of Personal Pronouns. Personal pronouns and the pronoun *who* show possession by changing form, not by adding an apostrophe.

This is **his** coat, but **whose** coat is that?

None of these possessive pronouns include apostrophes.

Possessive Pronouns

my, mine	his	its	their, theirs
your, yours	her, hers	our, ours	

NOTE: Do not confuse a contraction with a possessive pronoun. A possessive pronoun does not include an apostrophe, but a contraction does. *Its, your, their,* and *theirs* are possessive pronouns. *It's, you're, they're,* and *there's* are contractions. *(See page 148.)*

The Possessive Forms of Indefinite Pronouns. An indefinite pronoun forms its possessive in the same way a singular noun does—by adding *'s*. *(See page 7 for a list of common indefinite pronouns.)*

No one**'s** oral report will be given tomorrow.
Did you ask for anyone**'s** advice?

EXERCISE 3 Using the Possessive of Pronouns
Rewrite any incorrectly written possessive form of a pronoun. If all the pronouns in a sentence are written correctly, write *C* after the number.

1. You're research papers are due on Friday.
2. Everyones suggestions should be considered.
3. I think this cap is mine, but it could be his.
4. Who's telephone number is this?
5. Her's is the one with the purple stripes.
6. It's time to take the dog for it's checkup.
7. Someone's jacket was left in the bleachers.
8. Your's arrived the first thing this morning.
9. There time cards should be put over there.
10. Neither ones photograph won a prize.

Other Uses of Apostrophes

An apostrophe is used to write contractions, to form certain plurals, and to show joint and separate ownership.

Apostrophes with Contractions. An apostrophe is substituted for letters omitted in a contraction.

12c Use an apostrophe in a contraction to show where one or more letters have been omitted.

are n~~o~~t = aren't	that ~~i~~s = that's
we ~~ha~~ve = we've	let ~~u~~s = let's
I ~~wi~~ll = I'll	o~~f~~ ~~the~~ clock = o'clock

The only contraction in which any letters are changed or added is the contraction for *will not,* which is *won't.*

EXERCISE 4 Writing Contractions
Write the contraction for each pair of words.

1. do not
2. I have
3. did not
4. let us
5. we will
6. who is
7. they are
8. will not
9. I am
10. is not
11. were not
12. it is
13. you are
14. has not
15. I would
16. there is
17. does not
18. are not
19. we have
20. have not

Apostrophes to Show Joint and Separate Ownership. In written work apostrophes can signal either joint or separate ownership. One apostrophe is used to show joint ownership; two or more apostrophes are used to show separate ownership.

12d Add 's to only the last word to show joint ownership.
Add 's to each word to show separate ownership.

In the following example, the canoe belongs to Paul and Craig. Since both people own the canoe, an apostrophe is added to the second name only.

Paul and Craig**'s** canoe has been returned.

If one of the words showing joint ownership is a possessive pronoun, the noun must also show possession.

Paul**'s** and **his** canoe has been returned.

In the following example, Paul and Craig own separate canoes; therefore, an apostrophe is added to both names.

Paul**'s** and Craig**'s** canoes have been returned.

Apostrophes to Form Certain Plurals. The plural of certain items and words is formed by adding an apostrophe and an *s*.

12e Add *'s* to form the plural of numbers, letters, symbols, and words that are used to represent themselves.

Your *3***'s** look like backward *E***'s**.
Insert *$***'s** where necessary in the financial statement.
You used too many *very***'s** in your composition.

NOTE: Only the number *3*, the letter *E*, the dollar sign, and the word *very* are italicized in the examples above. The *'s* is not italicized. *(See page 278 for the use of italics.)*

EXERCISE 5 Using Apostrophes in Special Situations
Write each letter, symbol, or word that needs an apostrophe or an apostrophe and an *s*.

1. My typewriter types *&* but not *+*.
2. Their company uses Jones and Carey delivery service.
3. Does the word *referred* have two or three *r*?
4. Julie and Hernandez grades were the highest in our English class.
5. Lets get started no later than six oclock.
6. Points will be deducted if your *t* arent crossed and your *i* arent dotted.
7. Willie and her dog is only two months old.
8. Gary and Melinda photographs were exhibited at the fair.
9. Youve used 25 *however* in your report.
10. Theyll meet us at the town hall if they dont get delayed.

EXERCISE 6 Time-out for Review
Number your paper 1 to 10. Rewrite any incorrectly written letter or word. If a sentence is correct, write *C* after the number.

1. Beth's article was well written, was'nt it?
2. The Joneses and Taylors' apartments were painted.

3. The Queen of Englands picture seems to be everywhere in London.
4. There's their neighbor, waiting at the bus stop.
5. Teenager's interests certainly have changed over the past 50 years.
6. Gorman' advertisement in this mornings' *Herald* features sneakers and sweatshirts.
7. A student's life is very busy.
8. The Raidens' youngest son got two *A*'s and three *B*'s on his' report card.
9. Well need Dad's permission to go.
10. Aren't there two *c*s in *accumulate?*

SEMICOLONS AND COLONS

By using the semicolon (;) and the colon (:), you can create sentence variety in your writing.

Semicolons

Two independent clauses that are not properly joined result in a run-on sentence. A run-on sentence can be corrected in any of several ways. One way to correct a run-on sentence is to join the clauses with a coordinating conjunction and a comma. *(See pages 251–252.)*

Monday is my birthday**, and** Tuesday is my mom's birthday.

The clauses in a compound sentence can be joined by a semicolon when there is no conjunction.

12f Use a semicolon between the clauses of a compound sentence when they are not joined by a conjunction.

Monday is my birthday**;** Tuesday is my mom's birthday.
The earthworm has no lungs**;** it breathes through its skin.

NOTE: Only clauses that are closely related should be joined by a semicolon. If two ideas are not closely related, they should be put into two separate sentences.

Semicolons with Transitional Words. The clauses in a compound sentence can also be joined by a semicolon and a transitional word.

12g Use a semicolon between the clauses in a compound sentence when they are joined by certain transitional words.

The meeting was scheduled to begin at noon**;** **nevertheless,** it didn't start until one.

Following is a list of such common transitional words.

Common Transitional Words

accordingly	furthermore	moreover
as a result	hence	nevertheless
besides	however	otherwise
consequently	indeed	that is
for example	in fact	therefore
for instance	instead	thus

NOTE: Some of the transitional words in the preceding box can also be used as parenthetical expressions within a single clause. *(See page 257.)*

Notice in the following examples that the semicolon comes before the transitional word, and a comma follows the transitional word.

The loud speaker wasn't working properly**;** as a result**,** people in the balcony couldn't hear the music very well.

Jamaica is covered with beautiful vegetation**;** for example**,** tropical fruits and flowers grow everywhere.

Semicolons to Avoid Confusion. To make your meaning clear, you may have to substitute a semicolon for a comma.

12h Use a semicolon instead of a comma in certain situations to avoid possible confusion.

A semicolon is used instead of a comma between the clauses of a compound sentence if there are commas within a clause.

> Look for a jacket in yellow, blue, or green**;** for those are Ted's favorite colors. [Normally a comma would come before a conjunction separating the clauses in a compound sentence.]

Semicolons are also used instead of commas between items in a series if the items themselves contain commas.

> The President's schedule includes stops in London, England**;** Paris, France**;** Florence, Italy**;** Geneva, Switzerland**;** and New Delhi, India. [Normally commas would separate the items in a series.]

NOTE: See Chapter 11 for comma rules.

EXERCISE 7 Using Semicolons

Write each word that should be followed by a semicolon and then add the semicolon.

1. Poison ivy is not ivy it is a member of the cashew family.
2. The vegetable stand was out of fresh corn therefore, I bought some peas.
3. I want to write my research paper on the poetry of Shelley, Keats, or Wordsworth but I can't decide which poet interests me the most.
4. The site of the 1898 Klondike gold rush wasn't Alaska in fact, it was the Yukon Territory of Canada.
5. The county fair will be held on Saturday, June 8 Sunday, June 9 and Monday, June 10.
6. Geoffrey Chaucer wrote during the Middle Ages William Shakespeare wrote during the Elizabethan Age.
7. I completed my weekend chores several hours early thus, I had more time for leisure activities.
8. Pocahontas's real name was said to be Matoaka Pocahontas was a family name.
9. I will put away the milk, the yogurt, and the cottage cheese or they will turn sour.
10. In the Northern Hemisphere, water goes down drains counterclockwise in the Southern Hemisphere, it goes clockwise.

EXERCISE 8 Using Semicolons and Commas
Write the following sentences, adding semicolons and *commas* where needed.

1. The Sahara Desert covers an area of about 3,500,000 square miles Europe covers about 4,100,000 square miles.
2. I have lived in Detroit Michigan Lincoln Nebraska and Des Moines Iowa.
3. Every seat in the auditorium was filled in fact some people had to be turned away.
4. The temperature today reached 102 degrees it broke all existing records.
5. A queen bee never uses her stinger on workers drones or people but she will use it on another queen bee.
6. Our bake sale was a success we raised more than twenty-five dollars.
7. The test will cover Chapter 5 Sections 1 and 2 Chapter 6 Sections 5 and 6 and Chapter 7 Sections 3 and 4.
8. The traffic lights at Main and Belmont were not working during rush hour however not a single problem resulted.
9. Florida is not the southernmost state in the United States Hawaii is farther south.
10. You may have your senior picture taken at eight nine or ten but the earliest appointments are less crowded.

EXERCISE 9 Writing Sentences
Write compound sentences that follow the directions below.

1. Join the clauses with a comma and a conjunction.
2. Join the clauses with a semicolon only.
3. Join the clauses with a semicolon and the word *moreover*.
4. Join the clauses with a semicolon and the word *however*.
5. In the first clause, include a series of words. Then join the clauses with a semicolon.

Colons

A colon is used most often to introduce a list of items that is about to follow in a sentence.

12i Use a colon before most lists of items, especially when a list comes after an expression such as *the following*.

> When I applied for the job, the employer required the following**:** a résumé, two references, and a writing sample.

A colon, however, does not follow a verb or a preposition.

NO COLON	Required forms of identification include a driver's license, a passport, or a birth certificate.
COLON	You will need one of the following forms of identification**:** a driver's license, a passport, or a birth certificate.
NO COLON	Salt is used for making glass, building roads, and tanning leather.
COLON	Salt is used in the following processes**:** making glass, building roads, and tanning leather.

NOTE: Commas separate items in a series. *(See page 248.)*

A colon is also used to introduce a formal statement or a quotation that does not have a speaker tag.

> The question before the budget committee was this**:** How can property taxes be reduced? [The formal statement begins with a capital letter.]

> In Percy Shelley's "Ode to the West Wind," we read this line**:** "If winter comes, can spring be far behind?"

Colons are also used in several conventional situations.

BETWEEN HOURS AND MINUTES	6**:**30 P.M.
BETWEEN BIBLICAL CHAPTERS AND VERSES	Psalms 46**:**10
BETWEEN PERIODICAL VOLUMES AND PAGES	*Futura* 16**:**3–8
AFTER SALUTATIONS IN BUSINESS LETTERS	Dear Sir or Madam**:**

See page 599 for use of colons to introduce long quotations.

EXERCISE 10 Using Colons

Number your paper 1 to 10. Then write each word or number that should be followed by a colon and add the colon. If a sentence does not need a colon, write *C* after the number.

1. The following words are all twentieth-century creations *beautician, highbrow,* and *superhighway.*
2. The decision to be made is this Who will introduce the President at the convention?

3. That dealership sells cars, trucks, and vans.
4. Four women are represented in the U.S. Capitol's Statuary Hall Frances Willard, Maria Sanford, Florence Rena Sabin, and Esther Hobart Morris.
5. If we leave at 6 15, we should be at your house by 6 45.
6. Theodore Roosevelt is known for this saying "The only man who never makes a mistake is the man who never does anything."
7. To complete my coin collection, I need a 1963 penny, a 1940 dime, and a 1976 quarter.
8. The text for last Sunday's service was Joshua 1 9.
9. On our trip this summer, we plan to visit the following cities New Orleans, Montgomery, and Atlanta.
10. The question before the committee is this Should new members be installed twice a year?

EXERCISE 11 Time-out for Review

Write the following sentences, adding semicolons, colons, and *commas* where needed.

1. Benjamin Franklin played three instruments the harp the guitar and the violin.
2. I remembered the capitals of Georgia Texas and Utah but I had forgotten that Frankfort is the capital of Kentucky.
3. Some gorillas have learned sign language others have learned to read and write.
4. There are some places I have never visited in the city for example I have not yet been to the art museum.
5. Cities named after presidents are Jefferson City Nebraska Jackson Mississippi Lincoln Nebraska and Madison Wisconsin.
6. Sir Winston Churchill once wrote "History unfolds itself by strange and unpredictable paths."
7. It didn't take as long as I'd planned to plant the seeds Kate and I finished the work in three hours.
8. An insect has three parts head thorax and abdomen.
9. Katherine Lee Bates wrote "America the Beautiful" in 1893 she was inspired by the view from Pikes Peak in Colorado.
10. Most caterpillars change into butterflies inside a chrysalis however moths usually metamorphose inside a cocoon.

UNDERLINING

When words are printed in italics, they slant to the right *like this*. When you write, you can use underlining as a substitute for italics. Letters, numbers, words, and titles should be underlined in certain situations.

12j Underline letters, numbers, and words when they are used to represent themselves. Also underline foreign words that are not generally used in English.

LETTERS, NUMBERS	When you write your compositions, your capital q's look like 2's.
WORDS, PHRASES	In Shakespeare's time the word gentle meant "noble."
FOREIGN WORDS	In Hebrew shalom means "peace."

NOTE: Only the *q* and the *2* in the first example are underlined — not the *'s*.

12k Underline the titles of long written or musical works that are published as a single unit. Also underline the titles of paintings and sculptures and the names of vehicles.

Long works include books, periodicals, newspapers, full-length plays, and very long poems. Long musical compositions include operas, symphonies, ballets, and albums. Vehicles include airplanes, ships, trains, and spacecraft. Titles of movies and radio and TV series should also be underlined.

George Eliot wrote Silas Marner.

Henrik Ibsen's plays Hedda Gabler and A Doll's House were written in the latter part of the nineteenth century.

Wolfgang Amadeus Mozart composed the opera Don Giovanni in Italian and the opera The Magic Flute in German.

The Gudgeon was the first submarine to circle the earth.

We're now getting the Philadelphia Bulletin delivered to our house. [*The* is generally not considered part of the title of a newspaper or a periodical.]

NOTE: See pages 236–238 for the capitalization of titles.

EXERCISE 12 Using Underlining
Write and underline each letter, number, word, or group of words that should be italicized.

1. In our city Meet the Press airs on television every Sunday.
2. Charles Schulz, who created the character Charlie Brown, was once a cartoonist for the magazine Saturday Evening Post.
3. Leonardo da Vinci's painting The Last Supper is considered one of the great art treasures of the world.
4. In many of the world's languages, the word mother begins with the letter m.
5. The expression to bury the hatchet means "to make peace."
6. Of all Dickens' books that I have read, I enjoyed Oliver Twist the most.
7. The term First Lady wasn't widely used until a comedy about Dolley Madison, called The First Lady in the Land, opened in New York in 1911.
8. "Time flies" is the meaning of the Latin expression tempus fugit.
9. Kaddara, an opera produced in 1921, is about Eskimos.
10. Gus Grissom made the second United States manned space flight in Liberty Bell 7.

QUOTATION MARKS

Knowing how to use quotation marks correctly when you write fiction is important because conversations cannot be written without them. Authors often use conversation to reveal important information about the characters and to add realism to fiction.

Quotation marks are also essential in research papers. If you omit or incorrectly use quotation marks in a research paper, you may, unwittingly, be plagiarizing someone else's words. Quotation marks show that the words you are writing are not your own—that they belong to someone else.

One of the most important things to remember about quotation marks is that they come in pairs. They are placed at the beginning and at the end of uninterrupted quotations and certain titles.

Quotation Marks with Titles

The titles of long works of art and publications are underlined. These long works, however, are usually composed of smaller parts. A newspaper has articles, for example, and a book can include chapters, short stories, short plays, or poems. When the titles of these smaller parts are written, they should be enclosed in quotation marks.

12l Use quotation marks to enclose the titles of chapters, articles, stories, one-act plays, short poems, and songs.

Quotation marks are also placed around the titles of essays, compositions, episodes from TV series, and movements from long musical compositions.

> "A Voyage to Lilliput" is my favorite chapter in Gulliver's Travels by Jonathan Swift.
>
> "Facing the Future" was an informative article in Time.
>
> Yesterday in class we read Robert Browning's poem "My Last Duchess" in our anthology English Literature.

EXERCISE 13 Using Quotation Marks with Titles
Write each title, adding quotation marks and underlining where needed.

1. Automation on the Line was a recent article in the Detroit News.
2. The drama class recently presented the one-act play The Happy Journey to Trenton and Camden by Thornton Wilder.
3. The band played Yankee Doodle as we marched by.
4. You can find the short story The Bear in the book The Works of William Faulkner.
5. The Elizabethan Stage was the title of my essay for English class.
6. Are we supposed to read Keats's poem To Autumn or Shelley's poem To a Skylark for class tomorrow?
7. As Time Goes By is the famous song in the movie Casablanca.
8. Cloudburst is the last movement from Grofé's Grand Canyon Suite.

9. Have you read the chapter The Turning Point in our textbook The History of the World?
10. The article Buying a Used Car in Consumer Reports was very helpful.

Quotation Marks with Direct Quotations

Quotation marks are placed around a *direct quotation*—the exact words of a person. They are not placed around an *indirect quotation*—a paraphrase of someone's words.

12m Use quotation marks to enclose a person's exact words.

DIRECT QUOTATION	Bill said, "I'm almost ready."
INDIRECT QUOTATION	Bill said that he was almost ready. [The word *that* often signals an indirect quotation.]

A one-sentence direct quotation can be placed before or after a speaker tag, and it can also be interrupted by a speaker tag. In all three cases, quotation marks enclose *only* the person's exact words. Notice in the third sentence in the following examples that two sets of quotation marks are needed because quotation marks enclose only a person's exact words—not the speaker tag.

BEFORE	"The game was very suspenseful," he said.
AFTER	He said, "The game was very suspenseful."
INTERRUPTED	"The game," he said, "was very suspenseful."

Only one set of quotation marks is needed to enclose any number of sentences—unless the quotation is interrupted by a speaker tag.

He said, "The game was very suspenseful. We were tied in the last inning. Then Willie hit a home run."

Capital Letters with Direct Quotations. A capital letter begins a quoted sentence—just as it begins a regular sentence.

12n Begin each sentence of a direct quotation with a capital letter.

"**A**ways be sure to think before you speak," Priscilla stated.

Priscilla stated, "**A**lways be sure to think before you speak." [Two capital letters are needed: one for the first word of the sentence and one for the first word of the quotation.]

"**A**lways be sure to think," Priscilla stated, "before you speak." [*Before* does not begin with a capital letter because it is in the middle of the quotation.]

"**A**lways be sure to think before you speak," Priscilla stated. "**T**hat is the best advice I can give you." [*That* begins with a capital letter because it starts a new sentence.]

EXERCISE 14 Using Quotation Marks and Capital Letters with Direct Quotations

Write each sentence, adding quotation marks and capital letters where needed. In this exercise place a comma or an end mark that follows a quotation *inside* the closing quotation marks.

Happiness

1. happiness is not a state to arrive at, but a manner of traveling, commented Margaret Runbeck.
2. too often travel, observed Elizabeth Drew, instead of broadening the mind merely lengthens the conversation.
3. when one is happy, there is no time to be fatigued. being happy engrosses the whole attention, E. F. Benson said.
4. Don Marquis mused, happiness is the interval between periods of unhappiness.
5. when a happy moment, complete and rounded as a pearl, falls into the tossing ocean of life, Agnes Repplier said, it is never wholly lost.
6. happiness is not being pained in body or troubled in mind, commented Thomas Jefferson.
7. C. P. Snow said, the pursuit of happiness is a most ridiculous phrase. if you pursue it, you'll never find it.
8. if happiness truly consisted in physical ease and freedom from care, then the happiest individual, I think, would be an American cow, William Phelps mused.
9. the happy do not believe in miracles, Goethe stated.
10. happiness is not a matter of events. it depends upon the tides of the mind, Alice Meynell once said.

Commas with Direct Quotations. A comma is used to separate a direct quotation from a speaker tag.

12o Use a comma to separate a direct quotation from a speaker tag. Place the comma inside the closing quotation marks.

Notice in the following examples that when the speaker tag follows the quotation, the comma goes *inside* the closing quotation marks.

> "Today's mail is late**,**" she said. [The comma goes *inside* the closing quotation marks.]
>
> She said**,** "Today's mail is late." [The comma follows the speaker tag.]
>
> "Today's mail**,**" she said**,** "is late." [Two commas are needed to separate the speaker tag from the parts of an interrupted quotation. The first comma goes *inside* the closing quotation marks.]

End Marks with Direct Quotations. A period marks the end of a statement or an opinion, and it also marks the end of a quoted statement or opinion.

12p Place a period inside the closing quotation marks when the end of the quotation comes at the end of the sentence.

> He said, "I think I'll order lasagna**.**" [The period goes *inside* the closing quotation marks.]
>
> "I think I'll order lasagna," he said**.** [The period follows the speaker tag, and a comma separates the quotation from the speaker tag.]
>
> "I think," he said, "I'll order lasagna**.**" [The period goes *inside* the closing quotation marks.]

If a quotation asks a question or shows strong feeling, the question mark or the exclamation point goes *inside* the closing quotation marks. Notice that the question mark goes *inside* the closing quotation marks in the three examples that follow.

> She asked, "Where did you pick the apples**?**"
> "Where did you pick the apples**?**" she asked.
> "Where," she asked, "did you pick the apples**?**"

The exclamation point also goes *inside* the closing quotation marks in the following three examples.

He exclaimed, "I'm thrilled that I've been hired**!**"
"I'm thrilled that I've been hired**!**" he exclaimed.
"I'm thrilled," he exclaimed, "that I've been hired**!**"

A quotation of several sentences can include various end marks.

"Did you see the movie at Cinema I**?**" Lance asked. "It was the funniest movie I've ever seen**!**"

Question marks and exclamation points are placed inside the closing quotation marks when they are part of the quotation. Occasionally a question or an exclamatory statement will include a direct quotation. In such cases, the question mark or the exclamation point goes *outside* the closing quotation marks. Notice in the following examples that the end marks for the quotations themselves are omitted. Only one end mark is used at the end of a quotation.

Did Nancy say, "The class rings have arrived"**?** [The whole sentence—not the quotation—is the question.]

I was so relieved when my teacher said, "You've passed the exam"**!** [The whole sentence—not the quotation—is exclamatory.]

NOTE: Semicolons and colons go *outside* closing quotation marks.

Robert Browning wrote, "That's my last Duchess"**;** thus he began one of the most famous poems of all times.

Mrs. Rooney said that the following are "mandatory reading for seniors"**:** *Macbeth* and *Great Expectations.*

EXERCISE 15 Using Commas and End Marks with Direct Quotations

Write each sentence, adding commas and end marks where needed.

1. "Most baby seals must be taught how to swim by their mothers" Martha told us
2. Cheryl asked "Why should a right-handed bowler step out on the right foot"

3. "I was so cold, my teeth were chattering" Beth exclaimed
4. "The safest way to double your money" Frank Hubbard advised "is to fold it over once and put it in your pocket"
5. I was so proud when the bandleader announced to the band members "You've won second prize in the Chenango County competition"
6. "Did you get that summer job you applied for" Tara asked
7. Phillip called "We've run out of gas"
8. Norman Douglas observed "Life is full of untapped sources of pleasure Education should train us to discover them"
9. Did the principal say " The Senior Prom is on June 20 and graduation is on June 23"
10. "Those fresh tomatoes were delicious" Megan said "Did you grow them yourself"

EXERCISE 16 Time-out for Review

Write each sentence, adding capital letters, quotation marks, and other punctuation marks where needed.

Quotes by Famous Authors

1. the applause of a single human being is of great consequence Samuel Johnson said
2. the most beautiful adventures explained Robert Louis Stevenson are not those we go to seek
3. we need to restore the full meaning of the old word *duty* Pearl Buck remarked it is the other side of *rights*
4. Joseph Conrad stated an ideal is often but a flaming vision of reality
5. make up your mind to act decisively and take the consequences no good is ever done in this world by hesitation Thomas Huxley warned
6. Janet Erskine Stuart said to aim at the best and to remain essentially ourselves are one and the same thing
7. welcome everything that comes to you André Gide advised but do not long for anything else
8. can anything be sadder than work left unfinished Christina Rossetti asked yes, work never begun
9. did W. B. Yeats say good conversation unrolls itself like the dawn
10. I do not like arguments I seek harmony if it is not there, I move away Anaïs Nin stated

Other Uses of Quotation Marks

In long quotations in a report and conversations in a story, quotation marks require special applications.

Quoting Phrases. If you are quoting a phrase or the definition of a word, put quotation marks around the borrowed words only. Capital letters and commas are usually not needed. Notice in the following examples that the period goes *inside* the closing quotation marks when the phrase or the definition comes at the end of the sentence.

> During his inaugural address, John F. Kennedy said that the day should be spent as **"**a celebration of freedom**."**
>
> The word *mutual* means **"**given and received in equal amount**."**

NOTE: The word being defined in the previous example is italicized (underlined). *(See page 278.)*

Writing Dialogue. When you write dialogue—conversation between two or more people—begin a new paragraph each time the speaker changes. Each new paragraph will clearly indicate who is speaking.

The following dialogue from *A Christmas Carol* takes place between Scrooge's nephew Fred and Fred's wife Bell. Each quotation follows the rules you have just studied; but each time the speaker changes, a new paragraph begins. Notice also that actions or descriptions of the two characters are sometimes included within the same paragraph in which each one speaks.

> "Bell," said the husband, turning to his wife with a smile. "I saw a friend of yours this afternoon."
>
> "Who was it?"
>
> "Guess!"
>
> "How can I? Tut, don't I know?" she added in the same breath, laughing as he laughed. "Mr. Scrooge."
>
> —CHARLES DICKENS

NOTE: An ellipsis (three dots) is used to indicate the omission of part of a quotation. If an ellipsis comes at the end of a complete sentence, it is preceded by a period—making four dots.

> "I saw a friend of yours. . . ."

Quoting Long Passages. Quotation marks are not necessary when you write a quote of five or more lines in a research paper. Instead, skip two lines and indent ten spaces along the left margin. *(See page 599.)*

Quotations within Quotations. If a title or a quotation is included within another quotation, a distinction must be made between the two sets of quotation marks. To avoid any possible confusion, use single quotation marks to enclose a quotation or certain titles within a quotation.

> "Is the song '76 Trombones' from the movie *The Music Man?*" Janice asked.
>
> Lou asked, "I wonder what he meant when he said, 'You'll be seeing me soon.' "

A quotation within a quotation follows all the rules covered in this section. Notice, however, in the last example, that the closing single quotation mark and the closing double quotation mark come together.

EXERCISE 17 Time-out for Review
Correctly rewrite the following dialogue between Scrooge and Bob Cratchit. Add punctuation, capitalization, and indentation where needed.

From *A Christmas Carol*

Hallo growled Scrooge in his accustomed voice as near as he could feign it. What do you mean by coming here at this time of day? I am very sorry, sir said Bob. I am behind my time. . . . Yes. I think you are. Step this way, sir, if you please. It's only once a year, sir pleaded Bob, appearing from the tank. It shall not be repeated. I was making rather merry yesterday, sir. Now, I'll tell you what, my friend said Scrooge. I am not going to tolerate this sort of thing any longer. Therefore . . . I am about to raise your salary!

—CHARLES DICKENS

EXERCISE 18 Writing Dialogue
Taking the role of President of the United States, write a brief imaginary conversation in which you speak with the head of state of a foreign country. Punctuate and indent the dialogue correctly.

OTHER MARKS OF PUNCTUATION

Hyphens, dashes, parentheses, and brackets will be covered in this section.

Hyphens

A hyphen has several uses besides its most common use, dividing a word at the end of a line.

Hyphen with Numbers and Words. Certain numbers and fractions are written with a hyphen.

12q Use a hyphen when writing out the numbers *twenty-one* through *ninety-nine.* Also use a hyphen when writing out a fraction that is used as an adjective.

Eighty-four seniors from Delton will graduate in June.

A two-thirds vote of the House is needed.

A fraction used as a noun is *not* written with a hyphen.

Two thirds of the town voted for the referendum.

Hyphens with Compound Nouns and Adjectives. Compound nouns and adjectives can be written as two separate words, two combined words, or two or more hyphenated words. Since compound nouns and compound adjectives can take these different forms, it is always best to check the dictionary for the correct spelling.

12r Use a hyphen to separate the parts of some compound nouns and adjectives.

COMPOUND NOUNS	clock-watcher, flare-up, double-time
COMPOUND ADJECTIVES	skin-deep, long-term, run-of-the-mill

NOTE: Never hyphenate a compound adjective that includes an adverb ending in *ly.*

That **superbly talented** musician is my uncle. [no hyphen]

Hyphens with Certain Prefixes. Several prefixes and one suffix are always separated from their root words by a hyphen.

12s Use a hyphen after the prefixes *ex-*, *self-*, and *all-* and before the suffix *-elect.*

ex-champion, self-control, all-around, governor-elect

Also use a hyphen with all prefixes before a proper noun or a proper adjective.

mid-Atlantic, pre-Columbian, pro-American

EXERCISE 19 Using Hyphens

Number your paper 1 to 10. Then correctly write each word that should be hyphenated. If no word in the sentence needs a hyphen, write *C* after the number.

1. Is Madeline Nenno the stand in for the female lead in our school play?
2. The ex mayor of South Morrisville teaches at the University of Nebraska.
3. I still must type one third of my term paper.
4. Fifty six bushels of corn were picked today.
5. Can you name two mid Victorian poets?
6. The metal used in the sculpture is one fourth copper.
7. This report includes up to date statistics.
8. The solidly constructed house has already stood for over 200 years.
9. Jamie is unusually self reliant for a young person.
10. The principal commended the students for their all out effort in the fund raising drive.

Hyphens to Divide Words. When you write a research paper or a composition, you should, whenever possible, avoid dividing words at the end of the line.

12t Use a hyphen to divide a word at the end of a line.

If you must divide a word, use the guidelines listed on the following page.

Guidelines for Dividing Words

1. Divide words only between syllables.
   hu-morous or humor-ous
2. Never divide a one-syllable word.
   laugh brought save lead
3. Never separate a one-letter syllable from the rest of the word.
   DO NOT BREAK a-dore e-mit i-ris
4. Hyphenate after two letters at the end of a line, but do not carry a two-letter word ending to the next line.
   BREAK be-lieve re-call in-vite
   DO NOT BREAK tight-en shov-el over-ly
5. Usually divide words containing double consonants between the double consonants.
   shim-mer oc-cur ship-ping stag-ger
6. Divide hyphenated words only after the hyphens.
   spur-of-the-moment father-in-law self-confident
7. Do not divide a proper noun or a proper adjective.
   Olivero Yonkers Himalayan Polish

EXERCISE 20 **Using Hyphens to Divide Words**
Number your paper 1 to 20. Then write each word, using a hyphen or hyphens to show where the word can be divided. If a word should not be divided, write *no* after the number.

1. educate	6. octave	11. dress	16. oboe
2. squeeze	7. permit	12. teenage	17. plank
3. follow	8. planet	13. decent	18. Pacific
4. event	9. puzzle	14. Reggie	19. tip-top
5. governor	10. immune	15. method	20. able

Dashes, Parentheses, and Brackets

Dashes, parentheses, and brackets are used to separate certain words or groups of words from the rest of the sentence. Be careful that you do not overuse these marks of punctuation or substitute them for other marks of punctuation, such as commas or colons.

Dashes. Like a comma, a dash is used to separate words or expressions. A dash, however, indicates a greater separation than a comma does. Dashes should be used in the following situations.

12u Use dashes to set off an abrupt change in thought.

Several students—there were three—applied for the scholarship.

I've misplaced the envelope—oh, I see you have it.

12v Use dashes to set off an appositive that is introduced by words such as *that is, for example,* or *for instance.*

If your car gets mired—for example, in mud, snow, or soft sand—apply power slowly, keeping the front wheels in a straight position.

Mary Ann Evans' pseudonym—that is, her pen name—was George Eliot.

12w Use dashes to set off a parenthetical expression or an appositive that includes commas. Also use dashes to call special attention to a phrase.

You can call me Monday or Wednesday—or Friday, for that matter—right after school.

The names of four states—Alaska, Arizona, Arkansas, and Alabama—begin with the letter *A.*

12x Use dashes to set off a phrase or a clause that summarizes or emphasizes what has preceded it.

June 6, 7, and 8—these are the dates of the county fair.

A book, a picture frame, and a tee shirt—I got these gifts for my birthday.

NOTE: You can write or type a dash by placing two hyphens together, with no space before or after them.

Parentheses. Parentheses separate from the rest of the sentence additional information or an explanation that is added, but not needed. Definitions and dates, for example, are sometimes enclosed by parentheses.

12y Use parentheses to enclose additional information that is not needed in a sentence.

Dylan Thomas **(**1914–1953**)** read his own poetry brilliantly.

Samuel Clemens didn't invent the name Mark Twain **(**which means "a depth of 2 fathoms, or 12 feet"**)**.

NOTE: A period follows a closing parenthesis that comes at the end of a sentence.

Brackets. When you write a research paper that includes quoted passages, you may need to use brackets.

12z Use brackets to enclose an explanation within quoted material that is not part of the quotation.

Richard Ellmann wrote, "He **[**W. B. Yeats**]** displayed and interpreted the direction in which poetry was to go."

EXERCISE 21 Using Dashes and Parentheses

Write the following sentences, adding dashes and parentheses where needed.

1. The Impressionist painter Claude Monet 1840–1926 painted many pictures of the same lily pads to show varying effects of light.
2. Running, swimming, and riding a bicycle all these are good forms of exercise.
3. A number of countries in the world for example, Bolivia, Switzerland, and Austria have no seacoast.
4. I believe you are too young how shall I say it? to be on your own in a big city.
5. A provision in author Willa Cather's will she died in 1947 prohibited publication of her letters.
6. The dogwood grows well in many states for instance, New York, Maryland, and Virginia.
7. I cannot I repeat, cannot hear the people in the balcony.
8. In 1895, Lieutenant Peary later Admiral Peary found one of the world's largest iron meteorites in Greenland.

9. Los Angeles 464 square miles is more than one third the size of Rhode Island 1,214 square miles.
10. The dates for some of this year's events graduation, senior prom, and senior picnic have been established.

Application to Writing

Using the correct punctuation in a report or a composition is one of the best ways to guarantee that your readers will understand exactly the meaning you intended. When you finish writing, always take a few extra minutes to edit your work for correct punctuation. Consider that time an insurance policy for your efforts.

EXERCISE 22 Editing for Punctuation Marks
Write the following three paragraphs. Add any necessary punctuation.

It's OK

There arent any hard statistics nevertheless the expression OK is probably the most widely used American expression in the world. Some Spaniards probably say it more often than the word salud many English people have substituted it for right-o. OK is even used by people who dont understand any other words in English.

During World War II, there was a special soccer match. One team was composed of members from the following countries Poland, Czechoslavakia, Denmark, and Norway. The team eventually had serious difficulties because of the language differences. Finally one of Polands players shouted OK! Feeling confident that everyone finally understood the same thing, the team members went on to win the game.

Despite its international acceptance, OK is an all American expression. It first appeared in print in 1839 in a newspaper, the Boston Morning Post. It was used as an abbreviation for the expression all correct. A year later President Martin Van Buren he was born in Kinderhook, New York ran for a second term. He was called Old Kinderhook by his backers. The initials of his nickname were then used during the campaign by New Yorks Democratic OK Club. Later OK became a catchword meaning all is right.

CHAPTER REVIEW

A. Write the following sentences, adding any needed punctuation. (There are no direct quotations in this exercise.)

1. The conservation department puts rainbow trout into the streams the lakes are stocked with pickerel and perch.
2. The prop committee still hasnt found the following items a straw hat a wicker chair and a large desk.
3. Everyones enthusiasm at the pep rally encouraged the players on Newtons all star team.
4. In the code the 2s stood for es.
5. The 18th amendment the prohibition amendment was never ratified by Connecticut and Rhode Island.
6. Most insects have no eyelids thus their eyes are always open.
7. Six forty and ten these are the three correct answers.
8. Its time to apply for the dogs new license.
9. We have our choice of pink aqua or lavender but we dont know which color would be best for the room.
10. A tree snake appears to fly through the air however it merely glides on air currents.
11. We couldnt possibly be at your house by 7 30.
12. Shiny metals for example tin and copper turn into black powders when finely ground aluminum is an exception.
13. Gregor Mendel 1822–1884 was the Austrian botanist who developed the basic laws of heredity.
14. Bobs and Teds scores were the best theyve ever had.
15. Only two copies of the works of the Greek sculptor Myron are known to have survived one of those is the sculpture Discus Thrower.
16. Three people Nancy Alex and Claire will represent the school at the conference in Philadelphia.
17. There are no penguins at the North Pole in fact there are no penguins anywhere in the Northern Hemisphere.
18. The question before the finance committee is this Which of the two investments will yield the greater return?
19. The famous painting Mona Lisa by Leonardo da Vinci is a portrait of Lisa del Giocondo of Venice.
20. We will donate two thirds of the clubs earnings to a fund for famine relief.

B. Write the following quotations, adding capital letters, quotation marks, and other punctuation marks where needed.

1. were taking Rex with us to the store Chris announced
2. what an enthusiastic audience this is Beth remarked
3. why didnt someone answer the telephone she asked
4. the clerk said these shirts will be on sale next week youll save two dollars on each one if you wait
5. the television special I told you about Jake announced is about to begin
6. Gary asked does soccer practice start at three oclock
7. there is nothing better Katharine Butler Hathaway said than the encouragement of a good friend
8. what is the rhyme scheme in this poem by Lord Byron Ms. Otero asked
9. did you read the article Space Station Speculation in todays issue of the Washington Post Leila asked
10. show me what a man envies the least in others Josh Billings observed and I will show you what he has the most of himself
11. sixty nine people have signed up for the race on Sunday Kenneth explained
12. conversation is possible between two people John Erskine stated but it cant be much of an art unless there are at least three
13. I visited the ship Old Ironsides Martha stated when I was in Boston last summer
14. do you know the words to the old song Harvest Moon my dad asked
15. not what we have, but what we enjoy J. Petit-Senn stated constitutes our abundance
16. were having a party on Saturday said Betsy will you and Jim join us
17. Bryan said the dictionary definition of the word glint is a tiny bright flash of light
18. this years harvest was particularly good the corn crop was especially plentiful Mac told us
19. did Mr. Meyers say class reports arent due for another week
20. Mom told us I think it was Peter who said I dont plan to be home for dinner tonight

MASTERY TEST

Number your paper 1 to 10. Then write each sentence, adding apostrophes, semicolons, colons, hyphens, quotation marks, and all the punctuation marks needed with direct quotations. Only a sentence with a speaker tag should be considered a direct quotation.

1. Switzerland has four official languages French, German, Italian, and Romansch.
2. Seeds from plants are often dispersed by ingenious methods for example, the milkweed seed rides on a tiny parachute.
3. Anyones guess is as good as mine.
4. My research paper answered this question What is the main conflict in Shakespeares play Hamlet?
5. Andrea said His self assured manner impressed everyone.
6. At 5 30 A.M. Roy and I headed for Pier Ten.
7. True chameleons can change to green, yellow, or brown the American chameleon can turn only green and brown.
8. Are you taking an umbrella Rebecca asked It looks as if its going to rain.
9. Did Mozart ever write an opera Dwayne inquired.
10. You just scored the winning point he cheered.

STANDARDIZED TEST

MECHANICS

Directions: Each sentence may contain a capitalization or punctuation error in one of the underlined parts. On your answer sheet, fill in the circle containing the letter of the part that has an error. If there is no error in an underlined part, fill in *E*.

SAMPLE Do you know the senator (A) personally, (B) Aunt (C) Mae. (D) No error (E)

ANSWER Ⓐ Ⓑ Ⓒ ● Ⓔ

1. Hurry, (A) Pat; (B) or we'll (C) miss the bus to Long Island. (D) No error (E)
2. Whose (A) story is entitled "A Gift (B) For (C) Anne"? (D) No error (E)
3. Twenty-one (A) families have looked at the Bensons' (B) house; (C) however, (D) not one has offered to buy it. No error (E)
4. "Is you're (A) sister (B) Eva coming in May?" (C) he asked. (D) No error (E)
5. "Yes, (A) she's (B) arriving on Memorial (C) Day" (D) I replied. No error (E)
6. Both Cora's (A) and John's (B) *v*'s (C) look like *w*'s. (D) No error (E)
7. The only cities in the Northeast (A) I have visited are: (B) Boston, (C) New York, (D) and Bangor. No error (E)
8. Popocatépetl, (A) Mexico's famous volcano, (B) has a crater that is large, (C) deep (D) and bell-shaped. No error (E)
9. "Why?" (A) he asked, (B) "is the congresswoman (C) frowning?" (D) No error (E)
10. Shakespeare's (A) play *Hamlet,* (B) I believe (C) will be the next presentation of the Windsor Drama Society. (D) No error (E)

Directions: Each sentence has one underlined part. After the sentence there are five ways to write the underlined part. Choose the best way. If the sentence is correct as it stands, choose *A*. Fill in the circle containing the letter of your answer.

SAMPLE Leif Erikson a Norse Explorer discovered Labrador in 1000.

A Leif Erikson a Norse Explorer
B Leif Erikson, a Norse Explorer,
C Leif Erikson, a Norse explorer,
D Leif Erikson, a norse explorer,

ANSWER Ⓐ Ⓑ Ⓒ Ⓓ

11. Will your uncle drive, take the bus or just walk here?
A uncle drive, take the bus or
B Uncle drive, take the bus or
C Uncle drive, take the bus, or
D uncle drive, take the bus, or

12. The Caspian Sea is not really a sea; it is a land-locked lake.
A sea; it is a land-locked lake.
B Sea, it is a land-locked lake.
C Sea; it is a land-locked Lake.
D sea, it is a land-locked Lake.

13. Elyse, do you know who wrote the opera *Aïda?*
A Elyse, do you know who wrote the opera *Aïda?*
B Elyse, Do you know who wrote the opera "Aïda"?
C Elyse do you know who wrote the opera *Aïda?*
D Elyse, do you know who wrote the opera "*Aïda?*"

14. Jay sat down, but then fell asleep before we could talk.
A down, but then fell asleep before
B down but then fell asleep before
C down, but then fell asleep, before
D down but then fell asleep, before

15. On the other hand a person, who doesn't try, can never win.
A On the other hand a person, who doesn't try,
B On the other hand a person who doesn't try
C On the other hand, a person who doesn't try
D On the other hand, a person who doesn't try,

Unit 4

Vocabulary and Spelling

13

Vocabulary

Acquiring a good vocabulary is a challenge that will continue long after you leave school. Whether you go to college or take a job after high school graduation, you will constantly encounter unfamiliar words. Expanding your vocabulary will help you communicate more effectively, both in school and on the job.

WORD MEANING

The English language contains thousands of words. Most of them have more than one definition. Although you would be faced with a difficult task if you tried to learn all those words and definitions, there are several methods you can use to build your vocabulary. One way is to record each new word as you encounter it and to look up its meaning in the dictionary. Another way is to figure out the meaning of each new word by looking carefully at the words in the rest of the sentence. You can also determine the meaning of an unfamiliar word by defining its word parts. In addition, you can search the sentence for an obvious synonym or antonym that will give you a clue to the meaning of the unfamiliar word. This chapter covers some of the procedures you can use to unlock the meanings of words you do not recognize.

Context Clues

You have learned most of the words in your vocabulary through context. The *context* of a word is the sentence, surrounding words, or situation in which the word appears. One way to increase your vocabulary is to use verbal context—that is, the surrounding words and sentences—to help you define each new word. Sometimes the verbal context will supply a precise definition, as it does in the following sentence.

A *thermograph* is a self-recording thermometer.

Usually the context of a word provides only a clue to the meaning of a word, rather than an actual definition. Following are examples of familiar types of context clues.

RESTATEMENT The sun reached its *zenith,* or **highest point in the sky,** just as we began to eat lunch. [The word *or* introduces an appositive that defines the word *zenith.*]

EXAMPLE *Symmetry* often contributes to the beauty of architecture, as it does, for example, in the **perfect proportions and balanced forms of the Taj Mahal.** [By using the well-known Taj Mahal as an example, the writer makes clear what is meant by *symmetry.*]

COMPARISON A *prodigy* in music, she was **nearly the equal of Mozart, the composer who wrote a sonata at the age of eight.** [The comparison with Mozart shows that *prodigy* means "a highly talented child."]

CONTRAST Mark's **customized purple jeep, with a gilt crown for a hood ornament,** is as *gaudy* as Mr. Foster's gray sedan is plain. [The contrast between Mark's car and Mr. Foster's shows that *gaudy* means just the opposite of *plain:* "showy, garish, and possibly tasteless."]

PARALLELISM She was **determined,** he was **iron-willed,** and I was equally *resolute.* [The parallel sentence structure suggests that *resolute* is a synonym for *determined* and *iron-willed.*]

EXERCISE 1 Using Context Clues

Write the letter of the word or group of words closest in meaning to the underlined word.

1. Congress passed a statute, or law, to provide for federal enforcement of the Constitutional amendment.
   (A) request (B) written rule (C) sculptured likeness
   (D) book (E) statement
2. The king decided to abdicate, as King Edward VIII did when he gave up the throne of England in 1936.
   (A) relinquish power (B) be crowned (C) control
   (D) marry (E) escape
3. Amity exists between Switzerland and its neighbors, in contrast to the bitterness that exists between some other nations of the world.
   (A) rivalry (B) hostility (C) borders (D) friendship
   (E) helplessness
4. Inquiring about his son's career, the man naturally took a paternal interest in the boy's success.
   (A) brotherly (B) long-term (C) fatherly
   (D) excessive (E) mild
5. The recent political caucus, unlike those old-time small gatherings, was well reported by the press.
   (A) defeat (B) meeting (C) campaign (D) dinner
   (E) platform
6. A referee should be completely impartial, favoring neither one side nor the other.
   (A) businesslike (B) enthusiastic (C) outspoken
   (D) cordial (E) fair
7. This is a facsimile, or replica, of a $500 bill issued by the Confederate States of America.
   (A) reproduction (B) variety (C) counterfeit
   (D) bonanza (E) display
8. When the foreman was warned about his laxity, he changed overnight and became a complete perfectionist.
   (A) extravagance (B) appearance (C) negligence
   (D) ignorance (E) temper
9. Although the candidate failed to win a majority of votes in the primary, he did have a sizable plurality over the first runner-up.
   (A) loss of votes (B) excess of votes (C) celebration
   (D) concern (E) surprise

10. Among the other pleasant smells in the village was the savory odor of chili coming from a small café.
(A) appetizing (B) sturdy (C) flowery (D) gracious (E) rural
11. In some countries military service is compulsory; in others, it is voluntary.
(A) enjoyable (B) unnecessary (C) disagreeable (D) required (E) illegal
12. He holds the orthodox, or customary, view of what the company should do to increase sales.
(A) modern (B) religious (C) thoughtful (D) unpopular (E) traditional
13. Dr. Elroy tried to ascertain the cause of the illness, but he was never sure he was right.
(A) cure (B) destroy (C) treat (D) determine (E) dismiss
14. The lake was placid after the storm, its surface as smooth as a tabletop.
(A) peaceful (B) transparent (C) choppy (D) muddy (E) cold
15. Every recipient of the award gives an acceptance speech.
(A) promoter (B) loser (C) receiver (D) giver (E) producer
16. A handwritten note is not enough; you must have an affidavit, a document signed and witnessed.
(A) instruction (B) explanation (C) alibi (D) oral oath (E) sworn statement
17. Sally is so meticulous in her work that she will rewrite a whole page to correct one small error.
(A) prompt (B) careful (C) excitable (D) remarkable (E) indifferent
18. Some board games require very little thought or intelligence, but chess is quite cerebral.
(A) simple (B) intellectually demanding (C) thrilling (D) socially impressive (E) ancient
19. It is almost as hard to decipher Mr. Cook's handwriting as it would be to crack a tough foreign code.
(A) study (B) copy (C) see (D) interpret (E) print
20. Emily Dickinson's renown, or fame, is based on a collection of short, brilliant poems.
(A) pen name (B) gentleness (C) technical mastery (D) obituary (E) honored status

Prefixes, Suffixes, and Roots

Besides using the context of a word, you can use a word's structure, or parts, to find clues to its meaning. The word parts—prefixes, roots, and suffixes—of many English words come from Latin and Greek, although some are from Old English, French, and other languages.

A *root,* as you will recall, is the part of a word that carries the basic meaning. A *prefix* is one or more syllables placed in front of the root to modify the meaning of the root or to form a new word. A *suffix* is one or more syllables placed after the root to help shape its meaning and often to determine its part of speech.

The English language contains hundreds of roots, prefixes, and suffixes. With a knowledge of even a few examples of each kind of word part, you should be able to make reasonable guesses about the meanings of words that contain these parts. Knowing, for instance, that the root *duc* means "lead" will help you figure out the meanings of such words as *deduction, abduct,* and *aqueduct.* The following examples illustrate how the meaning of each word part contributes to the meaning of the word as a whole.

Word Parts with Latin Origins

WORD	PREFIX	ROOT	SUFFIX
abrasive	ab-	-rase-	-ive
	(away)	(erase)	(toward action)
component	com-	-pon-	-ent
	(together)	(put)	(one that performs)
inaccessible	in-	-access-	-ible
	(not)	(approach)	(capable of)

Word Parts with Greek Origins

WORD	PREFIX	ROOT	SUFFIX
amorphous	a-	-morph-	-ous
	(without)	(form)	(qualities of)
ejection	e-	-ject-	-ion
	(out)	(throw)	(act or process)
precedence	pre-	-ced-	-ence
	(before)	(go)	(act or process)

As you can see, the meanings of prefixes, roots, and suffixes seldom give a complete definition of a word. Rather, they give clues to the meaning of a word. Following are dictionary definitions of the previous examples.

abrasive: tending to rub or wear away
component: simple part or element of a system
inaccessible: not capable of being approached
amorphous: having no definite form, shapeless
ejection: act of throwing out or off from within
precedence: act of going before in order, rank, or importance

By learning the prefixes, suffixes, and roots in the lists that follow, you will be able to determine the meanings of a number of unfamiliar words.

Prefixes. Many prefixes have clear-cut and familiar meanings. The number prefixes, such as *mono-*, *bi-*, *tri-*, and *quad-*, are good examples. Other prefixes, however, have more than one meaning and more than one spelling. The prefix *ad-*, for example, may mean "to" or "toward." It may be spelled *ad-* (*ad*jacent), *ac-* (*ac*quire), or *al-* (*al*lure), according to the first letter of the root to which it is attached. The two charts that follow show some common Latin and Greek prefixes.

Prefixes from Latin

PREFIX	MEANING	EXAMPLE
ab-, a-	from, away, off	ab + errant: wandering away from the right or normal way
ad-, ac-, af-, ag-, al-, ap-, as-, at-	to, toward	ad + jacent: nearby ac + quire: get as one's own al + lure: entice by charm as + sure: make certain or safe
ante-	forward, in front of, before	ante + chamber: outer room, such as a waiting room
bi-	two, occurring twice	bi + lingual: using two languages with equal skill bi + nomial: mathematical expression consisting of two terms
circum-	around, about	circum + navigate: sail completely around

com-, col-, con-	with, together	com + press: squeeze together con + cur: happen together, agree
contra-	opposite, against	contra + dict: resist or oppose in argument
de-	do the opposite of, remove	de + activate: make inactive or ineffective
dis-	opposite of, not	dis + assemble: take apart
ex-	out of, outside	ex + clude: shut out
in-, il-, im-, ir-	not, in, into	in + animate: not lively or spirited im + press: affect deeply
inter-	between, among	inter + stellar: located among the stars
intra-, intro-	within, during	intra + venous: within or entering by way of a vein
non-	not	non + committal: not giving a clear indication of attitude
ob-	against, in the way	ob + stacle: something that stands in the way
post-	after, behind	post + script: writing added after a completed work
pre-	earlier than, before	pre + determine: decide or establish in advance
re-	again, back	re + organize: arrange or systematize again
retro-	backward, back, behind	retro + spect: review of past events retro + flex: turned or bent abruptly backward
semi-	half of	semi + circle: half of a circle
sub-	beneath, under	sub + plot: secondary series of events in a literary work
super-	over and above, more than	super + human: exceeding normal human power, size, or capability
trans-	across, beyond, through	trans + atlantic: extending across the Atlantic Ocean
ultra-	beyond in space, beyond limits of	ultra + violet: a violet beyond that visible in the spectrum
vice-	one that takes the place of	vice + principal: person who acts in place of the principal

Prefixes from Greek

PREFIX	MEANING	EXAMPLE
a-, an-	without, not	a + typical: not regular or usual
anti-	against	anti + pathy: dislike, distaste
cata-, cat-, cath-	down	cata + comb: underground passageway or tomb
dia-, di-	through, across	dia + gonal: extending from one edge of a solid figure to an opposite edge
dys-	difficult, impaired	dys + lexia: disturbance of the ability to read
epi-	over, after, outer	epi + dermis: outer layer of skin
hemi-	half	hemi + sphere: half a sphere
hyper-	above, excessive	hyper + tension: abnormally high blood pressure
para-	beside, closely related to	para + phrase: restate a text in another form or in other words
peri-	all around, surrounding	peri + pheral: relating to the outward bounds of something
pro-	earlier than, in front of	pro + logue: introduction to a literary work
syn-, sym-	with, at the same time	syn + thesize: combine to form a new, complex product

EXERCISE 2 Combining Prefixes and Roots

Write the Latin or Greek prefix that has the same meaning as the underlined word or words. Then write the complete word defined after the equal sign.

EXAMPLE *between* + cede = act as mediator in a dispute
ANSWER inter—intercede

1. two + lingual = using two languages
2. back + active = extending to a prior time or to conditions that existed in the past
3. against + toxin = substance that counteracts poison
4. with + league = associate in a profession
5. opposite of + continue = cease to operate or use
6. not + fallible = not capable of making mistakes
7. before + bellum = existing before a war
8. around + ference = perimeter of a circle

9. excessive + active = excessively energetic
10. after + mortem = occurring after death
11. beside + graph = distinct division in written composition, often shown by indentation
12. again + generate = form or create again
13. across + fuse = cause to pass from one to another
14. down + clysm = momentous event marking demolition
15. remove + moralize = weaken the morale of
16. away + stain = keep oneself away from indulging in
17. under + merge = cover or overflow with water
18. without + morphous = having no definite shape or form
19. beyond + modern = having the very latest ideas, styles, or tendencies; futuristic
20. half + skilled = having less training than skilled labor and more than unskilled labor

Suffixes. There are two kinds of suffixes. One kind, called an inflexional suffix (or grammatical suffix), serves a number of purposes. This suffix changes number in nouns *(computer, computers)*, possession in nouns *(woman, woman's)*, degree of comparison in modifiers *(soft, softer, softest)*, and the form of verbs *(care, cared, caring)*. An inflexional suffix does not change either the essential meaning of the word or its part of speech.

A second kind of suffix is the derivational suffix, which is more important than the inflectional suffix in vocabulary study. The derivational suffix changes the meaning and very often the part of speech of the word to which it is added. Look at the changes that the derivational suffixes make when they are added to the verb *observe*.

WITH NO SUFFIX	*observe:* verb
WITH *-ANCE*	*observance:* noun
WITH *-ABLE*	*observable:* adjective
WITH *-LY*	*observably:* adverb (*-ly* added to the adjective form)

As the previous examples show, some suffixes form nouns, some form adjectives, some form verbs, and some form adverbs. (The only common adverb-forming suffix is *-ly*.) The following chart shows a number of suffixes and the part of speech formed by each.

Suffixes

NOUN SUFFIX	MEANING	EXAMPLE
-ance, -ence	action, process, quality, state	exist + ence: state or fact of being
-ard, -art	one that does to excess	bragg + art: one that boasts excessively
-cy	action, state, quality	normal + cy: state of being average or regular
-dom	state, rank, or condition of	free + dom: state of having liberty or independence
-er, -or	one that is, does, makes, is resident of	retail + er: one who sells directly to consumers
-ion	act, process, result, state	react + ion: act of responding
-ism	act, state, or characteristic of	critic + ism: act of considering merits and demerits
-ity	state, quality, degree	moral + ity: doctrine or system of standard or correct conduct
-ness	state, quality	brisk + ness: state of being keenly alert and lively
-ure	act, process, function	post + ure: position or bearing of the body
-able, -ible	capable of, fit for, tending to	expend + able: capable of being consumed by use
-al	characterized by, relating to	tradition + al: relating to the handing down of customs
-en	belonging to, made of	earth + en: made of soil or clay
-ful	full of, having the qualities of	master + ful: having the power and skill of a qualified worker
-ic	having the character of	hero + ic: being courageous and daring
-ish	characteristic of, inclined to	clown + ish: having characteristics of a clown
-less	not having, unable to act	purpose + less: lacking goals or aims
-ly	like in appearance, manner, or nature	friend + ly: of, relating to, or befitting a friend

-ory	of, relating to, producing	transit + ory: of brief duration
-ous	full of, having the qualities of	clamor + ous: marked by a confused din or outcry
-some	characterized by action or quality	burden + some: characterized by being a heavy load to bear
-ate	act on, cause to become	captiv~~e~~ + ate: influence by special charm
-en	cause to be or have	height + en: cause to have increased amount or degree of
-fy, -ify	make, form into, invest with	spec + ify: make clear and state explicitly
-ize	become like, cause to be	character + ize: cause to be a distinguishing trait of

Notice that some suffixes can be used to make more than one part of speech. The suffix *-en,* for example, appears on both the adjective list and the verb list. The suffix *-ate,* although it is shown only on the verb list, can also form nouns *(candidate, nitrate)* and adjectives *(temperate, proportionate).*

EXERCISE 3 Adding Suffixes to Words

Write the suffix that has the same meaning as the underlined word or words. Then write the complete word defined after the colon. Make spelling changes if necessary.

EXAMPLE *category* + cause to be: classify
ANSWER ize—categorize

1. zeal + full of: full of eagerness and enthusiasm
2. convention + characterized by: relating to established practices or customs
3. survey + doer: one who measures tracts of land
4. complicate + act of: act of making complex or difficult
5. enlight + cause to be: cause to receive knowledge or instruction in something
6. gull + capable of: capable of being easily deceived or cheated
7. serf + state of: state of being in a servile feudal class
8. amalgam + act on: merge into a single body
9. lag + one who does to excess: one who lingers too much
10. flavor + full of: full of pleasant taste

11. tire + <u>characterized by</u>: characterized by the quality of being wearisome and tedious
12. pleasure + <u>capable of</u>: capable of gratifying
13. daunt + <u>not having</u>: not having fear
14. material + <u>cause to be</u>: cause to come into existence or to assume bodily form
15. sheep + <u>characteristic of</u>: resembling a sheep in meekness
16. break + <u>capable of</u>: capable of being cracked or smashed
17. orate + <u>one that does</u>: one who delivers a formal, elaborate speech
18. angel + <u>having the character of</u>: having the goodness of an angel
19. malice + <u>full of</u>: full of spite and ill will
20. bounty + <u>full of</u>: characterized by providing abundantly

Roots. The root of a word—the part that carries the basic meaning—may be well known in English; or it may be less obvious, having come from Latin or Greek. Sometimes a root may stand alone, as in the word *self*. A root may be combined with a prefix (re*tract*), a suffix (*port*able), or even another root *(autograph)*. The following chart contains some of the common Latin and Greek roots that are the basic elements of many English words.

Latin Roots

ROOT	MEANING	EXAMPLES
-aqua-, -aqui-	water	aquarium, aqueous
-aud-	hear	audience, auditorium
-bene-	good, well	benefit, benevolence
-cred-	believe	credential, credit
-cid-	kill	germicidal, insecticide
-fid-	faith, trust	bona fide, infidel
-fract-, -frag-	break	fraction, refract fragile, fragment
-grat-	pleasing, thankful	grateful, gratitude, gratuity
-loqu-	speak	eloquent, loquacious
-mor-, -mort	death	immortal, mortally, mortuary
-omni-	all, every	omniscient, omnivorous

-ped-	foot	pedestrian, centipede
-port-	carry	portable, import
-rupt-	break, burst	rupture, interrupt
-scrib-, -script-	write	describe, prescribe inscription, manuscript
-sequ-	follow	sequel, subsequent
-tort-	twist	distort, tortuous
-tract-	draw, pull	traction, retract
-vert-, -vers-	turn	invert, subvert versatile, reverse
-vic-, -vinc-	conquer	victory, convince, invincible
-viv-, -vit-	life, live	survive, vivacious vitality, vitamin

Greek Roots

ROOT	MEANING	EXAMPLES
-anthrop-	man, human	anthropology, philanthropy
-arch-	rule	monarch, hierarchy
-auto-	self	autograph, automobile
-biblio-	book	bibliography, bibliophile
-bio-, -bi-	life	biology, antibiotic
-chrom-	color	chromatic, monochrome
-cosm-	world, order	cosmic, macrocosm
-geo-	earth, ground	geography, geology
-gram-	drawing, writing	grammatical, program
-graph-	write	graph, typography
-log-, -logy-	speech, reason, study, science	catalog, monologue bacteriology, technology
-micro-	small	microfilm, microwave
-mono-	one, single	monopoly, monograph
-morph-	form	amorphous, metamorphosis
-neo-	new	neon, neoclassical
-path-	suffering	pathetic, apathy
-phon-	sound	phonetic, telephone
-pod-	foot	podiatrist, tripod
-poly-	many	monopoly, polytechnic
-psych-	mind	psychology, psychic
-tele-	far off	telescope, telegraph
-therm-	heat	thermal, thermometer

EXERCISE 4 Recognizing Latin and Greek Roots
Write the root of each of the following words. Then use the charts in this chapter to write a definition for each word. Refer to a dictionary if necessary.

EXAMPLE audible
ANSWER aud—capable of being heard

1. disruption
2. subscription
3. gratify
4. convertible
5. graphic
6. colloquial
7. transport
8. convivial
9. infraction
10. sequential

EXERCISE 5 Using Roots, Prefixes, and Suffixes
Write the letter of the phrase closest in meaning to the word in capital letters. What you have learned in this chapter will help you determine the meaning of each capitalized word.

1. MERITORIOUS (A) without value (B) having worthy qualities (C) state of being wise
2. COMPATIBLE (A) capable of getting along together (B) in the manner of a friend (C) well qualified
3. EMANCIPATE (A) relating to a king (B) cause to become free (C) one who wins great acclaim
4. POLYCHROMATIC (A) the science of color (B) a metal alloy (C) having many colors
5. ILLOGICAL (A) between reason and knowledge (B) within reason (C) not valid, or unskilled in reasoning
6. TRANSITION (A) underground passage (B) process of going across from one place to another (C) loss of credibility
7. BIPED (A) able to walk backward (B) bicycle (C) two-footed animal
8. RETROGRESS (A) lack of progress (B) in need of repairs (C) go backward
9. COMMUNICABLE (A) capable of being transmitted (B) full of information (C) condition of being infected
10. RECOIL (A) jump forward suddenly (B) draw back (C) lose sight of

Synonyms and Antonyms

Another way of expanding your vocabulary is to have a thorough understanding of synonyms and antonyms. A *synonym* is a word that has the same, or nearly the same, meaning as another word. An *antonym* is a word that means the opposite, or nearly the opposite, of another word.

There are often several synonyms for a word. For instance, among the synonyms for the word *candor* are *sincerity* and *forthrightness.* Notice that these words have slightly different shades of meaning. Dictionary entries often explain the slight differences between synonyms. *(See page 345.)*

You have probably used the specialized dictionary for synonyms called a *thesaurus.* Usually a thesaurus is indexed to help users find the synonyms they need. *(See page 359.)*

EXERCISE 6 Recognizing Synonyms

Write the letter of the word or group of words closest in meaning to the word in capital letters. Check your answers in a dictionary.

1. ADAMANT (A) skillful (B) unworthy (C) unyielding (D) distressing (E) faithful
2. INDICT (A) accuse (B) show (C) imprison (D) warn (E) release
3. ULTIMATE (A) preliminary (B) substitute (C) rewarding (D) eventual (E) concealed
4. NOTORIOUS (A) legal (B) fortunate (C) unfavorably known (D) unfamiliar (E) industrious
5. BESTOW (A) discard (B) give (C) restore (D) darken (E) gamble
6. PREDATORY (A) entertaining (B) tragic (C) corrupt (D) preying (E) lackluster
7. LATERAL (A) potential (B) upward (C) sluggish (D) afterward (E) related to the side
8. ARBITRATION (A) authority (B) mystery (C) concern (D) mediation (E) treatment
9. BEGUILE (A) deceive (B) begin (C) explain (D) reject (E) learn
10. ARABLE (A) feathery (B) fashionable (C) tillable (D) windy (E) livable

EXERCISE 7 Recognizing Antonyms
Write the letter of the word most nearly opposite in meaning to the word in capital letters. Check your answers in a dictionary.

1. FEASIBLE (A) faulty (B) impossible (C) impoverished (D) fatigued (E) insecure
2. ACCENTUATE (A) de-emphasize (B) protest (C) regulate (D) disagree (E) relinquish
3. ERRONEOUS (A) mistaken (B) possible (C) skillful (D) tardy (E) correct
4. VULNERABLE (A) unsusceptible (B) cheerful (C) greedy (D) ridiculous (E) modest
5. EMANCIPATE (A) forget (B) strengthen (C) disallow (D) enslave (E) forget
6. CYNICAL (A) soothing (B) stable (C) trustful (D) square (E) charming
7. OBLIQUE (A) brilliant (B) questionable (C) direct (D) passive (E) painful
8. ALLEVIATE (A) forget (B) associate (C) persuade (D) improve (E) aggravate
9. HERETIC (A) villain (B) conformist (C) saint (D) traitor (E) critic
10. EQUILIBRIUM (A) disapproval (B) observation (C) hope (D) imbalance (E) high pitch

WORD ETYMOLOGY

Every word has a history. The *etymology* of a word is the history of that word from its earliest recorded use. Some dictionaries list the meanings of each word in chronological order—that is, with definitions arranged from the earliest recorded meaning to the present meaning. For example, from the Greek word *koronos,* meaning "curved," came the Latin word *corona,* meaning "wreath or crown." That word became the Old French word *corone,* then the Middle English word *coroune* or *crowne*. Eventually, the word took its present form, *crown*. Many dictionaries include brief etymologies. *(See page 343.)*

Tracing Word Histories

This chapter has concentrated on the Latin and Greek elements in English words. However, the English language has roots that go back to a time before Latin and Greek existed.

English—like Latin, Greek, and many other languages—goes back to a parent language called Indo-European. Although Indo-European was an unwritten language, comparative linguists have been able to reconstruct it to some extent. To do so, they have studied relationships such as the following, which show English to be closely connected with Dutch, German, Latin, and Greek.

ENGLISH	brother	GERMAN	bruder	LATIN	frater
DUTCH	broeder	IRISH	brathair	GREEK	phrater

The English that people use today has gone through three principal stages, the first of which began about 1,500 years ago.

Old English (450–1150). This earliest form of English was the language of the three German tribes that invaded England and settled there. These tribes were the Angles, the Saxons, and the Jutes. They seem to have called their language *Englisc* (from *Engle,* "the Angles"). Although the Old English vocabulary was extensive—more than 40,000 words exist in the old documents—only a small fraction of those words have survived. Among them are some of the most common words in the modern English language.

FAMILIAR OBJECTS	horse, cow, meat, stone, earth, home
PARTS OF THE BODY	head, hand, foot, arm, elbow, knee
FAMILY MEMBERS	father, mother, brother, sister, wife
IRREGULAR VERBS	buy, sell, speak, ride, sing, drink, swim
PRONOUNS	I, you, he, she, we, they, who
NUMBERS	one, two, three, four, five, six, seven

Middle English (1150–1500). In 1066, England was invaded by the French from Normandy under William the Conqueror. This invasion, known as the Norman Conquest, had far-reaching effects on the language. For centuries the rulers and the upper classes of England spoke French, although religious and legal documents were still written in Latin. During this Middle English period, Old English, French, and Latin gradually became intermixed. A number of synonyms were contributed from all three languages: *old* from Old English, *ancient* from French, *venerable* from Latin. The richness of our present-day English vocabulary stems in part from its variety of sources.

Modern English (1500 to present). By 1500, the assimilation of the contributing languages was largely complete. William Shakespeare wrote his great works early in the Modern English period. The documents of our American Revolution were written in Modern English. Yet substantial changes have occurred in English between 1500 and the present. Anyone who has struggled with the unfamiliar words and constructions in the works of Shakespeare will observe how much the language has changed, even within this period.

Other cultural groups have contributed words to American English. The various American Indian languages had a significant influence on place names in the United States—*Omaha, Wichita,* and *Niagara,* for example. Some of the other Indian contributions include *succotash, raccoon,* and *opossum.*

As explorers, settlers, and visitors came to this country, they brought their own contributions to the English language. For example, the words *Los Angeles* and *tornado* are Spanish; *bureau* and *prairie* are French; *hamburger* and *noodle* are German; *Brooklyn* and *yacht* are Dutch; and *opera* and *spaghetti* are Italian. This process of borrowing words from other cultures continues, for the English language is always changing.

Words with Unusual Origins

Although many English words come from Old English, French, Latin, Greek, and other languages, some have more unusual origins. The names of characters in literature and mythology and the names of real people, places, and historical events have occasionally become familiar English words. The word *quixotic,* meaning "idealistic to an impractical degree," derives from Don Quixote, hero of the seventeenth-century novel *Don Quixote de la Mancha,* by Cervantes. Some words have their origins in mythology—*cereal,* for example, named for Ceres, the Roman goddess of the harvest and grain. An internal-combustion engine, the *diesel,* is named for its inventor, Rudolf Diesel. The word *cologne,* "perfumed water," is named after a city in West Germany. The word *waterloo,* "decisive defeat," is usually used in the phrase "meet one's waterloo" and derives from the battle that marked Napoleon's defeat in 1815. Following are a few additional examples of words with unusual origins.

WORD	MEANING	ETYMOLOGY
malapropism	humorous misuse of a word	from Mrs. *Malaprop,* a character noted for misusing words in Richard Sheridan's 1775 comedy *The Rivals*
martinet	strict disciplinarian	from Jean *Martinet,* a seventeenth-century French army officer
saga	long, heroic narrative	from the Old Norse word in twelfth- and thirteenth-century Norway and Iceland

EXERCISE 8 Recognizing Etymologies

Write the letter of the phrase that matches the etymology of the numbered word. Check your answers in a dictionary.

1. bunkum	a. cotton cloth; named after city in India
2. calico	b. teaching method used by Greek philosopher and his followers
3. canyon	c. chemical element; named for god in Roman myth
4. lethargic	d. corn and beans; from American Indian word
5. martial	e. insincere talk; named after North Carolina county
6. mercury	f. a comfortable railroad sleeping car; named for its inventor
7. Pullman	g. lazy or indifferent; word based on Greek "river of forgetfulness"
8. Socratic	h. electrical unit; named for Scottish engineer and inventor
9. succotash	i. narrow valley; from Spanish word for "tube"
10. watt	j. warlike; from name of god of war in Roman myth

EXERCISE 9 Exploring Etymologies
Write the letter of the phrase that matches the etymology of the numbered word. Check your answers in a dictionary.

1. crypt	a. expression of great joy; from Latin word meaning "leap up"
2. decrepit	b. underground vault; from Greek word *kryptein,* meaning "hide"
3. enthrall	c. wander aimlessly; from Greek word for the Menderes River in Asia Minor
4. exultation	d. county official; from Old English words *shire* and *reeve*
5. imperative	e. weakened by old age; from Latin word for "crack" or "creak"
6. inquisition	f. hold spellbound; from Old Norse word meaning "person in bondage"
7. meander	g. urgent or obligatory; from Latin word *imperare,* meaning "command"
8. sardonic	h. relating to the senses; from Latin word *sentire,* meaning "perceive" or "feel"
9. sensory	i. investigation or questioning; from Latin word meaning "seek"
10. sheriff	j. scornful or mocking; from Latin word for "bitter herb that distorts the face of the eater"

INCREASING YOUR VOCABULARY

The more you read, the more your vocabulary is likely to expand. In addition, you will find it helpful to increase your word power in a more systematic way. When you come across an unfamiliar word, look it up in a dictionary. Read the definition and check the spelling and the syllabication. Also pay attention to prefixes, suffixes, and roots as well as the etymology of each word. This method can help you understand the meaning, not only of the word you are looking up but also of other words.

If you are serious about adding new words to your vocabulary, you can keep a vocabulary notebook. Jot down new words and their meanings and study this list from time to time. As your list of words grows, so will your vocabulary.

Vocabulary List

The following vocabulary list contains words that you are likely to come across in your reading. Review the words and try to define each one. Check the dictionary if you are unsure of any of the meanings. Enter the words you are unsure of in your vocabulary notebook and review them often.

Vocabulary List

abdicate	credential	inquisition	precedence
aberrant	crypt	intercede	predatory
accentuate	cynical	lateral	prodigy
adamant	dauntless	laxity	prologue
affidavit	decipher	lethargic	recipient
alleviate	decrepit	malapropism	regenerate
amity	ejection	malicious	renown
amorphous	emancipate	meritorious	resolute
arable	epilogue	meticulous	retrospect
arbitration	equilibrium	microcosm	saga
ascertain	erroneous	monologue	sardonic
beguile	exultation	noncommittal	savory
bestow	facsimile	notorious	sensory
captivate	feasible	oblique	sequential
caucus	gaudy	omniscient	statute
cerebral	heretic	orator	symmetry
colloquial	impartial	orthodox	synthesize
compatible	imperative	paraphrase	transition
component	inaccessible	paternal	ultimate
compulsory	inanimate	physiology	vulnerable
conventional	indict	placid	zealous
convivial	infallible	plurality	zenith

CHAPTER REVIEW

A. Write the letter of the word or group of words closest in meaning to the word in capital letters.

1. EMANCIPATE (A) free (B) jeopardize (C) uphold (D) revise (E) penalize
2. ULTIMATE (A) fussy (B) initial (C) hidden (D) eventual (E) amusing

3. ALLEVIATE (A) depart (B) raise (C) undertake (D) relieve (E) assign
4. RECIPIENT (A) receiver (B) improvement (C) appearance (D) revival (E) critic
5. STATUTE (A) equation (B) likeness (C) law (D) prestige (E) stable
6. NONCOMMITTAL (A) trivial (B) disturbed (C) unlikely (D) indefinite (E) unreliable
7. OMNISCIENT (A) impressive (B) sympathetic (C) stylish (D) resentful (E) all-knowing
8. FACSIMILE (A) writing (B) reproduction (C) understanding (D) code (E) reply
9. BEGUILE (A) annoy (B) disappear (C) advance (D) deceive (E) explain
10. LAXITY (A) negligence (B) legality (C) genius (D) insistence (E) worth

B. Write the letter of the word or group of words most nearly opposite in meaning to the word in capital letters.

1. METICULOUS (A) unusual (B) kindly (C) careless (D) violent (E) mischievous
2. IMPERATIVE (A) fading (B) unessential (C) mysterious (D) eminent (E) tactless
3. FEASIBLE (A) casual (B) repeatable (C) impossible (D) praiseworthy (E) sensible
4. MALICIOUS (A) charitable (B) spiteful (C) foul-smelling (D) gaudy (E) lazy
5. CONVENTIONAL (A) extravagant (B) handy (C) talkative (D) invaluable (E) untraditional
6. ADAMANT (A) yielding (B) exciting (C) flavorful (D) reasonable (E) obscure
7. ZEALOUS (A) fertile (B) difficult (C) upset (D) unforgiving (E) unenthusiastic
8. AMITY (A) generosity (B) talent (C) hostility (D) purity (E) coolness
9. INANIMATE (A) leafy (B) forgotten (C) partial (D) foolhardy (E) lively
10. RESOLUTE (A) unfamiliar (B) undecided (C) defensive (D) outdated (E) lethal

14

Spelling

Learning to spell correctly is a lifelong task. Even the best spellers continue to find words that give them difficulty. While there are no magic techniques for improving your spelling, there are some rules to keep in mind. This chapter covers some of the techniques that will help you become a better speller.

SPELLING RULES

Spelling improvement is made easier by a knowledge of spelling rules. Although some spelling rules look complicated, they do not seem as complicated if you study them step by step.

There are three kinds of spelling rules. The first kind applies to spelling patterns, such as those involving the choice between *ie* and *ei*. The second set of rules concerns the formation of plurals. The third set deals with the addition of prefixes and suffixes to roots.

Even though many of the rules have exceptions, you will find that a knowledge of, and an adherence to, the rules will help you in many spelling situations. The rules and their exceptions are well worth mastering.

Spelling Patterns

The best-known rule of spelling is the "*i* before *e*, except after *c*" rule. The second rule, almost as familiar, covers the spelling of the "seed" sound.

Words with *ie* or *ei*. When the sound is long *e* (ē), the spelling is *ie*. After the letter *c*, however, the spelling is *ei*.

Put *i* before *e*:	chief	fierce	piece	relieve
Except after *c*:	ceiling	deceit	perceive	receive

When the sound is long *a* (ā), the spelling is *ei*.

Long *a* sound:	feign	freight	heinous	reign
	rein	sleigh	veil	weight

Although these *ie/ei* rules cover most words, there are a number of exceptions, such as the following words.

ancient	counterfeit	height	seize
conscience	either	leisure	sovereign
efficient	foreign	neither	their
species	sheik	protein	weird

NOTE: These rules do not apply if the *i* and *e* are in different syllables.

be ing	de ice	pi ety	sci ence

Words with the "Seed" Sound. The "seed" sound is spelled three ways: *-sede, -ceed,* and *-cede*. The following points will help you spell correctly the words that end in the "seed" sound.

1. Only one word in English ends in *-sede: supersede.*
2. Only three words end in *-ceed: exceed, proceed,* and *succeed.*
3. All other words that end in the "seed" sound have the ending *-cede*. These words include *accede, concede, precede, recede,* and *secede.*

EXERCISE 1 Using Spelling Patterns
Write each word, adding either *ie* or *ei*.

1. br__f	6. p__ce	11. s__ge	16. dec__ve
2. for__gn	7. l__sure	12. hyg__ne	17. n__ther
3. th__r	8. perc__ve	13. s__zure	18. med__val
4. n__ce	9. w__gh	14. rec__ve	19. rel__ve
5. rec__pt	10. y__ld	15. conc__t	20. counterf__t

EXERCISE 2 Using Spelling Patterns
Write each word, adding *-sede, -ceed,* or *-cede.*

1. re___	3. ex___	5. pro___	7. ac___	9. super___
2. con___	4. inter___	6. se___	8. suc___	10. pre___

Plurals

There are a number of useful rules that will help you spell the plural form of most nouns.

Regular Nouns. To form the plural of most nouns, add *s.*

SINGULAR	geologist	frog	bicycle	rose
PLURAL	geologists	frogs	bicycles	roses

To form the plural of nouns ending in *s, ch, sh, x,* or *z,* add *es.*

SINGULAR	moss	church	dish	tax
PLURAL	mosses	churches	dishes	taxes

Nouns Ending in *y*. Add *s* to form the plural of a noun ending in a vowel and *y.*

SINGULAR	payday	journey	alloy	monkey
PLURAL	paydays	journeys	alloys	monkeys

Change the *y* to *i* and add *es* to a noun ending in a consonant and *y.*

SINGULAR	baby	fallacy	category	sixty
PLURAL	babies	fallacies	categories	sixties

EXERCISE 3 Forming Plurals
Write the plural of each of the following nouns.

1. family	6. fox	11. casualty	16. birthday
2. editor	7. ally	12. bench	17. melody
3. latch	8. phrase	13. caddy	18. sketch
4. thistle	9. hoax	14. railway	19. melee
5. tragedy	10. blueberry	15. grass	20. query

Nouns Ending in *o*. Add *s* to form the plural of a noun ending in a vowel and *o.*

SINGULAR	curio	ratio	stereo	rodeo	cuckoo
PLURAL	curios	ratios	stereos	rodeos	cuckoos

Also add *s* to form the plural of a musical term ending in *o*.

SINGULAR	alto	piano	maestro	trio	piccolo
PLURAL	altos	pianos	maestros	trios	piccolos

Plurals of nouns ending in a consonant and *o* follow no regular pattern. They may end in either *s* or *es*.

SINGULAR	burro	credo	echo	potato	tornado
PLURAL	burros	credos	echoes	potatoes	tornadoes

A number of words ending in a consonant and *o* can form their plural with either *s* or *es*. The plural of *zero*, for example, can be spelled *zeros* or *zeroes*. When you are in doubt about the spelling of a plural, consult the dictionary. *(See page 339.)* If the dictionary shows more than one plural form, use the first form listed. If the dictionary shows no plural form, check to make sure you are looking under the noun entry. Many words can be used as more than one part of speech. If no plural is shown for the word as a noun, simply add *s* or *es*.

Nouns Ending in *f* or *fe*. To form the plural of some nouns ending in *f* or *fe*, simply add *s*.

SINGULAR	chef	staff	roof	safe	fife
PLURAL	chefs	staffs	roofs	safes	fifes

For other nouns, change the *f* to *v* and add *s* or *es*.

SINGULAR	shelf	leaf	hoof	wife	knife
PLURAL	shelves	leaves	hooves	wives	knives

When you are in doubt about how to form the plural of a noun ending in *f* or *fe*, consult the dictionary.

Foreign Plurals. Some foreign words keep their original form.

SINGULAR	alga	alumnus	bacterium	ellipsis
PLURAL	algae	alumni	bacteria	ellipses

The plural form of some Italian musical terms take either the English *s* ending or the original Italian *i* ending. For example, the plural of *concerto* can be *concertos* or *concerti*.

Plurals of Numbers, Letters, Symbols, and Words Used as Words. Add an apostrophe and an *s* to form the plural of numbers, letters, symbols, and words used as words.

NUMBERS	The 7's in this column of figures should be *4*'s.
LETTERS	If *e*'s are closed at the top, they look like *i*'s.
SYMBOLS	Ampersands—that is, *&*'s—are used in some company names.
WORDS AS WORDS	When used, these ampersands replace *and*'s.

EXERCISE 4 Forming Plurals
Write the plural of each of the following nouns. Then check your answers in a dictionary.

1. scenario	6. stereo	11. belief	16. gulf
2. cello	7. hero	12. half	17. proof
3. tomato	8. soprano	13. sheriff	18. self
4. *the*	9. pimiento	14. basis	19. *12*
5. analysis	10. folio	15. alumna	20. chief

Other Plural Forms. A number of familiar nouns form their plural in irregular ways.

SINGULAR	child	man	woman	tooth	foot	mouse
PLURAL	children	men	women	teeth	feet	mice

Some nouns do not change form.

SINGULAR	sheep	moose	corps	scissors	Chinese
PLURAL	sheep	moose	corps	scissors	Chinese

Compound Nouns. The plurals of most compound nouns are formed in the same way that other plural nouns are.

SINGULAR	stepchild	wristwatch	musk-ox
PLURAL	stepchildren	wristwatches	musk-oxen

In hyphenated compounds and in nouns of more than one word, the main word is often made plural.

SINGULAR	mother-in-law	knight-errant	bill of sale
PLURAL	mothers-in-law	knights-errant	bills of sale

EXERCISE 5 Forming Plurals
Write the plural of each of the following nouns.

1. buildup
2. Sioux
3. teaspoonful
4. headquarters
5. rosebush
6. sergeant at arms
7. eyetooth
8. day lily
9. chairperson
10. pliers
11. attorney-at-law
12. Portuguese
13. midwife
14. notary public
15. onlooker

Prefixes and Suffixes

A *prefix* is one or more syllables placed in front of a root to modify the meaning of the root or to form a new word. When you add a prefix, do not change the spelling of the root.

anti + toxin = antitoxin   pre + industrial = preindustrial

By remembering to keep the spelling of the root unchanged, you will be able to spell a number of words that sometimes cause confusion.

co + ordinate = coordinate   pre + exist = preexist

A *suffix* is one or more syllables placed after a root to help shape its meaning. The spelling of the root does not change when the suffixes *-ness* and *-ly* are added.

even + ness = evenness   usual + ly = usually

When you add a suffix other than *-ness* and *-ly,* you may have to change the spelling of the root.

Words Ending in e. Drop the final *e* before adding a suffix that begins with a vowel.

care + ing = caring   note + able = notable

Keep the final *e* before adding a suffix that begins with a consonant.

excite + ment = excitement   tame + ness = tameness

If a word ends in *ce* or *ge* and the suffix begins with *a* or *o,* keep the final *e.*

advantage + ous = advantageous
manage + able = manageable

Following are some exceptions to these rules.

true—truly judge—judgment die—dying

EXERCISE 6 Adding Prefixes and Suffixes
Write each word, adding the prefix or the suffix shown. Remember to make any necessary spelling changes.

1. dis + appear
2. re + enact
3. nerve + ous
4. operate + ion
5. grieve + ous
6. ir + regular
7. use + able
8. im + mobile
9. final + ly
10. true + ly

Words Ending in *y*. When adding a suffix to most words ending in a vowel and *y*, keep the *y*.

display + ing = displaying repay + ment = repayment

For most words ending in a consonant and *y*, change the *y* to *i* before adding a suffix.

ally + ance = alliance merry + ly = merrily

Following are some exceptions to these rules.

SUFFIX BEGINNING WITH *i*	relying	hobbyist	gratifying
ONE-SYLLABLE ROOT WORDS	daily	paid	shyness

Doubling the Final Consonant. Sometimes you double the final consonant when adding a suffix beginning with a vowel. Do so only if the root word has *both* characteristics.

- The word has only one syllable or is stressed on the final syllable.
- The word ends in one consonant preceded by one vowel.

ONE-SYLLABLE WORD	tap + ing tapping	run + er runner	slim + est slimmest
FINAL SYLLABLE STRESSED	defer + al deferral	recur + ence recurrence	upset + ing upsetting

Words Ending in *c*. There is a special rule for words that end in *c* preceded by a single vowel. If the suffix begins with *e* or *i*, do not double the final *c*. Instead, add *k* before the suffix.

picnic, picnicking shellac, shellacked frolic, frolicking

EXERCISE 7 Adding Suffixes
Write each word, adding the suffix shown. Remember to make any necessary spelling changes.

1. lobby + ist
2. offer + ed
3. grace + ous
4. vary + ance
5. imply + ing
6. transmit + al
7. clear + ance
8. regret + able
9. politic + ing
10. bag + age
11. plan + er
12. profit + able
13. apply + ance
14. concur + ent
15. knit + ed
16. amateur + ish
17. deter + ence
18. clamor + ous
19. drift + ing
20. admit + ance

COMMONLY MISSPELLED WORDS

The words on the following list are frequently used but commonly misspelled. Study them carefully.

Spelling Demons

abundance	crystal	mammoth	rendezvous
accessible	curriculum	manageable	requisition
accuracy	descendant	melancholy	sacrifice
aesthetic	dilemma	miscellaneous	schism
allege	dilettante	mosquito	severely
allegiance	exorbitant	mustache	shellacked
ambiguous	extraordinary	naïve	sieve
apparatus	exuberant	obedient	similarity
apparent	financier	obsolete	simultaneous
appetite	finesse	ordinarily	subsidiary
bankruptcy	gauge	overture	succession
behavior	grievous	pantomime	superintendent
bizarre	hypocrisy	parallelism	symmetrical
buoyant	immense	perennial	terrestrial
catastrophe	incessant	phenomenon	testimonial
changeable	initiative	pinnacle	theoretical
chassis	interference	plagiarism	thesaurus
collaborate	leisurely	prestige	thesis
colossal	liaison	prophecy	transcend
competent	license	psychiatrist	unmistakable
convalescent	livelihood	rehearsal	unwieldy
coupon	luscious	relieve	vacillate

CHAPTER REVIEW

Write the letter preceding the misspelled word in each group. Then write the word, spelling it correctly.

1. (A) proceed (B) sharing (C) stereos (D) acurracy (E) rendezvous
2. (A) deceive (B) occurred (C) managable (D) eyeglasses (E) forgettable
3. (A) piece (B) excede (C) feign (D) fifes (E) echoes
4. (A) thesaurus (B) usualy (C) descendant (D) gauge (E) notaries public
5. (A) rarity (B) chefs (C) alloys (D) rein (E) rehersal
6. (A) apparant (B) concede (C) referral (D) patios (E) outrageous
7. (A) releive (B) seize (C) veil (D) wives (E) thesis
8. (A) leisure (B) overrule (C) alumnuses (D) obedient (E) bizarre
9. (A) changeable (B) disimilar (C) loneliness (D) mosquito (E) bushes
10. (A) recurence (B) license (C) overture (D) sieve (E) neither
11. (A) believing (B) sopranos (C) mistatement (D) hooves (E) superintendent
12. (A) rustiest (B) onlookers (C) allegiance (D) accede (E) sacrafice
13. (A) prestige (B) supplier (C) location (D) heinous (E) bill of sales
14. (A) thier (B) alga (C) trios (D) naïve (E) corps
15. (A) incurred (B) soloes (C) fierce (D) steadily (E) unmistakable
16. (A) quotable (B) happiness (C) immense (D) overun (E) roofs
17. (A) obsolete (B) fateful (C) chrystal (D) remittance (E) coupon
18. (A) secede (B) shelves (C) churchs (D) satisfying (E) hypocrisy
19. (A) mammouth (B) freight (C) ordinarily (D) competent (E) fathers-in-law
20. (A) dryness (B) advantageous (C) financier (D) dilemna (E) plentiful

STANDARDIZED TEST

VOCABULARY AND SPELLING

Directions: Decide which underlined word in each sentence is misspelled. On your answer sheet, fill in the circle containing the same letter as your answer. If no word is misspelled, fill in *e*.

SAMPLE The weather was changeable, and our hiking
a
apparatus was unweildy; but we reached the
b **c**
pinnacle by noon. No error
d **e**

ANSWER ⓐ ⓑ ⓒ ⓓ ⓔ

1. Relieved that the rehersal had ended early, Cora enjoyed
a **b**
a leisurely lunch at the Crystal Room. No error
c **d** **e**
2. Ordinarily the financeer did not fear bankruptcy, but the
a **b** **c**
present situation was extraordinary. No error
d **e**
3. Buzzing around the picnickers, the mosquito searched
a
incessantly for luscious, accessable targets. No error
b **c** **d** **e**
4. Apparently Frances and the man with the thick mustache
a **b**
had collaborated on a colossal business deal. No error
c **d** **e**
5. According to Ms. Bigby, the theoretical dilemma arose
a **b**
from the ambiguos nature of the thesis. No error
c **d** **e**
6. She alledged that the witness had vacillated and that the
a **b**
accuracy of his testimony was doubtful. No error
c **d** **e**
7. Their arrivals were simultaneous; the exuberant friends had
a **b**
a rendezvous at the immence terminal. No error
c **d** **e**
8. As the overture was played, three dancers, in succession,
a **b**
acted out the prophecy in pantomine. No error
c **d** **e**

9. Judged competent (a) by everyone, Lee took the initiative (b) and acted as liason (c) without any interference (d). No error (e)

10. The similarity (a) in behavior (b) of the two buoyant (c) children was unmistakeable (d). No error (e)

Directions: Choose the word that is most nearly *opposite* in meaning to the word in capital letters. Fill in the circle containing the same letter as your answer.

SAMPLE COMPULSORY (a) illegal (b) voluntary (c) required (d) legal (e) unfair

ANSWER ⓐ ⓑ ⓒ ⓓ ⓔ

11. ALLEVIATE (a) worsen (b) approve (c) disapprove (d) improve (e) raise
12. NONCOMMITTAL (a) notorious (b) definite (c) indefinite (d) unfamiliar (e) known
13. EMANCIPATE (a) punish (b) enslave (c) disappear (d) appear (e) free
14. BESTOW (a) accuse (b) suffer (c) give (d) enjoy (e) receive
15. SAVORY (a) preventive (b) damaging (c) unappetizing (d) failing (e) appetizing
16. ORTHODOX (a) modern (b) illegal (c) unpopular (d) legal (e) untraditional
17. RECIPIENT (a) leader (b) instructor (c) giver (d) believer (e) receiver
18. ABERRANT (a) implied (b) stated (c) unusual (d) normal (e) innocent
19. IMPARTIAL (a) biased (b) unrewarding (c) satisfying (d) unerring (e) sure
20. LAXITY (a) laziness (b) hysteria (c) certainty (d) carefulness (e) negligence

Unit 5

Reference Skills

15

The Dictionary

Whether you are studying George Orwell's novel *1984* or developing a character analysis of the key figure in Shakespeare's *Hamlet,* the dictionary is a valuable resource tool. As you read, the dictionary can help define unfamiliar words. As you write, it can help you make accurate word choices. Today there are many different kinds of dictionaries. Whatever your purpose, there is a dictionary available to help you find the information you need.

KINDS OF DICTIONARIES

The most widely used dictionaries are general dictionaries. These contain many different kinds of information, including abbreviations, names, places, and technical words. General dictionaries are classified according to their size. The largest are the *unabridged,* or unshortened, dictionaries, which contain more than half a million words. Unabridged dictionaries usually sit open on a dictionary stand or table in the reference room of the library. These dictionaries provide longer definitions and more complete information than do smaller dictionaries. Following are several of the best-known unabridged dictionaries.

UNABRIDGED DICTIONARIES

Oxford English Dictionary

Random House Dictionary of the English Language, Unabridged Edition

Webster's Third New International Dictionary of the English Language

The organization of the *Oxford English Dictionary* is different from that of the other unabridged dictionaries listed above. This dictionary, commonly referred to as the O.E.D., is a historical dictionary. Its contents fill twelve volumes. Although the entries are arranged alphabetically, the meanings of each word are organized by dates. This arrangement allows the reader to see when a word was introduced into the English language and how it was first used. This dictionary also helps the reader to see how the definition and use of some words have changed over the years.

Abridged, or shortened, dictionaries are called *college* or *school* dictionaries. They contain fewer words than unabridged dictionaries, and their definitions are usually shorter and more concise. They are also much more convenient and easier to handle. These dictionaries contain most of the words you will encounter in your everyday reading and conversation. The following list shows some of the most popular shortened dictionaries classified by size.

COLLEGE DICTIONARIES

American Heritage Dictionary of the English Language

Random House College Dictionary

Webster's New Collegiate Dictionary

Webster's New World Dictionary, Second College Edition

SCHOOL DICTIONARIES

The Macmillan Dictionary

Scott, Foresman Advanced Dictionary

Webster's New World Dictionary, Student's Edition

Compare the following entries. The first is from an abridged dictionary. The second is from an unabridged dictionary. Notice that each entry includes the same main parts but that the unabridged version is more thorough.

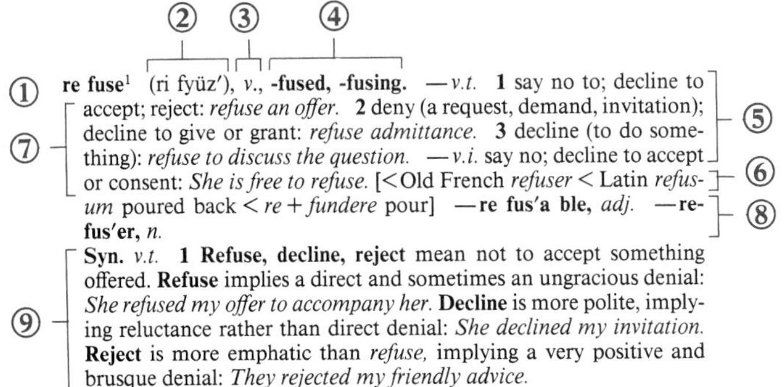

re fuse[1] (ri fyüz′), *v.*, **-fused, -fusing.** —*v.t.* **1** say no to; decline to accept; reject: *refuse an offer.* **2** deny (a request, demand, invitation); decline to give or grant: *refuse admittance.* **3** decline (to do something): *refuse to discuss the question.* —*v.i.* say no; decline to accept or consent: *She is free to refuse.* [<Old French *refuser* < Latin *refusum* poured back < *re* + *fundere* pour] —**re fus′a ble,** *adj.* —**re-fus′er,** *n.*

Syn. *v.t.* **1 Refuse, decline, reject** mean not to accept something offered. **Refuse** implies a direct and sometimes an ungracious denial: *She refused my offer to accompany her.* **Decline** is more polite, implying reluctance rather than direct denial: *She declined my invitation.* **Reject** is more emphatic than *refuse,* implying a very positive and brusque denial: *They rejected my friendly advice.*

From SCOTT, FORESMAN ADVANCED DICTIONARY by E. L. Thorndike and Clarence L. Barnhart. Copyright © 1983, 1979, 1974 by Scott, Foresman & Co. Reprinted by permission.

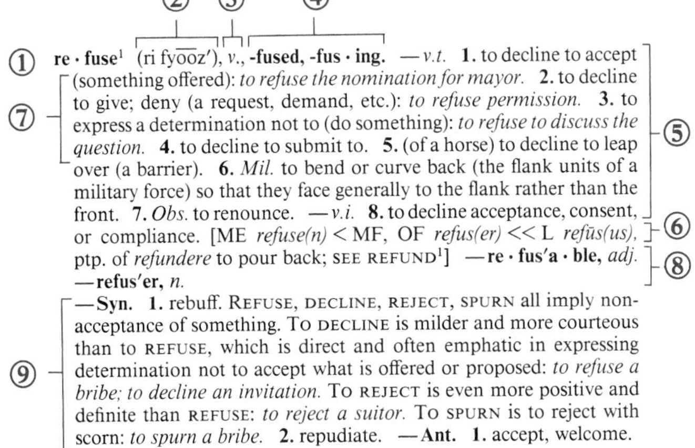

re · fuse[1] (ri fyōōz′), *v.*, **-fused, -fus · ing.** —*v.t.* **1.** to decline to accept (something offered): *to refuse the nomination for mayor.* **2.** to decline to give; deny (a request, demand, etc.): *to refuse permission.* **3.** to express a determination not to (do something): *to refuse to discuss the question.* **4.** to decline to submit to. **5.** (of a horse) to decline to leap over (a barrier). **6.** *Mil.* to bend or curve back (the flank units of a military force) so that they face generally to the flank rather than the front. **7.** *Obs.* to renounce. —*v.i.* **8.** to decline acceptance, consent, or compliance. [ME *refuse(n)* < MF, OF *refus(er)* << L *refūs(us),* ptp. of *refundere* to pour back; SEE REFUND[1]] —**re · fus′a · ble,** *adj.* —**refus′er,** *n.*

—**Syn. 1.** rebuff. REFUSE, DECLINE, REJECT, SPURN all imply nonacceptance of something. To DECLINE is milder and more courteous than to REFUSE, which is direct and often emphatic in expressing determination not to accept what is offered or proposed: *to refuse a bribe; to decline an invitation.* To REJECT is even more positive and definite than REFUSE: *to reject a suitor.* To SPURN is to reject with scorn: *to spurn a bribe.* **2.** repudiate. —**Ant. 1.** accept, welcome.

From *The Random House Dictionary of the English Language,* published by Random House, Inc., copyright © 1967, 1966 by Random House, Inc. Reprinted by permission of the publisher.

1 word shown in syllables
2 pronunciation
3 part of speech
4 inflected forms
5 definitions
6 etymology
7 word used in a phrase or sentence
8 derived words
9 synonyms and antonyms

INFORMATION IN A DICTIONARY

The largest part of any dictionary is the main alphabetical listing of words. In addition to this list of entries, most dictionaries also include some special entries. The placement of these special entries varies from dictionary to dictionary. Learning the content and arrangement of one particular dictionary will help you use it efficiently.

Special Sections

At the beginning of each dictionary is a collection of information called *front matter.* Front matter consists of charts, tables, and short articles that explain the dictionary's system of organization, the symbols it uses, and how the English language developed through history. A complete pronunciation key and a list of abbreviations are also provided.

Special entries, such as biographical and geographical names, foreign words and phrases, and abbreviations may also be placed in separate sections. To find where these unusual entries are located, check the dictionary's contents page or index.

Entries Often Placed in Special Sections

Type of Entry	Example
abbreviations and acronyms	etc., GNP, S.A.T. radar
biographical names	George Orwell, Kurt Vonnegut
charts, tables	periodic table of elements
colleges, universities	Iona College, Drew University
foreign phrases	*errare humanum est*
geographical names	Zaire, Glacier Bay
new words	Pascal, floppy disk
signs, symbols	⊥ perpendicular, π pi
style	manuscript form

EXERCISE 1 Learning about Your Dictionary
Write the title of the dictionary you use most often. Then tell where each of the following is located by writing *front, back,* or *main alphabetical listing.*

1. list of abbreviations used in the dictionary
2. geographical names
3. proofreader's symbols
4. metric system table
5. information on the history of the English language
6. biographical names
7. foreign words and phrases
8. symbols used in mathematics
9. the parts of a dictionary entry
10. complete pronunciation key

EXERCISE 2 Using Your Dictionary
Use a dictionary to answer the following questions.

1. What does the abbreviation *ENE* stand for?
2. What four words are represented in the word *COBOL?*
3. Who is Andrew Wyeth?
4. Approximately how many miles would you run in a ten-kilometer road race? (Hint: Find the table of weights and measures.)
5. To which European country do the Canary Islands belong?
6. Between what two states along the Colorado River was the Hoover Dam built?
7. What is a quahog?
8. What is the definition of the combining form *geo-?*
9. When was the Bronze Age?
10. What does *noblesse oblige* mean?
11. Where is Mount Kilimanjaro?
12. What is the definition of the prefix *syn-?*
13. What was Excalibur?
14. What does the abbreviation *S.P.C.A.* stand for?
15. What is the meaning of the phrase *en famille?*
16. What is a regatta?
17. What is the Richter scale used to measure?
18. What is a billet-doux?
19. What is the atomic number of the element chlorine?
20. What are the names of the five Great Lakes?

Information in an Entry

All words listed in a dictionary are called *entry words.* Entry words are printed in heavy type and are broken into syllables to show how the word divides. In addition to the entry word itself, the dictionary includes the word's part of speech, other forms of the word, the meaning of the word, the word's history, and often synonyms and antonyms. All of this information about each word is called a *main entry.*

Most entry words are single words. Some, however, are parts of words, abbreviations, or compound words. Whatever their type, entry words are listed in strict letter-by-letter alphabetical order. The following list shows different types of entry words in the order they would appear in a dictionary.

Entries Placed in the Main Listing

Single word	mercy
Suffix	-mere
Prefix	meso-
Compound word	mess kit
Abbreviation	Messrs.

Preferred and Variant Spellings. Some words have more than one correct spelling. The spelling most commonly used, called the *preferred spelling,* is usually listed first. Less common spellings, called *variants,* follow the preferred spelling.

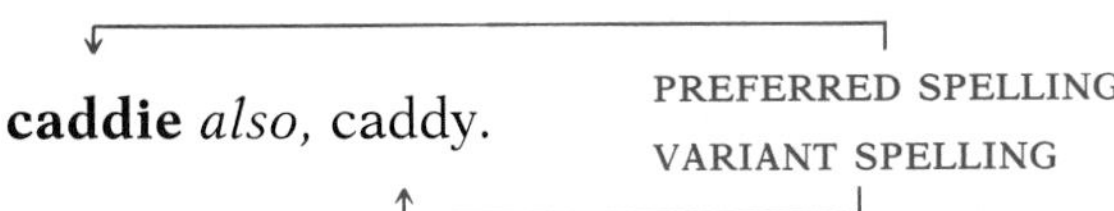

Sometimes a variant spelling will be listed separately. The entry for it, however, will not include a full definition. Instead it will refer the reader to the preferred spelling for the complete information about the word. Use the preferred spelling of words in your writing.

EXERCISE 3 Finding Preferred Spellings
Find each of these variant spellings in a dictionary. Then write the preferred spelling for each word.

EXAMPLE disc
ANSWER disk

1. pilaff
2. cooky
3. aeon
4. sulphur
5. briquet
6. cony
7. chlorophyl
8. adze
9. dialog
10. abridgement

Dividing Words into Syllables. Sometimes when you write a composition, you may need to divide a word with a hyphen. *(See pages 289–290.)* The dictionary shows the correct division of syllables for each entry word.

re · sus · ci · tate **ret · i · cence** **re · vers · i · ble**

EXERCISE 4 Dividing Words into Syllables
Find each word in a dictionary. Then write the word, placing a small dot between each syllable.

EXAMPLE corporeal
ANSWER cor · po · re · al

1. bourgeoisie
2. calypso
3. desperation
4. despond
5. epistle
6. geotropic
7. geotropism
8. Liechtenstein
9. piranha
10. superfluity

Pronunciation. Following the entry word is the phonetic spelling of the word, which shows how the word is pronounced.

in · au · gu · rate (in ȯ′ gyə rāt′)

A chart at the front of the dictionary contains a complete list of symbols used in the phonetic spellings. Most dictionaries also show a partial pronunciation key on the pages of the dictionary itself.

\ə\abut \ᵊ\kitten, F table \ər\further \a\ash \ā\ace \ä\cot, cart \au̇\out \ch\chin \e\bet \ē\easy \g\go \i\hit \ī\ice \j\job \ŋ\sing \ō\go \ȯ\law \ȯi\boy \th\thin \th\the \ü\loot \u̇\foot \y\yet \zh\vision \à, k̲, ⁿ, œ, œ̄, ue, ue̅, ʸ\ *see* Guide to Pronunciation

To find out how to pronounce the vowel sound in the second syllable of *inaugurate,* find the symbol *ȯ* in the key. You can see that it is pronounced like the *aw* in the word *law.*

To distinguish one vowel sound from another, dictionaries use diacritical marks above the vowels. *Webster's Ninth New Collegiate Dictionary* shows two different ways to pronounce the letter *o.*

ō as in g**o** ȯ as in l**aw** DIACRITICAL MARKS

All vowels can sometimes be pronounced *uh.* This sound is represented by a symbol called the *schwa.* In the word *inaugurate,* the third syllable contains the schwa sound.

in ȯ′ gyə rāt′ SCHWA

Phonetic spellings also show which syllables are stressed. A heavy accent mark, called a *primary stress,* shows which syllable receives the most emphasis. A *secondary stress* is marked with a lighter accent.

in ȯ′ gyə rāt′ PRIMARY STRESS SECONDARY STRESS

Some words can be pronounced more than one way. The dictionary will show each pronunciation. The first one shown, however, is the more common. In some dictionaries only those parts of an alternate pronunciation that differ will be given.

ALTERNATE PRONUNCIATIONS

ro · deo (rō′dē ō′, rō dā′ ō)
en · ve · lope (en′və lop, än′—)

Phonetic symbols and the placement of accent marks differ from dictionary to dictionary. Check the front of your dictionary to learn the symbols used in pronunciation.

EXERCISE 5 Using a Pronunciation Key

Using the following partial pronunciation key, write the word that each phonetic spelling represents.

a hat	**i** it	**oi** oil	**ch** child		a in about
ā age	**ī** ice	**ou** out	**ng** long		e in taken
ä far	**o** hot	**u** cup	**sh** she	ə =	i in pencil
e let	**ō** open	**u̇** put	**th** thin		o in lemon
ē equal	**ô** order	**ü** rule	**ᴛʜ** then		u in circus
ėr term			**zh** measure	< = derived from	

1. fyü′ dl iz′əm — a. phenomenon
2. ter′ə dak′ təl — b. Pythagoras
3. süd′ən im — c. pterodactyl
4. sib′ə lənt — d. psychology
5. fus′ chən — e. pseudonym
6. fə nom′ə non — f. feudalism
7. sing′ krə nīz — g. fusion
8. fyü′ zhən — h. fustian
9. sī kol′ə jē — i. sibilant
10. pə thag′ər əs — j. synchronize

Part of Speech Labels. Following the phonetic spelling of an entry word is an abbreviation that indicates the word's part of speech. If the word can be used as more than one part of speech, its most common usage will usually be listed first.

sharp (shärp) *adj.* **sharper, sharpest. 1.** Having a thin, keen edge or a fine, acute point; suitable for or capable of cutting or piercing: *a sharp knife.* **2.** Having an acute edge or point; not rounded or blunt; peaked: *a sharp nose.* **3.** Abrupt or acute; not gradual; sudden. **4.** Clear or marked; distinct. **5.** Shrewd; astute. **6.** Artful; underhand. **7.** Vigilant; alert. **8.** Brisk; ardent; vigorous. **9.** Harsh; biting; acrimonious. **10.** Fierce or impetuous; violent. **11.** Intense; severe. **12.** Sudden and shrill. **13.** Composed of hard, angular particles: *sharp sand.* **14.** *Music.* **a.** Raised in pitch by a semitone. **b.** Above the proper pitch. **c.** Having the key signature in sharps. Compare **flat. 15.** *Phonetics.* Voiceless. Said of a consonant. **16.** *Slang.* Pleasing in appearance or personality; attractive or stylish; *a sharp jacket.* —*adv.* **1.** In a sharp manner. **2.** Punctually; exactly. **3.** *Music.* Above the true or proper pitch. —*n.* **1. a.** A musical note or tone raised one semitone above its normal pitch. **b.** A sign (#) indicating this. Compare **flat. 2.** A slender sewing needle with a very fine point. **3.** *Informal.* A shrewd cheater; a sharper. —*v.* **sharped, sharping, sharps.** *Music.* —*tr.* To raise in pitch by a half step. —*intr.* To sound above the proper pitch. [Middle English *s(c)harp,* Old English *scearp.* See **sker-**[1] in Appendix.*] —**sharp′ly** *adv.* —**sharp′ness** *n.*

ADJECTIVE
ADVERB
NOUN
VERB

Inflected Forms and Derived Words. Inflections are endings that change the form of the word but not its part of speech. Verbs, for example, can be inflected with the endings *-ed* or *-ing* to show a change from one principal part to another. Adjectives can be inflected with *-er* or *-est* to show degrees of comparison. Nouns can be inflected by adding *-s* or *-es* to make them plural. Most dictionaries show the inflected forms only when they are formed irregularly.

Derived words are also formed by adding endings, but in such cases the word's part of speech also changes. For example, adding the suffix *-ly* turns the adjective *hungry* into the adverb *hungrily*.

juic · y (jo͞o′sē) **juic · i · er, juic · i · est.** *adj.* **1.** having much juice; succulent: *a juicy orange.* **2.** full of interest; colorful; lively: *some juicy gossip.* **—juic′i · ly,** *adv.* **—juic′i · ness,** *n.*

INFLECTED FORMS

DERIVED WORDS

Etymologies. The etymology of a word is an explanation of its origin and history. Dictionaries use symbols and abbreviations to explain the source of each word. In an etymology the most recent source word is listed first. The symbols often stand for such phrases as "derived from" (<) or "equivalent to" (=). The abbreviations stand for the languages from which the word is derived. A chart at the beginning of the dictionary lists all the symbols and abbreviations needed to understand a word's etymology.

pre · am · ble (prē′ăm′bəl) *n.* **1.** A preliminary statement; especially, the introduction to a formal document, explaining its purpose. **2.** An introductory occurrence or fact; preliminary. [Middle English, from Old French *preambule,* from Medieval Latin *praeambulum,* from Late Latin *praeambulus,* walking in front: *prae,* in front + *ambulāre,* to walk] **—pre · am′bu · lar′y** *adj.*

ETYMOLOGY

The etymology for *preamble* can be translated as follows: The word *preamble* comes from the Middle English, which came from the Old French *preambule. Preambule* came from the Medieval Latin word *praeambulum,* which was taken from the Late Latin word *praeambulus,* which meant "walking in front." *Praeambulus* was from the Latin prefix *prae* meaning "in front" and *ambulare,* meaning "to walk."

EXERCISE 6 Tracing Word Origins
Use a dictionary to discover the etymology of each of the following words. Then choose five etymologies and write their translations. Use the example of the translation for *preamble* on page 343 as a model.

1. bellicose
2. chromosome
3. forceps
4. geranium
5. guitar
6. hominy
7. menace
8. nightmare
9. philodendron
10. verdict

Multiple Meanings. Many words have more than one meaning. Dictionaries will usually list the most common meaning first. Dictionaries use labels to indicate these differences in meaning. These are called *restrictive labels,* since they restrict the meaning of a word to a certain geographic area, a certain subject area, or a certain level of usage. Some dictionaries, like the *Oxford English Dictionary,* list word meanings in historical order. *(See page 335.)* Read the entry for *honor* below and notice the various meanings.

hon · or (ŏn′ər) *n.* Also *chiefly British* **hon · our. 1.** Esteem; respect; reverence: *the honor shown to him.* **2. a.** Reputation; good name. **b.** Credit: *It was to his honor that he refused the award.* **3. a.** Glory; fame; distinction. **b.** A mark, token, or gesture of respect or distinction: *the place of honor at the table.* **c.** A decoration, as the Navy Cross. **d.** A title conferred for achievement, as a knighthood. **4.** Nobility of mind; probity; integrity. **5.** High rank. **6. a.** The dignity accorded to position: *He is awed by the honor of his office.* **b.** One that imparts distinction by association: *He is an honor to our organization.* **7.** Great privilege: *I have the honor to present the governor.* **8.** *Capital* H. A title of address often accorded to mayors and judges. Preceded by *Your, His,* or *Her.* **9. a.** A code of principally male dignity, integrity, and pride, maintained in some societies, as in feudal Europe, by force of arms. **b.** Personal integrity maintained without legal or other obligation. **c.** A woman's chastity; a reputation for chastity. **10.** *Plural.* Courtesies offered to guests. **11.** *Plural.* **a.** Special recognition for unusual academic achievement: *graduate with honors.* **b.** A program of individual advanced study for exceptional students: *Four students are in honors this year.* **12.** *Golf.* The right of being first at the tee. **13.** *Plural. Card Games.* The four or five highest cards in trump or in all suits. —See Synonyms at **honesty.** —**do the honors.** To perform the social courtesies required of a host. —**on** (or **upon**) **one's honor.** With one's good name as a pledge. —*tr.v.* **honored, -oring, -ors.** Also *chiefly British* **hon · our. 1. a.** To esteem; hold in respect. **b.** To show respect for. **2.** To confer distinction upon: *The ambassador honored us with his presence.* **3.** To accept or pay as valid (a credit card or check, for example). [Middle English *hono(u)r,* from Old French *honor,* from Latin *honor, honōs*† (stem *honōr-*).] —**hon′or · er** *n.*

USAGE LABEL (8. *Capital*)
USAGE LABEL (10. *Plural.*, 11. *Plural.*)
SUBJECT LABEL (12. *Golf.*, 13. *Plural. Card Games.*)
IDIOMS (do the honors; on (or upon) one's honor)

Meanings of a word also vary if the word is used in an idiom. An *idiom* is an expression such as *do the honors* in the entry on page 344. The literal meaning of the individual words does not always match the meaning of the phrase.

Synonyms and Antonyms. The last part of an entry is often a list of synonyms (words with similar meanings) and antonyms (words with opposite meanings). Synonyms are listed more frequently than antonyms.

EXERCISE 7 Recognizing Multiple Meanings

Use the following entry for *quarter* to write the definition that suits the use of the underscored word in each sentence below.

quar ter (kwôr′tər), *n.* **1** one of four equal or corresponding parts into which a thing may be, or is, divided; half of a half; one fourth. **2** a copper and nickel coin of the United States and Canada, worth 25 cents. Four quarters make one dollar. **3** one of four equal periods of play in football, basketball, soccer, etc. **4** one fourth of a year; 3 months: *Many savings banks pay interest every quarter.* **5** one fourth of a school year. **6** one of the four periods of the moon, lasting about 7 days each. **7** one fourth of an hour; 15 minutes. **8** one fourth of a yard; 9 inches. **9** section; district: *the French quarter.* **10 at close quarters,** very close together; almost touching. **11 quarters,** *pl.* **a** place to live or stay. **b** positions or stations assigned to members of a ship's company, as for battle, drill, alerts, etc.: *a call to quarters.* **12** the part of a ship's side near the stern.
—*v.t.* **1** divide into quarters. **2** divide into parts: *quarter a chicken for frying.* **3** give a place to live in; station; lodge.
—*adj.* being one of four equal parts; being equal to only about one fourth of full measure.
[< Old French *quartier* < Latin *quartarius* a fourth < *quartus* fourth]
—**quart′er er,** *n.*

EXAMPLE In the last quarter of the game, the team came from behind and won.

ANSWER *n.*, 3. one of four equal periods of play in football, basketball, soccer, etc.

1. My favorite restaurant is in the Italian quarter.
2. Would you lend me a quarter?
3. Since I did well on the physics exam, my grade this quarter should be a B+.
4. We are going to quarter our friends' Great Dane, Hamlet, for two weeks this summer.
5. Business was brisk in the first quarter.

CHAPTER REVIEW

Using the entries on page 347, answer the following questions.

1. What is the variant spelling of *epilogue?*
2. What parts of speech can the word *epidemic* be used as?
3. What is a translation for the etymology of *epidemic?*
4. What syllable receives a secondary stress in the word *epidemiology?*
5. How many schwas are in the phonetic spelling of the word *epidemiology?*
6. Under what word would you find the complete definition for *epinephrine?*
7. What words are derived from *epic?*
8. What are the inflected forms of the word *epitomize?*
9. When would the word *epiphany* be capitalized?
10. What is the meaning of the prefix *epi-?*
11. What are three synonyms for the word *epigram?*
12. When did Epicurus die?
13. What were the teachings of Epicurus?
14. What do the letters *EPA* stand for?
15. Where is the *epiglottis?*
16. What is the meaning of the Latin phrase *e pluribus unum?*
17. *E pluribus unum* was the motto of the United States until 1956. What is the current motto of the United States?
18. What definition of the word *episode* suits its meaning in the following sentence?
    My favorite part of the movie was the <u>episode</u> in the lunar spacecraft.
19. Where is an epitaph usually written?
20. What are two examples of an epic?

EPA, Environmental Protection Agency.

epi-, *prefix.* on; upon; above; among: *Epicalyx = on the calyx. Epidermis = upon or above the dermis.* [< Greek *epi*]

ep ic (ep′ik), *n.* **1** a long narrative poem that tells the adventures and achievements of one or more great heroes, written in a dignified, majestic style, and often giving expression to the ideals of a nation or race. The *Odyssey* and *Beowulf* are epics. **2** a long novel, etc., having the qualities of an epic. **3** story or series of events worthy of being the subject of an epic. —*adj.* **1** of an epic. **2** majestic in style; heroic: *epic deeds.* [<Latin *epicus* < Greek *epikos* < *epos* story, word] —**ep′i cal,** *adj.* —**ep′ic like′,** *adj.*

Ep i cur us (ep′ə kyůr′əs), *n.* 342?-270 B.C., Greek philosopher who taught that pleasure is the highest good, but that true pleasure depends on self-control, moderation, and honorable behavior.

ep i dem ic (ep′ə dem′ik), *n.* **1** the rapid spread of a disease so that many people have it at the same time: *a flu epidemic.* **2** the rapid spread of an idea, fashion, etc. —*adj.* affecting many people at the same time; widespread: *an epidemic disease.* [<Greek *epidēmia* a stay, visit, prevalence (of a disease) < *epi-* among + *dēmos* people] —**ep′i dem′i cal,** *adj.* —**ep′i dem′i cal ly,** *adv.*

ep i de mi ol o gy (ep′ə dē′mē ol′ə jē), *n.* branch of medicine dealing with the causes, distribution, and control of the spread of diseases in a community.

ep i glot tis (ep′ə glot′is), *n.* a thin, triangular plate of cartilage that covers the entrance to the windpipe during swallowing, so that food and drink do not get into the lungs.

ep i gram (ep′ə gram), *n.* **1** a short, pointed or witty saying. EXAMPLE: "Speech is silver, but silence is golden." See synonym study below. **2** a short poem ending in a witty or clever, and often satirical, turn of thought. EXAMPLE:

"Here lies our Sovereign Lord the King,
Whose word no man relies on,
Who never said a foolish thing,
Nor ever did a wise one."

[<Greek *epigramma* < *epigraphein* inscribe < *epi-* on + *graphein* write]

Syn. *n.* **1 Epigram, paradox, aphorism, proverb** are all short, thoughtful sayings. An **epigram** is usually witty: *Some people know the cost of everything, but the value of nothing.* A special type of epigram is the **paradox,** which makes a statement that, as it stands, contradicts fact or common sense or itself, and yet suggests a truth or at least a half truth: *All generalizations are false, including this one.* Closely related to the epigram is the **aphorism,** which is likely to be abstract and not necessarily witty: *Fools rush in where angels fear to tread.* A **proverb** is likely to make an observation on character or conduct and is the often-quoted, concrete expression of popular wisdom: *Still waters run deep.*

ep i logue or **ep i log** (ep′ə lôg, ep′ə log), *n.* **1** a concluding section added to a novel, poem, etc., that rounds out or interprets the work. **2** speech or poem, addressed to the audience by one of the actors at the end of a play. **3** any concluding act or event. [<Greek *epilogos,* ultimately < *epi-* above + *legein* speak]

ep i neph rine (ep′ə nef′rən, ep′ə nef′rēn′), *n.* adrenalin. [<*epi-* + Greek *nephros* kidney]

e piph a ny (i pif′ə nē), *n.* **1 Epiphany,** January 6, the Christian festival commemorating the coming of the Magi to honor the infant Jesus at Bethlehem. **2** the appearance or manifestation of a divine being. **3** a moment of enlightenment when the underlying truth or essence of a thing is suddenly made clear. [<Late Latin *epiphania,* ultimately < Greek *epi-* + *phainein* to show]

ep i sode (ep′ə sōd), *n.* **1** an outstanding incident or experience in a person's life, in the history of a country, the world, an institution, etc. **2** an incidental set of events or actions separate from, but essential to, the main plot of a novel, story, etc. **3** (in music) a passage separated from and in contrast to the principal themes, especially in a sonata or fugue. [<Greek *epeisodion,* literally, accidental, coming in besides < *epi-* besides, on + *eis* in, into + *hodos* way]

ep i taph (ep′ə taf), *n.* a short statement in memory of a dead person, usually put on a gravestone or tombstone. [<Greek *epitaphion* funeral oration < *epi-* upon + *taphos* tomb]

e pit o mize (i pit′ə mīz), *v.t.,* **-mized, -mizing.** **1** give an epitome of; summarize. **2** be typical or representative of: *Helen Keller epitomizes the human ability to overcome handicaps.* —**e pit′o mi za′tion,** *n.* —**e pit′o miz′er,** *n.*

e plu ri bus u num (ē plůr′ə bəs yü′nəm), LATIN. out of many, one. It is the motto inscribed on the official seal of the United States. It was once the official motto of the United States, but since 1956 the official motto has been "In God We Trust."

16
The Library

The library is an unequaled resource for information and ideas. Books, magazines, newspapers, and pamphlets contain information on thousands of subjects. Most libraries also provide nonprint materials such as records, films, videotapes, and computer software. Understanding the library's arrangement and the wide variety of sources available will help you efficiently locate the materials you need.

LIBRARY ARRANGEMENT

The thousands of books and other materials in a library are classified so they are easy to locate. For many years the most popular system of organizing books was the Dewey decimal system, developed by American librarian Melvil Dewey in the 1870s. As library collections grew to include more than 30,000 titles, another system became necessary. The Library of Congress developed a system that can classify *millions* of books. Although the Dewey decimal system is still widely used today, most large libraries, such as those at colleges and universities, use the Library of Congress system.

The Dewey Decimal Classification System

Most school and local libraries use the Dewey decimal system. In this system works of fiction are kept separate from nonfiction works.

Fiction. Works of fiction are arranged alphabetically by the author's last name. When searching for a work of fiction, remember the following guidelines for alphabetizing.

- Two-part names are alphabetized by the first part of the name. (**De** Soto, **O'**Connor)
- Names beginning with *Mc* and *St.* are alphabetized as if they began with *Mac* and *Saint.*
- Books by authors with the same last name are alphabetized by the author's first name.
- Books by the same author are alphabetized by title, skipping *a, an,* and *the.*
- Numbers in titles are alphabetized as if they were written out. (40,000 = forty thousand)

Nonfiction. Nonfiction works in the Dewey decimal system are assigned a number according to their subject.

Main Subject Areas in the Dewey Decimal System

000–099	General Works (reference works)
100–199	Philosophy
200–299	Religion
300–399	Social Sciences (law, education, economics)
400–499	Language
500–599	Science (mathematics, biology, chemistry)
600–699	Technology (engineering, medicine)
700–799	Fine Arts (painting, music, theater)
800–899	Literature
900–999	History (biography, geography, travel)

For each main subject area, there are ten smaller divisions. The following subdivisions show how the main subject *Language* is classified by number.

400–499 Language	
400–409	Philosophy and Theory
410–419	Linguistics
420–429	English and Anglo-Saxon
430–439	Germanic languages
440–449	Romance languages
450–459	Italian, Romanian, and Swiss languages
460–469	Spanish and Portuguese
470–479	Italic languages (mainly Latin)
480–489	Hellenic languages (mainly Greek)
490–499	Other languages

The subdivisions are divided further with the use of decimal points and other identifying symbols. The shelves are also marked with numbers so that books can be easily located.

EXERCISE 1 Finding Fiction

Number your paper 1 to 10. List the following fiction books in the order in which you would find them on the shelves.

A Member of the Wedding by Carson McCullers
Frankenstein by Mary Shelley
The Money Stones by Ian St. James
The Last Crusader by Louis De Wohl
Mountain Time by Bernard De Voto
Agent in Place by Helen MacInnes
Wind in the Pampas by Betty De Sherbinin
Ghost Town by W. C. MacDonald
The Stone Fish by John McIntosh
O Western Wind by John Anthony Devon

EXERCISE 2 Understanding the Dewey Decimal System

Using the list of classifications on page 349, write the subject numbers for each of the following books.

EXAMPLE *Shaw on Music*
ANSWER 700–799

1. *This Chemical Age*
2. *Engineering Technology*

3. *Drawing the Human Head*
4. *New Church Programs for the Aging*
5. *Conversational French*
6. *20th Century French Literature*
7. *The British Empire before the American Revolution*
8. *Guide to Philosophy*
9. *The Complete Book of Ceramic Art*
10. *Principles of Political Economy*

The numbers identifying the book make up the *call number*. Every book has a different call number. In addition to the call number, some books carry a special label to show the section of the library in which they are shelved. Biographies, for example, are often marked with a B or 92 (short for 920 in the Dewey decimal system). The following chart shows some other special labels.

Categories	**Special Labels**
Juvenile books	J or X
Reference works	R or REF
Records	REC
Filmstrips	FS

Biographies and autobiographies are often shelved in a section of their own. They are arranged in alphabetical order according to the name of the person they are about. Books about the same person are arranged according to the author's last name.

The Library of Congress System

Three main features differentiate the Library of Congress system from the Dewey decimal system. First, the Library of Congress system assigns letters to the books instead of numbers. Second, the Library of Congress system uses 20 subject divisions instead of 10. Finally, the Library of Congress system does not separate fiction and biography from other kinds of works.

The 20 main subject categories in the Library of Congress system are shown in the following chart.

Main Categories in the Library of Congress System

A	General works	**M**	Music
B	Philosophy, religion	**N**	Fine Arts
C	Sciences of history	**P**	Language and Literature
D	Non-American history and travel	**Q**	Science
		R	Medicine
E	American history	**S**	Agriculture
F	U.S. local history	**T**	Technology
G	Geography, anthropology	**U**	Military science
H	Social sciences	**V**	Naval science
J	Political science	**Z**	Library science
L	Education		

The 20 main categories can be further divided by using a second letter. Even smaller divisions are possible with the use of numbers, including decimals, and letters that stand for the author's last name. Books classified by the Library of Congress system are shelved in alphabetical order according to their call number. Books with the same identifying letters are shelved in numerical order according to the numbers that follow the letters. The following list shows the order in which Library of Congress call numbers are shelved.

M 7309
N 621
P 414
PE 8037
PE 8037.T2

EXERCISE 3 Understanding the Library of Congress System Number your paper 1 to 10. Using the list of classifications on page 352, write the first letter of the call number for each of the books listed in Exercise 2.

EXAMPLE *Shaw on Music*
ANSWER M

The Card Catalog

The card catalog is a listing of all the books a library holds. Most catalogs are made up of small file drawers that contain typed cards with information about each book. Some libraries, however, list their holdings on microfilm or in a computer. A librarian will show you how to use electronic card catalogs.

Most books have three cards in the card catalog: the *author card, title card,* and *subject card*. In some libraries each type of card is filed in a separate cabinet.

The author card is sometimes called the main entry because it contains the fullest information. When you need a particular book by an author, look under the author's last name in the catalog.

Author Card

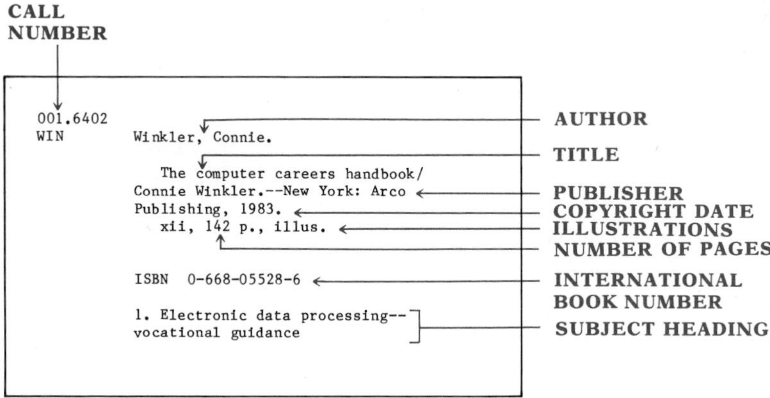

Title cards list the title of the book at the top of each card. Title cards are alphabetized by the first word in the title except *a, an,* and *the*.

Title Card

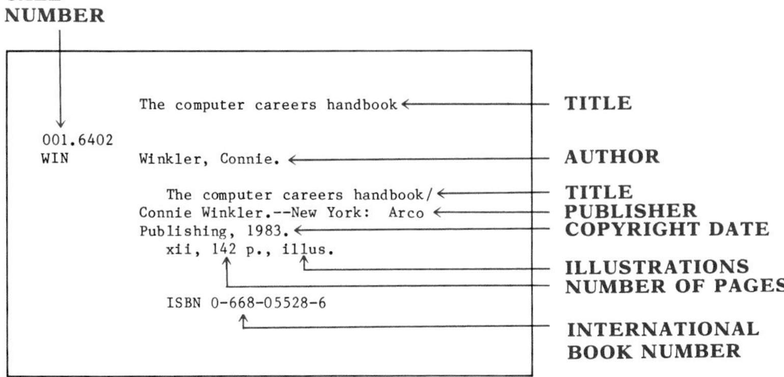

Subject cards are especially useful if you do not know the title or author of a specific book or if you do not even have a specific book in mind. These cards are arranged alphabetically according to the first main word in the subject heading. Subject headings under history, however, are filed in chronological order.

Subject Card

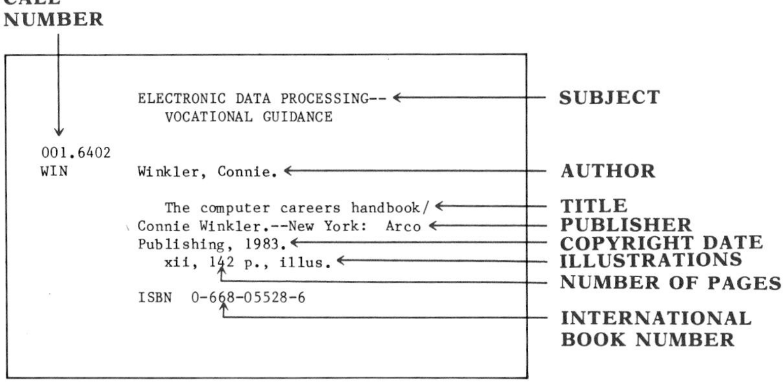

In addition to the author, title, and subject cards for each book, the catalog contains "see" and "see also" cards. These are called *cross-reference cards* because they refer you to other listings in the catalog. A "see" card tells you that the subject you have looked up is under another heading. A "see also" card refers you to additional headings you could look up to find relevant titles about your subject.

Cross-Reference Cards

Computers--Careers see Electronic data processing Vocational guidance	Electronic data processing see Word processing Telecommunications

If you are searching for a work that is part of a collection, an *analytic card* will help you find it. These cards are alphabetized according to the specific work you are seeking. They also, however, list all the other pieces contained within the collection. Each piece in the collection will have a separate analytic card of its own.

Analytic Card

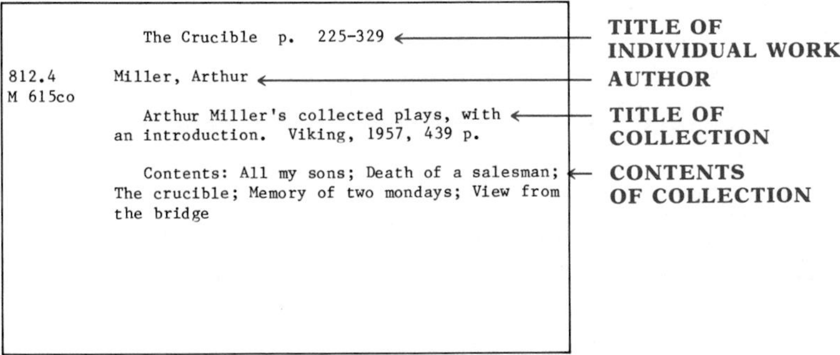

Most card catalogs arrange their contents by alphabetizing word by word rather than letter by letter. The entry *car safety,* for example, would come before the entry *Caracas.*

EXERCISE 4 Understanding the Card Catalog
Write the first three letters you would look under to find each of the following in the card catalog.

1. *The Once and Future King*
2. selecting a college
3. Sandra Day O'Connor
4. the experiments of Ivan Pavlov
5. the French constitution
6. *Gulliver's Travels*
7. how to maintain a car
8. the Iroquois League
9. Phillis Wheatley
10. training dolphins

EXERCISE 5 Understanding Catalog Cards
Using the catalog card below, write the answer to each of the questions that follow it.

```
BW          Harlan, Louis R.
276 Ha 2
               Booker T. Washington: the wizard of
            Tuskegee, 1901-1915/Louis R. Harlan.--
            New York: Oxford Univ. Press, 1983.

               xiv, 548 p.

            ISBN 0-19-503202-0

               1. Washington, Booker T., 1856-1915
          2. Afro-Americans--Biography  3. Educators--
          United States--Biography
```

1. Is this catalog card an author, subject, or title card?
2. Who is the author of this book?
3. What is the call number for this book?
4. What symbol in the call number tells you this book is a biography?
5. Who is the publisher?
6. Does this book contain illustrations?
7. Under what subject headings are books about this subject listed?
8. What is the book's copyright date?
9. What is the international code number for this book?
10. What do the letters *Ha* stand for in the call number?

REFERENCE MATERIALS

In most libraries reference materials are kept in a separate room. Since these materials cannot be removed from the library, a study area is usually provided.

Encyclopedias

Encyclopedias provide information on a wide variety of subjects. The articles they contain are separated into volumes and arranged alphabetically. Many encyclopedias also contain a bibliography, or list, of further readings at the end of each article. For this reason encyclopedias are good sources to start with if you are gathering information for a report.

GENERAL ENCYCLOPEDIAS

Collier's Encyclopedia
Encyclopaedia Britannica
Encyclopedia Americana
The Random House Encyclopedia
Compton's Encyclopedia
World Book Encyclopedia
The New Columbia Encyclopedia

The most recent edition of the *Encyclopaedia Britannica* comes in 20 volumes organized into three parts. The first volume, called the *Propaedia,* is an overview of the rest of the work and a guide to users of the encyclopedia. The next 10 volumes are called the *Micropaedia*. The *Micropaedia* contains short articles on its subjects. It also provides references to longer articles in the remaining 19 volumes. These last volumes are called the *Macropaedia*. The *Macropaedia* contains in-depth articles on many subjects.

Specialized References

Specialized references are limited to a certain subject area or a certain kind of information. Most libraries have at least one of each type of the following specialized sources.

Specialized Encyclopedias. These sources include information on only one main subject area, such as chemistry, zoology, or music. Like the general encyclopedias, they are organized alphabetically.

SPECIALIZED ENCYCLOPEDIAS

Encyclopedia of Space Travel and Astronomy
International Encyclopedia of the Social Sciences
The Encyclopedia of Chemistry
The Encyclopedia of Dance and Ballet
The McGraw-Hill Encyclopedia of Science and Technology

Biographical References. Researchers use these reference sources for brief information about famous people past and present. Some biographical references include long articles, while some have only brief sketches. All, however, include vital statistics such as date of birth, education, occupation, and an explanation of why the person is famous. The following excerpt about conductor and composer John Williams is from *Who's Who in America, 1982–1983.*

> **WILLIAMS, JOHN T.,** composer, condr.; b. Flushing, N.Y., Feb. 8, 1932; attended Juilliard Sch. Composer film scores: The Secret Ways, 1961, Diamond Head, 1962, None But the Brave, 1965, How to Steal a Million, 1966, Valley of the Dolls, 1967, The Cowboys, 1972, The Poseidon Adventure, 1972, Tom Sawyer, 1973, Earthquake, 1974, The Towering Inferno, 1974, Jaws, 1975, The Eiger Sanction, 1975, Family Plot, 1976, Midway, 1976, The Missouri Breaks, 1976, Raggedy Ann and Andy, 1977, Black Sunday, 1977, Star Wars, 1977, Close Encounters of the 3d Kind, 1977, The Fury, 1978, Jaws 2, 1976, Superman, 1978, Dracula, 1979, 1941, 1980, Raiders of the Lost Ark, 1981; condr. Boston Pops Orch., 1980—. Recipient Emmy award for outstanding achievement in music composition for a spl. program Jane Eyre, 1972, Grammy award best original score for motion picture or TV spl. Jaws, 1976, Grammy awards for Star Wars: best instrumental composition, best pop instrumental recording, best original score written for motion picture or TV spl., 1978, Golden Globe award, 1978, Acad. award for arrangement Fiddler on the Roof, 1971, original score Jaws, 1975, Star Wars, 1977.

BIOGRAPHICAL REFERENCES

Current Biography
Who's Who
Who's Who in America
Who's Who of American Women
Who's Who in American Politics
Dictionary of National Biography
New Century Cyclopedia of Names
The New York Times Obituaries Index

Atlases. These books of maps include a variety of information about the regions and countries of the world. Special-purpose maps, charts, and tables show a region's cities, population, climate, products, and development throughout history.

ATLASES

Goode's World Atlas
Grosset World Atlas
The World Book Atlas
The Times Atlas of the World
Hammond Medallion World Atlas
Rand McNally International World Atlas

Almanacs and Yearbooks. Published once a year, almanacs and yearbooks are good sources for up-to-date information. Some are organized chronologically, while others are organized alphabetically by topic. The following excerpt is from the *World Almanac & Book of Facts.*

A Collection of Animal Collectives

The English language boasts an abundance of names to describe groups of things, particularly pairs or aggregations of animals. Some of these words have fallen into comparative disuse, but many of them are still in service, helping to enrich the vocabularies of those who like their language to be precise, who tire of hearing a group referred to as "a bunch of," or who enjoy the sound of words that aren't overworked.

band of gorillas
bed of clams, oysters
bevy of quail, swans
brace of ducks
brood of chicks
cast of hawks
cete of badgers
charm of goldfinches
chattering of choughs
cloud of gnats
clowder of cats
clutch of chicks
clutter of cats
colony of ants
congregation of plovers
covey of quail, partridge
cry of hounds
down of hares
drift of swine
drove of cattle, sheep
exaltation of larks
flight of birds
flock of sheep, geese
gaggle of geese
gam of whales
gang of elks
grist of bees
herd of elephants
hive of bees
horde of gnats
husk of hares
kindle or **kendle** of kittens
knot of toads
leap of leopards
leash of greyhounds, foxes
litter of pigs
mob of kangaroos
murder of crows
muster of peacocks
mute of hounds
nest of vipers
nest, nide of pheasants
pack of hounds, wolves
pair of horses
pod of whales, seals
pride of lions
school of fish
sedge or **siege** of cranes
shoal of fish, pilchards
skein of geese
skulk of foxes
sleuth of bears
sounder of boars, swine
span of mules
spring of teals
swarm of bees
team of ducks, horses
tribe or **trip** of goats
troop of kangaroos
volery of birds
watch of nightingales
wing of plovers
yoke of oxen

ALMANACS AND YEARBOOKS

Information Please Almanac
The World Almanac & Book of Facts
Guinness Book of World Records
Britannica Book of the Year
Collier's Yearbook

Specialized Dictionaries. In addition to the abridged and unabridged dictionaries discussed in Chapter 15, the library also has a number of specialized dictionaries. One such work is a dictionary of synonyms, called a thesaurus. Specialized dictionaries are also available for most subject areas.

SPECIALIZED DICTIONARIES

Roget's Thesaurus in Dictionary Form
Webster's New Dictionary of Synonyms
Congressional Dictionary
Dictionary of Science and Technology
Harvard Dictionary of Music

Readers' Guide to Periodical Literature. Every year, thousands of articles are published in magazines and newspapers. Indexes help readers locate articles by naming the author, title, date, and periodical. Most indexes are arranged alphabetically by both subject and author and contain listings of all those articles written on a subject within a certain period of time. The *Readers' Guide to Periodical Literature* is one of the most useful and popular indexes. It indexes articles, short stories, and poems published in more than 175 magazines. It is issued in paperback form once in February, July, and August and twice during all other months. The following excerpt is from the February 1984 publication.

College education, Value of
Education's earning power [how college education relates to salaries for men and women] S. Guinzburg. *Psychol Today* 17:20-1 O '83
College enrollment *See* Colleges and universities—Attendance
College Entrance Examination Board
The Educational Equality Project: focus on results. A. Y. Bailey. *Phi Delta Kappan* 65:22-5 S '83
College fraternities
New wave networkers [black fraternities and sororities] P. King. *Black Enterp* 14:89-90+ D '83
College graduates
See also
Business schools and colleges—Graduates
College education, Value of
Colleges and universities—Graduate work
For 10,000 sons of Harvard and Yale, the schools' 100th football reunion will, as always, be more than a game. R. Drake. il *People Wkly* 20:179+ N 21 '83
The reunion [male college friends] P. Gottlieb. il *N Y Times Mag* p25 D 25 '83

Employment

College graduates and the market. S. M. Ehrenhalt. *Current* 257:15-24 N '83
Turn for better in job prospects for '84 grads. C. W. English. il map *U S News World Rep* 95:32-3 D 12 '83

Dismissal

The president who did not leave [dismissal of H. J. Perkins from Manitoba's Brandon University] E. Mills. *Macleans* 96:14-15 D 19 '83
College sports *See* College athletics
College students
See also
Black students
College fraternities
College graduates
Foreign students
College students in the 1990s: a demographic portrait. H. L. Hodgkinson. *Educ Dig* 49:28-31 N '83
What they should have told me when I was a senior [address, September 13, 1983] R. C. Jann. *Vital Speeches Day* 50:51-2 N 1 '83

Many newspapers also publish an index to the articles that have appeared within their pages. Large papers like the *New York Times* and the *Chicago Tribune* publish their own indexes. A more general index that includes articles from many newspapers is called *The Newspaper Index.*

EXERCISE 6 Understanding the *Readers' Guide*

Using the excerpt from the *Readers' Guide* on page 360, write the answers to the following questions.

1. What are the three subheadings listed under the heading *College Graduates?*
2. Who is the author of the article about the College Entrance Examination Board?
3. Under what subject heading would articles about college sports be listed?
4. What are the titles of the two articles concerning employment for college graduates?
5. Which magazine published an article about the 100th Harvard-Yale football reunion?
6. Who is the author of the article "College students in the 1990s: a demographic portrait"?
7. What is the title of the article about the dismissal of H. J. Perkins from Manitoba's Brandon University?
8. What year were all of the articles in this *Readers' Guide* published?
9. Under what other subject headings would articles about college students be found?
10. What is the title of the article listed under the heading *College Education* about?

The Vertical File. Some pamphlets, catalogs, newspaper clippings, and other printed matter are stored in a filing cabinet called the vertical file. These materials are kept in folders and are arranged alphabetically by subject. Most libraries print a listing of the materials included in their vertical file.

EXERCISE 7 Using Specialized References

Write one kind of reference work other than a general encyclopedia that would contain information about the following.

EXAMPLE the world's largest swamp
POSSIBLE ANSWER almanac

1. newspaper articles about space shuttles
2. information about a senator's life
3. how ocean currents affect climate
4. pamphlet on obtaining a lifesaver's certificate

5. the meaning of the computer term *interface*
6. the highest mountain peak in the Himalayas
7. synonyms for the word *imagination*
8. pamphlets on windsurfing or board sailing
9. magazine articles about job opportunities in Alaska
10. college and university catalogs

Reference Materials about Language and Literature

Libraries also keep specialized reference works that focus on only one subject area. These specialized references are usually shelved with the general works of the same type. Both general and specialized dictionaries, for example, are shelved in the same location. All of the following reference works provide information about language and literature.

SPECIALIZED DICTIONARIES	*Webster's Dictionary of Synonyms* *Roget's International Thesaurus* *Funk and Wagnall's Dictionary of Synonyms* *A Dictionary of Literary Terms* *Wood's Unabridged Rhyming Dictionary*
SPECIALIZED ENCYCLOPEDIAS	*Cassell's Encyclopedia of World Literature* *The Reader's Encyclopedia of American Literature* *Encyclopedia of World Literature in the 20th Century*
BIOGRAPHICAL REFERENCES	*Contemporary Authors* *Twentieth Century Authors* *Author's and Writer's Who's Who* *British Authors of the Nineteenth Century* *Contemporary Poets of the English Language* *Black American Writers Past and Present: A Biographical and Bibliographical Dictionary*

The handbook is another kind of literary reference work. A handbook can explain literary terms, give plot summaries, or describe characters.

HANDBOOKS	*The Reader's Encyclopedia* *American Authors and Books* *The Oxford Companion to American Literature*

The Oxford Companion to English Literature
Penguin Companion to European Literature
Crowell's Handbook of Contemporary American Poetry

A book of quotations can tell you the source of a particular quotation. In addition to printing the complete quotation, it will list other quotations about the same subject. Quotations are arranged by the subject or the author. To help lead you to the correct page, an index of first lines is provided.

BOOKS OF QUOTATIONS
Bartlett's Familiar Quotations
The Home Book of Quotations
Dictionary of Quotations
The Quotable Woman
Quotations in Context

Indexes are useful references when you are looking for a specific poem, short story, or play. An index will list the books that contain the particular selection you are looking for.

INDEXES
Granger's Index to Poetry
Ottemiller's Index to Plays in Collections
Short Story Index
Play Index

EXERCISE 8 Understanding Literary Reference Works
After each question write the name of one source listed on pages 362–363 in which you could find the answer.

EXAMPLE What words rhyme with *scald?*
POSSIBLE ANSWER *Wood's Unabridged Rhyming Dictionary*

1. In what year did the Russian author Leo Tolstoy write *War and Peace?*
2. Where could you find a short story called "Flowering Judas" by Katherine Anne Porter?
3. What American novelists were at work during the Civil War period?
4. What poem begins with the line "The time you won your town the race"?
5. What does the term *picaresque* mean in literature?
6. What other British playwrights were at work in Shakespeare's time?

7. What are two synonyms for *elan?*
8. What Japanese novelists achieved fame in the mid-1900s?
9. Where could you find the title of a publication that includes the play *She Stoops to Conquer?*
10. Where could you find a list of books about black American writer Lorraine Hansberry?

CHAPTER REVIEW

A. Using the following list of library sources, write the best resource for finding the answer to each question.

card catalog	*Readers' Guide*
general encyclopedia	atlas
specialized encyclopedia	almanac
biographical reference	vertical file
specialized dictionary	index

1. In what year was Ernest Hemingway born?
2. What are two synonyms for *ambivalent?*
3. When was Richard Wright's novel *Native Son* published?
4. What three European countries begin with the letter *A*?
5. Who won the Pulitzer Prize for fiction in 1932?
6. How many moons does Jupiter have?
7. Who wrote the poem "Ozymandias"?
8. Through what three states does the Snake River flow?
9. Which work by American playwright Eugene O'Neill is said to be autobiographical?
10. What four food groups are part of good nutrition?
11. What are the entrance requirements for Florida State University and the University of Miami?
12. Who holds the world record for the high jump?
13. What events led up to statehood for Hawaii?
14. How many novels by John Steinbeck does your library have?
15. What recent magazine articles have been published on the subject of airplane safety?

B. Use the resources of your library to answer the first ten questions in part A.

Unit 6

Composition

17

Words and Sentences

Writing is a way of expressing ideas, but it is also a way of discovering ideas. Many writers, beginning with a general idea of what they want to say, find that each new word or sentence they compose leads to new thoughts and new ideas. A well-chosen word can lead a writer down new avenues of thought. A concise sentence can untangle a mental knot. This chapter will help you choose words effectively and combine them into orderly, expressive sentences.

WORD CHOICE

The following passage describes the scene in which Dr. Frankenstein brings his famous creation to life.

> It was on a dreary night of November that I beheld the accomplishment of my toils. With an anxiety that almost amounted to agony, I collected the instruments of life around me, that I might infuse a spark of being into the lifeless thing that lay at my feet. It was already one in the morning. The rain pattered dismally against the panes, and my candle was nearly burnt out. Then, by the glimmer of the half-extinguished light, I saw the dull yellow eye of the creature open. It breathed hard, and a convulsive motion agitated its limbs.
>
> —MARY SHELLEY, *FRANKENSTEIN*

Just as Frankenstein sparks life into his creature, Shelley sparks life into her writing by using carefully chosen words with precise and rich meanings. Choosing words that paint vivid mental pictures will help bring your writing to life.

Specific Words

In most cases, the more specific the word, the clearer the mental image it creates. Study the following examples in which general words are replaced with specific words to sharpen the meaning of the sentence.

GENERAL VERB	The guests **ate** their salads and eagerly awaited the next course.
SPECIFIC VERB	The guests **wolfed** their salads and eagerly awaited the next course.
GENERAL NOUN	Ted took some **books** out of the library to take along on his vacation.
SPECIFIC NOUN	Ted took some **mysteries** out of the library to take along on his vacation.
GENERAL ADJECTIVE	Ella's hair is so **pretty.**
SPECIFIC ADJECTIVE	Ella's hair is so **lustrous.**
GENERAL ADVERB	Mikhail dances **well.**
SPECIFIC ADVERB	Mikhail dances **gracefully.**

All words have a literal meaning, or *denotation.* In addition to their denotation, many words also convey meanings that come from emotions or ideas associated with the words. This level of meaning is called *connotation.* The connotation of a word is often either positive or negative. Specific words are usually richer in connotation than are general words. In the following example, the denotation of all the words is essentially the same. The first two specific words, however, carry a positive feeling. The last two convey a negative impression.

GENERAL WORD	work	
SPECIFIC WORDS	vocation profession	positive connotations
	drudgery toil	negative connotations

The connotations of words are not always emotional. The connotations of the words *delicate* and *fragile*, for example, are neutral emotionally. Yet we tend to think of *fragile* as more extreme than *delicate*.

17a Use **specific words** with **connotations** that suit your meaning.

EXERCISE 1 Choosing Specific Words

Choose 10 of the following general words. Then write two specific words for each word you chose.

1. talked
2. saw
3. sad
4. dish
5. dance
6. help
7. awful
8. quickly
9. beautiful
10. great
11. happy
12. calm
13. walked
14. strong
15. shy
16. eat
17. bright
18. bad
19. school
20. win

EXERCISE 2 Thinking of Words with Different Connotations

In each of the following sentences, a general word is underlined. Write two specific words that could replace the general word. One should have a positive connotation; the other should have a negative. Use a thesaurus if you wish.

EXAMPLE He took off in his car.
POSSIBLE ANSWER sedan [positive] jalopy [negative]

1. A child wandered the empty street.
2. She smiled at the mention of his name.
3. The garden was filled with plants.
4. Thomas Retherford lived along a roadway.
5. The locomotive pulled out of the station.
6. Preston has an unusual face.
7. The room was filled with interesting furnishings.
8. The wind was cold on that late November day.
9. The hallways were crowded with students hurrying to class.
10. Wait until you hear the latest information!

Writing Extra

Jargon means the specialized, often wordy language of a certain field, such as business, physics, or computer technology. Jargon presents two main problems in clear thinking and writing. One is that a reader unfamiliar with the subject area may not understand the meaning of some jargon. The other is that even readers familiar with the words may have become so used to them that the jargon will fail to convey a precise meaning. Notice in the following example how much clearer the simple statement is than the one that contains jargon.

> The psychological complexes of the youth prevented him from overcoming his acrophobia. [jargon]
>
> The troubled youth could not overcome his fear of heights. [simple, direct language]

EXERCISE 3 Translating Jargon
Translate each of the following jargon-filled sentences into simple, direct language. Use a dictionary to look up any unfamiliar words.

1. The maternal instinct in dolphins is developed to such a degree that a female dolphin is believed to experience an emotional trauma at the death of her young.
2. The negotiations to end the military conflict were insufficient to develop an agreement that fairly laid out the terms of the demilitarization of the area.
3. The chief attending physician consulted with the patient's nearest of kin to explain the prognosis.
4. One of the curriculum objectives is to develop students' written and oral communication skills.

Figurative Language

Some expressions, called figures of speech, ask a reader to stretch the literal meaning of words in order to understand an imaginative meaning. For example, the expression "lend a hand" is a figurative way of saying "help out." Figurative language is often more powerful than literal language in creating strong mental pictures.

17b Use **figurative language** to appeal to your reader's imagination.

Similes and Metaphors. Similes and metaphors are probably the most common figures of speech. They both use comparisons to strike the reader's imagination.

SIMILE Here he stopped again, and glanced suspiciously to right and left, **like a rabbit that is going to bolt into its hole.** —E.M. FORSTER

METAPHOR The days ahead **unroll in the mind, a scroll** of blessed events in the garden and the barn. —E.B. WHITE

Similes use the word *like* or *as* to compare two essentially different things. Metaphors, on the other hand, imply a comparison without using *like* or *as*, or they simply say that one thing *is* another.

Thoughtful use of similes and metaphors can enrich writing and help readers understand ideas in fresh ways. Careless use of comparisons, however, can confuse readers. One type of careless comparison is called a mixed metaphor. In a mixed metaphor, the writer illogically combines two or more different comparisons.

MIXED METAPHOR She forced herself to climb the ladder of success by putting her nose to the grindstone.

IMPROVED She forced herself to climb the ladder of success by never failing to take some significant step each year.

In the mixed metaphor, the two comparisons combined to describe the woman's effort—climbing a ladder and working hard at a grindstone—are inconsistent and confusing. In the improved metaphor, the idea of climbing is extended logically with the idea of taking steps.

Another hazard in using figurative language is the cliché. A cliché is a comparison that has been used so often that it has lost its power to evoke a strong mental image. Following are some examples of overused comparisons.

happy as a lark	stubborn as a mule	good as gold
strong as a bull	old as the hills	busy as a bee

17c Avoid **mixed metaphors** and **clichés.**

Personification. This figure of speech transfers a quality of a living person to a lifeless object or idea.

PERSONIFICATION The unsealed envelope beckoned me to read the letter.
The trees danced to the rhythm of the wind.
The mountain dared me to try its slopes.
Darkness stole into the old house.

Envelopes cannot beckon, and trees cannot dance. Yet the meaning of these sentences is completely clear to a reader, since the actions described are understandable human actions. Personification, like metaphor and simile, invites readers to see objects and ideas in fresh, new ways.

Sound Effects. Some figures of speech rely on the sounds of words to create vivid impressions. *Onomatopoeia,* for example, is a figure of speech in which the word's sound matches its meaning. The following are examples of onomatopoeia.

crash	slither	cough
thump	hiss	quiver
boom	whistle	jangle

Another figure of speech that relies on sound effects is called *alliteration.* In a passage with alliteration, several words begin with the same sound, and often the sound echoes the meaning of the phrase.

ALLITERATION *B*ooth led *b*oldly with his *b*ig *b*ass drum . . . —VACHEL LINDSAY

The repeated *b* sound in the line above vividly recreates the sound of a drumbeat.

Both onomatopoeia and alliteration are more widely used in poetry than in prose. Used sparingly, however, they can enrich prose writing by calling on the reader's sense of hearing to bring a passage to life.

EXERCISE 4 Identifying Figures of Speech
All of the following excerpts are from a novel by Stephen Crane. Next to the proper number on your paper, identify the

underlined figure of speech by writing *simile, metaphor, personification,* or *onomatopoeia.*

The Red Badge of Courage

1. The trees began softly to sing a hymn of twilight.
2. The regiment was like a firework that once ignited, proceeds superior to circumstances until its blazing vitality fades.
3. There was a little flower of confidence growing within him.
4. The red sun was pasted in the sky like a wafer.
5. The regiment was a machine run down.
6. War, the red animal, war, the blood-swollen god, would have bloated full.
7. The voices of the cannon were clamoring in interminable chorus.
8. The guns belched and howled . . .
9. As the youth looked at them the black weight of his woe returned to him.
10. Thus, many men of courage, he considered, would be obligated to desert the colors and scurry like chickens.

EXERCISE 5 Experimenting with Sound Effects

Write one sentence about each of the following subjects. Use onomatopoeia and/or alliteration to add sound effects that match the subject.

EXAMPLE a snake

POSSIBLE ANSWER The snake hissed and slithered and slinked away.

1. a dancer
2. a racing car
3. church bells
4. a parade
5. a busy newspaper office
6. a hurricane
7. the surf on the shore
8. a pianist
9. the space shuttle
10. a stampede of caribou

EXERCISE 6 On Your Own

Choose one subject from Exercise 5 and write the following sentences to describe it.

1. Write one sentence using precise, literal language.
2. Write one sentence using a simile or metaphor.
3. Write one sentence using personification.

CONCISE SENTENCES

Just as a backpacker carries only essentials, a writer uses only enough words to communicate clearly. Learn to omit needless words to lighten the load for your readers.

17d Keep your sentences concise by eliminating needless words and phrases.

Redundancy

One form of excess baggage is redundancy, or unnecessary repetition. The following examples show how the idea in a redundant sentence can be expressed in fewer words.

REDUNDANT Our trip to the Olympic Games was memorable and unforgettable.
CONCISE Our trip to the Olympic Games was unforgettable.

REDUNDANT Animals who are members of the mammal family are warm-blooded.
CONCISE Mammals are warm-blooded.

EXERCISE 7 Eliminating Redundancy
Revise each sentence by eliminating the redundant words or phrases.

Sports in Japan

1. Many of the popular sports in Japan are contests of strength and power.
2. *Sumo* wrestling, for example, pits two huge and giant men against each other.
3. The loser in a *sumo* match is the first wrestler to touch the floor before the other with anything besides his feet.
4. Before the wrestling begins, the contestants go through a traditional ritual that precedes the match itself.
5. After clapping their hands, they extend their arms with open and unfisted hands to show that they carry no weapons.
6. Finally they stamp their feet on the ground as a symbol of driving away evil.
7. *Kyudo,* a centuries-old form of archery, dates back hundreds of years.
8. Fencing with swords, or *kendo,* is hundreds of years old.

9. *Kendo* is taught in Japan's junior and senior high schools where students can learn it.
10. Japanese police and law enforcement officers are experts in *kendo* and *judo,* and they carry no firearms.

Empty Expressions

Another way to reduce the number of words in a sentence is to eliminate expressions that add no meaning. Called *empty expressions,* these fillers do nothing more than take up space. If you find an empty expression in your writing, replace it with a single word or eliminate it entirely.

EMPTY It is truly something wonderful to gaze at the stars.
CONCISE Stargazing is wonderful.

EMPTY The thing of it is that I cannot turn in my paper due to the fact that I forgot it.
CONCISE I cannot turn in my paper because I forgot it.

EMPTY It seems there were twenty people at the party.
CONCISE Twenty people attended the party.

Empty Expressions

on account of	so, as you can see
what I want/believe/ think is	the reason that
it seems as if	the thing of it is that
in my opinion	there is/are/was/were
due to the fact that	I believe/feel/think that

EXERCISE 8 Eliminating Empty Expressions
Revise each sentence to eliminate the empty expression.

EXAMPLE There are many architects who have designed space-age cities.
POSSIBLE ANSWER Many architects have designed space-age cities.

Cities of the Future

1. Due to the fact that he believed each person should have a large amount of land, Frank Lloyd Wright designed a futuristic city called Broadacre.

2. In Broadacre it seems as if every person would have at least one acre of land.
3. As far as I can see, the plans of Paolo Soleri seem to be in sharp contrast to those of Wright.
4. I believe that Soleri designed one future city that is part underground and part above ground, soaring one mile into the air.
5. The thing that Soleri planned was a city with a population density of 200,000 per square mile.
6. Architect Moshe Safdie offered a compromise between Wright and Soleri, due to the fact that he saw value in both approaches.
7. It was in Montreal at Expo '67 that Safdie's city structure called Habitat was exhibited.
8. Many people applauded Safdie's 158-unit complex, the reason being that each unit was designed to receive plenty of sunlight and to have a clear view of outdoors.
9. On account of the severe overcrowding in Hong Kong and Singapore, many people live in boats on the water.
10. It may be that floating cities will become popular in the future.

Wordiness

The expression "less is more" may sound like a contradiction, but it makes good sense when applied to writing. If the same idea can be expressed in more than one way, choose the way that uses the fewest words. Constructions that use more words than necessary are called wordy.

In each of the following examples, a wordy construction is reduced to a shorter phrase or a single word.

WORDY Winds on Greenland's ice cap howl **in a fierce way.** [prepositional phrase]
CONCISE Winds on Greenland's ice cap howl **fiercely.** [adverb]

WORDY The snow on the ice cap is dry, **having the quality of sand.** [participial phrase]
CONCISE The snow on the ice cap is dry and **sandlike.** [adjective]

WORDY Because of the winds, some scientists **who are in Greenland** have never traveled more than 100 yards from their stations. [adjective clause]

CONCISE Because of the winds, some scientists **in Greenland** . . . [prepositional phrase]

or

. . . some scientists **living in Greenland** . . . [participial phrase]

WORDY The ice cap, **which is a treacherous wilderness,** appears from the air as a rainbow of soft blues and greens. [adjective clause]

CONCISE The ice cap, **a treacherous wilderness,** appears from the air as a rainbow . . . [appositive phrase]

WORDY A glare **that is blinding** rises from the ice cap on a sunny day. [adjective clause]

CONCISE A **blinding** glare . . . [adjective]

EXERCISE 9 Reducing Wordy Sentences

Revise each sentence by shortening the underlined wordy phrase or clause.

Going on a Dig

1. Kampsville, which is a center for archaeological research and training, is located in west central Illinois.
2. Every year, junior and senior high school students who are interested in archaeology go to Kampsville to learn how to dig up the past.
3. The study program, which is an offshoot of Northwestern University and the Foundation for Illinois Archaeology, is uncovering the remains of 2,000 prehistoric communities of American Indians.
4. Since the buried remains are precious, students are taught to dig in a very careful way.
5. The site is divided into areas measuring six feet square, each of which is assigned a number.
6. Items that are excavated are identified by the number of the square in which they were found.
7. Students look for points, notches, and grooves, which are signs of human handiwork, on the bones and shells that they unearth.
8. A student who is at Kampsville learns much about the everyday life of ancient peoples.

9. Bones that are from animals also tell much about prehistoric wildlife.
10. Zooarchaeologists, who are experts in animal bones, surmise that early American Indians kept dogs as pets.

EXERCISE 10 On Your Own
Write one paragraph explaining your definition of the word *adult*. Revise your paragraph to eliminate redundancy, empty expressions, and wordiness. Exchange papers with a classmate. Discuss the content and style of your partner's paragraph.

SENTENCE VARIETY

Clothing with an appealing style flatters and enhances the human shape. In the same way, an appealing writing style dresses ideas so they are shown at their best advantage. One important quality of writing style is sentence construction. Interesting and varied sentences appeal to the reader's ear and give a graceful shape to ideas.

17e Vary the length and structure of your sentences.

Sentence Combining

Writing made up of short, choppy sentences usually suffers from two problems. One is that the rhythm soon becomes tiresome to the reader. The other is that closely related ideas are unnaturally separated from one another. Consider the following example of choppy sentences.

> Alfonso beat John in the race. John was Alfonso's best friend. John was also Alfonso's chief rival in track. Alfonso was proud to win. Alfonso felt sorry that John lost.

The story of Alfonso and John, while simple on the surface, is actually layered with complexities that the short, simple sentences do not adequately convey. Notice how clearly the following sentence relates the separate ideas.

> Alfonso won the race, proud of his victory but sorry for the defeat of his best friend and chief rival, John.

Learning the techniques of sentence combining will help you compose sentences that clearly link related ideas. Sentence combining is also a useful strategy for varying sentence lengths and developing a smooth style.

Combining Sentences with Phrases. In the example about Alfonso and John on page 377, the most important idea (that Alfonso won the race) is used as the base of the new sentence. The additions to the sentence are details that modify or clarify that main idea. In each of the following examples, an idea from a separate sentence is turned into a phrase that modifies the main idea.

A. Police departments use computers. The computers store important information about suspects.

Police departments use computers to store important information about suspects. [infinitive phrase]

B. In 1967, the first computer system used against crime was developed. The FBI developed it.

In 1967, the first computer system used against crime was developed by the FBI. [prepositional phrase]

C. The National Crime Information Center provides valuable information by computer. It helps police departments all over the United States, Canada, the Virgin Islands, and Puerto Rico.

The National Crime Information Center provides valuable information by computer, helping police departments all over the United States, Canada, the Virgin Islands, and Puerto Rico. [participial phrase]

D. CATCH is a program that can call up a picture of a suspect on the computer screen. CATCH is one of the most advanced systems in the country.

CATCH, one of the most advanced systems in the country, is a program that can call up a picture of a suspect on the computer screen. [appositive phrase]

EXERCISE 11 Combining Sentences with Phrases
Combine each set of short sentences using one or more of the techniques shown above. Use commas correctly.

A Long Flight

1. Birds somehow navigate the long distances of their migration routes. They use innate compasses and clocks as a guide.
2. The golden plovers of eastern Canada cover enormous distances. They travel up to 2,400 miles nonstop.
3. The Arctic tern holds the distance record. The tern is an amazing bird. It flies a round-trip distance of about 23,000 miles. It flies from the Arctic to the Antarctic every year.
4. The summer solstice is the midpoint of the birds' arrivals and departures in the Northern Hemisphere. The summer solstice is the longest day of the year.
5. Bluethroats follow a 14-week pattern. They arrive 14 weeks before the solstice. They depart 14 weeks after the summer solstice.
6. The birds use the sun. They navigate their long journeys by the sun.
7. Tens of millions of shearwaters all arrive on islands off Australia. The day they arrive is a late November day.
8. The shearwaters all arrive within a 20-minute period. They have come from such different points as Japan, the North Pacific Ocean, and Canada.
9. Adélie penguins migrate hundreds of miles over land and water in Antarctica. Adélie penguins are flightless birds.
10. Some of the most famous migrating birds are the swallows of Mission San Juan Capistrano, California. They arrive from Central America every year on April 19.

Combining Sentences by Coordinating. Ideas of equal importance can be joined in one sentence with the use of coordinating conjunctions *(and, but, or, for, yet,* and *so).* The resulting sentences will contain compound elements.

A. *I, Robot* is a work of fiction by Isaac Asimov. *The Rest of the Robots* is a work of fiction by Isaac Asimov.

   I, Robot* and *The Rest of the Robots are works of fiction by Isaac Asimov. [compound subject]

B. In many science-fiction novels, robots grow too powerful. They try to take over the world.

   In many science-fiction novels, robots **grow** too powerful **and try** to take over the world. [compound verb]

C. Early portrayals of robots influenced film director Stanley Kubrick. Early portrayals of robots also influenced film director George Lucas.

Early portrayals of robots influenced film directors **Stanley Kubrick and George Lucas.** [compound object]

D. Robots in most early works were dangerous. In *Star Wars* C3PO and R2D2 are friendly.

Robots in most early works were dangerous, **but** in *Star Wars* C3PO and R2D2 are friendly. [compound sentence]

E. The two droids in the movie *Star Wars* were comic. They were courageous.

The two droids in the movie *Stars Wars* were **comic but courageous.** [compound predicate adjective]

F. One famous movie robot is Gort in *The Day the Earth Stood Still.* Another famous movie robot is Robbie the Robot in *Forbidden Planet.*

Two famous movie robots are **Gort** in *The Day the Earth Stood Still* **and Robbie the Robot** in *Forbidden Planet.* [compound predicate nominative]

EXERCISE 12 Combining Sentences by Coordinating

Combine the following pairs of sentences, using the models on pages 379–380 as a guide. The conjunction to be used is provided in parentheses.

EXAMPLE Beavers use their tails to warn their group of nearby danger. Giraffes use their tails to warn their group of nearby danger. [and]

ANSWER Beavers and giraffes use their tails to warn their groups of nearby danger.

Last but not Least

1. Tails are used for communication. Tails are used for locomotion. [and]
2. The position in which an animal holds its tail often shows aggression. It often shows social rank. [or]
3. A bird that has lost its tail can still fly. Its movements will be difficult. [but]
4. For many animals tails are rudders. For many animals tails are balances. [both/and]

5. Kangaroos need their tails for balance in hopping. Lizards need their tails for balance in running. [and]
6. Running cheetahs bend their tails in the direction they want to turn. Running wolves bend their tails in the direction they want to turn. [and]
7. Another function of tails is regulating heat. Another function of tails is expressing emotion. [and]
8. Australian rat kangaroos sweat through their tails. They are kept cool by the evaporation. [and]
9. Dogs wag their tails to show happiness. Wolves wag their tails to show happiness. [and]
10. The tails of some rodents can save the animals' lives by breaking off if caught by predators. The tails of some lizards can save those animals' lives in the same way. [and]

Combining Sentences by Subordinating. Ideas of unequal importance can be combined into one sentence by turning the less important idea into a subordinate clause. This technique is called subordinating. The following words are often used to introduce subordinate clauses. *(For a complete list of subordinating conjunctions, see page 77.)*

RELATIVE PRONOUNS		SUBORDINATING CONJUNCTIONS	
who	that	after	because
whom	which	until	whenever
whose	whoever	unless	although

The following examples use the technique of subordinating to combine sentences. Note that each revised sentence contains a subordinate clause.

A. Capitol pages have a chance to see government in action. Capitol pages are aides and messengers to lawmakers.

   Capitol pages, **who are aides and messengers to lawmakers,** have a chance to see government in action. [adjective clause]

B. The Supreme Court uses only three high school students as pages. The chances of becoming a Supreme Court page are slim.

   Because the Supreme Court uses only three high school students as pages, the chances of becoming a Supreme Court page are slim. [adverb clause]

C. A person may want to become a Capitol page. That person should write to his or her senator and representative for information.

Whoever wants to become a Capitol page should write to his or her senator and representative for information. [noun clause]

EXERCISE 13 Combining Sentences by Subordinating
Combine the following sentences, using the models on pages 381–382. The joining word to be used is given in brackets.

A Capitol Page

1. The tasks of Capitol pages demand discipline and energy. The tasks of Capitol pages include preparing desks for lawmakers, handling phone calls, and running errands through the long hallways of Congress. [which]
2. The parliamentary rules must be followed to the letter. Capitol pages carefully sound the bells that call House members to a vote. [because]
3. Capitol pages serve out their appointed terms. They must also attend school. [while]
4. The school that pages attend is part of the Washington, D.C., public-school system. The school schedule is shifted to meet the pages' special needs. [although]
5. Regular classes are just beginning. The capitol pages have already finished their early-morning schooling. [when]
6. Pages attend school. They rush to Capitol Hill to begin a full day's work. [after]
7. Pages in the Senate may be between 14 and 17 years old. Pages in the House must be high-school juniors or seniors. [while]
8. The *Capitol Page School Handbook* helps new pages understand their jobs. It is issued by the House of Representatives. [which]
9. A person may come from a state far away to work as a page. He or she must arrange for housing and meals. [whoever]
10. Pages are well paid. Living expenses are high. [although]

Varying Sentence Structure

Besides creating sentences of varying lengths, sentence-combining techniques help you achieve a variety of sentence structures. Experienced writers use a healthy mixture of the four basic sentence types: simple, compound, complex, and compound-complex. *(See pages 87–88.)*

SIMPLE	Rita read the letter.
COMPOUND	Rita read the letter, and Sam tried to guess its contents by watching her face.
COMPLEX	While Rita read the letter, Sam tried to guess its contents by watching her face.
COMPOUND-COMPLEX	While Rita read the letter, Sam tried to guess its contents by watching her face, but her expression revealed nothing.

Expanding Sentences with Details. In addition to using a mixture of the four sentence types, you can vary each type by adding amplifying words or phrases to different parts of your sentences. In the following examples, details are added first to the subject, then to the verb, and finally to the object. Each of the sentences is based on the simple sentence *Rita read the letter.*

DETAILS AMPLIFYING THE SUBJECT	Rita, **perspiring with tension,** read the letter.
DETAILS AMPLIFYING THE VERB	Rita, **after a deep sigh,** read the letter.
DETAILS AMPLIFYING THE OBJECT	Rita read the letter, **a jumble of words scribbled on torn paper, a message that could change her life.**

EXERCISE 14 Expanding Sentences with Details

Revise each of the following sentences, adding details to the part of the sentence indicated in brackets. Use your imagination to make up the details.

EXAMPLE	Tamara swam to shore. [subject]
POSSIBLE ANSWER	Tamara, gasping for breath in the icy water, swam to shore.

1. The spring rain brought the tulips to life. [subject]
2. Abebe studied until he had the formulas memorized. [verb]
3. Romeo and Juliet were victims of a deadly misunderstanding. [subject]

4. Marilyn found a cat. [object]
5. Eleanor decided to go to medical school. [verb]
6. Marcia sat at the edge of her seat during the entire movie. [subject]
7. Ben drove the long stretch of desert highway. [verb]
8. Alex took pride in his bike. [object]
9. The plane streaked through the sky. [subject]
10. Time heals all wounds. [object]

Varying Sentence Beginnings. The most natural word order places the subject at the beginning of a sentence. Overused, however, that pattern soon becomes monotonous. Each of the following sentence starters offers a good change of pace.

ADVERB	**Probably** the largest meteor to fall within recorded history landed in Siberia in 1947.
ADJECTIVE	**Brittle** as glass, the meteor broke on its path to Earth into thousands of smaller pieces.
PREPOSITIONAL PHRASE	**In its original form,** it probably weighed 200 tons.
INFINITIVE PHRASE	**To trace the source of the meteor,** scientists studied the debris at the site.
PARTICIPIAL PHRASE	**Landing with great destructive force,** the meteor felled all trees within 40 miles.
ADVERB CLAUSE	**If the event had happened two hours later,** the earth's movement would have made St. Petersburg the target.

EXERCISE 15 Varying Sentence Beginnings

Vary the beginnings of the following sentences. Use the openers in brackets.

Spiders

1. Most spiders have poisonous fangs to stun their prey. [infinitive phrase]
2. Spiders are different from other insects, having eight legs and eight eyes. [participial phrase]
3. All spiders have spinnerets, although not all spiders make webs. [adverb clause]
4. A female black widow spider has a bold red mark on its underside. [prepositional phrase]
5. A black widow's bite is occasionally fatal. [adverb]

6. Naturalists have given the name *parachuters* to young spiders. [prepositional phrase]
7. These spiders travel on long silky threads that they have spun, letting the wind transport them. [participial phrase]
8. Daddy longlegs are not really spiders, although most people think otherwise. [adverb clause]
9. Wolf spiders make a pouncing movement to catch their prey. [infinitive phrase]
10. The spider's sturdy silk is used for a variety of purposes. [adjective]

EXERCISE 16 On Your Own
Write your favorite joke or an amusing incident. (Make sure it is a story joke, not a riddle or a one-liner.) Read over what you have written and revise it as necessary to include a variety of sentence lengths, types, and structures.

FAULTY SENTENCES

Even for experienced writers, composing is a challenge that requires great concentration. Most writers find that they must concentrate on one stage of the writing process at a time. When they write their first draft, for example, their primary concerns are content and organization. Later, when the rough draft is finished, they go back and concentrate on polishing their sentences and correcting any mistakes. The sections that follow will help you revise your sentences to eliminate some common sentence faults.

17f Revise your sentences to eliminate **faulty coordination** and **faulty subordination, rambling sentences, faulty parallelism,** and **overuse of the passive voice.**

Faulty Coordination and Faulty Subordination

Coordination and subordination are useful techniques for varying sentences and clarifying ideas. If you use the wrong conjunction, however, the resulting sentence can leave a reader puzzling over the relationship between ideas.

FAULTY COORDINATION	I'd love some dessert, and I don't want to go off my diet.
PRECISE COORDINATION	I'd love some dessert, but I don't want to go off my diet.

The following chart lists some common coordinators according to their use.

Common Coordinators Listed According to Use

Similarity	Contrast	Alternative	Result
and	but	either/or	so
both/and	still	neither/nor	therefore
furthermore	nevertheless	or, nor	as a result

Faulty coordination also results if you try to combine two unrelated ideas. To correct this problem, express the ideas in separate sentences.

FAULTY COORDINATION	Many people continue working past the age of 65, and my grandfather still works as a carpenter.
CORRECT	Many people continue working past the age of 65. My grandfather still works as a carpenter.

Another problem occurs if you coordinate ideas that are not of equal importance. Use subordination to express ideas of unequal importance, making the less important idea into a phrase or a subordinate clause.

FAULTY COORDINATION	Geneva heard the fire alarm, and she was studying at the time.
CORRECT	While studying, Geneva heard the fire alarm. [phrase]
CORRECT	While she was studying, Geneva heard the fire alarm. [subordinate clause]

Faulty subordination is another possible problem. To avoid it, express your most important idea in an independent clause.

FAULTY SUBORDINATION	Although she finished the book, it was long.
CORRECT	Although it was long, she finished the book.

When subordinating, use the connecting word that best shows the relationship of your ideas.

FAULTY SUBORDINATION The athlete trained for months even though he would be ready for trials.

PRECISE SUBORDINATION The athlete trained for months so that he would be ready for trials.

Following are some common subordinators, listed according to their use.

Common Subordinators Listed According to Use

Time	Cause	Purpose	Condition
after	because	that	if
before	since	so that	even though
whenever	as	in order that	unless

The following guidelines will help you correct problems in coordination and subordination.

17g

Correcting Faulty Coordination and Faulty Subordination

1. Use the connecting word that best shows the relationship of your ideas (similarity, contrast, alternative, result; time, cause, purpose, condition).
2. Express unrelated ideas in separate sentences.
3. If related ideas are of unequal importance, change the less important idea into a phrase or a subordinate clause.
4. Always express your most important idea in an independent clause.

EXERCISE 17 Correcting Faulty Coordination and Faulty Subordination

Use the guidelines above to revise each sentence.

Early Cowboys

1. Tales of Western cowboys depict adventurous heroes, and their lives were both dangerous and exhausting.
2. Because cowboys on the open range endured many hardships, the winds were fierce, water was scarce, and raiders were many.

3. The cowboy's most precious possession was his horse; also, the horse was his only means of transportation.
4. If necessary a cowboy might give the water in his canteen to his horse since he himself was thirsty.
5. A Western saddle was designed for support because a cowboy could even take a short nap in the saddle without fear of falling off.
6. A cowboy had to be skilled at using the rope; furthermore, it was his most important tool.
7. Cowboys in different regions of the country used different names for the rope, and those in the Southwest called it a lariat while those along the Pacific Coast called it a lasso.
8. The cattle roundup was an important part of a cowboy's work, so it was also a social gathering.
9. Cowboys held after-work contests called rodeos; furthermore, they competed in bareback riding, trick riding, trick roping, and other exhibitions of skill.
10. Because rodeos still take place today, they are more commercialized than they were in the days of the early cowboys.

Rambling Sentences

Sentences that ramble on and on are usually the victims of excessive coordination. To break up rambling sentences, separate the ideas into shorter sentences of their own.

RAMBLING Lions who live in groups are the lucky ones, because the group, called a pride, shares many important jobs, and these jobs include hunting, protecting the turf, and caring for the young, while solitary lions must hunt on their own, and they have no one to help protect them.

IMPROVED Lions who live in groups called prides are luckier than solitary lions. The group shares such important jobs as hunting, protecting the turf, and caring for young. Solitary lions must hunt on their own, and they have no one to help protect them.

EXERCISE 18 Correcting Rambling Sentences

Revise the following rambling sentences by breaking them into shorter sentences. Remember to capitalize and punctuate the new sentences correctly.

1.

The Beatles were an immensely popular singing group in the 1960s and 1970s, and they expressed in their words and music the feelings of young people of those times, but they were controversial too, and their records and appearances were banned in some places, but their popularity held steady for many years, and at least one university now offers a full-credit college course on the music and impact of the Beatles.

2.

People interested in a research career in chemistry must choose between basic research and applied research, and the choice is an important one because there are big differences between the two types, since in basic research, the chemists' main goal is to expand knowledge about nature, while in applied research, chemists work to improve or develop specific products and services, and there are usually more job openings in applied research.

3.

The word *Chicano* is a shortened version of the word *Mejicano,* because originally the Spaniards pronounced the word like "Me*sh*icano," and later the *sh* sound was changed to a *ch* sound, although that sound was represented by the letter *j*, and finally the longer form, *Mejicano,* was simply shortened to *Chicano.*

4.

The sign language used by deaf people is very descriptive, and the signs for animals are especially so, since *elephant,* for example, is signed with the hand extending from the nose, like an elephant's trunk, and the sign for *monkey* is the famous chest-scratching motion, while the sign for *dog* says more about that animal's behavior than appearance, because that sign is a series of repeated snaps on the knee followed by the snapping of fingers, motions one would use to call a dog.

Faulty Parallelism

A parallel structure is one in which two or more ideas linked with coordinate or correlative conjunctions are expressed in the same grammatical form. Ideas being contrasted should also be parallel. Parallelism helps readers group related ideas together. Faulty parallelism adds a jarring effect to a sentence. The following examples show how coordinated ideas should be expressed in parallel form.

FAULTY The committee members were **enthusiastic, energetic,** and **of great diplomacy.** [two adjectives and one prepositional phrase]

PARALLEL The committee members were **enthusiastic, energetic,** and extremely **diplomatic.** [three adjectives]

FAULTY Success in school requires good **study habits** and **wanting** to succeed. [one noun and one gerund]

PARALLEL Success in school requires good **study habits and a desire** to succeed. [two nouns]

In the following examples, ideas connected with correlative conjunctions (*either/or, neither/nor, both/and,* etc.) are made parallel.

FAULTY Neither soft **words** nor **offering** treats would coax the frightened kitten down from the tree. [one noun and one gerund]

PARALLEL Neither soft **words** nor **treats** would coax the frightened kitten down from the tree. [two nouns]

FAULTY The vacation was not only **exciting** but also **a trip** filled with surprises. [one adjective and one noun]

PARALLEL The vacation was not only **exciting** but also **full of surprises.** [two adjectives]

When using correlative conjunctions, remember to place them right before the parallel items, not elsewhere in the sentence.

FAULTY Either Ellen will call you or me.

CORRECT Ellen will call either you or me.

Contrasting ideas are made parallel in the following examples.

FAULTY **Doing** your best is more important than **to win.** [one gerund and one infinitive]

PARALLEL **Doing** your best is more important than **winning.** [two gerunds]

FAULTY **How well newscasters read** is as important as **their ability to gather the news.** [one clause and one phrase]

PARALLEL **How well newscasters read** is as important as **how well they gather the news.** [two clauses]

EXERCISE 19 Correcting Faulty Parallelism

Revise the following sentences so that linked ideas are expressed in parallel form.

1. Michael is loyal, trustworthy, and an industrious person.
2. Police dogs must be both good retrievers and good at barking.
3. The sense of smell is more powerful in evoking memories than how things sound.
4. Some toys are neither safe nor of any educational value.
5. As we watched the sailboat race from the shore, we saw billowing sails, rippling waves, and that the gulls swept by.
6. The club members discussed how to recruit new members, where to go for the annual outing, and the pros and cons of raising dues.
7. Tom felt both disappointed and relief when he learned he had not been chosen to give the farewell speech.
8. Vernetta's goals are to study law, to find a good job, and saving money for the future.
9. Neither raking nor to sweep can remove all the fallen leaves.
10. The acting in the movie was better than the people who wrote the script.

Passive Voice

The passive voice places emphasis on the receiver of the action rather than on the doer.

PASSIVE The dinner **was relished by me.**

ACTIVE **I relished** the dinner.

The passive voice usually requires more words than the active voice, so it is rarely the most economical way to express an idea. Even worse, overuse of the passive voice dulls a written passage by robbing it of its action. In some cases the doer of the action is missing entirely.

PASSIVE The giant trout **was held up.**

When the doer of the action is restored to the scene, the picture comes to life.

ACTIVE The proud **angler held up** the giant trout.

In some cases, however, the doer of the action is either understood or unimportant. In these cases passive voice is proper and useful.

PASSIVE The old library was completely remodeled.
PASSIVE Jimmy Carter was elected president in 1976.

EXERCISE 20 Changing the Passive to the Active Voice
Revise each of the following sentences by using the active voice instead of the passive voice.

EXAMPLE The car was driven by me while the maps were consulted by my sister.
ANSWER I drove the car while my sister consulted the maps.

1. A yard full of holes was dug by the persistent husky.
2. A decision was made by the company president to offer all employees bonuses.
3. A foul ball was called by the first-base umpire.
4. The plan for a new shopping mall was vetoed by the mayor.
5. The World's Fair was attended by thousands of people.
6. The telephone bill was handed to me by my mother with a stern look in her eyes.
7. A donation was made by our graduating class to the school library.
8. Survival techniques were learned by the Pilgrims from the Indians.
9. The cool midsummer evening was ushered in by the passing thunderstorm.
10. An enormous amount of money was being spent by executives on unnecessary travel.

EXERCISE 21 On Your Own
Write a paragraph explaining an important decision you made. When you have finished, exchange papers with a classmate and comment on the following questions.

1. Are there any sentences with faulty coordination or faulty subordination?
2. Are there any rambling sentences?
3. Are there any sentences with faulty parallelism?
4. Has the passive voice been overused?

CHAPTER REVIEW

A. Specific Words
Revise each of the following sentences to eliminate the problem indicated in brackets.

1. The entertainer left the audience howling with laughter. [general noun]
2. From our study hall we could smell the food cooking in the cafeteria. [general noun]
3. Eleanor went to answer the telephone on the first ring. [general verb]
4. The eager aunt stared into the new baby's room. [wrong connotation]
5. Before the guests came, we each gobbled the frosting on the cake. [wrong connotation]

B. Figurative Language
Identify the figure of speech used in each of the following sentences by writing *simile, metaphor, personification, onomatopoeia,* or *alliteration.*

6. The heat of the summer night was an itchy blanket.
7. The bundle of balloons bounced buoyantly from clown to clown.
8. The skies growled at the cowering sailor, out in his new boat for the first time.
9. Cynthia's eyes glistened like a northern lake at sunrise.
10. The cat whined and meowed, scratching at the back door.

C. Effective Sentences
Revise each sentence to eliminate the problem indicated in brackets.

11. Stan repeated the phrase in his mind over and over again. [redundancy]
12. Everyone should drive defensively, the reason being that the "other guy" may be careless. [empty expression]
13. The main point of what I'm trying to say is that an understanding friend will forget words spoken in anger. [empty expression]
14. The book that is sitting on my desk is about people who work as archaeologists. [wordiness]
15. My neighbor who lives next door is a professional doctor. [redundancy]
16. Max faced his classmates. He cleared his throat and began to deliver his speech. [needs combining with a phrase]
17. Carla spent all her money. Jeanna still had money left for a few trinkets. [needs combining with coordination]
18. The last song was played. The weary dancers sat quietly fanning themselves in the open courtyard. [needs combining with subordination]
19. Becky wanted the job more than anything else in her life, but she knew she could do it well. [faulty coordination]
20. Graduation day is both a sad and a happy time, because it is a time to say good-bye to old friends and routines, and it is also a time to look forward to new challenges, for the years ahead are filled with promise, but the years behind are filled with fond memories. [rambling]
21. Rhoda has always had an easy time making conversation with strangers, helping others feel at ease, and to bring out the best in people around her. [faulty parallelism]
22. Rick was sure that the book would both be entertaining and very well written. [incorrect placement of correlative conjunction]
23. The gymnasium was emptied by the spectators after the disappointing defeat. [misuse of passive]
24. A meal was eaten by us before we set out on the hike. [general noun and misuse of passive]
25. The controls were checked by the pilot. The jumbo jet began to glide away from the gate. [misuse of passive and needs combining]

Chapter Summary

Words and Sentences

Word Choice

1. Use specific words with connotations that suit your meaning.
2. Use figurative language to enliven writing.
3. Avoid mixed metaphors and clichés.

Concise Sentences

4. Express your meaning in as few words as possible by
   - eliminating redundancy.
   - avoiding empty expressions.
   - revising wordy sentences.

Sentence Variety

5. Vary the length of your sentences. Combine sentences to avoid too many short, choppy sentences in a row.
6. Use a mixture of simple, compound, complex, and compound-complex sentences.
7. Vary your sentences by adding amplifying details to different parts of your sentences.
8. Vary the beginnings of your sentences.

Faulty Sentences

9. Revise faulty sentences by
   - eliminating faulty coordination and subordination.
   - breaking up rambling sentences.
   - using parallel constructions.
   - avoiding overuse of passive voice.

18

Clear Thinking

Clear writing is impossible without clear thinking. Even if it is correct in form and grammar, a composition without a strong, clear idea is an empty shell. A good idea, carefully reasoned, is the essence of writing. Although the act of writing can help you discover ideas, only careful and deliberate thinking can help you shape those ideas into a meaningful expression. This chapter will show you how to keep your thinking sharp and clear.

FACTS AND OPINIONS

Facts are statements that can be proved true. That one plus one equals two can be demonstrated, or proved, time after time within your own experience. You can count the number of pencils or oranges or shoes you have if you add one to one: You will always have two.

Some facts, however, cannot be verified by your experience alone. Consider the following statement.

> During a solar eclipse, the moon's shadow appears to cover the sun.

Your own experience may tell you that the sky darkens during a solar eclipse, but it probably cannot tell you for certain that the moon's shadow is the cause of the darkness. Astronomers, however, use measurements and calculations that *can* verify the cause of the eclipse. Consulting reliable sources is one way to verify facts that lie outside your experience.

18a Use your own experience and reliable authorities to verify facts.

Opinions are judgments, interpretations, predictions, or preferences that can vary from person to person.

OPINIONS *The Empire Strikes Back* was a better movie than *Star Wars.*

In every new automobile, car manufacturers should be required to install air bags that protect people in an accident.

The poems of Carl Sandburg reflect the ruggedness of the American character.

Summer is more fun than winter.

By the early twenty-first century, robots will be performing routine household tasks.

Opinions, by definition, cannot be proved. Some, however, can at least be supported with convincing evidence. Opinions that can be backed up with facts are called *arguable propositions.* Opinions that express preference only are not worth arguing, since no facts are available to prove the point.

ARGUABLE PROPOSITION The actors' waiting room should be painted green, since green is a color known to have a calming effect on the nerves. [Tests and experiments have provided factual evidence that people tend to relax in a green room.]

PREFERENCE Green is a more pleasing color than blue. [No facts available to back up preference.]

18b Build your compositions on **arguable propositions** and collect the factual evidence needed to argue convincingly.

EXERCISE 1 Verifying Facts

For each statement, decide if the fact can be verified by your experience or if reliable authorities must be consulted. Indicate your answer by writing *experience* or *authorities* next to the proper number.

EXAMPLE Pittsburgh received 1.5 inches of rain yesterday.

ANSWER authorities [Pittsburgh residents might be able to verify that it rained yesterday, but they would not be able to verify the precise amount.]

1. Yellow (or amber) is the color used to indicate caution on a traffic light.
2. Thomas Jefferson founded the University of Virginia.
3. High school ends with the twelfth grade.
4. Johann Sebastian Bach lived from 1685 to 1750.
5. One job of police officers is enforcing speed limits.
6. Litmus paper turns red in acid solutions.
7. The English alphabet has 26 letters.
8. Under the Treaty of Versailles signed in 1919, Poland regained lost territory.
9. Half of the women in the United States work at a job outside the home.
10. The gross national product of the United States was nearly three trillion dollars in 1981.

EXERCISE 2 Identifying Arguable Propositions

Indicate what type of opinion each sentence asserts by writing *arguable proposition* or *preference.*

Getting Around

1. Riding in an airplane is more exciting than riding on a train.
2. Airline safety could be improved with more rigorous training for flight mechanics.
3. Aircraft of the future will be controlled almost entirely by computers.
4. The meals on Trans Pacific Airways flights are better than the meals on Air America flights.
5. Because of the stressful nature of their jobs, air traffic controllers should have more time off to relax.
6. No thrill can compare to that of watching the engine of your train steaming around a bend on a mountainside.

7. Take-off is the best part of any flight.
8. Take-off is one of the most risky parts of any flight.
9. Passengers should listen carefully to the safety instructions at the beginning of each flight.
10. The romance of riding the rails has faded in the last twenty years.

EXERCISE 3 Supporting Opinions with Facts

For each of the following arguable propositions, write one fact that could be used to back it up.

EXAMPLE Football is a more dangerous game than baseball.

POSSIBLE ANSWER Football injuries are more numerous and serious than baseball injuries.

1. Excessive television-watching may be harmful to one's success in school.
2. People who illegally park in front of fire hydrants should face a stiffer fine than the one now in force.
3. Americans should increase their intake of fruits.
4. People should never use an electrical appliance near water.
5. New sources of energy should be developed.
6. On hot days joggers should run only in the morning or in the evening.
7. Green plants in a window should be moved a quarter-turn each week so they do not grow up crooked.
8. Police work is dangerous.
9. The years of World War II were a time of sacrifice for Americans.
10. John F. Kennedy had a brilliant but tragic life.

EXERCISE 4 On Your Own

In one sentence, write an arguable proposition on the general subject of high school graduation. Then list three facts you could use to back up your proposition. Exchange papers with a classmate and check the following points in each other's work.

1. Is the proposition arguable?
2. Is it supported by facts and not more opinions?
3. Are the facts verifiable?

LOGICAL THINKING

Every writer tries to discover the truth about his or her subject. Firsthand experience and reliable authorities are two good sources for discovering a truth. A third source is your own reasoning power. By combining facts you already know, you can use your reasoning skills to discover new facts and to draw logical conclusions.

Inductive Approach

One approach to discovering new facts and drawing conclusions is called inductive reasoning. The inductive approach builds on specific facts to draw a general conclusion. The following chain of thoughts about naval officers is an example of inductive reasoning.

SPECIFIC FACT	A Fleet Admiral is the highest officer in the Navy.
SPECIFIC FACT	A Fleet Admiral wears one large gold stripe and four smaller gold stripes.
SPECIFIC FACT	An Admiral is lower in rank than a Fleet Admiral.
SPECIFIC FACT	An Admiral wears one large gold stripe and three smaller gold stripes.
GENERAL CONCLUSION	The rank of Navy officers can probably be determined by the number of gold stripes on their uniforms.

Note the word *probably* in the general conclusion. Unless the stripes of every naval officer are examined, the general conclusion cannot be stated with absolute certainty. The conclusions reached by the inductive method of reasoning must always be qualified, or limited, to provide for exceptions.

18c Use **inductive reasoning** to form a qualified general conclusion based on known facts about particulars.

Based on the four facts provided about specific navy officers, the general conclusion seems reasonable. If you suddenly learned the following new facts, however, you would need to revise your thinking and form a new general conclusion.

NEW FACT A commodore wears one two-inch gold stripe.
NEW FACT An ensign wears one half-inch gold stripe.
NEW FACT A commodore has a much higher rank than an ensign.

The old conclusion that equated rank with the *number* of gold stripes on a uniform no longer holds, since both commodores and ensigns wear one stripe. You can, however, draw another reasonable conclusion based on the expanded body of facts at hand.

NEW CONCLUSION The rank of Navy officers can probably be determined by the number and size of the gold stripes on their uniforms.

The main pitfall in using the inductive approach is failing to base your conclusion on a sufficient number of particulars. The result is a hasty generalization, a conclusion that leaves too much room for error and exceptions. The writer of the following paragraph uses inductive reasoning but arrives at a hasty generalization.

SPECIFIC FACTS

HASTY GENERALIZATION

Everybody thinks the nation's "hot spots" are in the southwest or south, but the temperature can also soar in the northeast. I've been to Boston three times, and every single time I've been there, the temperature has been 90° or above. The first time was in May of 1979. On that day, the mercury reached 95°. One other time was in the summer of 1981. That time the temperature was 98°. In September of 1983, I passed through Boston again, and even in the late part of the month the temperature reached 91°. *Boston must be one of the hottest cities in the country.*

The writer of this paragraph bases a general conclusion on only three days over a four-year period. The fact that Boston experiences cold winters is also not taken into account. In addition, the writer fails to check the record of temperatures in other cities. All of these failings could have been avoided if the writer had used the following guidelines.

18d

How to Avoid Hasty Generalizations

1. Examine a sufficient number of particulars.
2. Check reliable authorities to confirm your analysis of particulars.
3. Be able to explain any exceptions.

Even many sound generalizations are, at best, theories. Use words like *some, many, most,* and *probably* to limit generalizations. Beware of such words as *all, total, complete, always, never,* and *none,* which suggest that there are no exceptions.

EXERCISE 5 Using Inductive Reasoning to Draw Conclusions

Read each set of facts below. Then form a general conclusion that answers the question following the facts. Be sure to limit your conclusion with the word *probably, some, many,* or *most.*

EXAMPLE FACTS Two weeks ago my new computer jammed.
On the day it jammed, the weather was very hot and humid.
Last week on a hot and humid day my computer jammed again.
QUESTION What are two factors that probably affect the performance of computers?
ANSWER Two factors that probably affect the performance of computers are temperature and humidity.

1. FACTS At my brother's college, students majoring in business outnumber students majoring in liberal arts.
At my cousin's college, students majoring in business outnumber students majoring in liberal arts.
QUESTION Which field probably attracts more students, business or liberal arts?

2. FACTS *The Day the Earth Stood Still* is a science-fiction movie in which visitors from outer space come to Earth. It is set in the present.

E.T. is also a science-fiction movie in which a visitor from outer space comes to Earth. It is set in the present.
Close Encounters of the Third Kind is another science-fiction movie about visitors from outer space. It is also set in the present.

QUESTION What is one characteristic of many science-fiction movies in which visitors from outer space come to Earth?

3. FACTS When the Chicago Cubs meet the Montreal Expos in Chicago, "The Star-Spangled Banner" is played before "O Canada."
When the Chicago Cubs meet the Montreal Expos in Montreal, "O Canada" is played before "The Star-Spangled Banner."

QUESTION What factor probably determines the order in which national anthems are played at baseball games?

4. FACTS In winter, goats, sheep, and antelope leave the alpine zone of mountains for lower snow-free slopes.
In winter, squirrels and marmots in the alpine zone hibernate.

QUESTION How do the conditions for most animal life in the alpine zone change in winter?

Deductive Approach

In deductive reasoning, you start with a generalization assumed to be true and then apply it to a particular case. Because deduction moves from the general to the particular, it is often considered the opposite of induction. The following chain of thoughts demonstrates the deductive process.

GENERALIZATION No mail is delivered on legal holidays.
PARTICULAR Today is a legal holiday.
CONCLUSION No mail will be delivered today.

18e Use **deductive reasoning** to prove that what is true about a group (generalization) will be true about an individual member of that group (particular).

The steps in the deductive process can be expressed in a three-part statement called a *syllogism*. Each part of the syllogism has a name.

MAJOR PREMISE	All members of the jazz band are seniors.
MINOR PREMISE	Kristin is a member of the jazz band.
CONCLUSION	Kristin is a senior.

The following diagram shows how the conclusion must follow from the premises.

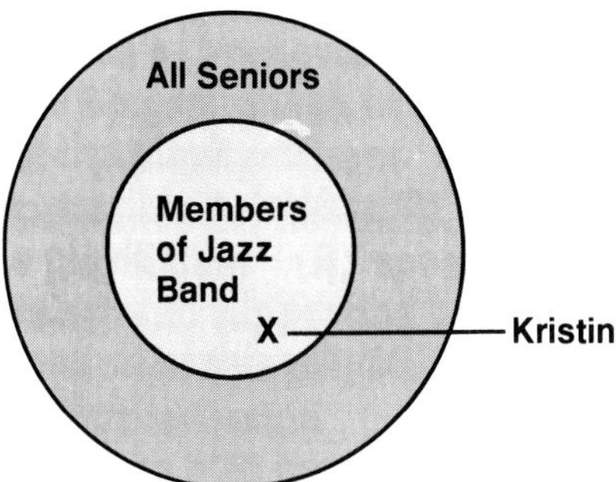

As long as the premises are true, the conclusion about Kristin must also be true, or *sound*. If either or both of the premises are false, however, the conclusion is automatically false, or *unsound*.

In the following example, the conclusion is illogical even if the premises are both true.

MAJOR PREMISE	All members of the jazz band are seniors.
MINOR PREMISE	Kristin is a senior.
CONCLUSION	Kristin is a member of the jazz band.

Another diagram will show why this reasoning is not logical.

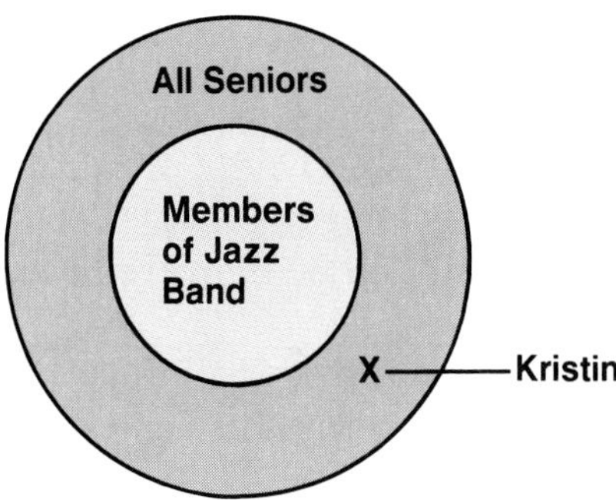

The fact that Kristin belongs to the larger group, seniors, does not guarantee that she will belong to the smaller group, members of the jazz band. Unless the particular in the minor premise is shown to be a member of the smaller group in the major premise, the conclusion is illogical, or *invalid*.

18f A syllogism is **sound** if its premises are true.
A syllogism is **valid** if the reasoning is logical.

EXERCISE 6 Using Deductive Reasoning to Draw Conclusions

Supply the logical conclusion for each of the following sets of premises.

EXAMPLE **MAJOR PREMISE** All city officials live within the city boundaries.
MINOR PREMISE Sal Savetti is a city official.
ANSWER Sal Savetti lives within the city boundaries.

1. **MAJOR PREMISE** All triple-crown winners have won the Kentucky Derby.
   MINOR PREMISE Seattle Slew was a triple-crown winner.
2. **MAJOR PREMISE** All members of the bowling team must have an average of at least 175.
   MINOR PREMISE Carl is a member of the bowling team.
3. **MAJOR PREMISE** All fruits in this basket are either apples or oranges.
   MINOR PREMISE This fruit from the basket is not an apple.
4. **MAJOR PREMISE** All Marx Brothers movies are comedies.
   MINOR PREMISE *A Day at the Races* is a Marx Brothers movie.
5. **MAJOR PREMISE** Saturdays are not school days.
   MINOR PREMISE Today is Saturday.

EXERCISE 7 Recognizing Flaws in Deductive Reasoning

Each of the following syllogisms is either *unsound* or *invalid*. If the premises are not true, write *unsound* after the proper number. If the reasoning is illogical, write *invalid*.

1. All four-legged animals are cows.
   My cat is a four-legged animal.
   My cat is a cow.

2. All cats are four-legged animals.
   My cow is a four-legged animal.
   My cow is a cat.
3. All late papers will be given failing grades.
   Bill's paper was given a failing grade.
   Bill's paper was late.
4. All seniors are on the honor roll.
   Sondra is a senior.
   Sondra is on the honor roll.
5. All southern states begin with the letter *M*.
   Florida is a southern state.
   Florida begins with the letter *M*.

Writing Extra

Many a tricky reasoning problem has been solved by the "process of elimination." That familiar reasoning process is another example of deduction. On multiple-choice tests, for example, you might arrive at the correct answer only by eliminating the incorrect choices. Your reasoning is as follows:

The correct answer is either a, b, c, or d.
The correct answer is not a, c, or d.
The correct answer must be b.

The deductive process of elimination is sometimes used in brain teasers. Test your skill at deduction by trying the following puzzle.

EXERCISE 8 Deducing the Answer to a Brain Teaser
Read the following puzzle and write the logical steps that explain the answer.

Mr. Peters conducted a logic test in his class. He called up Henry, Jim, and Paul and asked them to face each other around a circle. Then he blindfolded the three boys and said, "I am going to move my finger across your foreheads. I can choose to use this finger with soot on it or this clean finger. You won't know whether you have a black mark on your forehead or not. When I remove the blindfolds, it will be your task to discover whether or not you have a black mark. However, I will give you one hint. At least one of you will have a black mark."

He proceeded to make a black mark on Henry and Jim but not on Paul and then removed the blindfolds. Henry looked at the others and noticed that Jim had a black mark but Paul did not. In a few seconds he shouted, "I have a black mark!" How did he make this deduction? —HY RUCHLIS, *CLEAR THINKING*

HINT Henry started with the following premise.
"Either I have a black mark on my forehead or I do not."
He then observed the reactions of Jim and Paul to arrive at his conclusion. What were the steps in his process?

Combining Induction and Deduction

Computer specialists have long been studying the workings of the human brain to learn how to build machines that can copy human thought processes. Although researchers have identified some patterns of thought, such as induction and deduction, they remain mystified at the variety and complexity of human thought. More often than not, humans combine different patterns of thought. Scientists, for example, combine induction with deduction to develop and test hypotheses.

The following passage by naturalist Konrad Lorenz explains how he made some discoveries about duck behavior. Notice how his thinking process moves back and forth from induction to deduction.

> (1) I was experimenting at one time with young mallards to find out why artificially incubated and freshly hatched ducklings of this species, in contrast to greylag goslings, are unapproachable and shy. Greylag goslings unquestioningly accept the first being whom they meet as their mother, and run confidently after her. The mallards, on the contrary, always refused to do this. If I took from the incubator freshly hatched mallards, they invariably ran away from me and pressed themselves in the nearest dark corner. Why?
>
> (2) I remembered that I had once let a muscovy duck hatch a clutch of mallard eggs and that the tiny mallards had also failed to accept this foster-mother. As soon as they were dry, they had simply run away from her, and I had trouble enough to catch these crying, erring children. On the other hand, I

once let a fat white farmyard duck hatch out mallards, and the little wild things ran just as happily after her as if she had been their real mother. The secret must have lain in her call note, for, in external appearance, the domestic duck was quite as different from a mallard as was the muscovy. What she had in common with the mallard (to which she is related) were her vocal expressions . . . The inference was clear: I must quack like a mother mallard in order to make the little ducks run after me. —KONRAD LORENZ, *KING SOLOMON'S RING*

In paragraph one, Lorenz uses induction to come to the general conclusion that baby mallards and baby greylags behave in different ways. He bases his reasoning on observations of specific ducks. In paragraph two, he starts with induction as he recalls specific instances involving muscovy ducks and mallards. He then uses deduction to arrive at a possible explanation for the success of the farmyard duck in passing for a mallard mother. He bases this reasoning on known general truths about mallards, farmyard ducks, and muscovys. He then applies these facts to his specific ducks and is able to reason how to make them follow him.

18g Use a mixture of induction and deduction to formulate and test your ideas.

EXERCISE 9 Analyzing a Mixture of Induction and Deduction

The following paragraphs continue the story of Lorenz's discoveries about ducks. As you read them, look for examples of induction and deduction. Then write answers to the questions that follow.

(1) My theory was indisputably proved . . . Anything that emits the right quack will be considered as mother, whether it is a fat Pekin duck or a still fatter man. However, the substituted object must not exceed a certain height. At the beginnings of these experiments I had sat myself down in the grass amongst the ducklings and, to make them follow me, had dragged myself, sitting, away from them. When I tried to lead them on from a standing position, however, they gave up, peered searchingly on all sides, but not upwards towards me, and before long they began "crying." They were unable to adapt themselves to the fact that their foster-mother had

become so tall. So I was forced to move along, squatting low, if I wished them to follow me. This was not very comfortable.

(2) Still less comfortable was the fact that the mallard mother quacks continuously. If I stopped for even half a minute my melodious "Quahg, gegegegeg, Quahg, gegegegeg," the necks of the ducklings became longer and longer, just like "long faces" in human children. If I did not begin quacking again immediately, the shrill weeping began anew. As soon as I was silent, they seemed to think that I had died, or perhaps that I loved them no more: cause enough for crying! Imagine a two-hour walk, all the time squatting low and quacking without interruption! In the interests of science, I submitted myself literally for hours on end to this ordeal.

(3) One Sunday I was wandering about, squatting and quacking, in a May-green meadow at the upper part of our garden. I was congratulating myself on the obedience and precision with which my ducklings came waddling after me. Then I suddenly looked up and saw the garden fence framed by a row of dead-white faces. A group of tourists was standing at the fence and staring horrified in my direction. Forgivable! For all they could see was a big man with a beard dragging himself, crouching, round the meadow, glancing over his shoulder and quacking. The ducklings, the all-revealing and all-explaining ducklings, were hidden in the tall spring grass from the view of the astonished crowd.

—KONRAD LORENZ, *KING SOLOMON'S RING*

1. By which method, induction or deduction, does Lorenz arrive at the conclusion that the ducklings could not adapt to the full height of their foster mother?
2. At the beginning of paragraph 2, Lorenz starts his reasoning about mallard quacking with the premise that "mother mallards quack continuously." Implied in the rest of the paragraph are the following logical extensions of that idea: "I am a mother mallard. Therefore I must quack continuously." Which logical method does this reasoning represent, induction or deduction?
3. In paragraph 2, Lorenz tests his conclusion about the need for quacking. As Konrad Lorenz observes the ducklings' reactions, which method of reasoning is he using, induction or deduction?
4. In paragraph 3, Lorenz relates the reactions of "horrified" onlookers who seem to regard him as a highly abnormal

person. By what method of reasoning did the onlookers arrive at this conclusion? (For a hint, see question 5.)

5. The onlookers used the following premises to arrive at their conclusion about Lorenz.

   People who squat and quack without any understandable reason are abnormal.

   This man is squatting and quacking without any understandable reason.

   What is the logical conclusion from these premises?

EXERCISE 10 On Your Own

Using the general subject of cars and driving as a starting point, write the logical steps in arriving at one inductive conclusion and one deductive conclusion. Use the following models as a guide.

Inductive

Beth, Ann, and Flora passed their driving tests on the first try.
Mike, Conrad, and Dan passed their tests on the second try.
Girls probably pass their driving tests on the first try more often than boys do.

Deductive

All new cars must have a catalytic converter.
My car is a new car.
My car must have a catalytic converter.

FALLACIES

A fallacy is a flaw in reasoning. You have already seen how to avoid some flaws, such as the hasty generalization and the faulty syllogism. In addition to these, the following six fallacies need special attention, since they frequently surface in a poorly reasoned argument.

Attacking the Person Instead of the Issue. This fallacy is often called *argumentum ad hominem,* which is Latin for "argument against the man." Writers who commit this fallacy attack the character of their opponent instead of addressing the real issue. The fallacy in the following example is the effort to discredit the *character* of Senator Moreland instead of the specific proposals that may be contained within the bill.

AD HOMINEM FALLACY — Senator Moreland has missed every important vote this year. How could his new bill have any merit?

Although Moreland's voting record may be irresponsible, his new bill may be very worthy.

It is illogical to argue from irrelevant, negative character traits. It is also illogical to use irrelevant, positive personal qualities as the basis of an argument.

AD HOMINEM FALLACY — Sally Jones has never been late to work. She's the sort of person we need as mayor of our city.

Promptness is admirable, but it is not the only quality a mayor should have.

Fallacy of *Either-Or/If-Then*. Writers guilty of this fallacy assume that there are only two sides to an issue, ignoring all alternative viewpoints. Notice how in the following examples the issues are illogically limited to two choices.

EITHER–OR FALLACY — Either we stop using nuclear power for energy or we face certain disaster in the future.

IF–THEN FALLACY — If I can't buy that dress, then I'm not going to the dance.

In the first example, another reasonable alternative to "certain disaster" might be better systems of waste management. In the second example, another alternative to not going to the dance would be wearing something else. Between the two extreme positions on most issues lie a number of interesting and worthwhile viewpoints.

The Fallacy of *Non Sequitur*. In Latin, the words *non sequitur* mean "it does not follow." You have already seen examples of conclusions that do not necessarily follow from the evidence. Most *non sequiturs* are the result of illogical deductive thinking.

NON SEQUITUR — My sister recommended this book; it must be good.
John's car was more expensive than mine; he must be richer than I.

Like the fallacy of either-or, the *non sequitur* omits possible alternatives. Judgments about the quality of books vary greatly, and your sister's taste may not match your own. John may have spent more money on his car, but his overall wealth is impossible to determine from this one fact.

Confusing Chronology with Cause and Effect. This fallacy assumes that whatever happens after an event is the *result* of that event. In many cases, the relationship between the two events is entirely coincidental.

CAUSE–EFFECT FALLACY

I made a wish on my birthday that I would win a prize. The following week I won two concert tickets in a raffle. Wishing really works!

The cause of the roof's collapse was yesterday's heavy snowfall.

In the first example, only coincidence relates the two events. In the second example, however, the heavy snowfall may indeed have been a *contributing* cause to the collapse of the roof. The fallacy lies in assuming it was the *only* cause. A sound roof could have withstood a snowfall, so another cause could have been rotted supports. Most errors in cause-and-effect reasoning are the result of failing to admit a number of causes.

False Analogies. An analogy is a comparison between two things that are alike in some significant ways. The assumption behind an analogy is that things that are similar in some ways are similar in *most* ways. A false analogy attempts to compare two things that are not enough alike for that assumption to be sound. Analogies are useful tools for explaining, but they are rarely effective in proving a point.

FALSE ANALOGY

The phone company's discontinuation of my telephone service was unfair, because even a criminal gets one phone call.

Inviting Charlie and Rita to the same party would be a big mistake, because oil and water don't mix.

There are no logical grounds for comparing the situation of a free citizen who has not paid the telephone bill and that of an imprisoned criminal. The second false analogy is less obvious.

It may be true that Charlie and Rita get along as poorly as oil and water. The analogy is nevertheless false because the two could attend a party without interacting with one another like a mixture of oil and water.

Begging the Question. A writer who "begs the question" builds an argument on an unproved assumption.

BEGGING THE QUESTION That unethical doctor should not be allowed to practice medicine.

Fireworks are illegal in our town because there is a law forbidding them.

In the first example, the writer *assumes* (takes as a given fact) that the doctor is unethical, when in fact the doctor's character is the real question being decided. The second example shows the *circular reasoning* process that makes question-begging a fallacy. All that sentence is saying is: Fireworks are illegal because they are illegal.

18h Eliminate **fallacies** from your thinking and writing.

EXERCISE 11 Recognizing Fallacies

After the proper number on your paper, write the name of the fallacy committed in each of the following statements.

attacking the person instead of the issue	confusing chronology with cause and effect
either-or/if-then	false analogy
non sequitur	begging the question

1. Either you allow the hunting of wolves or you end up with slaughtered farm animals.
2. The dog is barking; there must be someone at the door.
3. The sun reappeared after the cave dwellers chanted a hymn during the eclipse. The chanting of the hymn must have caused the sun to reappear.
4. I didn't hear Kathleen's speech, but I know I disagree with it. She's always so disorganized!
5. These unnecessary taxes are a burden on taxpayers.
6. Just as a car needs gasoline to keep running, a hospital needs volunteers.

7. If you don't clean your room, then you obviously do not care what people think about you.
8. The show was a flop; the actors must not have rehearsed long enough.
9. Every time I go running I get thirsty. Running must cause thirst.
10. The shortsighted plan to cut the trees down will have unpleasant future consequences.
11. That extra game we played during the regular season caused us to lose in the semifinals of the play-offs.
12. Dyer aspirin gets rid of your headache in minutes; it's a wonder drug.
13. Electing an inexperienced citizen to the United States Senate is like putting a hero from a science-fiction movie at the controls of the real space shuttle.
14. Since Luis received only average grades his first year at college, he cannot become a lawyer.
15. Jon Albano is the youngest candidate; I wouldn't trust him as class president.
16. Living in the United States without a car is like cooking bread without flour.
17. Jim Miller's illogical plan does not make sense and will not help.
18. Either you are for raising taxes or you are against providing people with important services.
19. If I don't make it as a jazz musician, my life will be empty.
20. Demetrius Pappas has always been kind enough to look after our house when we're away. He's got my vote.
21. No sooner did the Dagerwoods move into the neighborhood than we began having more crime around here. I bet they are involved in illegal activities.
22. Plato is a famous philosopher; his argument about the human soul must be correct.
23. Getting *A*'s and *B*'s in school is as easy as doing your chores at home.
24. Jim Dine plays the lottery all the time, hoping to get rich in a hurry. Should we seriously consider making him a partner in our business?
25. Buy a *Little Flowers* dress and add the magic of romance to your life.

EXERCISE 12 On Your Own
Write five sentences agreeing or disagreeing with the following statement.

A college education is worth pursuing.

Exchange papers with a classmate and check each other's work for fallacies.

CHAPTER REVIEW

A. Facts and Opinions
Identify each of the following statements as *fact, preference,* or *arguable proposition.*

1. Geometry is more interesting than algebra.
2. The Declaration of Independence was signed on July 4, 1776.
3. Many national trends begin in California.
4. The speed limit on interstate highways is 55 miles per hour.
5. The competition in the telephone industry has benefited consumers.
6. Watching baseball is much more exciting than watching football.
7. Because they are faced with life and death decisions, nurses should be paid more.
8. You should wait one hour after eating to go swimming.
9. Students must get high scores on the S.A.T.'s to be accepted at a good college or university.
10. A United States president serves a term of four years.

B. Logical Thinking
Identify each of the following statements as an example of either *inductive* or *deductive* reasoning.

11. Five people I know are sick with the flu. The flu must be going around.
12. Bernadette based her decision to become a lawyer on the facts that lawyers earn good pay and perform a useful service.

13. Most redheads I know also have freckles. Red hair and freckles are probably related genetically.
14. The last time I picked up a glass with wet hands, I dropped it. I'd better dry my hands this time.
15. People who park illegally run the risk of getting a ticket. I don't want to get a ticket, so I'll keep looking for a legal space.
16. Sam Adams is a good athlete. He will probably make the soccer team.
17. I have never seen anyone at the Taft School wearing jeans. Wearing jeans must be against the school dress code.
18. I want to become a journalist. Journalists must have strong writing skills, so I work hardest in English class.
19. Dan wants to be a mechanic, but he doesn't like getting his hands dirty. You have to get your hands dirty to fix a car. Dan should consider another career.
20. Many new apartments have been built in the city recently. There must be a housing shortage.

C. Fallacies

Identify the fallacy in each of the following statements.

21. This difficult assignment should be simplified.
22. I don't know why anyone would vote for Antonia; she wasn't even born in this country.
23. Music should be a required course in high school. People do not live by bread alone.
24. I remembered to take my umbrella today. That's why it didn't rain!
25. If you don't approve this plan, then you have no regard for the disadvantaged.
26. If you can put together a jigsaw puzzle, you can build a motorcycle.
27. If people will pay exorbitant prices for designer clothes, designers should continue to set prices high.
28. Ever since I became student-council president, the student body has shown members of the council more respect—a direct result of my leadership.
29. If you do not support increased military spending, then you advocate a defenseless United States.
30. Jeanne Gibbons, a marvelous mother and homemaker, is the best choice for city councilor.

Chapter Summary

Clear Thinking

Facts and Opinions

1. Use your own experiences and reliable authorities to verify facts.
2. Build your compositions on arguable propositions and collect the evidence needed to argue convincingly.

Logical Thinking

3. Use inductive reasoning to form a qualified general conclusion based on known facts about particulars.
4. Avoid hasty generalizations.
5. Use deductive reasoning to prove that what is true about a group will be true about an individual member of that group.
6. Avoid unsound and invalid syllogisms.
7. Use a mix of induction and deduction to formulate and test your ideas.

Fallacies

8. Rid your thought of fallacies, especially:
   - attacking the person instead of the issue
   - the fallacy of either-or/if-then
   - non sequiturs
   - confusing chronology with cause and effect
   - false analogies
   - begging the question

19

Paragraphs

In a longer piece of writing, paragraphs help break up thoughts so that readers can easily follow them. The indented line at the beginning of a paragraph tells readers that a new idea is about to be developed. When it stands alone, a paragraph is a short composition, complete with an introductory sentence, a body of supporting sentences, and a concluding sentence. Many essay tests call for answering a question with such a paragraph composition.

Although you may come across a variety of paragraph styles in your reading, most good paragraphs have some common features that ensure clarity. As in all writing, the main purpose of a paragraph is to help readers understand your message, clearly and simply.

19a A **paragraph** is a group of related sentences that present and develop one main idea.

FEATURES OF A GOOD PARAGRAPH

You have heard people say after reading something, "I really didn't get much out of it." Although sometimes the fault lies with the reader, the writer must bear the responsibility for providing a message with substance and an easy-to-follow structure. Notice how much you can "get out of" the following paragraph.

Stellar Compromises

TOPIC SENTENCE: STATES MAIN IDEA

Director George Lucas considers *Star Wars* a "real low-budget movie."

BODY OF SUPPORTING SENTENCES: DEVELOPS MAIN IDEA WITH SPECIFICS

He had to pare down his original budget estimate of $18 million, and, as a result, the film is full of compromises. He cut out over a hundred special-effects shots. New sets were made from old sets. Space weapons were made out of cut-down machine guns. On such a low budget, the robots didn't work right at first. The original R2-D2 couldn't go more than three feet without running into something. (Extra footage had to be shot later for some scenes in the beginning.) Even the cantina scene, in which Luke and Ben Kenobi hire Han Solo and Chewbacca from among a roomful of bizarre, other worldly creatures, is only a shadow of what was in Lucas's imagination. The designer fell sick, and the studio wouldn't give Lucas enough money to have someone fully complete it.

CONCLUDING SENTENCE: REINFORCES MAIN IDEA

"The film is about 25 percent of what I wanted it to be," he has said.

—DIAN G. SMITH, *AMERICAN FILMMAKERS TODAY* (ADAPTED)

This paragraph is effective for a number of reasons. Its clear structure is easy to follow. The main idea is amply supported with specific details. All the sentences stick to the main idea, and they are presented in a smooth, logical order. In short, it has all the features of a good paragraph.

Paragraph Structure

A paragraph that stands alone has three main parts: a topic sentence, a body of supporting sentences, and a concluding sentence. The following chart summarizes the function of each element in a paragraph.

19b

Elements in a Paragraph

1. The **topic sentence**
   - states the main idea.
   - limits the main idea to one aspect of the subject that can be covered in one paragraph.
   - controls all the other sentences in the paragraph.
   - is more general than the sentences that develop it.
2. The **supporting sentences** explain, develop, or prove the topic sentence with specific details, events, facts, examples, or reasons.
3. The **concluding sentence,** often called a clincher, adds a strong ending by restating, re-emphasizing, or summarizing the main idea.

The topic sentence can come at the beginning, middle, or end of a paragraph. In some paragraphs the main idea is expressed in two sentences instead of one. In other cases it is implied rather than stated directly. All of these choices are available to writers as long as the main idea is clear. The following examples show variety, but in each paragraph the development of one main idea is clear.

TOPIC SENTENCE AT BEGINNING

The automobile is a fixture of American life and seems certain to remain so. Eighty percent of all American families own at least one car. In urban areas, the percentage of car-owning families ranges from a low of 72 percent in Chicago to a high of 91 percent in San Jose, California. In the latter city, 37 percent own more than one car. Owning a car is an American birthright—and a necessity. Sixty-four percent of the population use the car to get to and from work. The car is a symbol of affluence, a source of pleasure, and an island of privacy in a crowded world. It supports several giant industries, such as automobile manufacturers and makers of rubber and petroleum. The car *is* now and *will be* in the future.

—ROBERT A. LISTON, *DOWNTOWN*

TOPIC SENTENCE IN MIDDLE

Japan is a collection of large islands, strung along the eastern shore of the mainland of Asia. The islands are very rugged and very mountainous. High over all the other peaks rises the one supreme peak—the perfect cone of snow-clad Fuji. Like most of the high mountains of Japan, Fuji is a volcano, sleeping, but far from dead. Compared to the Alps and the Himalayas, Fuji is not especially high. It seems high, however, because it rises in one superb sweeping curve right from the shore to the sky, a curve that can be seen for a hundred miles on every side.

—RICHARD HALLIBURTON, *COMPLETE BOOK OF MARVELS*

TOPIC SENTENCE AT END

On July 14, 1853, the early morning sun shone brilliantly on the four American warships as they lay at anchor in Yedo Bay, now called Tokyo Bay. The weather was perfect, the sea calm, and even the warships looked tranquil. The looks, however, were deceiving. Aboard the vessels sailors and marines were busily preparing for one of the most spectacular diplomatic efforts in the history of the United States. Commodore Matthew Calbraith Perry, Commander-in-Chief of U.S. Naval Forces in the Far East, India, China, and Japan seas, was about to make the first American landing in Japan.

—JOSEPH D. ICENHOWER, *PERRY AND THE OPEN DOOR TO JAPAN* (ADAPTED)

MAIN IDEA IMPLIED

When the newborn seal pup slips from the warmth of his mother's body onto the ice, crystals form on his wet little body and his skin temperature falls to 70° F. He shivers so vigorously that in about 45 minutes he has produced enough heat to bring his skin temperature to 93.4° F. Only a light coat of baby fur, the lanugo, protects him from the zero temperatures of the Antarctic spring. His metabolism, however, is exceedingly high during his early life, and he can take in great quantities of milk. Seal mothers' milk is richer than heavy cream; it is half butterfat. On this creamy diet the pup gains about 250 pounds in six weeks and has a good coating of fat.

—LUCY KAVALER, *LIFE BATTLES COLD* (ADAPTED)

Implied main idea: Seal pups have innate mechanisms to help them survive infancy in extreme cold weather.

EXERCISE 1 Identifying the Main Idea
Copy the topic sentence from each of the following paragraphs. If the main idea of a paragraph is implied rather than stated directly, write a sentence expressing the main idea in your own words.

1. Starry Neighbors

Easter Island is the loneliest inhabited place in the world. The nearest solid land the islanders can see is above, in the firmament, the moon and the planets. They have to travel farther than any other people to see that there really is land closer. Therefore, living nearest the stars, they know more names of stars than of towns and countries in our own world.

—THOR HYERDAHL, *AKU-AKU*

2. Future Travel

By the year 2025, very wide planes will be in use and will be very different from those of today. Even your preflight arrangements will be made in an entirely new way. You will buy your ticket using your home or office computer. By pushing some buttons, you will get a printout of airline schedules and be able to make your reservation. You will also receive a printout confirmation of your flight number, seat number, and your destination. When you arrive at the airport, you will put this printout card in a check-in machine. It will check your identity, check your reservations, and record your name on the list of passengers. It will charge your bank account the correct amount for the fare. This will all be done by a mechanical computerized voice. It will even greet you by name.

—HARRIETTE S. ABELS, *FUTURE TRAVEL* (ADAPTED)

3. Forest Rangers

Park rangers' work includes planning and carrying out conservation efforts to protect plant and animal life in the parks from fire, disease, and heavy visitor traffic. Rangers plan and conduct programs of public safety, including law enforcement and rescue work. They set up and direct interpretive programs such as slide shows, guided tours, displays, and occasionally even dramatic presentations. These programs are designed to help visitors become aware of the natural and historic significance of the areas they visit.

—WALTER OLEKSY, *CAREERS IN THE ANIMAL KINGDOM*

4. Two Kinds of Twilight

Civil twilight lasts until the sun's center is 6° below the horizon, when the light has become too dim for outdoor activities. It is, however, still twenty times brighter than the light of the full moon. Astronomical twilight ends when the sun's center is 18° below the horizon, when the sky is so dark that the faintest stars can be seen. The same phenomena recur in reverse order before sunrise.

—KENNETH HEUER, *RAINBOWS, HALOS, AND OTHER WONDERS*

5. Opening the Door to the Heart

On July 9, 1893, a skillful black surgeon named Daniel Hale Williams made a six-inch incision in the chest of a wounded patient at Provident Hospital in Chicago. Detaching the fifth rib from the patient's breastbone and working through a 1½-by-2-inch opening into the chest cavity, he repaired a torn artery. He also stitched up the pericardium, or membranous sac enclosing the heart, which had been punctured by a knife wound. The patient survived the delicate operation and regained full health. Dr. Williams had achieved a landmark in the history of surgery and opened the door to a new epoch in medicine.

— BEN RICHARDSON AND WILLIAM A. FAHEY, *GREAT BLACK AMERICANS* (ADAPTED)

Adequate Development

As you have seen, the job of the supporting sentences in a paragraph is to develop the main idea with specifics. The specifics may be in the form of facts, examples, reasons, events, descriptive details, or comparisons and contrasts.

Whatever their form, the supporting ideas should be sufficiently numerous and specific to fulfill their job of adequately developing the main idea.

The following paragraph lacks adequate development. The sentences that form the body of the paragraph are too general and too few to support the full weight of the main idea.

INADEQUATE DEVELOPMENT

Around the turn of the last century, child labor practices led to a grueling life for many American children. Many children worked instead of going to school, and they had hard jobs. They also worked long hours for little pay. Since their families often needed the money, these children had little choice but to work hard. Eventually some laws were passed that put an end to some of the child labor practices.

In the following paragraph, vivid and specific facts and examples supply adequate development of the main idea.

ADEQUATE DEVELOPMENT

Around the turn of the last century, child labor practices led to a grueling life for many American children. In 1900, at least 1.7 million children under the age of sixteen worked for wages. Children working at night were kept awake by having cold water splashed in their faces. Some girls under sixteen worked sixteen hours a day in canning factories, capping forty cans per minute. Ten-year-old boys crouched over dusty coal chutes for ten hours a day to pick slate out of the coal sliding past. In city tenements many children seven years and younger made artificial flowers at night to be sold the next day at street stands. Some states began passing laws protecting child laborers after 1905. Not until 1938 was a federal law passed that prevented employers in most industries from hiring children under the age of sixteen.

—CLARENCE L. VER STEEG, *AMERICAN SPIRIT* (ADAPTED)

19c Use numerous and specific facts, examples, and other details to provide adequate development of your main idea.

EXERCISE 2 Revising a Paragraph with Inadequate Development

The supporting sentences in the following paragraph are too general. Using the facts that follow it, revise the paragraph to include specifics that ensure adequate development. Use the first sentence (topic sentence) and concluding sentence as they are.

Cities Take Over

Between the years of 1860 and 1910, the nation's population increased enormously. Many people came from Europe. The new population moved to both rural and urban areas, but more people moved to cities. The number of cities increased dramatically. Ever since the early 1900s, the United States has been a nation of cities.

FACTS	1860	1910	% change
overall population	31 million	92 million	200
rural population	25 million	50 million	100
urban population	6 million	42 million	600
number of cities	400	2200	450

number of immigrants from Europe (1865–1910): 19 million

Unity

In a paragraph with unity, all of the sentences support and develop the main idea. A paragraph with unity is easy to follow, since the reader is not distracted by ideas or details that stray from the subject.

19d Achieve **unity** in a paragraph by making sure that all of the supporting sentences relate directly to the main idea.

The crossed-out portions of the following paragraph stray from the main idea. Notice that the paragraph is easier to follow without them.

Sammy Lee

Sammy Lee, a second-generation Korean-American, has devoted his life to athletic excellence and physical fitness. In 1948, he won the Olympic medal for high diving. When he repeated his success at the following Olympics four years later, he became the first male diver to win two consecutive times. ~~Another Korean-American, Richard You, was an Olympic weight lifting coach.~~ Lee also won the James E. Sullivan award for outstanding sports achievement in 1958. Lee now practices medicine and is a member of the President's Council on Physical Fitness. ~~Richard You is also a doctor.~~

At first glance the sentences about Richard You may seem related to the idea of the paragraph. Like Sammy Lee, You is a Korean doctor who achieved athletic fame. The main idea of the paragraph, however, is limited by the topic sentence to Sammy Lee only.

EXERCISE 3 Understanding Unity

Write the sentences in each paragraph that stray from the main idea and weaken the paragraph's unity.

1. Science or Magic?

Although the alchemists of earlier centuries are often regarded as superstitious magicians, they did help pave the way to some important discoveries. In their vain search for a way to turn base metals into gold and develop an elixir of life, they discovered chemicals that we now use every day in such products as dyes, varnish, medicine, glass, and steel. Some alchemists, however, were frauds. They also developed methods for waterproofing, smelling salts, and some pain killers. One famous alchemist, Merlin, may have existed only in legend. One early alchemist developed a theory of gas, and others led the way to an understanding of blood circulation and enzymes and hormones. Although their work was limited by the lack of good knowledge, many alchemists were serious scientists whose discoveries opened new doors.

2. Chocolate on the Waterfront

San Francisco's Ghirardelli Square is a good example of urban creativity. Once the site of run-down factory buildings, including the famous chocolate factory that gives the square its name, this waterfront area was slated for the wrecker's ball. Hershey, Pennsylvania, is another famous chocolate-making city. Creative architects and designers, however, took to remodeling the factory buildings, bringing out the beauty of their old brick archways and decorative ironwork. Now Ghirardelli Square is a pleasant shopping area with restaurants, fountains, and parks. Fanueil Hall, an old structure in Boston, was also remodeled and converted into a highly successful shopping area. The waterfront once again carries the aroma of chocolate, and the square attracts thousands of tourists each year.

3. Director of Volunteer Services

Volunteers are extremely important in the smooth running of a hospital. For this reason, the Director of Volunteer Services is usually a well-paid professional. The requirements for this position often include a college education, usually in sociology, psychology, or management. Hospital volunteers of all ages perform a number of tasks, from working in the gift shop to writing letters for people too sick to write for themselves. The salary of the volunteer director varies according to the worker's previous experience and the size and resources of the hospital. Most doctors earn more money than the volunteer director. The job is so important, however, that most volunteer directors earn a good wage.

4. Seven Wonders

The Seven Wonders of the ancient world were remarkable human creations, scattered around the Mediterranean lands. The oldest of the Seven Wonders was the pyramid of Cheops in Egypt, a monument that was ancient when most of the other marvels were just being constructed. The second wonder was located in Babylon. There the famed hanging gardens brought luxuriant plants and flowers to a dry land. At Halicarnassus, in what is now Turkey, stood the third wonder, the tomb erected by the queen Artemisia in honor of her husband, Mausolus. That portion of Asia Minor, which is now Turkey, was once settled by the Greeks. The fourth wonder was the Colossus of Rhodes, a bronze statue of the sun-god Helios, which towered a hundred feet over the point of the harbor of Rhodes. The fifth wonder was another famous beacon, the Pharos, or lighthouse of Alexandria, a guide for sea-weary travelers. Lighthouses are useful guides, located as they often are on cliffs and capes. The sixth wonder, the statue of Zeus by the artist Phidias, was a superb image of ivory and gold. There were also temples in honor of Hera, the wife of Zeus, but these were not so important as the temples of Zeus. The final wonder was the magnificent temple at Ephesus in honor of Artemis, goddess of the hunt. These Seven Wonders charmed travelers for centuries, but today only the pyramid has survived.

Coherence

Coherence is the quality of a paragraph that makes each idea seem logically and smoothly related to all the others. Two keys to coherent paragraphs are a logical organization and effective connecting devices.

19e Achieve **coherence** by using a logical organization and effective connectives.

Logical Organization. The following chart shows the most common ways to organize paragraphs and longer pieces of writing. Almost all subjects can be logically organized by one of the following methods.

19f

Methods of Organization

CHRONOLOGICAL ORDER	Items are arranged in the order in which they happened (time order).
SPATIAL ORDER	Items are arranged according to their location (near to far, top to bottom, left to right, etc.).
ORDER OF IMPORTANCE	Items are arranged in order of most to least or least to most important, interesting, or sizable.
DEVELOPMENTAL ORDER	Items are arranged in a logical progression, in which one idea grows out of another.

EXERCISE 4 Recognizing Methods of Logical Organization Identify the type of order used in each of the following paragraphs by writing *chronological, spatial, order of importance,* or *developmental order.*

1. The Distant Past

Throughout most of the Mesozoic Era, sometimes called the Age of Reptiles, primitive mammals scurried about, lost in the shadows of the mighty dinosaurs who lumbered through the gloomy swamps and giant softwood forests. In the beginning of the Cretaceous, the period which marks the last chapter in the reign of the giant reptiles, the earth cooled. Inland seas receded, marshes dried up, and the monster dinosaurs clambered out onto the trembling uplands and began to live on open ground. Great hardwood forests of oak, walnut, beech, and laurel bloomed and soon covered the land. Life for the small, ancestral mammals was perilous, and while the terrible dinosaurs ruled, the little animals hurried about in the deep green shade of the forests or took refuge in the branches of bushes and trees, often venturing forth only at night. They waited, unaware of the kingdom they were soon to inherit, and used their wits and mammalian advantages to survive. —JUDITH GROCH, *YOU AND YOUR BRAIN*

2. Packaging the Human Brain

Without the skull to hold it together, the moist, rubbery brain would lose its familiar shape. The cortex of the bulging cerebrum is deeply wrinkled, or convoluted, while parallel and curved furrows divide the smaller cerebellum onto leaves that resemble the sections of a tangerine. This is nature's ingenious answer to the problem of how to pack approximately three and a half square feet of valuable brain surface into an area five to six inches in diameter. A deep cleft, running from front to back, divides the cerebrum into left and right halves. These are known as the cerebral hemispheres. Each of the hemispheres is divided by other crevices which produce the four familiar lobes of the cerebral landscape—frontal, temporal, parietal, and occipital.

—JUDITH GROCH, *YOU AND YOUR BRAIN*

3. A Man of Many Talents

Benjamin Franklin accomplished many things in his eighty-four years. He was a recognized inventor. Franklin gave to the world the stove, bifocals, and the lightning rod. He invented a draft for fireplaces and a combination chair and stepladder for the kitchen. He was also a city-planner. Franklin reorganized the British Post Office, established a city police system in Philadelphia, and an efficient fire control organization. He was instrumental in providing his city with a public hospital and a subscription library. Furthermore, Franklin was a military strategist. He organized a successful defense of his colony when it was threatened by attack by the French. He led a force of men into the wilderness near Bethlehem and supervised the building of three important forts in that area. Finally, Franklin was an active statesman. He was a member of the committee which drew up the Declaration of Independence, a delegate to the Constitutional Convention, and a very popular and valuable ambassador to England and France for over twenty-five years.

—P. JOSEPH CANAVAN

4. Memory Mosaic

However it operates, wherever are hidden the multiplication tables, the faces of friends, the catalogues of pleasure and pain, it is clear that human memory requires space. No single region of the brain could possibly serve as the specialized storehouse of memory. It has been estimated that millions of neurons are involved in the recall of a single memory, for so intricate is the storage system that each bit of information is itself broken into smaller pieces and stored at different points in the brain. The color, shape, texture, taste, meaning, feeling, and other associations which belong to the word *apple* are scattered like the pieces of a jigsaw puzzle throughout the storage units of the brain. Yet upon request they spring together so that immediately the familiar fruit is seen drifting across a mental screen, hanging with companions in a mental orchard, or resting in a fruit bowl similarly conjured from the scattered fragments of a memory mosaic.

—JUDITH GROCH, *YOU AND YOUR BRAIN*

Effective Connectives. The most important connective, or linking device, is the transition. *Transitions* are words or phrases that show how ideas are related to one another. The following chart lists some common transitions and the type of logical order with which they are often used.

Chronological Order	Spatial Order	Order of Importance	Developmental Order
first, second	above	first, second	furthermore
then	below	more important	besides
at first	right	most important	however
by evening	next to	the largest	nonetheless
as soon as	beyond	above all	despite
after	inside	besides	another
finally	behind	another	in addition

Some other devices that accomplish the same purpose as transitions are summarized in the following chart.

19g

Ways to Connect Ideas

1. Use transition words and phrases.
2. Repeat key words occasionally.
3. Use synonyms in place of some key words.
4. Use pronouns in place of some key words.

EXERCISE 5 Identifying Connectives
Identify each connective in the following paragraph by writing *transition, repeated key word, synonym,* or *pronoun.*

Bicycles Go to War

When the American army moved into Europe during World War I, it brought with it 29,000 bicycles. (1) *During* World War II, fighting on many more fronts, the American (2) *armed forces* went overseas with a total of over 60,000 bicycles. (3) *As in World War I,* none of the (4) *two-wheelers* were assigned to combat organizations to be used as weapons. (5) *Instead,* the (6) *bicycles* filled subsidiary roles in personal transportation, message carrying, and other utility functions. In one of the paradoxes of the bicycle's employment during the war, (7) *American soldiers* in Europe ended up using the two-wheelers in pursuit of the Germans—on captured enemy (8) *machines.* Wherever (9) *G.I.s* found bicycles abandoned by hastily retreating Germans, (10) *they* snatched up their loot on the basis that it's better to be riding than walking.

—MARTIN CAIDIN AND JAY BARBREE, *BICYCLES IN WAR*

EXERCISE 6 On Your Own
Select for study one of the four paragraphs in Exercise 4 on pages 429–430. Label your paper with the title of the paragraph, and then write answers to the following questions.

1. What is the topic sentence (or implied main idea)?
2. What specifics provide adequate development of that idea?
3. What gives the paragraph unity?
4. What is one transition used in the paragraph?
5. Locate three other devices used to achieve coherence.

KINDS OF PARAGRAPHS

Millions of pages of prose have been written since humans first invented writing. Virtually all of them, however, can be classified into one of four main types of writing. The type is determined by the author's purpose. The four main purposes are to tell a story, to describe, to explain, and to persuade. Each type of writing calls for special techniques that suit the writing purpose.

Narrative Paragraphs

Writing that tells what happens is called narration. Narration is used in letters, news stories, short stories, novels, histories, and biographies.

19h

A **narrative paragraph** tells a real or imaginary story with a clear beginning, middle, and ending.

Most stories have a *conflict* of some sort at their core. In the following narrative paragraph, the conflict is between the crew of a coast-guard vessel and a polar bear. As you are reading the paragraph, notice the features of narration. Transitional words and phrases are in heavy type.

A Curious Clown

TOPIC SENTENCE: MAKES A GENERAL STATEMENT ABOUT THE STORY

The polar bear has an insatiable curiosity, and sometimes he can be quite a clown. **In 1969,** a coast-guard vessel in the Canadian Arctic received a visit from an adult male polar

SUPPORTING SENTENCES: TELL STORY EVENT BY EVENT

EVENTS IN CHRONOLOGICAL ORDER

bear traveling atop a drifting ice-floe. The animal was obviously bent on a shopping expedition, and the crew obliged by throwing it a carton full of black molasses which the bear **soon** spread all over itself and the ice. This was **followed by** some jam, salt pork, two salami sausages, an apple which it spat out in disgust, and a jar of peanut butter which disappeared in about two seconds flat. It refused to touch bread or potatoes but loved chocolate bars. **Eventually** the food supply ran out, but the 363 kg (800 lb) bear, its appetite now thoroughly whetted, decided to investigate further. It stuck its head through one of the port-holes in search of further nourishment. **When** nothing turned up, it decided to climb aboard, much to the alarm of the crew, who decided to open up the hoses on it. This was a big mistake, however, because the bear absolutely loved the drenching and raised its paws in the air to get the jet of water under its armpits. **In the end** the coastguards were forced to fire a distress rocket rather close to the interloper **before** it reluctantly moved away.

CONCLUDING SENTENCE: GIVES THE OUTCOME OF THE STORY

—GERALD L. WOOD, *ANIMAL FACTS AND FEATS*

The following chart summarizes the features of a narrative paragraph.

19i

Features of a Narrative Paragraph

1. The topic sentence captures attention, sets the scene, or makes a general statement about what the story relates.
2. The supporting sentences relate the events of the story leading to and following the conflict.
3. The supporting sentences are organized in chronological order with transitions that clearly show when each event happened.
4. The concluding sentence resolves the story's conflict or makes a general statement about the meaning of the story.

Point of View. The person whose "voice" is telling the story in narrative writing is called the *narrator.* A first-person narrator is directly involved in the story and uses personal pronouns such as *I, we, us,* and *our.* In contrast, a third-person narrator stands back from the story and tells what happens to others, using third-person pronouns such as *she, he, they, their,* and *his.* These different narrative styles are called *points of view,* because they indicate through whose eyes the story is told.

FIRST PERSON	**I** filmed the tiger, attempting to keep still the mixture of pleasure and fear in **my** stomach.
THIRD PERSON	**Henry** filmed the tiger, attempting to keep still the mixture of pleasure and fear in **his** stomach.

Once you choose a point of view, you should use it consistently throughout the narrative.

19j Use **first-person point of view** if you are a character in the story. Use **third-person point of view** if you are reporting what happened to others.

EXERCISE 7 Analyzing a Narrative Paragraph
Read the paragraph and then write answers to the questions that follow it.

Cave Art

In the last century, a young Spanish girl made a discovery that would become world famous. One day in 1879, Don Marcelino de Sautuola and his young daughter Maria set out to explore a deep cave near their home in northern Spain. Once inside the cave, Maria watched for a while as her father, an archeologist, dug for stones and other relics in the cave floor by the light of an oil lamp. Soon she tired of watching her father and wandered a short way off until she found a ledge where she could stretch out and rest. As she was looking around casually, she suddenly saw something that made her cry out. After her father came running with his oil lamp, they both stared in amazement at their colorful, mysterious find. On the walls of the cave above Maria were painted pictures of bison and wild boars, animals that had not been seen in Spain for hundreds of years. Maria, quite by accident, became the first to discover cave paintings from prehistoric times, and the Altamira Caves have been famous ever since.

—WILLIAM AND RHODA CAHN, *THE STORY OF WRITING* (ADAPTED)

1. What is the topic sentence?
2. What is the function of the topic sentence: to set the scene, or to make a general statement about what the story relates?
3. What transitions are used in this paragraph to show the passing of time? List them.
4. What sentence in the paragraph creates suspense as the conflict unfolds?
5. What is the function of the concluding sentence: to resolve the conflict, or to make a general statement about the meaning or significance of the story?

EXERCISE 8 Using Points of View

The paragraph in Exercise 7 is written in the third-person point of view. Rewrite the paragraph from a first-person point of view by pretending it was you, rather than Maria de Sautuola, who discovered the cave painting.

Descriptive Paragraphs

Descriptive writing uses sensory details to bring a subject to life. The purpose of description is to recreate for the reader the sights, sounds, and other sensory impressions of people, places, and objects.

19k A **descriptive paragraph** paints a vivid picture of a person, scene, or object by stimulating the reader's senses.

Like a photographer, the writer of description cannot possibly record everything in sight. Instead, the writer must focus on a single person, object, or scene and strive to convey one overall impression of it. In most descriptive paragraphs, this overall impression is stated in the topic sentence. The following are topic sentences for descriptive paragraphs, each conveying a different type of overall impression of the subject.

The school yard was a grab bag of running, throwing, yelling, and crying. [overall impression of liveliness]

The aged tree brooded over the pond like a father over an ill child. [overall impression of gloom and darkness]

Optimism showed in every feature of the man's face. [overall impression of happiness and hope]

The supporting sentences in a description provide specific details that *show* how the overall impression was formed.

Spatial order is the most common method of organizing the details in a description. The details may be presented in the order of top to bottom, right to left, outside to inside, near to far, or the reverse of one of these. A writer may also choose to record the details in the order in which they strike him or her. This unique spatial order is especially useful for descriptions that involve several senses such as sights, sounds, and smells. In any description organized spatially, transitions help the reader piece the details together.

Notice the abundance of specific and sensory details in the following examples. The first paragraph uses an outside-to-inside spatial order, beginning with the room as a whole and eventually centering on the figure in the room. The second paragraph presents the details in the order they strike the writer. Transitions in both examples are in heavy type.

OUTSIDE-TO-INSIDE SPATIAL ORDER

Imagine, if you can, a small room, hexagonal in shape, like the cell of a bee. It is lighted neither by window nor by lamp, yet it is filled with a soft radiance. There are no apertures for ventilation, yet the air is fresh. There are no musical instruments, and yet, at the moment that my meditation opens, this room is throbbing with melodious sounds. An armchair is **in the center, by its side** a reading-desk—that is all the furniture. And **in the armchair** there sits a swaddled lump of flesh—a woman, about five feet high, with a face as white as a fungus. It is to her that the little room belongs.

—E. M. FORSTER, "THE MACHINE STOPS"

UNIQUE SPATIAL ORDER (DETAILS PRESENTED AS THEY STRUCK WRITER'S MEMORY)

The memories of Beach Haven run all to smells and sounds and sights; they are physical, of the blood and appetite, as is natural to summertime. **At the west end** of Coral Street the marshes began, turning soft with color at sunset, pink and lilac and golden green. The ocean beach at low tide lay hard **underfoot,** wet sand dark below the waterline. **On the dunes**—we called them sandhills—we played King of the

Castle or slid down on our bloomer seats, yelling with triumph and pure joy. The floors of Curlew Cottage, the chairs, even the beds were sandy. Always a lone sneaker sat **beneath the hall sofa; by August** our city shoes were mildewed in the closets, and towels were forever damp.

—CATHERINE DRINKER BROWN, "BEACH HAVEN"

The following chart summarizes the features of a descriptive paragraph.

19l

Features of a Descriptive Paragraph

1. The topic sentence suggests an overall impression.
2. The supporting sentences provide specific and sensory details that bring the scene to life.
3. The supporting details are organized in spatial order with appropriate transitions to guide the reader through the description.
4. The concluding sentence reinforces the overall impression conveyed in the paragraph.

EXERCISE 9 Analyzing a Descriptive Paragraph

Read the paragraph below and then write answers to the questions that follow it.

Maycomb was an old town, but it was a tired old town when I first knew it. In rainy weather the streets turned to red slop; grass grew on sidewalks, the courthouse sagged in the square. Somehow, it was hotter then; a black dog suffered on a summer's day; bony mules hitched to Hoover carts flicked flies in the sweltering shade of the live oaks on the square. Men's stiff collars wilted by nine in the morning. Ladies bathed before noon, after their three o'clock naps, and by nightfall were like soft tea-cakes with frostings of sweat and sweet talcum.

—HARPER LEE, *TO KILL A MOCKINGBIRD*

1. What is the topic sentence?
2. Is the overall impression conveyed by the topic sentence positive or negative?

3. What are five sensory details in the paragraph that show how the overall impression was formed? List them.
4. What type of spatial order is used in this paragraph: right to left, top to bottom, near to far, outside to inside, or the reverse of one of these, or unique?
5. Name two transitions that show location; name two others that show time.

Expository Paragraphs

Expository, or explanatory, writing is probably the most common and practical kind of writing. It is used to convey information in textbooks, on essay exams, and in the business world. Whenever your writing purpose is to explain, you will be writing exposition.

19m An **expository paragraph** explains, gives directions, or informs.

There are many different ways to explain. Usually the topic sentence holds the key to the best method of explaining. Study the following examples of expository topic sentences.

1. Many areas of the country have colorful and unusual traditions for celebrating the Fourth of July.
   WAY TO EXPLAIN Facts and examples
2. The process by which the Declaration of Independence was written and finally approved shows the nature of democracy.
   WAY TO EXPLAIN Steps in a process
3. At the end of the Independence Day holiday, the flag should be folded properly.
   WAY TO EXPLAIN Set of directions
4. I discovered how patriotic I was when I visited a foreign country for the first time.
   WAY TO EXPLAIN Incident
5. Patriotism involves both emotions and actions.
   WAY TO EXPLAIN Definition
6. The British government of today, while based on earlier traditions, is different from the British government of colonial times.
   WAY TO EXPLAIN Comparison/contrast

7. In some ways, the British government treated the colonies in America as a parent treats a child.
   WAY TO EXPLAIN Analogy
8. The constitution of the new United States created a government with three distinct branches.
   WAY TO EXPLAIN Analysis of parts
9. A long series of grievances with the British crown led to the final break and the creation of a new country.
   WAY TO EXPLAIN Cause and effect
10. The grievances can be classified into concerns of economics, politics, and ideals.
    WAY TO EXPLAIN Classification

The organization of details in an expository paragraph is determined in part by the paragraph's method of explaining. If the supporting details are steps in a process or a set of directions, chronological order is usually the most logical. In some paragraphs of analysis, in which the parts of an object are explained in relation to the whole, spatial order may be the most useful. Most expository paragraphs, however, use order of importance or developmental order, with transitions clearly showing the relationship of ideas. *(See page 431.)*

The following examples show two different ways to explain. The first uses facts and examples to explain and is organized in order of importance. The second explains by defining and is organized in developmental order. Transitions are printed in heavy type.

FACTS AND EXAMPLES IN ORDER OF IMPORTANCE

The Tennessee Valley Authority (TVA), a federal agency set up in 1935, has brought significant progress to the people of the region. First, before 1935, flood damage in the area averaged two million dollars a year. The TVA dams have been successful in controlling floodwaters and putting them to good use. **Another** accomplishment of TVA was the education of the region's farmers to methods of soil conservation. Downhearted farmers, certain that their land was forever ruined, learned how contour plowing, strip-cropping, and tree planting could protect their soil. Today the region's soil is restored. Probably **the most important** benefit of the TVA, **however,** was the generating of electric power. Without electricity, the once-depressed region could never have kept pace with the rest of the country. **Now** people from all over the world visit the region to learn how to improve river valleys in their own countries.

DEFINITION IN DEVELOPMENTAL ORDER

Artificial Intelligence is the study of ideas that enable computers to be intelligent. Note that wanting to make computers *be* intelligent is not the same as wanting to make computers *simulate* intelligence. Artificial Intelligence seeks to uncover principles that all intelligent information processors use, not just those made of wet neural tissue (human brains) instead of dry electronics (computers). **Consequently,** there is neither an obsession with mimicking human intelligence nor a prejudice against using methods that seem involved in human intelligence. **Instead,** there is a new point of view that brings along a new methodology and leads to new theories.

— PATRICK HENRY WINSTON,
ARTIFICIAL INTELLIGENCE

The following chart summarizes the features of an expository paragraph.

19n

Features of an Expository Paragraph

1. The topic sentence states a factual main idea, making clear an expository purpose.
2. The supporting sentences use facts, examples, incidents, comparisons/contrasts, analogies, definitions, analysis, steps in a process, or classification to explain the main idea.
3. The paragraph may be organized in order of importance, developmental order, chronological order, or spatial order, depending on the type of details used in the paragraph. Transitions show the relationship of ideas.
4. The concluding sentence summarizes, adds an insight, or evaluates the details in the paragraph.

EXERCISE 10 Analyzing Expository Paragraphs
Write which of the listed methods of explaining each of the following paragraphs uses:

analysis of parts or qualities	steps in a process
comparison/contrast	incidents

1. Police Officer with the K-9 Unit

Dogs and the officers who handle them are carefully trained from the start. Dogs are obtained from the public, preferably between the ages of 6 months and 16 months. They are, in the first instance, kept at the Dog Training Establishment for a period varying from one week to three weeks in order to assess their health, physique, and working abilities. On completion of this period, if found satisfactory, they are given to a handler, who takes a five days' course of instruction. The dog is then taken to the home of the handler to begin a period of familiarization, which is very important as it is essential to build trust and understanding between dog and handler before serious training is undertaken.

—"METROPOLITAN POLICE DOGS," *SCOTLAND YARD OF LONDON* (ADAPTED)

2. Qualities of a Good Broadcaster

To help broadcasters decide which candidates to hire for a position in radio or television, the National Association of Broadcasters drew up a list of qualities to look for in job applicants. The most successful broadcasters have most, if not all, of these qualities. One important trait is enthusiasm. Another is a sense of public relations, since broadcasters must anticipate the needs and interests of viewers and listeners. Creativity is also a desired trait; developing entertaining programming amidst fierce competition requires a lively imagination. A balanced temperament and reliability are two other important qualities that go hand in hand. The pressures in the field of broadcasting can be very strong, and a person who can get the job done and work well with others is very valuable. While cooperation is important, so is initiative, since employees in responsible positions are expected to monitor their own work schedules and progress. Finally, a good broadcaster has a good business sense. Without the ability to manage budgets and handle other financial matters, a broadcaster is not likely to rise very high in the professional ranks.

3. Zookeepers Then and Now

Until fairly recently, the job of animal keeper in a zoo required no advanced education. In the past, the main job of an animal keeper was to feed the animals and keep their cages clean. Although some animal keepers today have a high school education, more and more zoos are hiring college graduates. In contrast to earlier times, the job of animal keeper today has grown to include presenting educational programs to the public and studying the natural habitat of animals. Furthermore, a growing number of people interested in working with animals are now seeking work. Zoos are deluged with applications for keepers, and they are thus able to find college-educated people to fill these jobs. Most keepers today have had at least three years of college.

Writing Extra

Paragraphs developed with comparisons and contrasts can be organized in one of several ways. One way is called *whole by whole.* In this approach each of the things being compared or contrasted is treated separately, one after the other. In another way, called *point by point,* items are compared and contrasted with respect to specific points which are discussed one at a time.

EXERCISE 11 Experimenting with Order in Comparisons/ Contrasts

Using the following unsorted facts about Asiatic and African elephants, draw up two lists showing how you would organize the facts in a whole by whole comparison/contrast and a point by point comparison/contrast.

- Asiatic elephants have smallish ears
- Average African male elephant stands 10½ feet high at shoulders and weighs 12,000 pounds
- Asiatic elephants have backs that arch up in the middle
- African elephants have large ears
- Average Asiatic male elephant is 9 feet high and weighs 10,000 pounds
- African elephants have backs that arch down in the middle

Persuasive Paragraphs

The purpose of persuasion is to convince readers to share your opinion or to take a certain course of action. Advertisers use persuasion to sell products. Book reviewers use persuasion to defend their opinion of a book. Job hunters use persuasion in letters to convince prospective employers of their qualifications. If your writing purpose is to assert and support an opinion, you will be writing persuasion.

19o A **persuasive paragraph** states an opinion and uses facts, examples, reasons, and opinions of experts to convince readers.

In contrast to exposition, the topic sentence of a persuasive paragraph states an opinion, not a fact. The best paragraphs rest on arguable propositions rather than simple preferences. *(See page 397.)* The test of a good opinion for a persuasive topic sentence is the availability of reliable facts, examples, and expert opinions to back it up. Most writers of persuasion present their arguments in order of importance, building the argument from the least important point to the most important or starting with the strongest point and finishing with the weakest. As in other types of paragraphs, transitions show how ideas are related. *(See page 431.)*

How persuasive a writer is depends in part on how well he or she uses the tools of persuasion summarized in the following chart.

19p

Tools of Persuasion

1. Use logic that is free of fallacies that readers could attack. *(See pages 410–413.)*
2. Use reliable facts, examples, and statistics as support instead of more opinions.
3. Use the testimony of experts in the field.
4. Use polite and reasonable language rather than charged emotional words.
5. Anticipate arguments on the other side of the issue and concede the opposition's good points, but then show why your general opinion is unchanged.

Conceding a Point. Trying to ignore opposing viewpoints in a persuasive paragraph will only weaken the appeal. For this reason, the fifth tool of persuasion is especially important. Admitting that the opposition has a good point helps establish the writer's credibility, or believability. At the same time, however, the writer must show why that good point is not sufficiently important to tip the argument in the opponent's favor. Certain transitions are often used in this process of conceding a point. They include *while it is true that, nevertheless, however, notwithstanding, granted that, despite,* and *although.*

The following paragraph demonstrates the tools of persuasion. The transitions are printed in heavy type.

The Fall of Rome

TOPIC SENTENCE: STATES AN OPINION

SUPPORTING SENTENCES: PRESENT FACTS, EXAMPLES, TESTIMONY OF EXPERTS

CONCEDING A POINT

CONCLUDING SENTENCE: DRIVES HOME MAIN IDEA

Historians have long been fascinated by the fall of the Roman Empire and the causes of the fall. **Although** at one time most historians blamed the invasion of barbarians for Rome's collapse, a more careful study shows that Rome had long contained the seeds of its own destruction. **For one** thing, the economy of Rome was in serious disorder. Historian Max Weber argues that the decline of slavery and cities coupled with the development of self-sufficient manors left the city-based governments in poverty. **At the same time,** wealthy Romans indulged in unheard-of luxury, widening the gap between the social classes. **Another** historian, Mikail Rostovtzeff, adds to the causes of Rome's collapse an intellectual crisis. He claims that the influx of conquered nationalities "barbarized" Rome, sapping it of its intellectual vigor. **Perhaps most important,** Rome's political structure was in disarray. Uncertainty over who held the ruling power, the people or the nobles in the Senate, led to revolutions and massacres. **Although** no one of these forces could have toppled the great empire alone, the combination of internal weaknesses left the Empire defenseless against the final blow of the barbarian invaders.

The following chart summarizes the features of a persuasive paragraph.

19q

Features of a Persuasive Paragraph

1. The topic sentence states an opinion.
2. The supporting sentences use facts, examples, reasons, and the tools of persuasion to convince readers of the soundness of the opinion.
3. The ideas in the supporting sentences are usually organized in order of importance. Transitions show how the ideas are related.
4. The concluding sentence reinforces the main idea or summarizes the argument.

EXERCISE 12 Analyzing a Persuasive Paragraph

The following paragraph presents a different view on the fall of Rome. The sentences have been numbered for easy reference. Read it carefully and then write the answers to the questions that follow it.

Was Rome Really in Decline?

(1) The now-popular belief that weaknesses within Rome led it along a doomsday path needs to be reconsidered. (2) While it is true that the Late Empire was in the midst of a crisis, it is also true that under favorable conditions growth and progress can emerge from a crisis. (3) Historian André Piganiol points out three examples of such progress in the supposedly declining Empire. (4) First, the decline of slavery, while causing economic disruption, gave way to a new respect for the rights of people and the toil of laborers. (5) Second, the new subjects that included conquered nationalities ushered in a revival of native languages and folk art. (6) Far from being sapped, the intellectual life of Rome continued to grow. (7) The first modern book was developed in fourth-century Rome, and old Greek texts were studiously edited. (8) Third, the political crisis of the Late Empire, suggests Piganiol, was remedied by Diocletian and Constantine. (9) Rome in the Late Empire was, without a doubt, in a critical period. (10) Byzantium in the east, however, experienced similar crises, yet it managed to flourish. (11) The one crisis Byzantium did not share with Rome was the barbarian

invasions. (12) Although Rome's poverty left it unable to raise a defending army, the real enemy of Rome and the cause of its collapse was the wave of barbarian invasions, not a general internal weakness.

1. What is the topic sentence?
2. What tool of persuasion is used in the second sentence?
3. What tool of persuasion is used in the third sentence?
4. What kinds of supporting details are used in the seventh sentence?
5. Write all the transitions used in this paragraph.
6. What is the function of the concluding sentence?
7. Which paragraph on Rome was the more convincing to you? Why? Explain your position in two or three sentences.

EXERCISE 13 On Your Own
Review pages 432–445. Then, using the following questions as starting points, think about subjects on which you could write a paragraph. Write down ideas as you think of them.

1. What is the funniest thing that ever happened to me? What conflict have I faced and resolved?
2. What places have left a lasting impression on me? What objects do I find beautiful?
3. What do I know about that I could explain to others? What would I like to know more about?
4. What opinions do I hold that I could defend with the tools of persuasion? What advice would I give to a younger person about achieving important goals?

THE PROCESS OF WRITING PARAGRAPHS

Good writing may appear to have been composed effortlessly. Its smoothness seems natural and spontaneous, as if the writer transferred his or her thoughts in final form to the paper in one sitting. In fact, however, most writers work through a careful and deliberate process of planning, drafting, revising, and polishing until the final result *seems* effortless.

In the following pages, you will review the four main stages of the writing process and the specific steps involved in writing a paragraph.

Prewriting

Prewriting includes all of the planning steps that come before writing the first draft. During this stage, writers find and shape their subjects and plan the substance and organization of their compositions.

Finding Ideas. The first step in prewriting is to explore your own storehouse of knowledge and experiences for a good idea to write about. The following exercise will help remind you of the many things you already know that could form the basis of a paragraph.

EXERCISE 14 Finding Ideas
Number your paper 1 to 5, leaving 10 blank lines between numbers. Then write down everything that comes to mind to complete each of the following statements.

1. Aside from my parents, the people who have influenced me the most are . . .
2. In the next five years of my life, I would like to . . .
3. Of all the reports and projects I have done in high school, the ones that still interest me include . . .
4. If people, like states, had official songs, mottos, birds, flowers, and animals, mine would be . . .
5. Of all the controversies debated in the newspaper and on radio and television, those that have touched my life directly are . . .

Choosing and Limiting a Subject. After you discover a variety of ideas, the next step is to choose and shape a subject to write about. The following guidelines will help you to choose a subject from your prewriting notes.

19r

Guidelines for Choosing a Subject

1. Choose a subject that interests you.
2. Choose a subject that will interest your readers.
3. Choose a subject you know enough about or can learn enough about to cover adequately.

Suppose in your prewriting notes that you discovered that you were still interested in the mock trial you were part of in civics class. To shape that general idea into a workable subject, you must first decide what your writing purpose will be. A narrative paragraph, for example, would tell a story about the mock trial. A descriptive paragraph might attempt to recreate the tension of the scene. An expository paragraph might explain the process by which the participants prepared for the trial. A persuasive paragraph might assert an opinion on the value of such an activity or on a legal issue raised by the trial.

To help you decide on a writing purpose, you may wish to brainstorm on your subject. *Brainstorming* means writing down everything that comes to mind when you think about your subject. The brainstorming notes on the mock trial might look like the following:

SUBJECT mock trial

BRAINSTORMING NOTES
- I was chosen as witness
- use of real court transcript
- details of case
- real lawyer served as judge
- comments stricken from record
- how lawyers convince jury
- kinds of objections made
- different kinds of evidence
- other students in trial
- how we all got caught up in it
- closing arguments
- witness who forgot her lines

As you looked over your notes, you might have decided that you were most interested in writing an expository paragraph about how lawyers convince juries. That subject, however, is too broad to be covered in one paragraph. The next step, then, is to limit your subject to a manageable size. The following are three suitably limited versions of the broad subject.

BROAD SUBJECT how lawyers convince juries

LIMITED SUBJECTS
- what the mock trial taught me about how lawyers convince juries
- how lawyers present their witnesses to best advantage
- theatrics in the courtroom

There are many techniques you can use to limit a broad subject. One is to ask yourself *What about (your broad subject)?* until you arrive at a subject suitably limited. Another simple technique is to draw a tree diagram, making your broad subject the trunk and identifying as branches several aspects of that subject that will be suitably limited.

EXERCISE 15 Choosing and Limiting a Subject
Number your paper 1 to 5, leaving 10 blank spaces after each number.

a. After each number, write a possible subject for a paragraph. You may wish to use ideas from Exercise 14.
b. On the lines after each subject, brainstorm to help you decide on a writing purpose.
c. Circle the two subjects that interest you the most. Then write a suitably limited subject for each broad subject you have circled.

Listing Supporting Details. Once you have narrowed your subject to a suitable size, you can begin listing supporting details that you will use in the body of your paragraph. A good paragraph uses numerous and specific supporting details, so be sure to list between five and ten items. *(See pages 423–425.)*

The following chart shows the types of supporting details used with the four different kinds of paragraphs.

19s

Types of Supporting Details

Narrative paragraphs	Events *(See page 433.)*
Descriptive paragraphs	Sensory details *(See pages 436–437.)*
Expository paragraphs	Facts, examples, reasons, definitions, analogies, etc. *(See pages 439–440.)*
Persuasive paragraphs	Facts, examples, reasons, testimony of experts *(See pages 444–445.)*

EXERCISE 16 Listing Supporting Details
Write each subject and purpose on your paper. Under each one, list four supporting details that would help you develop

the paragraph. Make sure that the type of detail matches the writing purpose. Save your work for Exercise 17.

EXAMPLE SUBJECT theatrics in the courtroom
PURPOSE expository
DETAILS
- with credible witness, lawyer takes backstage
- with doubtful witness, lawyer draws attention to himself or herself
- the importance of gestures
- the importance of dress

1. SUBJECT my most disastrous experiment
   PURPOSE narrative
2. SUBJECT who should go to college
   PURPOSE persuasive
3. SUBJECT a church and churchyard
   PURPOSE descriptive
4. SUBJECT training needed for your future career
   PURPOSE expository
5. SUBJECT sacrifices required in friendships
   PURPOSE expository

Organizing Details in Logical Order. The last step in the prewriting stage is to arrange your list of supporting ideas in a logical order. The following chart reviews the methods of organization commonly used in the four types of paragraphs.

Type of Paragraphs	Method of Organization
Narrative	Chronological order
Descriptive	Mainly spatial order
Expository	Order of importance, developmental order; sometimes chronological or spatial order *(See page 431.)*
Persuasive	Mainly order of importance

EXERCISE 17 Arranging Details in Logical Order

Using your notes from Exercise 16, organize the details under each subject in a logical order. Underneath your list, indicate which method of organization you have used. Save your work for Exercise 18.

Writing

When you write the first draft, you develop your prewriting notes into a paragraph with a topic sentence, supporting sentences, and a concluding sentence. Concentrate on expressing your message as clearly as possible.

Writing the Topic Sentence. The following chart outlines the steps for writing a clear topic sentence.

19t

Steps for Writing a Topic Sentence

1. Look over your prewriting notes.
2. Express your main idea in one sentence.
3. Rewrite that sentence until it
   - makes your writing purpose clear, and
   - covers all your supporting details.

Study the following notes on theatrics in the courtroom. They have been arranged in order of importance. Then notice how the topic sentence is written and then revised for clarity.

SUBJECT theatrics in the courtroom

PURPOSE expository

DETAILS
- the importance of dress
- the importance of gestures
- with credible witness, the lawyer takes backstage
- with doubtful witness, lawyer draws attention to himself or herself

FAULTY TOPIC SENTENCE I'll never forget the day my class conducted a mock trial and the theatrics we had to learn. [suggests that the paragraph will be narrative instead of expository]

FAULTY TOPIC SENTENCE Lawyers rely on appearance and gestures to make a good impression on juries. [fails to cover all of the supporting details]

STRONG TOPIC SENTENCE Many lawyers use an array of theatrical techniques in the courtroom to help them win their cases. [makes the expository purpose clear and covers all the supporting details]

EXERCISE 18 Writing Topic Sentences
Using the organized lists of details from Exercise 17, write a topic sentence for each subject. Use the steps on page 451 as a guide.

Writing the Paragraph Body. To turn your list of supporting details into smoothly flowing sentences, take the following steps.

19u

Steps for Writing the Paragraph Body

1. Write a complete sentence for each detail on your list.
2. Combine sentences that seem to go together.
3. When necessary, add transitions to help one sentence lead smoothly into the next and to show the relationship of your ideas.

Notice how the transitions in the following paragraph on theatrics in the courtroom keep the reader on course.

Many lawyers use an array of theatrical techniques in the courtroom to help them win their cases. **One** useful technique has to do with the appearance of the witnesses. Clothes do make an impression, so lawyers often advise their witnesses to dress in crisp, attractive but conservative clothing. A **more powerful** technique than "costuming" is the use of accusatory gestures in cross-examinations. If a lawyer, **while** asking tough questions, repeatedly points his or her finger at the witness, the witness may begin to act nervous and guilty, which weakens the testimony. Perhaps the **most important** theatrical techniques are those that manipulate the jury's attention. A witness who looks trustworthy, is well-dressed, and has a confident speaking manner is every lawyer's dream. **When** such a person is testifying, the lawyer remains "backstage," keeping movement and gesturing to a minimum **so** the jury's attention will stay on the witness. Many witnesses, **however,** are nervous, inarticulate, and suspicious looking. **Although** their appearance may have nothing to do with their guilt or innocence, a lawyer may try to distract the jury from such witnesses by moving around a lot and gesturing in large movements.

EXERCISE 19 Writing the Body of an Expository Paragraph Write the body of an expository paragraph using the notes provided. Include the topic sentence and concluding sentence on your paper. Save your work for Exercise 21.

TOPIC SENTENCE	The side stitch experienced by many beginning runners is nothing serious and can be relieved by a few simple techniques.
DETAILS	• side stitch is a sharp pain usually felt just under rib cage • believed to be a cramped abdominal muscle • can be relieved sometimes by a change in stride • can be relieved sometimes by letting all the air out of your lungs, by yelling or singing • deep breathing also helps • best technique is to keep running and not worry
CONCLUDING SENTENCE	Although the side stitch is only a temporary discomfort, it can be prevented by building up speed and time gradually rather than pushing too hard too fast.

Writing the Concluding Sentence. A concluding sentence serves one or more of the following purposes.

19v

Purposes of a Concluding Sentence

A concluding sentence may
- restate the topic sentence in fresh words.
- summarize the paragraph.
- evaluate the supporting details.
- add an insight to show the importance of the main idea.

The following concluding sentence to the paragraph on courtroom theatrics adds an insight.

> Most jury members do their very best to remain objective and consider only the evidence itself, but, in defense of their clients, lawyers try to cover all bases that may affect the verdict.

EXERCISE 20 Writing Concluding Sentences
Write two more possible concluding sentences for the paragraph on courtroom techniques. Each one should serve one or more of the purposes shown in the box.

Revising

When writers revise their first drafts, they try to stand apart from their work and see it as a reader would see it. This distance helps writers know what needs to be strengthened or clarified. Use the following checklist to revise your paragraphs step-by-step.

19w

Revision Checklist

Checking Your Paragraph

1. Do you have a strong topic sentence? *(See pages 420–422.)*
2. Do you have adequate and appropriate supporting sentences? *(See pages 423–425.)*
3. Does your paragraph have unity? *(See pages 425–426.)*
4. Does your paragraph have coherence? *(See page 428.)*
5. Did you use appropriate transitions where needed? *(See pages 430–431.)*
6. Do you have a strong concluding sentence? *(See page 420.)*

Checking Your Sentences

7. Do your sentences have variety? *(See pages 377–384.)*
8. Did you combine sentences that go together? *(See pages 377–382).*
9. Are your sentences concise? *(See pages 373–376.)*
10. Have you avoided faulty parallelism and overuse of the passive voice? *(See pages 390–392.)*

Checking Your Words

11. Did you use specific words with appropriate connotations? *(See pages 367–368.)*
12. Did you use figurative language where appropriate? *(See pages 369–371.)*

EXERCISE 21 Revising
Using the Revision Checklist, revise the paragraph you wrote for Exercise 19.

Editing

The final stage in the writing process is editing. A neat, easy-to-read paper will focus all your reader's attention on your message. Use the following editing checklist to polish your final draft. You may want to use the proofreading symbols on page 662 when you edit.

19x

Editing Checklist

1. Are your sentences free of errors in grammar and usage?
2. Did you spell each word correctly?
3. Did you capitalize and punctuate correctly?
4. Did you use correct manuscript form? *(See page 659.)*
5. Is your typing or handwriting clear?

EXERCISE 22 On Your Own
Review pages 446–455. Then using what you have learned about prewriting, writing, revising, and editing, write a paragraph on a subject of your choice.

CHAPTER REVIEW

A. Read the following paragraph and answer the questions that follow it.

Astronomers are becoming concerned over the brightness of the earth's night sky, sometimes called light pollution, which can ruin the observation of faint stars. The worst offenders are densely populated areas whose electric lights reduce visibility in the eastern United States, western Europe, and Japan. Even over less populated regions, however, lights from the earth pollute the night sky. In parts of Asia and Indonesia, fires started to clear forests and fields glow in the night. In North Africa and the Middle East, flares used to burn off gas disturb the night sky over oil fields. To a smaller degree, lights in the towns along the Trans-Siberian Railroad affect astronomical observations. Astronomer Woodruff T. Sullivan III is so concerned about the loss of good viewing that he refers to the problem as "our endangered night sky."

1. What is the topic sentence of this paragraph?
2. Is this paragraph narrative, descriptive, expository, or persuasive in purpose?
3. Are the supporting details events, sensory details, or facts and examples?
4. Is this paragraph organized in chronological order, spatial order, or order of importance?
5. What transitions in the second, third, and sixth sentences show the organizational method used in this paragraph?

B. Using what you have learned about prewriting, writing, revising, and editing, write a paragraph on one of the following subjects or on one of your own choosing. Use the Steps for Writing Paragraphs on page 458 as a guide.

Subjects for a Narrative Paragraph

1. your first job interview
2. a surprise party
3. a brush with danger
4. how you met your best friend
5. an exciting end to a ball game
6. visiting a college campus
7. auditioning for a performance
8. forming a rock band
9. working on a farm
10. campaigning for class office

Subjects for a Descriptive Paragraph

11. a picnic
12. rush hour
13. your kindergarten classroom
14. a wedding
15. the runners in a 100-meter dash

16. a fire
17. a hurricane
18. a concert
19. an old piece of clothing
20. a mountain view

Subjects for an Expository Paragraph

21. a definition of *ecosystem*
22. inside an atom
23. how lobby groups influence the passage of a bill
24. how to plan a successful party
25. how to tune an engine
26. how to make a pizza
27. the dangers of asbestos
28. the effects of caffeine on the nervous system
29. the effectiveness of the fifty-five mile an hour speed limit
30. the latest developments in artificial heart transplants

Subjects for a Persuasive Paragraph

31. a disagreement you had with a movie review you read or heard
32. privileges seniors should have
33. the importance of taxes
34. the right of the oil industry to drill in fishing waters
35. juvenile rights
36. public vs. private school
37. recruitment of high school athletes by colleges
38. mandatory sentencing in the court system
39. methods used by advertising agencies to sell products
40. the validity of the Scholastic Aptitude Test for college entrance

Steps for Writing

Paragraphs

✓ **Prewriting**

1. Find ideas by examining your interests, knowledge, and experience. *(See page 447.)*
2. Make a list of subjects and choose one that interests you the most. *(See pages 447–448.)*
3. Determine the purpose of your paragraph. *(See pages 448–449.)*
4. Limit your subject so that it can be covered in one paragraph.
5. Write a list of supporting details.
6. Arrange your details in a logical order.

✓ **Writing**

7. Write a topic sentence appropriate for your purpose. *(See page 451.)*
8. Use your prewriting notes to write the supporting sentences. *(See page 452.)*
9. Add a concluding sentence. *(See page 453.)*

✓ **Revising**

10. Using the appropriate checklist on page 459 and the Revision Checklist on page 454, check your paragraph's structure, unity, coherence, and words.

✓ **Editing**

11. Using the Editing Checklist on page 455, check your grammar, usage, spelling, mechanics, and neatness.

Checklists for Revising

Paragraphs

✓ **Narrative Paragraphs**

1. Does your topic sentence set the scene or get the story moving and make your narrative purpose clear?
2. Do the supporting sentences tell the story event by event?
3. Did you use chronological order with transitions?
4. Does the concluding sentence tell the story's outcome or make a point about the story's meaning?

✓ **Descriptive Paragraphs**

1. Does your topic sentence make a general statement that suggests an overall impression of the subject?
2. Do the supporting sentences supply sensory details?
3. Did you use figurative language?
4. Did you use spatial order and appropriate transitions?
5. Does your concluding sentence reinforce the overall impression?

✓ **Expository Paragraphs**

1. Does your topic sentence state a factual main idea and make your purpose clear?
2. Did you use the method of development most appropriate for your topic sentence?
3. Did you use an appropriate method of organization?
4. Did you use transitions?
5. Does your concluding sentence summarize, add an insight, or evaluate the supporting details?

✓ **Persuasive Paragraphs**

1. Does your topic sentence state an opinion?
2. Do supporting sentences use the tools of persuasion?
3. Did you use logical order with correct transitions?
4. Does your concluding sentence reinforce the main idea or summarize the argument?

20

Expository Essays

Like your signature, everything you write bears your unique stamp. When you write an *essay*—a composition of three or more paragraphs—your task is to find the best way of expressing your ideas. No two writers would make the same choices and find the same solutions. Although the thousands of essays written in books and magazines have some common features, each is "signed" with the writer's unique outlook.

The expository essay is probably the most common type of essay. It can be used to explain factual subjects, such as how to land the space shuttle or why the sky is blue. It can also be used to explain ideas and insights, such as why people laugh or what freedom means. In all cases, the success of the essay depends on how clearly the writer explains and communicates.

20a An **expository essay** explains a factual main idea or a personal insight.

ESSAY STRUCTURE

Virtually all forms of communication have the same basic parts: a beginning, a middle, and an ending. Just as a phone call begins with a "hello" and ends with a "good-bye," a complete piece of writing is framed by introductory and concluding sections. In the following chart, the structure of a formal essay is compared with the structure of a paragraph.

20b

Paragraph Structure	Essay Structure
topic sentence that expresses the main idea of the paragraph	introductory paragraph(s) that include a thesis statement expressing the main idea of the essay
body of supporting sentences	body of supporting paragraph(s)
concluding sentence	concluding paragraph(s)

In the following essay, the three basic parts and the thesis statement are labeled at the left.

Alone

INTRODUCTION

Bolling Advance Weather Base, which I manned alone during the Antarctic winter nights of 1934, was planted in the dark immensity of the Ross Barrier on a line between Little America and the South Pole. It was the first inland station ever occupied in the world's southernmost continent. My decision to winter there was harder, perhaps, than even some of the men at Little America appreciated. For the original plan had been to staff the base with several men; but . . . this had proved impossible. In consequence, I had to choose whether to give up the base entirely—and the scientific missions with it—or to man it by myself. I could not bring myself to give it up.

THESIS STATEMENT

This much should be understood from the beginning: Above everything else, and beyond the solid worth of weather and auroral observations in the hitherto-unoccupied interior of Antarctica and my interest in these studies, I really wanted to go for the experience's sake.

So the motive was in part personal. Aside from the meteorological and auroral work, I had no important purposes. There was nothing of that sort, nothing except one man's desire to know that kind of experience to the full, to be by himself for a while and to taste peace and quiet and solitude long enough to find out how good they really are.

BODY It was all that simple. It is something, I believe, that people beset by the complexities of modern life will understand instinctively. We are caught up in the winds that blow every which way. In the hullabaloo, thinking people are driven to ponder where they are being blown and to long desperately for some quiet place where they can reason undisturbed and take inventory . . . For fourteen years or so, various expeditions, one succeeding the other, had occupied my time and thoughts to the exclusion of nearly everything else. In 1919, it was the Navy's transatlantic flight; in 1925, Greenland; in 1926, the North Pole; in 1927, the Atlantic Ocean; 1928–30, the South Pole; and 1933–35, the Antarctic again. In between there was no rest. An expedition was hardly finished before I was engaged in putting a new one together. Meanwhile I was lecturing from one end of the country to the other in order to make a living and pay off the debts of the completed expedition, or else scurrying around to solicit money and supplies for a new one.

CONCLUSION I wanted something more than just privacy in a geographical sense. I wanted to sink roots into some replenishing philosophy. So it occurred to me, as the situation surrounding the Advance Base evolved, that here was the opportunity. Out there on the South Polar barrier, in cold and darkness as complete as that of the Pleistocene, I should have time to catch up, to study and think and listen to the phonograph. For maybe seven months, I should be able to live exactly as I chose, obedient to no necessities but those imposed by wind and night and cold, and to no one's laws but my own.

—RICHARD E. BYRD, *ALONE* (ADAPTED)

Introduction

The introduction to an essay does just what its name implies: It introduces the reader to the subject and the tone of the essay. While the title of an essay may give the reader a general idea of what is to come, the thesis statement contained in the introduction expresses the specific main idea that the author is going to explain. Depending on the length of the essay, the introduction can be one or two paragraphs. In many essays, the thesis statement is the last sentence in the introduction, although it may appear any place in the introduction.

In addition to containing the thesis statement, the introduction sets the tone of the essay. *Tone* is the writer's attitude toward his or her subject and audience. The number of possible tones, therefore, is as great as the number of different attitudes. The tone may be straightforward, reflective, casual, bitter, comic, joyous, or any other human attitude. The tone of the essay by Richard Byrd on pages 461–463, for example, is serious and reflective. The reader understands from the start that Byrd takes his subject and readers seriously.

20c The **thesis statement** states the main idea of the essay and makes clear the writer's purpose.

20d The **tone** of an essay is the writer's attitude toward his or her subject and audience.

Read the following introductions to essays, noting the tone and thesis statement of each one.

STRAIGHT-FORWARD TONE

Everyone knows that a well-used city street is apt to be safe. A deserted one is apt to be unsafe. How does this work, really? What makes a city street well used or shunned? Why is the inner sidewalk mall in Washington Houses—which is supposed to be an attraction—shunned when the sidewalks of the old city just to its west are not? What about streets that are busy part of the time and then empty abruptly? A city street equipped to make a safety asset out of the presence of strangers, as successful city neighborhoods always do, must have three main qualities.

THESIS STATEMENT

—JANE JACOBS, *THE DEATH AND LIFE OF GREAT AMERICAN CITIES*

CASUAL TONE

THESIS STATEMENT

When it comes to fried chicken, let's not beat around the bush for one second. To know about fried chicken you have to have been weaned and reared on it in the South. Period. The French know absolutely nothing about it, and Julia Child and James Beard very little. Craig Claiborne knows plenty. He's from Mississippi. To set the record straight before bringing on regional and possible national holocaust over the correct preparation of this classic dish, let me emphasize and reemphasize the fact that I'm a Southerner, born, bred, and chickenfried for all times. We Southerners take our fried chicken very seriously, having singled it out years ago as not only the most important staple worthy of heated and complex debate but also as the dish that non-Southerners have never really had any knack for. The truth remains that once you've eaten real fried chicken by an expert chicken fryer in the South there are simply no grounds for contest.

—JIM VILLAS, "FRIED CHICKEN"

EXERCISE 1 Analyzing Essay Introductions

Copy the thesis statement from each essay introduction. Then after each thesis statement, identify the tone established in the introduction by writing *reflective, straightforward,* or *casual.*

1.

What do you do with all the owner's manuals, warranties and pieces of paper that come in the box when you buy something new? I never know what to do with them.

I bought a new blender last week, and there were eight separate things to read in there. I'm having a good time opening my new toy, and the first thing I get is a warning: "Stop!" They don't want me to hurt myself. "To avoid injury," it says, "see your recipe book for assembly instructions."

—ANDREW A. ROONEY, "WARRANTIES"

2.

Tension filled the crowded auditorium. Houselights dimmed, voices were stilled, and the audience readied itself for what was to follow. It was one of those tantalizing moments that occur just before any live performance, whether it be musical comedy, drama, opera, dance, even the circus. This audience, however, was about to experience a new type of theater, a very special blend of words and movement unlike any other seen before. The National Theater of the Deaf was about to present its new production, *Parade,* and any skepticism in the audience regarding deaf actors would soon dissolve in enthusiasm for the entertainment's swirl of color and movement and its panache.

—JEAN STRATTON, *SMITHSONIAN*

3.

For the Indians the world of nature itself was their temple, and within this sanctuary they showed great respect to every form, function, and power. That the Indians held as sacred all the natural forms surrounding them is not unique, for other traditions (Japanese Shinto, for example) respect created forms as manifestations of God's works. But what is almost unique in the Indians' attitude is the fact that their reverence for nature and for life is *central* to their religion: Each form in the world around them bears such a host of precise values and meanings that taken all together they constitute what one could call their "doctrine."

—JOSEPH EPES BROWN, "THE SPIRITUAL LEGACY OF THE AMERICAN INDIAN"

Body

The supporting paragraphs in the body of an essay, like the supporting sentences in a paragraph, back up the main idea with specifics. These specifics can be facts, examples, incidents, comparisons and contrasts, or any of a variety of details that help explain the main idea. Like paragraphs, essays are most successful when they are adequately developed with numerous and specific details.

20e The **supporting paragraphs** in the body of an essay develop the main idea with specific and numerous details.

Each paragraph in the body of an essay develops one main supporting point. In the following essay about a unique high-jumping technique, the supporting points are (1) what the technique is, (2) how the technique developed, and (3) how experts responded to the new technique.

The Fosbury Flop

In Mexico's Estadio Olímpico, a crowd of 80,000 gasped as high jumper Dick Fosbury flew over the bar at seven feet, four and a half inches to win a gold medal in the 1968 Olympics and set an Olympic record. It was not only the height that astounded them but also Fosbury's novel approach: head first and flat on his back.

Before jumping, Fosbury would stand at the start of the runway, sometimes for several minutes, meditating, worrying, visualizing himself clearing the bar. "I have to psych myself up," said the nervous jumper. "It's positive thinking, convincing myself that I'll make it." Then he would bolt down the runway, just left of center, plant his right (outside) foot firmly parallel to the bar, and spring up, pivoting quickly so his back was to the bar, which he glimpsed behind, then beneath him from the corner of one eye. With his back parallel to the ground and crosswise to the bar, his legs dangled down on the starting side, till he jackknifed them up to clear the bar and land—appallingly enough—on his back or the nape of his neck. The usual pile of sawdust did not make for a welcoming base, so Fosbury finished his backward flight on three feet of foam.

Fosbury did not deliberately set about to revolutionize the world of high jumping, nor even to invent a sensational method for himself. The Fosbury Flop, as the jump is commonly called, evolved over time. "I didn't change my style," Fosbury told *Sports Illustrated*'s Roy Blount. "It changed inside me." Fosbury started jumping in fifth grade and was still using the scissors method in high school to clear five-four. (This is a sideways jump in which the athlete kicks up the leg nearer the bar, crosses in a sitting position, and then brings the trailing leg up and over as the other leg comes down.) He tried the conventional straddle (crossing the bar on one's stomach, with one's body parallel to the bar), but it just didn't feel right, so he went back to the scissors. "As the bar's height increased," Fosbury recollects, "I started lying out more, and pretty soon I was flat on my back." He cleared five-ten at the time and the seed was planted for the Fosbury Flop.

Fosbury met with a lot of resistance from skeptical coaches along the way. It took a flying flop of about seven feet over a six-six bar to convince Fosbury's college coach Berny Wagner that the flop was more than a funny spectacle. "The physics of his jump are good," Wagner told *The New York Times.* "Dick exposes less of himself to the bar than any other high jumper."

Not only did Fosbury go on to glory with his backward, potentially hazardous leap, but the technique also became widely used among high jumpers. However, the innovator himself said in 1968, "Sometimes I see movies, and I really wonder how I do it."

—CAROLINE SUTTON, *HOW DID THEY DO THAT?* (ADAPTED)

A simple outline of this essay shows how the supporting paragraphs in the body develop the main idea expressed in the thesis statement.

THESIS STATEMENT It was not only the height that astounded them but also Fosbury's novel approach: head first and flat on his back.

I. His method
II. The evolution of his method
III. Response to his method

EXERCISE 2 Listing Supporting Points

Write each of the following thesis statements on your paper. Then list three supporting ideas in simple outline form that could serve as the basis for supporting paragraphs in the body. You may need to find information in the library to list supporting ideas for some of the thesis statements.

1. Politicians and citizens working together will have to solve some pressing social problems in the near future.
2. Few experiences are more embarrassing than a slip of the tongue.

3. Running for office is a laborious and exhausting process.
4. Students graduating from high school have to face a number of important decisions.
5. Without machines, most people would not know how to make it through a day.
6. Moviegoers can use a number of different guides to decide whether or not to see a new movie.
7. Television both reflects and shapes social attitudes.
8. Three books (or experiences) have changed the way I look at myself and the world.
9. Although mammals such as whales and dolphins resemble fish in some ways, they have significant differences.
10. There are three personality traits I have now that I would like to keep during my whole life.

Conclusion

If a person hangs up the telephone without saying good-bye to you, you would no doubt feel that you were cut off abruptly. In the same way, if a writer does not provide a satisfying ending, a reader will be left dangling. Once the supporting details have been presented, essayists usually return to more general comments—often referring to ideas in the introduction—to round off the essay. The length of the conclusion, like the length of the introduction, depends on the length of the essay itself. In most short essays, one paragraph is usually sufficient to complete the message.

20f The purpose of the **conclusion** is to complete the essay and drive home the main idea.

The following paragraph concludes an essay on the Theater of the Deaf. *(See the introduction to that essay on page 465.)* Notice how the main idea is restated.

CONCLUSION There is "eye music" in all National Theater of the Deaf performances—a ballet of darting fingers and a symphony of fluid motion. The theater is meant to be entertainment, but it is also communication, and true communication is more than just the transmittal of information from one person to another. To be truly effective it must connect and reach out, establish contact. Audiences who see *Parade* or are lucky enough to attend other National Theater of the Deaf performances will know that they have been reached. —JEAN STRATTON, *SMITHSONIAN*

EXERCISE 3 On Your Own
Over the next week, check your local newspaper and favorite magazines for short essays. When you find one that interests you, copy it (or cut it out if the paper or magazine belongs to you) and bring it to class. Be prepared to identify the essay's introduction, tone, thesis statement, supporting ideas offered in the body, and conclusion.

PREWRITING

The variety and individuality of essays is matched by a variety in the processes used to compose them. Most writers, however, follow the same general steps in composing an essay. The first step, called prewriting, begins with finding an idea to write about and ends with shaping that idea into an organized plan for the composition.

Finding Ideas

Some ideas seem to spring from unusual sources at unexpected times and places. Although you might rack your brain without success during study hall, later that evening while you are taking a relaxed walk, you might find an interesting idea. Countless ideas for subjects are in your head now; the task is to bring them to the surface by letting your mind relax or by asking yourself some probing questions.

Some writers use freewriting to help them relax and think of subjects. *Freewriting* means writing down anything and everything that comes to mind without stopping your pen or pencil or consciously thinking. Freewriting can consist of complete sentences, fragments, or unconnected words. Other writers prefer to ask themselves specific questions and then freewrite the answers to those questions. Still others prefer to skim books and magazines and ask themselves questions about what they read. All of these methods can unlock ideas for an essay.

EXERCISE 4 Finding Ideas by Freewriting
Using the short starter line provided, write freely for five minutes. Do not worry about correctness of spelling or grammar. Keep writing without pause. If you feel yourself running out of ideas, write "I can't think of anything" until a new idea comes to mind. Nobody will read this paper, so try to relax and have fun. Starter line: What you need to understand is . . .

EXERCISE 5 Finding Ideas by Asking Yourself Questions
Write the following questions on your paper, leaving ten blank lines after each. Write down any and all answers that come to mind.

1. What subjects do I enjoy talking about at school? At home? At parties?
2. Who in the news seems unworthy of fame, and who has genuinely earned it?
3. What places have I been to that seem harmonious and peaceful, and which have seemed hectic or unwelcoming?
4. What different directions might my future take?
5. Why do I have the friends that I do?

EXERCISE 6 Finding Ideas from Reading and Other Sources
Write the following questions on your paper, leaving ten blank lines after each one. Write down all answers that come to mind.

1. What have I been reading about in history class that interests me?
2. What have I been reading about in science or other classes that interests me?
3. What magazine articles or television shows have caught my attention recently?
4. What lessons or classes have I taken outside of school?
5. Which of the following quotations has a special meaning for me? What incidents in my life support or contradict the message in the quotation I chose?

a. ". . . every atom belonging to me as good belongs to you"—Walt Whitman
b. "Do good to thy friend to keep him, to thy enemy to gain him."—Benjamin Franklin
c. "Admiration is our polite recognition of another's resemblance to ourselves."—Ambrose Bierce

Writing Extra

"Everything I see or hear is an essay in bud. The world is everywhere whispering essays, and one need only be the world's recorder."

—ALEXANDER SMITH, *ON THE WRITING OF ESSAYS*

"A writer needs three things, experience, observation, and imagination. . . ."

—WILLIAM FAULKNER, INTERVIEW IN *THE PARIS REVIEW*

One way to record the "whisper" of essay subjects and develop the tools of writing is to keep a journal, a notebook in which you write something every day. Besides providing a source of possible subjects for writing assignments, journal writing will help you find your natural writing "voice" and will give you more practice in putting your ideas into words.

EXERCISE 7 Keeping a Journal
Every day for a month, make an entry in your journal. Write the day and date at the top of the page. Divide each entry into two parts. The first should be labeled *EXPERIENCES*. In this part you should write down the things that happened to you, your friends, and your family on that day. The second part should be labeled *OBSERVATIONS*. In this part you will record your thoughts and insights about the experiences of the day.

Choosing and Limiting a Subject

The following guidelines will help you choose a subject from the many possible ideas you discovered.

20g

Guidelines for Choosing a Subject

1. Choose a subject that you would enjoy writing about.
2. Choose a subject that will interest your readers.
3. Choose a subject you know enough about now or can learn enough about later to develop adequately in a short essay.
4. Choose a subject that might reveal an interesting insight about yourself or your world.

The next step is to limit your subject, to focus on one aspect of a broad subject that you wish to explain. A suitably limited subject will help you write a tight essay with no loose ends. Use the following questions to help you limit your subject.

20h

Questions for Limiting a Subject

1. What about my subject do I want to explain?
2. Who are my readers? What do they need to know to understand my subject?
3. What kind of tone is best suited to my message?
4. What insight can I draw from my subject?
5. How can I express my main idea in one sentence?

Suppose you chose a subject you learned about in psychology class: the boy found living in the wild in France in the early 1800s. The answers to the five questions for limiting a subject might look like the following.

Answer to question 1: I would like to explain the methods Dr. Itard used to help the wild boy and the influence his work had on later thinkers.

Answer to question 2: My readers have probably not heard of the wild boy, so they need some background information.

Answer to question 3: The tone best suited to my subject is straightforward.

Answer to question 4: Finding the wild boy provided scientists a chance to study the influences of heredity and environment on human development.

Answer to question 5: Dr. Itard's work with the wild boy of Aveyron led to new ideas in education and psychology.

Determining Your Audience. The second question for limiting a subject on page 472 has to do with *audience*, the people who will read your essay. How, for example, would the different audiences of a teacher, your parents, a friend, and a prospective employer each change the way you would write an essay? To understand how the audience for an essay may shape its content and style, read the following two essay introductions. Both are on the same general subject—mythical monsters. The first was published in *TV Guide;* the second in *Smithsonian,* a publication devoted to "the increase and diffusion of knowledge." As you read the selections, imagine what type of reader each one is directed toward.

The Monsters We Have Lived With

Humans have always lived with monsters. That fact dates back, no doubt, to the time when the early ancestors of humans moved about in constant fear of the large predators around them. Fearful as the mammoths, saber-toothed tigers, and cave bears may have been, it is the essence of the human mind that still worse could be imagined. —ISAAC ASIMOV

Fantastic Animals Prowl Tall Timber of our Mythology

The extent of the animal kingdom is almost beyond imagining. The total fauna amounts to some thousands of creatures which humans have loved, hated, feared, worshiped, eaten, exploited, and often exterminated. All the while, in addition, fable and legend have given us an apocryphal biology based on hearsay or faulty observation. We have the unicorn, the basilisk, the winged bulls of Assyria, the frightening griffin of the Hittites, the chimera, the phoenix, sphinx, sirens, and sea horses. This amounts to a vast archive of European and Oriental mythical animals. —GERALD CARSON

Both introductions mention real and imaginary animals, but the second introduction, from *Smithsonian,* contains more details and uses more difficult vocabulary. *Smithsonian* is directed toward well-educated readers who want specific and complete information, while *TV Guide* is directed toward a broader, more average audience.

EXERCISE 8 Choosing a Subject

Using your notes from Exercises 4–7 or any fresh ideas, make a list of ten possible subjects for an expository essay. Review the guidelines on page 472, and put a check next to the one subject that comes closest to following all four guidelines. Save your work for Exercise 13.

EXERCISE 9 Limiting a Subject
Write the following subjects on your paper one at a time. After each one, answer the five questions for limiting a subject on page 472. Use the model answers on page 472 as a guide.

1. winter
2. baseball
3. household chores
4. getting along with a boss
5. earning money

Listing Supporting Details

Once you have limited your subject, you can begin to list details that will help you explain it. *Brainstorming* will help you think of details. When you brainstorm, you write down all ideas that come to mind when you think of your subject, recording them in whatever order they occur to you. Later you will arrange them logically. Your list may include any of the following types of details that are appropriate to your limited subject. If you need more information, check the library or other sources for books or magazines that contain the information you need.

20i

Types of Supporting Details Used in Expository Essays

facts	steps in a process	comparisons/contrasts
examples	incidents	analogies
reasons	definitions	causes/effects

The following brainstorming notes are on the subject of the wild boy of Aveyron. They are not arranged in logical order.

LIMITED SUBJECT the wild boy of Aveyron

- Doctor's name was Jean-Marc-Gaspard Itard
- François Truffaut made a movie about the boy

- Itard named the boy Victor
- Victor was found in France in 1800, age 12 years
- had 23 scars all over him
- couldn't talk
- trotted instead of walked
- learned how to fetch water
- learned how to say *milk*
- had a nice smile
- expressed only joy and sorrow at first
- Itard first made sure the boy's needs were met before beginning to teach him
- Tarzan and Mowgli are fictional wild children
- Victor was insensitive to heat and cold and some sounds
- responded only to sounds related to foods
- Itard played games with him to develop thinking powers; games Victor was most interested in involved food
- Victor could reach into boiling water and not express pain
- Itard's work with Victor helped him develop ideas about how to teach deaf and mentally retarded people
- famous educator Maria Montessori was influenced by Itard's work

EXERCISE 10 Listing Supporting Details

Use the technique of brainstorming and your own memories and experiences to list at least five details for each of the following subjects.

1. how repetition helps people learn
2. how language changes with the times
3. communication between humans and animals
4. the qualities that make a television show good
5. rituals in high school
6. different kinds of comedy
7. how to be a safe driver
8. why endangered species are protected
9. how to prepare mentally for an athletic contest
10. the purpose of compliments

Outlining

The final step in prewriting is arranging ideas in a logical order. The disordered thoughts that occurred to you during brainstorming now need to be grouped into categories and arranged in an order that the reader can easily follow. Many writers use a two-step process to make an outline to use as a blueprint for their essay: (1) grouping notes into categories and (2) arranging those categories in a logical order with letters and numbers.

20j Organize your notes in an **outline** that shows how you will cover the **main topics, subtopics,** and **supporting details** of your subject.

Grouping Your Notes into Categories. Scan your list of supporting details, asking yourself what one idea might have in common with the other ideas on your list. Try to create three to five main categories of thought into which most of your details will fit. Details that do not easily fit into one of your main categories might be usable in the introduction or conclusion of your essay.

The following groupings show the categories that can be created from the notes about the wild boy of Aveyron.

Itard's methods and successes in helping Victor

- Itard first made sure the boy's needs were met before beginning to teach him
- Itard played games with him to develop thinking powers; games Victor was most interested in involved food
- learned how to fetch water
- learned how to say *milk*

How Itard's work influenced later educational practices

- Itard's work with Victor helped him develop ideas about how to teach deaf and mentally retarded people
- famous educator Maria Montessori was influenced by Itard's work

Boy's state when he was found

- had scars all over him
- trotted instead of walked
- had a nice smile
- expressed only joy and sorrow at first
- couldn't talk
- Victor was insensitive to heat and cold and some sounds
- Victor could reach into boiling water and not express pain
- only responded to sounds related to foods

Arranging Categories in a Logical Order. The categories you create when you group your prewriting details are the main topics that you will use to support your thesis statement. The next step is to arrange these topics in a logical order. If your essay explains steps in a process or uses an incident to explain something, *chronological order* is probably best. If your essay analyzes an object, *spatial order* might be the most logical. Most expository essays, however, use either *order of importance* or *developmental order.* *(See page 431.)*

The most logical arrangement for the main topics about the wild boy is developmental order. If a Roman numeral is assigned to each category, a simple outline would appear as follows.

I. Boy's state when he was found
II. Itard's methods and successes in helping Victor
III. Itard's influence on later educational practices

Notice that the wording of the third main topic is different from that on page 476. The change in wording was made so that the three main topics would be expressed in *parallel form.* *(See pages 390–391.)* The main topics and each group of subtopics in an outline must be expressed in parallel form.

After your simple outline is complete, you can continue the outlining process by arranging the items *within* each category into a logical order. This time each grouping, called a subtopic, is assigned a capital letter. As you draw up your outline, you may add new ideas as you think of them, provided you can find a logical place for them in your outline.

MAIN TOPIC I. Boy's state when he was captured
SUBTOPICS A. Physical appearance
B. Emotions
C. Insensitivities
MAIN TOPIC II. Itard's methods and successes in helping Victor
SUBTOPICS A. First step: meeting boy's needs
B. Second step: developing boy's sensitivities
C. Third step: playing thinking games
D. Fourth step: teaching language and chores
MAIN TOPIC III. Itard's influence on later educational practices
SUBTOPICS A. Idea of good learning environment
B. Education for deaf and mentally retarded
C. Influence on Montessori

After the subtopics are arranged in a logical order, the final step in outlining is to add supporting points under the subtopics if necessary. These are assigned Arabic numerals. If your supporting points can be broken down further, you can use lowercase letters to show the divisions. The pattern that follows is the correct form for an outline.

I. (Main topic)
    A. (Subtopic)
        1. (Supporting point)
        2. (Supporting point)
            a. (Detail)
            b. (Detail)
    B. (Subtopic)
    (etc.)

A final outline for the essay on the wild boy of Aveyron might look like this.

I. Boy's state when he was found
    A. Physical appearance
        1. Scars
        2. Method of walking

B. Emotions
  1. Smile
  2. Expression of only joy or sorrow
C. Insensitivities
  1. Heat and cold
  2. Certain sounds
    a. Failure to take notice of speech
    b. Ready notice of sounds relating to food

II. Itard's methods and successes in helping Victor
  A. First step: meeting boy's needs
  B. Second step: developing boy's sensitivities
  C. Third step: playing thinking games
  D. Fourth step: teaching civilized ways
    1. Language
    2. Chores

III. Itard's influence on later educational practices
  A. Idea of good learning environment
  B. Education for deaf and mentally retarded
  C. Influence on Montessori

After you have finished a draft of your outline, use the following questions to check its form.

20k

Questions for Checking an Outline

1. Did you use Roman numerals for main topics?
2. Did you use capital letters for subtopics?
3. Did you use Arabic numerals for supporting points?
4. If your supporting points can be broken down, did you use lowercase letters?
5. If you include subtopics under topics, do you have at least two?
6. If you include supporting points under subtopics, do you have at least two?
7. If you break down your supporting points, do you have at least two items in the break down?
8. Does your indentation follow the model of the final outline on pages 478–479?
9. Did you capitalize the first word of each entry?
10. Are your main topics and each group of subtopics expressed in parallel forms?

EXERCISE 11 Grouping Ideas into Categories
The following prewriting notes are on the subject of machines that have been celebrated or used in classical music. Find three categories into which you can group the ideas, and write each category on your paper. Then list the ideas under the proper category. All but one of the items should fit into one of the three categories you create. Save your work for use in Exercise 12.

- spinning-wheel sound imitated in Richard Wagner's opera *The Flying Dutchman* (1843)
- George Antheil composed the *Airplane Sonata* for piano in 1922
- Arthur Honegger portrayed sound of express train in *Pacific 231* (1923)
- Richard Strauss imitated sound of telephone ring in his opera *Intermezzo* (1924)
- Mikhail Glinka wrote "Song of the Railways" (1846)
- Alban Berg imitated telephone sound in his opera *Lulu* (1936)
- George Antheil used two aircraft propellers as instruments in his *Ballet Mécanique* (1924)
- Gian-Carlo Menotti wrote an opera called *The Telephone* (1947)

EXERCISE 12 Outlining
Following the steps on pages 476–479, use the categories you created for the items about machines in music in Exercise 11 to make an outline. The outline should show three main topics, with at least two subtopics under each one. The main topics and subtopics should be organized in a logical way. Save your work for Exercise 14.

EXERCISE 13 On Your Own
Using your work from Exercise 8, limit your chosen subject by asking yourself the five questions on page 472. Then brainstorm a list of supporting details and organize them into an outline. *(Review pages 474–479 for help.)* Save your work for Exercise 21.

WRITING

The next stage of the writing process is writing the first draft. Using your outline and other prewriting notes, you will express your thoughts in complete sentences and paragraphs. In the process of writing the first draft, you are likely to discover ideas that you did not include in your outline. You may include them in your first draft, as long as they relate to your main idea and help make it clearer or better developed. A first draft does not need to be polished or neat, but it should include all the parts of an essay: an introduction with a thesis statement, a body of supporting paragraphs, and a conclusion.

Writing the Thesis Statement

Your essay may not begin with the thesis statement, but writing it first will help you keep your main idea clearly in focus. Use the steps shown in the following chart to help you write an effective thesis statement.

201l

Steps for Writing a Thesis Statement

1. Look over your prewriting notes, especially your outline and the questions you answered to limit your subject.
2. Try to express your main idea in one sentence.
3. Revise your sentence until it covers all of your main topics.
4. Avoid such expressions as "In this paper I will . . ." or "This essay will be about . . ."

Reread the prewriting notes and outline on the wild boy of Aveyron on pages 474–479. Then study the problems in the following thesis statements.

WEAK THESIS STATEMENT When he was first captured in 1800, the wild boy of Aveyron was very different from a normal child. [too specific: does not cover details about Itard's work with him and the influence that work had on later practices]

Wild children exist in both fiction and fact. [too general: does not even mention the wild boy of Aveyron]

This essay will be about the wild boy of Aveyron. [focuses your reader's attention on the essay instead of on the wild boy]

The following thesis statement is appropriately specific and covers all the supporting details.

STRONG THESIS STATEMENT Dr. Itard's methods in attempting to civilize the wild boy from Aveyron led to ideas in education and psychology that we take for granted today.

EXERCISE 14 Identifying Problems in Thesis Statements
Reread your work from Exercises 11 and 12 on machines in music. Write the following thesis statements on your paper, leaving a blank line after each one. In the blank space, explain in one sentence what is wrong with the thesis statement. Use the models on pages 481–482 as a guide.

1. Airplanes and telephones have been celebrated in classical music.
2. In this essay I will show how composers have paid tribute to machines.
3. Composers often try to reflect in their music the social changes of the day.
4. This paper will be about music and machines.
5. George Antheil's *Airplane Sonata* is a good example of how composers celebrate machines.

EXERCISE 15 Writing a Thesis Statement
Following the steps on page 481, write a thesis statement for an essay about machines and music that is appropriately specific and that covers all of the main topics in the outline you wrote in Exercise 12.

Writing the Introduction

The purposes of the introduction are to make clear the subject and the thesis and to set the tone. The following suggestions may give you ideas for an introduction.

20m

Suggestions for Beginning an Essay

1. Begin with an incident that shows how you became interested in your subject.
2. Begin by giving some background information.
3. Begin with an example or incident that catches the reader's attention.

You may need to revise the thesis statement to work it in smoothly with the other sentences. The thesis statement about the wild boy has been reworked to fit smoothly into the introduction. Notice also that an idea left out of the outline is used in the introduction as part of the background information.

INTRODUCTION — The idea of a child growing up away from all other humans and being raised by animals has turned up again and again in popular tales. Tarzan of the apes, a creation of Edgar Rice Burroughs, and Rudyard Kipling's Mowgli the wolf boy are two famous examples. Wild children turn up in fact as well as in fiction, although there is no evidence that any were raised by animals. One of the most interesting and famous factual cases is that of Victor, the wild boy of Aveyron, France. The doctor who worked with the boy after he was captured from the wild in 1800 was Jean-Marc-Gaspard Itard.

THESIS STATEMENT — The young doctor's methods in trying to civilize the boy, whom he named *Victor,* led to new ideas in education and psychology, ideas that we take for granted today.

EXERCISE 16 Identifying Essay Beginnings

Read each of the following introductory paragraphs. Then write *personal incident, background information,* or *attention-getting example* to indicate how the essay begins.

1.

I remember, to start with, that day in Sacramento, in a California now nearly thirty years past, when I first entered a classroom—able to understand about fifty stray English words. The third of four children, I had been preceded by my older brother and sister to a neighborhood school. Neither of them, however, had revealed very much about their classroom experiences. They left each morning and returned each afternoon, always together, speaking Spanish as they climbed the five steps to the porch.

Their mysterious books, wrapped in brown shopping-bag paper, remained on the table next to the door, closed firmly behind them.

—RICHARD RODRIGUEZ, "ARIA: A MEMOIR OF A BILINGUAL CHILDHOOD"

2.

With his 47-pound bow drawn taut, a carbon graphite arrow held close to his cheek and EEG wires flowing from his scalp to monitor his brain, Rick McKinney seemed to be gazing absently at the majesty of Pikes Peak towering above the U.S. Olympic Training Center in Colorado Springs. Suddenly, he released the arrow and hit a perfect bull's eye that stood 98.6 yards downrange. Dr. Daniel Landers, an exercise scientist from Arizona State University, looked up from his EEG monitor, smiled and nodded with approval. McKinney had really not been thinking during the shot; the left side of his brain had shown diminished electrical activity.

—LEE TORREY, "HOW SCIENCE CREATES WINNERS"

3.

For almost three-quarters of a century, James Van DerZee has with rare artistry compiled a sweeping photographic survey of a way of life among black people of eastern America, particularly Harlem, that is unique and irreplaceable. It is both an historical record of value and an achievement of disciplined and feeling art. Van DerZee is only now beginning to be recognized as one of the notable photographers of middle-class people of the country.

—CLARISSA K. WITTENBERG, *SMITHSONIAN*

EXERCISE 17 Experimenting with Essay Beginnings

Read the following thesis statement. Then write two different introductory paragraphs that include the thesis statement. The first should provide background information; the second should use a personal incident or an attention-getting example. In each paragraph you may revise the thesis statement as needed to improve the flow.

THESIS STATEMENT Parks come in a variety of sizes and with a variety of attractions, from the neighborhood park to the sprawling national parks.

Writing the Body

Use your outline to help you draft the body of your essay, moving from point to point in the same order as the outline. You may add new ideas that would improve your essay. Check, however, to make sure each new idea relates directly to the main idea expressed in your thesis statement.

As you write the body of your essay, you will need to supply transitions to connect your thoughts within and between paragraphs. Use any transitional words or phrases that will help your reader follow your thoughts easily. *(See page 431 for lists of transitions.)*

Using transitions will help give your essay *coherence,* the quality that makes each sentence seem connected to the one before it. The following are other ways to achieve coherence.

20n

Tips for Achieving Coherence

1. Repeat a key word from an earlier sentence.
2. Repeat an idea from an earlier sentence using new words.
3. Use a pronoun in place of a word used earlier.

The following draft shows how ideas from the outline on the wild boy of Aveyron on pages 478–479 are fleshed out with transitions into complete sentences and paragraphs.

FROM I IN OUTLINE Itard and other scientists were interested in finding out how much of a human's development is inborn and how much is learned through the experiences of civilization. Victor provided an opportunity to study this question, for when he was captured at the age of twelve, he was in an extremely uncivilized state. Twenty-three scars from burns, bites, and scratches covered his dirty body, and he trotted instead of walked. He had a very pleasing smile, but he expressed only extremes of emotion: joy, especially when he was fed or taken on walks, and sorrow about not being free. He could not speak, and he appeared insensitive to heat and cold. He could reach into a pot of boiling water and show no pain while pulling out a potato. The only sounds that interested him were those related to food. For Itard, working with Victor was a rare chance to learn about humans raised in isolation and to try to succeed where others, with earlier wild children, had failed.

FROM II IN OUTLINE

Itard's first step in educating Victor was attending to his needs and desires. He gave Victor the foods he liked (mainly vegetables), plenty of rest, privacy, and exercise. Then he began developing the boy's sensitivities, such as sight and hearing, believing that no attempt to teach him to talk would succeed unless he was first sensitive to sound. Next, he tried to play games with Victor to stretch the boy's mental powers. He soon learned that only when food was involved did Victor pay any attention. To motivate Victor, Itard devised a game in which Victor would find a chestnut under one of three inverted cups. When he finally began teaching Victor to speak and read, however, Itard met with very little success. After years, the only words Victor learned were "milk" and "Oh God," the latter expression having been picked up by imitating his caretaker, Madame Guérin. Victor never learned to read. He did, however, learn some simple chores, including fetching water and sawing wood. He never became what most people would consider a normal person, although he did respond to the affectionate concern of those who surrounded him.

FROM III IN OUTLINE

Itard's methods, whatever their failings with Victor, opened new doors in education. First, the idea that a child can learn only after his or her needs are met showed the importance of a good learning environment. In addition, working with Victor enabled Itard to make discoveries about teaching deaf children to speak, and it helped him create a whole new field of study: teaching the mentally retarded. Finally, Maria Montessori, a pioneer in educating very young children, was influenced in her work by Itard's experiences with Victor.

EXERCISE 18 Analyzing the Body of an Essay
Refer to the supporting paragraphs about Victor, the wild boy of Aveyron, on pages 485–487 to write the answers to the following questions.

1. In the first supporting paragraph, the last sentence refers to an earlier idea. In what sentences in the paragraph is that earlier idea expressed?
2. What words from the last sentence of the first supporting paragraph are repeated in the first sentence of the second supporting paragraph?
3. What transitional words are used in the second supporting paragraph?
4. What key word is repeated in sentences eight, nine, and ten of the second supporting paragraph? What pronoun is used in sentences ten and eleven to aid coherence?
5. To what earlier idea does the phrase *whatever their failings with Victor* (first sentence in third supporting paragraph) refer?
6. What transitional words and phrases are used in the third supporting paragraph?

Writing the Conclusion

Like the introduction, the conclusion is usually more general than the supporting paragraphs in the body. The conclusion is a good place to express the insight that your subject inspired. Your prewriting notes, especially the questions you answered to limit your subject, may contain ideas for your conclusion. Any of the following is a good way to end an expository essay.

20o

Ways to End an Essay

1. Summarize the essay or restate the thesis statement in new words.
2. Refer to ideas in the introduction to bring the essay full circle.
3. Appeal to the reader's emotions.
4. Draw a conclusion based on the details in the essay body.

The following conclusion to the essay about Victor draws a conclusion based on the specifics in the body. The last sentence, often called a *clincher* because it fixes the message firmly in the reader's mind, adds a strong ending.

CONCLUSION After Itard stopped working with Victor, the French government paid for Victor's care for the rest of his life. He never fit into normal society. Itard concluded that the early years of human life are precious periods of learning and, if a child is deprived of a human environment, learning can never take place later. Although scientists and psychologists are still debating the influences of heredity and environment, Itard drew his own conclusion.

CLINCHER It is human society—civilization—that makes us what we are, and no amount of inborn humanity could make up for the loss of companionship that Victor endured in the wild.

Writing a Title. The final step in writing the first draft is thinking of a suitable title for your essay. Many titles are taken from words and phrases within the essays. Others are composed like a newspaper headline and express the main idea in an eye-catching way.

20p A good **title** should suggest the main idea and make your readers curious enough to want to read on.

EXERCISE 19 Analyzing a Concluding Paragraph

Reread the entire essay on Victor on pages 483, 485–487, and 488. Then write answers to the following questions.

1. Where else in the essay besides the concluding paragraph is the word *civilized* (or some form of it) mentioned?
2. To what sentence in the first supporting paragraph on page 485 do the last two sentences of the conclusion refer?
3. What words in the last sentence of the body are repeated in the first sentence of the conclusion?

EXERCISE 20 Thinking of Titles
Make a list of five possible titles for the essay about Victor.

EXERCISE 21 On Your Own
Using your outline from Exercise 13, write the first draft of an introduction, body, and conclusion. Then think of several good titles for your essay and write them at the top. Save your paper for Exercise 22.

REVISING

In the revising stage of the writing process, your purpose is to improve your first draft—to make it clearer, smoother, livelier, and more readable. After putting your paper away for a while and reading it later, you may think of new, better ways to express your meaning. You may need to write a second, third, or fourth draft until you are satisfied with the clarity of your message. Your main concern in the revising stage is your audience. Ask yourself over and over, "Will my readers understand exactly what I mean?"

Checking for Unity, Coherence, and Emphasis

In an essay with unity, all the ideas serve the purpose of developing and explaining the main idea. The topic sentence of each supporting paragraph should relate directly to the thesis statement. Similarly, each sentence within a particular paragraph should relate directly to the topic sentence. As you revise, watch for any ideas that stray off the main point and cross them out.

As you have seen, coherence is another important feature of a good essay. As you revise, look for ways to improve the organization and flow of your essay. Make sure your writing guides your readers along a logical path of thought.

Emphasis is another important feature of essays that should be checked in the revising stage. *Emphasis* is the quality in essays that makes the most important points stand out clearly in the reader's mind. You can achieve the emphasis you desire by devoting more space to important ideas, by using transitional words and phrases that show the importance of ideas, and by repeating important points.

20q A good essay has **unity, coherence,** and **emphasis.**

Use the following checklist to help you revise your essay.

20r **Checking for Unity, Coherence, and Emphasis**

Checking for Unity

1. Does every paragraph in the essay relate to your main idea?
2. Does every sentence in each paragraph support the topic sentence?

Checking for Coherence

3. Are the paragraphs in the body of your essay presented in a logical order? *(See page 428.)*
4. Do transitions smoothly connect the paragraphs? *(See page 431.)*
5. Are the sentences *within* each paragraph presented in a logical order?
6. Did you use the techniques for achieving coherence? *(See page 485.)*

Checking for Emphasis

7. Do your transitional words show the relative importance of your ideas?
8. Did you match the amount of space you gave to ideas in your essay with their relative importance?
9. Did you repeat key ideas to show their importance?

Revision Checklist

In addition to using the preceding checklist, you should ask yourself other questions about your essay's structure, sentences, and words. Use the following checklist.

20s

Revision Checklist

Checking Your Essay

1. Does the introduction set the tone and capture attention?
2. Does the thesis statement make your main idea clear?
3. Does your essay have unity, coherence, and emphasis?
4. Do you have a strong concluding paragraph?
5. Did you add a title?

Checking Your Paragraphs

6. Does each paragraph have a topic sentence? *(See pages 420–422.)*
7. Is each paragraph unified and coherent? *(See pages 425–431.)*

Checking Your Sentences and Words

8. Are your sentences varied? *(See pages 377–382.)*
9. Are your sentences concise? *(See pages 373–376.)*
10. Did you avoid faulty sentences? *(See pages 385–392.)*
11. Did you use specific words with correct connotations? *(See pages 367–368.)*
12. Did you use figurative language? *(See pages 369–371.)*

EXERCISE 22 On Your Own

Use the Revision Checklist to make a final revision of the essay you wrote for Exercise 21. Save your paper for Exercise 23.

EDITING

The final stage in the writing process is editing. Use the following checklist to edit your revised essay. You may want to use the proofreading symbols on page 662 as you edit.

20t

Editing Checklist

1. Are your sentences free of errors in grammar and usage?
2. Did you spell each word correctly?
3. Did you use capital letters where needed?
4. Did you punctuate sentences correctly?
5. Did you use correct manuscript form? *(See page 659.)*
6. Is your typing or handwriting clear?

EXERCISE 23 On Your Own
Use the editing checklist to edit your essay from Exercise 22.

CHAPTER REVIEW

Write an expository essay on one of the following subjects or on one of your own choosing. Use the Steps for Writing Expository Essays on page 493 as a guide.

Subjects Based on Personal Experience

1. why you decided to go (or not to go) to college
2. how to lose friends
3. how to plan a budget
4. what makes people buy on impulse
5. collecting as a hobby
6. puns
7. city life
8. solitude
9. fads in movies
10. a person in history you would like to be and why

Subjects Based on Outside Learning

11. Pavlov's experiments with dogs
12. Halley's comet
13. the process of electing a president
14. supply and demand in economics
15. using BASIC to program computers
16. how to put together a routine in gymnastics
17. the music of John Cage
18. James Earl Gideon and the Supreme Court
19. the process of carbon dating
20. Einstein's "twins" thought experiment

Steps for Writing

Expository Essays

✓ **Prewriting**

1. Find ideas by asking yourself questions and by reading. *(See pages 469–470.)*
2. From a list of possible subjects, choose one to develop into an essay. *(See pages 471–472.)*
3. Limit your subject by asking questions about your audience, tone, and focus point. *(See pages 471–473.)*
4. Brainstorm a list of supporting ideas. *(See page 474.)*
5. Organize your list of ideas into an outline. *(See pages 476–479.)*

✓ **Writing**

6. Write a thesis statement. *(See pages 481–482.)*
7. Write an introduction that includes your thesis statement. *(See pages 482–483.)*
8. Use your outline to write the paragraphs in the body. *(See pages 485–487.)*
9. Use connecting devices to link your thoughts. *(See page 485.)*
10. Add a concluding paragraph. *(See pages 487–488.)*
11. Add a title. *(See page 488.)*

✓ **Revising**

12. Using the Revision Checklist, revise your essay for structure, well-developed paragraphs, unity, coherence, emphasis, and varied and lively sentences and words. *(See page 491.)*

✓ **Editing**

13. Using the Editing Checklist, check your essay for errors in grammar, spelling, mechanics, and manuscript form. *(See page 491.)*

21

Other Kinds of Essays

An essay is a lens through which readers can peer into the mind of the writer. It focuses on one idea in that mind—a record of a personal experience, a remembered person or place, or a studied opinion. With smoothly organized ideas and carefully chosen words, essayists make public the experiences and outlooks that make them unique.

PERSONAL EXPERIENCE ESSAYS

The purpose of a personal experience essay is to relate a true story and to draw a general conclusion based on the events in the story. Since the material for the essay comes from the writer's personal experience, the natural way to relate the story is from the *first person point of view*. In a first person essay, the writer refers to himself or herself as "I."

21a A **personal experience essay** is a narrative that uses the first person point of view to tell a true story and draw a general conclusion.

Essay Structure

The following chart summarizes the structure of a personal experience essay.

21b

Structure of a Personal Experience Essay

1. The **introduction** sets the tone and leads into the story. It also contains a **thesis statement** that makes the narrative purpose clear.
2. The **supporting paragraphs** use the first person point of view and chronological order to tell a true story that backs up the thesis statement.
3. The **conclusion** tells the outcome of the story, revealing the significance of the personal experience.

In the following personal experience essay, the thesis statement is in heavy type. As you read the essay, notice the first person narrator and the way that the introduction and conclusion frame the incident related in the essay body. (The paragraphs are numbered for easy reference.)

The Lure of Islands

(1) Ever since boyhood the mere name, *island,* has had a peculiar fascination for me. An inland birth was, doubtless, partially responsible for that. Islands were far to seek on the prairies of Iowa, and yet they could be found, of a sort. A mudbank in the sluggish midstream of a prairie slough was enough. If at the season of the spring rains I found a large one with a tree or two, the roots undermined by the current, I asked nothing better than to halt and moor my flat-bottomed skiff to the roots of one of the trees. Try as I would, though, I could not imagine the sea—any sea. The fact that the earth is three-quarters water was not a fact to me. Neither the evidence furnished by maps in school geographies nor the assurance of my elders convinced me; or if I believed, it was only with the surface of my mind. Within was a solid core of doubt.

(2) **I finally came to believe in the sea on one wintry afternoon.** It must have been around my eleventh year: a memorable day that stands out with the entrancing roundness and clearness of objects seen through the stereoscopic

glasses our parents used to keep with the knickknacks on the parlor table. I remember the very weather of it: the fine, dry snow filling the wagon tracks in the frozen mud, sifting lightly along the board sidewalks, piling in drifts along the fronts of the store buildings, adding little by little to the grayness of a gray world. I was on my way to Mrs. Sigafoos's shop.

(3) She kept a small stationery and notions store not far from the C.R.I. & P. Railway Station. There she would sit by the window, a shawl pinned around her thin shoulders, keeping her rocker going when there was nothing to be seen out of doors, stopping it abruptly and peering out when someone passed. In her store she had a shelf of books: boys' books such as *Cudjo's Cave, Lost River,* and editions of the Henty and Alger books, all of which I read, taking great care not to soil them. There were also padded-leather editions of the poets: Bryant, Whittier, Longfellow, and Lowell, for birthday and school graduation gifts.

(4) There was another book on the shelf. I had noticed it before, but, somehow, it had failed to arouse my interest: *Typee,* by Herman Melville. It may have been the strange title that threw me off. On this afternoon I was tempted to take it down and open it. I read:

> Six months at sea! Yes, reader, as I live, six months out of sight of land; cruising after the sperm whale beneath the scorching sun of the Line, and tossed on the billows of the wide rolling Pacific—the sky above, the sea around, and nothing else!

(5) Who does not remember some day in childhood such as this one of mine, preserved—fragrant and memorable—between the covers of a book? *Typee* has my day safely hidden among its pages. It was my first authentic entrance, through literature, to the world of islands. What more fitting vantage-point or vantage-time could I have had for the experience than the back room of Mrs. Sigafoos's shop, in a little farming town on the prairies on the afternoon of a snowy winter day? For the first time I believed in the sea—emotionally, I mean. That opening paragraph spread it out before me as something not to be questioned, like the sea of land rolling away to the horizons that bounded my home town. However, as I followed Melville across it, in the imagination, to Nuku Hiva in the Marquesas Islands, I little realized that the first gossamer-like thread of Chance was being spun which was to take me to the South Pacific, with my friend Nordhoff, so many years later. —JAMES NORMAN HALL, "THE LURE OF ISLANDS" (ADAPTED)

EXERCISE 1 Analyzing a Personal Experience Essay
Reread the essay by James Norman Hall on pages 495–496, and write answers to the following questions.

1. What pronouns in the first paragraph show that the essay is written in the first person?
2. In what paragraph does Hall set the scene for his incident?
3. The events in the story are simple. Hall goes to the store on a wintry day, notices a title that catches his eye, takes the book down from the shelf, and reads the opening paragraph. What importance did this simple incident have for Hall?
4. How do the descriptive details in the second and third paragraphs contribute to the experience Hall is recounting?
5. In what sentence in the concluding paragraph does Hall tell the significance of the experience?

Developing and Organizing Narrative Details

The introduction and conclusion of a personal experience essay frame the story with insights or interpretations of the larger meaning of the story. The body presents the story itself.

At the heart of every good story is a conflict. In the essay by James Norman Hall, the conflict is between the writer and his imagination; he tries to imagine the sea. The supporting details in the essay body are the events leading up to and resolving the conflict, arranged in chronological order. The following chart offers some tips for writing effective narrative essays.

21c

Tips for Writing the Body of a Personal Experience Essay

1. Plan your story around a conflict that represented a turning point of great or small significance in your life.
2. Set the scene early in the story so the reader knows when and where the action takes place.
3. Use dialogue where appropriate to advance the action and reveal character.
4. Tell the story event by event, arranging the details in chronological order and using appropriate transitions. *(See page 431.)*
5. Resolve the conflict by showing how you overcame it or reached a new understanding about it.

EXERCISE 2 Thinking of Subjects for Personal Experience Essays

Each of the following represents a typical kind of conflict that may be used in a personal experience essay. Write each conflict on your paper, and then list at least three specific experiences from your life that illustrate that kind of conflict. Save your work for Exercise 3.

EXAMPLE Conflict with machines

POSSIBLE ANSWERS
- the time I first heard a talking camera
- the time the car broke down on the way back from the mountains
- my first attempt to use a computer

1. conflict with another person my age
2. conflict with a younger or older person
3. conflict with nature
4. conflict with conscience
5. conflict with a group (a business, a club, a class)

EXERCISE 3 Listing Events in Chronological Order

Choose one of the incidents that you identified in Exercise 2, and list all of the events leading up to and resolving the conflict. Arrange the events in chronological order. Save your work for Exercise 4.

EXAMPLE the time the car broke down on the way back from the mountains

EVENTS
- was returning home after a trip with friends to the mountains
- as night came on, the car's engine began sputtering and backfiring
- decided the car was running too roughly to drive further on the highway
- took the next exit and stopped on the side of a country road
- walked to the nearest telephone; picked up the phone to call the auto club for help
- before dialing noticed on my membership card that the expiration date had passed
- walked back to the car to find Ken closing the hood

- Ken started the engine and it purred
- I shook his hand in amazement and put us back on the road

EXERCISE 4 Drawing Conclusions from Personal Experiences

Look over your list of events from Exercise 3, and try to express in one sentence the significance of the conflict.

EXAMPLE the time the car broke down on the way back from the mountains

POSSIBLE ANSWER After having laughed at Ken when he enrolled in the vocational course, I realized for the first time the value of having enough basic skills to be self-reliant.

EXERCISE 5 On Your Own

Plan a personal experience essay by answering the following questions. (You may use your work from Exercises 2–4 if you wish.)

1. What incident in my life led to a new understanding of a conflict?
2. What events led up to and resolved the conflict?
3. Where and when did the events take place?
4. What background information should I provide in the introduction so the reader will understand the conflict?
5. What insights can I draw in the conclusion about the importance of this incident?

Writing Extra

When you write a personal experience essay, you use the *inductive method:* You examine a specific experience in your life and then draw a general conclusion about it. *(See page 400.)* A good way of finding a subject for a personal experience essay is to start with a general truth or insight and then search your memory for specific experiences that support or contradict that insight. If you use this approach, a good source of inspiration is a book of quotations, since memorable sayings often express a general truth.

EXERCISE 6 Finding Subjects for Personal Experience Essays

Choose one of the following quotations, and write it on your paper. Then think of one experience in your life that supports or contradicts the message in the quotation. Underneath the quotation, list the events of that experience in chronological order.

1. Advice is like snow; the softer it falls, the longer it dwells upon and the deeper it sinks into the mind.—Samuel Coleridge
2. Children have more need of models than of critics.
3. A liar ought to have a good memory.—Quintilian
4. Freedom is not worth having if it does not include the freedom to make mistakes.—Mahatma Gandhi
5. A person who has committed a mistake and does not correct it is committing another mistake.—Confucius
6. Truth is always exciting. Speak it, then. Life is dull without it.—Pearl S. Buck
7. Playing the game is an important achievement, but first you must know how to play and know all the rules. —Barbara Jordan
8. If anything can go wrong, it will.—Murphy's Law
9. Truth is stranger than fiction, but it is because fiction is obliged to stick to possibilities.—Mark Twain
10. Be silent always when you doubt your sense.—Alexander Pope

DESCRIPTIVE ESSAYS

In a descriptive essay, the writer's purpose is to help the reader create a mental image of a person, a place, or an object. No writer can capture the vast amount of sensory information an observer on the spot could perceive. A writer can, however, carefully select a sufficient number of details to convey an overall impression.

21d A **descriptive essay** creates a mood or impression by painting a vivid picture of a person, a scene, or an object.

Essay Structure

The following chart summarizes the structure of a descriptive essay.

21e

Structure of a Descriptive Essay

1. The **introduction** captures attention and contains the thesis statement. The **thesis statement** expresses an overall impression of the subject.
2. The **body of supporting paragraphs** presents specific and sensory details, arranged in a logical order with appropriate transitions.
3. The **conclusion** reinforces the overall impression by summarizing the specific details or by making a vivid comparison.

In the following descriptive essay, the writer's purpose is to recreate the view from an airplane over southernmost South America. The parts of the essay are labeled on the left.

The Plane and the Planet

INTRODUCTION: GETS THE READER'S ATTENTION AND SETS THE TONE

The pilot flying toward the Strait of Magellan sees below him, a little to the south of the Gallegos River, an ancient lava flow, an erupted waste of a thickness of sixty feet that crushes down the plain on which it has congealed. Farther south he meets a second flow, then a third. Thereafter every hump on the globe, every mound a few hundred feet high, carries a crater in its flank. No Vesuvius rises up to reign in the clouds. Instead there is, flat on the plain, a succession of gaping mouths.

THESIS STATEMENT: EXPRESSES MAIN IMPRESSION

This day, as I fly, the lava world is calm. There is something surprising in the tranquility of this deserted landscape where once a thousand volcanoes boomed to each other in their great underground organs and spat forth their fire. I fly over a world mute and abandoned, strewn with black glaciers.

FIRST BODY PARAGRAPH: GIVES SPECIFIC AND SENSORY DETAILS OF OLDER VOLCANOES FARTHER SOUTH

South of these glaciers there are yet older volcanoes veiled with the passing of time in a golden surface of grass. Here and there a tree rises out of a crevice like a plant in a cracked pot. In the soft and yellow light the plain appears as luxuriant as a garden. The short grass seems to civilize it, and round its giant throats there is scarcely any swelling to be seen. A hare scampers off; a bird wheels in the air. Life has taken possession of a new planet where the decent loam of our earth has at last spread over the surface of the star.

SECOND BODY PARAGRAPH: GIVES SPECIFIC AND SENSORY DETAILS OF POINTS STILL FARTHER SOUTH

Finally, crossing the line into Chile, a little north of Punta Arenas, one comes to the last of the craters, and here the mouths have been stopped with earth. A silky turf lies snug over the curves of the volcanoes, and all is smooth in the scene. Each fissure in the crust is sutured up by this tender flax. The earth is smooth, the slopes are gentle. One forgets the travail that gave them birth. This turf covers up from the flanks of the small hills the somber sign of their origin.

CONCLUSION: SUMMARIZES THE DETAILS; REINFORCES THE MAIN IMPRESSION OF CALM REBIRTH

We have reached the most southerly habitation of the world, a town born of the chance presence of a little mud between the timeless lava and the southern ice. So near the black cindery lava, how thrilling it is to feel the miraculous nature of humans! What a strange encounter! Who knows how, or why, humans visit these gardens ready to hand, habitable for so short a time—a geologic age—for a single day blessed among days?

—ANTOINE DE SAINT-EXUPÉRY, "THE PLANE AND THE PLANET"

EXERCISE 7 Analyzing a Descriptive Essay

Reread the essay "The Plane and the Planet" by Antoine de Saint-Exupéry on pages 501–502, and write answers to the following questions.

1. In the first paragraph, the writer uses the word *waste* instead of *residue* and *hump* instead of *bump*. Which connotations has he chosen, the more negative or the more positive? *(See pages 367–368.)*
2. To what are the craters compared in the last sentence of the first paragraph?
3. Is this image of the craters positive or negative?
4. Although the writer does not name any colors in the first paragraph, what color does your imagination supply?
5. What sounds are evoked in the second paragraph?
6. In what direction is the pilot flying?
7. To what are the trees rising out of crevices compared in the third paragraph?
8. What is different about the craters that are mentioned in the fourth paragraph?
9. The word *sutured* in paragraph four is borrowed from medicine. It means *sewn up to heal*. Name four other words in this paragraph that carry positive connotations.
10. What new sign of life appears in the last paragraph?

Selecting and Organizing Descriptive Details

The essay about flying over South America on pages 501–502 uses mainly visual impressions—sights—to recreate the scenes. Sight impressions are usually the first to come to mind when people recollect a place, a person, or an object. Other sensory impressions—smells, tastes, feelings, and sounds—are also useful in stirring the reader's imagination. To select sensory details that support the thesis statement of a descriptive essay, use the following brainstorming questions.

21f

Questions for Selecting Descriptive Details

1. What sights and sounds add to the overall impression?
2. What smells, tastes, or textures contribute to the overall impression?
3. What comparisons (similes and metaphors) would help a reader understand the overall impression? *(See pages 369–370.)*

After you have listed between 10 and 15 supporting details that help convey the overall impression of your subject, the next step is to plan the order in which you will present these details. Many descriptions, including "The Plane and the Planet" use spatial, or location, order. Spatial order can move from top to bottom (or the reverse), from side to side, inside out (or the reverse), near to far (or the reverse), or in a panoramic sweep (east to north to west to south, for example).

Other kinds of order are also possible in a descriptive essay. If your subject is a scene at different times of the day, chronological order would probably be the most logical arrangement of details. Order of importance and developmental order can also be used. *(See pages 428–431.)* Some writers of description use a unique order in which they record impressions in the order they are observed. *(See page 436.)* In all types of order, transitions guide the reader through the scene, pointing out the relationship of one supporting detail to another. *(See page 431.)*

EXERCISE 8 Selecting Descriptive Details

Write the following thesis statements one at a time. After each one, use your imagination to list one sight, one sound, one smell, and one feeling or texture that could contribute to the overall impression suggested in the thesis statement.

EXAMPLE The state fair was as exciting to us as it had been when we were younger.

POSSIBLE ANSWER the illuminated Ferris wheel [sight]
the cries of happy children [sound]
the livestock show [smell]
the jolts from riding the "bump" cars [feeling]

1. The auto repair shop throbbed with activity.
2. The new car that I took for a test drive was everything *my* car was not.
3. The dolphin show at the city's new aquarium was a joyous celebration.
4. The cabin had not been used for years; its unwelcoming appearance explained why.
5. When the temperature climbed above 90°, everyone headed for the pool in Memorial Park.
6. The street I grew up on is lined with warm memories.

7. The strangely decorated living room looked like a set for a science-fiction movie.
8. In the middle of a tent in the middle of a forest in the middle of the night, safety can seem just out of reach.
9. The attic, like the memory of an aging person, was crowded with old items.
10. At sunrise, even an otherwise busy city seems as tranquil as the wide-open spaces.

EXERCISE 9 Organizing Descriptive Details

The following details describe a potlatch, a gift-giving party held by the early Native Americans in the Pacific Northwest. The details are not in any order. Use the details to complete the outline that follows, assigning each detail a capital letter and placing it in a logical position in the outline.

- hosts gave away dried salmon and fish oil
- people wore robes made of otter, seal, or bearskins
- spread of food included smoked salmon
- some people wore headdresses carved with human faces
- bowls of wild berries were served
- hosts gave away fur robes
- other gifts were carved wooden bowls and chests
- meats served included roast duck or goose and deer or bear meat
- some gifts were blankets made from woven cedar fibers

I. Clothing
II. Foods served
III. Gifts

EXERCISE 10 On Your Own

Most descriptions are filtered through the eyes of the writer. The reader then pictures the scene from the vantage point of the writer. For practice in establishing a vantage point for your reader, try the following experiment. Write two paragraphs describing your living room. The first should be a record of what you see when you are in your favorite position in the room. The second should be from the vantage point of a pet in the room—a fish in an aquarium, a cat curled near the radiator, or a bird in a suspended cage. In the second paragraph, try to put yourself in the position of the pet you chose and describe the same scene from that vantage point. In both paragraphs, use such transitions as *to the left, above, next to,* etc.

PERSUASIVE ESSAYS

The purpose of a persuasive essay is to win readers over to your side of an argument or to motivate them to take actions they would otherwise not take. Underlying this purpose is the assumption that your readers do not already share your views. The clash of viewpoints and the essayist's art in winning readers over are what give the persuasive essay its bite.

21g A **persuasive essay** states an opinion on a subject and uses facts, examples, and reasons to convince readers.

The strongest persuasive essays are those built on arguable propositions rather than simple preferences. *(See pages 396–397.)* If you can back up your opinion with facts, examples, and logical reasons, then you probably have a suitable basis for a persuasive essay.

Essay Structure

The following chart shows the function of each main part of a persuasive essay.

21h

Structure of a Persuasive Essay

1. The **introduction** lays out the issue and contains the thesis statement, which expresses the author's opinion on the issue.
2. The **body of supporting paragraphs** presents reasons, facts, statistics, incidents, and examples that support the author's opinion.
3. The **conclusion** provides a strong summary or closing that drives home the author's opinion.

In the following persuasive essay, each part is labeled at the left. Notice the way the writer lays out the issue and his opinion in the introduction, supports his opinion in the body, and reinforces his main idea in the conclusion.

Controlling Alaska's Wolves

INTRODUCTION: PRESENTS THESIS STATEMENT; LAYS OUT ISSUE

The plan to eliminate humanely some of Alaska's soaring number of wolves makes good sense. Those who would deny Alaska's right to control its bourgeoning wolf population have failed to realize the ability of the wolf population to bounce back.

FIRST BODY PARAGRAPH: GIVES EXAMPLES AND FACTS

At one time, up to six federal varmint hunters ranged the Territory, poisoning, trapping, and shooting wolves from the air. As a result, at statehood few wolves remained. Since then, Alaska has worked hard to bring its wolves back. It added the wolf to its big game trophy and fur animal lists, which brought it under protection of bag limits and other regulations. It has shown flexibility in adjusting these regulations in response to wolf population changes. It has banned hunting wolves from an airplane as a sport. Finally, it has supported wolf research to learn how the animal lives.

SECOND BODY PARAGRAPH: GIVES STATISTICS

The wolf, with its remarkable resilience, has responded dramatically. In fact, there are so many wolves in some areas they are destroying their own food supply. In Alaska, the wolf's diet varies regionally but is mainly moose, deer, and caribou. Such prey is scarce in parts of the state now. The Arctic caribou herd crashed from 240,000 in 1970 to 60,000 in 1976; wolves may be killing up to 12,000 annually. The Tanana Flats near Fairbanks once supported 6,000 to 12,000 moose; now, the region contains only 3,000. In southeastern Alaska, deer herds thinned by severe winters have been kept at dangerously low levels by wolves. The wolves also starved, as deer became depleted.

THIRD BODY PARAGRAPH: CONCEDES THAT WOLVES ALONE ARE NOT RESPONSIBLE FOR TOTAL LOSS

Besides severe winters, there are a number of other reasons behind these alarming trends, including hunting by humans. Game is the main food for many wilderness residents. Nevertheless, in specific areas, there is little doubt that wolves have decimated moose, caribou, and deer.

CONCLUSION: REINFORCES MAIN IDEA

For many years, Alaska's game managers have demonstrated good wolf management. Now, unless the state can control soaring wolf numbers in specific areas, by humane and *strictly controlled* means, Alaska stands to lose many more caribou, moose, and deer—and, ultimately, its wolves.

—JIM REARDON, *NATIONAL WILDLIFE*

EXERCISE 11 Analyzing a Persuasive Essay

The essay that follows presents another view on the plan to eliminate some of Alaska's wolves. Read it carefully and answer the questions that follow it.

Wolves as Scapegoats

(1) The Alaska fish and game department has chosen the wolf as a scapegoat for its own disastrous mistakes in game management. In 1970, the Nelchina caribou herd numbered only 10,000 animals. Five years before, there had been 80,000. The same trend has been true of the Tanana moose herd. The great western Arctic caribou herd, which in 1972 contained 240,000 animals, numbered only 60,000 in 1977.

(2) Is this decimation of the western Arctic herd the wolf's doing? State game officials have declared that it is. However, they have no research to support that view. They do not even have a scientific count of how many wolves there are. Undaunted by what they do not know, they are determined to use aerial gunner teams to kill eight out of every ten western Arctic wolves. The caribou they want to defend, however, are the same ones they allowed hunters to kill without limits or closed seasons from 1959 until April of 1976. In 1976 alone, native hunters killed over 30,000 western Arctic caribou.

(3) In January of 1977, the fish and game department was caught trying to hush up the results of its own research on the Nelchina moose herd—research designed to demonstrate

scientifically, once and for all, what effect wolves have on calf survival. The research showed no significant wolf impact. So, instead, the department released to the press totally unscientific data.

(4) One department official in Anchorage said in April of 1977 that if every wolf in Alaska were killed, the western Arctic caribou herd would still not be helped. He added that, because the natives in the area were paying so little attention to the new seasons and limits set by the state, nothing could save the herd.

(5) In the spring of 1977, one house of the Alaska legislature passed a bill to ban all cow and calf moose hunting. We can hope that the blame for wildlife crises will now be placed where it belongs—on the shoulders of the Alaska fish and game department. —JAMES L. PITTS, *NATIONAL WILDLIFE*

1. What is the thesis statement of this essay?
2. What statistic in the introduction does Jim Reardon also use in his essay on pages 507–508?
3. Which of the following statements better summarizes the main idea of paragraph two?
   a. Wolves are not responsible for the decimation of the western Arctic herd.
   b. Game officials have insufficient evidence to blame wolves for the decimation of the western Arctic herd.
4. What statistic in paragraph two is omitted from the essay by Jim Reardon? What persuasive purpose does it serve in the essay by James L. Pitts?
5. One of Reardon's arguments is that the Alaska fish and game department has been doing a good job. What information in paragraph three of the essay by Pitts counters that argument?
6. To what authority does Pitts refer in paragraph four?
7. Which of the following statements better summarizes the main idea of paragraph four?
   a. Immoderate hunting is more a threat to the caribou than are wolves.
   b. Even one department official believes that immoderate hunting is more a threat to the caribou than are wolves.
8. What word from the last sentence of paragraph three is repeated in the first sentence of paragraph four as a transitional device?

9. The last sentence of the essay restates an earlier idea and adds a new emphasis. Write the earlier sentence to which it refers on your paper.
10. Which of the two essays about the Alaska wolves was more effective in persuading you? Explain your answer in a paragraph.

Developing and Organizing Strong Arguments

In between the two ends of the visible light spectrum are many different colors, sometimes distinguished from nearby colors by only a slight grade of hue. In the same way, most subjects of controversy spawn a wide range of possible viewpoints and interpretations; few issues are as simple as black and white.

One way to develop your own position on a controversial subject is to map out the whole spectrum of possible viewpoints in order to learn the subject well. On the subject of wolves, for example, the spectrum of ideas might appear as follows, with the strongly opposing views at either end.

- Eighty percent of wolves should be killed; hunting laws are adequate. [extreme view]
- Only wolves in certain areas should be killed; hunting laws are adequate. [moderate view]
- Wolves should be relocated, not killed; hunting laws should be tightened. [moderate view]
- No wolves should be killed; hunting laws should be greatly tightened. [opposite extreme view]

Once you have mapped out the possible viewpoints, you can formulate your own position. You may agree completely with one of the viewpoints, or you may see merits and weaknesses in several points of view and put together your own unique solution that borrows the strong points of several approaches.

After you have determined your position on an issue, your next task is to build a strong argument for your opinion, using specific facts and examples and logical ideas. The following guidelines will help you build the body of your essay into a strong argument.

21i

Guidelines for Building an Argument

1. List pros and cons (and positions in between) in your prewriting notes and be prepared to address the opposing views point by point.
2. Use facts and examples to support your opinion, rather than more opinions, since facts and examples are hard to dispute.
3. If those with an opposing view have a good point, admit it. Such an admission is called *conceding a point,* and it will strengthen your credibility.
4. Use polite and reasonable language rather than words that show bias or overcharged emotions.
5. Refer to well-respected experts and authorities who agree with your position.

After you have gathered the information you need to build your argument, the next step is to organize your ideas in a logical way. Many persuasive essays use *order of importance,* since this method clearly shows how the writer has evaluated the supporting facts, examples, and reasons. This technique also gives the most important points the most emphasis. *Developmental order* can also be effective, since in this method the reader can follow the logical thinking of the writer. *Chronological* and *spatial* order, while possible with certain kinds of subjects, do not usually serve the persuasive purpose as well as order of importance or developmental order. *(See page 431.)*

Whatever method of organization you choose, remember to use transitions to guide your readers through your points. *(See pages 430–431.)* Some transitions are especially useful when conceding a point or showing contrasting ideas.

21j

Transitions Showing Contrast or Concession

while it is true that	nonetheless
although	granting that
admittedly	still
nevertheless	despite
however	even though

EXERCISE 12 Developing an Argument

The following statements represent the spectrum of possible viewpoints on the subject of a college education. Read each one carefully. Then choose one with which you agree (or formulate your own viewpoint), and write it on your paper. Finally, list three central facts, examples, or reasons (or other kinds of evidence) that support your view. Save your work for Exercise 13.

1. College is a waste of time.
2. For some people, college is not useful or practical.
3. Even if it does not have direct use in preparing a student for a career, a college education is a worthwhile experience.
4. For many people, a college education is the most important investment for the future.
5. Everyone should go to college.

EXERCISE 13 Organizing Persuasive Ideas

Review your work from Exercise 12. Then do the following.

1. Write a thesis statement expressing your view (or, if you agreed with one statement in the text, copy that statement).
2. List the three ideas that support your position in the order of least to most important.
3. Assign each of your three points a Roman numeral as in an outline.
4. Add at least two supporting points under each of the Roman numerals. To develop your supporting points, try to anticipate what opposing views you may have to counter in order to persuade your reader. Your completed outline should look like the following.

    I. (Your least important point)
        A. (Supporting point)
        B. (Supporting point)
    II. (Your more important point)
        A. (Supporting point)
        B. (Supporting point)
    III. (Your most important point)
        A. (Supporting point)
        B. (Supporting point)

EXERCISE 14 On Your Own

The Declaration of Independence is an excellent example of persuasive writing. Find a copy of the document and study its use of deductive reasoning to prove the need for separation from Great Britain. Then answer the following questions.

1. How many paragraphs make up the introduction of the Declaration?
2. What two sentences in the introduction together form the thesis statement?
3. What type of supporting points are offered in the body: facts, examples, statistics, or expert opinions?
4. What method of organization is used in the body: spatial order, chronological order, order of importance, or developmental order?
5. Demonstrate your understanding of the deductive reasoning in the Declaration by completing the following representation of the colonists' argument. *(See pages 403–405 on deduction.)*

GENERAL STATEMENT	When a government deprives the governed of their natural rights, it is the right of the governed to change or abolish the government for one that upholds those rights.
PARTICULAR	______________________________
CONCLUSION	______________________________

INFORMAL ESSAYS

Although all essays are "signed" with their writers' unique style and approach, most have certain features in common. These include a three-part structure, a thesis statement, a logical order, and a clear purpose. Some essays, however, succeed in conveying their messages without one or more of these features. These are called informal essays, since the conventions of essay form are not strictly followed. They are also sometimes called familiar essays because their subject matter is usually highly personal.

21k An **informal essay** is a composition, usually on a personal subject, that presents ideas in an unconventional way.

Purpose in Informal Essays

In a formal essay, the writer's purpose is usually clear from the beginning. The introductory paragraph prepares the reader for a narrative, descriptive, expository, or persuasive purpose. In an informal essay, on the other hand, the purpose is often less clear. In some cases narration and description are combined; in others, narration and exposition or persuasion may work hand in hand. The main purpose of an informal essay is to share an experience or an understanding; any of the other writing purposes that may appear along the way are secondary. The informal essay allows you to express your own personality freely.

The following paragraph introduces an informal essay about an experience the writer had with Chet Atkins, a country musician. Notice, however, that the introduction does not limit the essay to a strictly narrative purpose.

> I don't have many friends who have done one thing so well that they're famous for it and could sit on their laurels if they wanted to, although I do know a woman who can touch her nose with her tongue, which she is famous for among all the people who have ever seen her do it. She doesn't do it often, because she doesn't need to, having proved herself. I also know a man who wrote a forty-one-word palindrome, which is about as far as you can go in the field of writing that reads the same forwards and backwards. And I know Chet Atkins, who is enplaqued in the Country Music Hall of Fame, in Nashville, and has a warm, secure spot in the history of the guitar. My own accomplishments fall into the immense dim area of the briefly remarkable, such as the play I made on a hot grounder off the bat of my Uncle Don, for which I felt famous one day in 1957. I backhanded the ball cleanly at third base and threw the aging speedster out at first, which drew quite a bit of comment at the time, but that was long ago and plays have been made since then that put mine in the shade. I was not quite fifteen and generally unaccomplished, so it meant a lot to me. The ball took a low bounce off the soft turf, and I had to pivot, get my glove down fast, then set my right foot to throw. The throw got him by a stride. If you had seen this, you would remember it.
>
> —GARRISON KEILLOR, *THE NEW YORKER*

Tone in Informal Essays

In most informal essays, the writer has a strong personal interest in the subject matter. For this reason, the straightforward, objective tone of many formal essays is replaced by a more personal, subjective tone in informal essays. Within this subjective range, however, a number of shades of tone are still possible. Compare the tones of the following two paragraphs from informal essays.

REFLECTIVE TONE

The sea answers all questions, and always in the same way; for when you read in the papers the interminable discussions and the bickering and the prognostications and the turmoil, the disagreements and the fateful decisions and the plans and the programs and the threats and the counter threats, then you close your eyes and the sea dispatches one more big roller in the unbroken line since the beginning of the world and it combs and breaks and returns foaming and saying: "So soon?"

—E. B. WHITE, "ON A FLORIDA KEY"

CONVERSATIONAL TONE

All last spring, the [fence] posts just sat around, though one day I did lug 30 or 40 in and stack them in the barn. Then, in June, I started a new project, which was to enlarge the woodshed. I needed some eight-foot pine boards for the new piece of roof. I *could* have gone to a lumberyard and bought some. But I didn't. Instead I called an old friend about 30 miles away who had just bought a little sawmill. We quickly made a deal whereby the next time I came down to visit I'd bring along a few eight-foot pine logs, plus twenty fence posts for him. He would saw me out 200 feet of boards in return.

—NOEL PERRIN, "BARTER"

The paragraph written by E. B. White uses a serious and poetic tone, contrasting the changing activities of humans with the unchanging rhythm of nature. The paragraph written by Noel Perrin, on the other hand, has the casual, warm tone of someone who is conversing over a fence with a neighbor.

Writers of informal essays may also choose an ironic tone. *Irony* is a literary device in which the author says one thing but means something else, often the opposite. Although an ironic essay plays on the reader's expectations, its message is often serious.

IRONIC TONE

Be respectful to your superiors, if you have any, also to strangers, and sometimes to others. If a person offends you, and you are in doubt as to whether it was intentional or not, do not resort to extreme measures; simply watch your chance and hit him with a brick. That will be sufficient. If you shall find that he had not intended any offense, come out frankly and confess yourself in the wrong when you struck him; acknowledge it and say you didn't mean to. Yes, always avoid violence; in this age of charity and kindliness, the time has gone by for such things. —MARK TWAIN, "ADVICE TO YOUTH"

In this example, Twain ironically advises the throwing of a brick in order to make a point about the folly of settling differences with violence.

Structure in Informal Essays

The most striking difference between formal and informal essays is their structures. While formal essays have an introduction, body, and conclusion, informal essays are not so neatly arranged. There is no single type of structure used in informal essays; each writer of an informal essay creates a structure most appropriate to the essay's message and tone.

The following informal essay is about the arrival of spring in Central Park, New York City. To capture the energy and newness of spring, John Updike chose to list the details he observed separately instead of trying to confine them in neatly "squared-off" paragraphs.

Central Park

On the afternoon of the first day of spring, when the gutters were still heaped high with Monday's snow but the sky itself was swept clean, we put on our galoshes and walked up the sunny side of Fifth Avenue to Central Park. There we saw:

Great black rocks emerging from the melting drifts, their craggy skins glistening like the backs of resurrected brontosaurs.

A pigeon on the half-frozen pond strutting to the edge of the ice and looking a duck in the face.

A policeman getting his shoe wet testing the ice.

Three elderly relatives trying to coax a little boy to accompany his father on a sled ride down a short but steep slope. After much balking, the boy did, and, sure enough, the sled tipped over and the father got his collar full of snow. Everybody laughed except the boy, who sniffled.

Four boys in black leather jackets throwing snowballs at each other. (The snow was ideally soggy, and packed hard with one squeeze.)

Seven men without hats.

Twelve snowmen, none of them intact.

Two men listening to the radio in a car parked outside the Zoo; Mel Allen was broadcasting the Yanks-Cardinals game from St. Petersburg.

A tehr *(Hemitragus jemlaicus)* pleasantly squinting in the sunlight.

An aoudad absently pawing the mud and chewing.

A yak with its back turned.

Empty cages labeled "Coati," "Orang-outang," "Ocelot."

A father saying to his little boy, who was annoyed almost to tears by the inactivity of the seals, "Father [Father Seal, we assumed] is very tired; he worked hard all day."

Most of the cafeteria's out-of-doors tables occupied.

A pretty girl in black pants falling on them at the Wollman Memorial Skating Rink.

"BILL & DORIS" carved on a tree. "REX & RITA" written in the snow.

Two old men playing, and six supervising, a checkers game.

The Michael Friedsam Foundation Merry-Go-Round, nearly empty of children but overflowing with calliope music.

A man on a bench near the carousel reading, through sunglasses, a book on economics.

Crews of shinglers repairing the roof of the Tavern-on-the-Green Restaurant.

A woman dropping a camera she was trying to load, the film unrolling in the slush and exposing itself.

A little boy in aviator goggles rubbing his ears and saying, "He really hurt me." "No, he didn't," his nursemaid told him.

The green head of Giuseppe Mazzini staring across the white softball field, unblinking, though the sun was in its eyes.

Water murmuring down walks and rocks and steps. A grown man trying to block one rivulet with snow.

Things like brown sticks nosing through a plot of cleared soil. A tire track in a piece of mud far removed from where any automobiles could be.

Footprints around a KEEP OFF sign.

Two pigeons feeding each other.

Two showgirls, whose faces had not yet thawed from the frost of their makeup, treading indignantly through the slush.

A plump old man saying "Chick, chick" and feeding peanuts to squirrels.

Many solitary men throwing snowballs at tree trunks.

Many birds calling to each other about how little the park has changed.

One red mitten lying lost under a poplar tree.

An airplane, very bright and distant, slowly moving through the branches of a sycamore.

—JOHN UPDIKE, "CENTRAL PARK"

As you can see, the structure of this essay is informal. In addition the writer allows himself to write fragments instead of complete sentences. In an informal essay, you have much more freedom than in a formal essay to express yourself in the way you see fit.

EXERCISE 15 Analyzing an Informal Essay

The following essay is about the writer's early experiences with Louis Armstrong, a famous jazz trumpeter whose nickname was *Satchmo* or *The Satch.* Read it carefully and answer the questions that follow it.

Louis Armstrong

Surely The Satch has forgotten, still, he was one of this writer's first friends, I met him when I was four, that would be around 1928, and he, a hard-plump and belligerently happy brown Buddha, was playing aboard a pleasure steamer that paddled between New Orleans and St. Louis. Never mind why, but I had occasion to take the trip very often, and for me the sweet anger of Armstrong's trumpet, the froggy exuberance of his come-to-me-baby-mouthings, bring memories to life: they make Mississippi moons rise again, summon the muddy lights of river towns, the sound, like an alligator's yawn, of river horns—I hear the rush of the mulatto river pushing by, hear, always, stomp! stomp! the beat of the grinning Buddha's foot as he shouts his way into "Sunny Side of the Street" and the honeymooning dancers, sweating through their talcum, bunny-hugging around the ship's saloony ballroom. The Satch, he was good to me, he told me I had talent, that I ought to be in vaudeville; he gave me a bamboo cane and a straw boater with a peppermint headband; and every night from the stand he announced; "Ladies and gentlemen, now we're going to present you one of America's nice kids, he's going to do a little tap dance." Afterward I passed among the passengers, collecting in my hat nickels and dimes. This went on all summer, I grew rich and vain; but in October the river roughened, the moon whitened, the customers lessened, the boat rides ended, and with them my career. Six years later, while living at a boarding school from which I wanted to run away, I wrote my former, now famous, benefactor, and said if I came to New York couldn't he get me a job at the Cotton Club or somewhere? There was no reply, maybe he never got the letter, it doesn't matter, I still loved him, still do. —TRUMAN CAPOTE (ADAPTED)

1. Which two of the four writing purposes (narrative, descriptive, expository, and persuasive) are combined in this essay?
2. What type of order is used in this essay: chronological, spatial, order of importance, or developmental order?
3. The first sentence and the last sentence each contain four main clauses, joined in an unconventional way with commas instead of separated by periods or semicolons. How might the subject matter (jazz, childhood memories, etc.) justify this unconventional punctuation? Explain your answer in two sentences.
4. What sensory details are brought to the writer's mind by the sound of Armstrong's trumpet?
5. Which of the following best describes the tone of this essay: reflective, conversational, ironic?

EXERCISE 16 On Your Own

Truman Capote, the author of the essay on Louis Armstrong on pages 518–519, was once asked if there were any devices writers could use to improve their technique. He replied, "Work is the only device I know of. Writing has laws of perspective, of light and shade, just as painting does, or music. If you are born knowing them, fine. If not, learn them. Then rearrange the rules to suit yourself."

For practice in "rearranging the rules to suit yourself," try the following exercise. Think of an experience from your early childhood that had importance for you. Write one paragraph relating that experience through the eyes of the young adult you are now. That paragraph should have a topic sentence, supporting sentences, and a concluding sentence. Write a second paragraph relating the same experience through the eyes of the child you were. Feel free in the second paragraph to abandon the formal conventions of the standard paragraph in order to express your message more personally.

CHAPTER REVIEW

A. Write a personal experience essay, formal or informal, on one of the following subjects or on one of your own choosing. (You may wish to use your work from Exercises 2–6.) Use the Steps for Writing Essays on page 522 as a guide.

1. your first day on the job
2. an unusual birthday celebration
3. taking charge of a group or an activity
4. standing apart from your friends for the first time
5. an accident
6. a struggle with your conscience
7. your first date
8. a misunderstanding
9. taking responsibility
10. helping someone in a crisis
11. working out a difference of opinion with an adult
12. being deeply moved by a book, piece of music, or film
13. realizing you know less than you thought you did

14. your first time in a foreign country or a different part of the United States
15. creating or building something of your own

B. Write a descriptive essay, formal or informal, on one of the following subjects or on one of your own choosing. Use the Steps for Writing Essays on page 522 as a guide.

1. an emergency room
2. a movie theater
3. a scenic park
4. a racetrack
5. the season's first snowfall
6. a college campus
7. a dentist's office
8. a cookout
9. a sculpture
10. a concert
11. a painting or photograph
12. an unusual outfit
13. a relative
14. an exciting part of an athletic contest
15. a piece of clothing you made or a dish you cooked

C. Write a formal persuasive essay on one of the following subjects or on one of your own choosing. Follow the Steps for Writing Essays on page 522.

1. conserving energy
2. Democratic vs. Republican programs
3. why people should vote
4. saving historic buildings
5. the excesses of television
6. suiting the punishment to the crime
7. the unwritten laws of friendship
8. preventive medicine
9. self confidence vs. egotism
10. the three best movies you've ever seen
11. television news vs. newspapers
12. improving the academic environment in your school
13. taxes
14. political advertisements on television
15. regulations for the senior prom

Steps for Writing

Essays

✓ **Prewriting**

1. Find ideas by asking yourself questions and reading for inspiration. *(See pages 469–470.)*
2. From a list of possible subjects, choose one and limit it. *(See pages 471–472.)*
3. Brainstorm a list of supporting ideas. *(See page 474.)*
4. Organize your list of ideas into an outline. *(See pages 476–479.)*

✓ **Writing**

5. Write a thesis statement. *(See pages 481–482.)*
6. Write an introduction that includes your thesis statement. *(See pages 482–483.)*
7. Use your outline to write the paragraphs in the body. *(See pages 485–487.)*
8. Use transitions and other connecting devices to link your thoughts. *(See page 485.)*
9. Write a concluding paragraph. *(See pages 487–488.)*
10. Add a title. *(See page 488.)*

✓ **Revising**

11. Does your formal essay have all of the elements shown in the appropriate checklist on page 523?
12. Does your essay have unity, coherence, and emphasis? *(See pages 489–490.)*
13. Do your sentences have variety? *(See pages 377–383.)*
14. Are your sentences concise and free of faulty constructions? *(See pages 373–376 and 385–392.)*
15. Did you use precise, vivid words? *(See page 367.)*

✓ **Editing**

16. Check sentences for errors in grammar or usage.
17. Check your spelling, capitalization, and punctuation.
18. Did you use correct manuscript form? *(See page 659.)*
19. Are your margins even?
20. Is your handwriting or typing clear?

Checklists for Revising

Essays

✓ **Personal Experience Essays**

1. Does your introduction set the tone, contain a thesis statement that makes the narrative purpose clear, and lead into the story?
2. Do the supporting paragraphs use the techniques of first-person narration to tell a story about a conflict?
3. Did you use dialogue where appropriate?
4. Did you use chronological order and transitions?
5. Does your conclusion draw an insight about the importance of the story?

✓ **Descriptive Essays**

1. Does your thesis statement express one main impression of your subject?
2. Do the supporting paragraphs in the body supply details that appeal to the senses?
3. Did you select details that support the overall impression you are trying to create?
4. Did you use logical order with appropriate transitions?
5. Does your concluding paragraph reinforce or summarize the overall impression?

✓ **Persuasive Essays**

1. Does your thesis statement express an opinion?
2. Do your supporting paragraphs use facts, examples, incidents, and reasons?
3. Did you concede the opposition's good points?
4. Did you use a type of logical order and appropriate transitions?
5. Does your concluding paragraph make a strong final appeal?

22

Writing about Literature

Writing is a process of making choices. In your own writing, you have made choices about what subject to cover, what organization to follow, what words to use, and what points to emphasize. Writers of literature — novels, short stories, plays, and poems — also make choices as they create their works. They choose stories, characters, images, settings, words, and themes. The purpose of literary essays is to analyze and interpret the choices that writers have made and to illuminate some aspect of the literary work. Because these essays depend on the critical powers of the essayist — powers of observation and evaluation — they are called critical essays.

22a A **critical essay** offers an interpretation of a work of literature and uses the techniques of exposition and persuasion to back up the interpretation.

Like other formal essays, the critical essay has an introduction, a body of supporting paragraphs, and a conclusion. The focus of the thesis statement and the kinds of details used to support it vary according to the type of work being analyzed. An analysis of a poem, for example, might focus on rhyme scheme or meter, while an interpretation of a novel or short story might focus on plot or narrative techniques. All critical essays share the purpose of examining the specific literary choices that created the work's overall effect on the reader.

ANALYZING LITERARY WORKS

When you first read a literary work, you take in the work as a whole. The separate elements within it may not be immediately obvious, since they work together to create certain overall responses in you. After you have read the work once, however, you can go back and study the separate parts within it to understand why you responded as you did.

Fiction

The following is a summary of the various elements in a novel or short story.

22b

Elements in a Work of Fiction

SETTING	when and where the story takes place; setting often creates a mood that parallels the thoughts of the characters
CHARACTERS	main and lesser characters whose thoughts and actions are the heart of the narrative
TONE	the writer's attitude toward his or her subject and characters
POINT OF VIEW	narrative "voice" telling the story; can be *first person, third person objective* (in which narrator tells only observable events), or *third person omniscient* (in which narrator can relate thoughts and feelings of one or more characters)
PLOT	the events leading up to and resolving a central conflict
SUBPLOT	a separate story line with minor characters that often parallels or contrasts with the main plot
DIALOGUE	conversation used to further action of the plot and to reveal character
THEMES	recurring ideas that contribute to the work's underlying meaning
IMAGERY	sensory details that enhance the mood and meaning of the work
SYMBOLISM	people, places, events, and objects that stand for a broader idea than themselves

EXERCISE 1 Analyzing Fiction

The following short story is by Anton Chekhov, a nineteenth-century Russian writer. Read it carefully and answer the questions that follow it.

A Nincompoop

A few days ago I asked my children's governess, Julia Vassilyevna, to come into my study.

"Sit down, Julia Vassilyevna," I said. "Let's settle our accounts. Although you most likely need some money, you stand on ceremony and won't ask for it yourself. Now then, we agreed on thirty rubles a month . . ."

"Forty."

"No, thirty. I made a note of it. I always pay the governess thirty. Now then, you've been here two months, so . . ."

"Two months and five days."

"Exactly two months. I made specific note of it. That means you have sixty rubles coming to you. Subtract nine Sundays . . . you know you didn't work with Kolya on Sundays, you only took walks. And three holidays . . ."

Julia Vassilyevna flushed a deep red and picked at the flounce of her dress, but—not a word.

"Three holidays, therefore take off twelve rubles. Four days Kolya was sick and there were no lessons, as you were occupied only with Vanya. Three days you had a toothache and my wife gave you permission not to work after lunch. Twelve and seven—nineteen. Subtract . . . that leaves . . . hmm . . . forty-one rubles. Correct?"

Julia Vassilyevna's left eye reddened and filled with moisture. Her chin trembled; she coughed nervously and blew her nose, but—not a word.

"Around New Year's you broke a teacup and saucer; take off two rubles. The cup cost more, it was an heirloom, but—let it go. When didn't I take a loss! Then, due to your neglect, Kolya climbed a tree and tore his jacket; take away ten. Also due to your heedlessness the maid stole Vanya's shoes. You ought to watch everything! You get paid for it. So that means five more rubles off. The tenth of January I gave you ten rubles . . ."

"You didn't," whispered Julia Vassilyevna.

"But I made a note of it."

"Well . . . all right."

"Take twenty-seven from forty-one—that leaves fourteen."

Both eyes filled with tears. Perspiration appeared on the thin, pretty little nose. Poor girl!

"Only once was I given any money," she said in a trembling voice, "and that was by your wife. Three rubles, nothing more."

"Really? You see now, and I didn't even make a note of it! Take three from fourteen . . . leaves eleven. Here's your money, my dear. Three, three, three, one and one. Here it is!"

I handed her eleven rubles. She took them and with trembling fingers stuffed them into her pocket.

"*Merci,*" she whispered.

I jumped up and started pacing the room. I was overcome with anger.

"For what, this—'*merci*'?" I asked.

"For the money."

"But you know I've cheated you, for God's sake—robbed you! I have actually stolen from you! *Why* this '*merci*'?"

"In my other places they didn't give me anything at all."

"They didn't give you anything? No wonder! I played a little joke on you, a cruel lesson, just to teach you . . . I'm going to give you the entire eighty rubles! Here they are in an envelope all ready for you . . . Is it really possible to be so spineless? Why don't you protest? Why be silent? Is it possible in this world to be without teeth and claws—to be such a nincompoop?"

She smiled crookedly and I read in her expression: "It is possible."

I asked her pardon for the cruel lesson and, to her great surprise, gave her the eighty rubles. She murmured her little "*merci*" several times and went out. I looked after her and thought: "How easy it is to crush the weak in this world!"

1. What is the setting of this story? How does the setting help show who is in charge in the story?
2. Who are the characters in the story? Who is the main character?
3. What is the point of view of this story?
4. What is the central conflict in the story?
5. Whose side of the conflict are you on at the beginning of the story? Why?
6. How does your attitude toward the children's father change toward the end of the story?

7. Several times in his dialogue the children's father says that Julia Vassilyevna says "not a word." Does she make any effort to stand up for herself?
8. What descriptions does the narrator offer that show how Julia Vassilyevna is reacting to the children's father's way of settling the account?
9. Why does the children's father get mad when Julia says "thank you" *("merci")*?
10. Do you think Julia learned anything from the "cruel lesson"? Explain your answer.
11. Does the children's father learn anything from the experience? Explain your answer.
12. What might the last line of the story have been if Julia Vassilyevna had been the narrator?
13. The children's father associates strength with "teeth and claws." Do you think he regards himself as a strong person? Explain your answer.
14. What do you think the story is saying about the theme of strength and weakness? Explain your answer in several sentences.
15. Do you think the title of the story refers to the children's father or to Julia Vassilyevna? Explain your answer in a few sentences.

Drama

Most of the elements of fiction also appear in dramatic literature. Both fiction and plays have settings, plots, characters, dialogue, themes, and imagery. If an analysis of a play focuses on one of these common elements, it can be similar to an analysis of a novel or short story.

Drama also, however, has its own unique elements. Drama is, after all, meant to be seen on a stage instead of read in a book. The costumes worn by the actors, the lighting, the props, and any incidental music used all contribute to the final effect of a play. If you have not seen a play you wish to analyze, be sure to read all the production notes and stage directions carefully to try to visualize the performance.

The following chart summarizes the elements unique to a dramatic performance.

22c

Elements in Dramatic Works

CHARACTERS' RELATION TO AUDIENCE	In some plays, characters do not relate to audience in any way; audience merely watches as if a fourth wall had been removed from the room in which action takes place. In other plays, characters sometimes speak directly to audience; some plays even have a narrator who establishes a clear point of view.
STAGING	In some plays, the staging, sets, and props are *realistic,* meant to convey life as it really is; in other plays, the staging is *expressionistic,* meant to convey feelings and moods through unusual lighting effects and stylized sets. In many plays, the staging is *minimal,* leaving the viewer's imagination to flesh out the settings.

EXERCISE 2 Analyzing a Dramatic Work

Read the following short play by Harold Pinter. Then write answers to the questions that follow it.

The Black and White

The FIRST OLD WOMAN *is sitting at a milk bar table. Small. A* SECOND OLD WOMAN *approaches. Tall. She is carrying two bowls of soup, which are covered by two plates, on each of which is a slice of bread. She puts the bowls down on the table carefully.*

SECOND You see that one come up and speak to me at the counter?

(She takes the bread plates off the bowls, takes two spoons from her pocket, and places the bowls, plates, and spoons.)

FIRST You got the bread, then?

SECOND I didn't know how I was going to carry it. In the end I put the plates on top of the soup.

FIRST I like a bit of bread with my soup.

(They begin the soup. Pause.)

SECOND Did you see that one come up and speak to me at the counter?

FIRST Who?

SECOND Comes up to me, he says, hullo, he says, what's the time by your clock? Bloody liberty, I was just standing there getting your soup.

FIRST It's tomato soup.

SECOND What's the time by your clock? he says.

FIRST I bet you answered him back.

SECOND I told him all right. Go on, I said, why don't you get back into your scraghole, I said, clear off out of it before I call a copper.

(Pause.)

FIRST I not long got here.

SECOND Did you get the all-night bus?

FIRST I got the all-night bus straight here.

SECOND Where from?

FIRST Marble Arch.

SECOND Which one?

FIRST The two-nine-four, that takes me all the way to Fleet Street.

SECOND So does the two-nine-one. *(Pause.)* I see you talking to two strangers as I come in. You want to stop talking to strangers, old piece of boot like you, mind who you talk to.

FIRST I wasn't talking to any strangers.

(Pause. The FIRST OLD WOMAN *follows the progress of a bus through the window.)*

That's another all-night bus gone down. *(Pause.)* Going up the other way. Fulham way. *(Pause.)* That was a two-nine-seven. *(Pause.)* I've never been up that way. *(Pause.)* I've been down to Liverpool Street.

SECOND That's up the other way.

FIRST I don't fancy going down there, down Fulham way, and all up there.

SECOND Uh-uh.

FIRST I've never fancied that direction much.

(Pause.)

SECOND How's your bread?

(Pause.)

FIRST Eh?

SECOND Your bread.

FIRST All right. How's yours?

(Pause.)

SECOND They don't charge for the bread if you have soup.
FIRST They do if you have tea.
SECOND If you have tea they do. *(Pause.)* You talk to strangers and they'll take you in. Mind my word. Coppers'll take you in.
FIRST I don't talk to strangers.
SECOND They took me away in the wagon once.
FIRST They didn't keep you though.
SECOND They didn't keep me, but that was because they took a fancy to me. They took a fancy to me when they got me in the wagon.
FIRST Do you think they'd take a fancy to me?
SECOND I wouldn't back on it.

(The FIRST OLD WOMAN *gazes out of the window.)*

FIRST You can see what goes on from this top table. *(Pause.)* It's better than going down to that place on the embankment, anyway.
SECOND Yes, there's not too much noise.
FIRST There's always a bit of noise.
SECOND Yes, there's always a bit of life.

(Pause.)

FIRST They'll be closing down soon to give it a scrubround.
SECOND There's a wind out.

(Pause.)

FIRST I wouldn't mind staying.
SECOND They won't let you.
FIRST I know. *(Pause.)* Still, they only close hour and half, don't they? *(Pause.)* It's not long. *(Pause.)* You can go along, then come back.
SECOND I'm going. I'm not coming back.
FIRST When it's light I come back. Have my tea.
SECOND I'm going. I'm going up to the Garden.
FIRST I'm not going down there. *(Pause.)* I'm going to Waterloo Bridge.
SECOND You'll just about see the last two-nine-six come up over the river.
FIRST I'll just catch a look of it. Time I get up there.

(Pause.)

It don't look like an all-night bus in daylight, do it?

1. If you were designing costumes for this play, how would you dress the women? Explain your answer.
2. How do you know what time of day the play takes place?

3. Does either of the characters talk directly to the audience?
4. Would you stage this play realistically or expressionistically? Explain your answer.
5. The old women disagree about whether or not the first was talking to strangers when the second walked in. How does this uncertainty add to the theme of the night world?
6. What does the dialogue about the police's ("coppers") picking up the second old woman reveal about the kind of life the women lead?
7. What does the dialogue about the closing of the diner show about the women's lives?
8. How does the central image of night buses contribute to the theme of the play?
9. Explain the possible relationship between the play's last line and the play's title.
10. Write one paragraph supporting or disproving the following interpretation of this play. Cite specific examples that back up your position.
    "The last line of the play (symbolically) says it all: In cities a sad night world exists totally unnoticed by most people."

Poetry

Poetry, like fiction and drama, has themes, imagery, and symbols. Some narrative poems also have a plot and dialogue. Poetry, however, also has special elements of expression.

22d

Elements in Poetry

PERSONA	like the narrator in a work of fiction, the persona in a poem is the "voice" the poet has assumed to tell the poem
METER	the patterns of stressed and unstressed syllables in a line of poetry
RHYME SCHEME	the patterns of rhymed sounds in a poem
FIGURES OF SPEECH	imaginative language, such as similes and metaphors *(See page 370.)*
VERSE STYLE	in conventional poetry, the regular pattern of meter and rhyme that makes up a stanza; or in much modern poetry, *free verse,* meaning no regular pattern

EXERCISE 3 Analyzing Poetry

Read the two poems below, looking up any unfamiliar words. The lines in each are numbered for easy reference. Think about ways in which the poems are alike and ways in which they differ. Then write answers to the questions that follow.

The Explorer

Somehow to find a still spot in the noise
Was the frayed inner want, the winding, the frayed hope
Whose tatters he kept hunting through the din.
A velvet peace somewhere.
A room of wily hush somewhere within.

So tipping down the scrambled halls he set
Vague hands on throbbing knobs. There were behind
Only spiraling, high human voices,
Wee griefs.
Grand griefs. And choices.
He feared most of all the choices, that cried to be taken.

There were no bourns.
There were no quiet rooms.

—GWENDOLYN BROOKS

The Road Not Taken

Two roads diverged in a yellow wood,
And sorry I could not travel both
And be one traveler, long I stood
And looked down one as far as I could
To where it bent in the undergrowth;

Then took the other, as just as fair,
And having perhaps the better claim,
Because it was grassy and wanted wear;
Though as for that the passing there
Had worn them really about the same,

And both that morning equally lay
In leaves no step had trodden black.
Oh, I kept the first for another day!
Yet knowing how way leads on to way,
I doubted if I should ever come back.

I shall be telling this with a sigh
Somewhere ages and ages hence;
Two roads diverged in a wood, and I—
I took the one less traveled by,
And that has made all the difference.

—ROBERT FROST

1. Which of the poems has a regular rhyme scheme?
2. Which poem has a regular meter and verse structure?
3. What is the explorer looking for in the first poem?
4. Do you think the "scrambled halls" in which the explorer searches are in a real building or in his mind? Why?
5. How do the rhythm and structure of lines 2–3 in "The Explorer" enhance the feeling of a frayed hope?
6. How does the explorer feel about the choices he has?
7. What is the choice in "The Road Not Taken"?
8. In what season is "The Road Not Taken" set? How do you know? How does the season affect the tone of the poem?
9. How different are the two roads from one another? In what lines is a difference noted? In what lines are they made to seem nearly the same?
10. What line explains why the persona will probably never come back to take the first road?
11. The dash at the end of line 18 suggests a pause. What might be going on in the persona's mind during that pause?
12. How does the persona feel about the choice he has made? How can you tell?
13. Which one of the following elements is most similar in the two poems: imagery, rhyme scheme, theme, or plot?
14. Which of the two poems has a darker (more gloomy) tone? Explain your answer.
15. Write a paragraph comparing and contrasting the explorer's view of life in "The Explorer" and the traveler's view of life in "The Road Not Taken."

EXERCISE 4 **On Your Own**

Choose a novel, short story, play, or poem about which you would like to write a critical essay. (You may wish to use the examples in Exercises 1–3.) Using the charts on pages 525, 529, and 532, reread the work you have chosen, jotting down notes on how each element contributes to your overall response to the work. Save your notes for Exercise 5.

WRITING A CRITICAL ESSAY

Literary works are open to a number of interpretations. When you write a critical essay, your purpose is to back up *your* interpretation with specific details from the work. Although you might find ideas by reading what others have written about the work you have chosen, the most important ideas for your essay should come from within the work itself.

Prewriting

The main purpose of a critical essay is to interpret a work of literature, not to summarize it. As you plan your essay, assume that your audience has already read the work. Concentrate on evaluating the details in the work and fitting them into a pattern that sheds light on the work's meaning.

Choosing and Limiting a Subject. In a short essay, you cannot cover all the elements that contribute to the work's overall effect. Instead you must limit your subject to some aspect of the work that holds particular interest for you. The charts on pages 525, 529, and 532 show the elements in fiction, drama, and poetry that you might choose as a focus point for your essay. Perhaps on your first reading of the work you were puzzled by a turn in the plot. Such a response would be a good starting point for a critical essay, since you could then search for an understanding of the puzzle as you developed your essay. Instead maybe you noticed a number of images of water, for example, or of stars. This would also be a good starting point, for then you could trace all the images and see if they form a pattern that enhances the work's meaning. Think about a number of possible focus points before choosing one.

EXERCISE 5 Choosing and Limiting a Subject
Use the following questions and your work from Exercise 4 to choose and limit a subject for a critical analysis. Write short answers to each question. Save your work for Exercise 7.

1. What meaning do I see in the work I have chosen?
2. What kind of feeling did the work leave me with?
3. What elements in the work contributed to the feeling and meaning of the work?

4. Which of those elements interests me the most?
5. How could I express in one phrase my limited subject for a critical essay?

Listing Supporting Details. Once you have narrowed your subject, you can begin to gather the details from the work that will help persuade your readers that your interpretation is sound and thoughtful. The following chart lists the steps you might take to list supporting details for your subject.

22e

Steps for Gathering Support for a Critical Analysis

1. Skim the work again, stopping each time you see a detail that would support your interpretation.
2. On a note card, write the detail you have found, indicating who said it (a character or the narrator or the persona), and the page number of the detail. (In drama, note the act and scene; in poetry, the line number.)
3. Make a separate card for each reference.

Suppose, for example, that you had decided to write about the imagery of light and darkness in the one-act play *The Glass Menagerie* by Tennessee Williams. Some sample note cards might appear as follows.

Tom: "Being a memory play, it is dimly lit." (opening speech, scene 1)
p. 487

Tom: "He [Jim, the gentleman caller] seemed to move in a continual spotlight." (opening of scene six)
p. 509

Laura, showing Jim the glass unicorn: "Hold him over the light, he loves the light! You see how the light shines through him?"
(scene seven), p. 526

EXERCISE 6 Listing Supporting Details

The following excerpts are from the novel *The Great Gatsby* by F. Scott Fitzgerald. Assume that you are listing supporting details on the subject of the symbolism of the green light in the novel and prepare a sample note card for each excerpt.

(1) Already it was deep summer on roadhouse roofs and in front of wayside garages, where new red gas-pumps sat out in pools of light, and when I reached my estate at West Egg I ran the car under its shed and sat for a while on an abandoned grass roller in the yard. The wind had blown off, leaving a loud, bright night, with wings beating in the trees and a persistent organ sound as the full bellows of the earth blew the frogs to life. The silhouette of a moving cat wavered across the moonlight, and turning my head to watch it, I saw that I was not alone—fifty feet away a figure had emerged from the shadow of my neighbor's mansion and was standing with his hands in his pockets regarding the silver pepper of the stars. Something in his leisurely movements and the secure position of his feet upon the lawn suggested that it was Mr. Gatsby himself, come out to determine what share was his of our local heavens.

I decided to call to him. Miss Baker had mentioned him at dinner, and that would do for an introduction. But I didn't call to him, for he gave a sudden intimation that he was content to be alone—he stretched out his arms toward the dark water in a curious way, and, far as I was from him, I could have sworn he was trembling. Involuntarily I glanced seaward—and distinguished nothing except a single green light, minute and far away, that might have been the end of a dock. When I looked once more for Gatsby he had vanished, and I was alone again in the unquiet darkness. (pp. 21–22)

(2) After the house, we were to see the grounds and the swimming-pool, and the hydroplane and the mid-summer flowers—but outside Gatsby's window it began to rain again, so we stood in a row looking at the corrugated surface of the Sound.

"If it wasn't for the mist we could see your home across the bay," said Gatsby. "You always have a green light that burns all night at the end of your dock."

Daisy put her arm through his abruptly, but he seemed absorbed in what he had just said. Possibly it had occurred to him that the colossal significance of that light had vanished forever. Compared to the great distance that had separated

> him from Daisy it had seemed very near to her, almost touching her. It had seemed as close as a star to the moon. Now it was again a green light on a dock. His count of enchanted objects had diminished by one. (p. 94)
>
> (3) And as I sat there brooding on the old, unknown world, I thought of Gatsby's wonder when he first picked out the green light at the end of Daisy's dock. He had come a long way to this blue lawn, and his dream must have seemed so close that he could hardly fail to grasp it. He did not know that it was already behind him, somewhere back in that vast obscurity beyond the city, where the dark fields of the republic rolled on under the night.
>
> Gatsby believed in the green light, the . . . future that year by year recedes before us. It eluded us then, but that's no matter—tomorrow we will run faster, stretch out our arms farther . . . And one fine morning——
>
> So we beat on, boats against the current, borne back ceaselessly into the past. (p. 182)

Organizing Supporting Details. After you have found all the details that relate to your limited subject, the next step is to look for patterns and groupings in the details. On the subject of light and darkness imagery in *The Glass Menagerie,* for example, you might group your notes according to the character to which the images refer. All the references to light and darkness surrounding Tom might be placed in one category; those about Laura in another; and those about Amanda, their mother, in a third. As you make your groupings, you are likely to discover ideas to bring out in your paper. For example, you might find that Tom is always associated with darkness, or Laura with a rare, transparent light. Try several approaches to grouping your supporting details, noting any new ideas.

In some cases, you may decide to present the details in the order in which they appear in the work. Many poems, for example, are short enough to be analyzed in their entirety, line by line. Such an analysis is called an *explication.* Even in a longer work of fiction, some subjects lend themselves to this arrangement. If you are analyzing the growth of a character, for example, you will trace that character's development from beginning to end, using a variant of chronological order.

Most subjects will not lend themselves to this arrangement, however. For most subjects, the step after grouping details is arranging the groups in a logical order. *(See page 428.)* The final prewriting step for any subject is to develop an outline based on the groups of details. The following is an outline for the essay on *The Glass Menagerie*.

I. Imagery associated with Tom
   A. As narrator
      1. Disdains "school for the blind"
      2. Tells audience that play is "dimly lighted"
   B. As character
      1. Dislikes "fluorescent tubes" in warehouse
      2. Escapes into dark movie houses
      3. Fails to pay electric bills
      4. Longs for lighted world of father
      5. Is haunted by "lighted window of a shop"
      6. Contrasts the lightning-lit sky with Laura's candles

II. Imagery associated with Laura
   A. Escapes from business school to the "Jewel-box"
   B. Contrasts with Jim's brightness
      1. "Spotlight"
      2. Write-up in *The Torch*
   C. Parallels her glass figures
      1. "Light shines through" unicorn
      2. Laura's beauty shines through candlelight

III. Imagery associated with Amanda
   A. Desire to "brighten things up" for gentleman caller
   B. Joke about Moses in the dark
   C. Use of melted-down candelabra
   D. Wish on the moon rising over Garfinkel's Delicatessen

EXERCISE 7 On Your Own
Using your work from Exercise 5, make note cards listing your supporting details and arrange your ideas logically in an outline. Save your work for Exercise 12.

Writing Extra

Another kind of literary essay is the *review*. Unlike a critical essay, a review attempts to evaluate the whole work rather than one element in it. A reviewer writes for a reader who has not yet read the work. Study the following book review.

Poland by James Michener, 1983
Reviewed by Harry Hurt III

INTRODUCTION: BACKGROUND ON AUTHOR

In a career spanning 36 years, James Michener has produced 31 titles ranging in subject from Japanese art to sports and politics. He has built his fame and fortune, however, on long and painstakingly detailed works of enormous scope. The typical Michener book blends fact and fiction into sweeping portraits of entire cultures.

BODY: EXPLAINS CONTENTS OF BOOK

Poland is true to form. Yet it is weighted with the sober realities of contemporary Poland, which the author suggests stem from a history of betrayal, plunder, and destruction. *Poland* begins and ends in 1982, but the body of its 556 pages recounts eight centuries of conquest, from Genghis Kahn to the consolidation of Communist control. "A Pole is born with a sword in his right hand and a brick in his left. When the battle is over, he starts to rebuild," he writes rather sadly.

QUOTATION: REVEALS AN IMPORTANT THEME

CONCLUSION: EVALUATES THE QUALITY OF THE AUTHOR'S WORK

In researching the book, Michener visited the country nine times and interviewed hundreds of Polish citizens and expatriates, including Karol Wojtyla, then Bishop of Krakow and now Pope John Paul II. He commissioned a dozen top Polish scholars to write factual reports, later translated into English, which provided him with "the best current thinking" on political, economic, and social matters. The result is a classic Michener book with a timely twist: a wide-ranging account of a country and people who have suddenly found themselves spotlighted on the world stage.

LAST SENTENCE: SUMS UP REVIEWER'S OPINION OF THE BOOK

EXERCISE 8 Writing a Review

Using the above example as a model, write a review of a literary work published within the last five years. Ask your teacher or school librarian for help in selecting a book. (You can find information about the writer, playwright, or poet in the front or back of the book containing the work, or you can use the library for information.) Remember to assume that your audience has not read the work, and to evaluate the work as a whole.

Writing

A critical essay combines expository and persuasive writing. As an analysis, it uses expository techniques to reveal the details of one element of the work and how that element fits into the work as a whole. Because the subject is a work of literature, however, the thesis statement expresses an interpretation that may differ from the interpretation of other readers. A critical essay then is persuasive, since the writer's goal is to convince readers that his or her interpretation is sound. The following are important guidelines for writing critical essays.

22f

Guidelines for a Critical Essay

1. Use an objective, serious tone rather than a subjective, casual tone in your essay.
2. Use third-person point of view. Avoid using *I* to make your interpretative points.
3. Use the present tense to discuss the literary work, approaching the work as if the author, the characters, and the events exist in the present. (For example, write: *Faulkner's hero Lena* ***succeeds*** *in . . . ;* or *In the poem "1929" Auden* ***tells*** *us . . .*)
4. Cite the sources of quotations.
   a. If all of your quotations are from the one work you are analyzing, indicate in a footnote which edition you are using. Then, for all quotations after the first, simply give the page numbers in parentheses directly following the quotation. For plays or long poems, also indicate main divisions, such as the act and scene of a play or the book or part of a poem, and the line numbers. *(See the model essay on pages 545–547.)*
   b. If your quotations are from two or more sources, fully cite each quotation with a footnote or endnote. *(See pages 601–602.)*

Writing the Thesis Statement. As in other kinds of formal essays, the thesis statement need not be the first sentence in the essay. Writing it first, however, will help keep your thoughts focused on your main idea. Use the following steps to write your thesis statement.

22g

Steps for Writing a Thesis Statement

1. Look over your prewriting note cards and the categories and outline you created.
2. Express in one sentence an interpretation of the details that sheds light on the meaning of the work.
3. Revise your thesis statement until it covers all the supporting details you plan to include.

Study the following thesis statements about the imagery of light and darkness in *The Glass Menagerie*. Note the reasons that the last thesis statement is better than the first two.

WEAK THESIS STATEMENTS

There are many references to light and darkness in *The Glass Menagerie*. [weak because it fails to express an interpretation of what those references mean]

Each character in *The Glass Menagerie* is surrounded by a different kind of imagery of light or darkness. [better because it is more specific, but still fails to interpret the significance of the imagery]

STRONG THESIS STATEMENT

The way each character copes with reality in *The Glass Menagerie* is reflected in the imagery of light and darkness. [best because it relates the imagery to a major theme of the play]

Writing the Introduction. The introduction to a critical essay should identify the author and the work that will be analyzed in the paper. It should also prepare the reader for the focus of your essay. Depending on your focus, you may wish to use one or more of the following ways to begin your essay.

22h

Ways to Begin a Critical Essay

1. Briefly review a significant theme or event in the plot that has bearing on the focus of your paper.
2. Offer some alternate interpretations as a prelude to showing why your interpretation is more sound than these others.
3. Introduce a general literary technique (plot, symbolism, etc.) as a preparation to showing its specific use in the work you are analyzing.
4. Offer some brief background on the author.
5. Include your thesis statement, revising it as necessary to make it connect smoothly with the other sentences in the introduction.

The following introduction to the essay on the imagery of light and darkness in *The Glass Menagerie* reviews a significant theme before presenting the thesis statement. Notice that the writer's original thesis statement from page 542 has been revised to make it flow smoothly from the preceding sentences in the introduction.

> *The Glass Menagerie* by Tennessee Williams is a play about illusion and reality, and about the misty overlap of past, present, and future. Each character has a unique way of relating to the "world of reality" represented by Jim, the gentleman caller. The relation each bears to this world is demonstrated through the recurring imagery of light and darkness.

EXERCISE 9 Analyzing Essay Beginnings

Write the thesis statement from each of the following introductions to critical essays. After the thesis statement, indicate which of the following introductory techniques the writer used. (One of the introductions uses a combination of two techniques.)

review of significant theme or event in plot
alternate interpretations
general literary technique
background of author

1.

The Glass Menagerie (1945) was Tennessee Williams' first major theatrical success. Over the years he has written a great deal, some of high quality indeed, but nothing better than this play which established him as an important post-war playwright. "The dramatist of frustration," John Gassner dubbed him in 1948 after *A Streetcar Named Desire*, but unlike most of his later plays, *The Glass Menagerie* projects not a series of violent confrontations leading to catastrophe but a vision of lonely human beings who fail to make contact, who are isolated from each other and from society, and who seem ultimately abandoned in the universe.

—ROGER B. STEIN, "*THE GLASS MENAGERIE* REVISITED: CATASTROPHE WITHOUT VIOLENCE"

2.

The heart of *Go Down Moses* (1942) by William Faulkner is "The Bear." The most widely acclaimed story of the seven in the volume, "The Bear" has received a variety of interpretations. One critic has emphasized the New Testament spirit, others its romantic and transcendental character, and still others its primitivism and myth. The variety of critical response testifies to the story's density of meaning. It is a rich, original story treating of a universal issue; nevertheless, it is distinctly American. Lionel Trilling has placed it in the romantic, transcendental tradition of Cooper, Thoreau, and Melville, while Malcolm Cowley has associated it with the work of Mark Twain. In its pastoral spirit "The Bear" does seem related to *Huck Finn;* and, in its development of the wilderness theme, to Cooper's *Leatherstocking Tales.* Yet because of the story's tendency to split into two parts—one part concerned with the wilderness, the other with the race issue—the structure of the story has seemed faulty and its meaning ambiguous. If "The Bear" is examined within the context of the other related stories of the *Go Down, Moses* volume, its meaning may be clarified.

—MELVIN BACKMAN, " 'THE BEAR' AND *GO DOWN, MOSES*"

3.

At the end of Edgar Allan Poe's "The Fall of the House of Usher," Madeline Usher escapes from her tomb and throws herself upon her brother, Roderick, bearing him to his death. The general interpretation of this scene accepts Madeline as alive. Yet this interpretation is erroneous, for the facts in the tale prove that Madeline is dead and, consequently, that the Madeline who hurls herself upon Roderick can only be a hallucination. Moreover, Poe was too conscientious a craftsman to ignore facts written into a story; and Poe's craftsmanship is the clue which, if followed, proves that Madeline's final appearance is made as a ghost.

—JOHN S. HILL, "THE DUAL HALLUCINATION IN 'THE FALL OF THE HOUSE OF USHER'"

4.

Plot—action—is usually the backbone of a play. Traditionally, drama comes from the tragic, comic, or tragicomic events the characters undergo. The backbone of Shakespeare's *Macbeth* is the murders planned and committed by Lady Macbeth and Macbeth; the backbone of Arthur Miller's *The Crucible* is the witch trials. In Harold Pinter's *The Black and White,* however, there is little or no plot, which is true of most Pinter plays. Drama in *The Black and White* comes only from what the old women's conversation—the only action—reveals about their lives.

Writing the Body. Once you are satisfied with your introduction, you can use your outline as a guide in writing the supporting paragraphs of the body. As in all essays, remember to use transitions to show your reader how the ideas in your essay are related and to move smoothly from one point to another. *(See pages 430–431.)* Notice how the body of the essay on light and darkness imagery in *The Glass Menagerie* follows the outline on page 539. Notice also how the quotations are worked into the sentences.

In his role as narrator, Tom introduces the imagery of light and darkness in his opening speech. He claims with some disdain that, in the 1930s, "the huge middle class of America was matriculating in a school for the blind."[1] Although he seems to condemn the darkness in which people choose to live, Tom himself escapes into darkness throughout the play. As narrator, he presents a memory play, "dimly lighted" (Sc. i; p. 277). As a character in that play, he despises the "fluorescent tubes" lighting the shoe warehouse where he works (Sc. iii; p. 290), and he seeks refuge night after night in the

[1] Tennessee Williams, *The Glass Menagerie,* in *Six Modern American Plays,* ed. Allan G. Halline (New York: Random House, 1951), Sc. i (p. 227). All further references to this work appear in the text.

darkness of a movie theater. In the climactic final scene, it is Tom's doing that the lights go out, since he failed to pay the electric bill. Tom's escape into darkness, however, is not satisfying. He longs to escape into the world of his father, who "skipped the light fantastic out of town" and whose portrait is always brightly lit (Sc. i; p. 278). Even when he enters that world of adventure, however, he is haunted by the past. The "lighted window of a shop . . . filled with pieces of colored glass" (Sc. vii; p. 340) brings his sister back to him, and again he tries to escape into the movies. The world of light he had hoped to enter is dark now with war, and Laura's soft candlelight is finally extinguished.

The light imagery associated with Laura also shows her delicate relation to reality. Instead of attending Rubicam's Business College, Laura escapes to the "Jewel-box, that big glass house where they raise the tropical flowers," where light and beauty combine in a delicate balance (Sc. ii; p. 285). The world of reality, as represented by Laura's secretly-loved Jim, is very bright. As Tom says, Jim "seemed to move in a continual spotlight" (Sc. vi; p. 307). Even the name of the school newspaper that gave Jim a "wonderful write-up," *The Torch,* suggests the bright light of reality (Sc. vii; p. 326). In contrast, Laura's world as revealed by her light images is subdued and transient. As Laura shows Jim her glass unicorn, she explains how "he loves the light! You see how the light shines through him?" (Sc. vii; p. 330). In the same way, the subdued candlelight in the final scene reveals Laura's beauty to Jim. Both the unicorn and Laura, however, are crushed by the exposure; their delicacy cannot stand up to the kind of reality Jim represents.

More than Tom or Laura, Amanda Wingfield seems to exist comfortably in both her own world and the world of reality. Although she revels in memories of her Mississippi home and gentlemen callers, she knows what she must do to survive in the present and the future. If she must sell magazine subscriptions to make money, then she does so, using the southern charm of her youth. If she must buy new furnishings on credit, then she does so, including a floor lamp and chintz covers that will "brighten things up" (Sc. v; p. 303). Although she may want a better life for her children, she sees reality for what it is. Her joke about Moses being in the dark when the lights go out (Sc. vii; p. 319) shows this understanding; she is not counting on any miracles. She does not pine for the candelabra that melted out of shape when the church was struck by lightning; instead, she puts it to practical use in setting the romantic scene for Jim and Laura. Laura and Tom both seek refuge from reality—Laura in beauty, Tom in adventure. Amanda, in contrast, can see beauty in reality. Although the moon rises over the unromantic Garfinkel's Delicatessen, Amanda sees the beauty of the "little slipper of a moon" and makes her wish on it (Sc. v; p. 301).

EXERCISE 10 Analyzing the Body of a Critical Essay
Reread the supporting paragraphs about light and darkness imagery on pages 545–547. Then write answers to the following questions.

1. Reread the introduction on page 543. What words from the last sentence of the introduction are repeated as a transition in the first sentence of the body?
2. Write one sentence from the first body paragraph that ends with a quotation.
3. Write one sentence from the first body paragraph that includes a quotation in the middle.
4. What transitional devices are used to connect the first and second body paragraphs?
5. What words in the first sentence of the final body paragraph serve as a transition from the rest of the body?

Writing the Conclusion. The concluding paragraph of a critical essay is a good place to draw together the separate threads you have analyzed in the body. Any of the following is a good way to end a critical essay.

22i

Ways to Conclude a Critical Essay

1. Restate your thesis statement in fresh words.
2. Suggest how the aspect of the work you analyzed in your paper relates to other aspects of the work.
3. Discuss ways in which the work sheds light on humans' lives and problems.

The conclusion of the essay about *The Glass Menagerie* shows how the tragedy of the Wingfields extends to other people as well.

> Amanda's wish, like that of so many parents, is for a better life for her children. Outside the Wingfields' apartment, however, the ominous flashes of "lightning" tell of the coming war, in which neither Tom's adventurousness, Laura's love for beauty, Jim's ambitions, nor Amanda's wishes will come to a happy ending. The tragedy of the Wingfields becomes a universal tragedy as "the world is nowadays lit by lightning" (Sc. vii; p. 340).

Adding a Title. The title of a critical essay should identify or suggest the focus of your paper. While you may wish to include the title of the work you are analyzing in your title, it should form only part of the title. Remember that you have fully identified the work and author in your introduction.

EXERCISE 11 Thinking of Titles
Review the titles of the essays excerpted in Exercise 9, pages 543–545. (You can find the titles at the end of the excerpts.) Then think of two possible titles for the essay about light and darkness imagery in *The Glass Menagerie.*

EXERCISE 12 On Your Own
Review what you have learned about writing a critical essay on pages 535–548. Then, using your work from Exercise 7, write the first draft of your essay. Add a title, and save your work for Exercise 13.

Revising

The most difficult task in revising something you have written is standing back from it so that you are able to see its flaws. Once you have completed your first draft, set it aside for a day or overnight. Then, looking at it from the point of view of your readers, revise it for *unity, coherence,* and *emphasis.* Also check your sentences for variety and conciseness and your words for clarity and liveliness. As you revise also keep in mind the special guidelines that a critical essay must adhere to, such as the use of third person point of view and present tense and the correct citation of quotations. Use the following checklist to help you revise.

22j

Revision Checklist

Checking Your Essay

1. Do you have a strong introduction that sets a serious tone, identifies the author and work you will analyze, and captures attention?
2. Does your thesis statement make the main idea of your interpretation clear?
3. Do the supporting paragraphs provide details from the work to support your interpretation?
4. Did you use third-person point of view and the present tense to discuss the literary work?
5. Did you cite the sources of quotations?
6. Does your essay have unity, coherence, and emphasis? *(See page 490.)*
7. Do you have a strong concluding paragraph?
8. Did you add a title that indicates the focus of your paper?

Checking Your Paragraphs

9. Does each paragraph have a topic sentence? *(See page 451.)*
10. Is each paragraph unified and coherent?

Checking Your Sentences and Words

11. Are your sentences varied? *(See pages 377–384.)*
12. Are your sentences concise? *(See pages 373–376.)*
13. Did you avoid faulty sentences? *(See pages 385–392.)*
14. Did you use specific words with correct connotations? *(See pages 367–369.)*
15. Did you use figurative language where appropriate? *(See pages 369–371.)*

EXERCISE 13 On Your Own

Using the Revision Checklist, revise your essay from Exercise 12. Save your work for Exercise 14.

Editing

The final stage in the writing process is editing. When you are satisfied with your final, revised draft, you need to edit and polish it so that it is neat and free from errors. Use the following checklist to edit your essay. You may wish to use the proofreading symbols on page 662 when you edit.

22k

Editing Checklist

1. Are your sentences free of errors in grammar and usage?
2. Did you spell each word correctly?
3. Did you capitalize and punctuate correctly?
4. Did you cite sources of quotations?
5. Did you use correct manuscript form? *(See page 660.)*
6. Is your handwriting or typing neat and clear?

EXERCISE 14 On Your Own
Use the Editing Checklist to edit your essay from Exercise 13.

CHAPTER REVIEW

Write a critical essay on one of the following literary works or on one of your own choosing. Use the Steps for Writing Critical Essays on page 551 as a guide.

Fiction
"Two Soldiers" by William Faulkner
"I Am an American" by James Alan McPherson
Pride and Prejudice by Jane Austen
"Winter Dreams" by F. Scott Fitzgerald
My Ántonia by Willa Cather

Plays
Amadeus by Peter Shaffer
Macbeth by William Shakespeare
All My Sons by Arthur Miller
Our Town by Thornton Wilder
The Caretaker by Harold Pinter

Poetry
"The Unbeliever" by Elizabeth Bishop
"My Last Afternoon with Uncle Devereux Winslow" by Robert Lowell
"The Tables Turned" by William Wordsworth
"The Hollow Men" by T. S. Eliot
"Driving to Town Late to Mail a Letter" by Robert Bly
"The Lovers of the Poor" by Gwendolyn Brooks
"Pied Beauty" by Gerard Manley Hopkins

Steps for Writing

Critical Essays

✓ **Prewriting**

1. Read the work once, and identify your overall response to it.
2. Read it a second time, jotting down notes on the various elements within it. *(See pages 525, 529, and 532.)*
3. Choose one element of the work as a focus point and try to express in one phrase your limited subject. *(See pages 535–536.)*
4. Skim the work again, stopping each time you find a detail that supports your main idea. Make a note card for each detail. *(See page 536.)*
5. Organize your notes in a logical order and make an outline. *(See pages 538–539.)*

✓ **Writing**

6. Write the thesis statement. *(See page 542.)*
7. Write an introduction that includes your thesis statement. *(See pages 542–543.)*
8. Use your outline to write the paragraphs in the body. *(See pages 545–547.)*
9. Write a concluding paragraph. *(See pages 547–548.)*
10. Add a title. *(See page 548.)*

✓ **Revising**

11. Use the Revision Checklist to revise for unity, coherence, emphasis, well-developed paragraphs, and varied and lively sentences and words. *(See page 549.)*

✓ **Editing**

12. Using the Editing Checklist, check your grammar, spelling, mechanics, and manuscript form. *(See pages 549–550.)*

23

The Summary

Summarizing is a valuable skill. If you are preparing a research paper, you may need to summarize information in your notes to provide important points for your readers. The ability to summarize also aids in preparing for tests. It allows you to focus on the most important information and to see clearly the main idea of a chapter or lesson. Writing a formal summary, or *précis,* is one way to learn the skills of summarizing.

23a The **summary** is a concise condensation of a longer piece of writing, covering only the main points of the original.

FEATURES OF A SUMMARY

The main task in writing a summary is to restate the information from an original work accurately and in your own words. A summary never includes personal comments, interpretations, or insights. Read the following original work and the summary that follows it. Notice that (1) the main ideas are presented in the same order as in the original, (2) most details are omitted, and (3) the summary uses different words.

ORIGINAL The networks and the sponsors determine what is aired on commercial television. They look for shows that many people want to see. More people watching the show means more people watching the commercials and perhaps buying the products. No one knows, however, which new series will turn out to be popular. When production companies come to the networks with their series ideas, the networks can only guess whether viewers will like these shows. The public's taste is impossible to predict, and network executives sometimes lose their jobs when they guess wrong.

Once a show is on the air, the number of viewers it attracts can be measured. The best-known way of measuring popularity is the Neilsen rating system. The A. C. Neilsen Company selects several hundred families that it feels represent the whole viewing audience. Some of these families have little boxes attached to their television sets to record which shows are watched. Others fill out weekly reports describing their viewing habits. Those shows which are most watched on a particular week get the highest ratings.

Every Tuesday, people who work in television anxiously await the results of the Nielsen ratings, and so do the sponsors. There are 81.5 million households in the United States that have television sets, and Neilsen rates approximately seventy shows each week. This is more than an interesting contest. The survival of a show depends on these ratings. A show that does not stay in the top third of the ratings is likely to be canceled.

It may seem that you, as an individual viewer, don't have any say in what programs stay on the air. Sponsors, however, care what you think. They sponsor shows because they want people to buy their products. If people write to the sponsor of a show, the sponsor pays attention. If enough people praise a show or complain about it, the sponsor may respond by keeping the show on the air or having it canceled. [323 words]

—MALKA DRUCKER AND ELIZABETH JAMES, *SERIES TV*

SUMMARY Networks and sponsors decide which television shows are broadcast. Sponsors like to back popular shows because their commercials then reach large audiences. Predicting the popularity of shows is therefore a key task of network executives. The Neilsen ratings measure how many people in a representative group are watching various shows. The ratings of about seventy shows are published every Tuesday and determine whether or not a show will stay on the air. Even viewers who are not part of the Neilsen group can influence broadcast decisions by writing to sponsors to express approval or displeasure. [95 words]

Read the summary a second time, looking for the following specific features.

23b

Features of a Summary

1. A summary is usually no more than one third the length of the original.
2. A summary provides the main ideas of the original, omitting all of the details except a few important ones.
3. A summary presents the main ideas in the same order as they are presented in the original.
4. Except for a few key words, the summary expresses the main ideas of the original in the summary writer's own words.

EXERCISE 1 Analyzing a Summary

Read both the original piece and the summary that follows it. Then write answers to the numbered questions.

ORIGINAL John Napier was a sixteenth-century Scottish mathematician whose neighbors feared he was a magician practicing the black arts. He was a believer in astrology and practiced divination. Fearful that Spain would invade the British Isles, he drew plans for all manner of strange defenses, from solar mirrors for burning ships at a distance to submarines and primitive tanks. However, his true fame rests on two great mathematical inventions: the decimal point and logarithms.

Today mathematicians take for granted these handy exponents of numbers that make it possible to multiply and divide by simple addition and subtraction. In Napier's day calculations were done laboriously in the old-fashioned way, and he fretted many hours over the time such arithmetic took . . .

In 1594, the thought struck Napier that all numbers could be written in exponential form, or as powers of a certain base number. For instance, 4 is 2^2, and 8 is 2^3. This alone is not startling, but Napier saw beyond it to a simple way of multiplying 4 times 8 without really multiplying. 2^2 plus 2^3 equaled 2^5 in Napier's new arithmetic, and 2^5 equals 32, the same as the product of 4 times 8. The same principle applies to exponents of *all* numbers, although there was a fantastic amount of work involved in computing these exponents extensively. In fact, it was not until 1614, twenty years after his revelation of the basic idea, that Napier published his logarithm tables. The result was something like the introduction of the electronic computer in our time. Logarithms drastically reduced the amount of work involved in mathematics and relieved scientists, particularly astronomers, from a great burden of mental drudgery.

—DAN HALACY, *CHARLES BABBAGE: FATHER OF THE COMPUTER*

SUMMARY John Napier, an eccentric Scottish mathematician of the sixteenth century, invented the decimal point and logarithms. Napier was concerned about the time-consuming calculations needed to multiply and divide. In 1594, Napier

> realized that the simpler tasks of addition and subtraction could be used with the same results if the numbers were expressed with exponents. Twenty years of testing followed this discovery. When Napier finally published his logarithm tables in 1614, the time savings were similar to the efficiency offered by electronic computers in our age.

1. Is the summary no more than one third the length of the original?
2. To how many sentences is the first paragraph in the original reduced in the summary?
3. Name three details about Napier omitted from the first paragraph.
4. What adjective in the summary hints at some of the details omitted from the first paragraph?
5. To how many sentences is the second paragraph in the original reduced in the summary?
6. Is the specific example provided in the third paragraph of the original retained in the summary?
7. Are all of the dates from the original included in the summary?
8. Consider your answers to questions 3, 6, and 7. What is the difference between original details omitted in the summary and those retained in the summary?
9. What detail about the effect of the logarithm tables has been omitted in the summary?
10. How are the main ideas of the original ordered in the summary?

EXERCISE 2 On Your Own
Look through magazines or books on subjects of interest to you for short articles or excerpts you could summarize. Choose one of particular interest and save it for Exercise 5.

PREWRITING

Most compositions begin with a main idea that you expand and develop into a detailed piece of writing. When you write a summary, however, your purpose is to reduce material to its main ideas by omitting details. During the prewriting stage, your most important task is to understand completely the selection you are summarizing. The following steps will ensure that you fully understand the original work.

23c

Prewriting Steps

1. Read the original work once to understand the general idea.
2. Read the work a second time, writing down unfamiliar words.
3. Look up each unfamiliar word and write a synonym for it or a definition in your own words.
4. Read the work a third time, writing down the main ideas in the order in which they are presented.
5. Determine the length of the original. Count words if the original is a short selection; count lines or pages if it is a long selection.

Understanding Vocabulary

A thorough understanding of all the words in a passage is a prerequisite to an accurate summary. Be sure to look up any words you do not know. Writing a synonym or a definition in your own words will help you remember the meanings.

23d For each unfamiliar word in a passage, write a definition in your own words or find a familiar synonym.

EXERCISE 3 Understanding Vocabulary
Use your dictionary to look up the numbered words in the following passage. For each word, write a synonym for the new word or a definition in your own words.

Because of their immediacy, it might seem that (1) *stimuli* present during sleep would have a greater influence upon dreaming and dream content than would those preceding the (2) *onset* of sleep. During sleep, external stimuli are by no means eliminated. It may happen, for example, that a housefly is captive in the bedroom. Not only does its buzzing provide a (3) *fluctuating* (4) *auditory* stimulus, but (5) *tactual* stimulation will also be produced if it chances to alight on one's forehead. Nor are bodily sensations entirely absent during sleep. Digestive processes may continue to apply themselves to an overly rich bedtime snack, for example, and a host of other stimulus-producing body processes (6) *persist* during sleep, as indeed they must.

(7) *Psychophysiological* studies of dream (8) *phenomena* have made it fairly clear that stimuli present during sleep, such as (9) *incidental* sounds or occasional bodily sensations, cannot account for the occurrence of dreaming nor explain dream content. The (10) *innervation* during sleep of a particular nervous structure in the base of the brain, however, does seem to be directly associated with the rapid-eye-movement that indicates that dreaming is occurring.

—DAVID FOULKES, *THE PSYCHOLOGY OF SLEEP* (ADAPTED)

Recognizing Main Ideas

Once you have looked up unfamiliar words and are certain you understand them, you can move on to the most important skill in summarizing: distinguishing between main ideas and supporting ideas. To find the main ideas, ask yourself, "Which idea is more general than all the others?" In many cases, the sentence expressing the most general idea will be the topic sentence of a paragraph or the thesis statement of an essay or article. In some writing the main idea will be implied instead of stated directly. If the main idea is implied, try to phrase a statement that expresses it.

In the first example that follows, the main idea is stated directly. In the second, it is implied.

MAIN IDEA STATED

Despite its apparent simplicity, or perhaps because of it, people have different ideas about what the sport of weight lifting should be. Some confine themselves to seeing how many pounds they can lift. Others feel that strength should be combined with speed. Still others think that what's most important is not what they lift but how their muscles look after they lift it.

—WILLIAM F. ALLMAN, "WEIGHT LIFTING: INSIDE THE PUMPHOUSE"

The main idea of this paragraph is stated directly in the first sentence, which is also the topic sentence. Compare Allman's paragraph with the following one.

MAIN IDEA IMPLIED

An outsider might look at a group of teenagers standing in front of a school and see only a confused and apparently random grouping of individuals. This interpretation, however, would be misleading, just as misleading as it would be to describe a colony of herring gulls as a bunch of birds. The gullery is, in reality, a highly structured society with leaders and followers, defined territories, and a whole host of subtle but very powerful symbols that keep each gull in its place. It is the same with the teenagers standing in front of their school. Generally everybody in the group knows who the leaders are, and a careful observer might be able to spot the leaders by the particular confidence in the way that they walk or stand and by the way others in the group act toward them.

—DANIEL COHEN, *HUMAN NATURE, ANIMAL NATURE: THE BIOLOGY OF HUMAN BEHAVIOR*

In this paragraph, although the main idea is clear, it is not stated in a single sentence. The main idea is: *However random they may seem, groups of people, like groups of certain animals, are highly structured.* All the other sentences in the paragraph support this idea.

23e Find the main ideas in a passage by identifying the most general statements or by expressing an implied main idea in your own words.

EXERCISE 4 Recognizing Main Ideas

Write the main idea of each paragraph. If the main idea is stated directly, copy it from the paragraph. If it is implied, write your own sentence that expresses the main idea.

1.

Some of the most important movies to come from postwar Europe were the Neo-Realist films from Italy. These films show life as it is lived, not as film studios imagine it to be. They show the streets, the houses, the vital everyday people of a struggling world; they neglect glamour, fancy houses and clothes, and movie stars. They argue against poverty, unemployment, inadequate housing, and the moral chaos caused by the war; and they offer realistic approaches, if not solutions, to realistic problems. The postwar Neo-Realist movement was short-lived, but it contributed some film masterpieces and left a distinct influence on future film-making.

2.

The producer works closely in the selection of actors and actresses, and he or she makes sure that the length of their contracts fits the overall shooting schedule. He or she goes over the shooting script (the screenplay broken down into shots, scenes, and locations) to plan indoor sound-stage settings and outdoor shooting locations. The locations must be scouted for such all-important variables as weather, geography, local facilities, transportation, and accessibility. The shooting schedule must be planned around another set of variables, which includes shooting "out of continuity" (in other words, a film in which the last scene might be shot before the first) and weather (when the script calls for sun, the schedule must be planned for a time of year when the sun is likely to shine). When the movie is completed, the producer is in charge of selling it to distributors, of planning advertising and publicity, and of other agreements, such as sales to television. If the film is successful at the box office, the producer takes a large share of the profits. If it wins awards, such as the Academy Award for the best picture, it is the producer, not the director, who receives it.

3.

Movie photography is the responsibility of two people: the director of photography and the camera operator. The director of photography (also called the cinematographer) attends the story conference and plans the shots to be filmed in consultation with the director, writer, and other members of the unit. The camera operator is the person responsible for overseeing the lighting and operating the camera used in shooting the film. In many films the two roles are performed by the same person.

4.

Some actors and actresses are famous for their low-keyed approach to roles; others are popular because they overact (or "chew up the scenery," as such a performance is known). Some are famous for their singing (Elvis Presley), swimming (Esther Williams), or dancing (Fred Astaire). Still others, like Henry Fonda, have become stars for their association with certain historical persons whose lives they have portrayed. Some, like Katherine Hepburn, are popular for the simple reason that they perform year after year, in movie after movie, and always give a good performance. There are no easy rules and no easy answers in the subject of acting.

5.

When Robert Redford gets into a fight in *Butch Cassidy and the Sundance Kid* (1969), the chances are that he is not in the fight at all but that a "double" is performing for him. Stunt performers act as doubles for actors and actresses when the action called for in the script is dangerous. Other stunt performers are experts at various sports or at driving fast cars or at falling off horses without getting hurt. Great skill is used in photographing these performers so that the audience sees their work but not their faces. When the film is edited, we are fooled into thinking that the stars of a picture are also excellent skiers or boxers or motorcyclists. François Truffaut's delightful film *Day for Night* (1973) shows many of the behind-the-scenes activities of special effects experts, stunt performers, and other movie magicians.

—ALL EXCERPTS FROM RICHARD MERAN BARSAM, *IN THE DARK: A PRIMER FOR THE MOVIES*

EXERCISE 5 On Your Own

Using the article or excerpt you selected in Exercise 2, complete the following prewriting steps. These prewriting steps will help you fully understand the original work.

1. Reread the passage and make a list of unfamiliar words.
2. For each unfamiliar word you listed, write a synonym or a definition in your own words.
3. Read the passage a third time and make a list of the main ideas in the order they appear in the original.
4. Count and write the number of words in the passage.

WRITING

Your prewriting notes will help you write the first draft of your summary. The first draft should contain all the important ideas from the original stated in your own words and presented in a shortened form. The chart that follows shows the steps for writing the first draft.

23f

Steps for Writing the First Draft

1. Present the main ideas in the same order in which they appear in the original.
2. Condense the original to approximately one third its length by
   - omitting unnecessary details.
   - combining ideas from several sentences into one.
   - replacing long phrases, clauses, and sentences with shorter phrases or even single words.
3. Paraphrase (restate the ideas from the original in your own words) by
   - using synonyms.
   - varying sentence structure.

Condensing

The omission of unnecessary details, the combining of several sentences into one, and the reduction of long phrases and clauses into shorter expressions are ways to shorten a passage into summary form. Study the following examples. The sentences in both the original and the summary are numbered for easy reference.

ORIGINAL (1) Rushmore got a great deal of free publicity in 1934 when the Hearst newspapers sponsored a contest for a six-hundred word history to be carved on Mount Rushmore. (2) An inscription had been part of Gutzon Borglum's design for a long time. (3) At one point he had asked Coolidge to write the inscription, but he and Coolidge disagreed over the wording, so nothing came of that. (4) Eight hundred thousand entries were submitted in the Hearst contest, and many cash prizes were given. (5) No entries were ever used because eventually Gutzon abandoned the inscription idea in favor of a great Hall of Records to be cut in the stone of the canyon behind the faces. (6) Gutzon felt that records carved or placed in a room in the mountain would last much longer than any identifying inscription on the surface of the mountain.

SUMMARY (1) In 1934, the Hearst newspapers sponsored a contest for an inscription for Mount Rushmore, which had been part of artist Gutzon Borglum's original plan. (2) Eight hundred thousand people responded. (3) Although many won cash prizes, their inscriptions were abandoned when Borglum decided instead to create a Hall of Records, a room carved into the stone, which he felt would be more permanent than a carved inscription.

The following chart shows how the sentences from the original were condensed in the summary.

Original Sentences		Summary
1 & 2	→	1
3	→	omitted (unnecessary detail)
4	→	2
5 & 6	→	3

23g Condense information from the original by omitting repetition and unnecessary details and by reducing several sentences into one.

EXERCISE 6 Condensing

Condense each paragraph in the following passage to no more than two sentences. Write those sentences next to the number of the paragraph.

(1)Writers exclaim over the coast of Maine so often that their descriptions lose meaning. "Rugged," "rockbound," and "pine-clad" generally fail to stir up any visions of this northeastern shore. Yet the Maine coast is all of them and much more, too. It is a splendid part of the country—shaped and hammered by vast natural forces, softened by forests, haunted by human history. People cannot visit these coves and harbors without falling hopelessly in love with the feeling of morning fog burning off under a warm sun, the scent of pine needles in the cool shade of the forest, the taste of wild blueberries, the muffled thunder of waves, the crisp hue of sunset on a cool evening. The best example of the 3,478-mile Maine coast (including the islands) is Acadia National Park, which became the first great park in the east.
(2)During the last Ice Age, this shoreline was pressed down by the huge weight of ice and snow. Glaciers scraped the rocky land, smoothed the hills, cracked loose rock away from parent ledges. The result is a sunken coast where what were once valleys are now sounds and inlets, where little granite islands jut from the ocean, where tumbled boulders clog the shore. Most of Maine is like this: Acadia typifies it. For here rise the heights of Mount Desert Island, the round-sculptured remnants of the pre-Ice Age mountain ridge. Its tallest summit is still the highest point in the United States that overlooks the Atlantic, and one of the first to catch the rising sun's rays.
(3)A deep, narrow sound cuts Mount Desert Island almost in two: Somes Sound, the only true fjord on the New England coast. On either side the hills rise, covered with tough, stunted pine and spruce—some not so stunted—and rich with wildflowers. Cadillac Mountain, 1,530 feet, marks the high point. Below it spreads Frenchman Bay and the old summer resort of Bar Harbor.
(4)Acadia was donated to the Federal government by the summer residents (once called "rusticaters" by the locals) who, between them, owned most of Mount Desert Island. That's why the park boundaries are strangely uneven—they follow the property lines. Most of the 48-square-mile park lies on Mount Desert Island; some is across Frenchman Bay on the Schoodic Peninsula; some occupies part of the Isle au Haut, an offshore island southwest of Mount Desert. All these park lands contain choice elements of scenery. Fresh-water ponds and lakes gleam among the dark evergreens on Mount Desert. Trout, salmon, and bass flirt with the angler, while

salt-water fishing invites visitors to brave the gray Atlantic in chartered vessels.

—ALL EXCERPTS FROM PAUL JENSEN, *NATIONAL PARKS*

Paraphrasing

Condensing, or shortening, original material is one technique to use when writing a summary. Another valuable skill when summarizing material is *paraphrasing.* When you use your own words to express the main ideas and essential details from an original selection, you are paraphrasing. In a paraphrase you must include all of the author's original ideas, even though you have rephrased them. For this reason, any material that you paraphrase will often be close to the length of the original. Two methods will help you paraphrase information from an original source. One method is to use synonyms to help replace words used in the selection. The second method is to vary the structure of the sentences in the original work. *(See pages 382–384.)*

23h **Paraphrase** the original work by using synonyms and by varying the sentence structure.

Notice in the following example how synonyms and a different sentence structure were used to paraphrase.

ORIGINAL Ralph Bunche was awarded the Nobel Peace Prize in 1950 for negotiating a resolution to the end of the Israeli-Egyptian conflict of 1948–49.

PARAPHRASE For his success in mediating a peace agreement between warring Israel and Egypt in 1948–49, Ralph Bunche won the Nobel Peace Prize in 1950.

The synonyms in the paraphrase are *mediating* for *negotiating, peace agreement* for *resolution,* and *warring* for *conflict.* The passive construction *was awarded* in the original has been changed to the active voice *won* in the paraphrase. In addition, the paraphrase begins with a prepositional phrase, while the original begins with the subject.

EXERCISE 7 Paraphrasing

Read the following passage about the camel. Then paraphrase each sentence in the excerpt by using synonyms and varying sentence structure. Look up any unfamiliar words. Use the example on page 537 as a guide.

(1) The camel has long had a reputation for being able to go for long periods of time without drinking any water. (2) Ancient writers believed that the camel had some mysterious internal water reservoir—a story that was told for so many centuries that it came to be believed. (3) No such reservoir, however, has ever been found. (4) Nevertheless, the camel is remarkably suited to getting along well on a minimum of water.

(5) When green vegetation is available, camels can live for months without drinking water at all. (6) Their food provides all the water they need. (7) Even in the Sahara's dry summer, when little natural food is available, camels can go for a week or more without water and for ten days without food.

(8) Camels accomplish this feat by drawing on water from their body tissues and on water produced chemically as a breakdown product of fat. (9) The camel's hump contains up to 50 pounds of fat, which is accumulated when food and water are plentiful. (10) As the fat is used up to supply the camel's energy needs, about 1.1 pounds of water are produced for every pound of fat used up. (11) This is made possible because hydrogen is given off as a by-product in the breakdown of fat. (12) Oxygen from breathing is then combined with the hydrogen to produce water. (13) Because oxygen is much heavier than hydrogen, it does not take much hydrogen, by weight, to make a pound of water.

(14) With the help of this water-producing system, a camel can function well for a good many days, even when carrying a load. (15) When water is again available, the camel gulps down as much as 25 gallons at one time to compensate for the water lost during the period of deprivation.

—WILLIAM C. VERGARA, *SCIENCE IN THE WORLD AROUND US*

EXERCISE 8 On Your Own

Using the work you selected from Exercise 2 and your prewriting notes from Exercise 5, write the first draft of a summary by following the steps outlined on page 562. Save your work for Exercise 10.

Writing Extra

In the example about John Napier on pages 554–555, the many details about the mathematician's life in the first paragraph of the original were condensed into one new word in the summary: *eccentric*. The process of finding a general word to replace specific details calls for the skills of classifying and generalizing. Study the following example.

ORIGINAL The tiny company was having trouble **paying its employees, meeting its debts to suppliers, and raising money through sales of its products.**

The specific details are omitted in the following condensed version. They have been replaced by a more general adjective.

CONDENSED The small company was struggling with **financial problems.**

EXERCISE 9 Classifying Details in Larger Categories
Write a condensed version of each of the following sentences. The details to be classified in one group are in italics.

1. *Presidents Kennedy, Johnson, Nixon, Ford, Carter, and Reagan* have all used the power of television to help them win popular support for their programs.
2. At the Air and Water Show, *bi-planes, jets, and helicopters* as well as *tugs, cruisers, and fireboats* put on a thrilling display.
3. Venita does well in *math, biology, physics,* and *chemistry.*
4. *Army, Navy, Air Force,* and *Marine* leaders met today with the secretary of state.
5. Books on *how to repair your car, your furniture,* and *your electrical appliances* lined the shelf.

REVISING

The two main features to look for as you revise your summary are accuracy and conciseness. Reread the original to make sure you have represented its ideas accurately. Also try to reduce your summary to the most economical version possible. The following checklist will help you.

23i

Revision Checklist

1. Compare your summary to the original. Are the ideas presented accurately?
2. Are the ideas in your summary presented in the same order as in the original?
3. Count the number of words in your summary. Is your summary no more than one third the length of the original? If not, condense your work further by repeating step 2 in the process of writing the first draft. *(See page 562.)*
4. Did you use synonyms and vary the sentence structure to paraphrase?
5. Did you use transitions and other connecting devices to make your summary flow smoothly? *(See pages 430–431.)*

EXERCISE 10 **On Your Own**
Use the Revision Checklist to revise your summary from Exercise 8. Save your work for Exercise 11.

EDITING

The final stage in the process of writing a summary is editing. Use the following checklist to prepare a neat, finished draft of your summary. You may wish to use the proofreading symbols on page 662 as you edit.

23j

Editing Checklist

1. Are your sentences free from errors in grammar and usage?
2. Did you spell each word correctly?
3. Did you capitalize and punctuate correctly?
4. Did you use correct manuscript form? *(See page 659.)*
5. Is your handwriting or typing clear?

EXERCISE 11 **On Your Own**
Use the Editing Checklist to edit the revised draft of your summary from Exercise 10.

CHAPTER REVIEW

Use the Steps for Writing Summaries on page 543 as a guide to help you write a summary of each of the following original passages.

1.

Neoteny is a process that produces an organism whose fixed muscular responses and instincts have never been locked into the adult stage. Such an organism has a great range of possible combinations and recombinations, both in determining the sequence of muscle contractions and in coupling these contractions with incoming stimuli. Neoteny produces an individual who can do all sorts of things in a great many different ways, and whose behavior in any given situation is neither rigid nor stereotyped. The ease with which dolphins and human beings can be conditioned, and the great variety of their behavior, can be seen as examples of neoteny.

Dolphins have many neotenic characteristics. An obvious example is their undisguised joy and interest in play. In fact, it was the first captive dolphins themselves who took the initiative in a great many of the simple games now played between humans and dolphins in aquariums all over the world. Dolphins, even adults, can play for hours with a ball or a feather. They are as tireless as human children in this respect.

Dolphins appear to play even in the wild state. They have been observed innumerable times riding the wakes of ships in a way that can hardly be classified as other than playful. On two separate occasions scientists on the beach have watched dolphins surfing. On one of these occasions it could be seen quite clearly that individual dolphins returned repeatedly to the same starting point in order to catch a new wave.

—KARL-ERIK FICHTELIUS & SVERRE SJOLANDER,
SMARTER THAN MAN?

2.

The much discussed turtle of *The Grapes of Wrath* is the one notable survivor in Steinbeck's animal kingdom. More than any other he resembles the stoic, independent animals found elsewhere in American literature. Like most of them, he sets off across the frontier *alone*. The interchapter devoted to this memorable character stands as one of the most striking in the novel.

> And over the grass at the roadside a turtle crawled, turning aside for nothing, dragging his high-domed shell over the grass: His hard legs and yellow-nailed feet threshed slowly through the grass, not really walking, but boosting and dragging his shell along. The barley beards slid off his shell, and the clover burrs fell on him and rolled to the ground. His horny beak was partly open, and his fierce, humorous eyes, under brows like fingernails, stared straight ahead. He came over the grass leaving a beaten trail behind him, and the hill, which was the highway embankment, reared up ahead of him. For the moment he stopped, his head held high.

Taken as a symbol, the turtle embodies the enduring qualities of the Okies who travel the same road in a southwestward direction. Like them, he is vulnerable to the elements, the machine and man, but he is not destroyed. His carrying of the wild oat seeds, however, is accidental: He is not a homesteader. The analogy also breaks down in more significant ways. Tom Joad, who collects a land turtle along that road, cannot be compared to the animal that eats an ant for survival; Joad crushed another's head in a bar brawl. The ex-convict's repeated observation of the directedness of the turtle marks a discrepancy with the man's misdirected life. The primary quality of the Okies that makes not only for spiritual strength but for physical survival, their brotherhood —sharing, bonding, and the compassion that extends beyond their family to other sufferers—is distinctly opposed to the self-reliance of the solitary turtle. Steinbeck's intent to show the turtle as a parallel to the Joad family is not accomplished. Unlike the Joads, the turtle survives because of self-interest.

—MARY ALLEN, *ANIMALS IN AMERICAN LITERATURE*

Steps for Writing

Summaries

✓ **Prewriting**

1. Read the original work once to understand the general idea.
2. Read the work a second time and make a list of unfamiliar words.
3. Look up each unfamiliar word and write a synonym for it or a definition in your own words.
4. Read the work a third time, jotting down the main ideas in the order in which they appear in the original work.
5. Determine the length of the original work. Count words if the original is a short selection; count lines or pages if it is a long selection.

✓ **Writing**

6. Present the main ideas in the same order in which they appeared in the original.
7. Condense the original to approximately one third its length by
   - omitting unnecessary details.
   - combining ideas from several sentences into one.
   - replacing long phrases, clauses, and sentences with shorter phrases or even single words. *(See pages 377–382.)*
8. Restate the ideas from the original in your own words by
   - using synonyms.
   - varying sentence structure. *(See pages 382–384.)*

✓ **Revising**

9. Use the Revision Checklist on page 568 to check for accuracy and length.

✓ **Editing**

10. Use the Editing Checklist on page 568 to check the accuracy of your grammar, usage, spelling, mechanics, and manuscript form.

24

Research Papers

The research paper is an effective learning tool. Writing one is perhaps the best way to gain new, useful knowledge. When you begin your reading on a subject of interest, you learn much that you did not know before. When you go further than reading and begin to evaluate and reorganize what you have read, you learn even more. If you take the final step and write what you have learned so that others will understand it, you have made the subject "yours." You have moved from being interested in your subject to being an expert on it.

24a A **research paper** is a composition based on research drawn from books, periodicals, and interviews with experts.

In the course of writing a research paper you will be drawing on many different skills. First, since you will need to find appropriate information in books and magazines, you will need good library skills. *(You may wish to review Chapters 15 and 16 on library skills.)* Second, when you are gathering information and taking notes from library sources you will use your skills of summarizing and paraphrasing. *(See Chapter 23.)* Finally, since the main purpose of a research paper is to convey information, you will use your skill of expository writing to help you present the information clearly and concisely.

PREWRITING

The main goals of the prewriting stage are gathering and synthesizing information. As you gather information, you will need a good system of keeping track of bits and pieces from different sources. A folder with pockets, index cards, paper clips, and rubber bands will make your job easier. As you *synthesize,* or put back together, the pieces of information you have gathered, you will use your critical thinking skills to arrange and evaluate your information and to draw your own conclusions. *(See Chapter 18.)*

Finding Ideas

Whenever you need ideas to write about, you can explore two avenues of thought. One is your own imagination, where your collected experiences and thoughts about them may lead you to a subject of interest. The other is sources outside you— classes you are taking, books you have read, or unfolding news stories. Asking yourself questions and jotting down answers will often direct your mind to an interesting subject.

EXERCISE 1 Finding Ideas from Personal Experience
Ask yourself the following questions and write answers to them.

1. What dangerous situation have I been in? What information could I give to others to help them avoid similar danger?
2. Who are my personal heroes? What function do heroes serve in a society?
3. What career do I intend to have? What are some of the interesting aspects of that career? What, if any, are the drawbacks?
4. Who are some of the people who are professional experts in my hobby? What have they contributed to the hobby?
5. What information would I like to have about computers?
6. How do I spend my leisure time? Are my recreations typical of other people my age? Does where one lives determine in part the way leisure time is spent?
7. Where have I been that other people probably have not been?

8. At what activity am I becoming expert?
9. How do the attitudes of my generation differ from those of my parents or older family members? What accounts for the difference? What similarities are there?
10. How do I take care of my health and safety? What knowledge can people use to prevent illness and injury?

EXERCISE 2 Finding Ideas from Outside Sources
Ask yourself the following questions and write answers to them.

1. What topics in my elective classes would I like to know more about?
2. Who is my favorite composer or musician?
3. What books or poems have I read and enjoyed in English class this year?
4. What are some trends in motion pictures today?
5. What changes came about as a result of the last national or local election?
6. What have I learned about recently from books, magazines, and television and radio shows?
7. What classes or lessons do I take outside of school?
8. What have I learned from an older relative?
9. In what part of the world are dramatic events happening?
10. What unusual happenings have occurred recently (birth of quintuplets, volcanic eruption, etc.)?

Choosing and Limiting a Subject

Use the following guidelines to help you choose one subject from among the several possible ones you have discovered in your search for ideas.

24b

Guidelines for Choosing a Subject

1. Choose a subject you would like to know more about.
2. Choose a subject that would interest your audience.
3. Choose a subject that can be covered in a research paper approximately 2,000 words (7 typed pages) long.
4. Choose a subject on which the library is likely to have sufficient information.

To follow the fourth guideline, you will need to check the library's card catalog and some recent issues of the *Readers' Guide to Periodical Literature*. If you cannot find at least two books and two magazine articles on your subject, you should try another subject.

When you are satisfied that you can find enough information, the next step is to limit your subject to a workable size and a clear focus. If your subject is too broad, you could spend valuable time collecting information that you will never use in your final paper. The subject of black holes in space, for example, is broad enough to fill a whole book. Within that subject, though, are smaller aspects of it that could be covered adequately in a 2,000-word paper. Some of these more limited subjects might be the following: "how Einstein's work predicted the possibility of black holes"; "where black holes are likely to be discovered"; "how black holes are created"; and "instruments astronomers use to search for black holes." Any of these smaller, more specific subjects would be suitable for a short research paper.

One useful way to limit your subject is to ask yourself a series of "what about" questions. Each question should produce a more specific version of your original broad subject.

BROAD SUBJECT	computers
FIRST QUESTION	*What about* computers?
MORE LIMITED	how computers help the handicapped
SECOND QUESTION	*What about* computers and the handicapped?
MORE LIMITED	how computers help the handicapped with language, vision, and motion
THIRD QUESTION	*What about* computers helping with language, vision, and motion?
SUITABLY LIMITED	recent developments and successes in the procedures by which computers help speechless, sightless, and immobilized people

Since most suitably limited subjects cannot be clearly expressed in just a few words, continue your "what about" questions until your answer is a phrase or partial sentence. Only then will the focus be sufficiently clear to guide you through your research and writing.

24c Limit your subject by asking "What about (the subject)?" until you can express the focus of your research paper in a phrase or partial sentence.

EXERCISE 3 Choosing a Subject
Decide which of the following subjects are suitable for a short research paper and which are too broad. Indicate your answer by writing *suitable* or *too broad* for each subject.

1. the Japanese language
2. American Indian words that have become part of the English language
3. how the space shuttle serves business and research
4. baseball
5. physical fitness
6. what to do when you encounter potentially dangerous animals while backpacking or hiking through a wilderness
7. Martin Luther King, Jr.
8. Poland
9. how engineers solved the problems in building the Brooklyn Bridge
10. the Ming dynasty

EXERCISE 4 Limiting a Subject
For each broad subject listed, write a series of "what about" questions until you have arrived at a suitably limited subject. Use the model on page 575 as a guide.

1. automobile safety
2. World War II
3. horses
4. the media
5. the United States government

Gathering Information

Once you have limited your subject, you can begin formulating questions that you will need to answer in your paper. These guide questions will help you find the specific information you need. If you had decided to write a paper on computers helping the handicapped, your guide questions might include the following questions.

- How do computers aid people with language disabilities? For different kinds of disabilities, are there different kinds of computers?
- How do computers help blind people? Can sightless people actually see again, or do computers help guide them as a trained dog might do?
- How do computers help people who have lost a limb or who are paralyzed? How far advanced is the technology in this area?
- Who are some of the pioneers in the field of computers helping the handicapped?
- What are the costs of these machines?
- How else are computers helping disabled people?

Once you have a list of between five and ten questions, you should place it in your folder for future use. Later, the questions will help you determine which passages in the sources you consult are relevant to your subject and worthy of note-taking.

The following steps will guide you through the process of collecting information from the library.

24d

Steps for Gathering Information

1. Begin by consulting a general reference work such as an encyclopedia or a handbook to gain an overview of your subject. You will also often find a list of additional sources at the end of these articles.
2. Use the subject catalog in the library to find more books on your subject.
3. Use the *Readers' Guide to Periodical Literature* to find magazine articles on your subject.
4. Use a newspaper index to find newspaper articles on your subject.
5. Make a note card for each available source. Include the author, title, date of publication, publisher and location, and call number. For magazines include the name of the magazine and the number and date of the issue.
6. Assign each source a number with which you can identify it in your notes.

EXERCISE 5 Gathering Information
Choose three of the following subjects. Then use the library to list five sources for each subject you chose. At least two sources for each subject should be magazine articles. Be sure to include all the information named in steps 5 and 6 on page 577.

1. violence on television
2. pros and cons of nuclear power plants
3. improving public housing
4. new car designs
5. fighting air and water pollution

Evaluating Sources

Some of the sources you come across in your research may be inadequate. Reviewing your sources for up-to-dateness, accuracy, and objectivity is an essential part of research. If a book has an old publication date, for example, it may be missing critical new information that you would need for your paper. If the author of a book or magazine article does not seem qualified in the subject, the source may suffer from inaccuracies. Another possible weakness in a source is bias. *Bias* is a strong leaning toward one viewpoint on a subject based more on emotion or self-interest than on objective evidence. In a biased source, you may not find complete information, since the author may have selected only the information that supports his or her viewpoint. The following checklists will help you screen your sources.

24e

Checklist for Evaluating Books

1. What is the publication date? If it is more than a few years old, will the book be missing too much new information?
2. Who is the author? What are his or her credentials? (You can find these by reading the notes on the book jacket or by looking the author up in a bibliographical reference work such as those listed on pages 358 and 362.)
3. Is there anything in the author's background that might suggest a biased viewpoint?
4. Check the table of contents and the index. Is there information on your limited subject in the book?

24f

Checklist for Evaluating Magazine and Newspaper Articles

1. When was the article published? If it was published more than a few years ago, do you think it may be missing important new information?
2. Who is the author? What are his or her credentials? (You can usually find these in a note at the bottom of the first or last page of the article.)
3. Does the magazine appeal to a special interest group that may have a biased viewpoint on your subject? (For example, a magazine called *Saving the Planet* would probably have a bias toward preserving the environment at all costs. One called *Industrial Progress,* on the other hand, might have a bias toward serving the needs of business over the needs of the environment.)
4. Does the article contain specific information on your limited subject?

Use only those sources you can rely on for accuracy and objectivity. Five to ten good sources should supply you with enough information to build a strong research paper.

EXERCISE 6 Evaluating Sources

Each of the following sources for a report on consumer safety suffers from one of the weaknesses listed below. Write the weakness of each source.

Weaknesses

probably outdated
probably biased
lack of strong author credentials
does not relate to subject

1. "Unnecessary Safety Controls Will Raise Prices," article in *Toymaker's Trade,* written by Lara Scranton, director of public relations at Smile-a-While Toy Company, published in 1984.
2. "Consumer Price Index Holds Steady," article in *Today* magazine, written by Dustin Calderon, chief economist at First National Bank, published in 1984.
3. *Consumer Rights and Safety,* a book published in 1953, written by William Hertz, Director of Consumer Affairs in Peoria, Illinois.

4. "The Need for Warning Labels," an article in *Home* magazine, written in 1983 by Helene Mayer, magazine writer with a regular column on household hints.
5. *Harmful Additives,* a pamphlet published in 1983 by NatureFoods Industries, written by Kyle Gardner, Executive Vice President of NatureFoods Industries.

Writing Extra

Some of the sources you use for your research paper may be statistical studies. Statistics are simply facts expressed in numbers. In most cases, the job of interpreting those statistics will be yours. Suppose you were preparing a paper on the effect of home computers on family activities. You could simply cite the following statistics, based on a study of 130 computer users in California. They reported the following changes in their family activities after buying a home computer.

Television watching dropped by about 75%
Time spent on hobbies dropped by about 40%
Sleeping time dropped by about 37%
Leisure time spent with family dropped about 20%
Study or work time increased by about 28%
Time spent alone increased by about 40%

—SOURCE: *PSYCHOLOGY TODAY*

In addition to citing the statistics, however, you may want to go a step further and interpret them, or draw some conclusions and judgments about them. Recognizing that the sample of people responding to the survey was limited, you can nonetheless make some qualified generalizations about the positive and negative effects of home computers. To do so you need to rate the importance of each activity mentioned in the survey and decide whether the changes were for the better or for the worse in terms of a happy and healthy family life.

EXERCISE 7 **Drawing Conclusions from Statistics**
Write a paragraph setting forth your views on the positive and/or negative effects of buying a home computer based on the statistics above. Be sure to use such words as *may, might, perhaps,* or *possibly* to qualify your views.

Taking Notes and Summarizing

Reviewing the guide questions you developed at the beginning of your work will help direct you to the information you need in each source. Use your index cards for note-taking. As you begin, write the identifying number of each source in the upper right-hand corner of the note card. *(See page 582.)* In the upper left-hand corner, identify the aspect of your subject that you are taking notes on. In most cases, the aspects of your subject will match or correspond to your research guide questions. On the subject of computers helping the handicapped, for example, notes taken to answer the question "How do computers help people who have lost a limb?" might be labeled *loss of limb.*

Although you should avoid taking notes on information that does not directly answer one of your guide questions, you should also be open to revising your guide questions as you acquire more information. You may find that an aspect of your subject you have not previously considered would strengthen and clarify your paper. In such a case, write an appropriate new guide question and proceed to take notes as usual on the question, using an appropriate label on note cards.

24g The goals of note-taking are to summarize main points in your own words and to record quotations that you might use in your research paper.

The following paragraphs are from a *Time* magazine article published on December 13, 1983. The writer of the paper on computers and the handicapped has assigned this source the identifying number 10. Read the excerpt carefully and compare it to the sample note card that follows.

> The ultimate hope of every spinal cord-injury victim is that crippled limbs will work again. That dream seems tantalizingly close for a 22-year-old paraplegic in Dayton. Using a computer-based locomotion system, Nan Davis, a senior at Wright State University, recently stood up in front of television news cameras and took half a dozen halting strides and said with a laugh, "One small step for mankind." Davis has been paralyzed from the rib cage down as a result of an auto crash in 1978, on the night of her high school graduation.

Throughout her programmed "walk" at the Wright State biomedical engineering lab, Davis was bolstered by props. She was strapped to a parachute harness that supported a third of her 130 pounds, and she gripped a pair of parallel bars as her legs stepped ahead of her down the 10-foot walkway. Nonetheless, her achievement marked an important development: the marriage of 200-year-old electrical stimulation techniques to today's high-speed computers.

To get Nan going, Dr. Jerrold Petrofsky, director of the lab, taped some 30 electrodes and sensors over the major muscle groups in her legs. Then he instructed a small desktop computer to fire successive bursts of electricity, each carefully orchestrated to trigger the right muscles at the proper time. A feedback system monitored the movements of Davis's ankles, knees, and hips, making corrections as necessary.

The resulting movements were crude and jerky. Moveover, extending the program so that Nan can turn, sit, squat, or climb steps will pose enormous difficulties. At present, the $200,000 system can only direct one foot to move in front of the other. Before it can be put to practical use, Petrofsky's 150-pound device must be streamlined and miniaturized. "It's a mass of wires right now," says Wright State Technician Harry Heaton. "But it will eventually be a small microprocessor capable of being implanted pacemaker-style." Petrofsky says his system might be ready for commercialization within a decade.

Sample Note Card

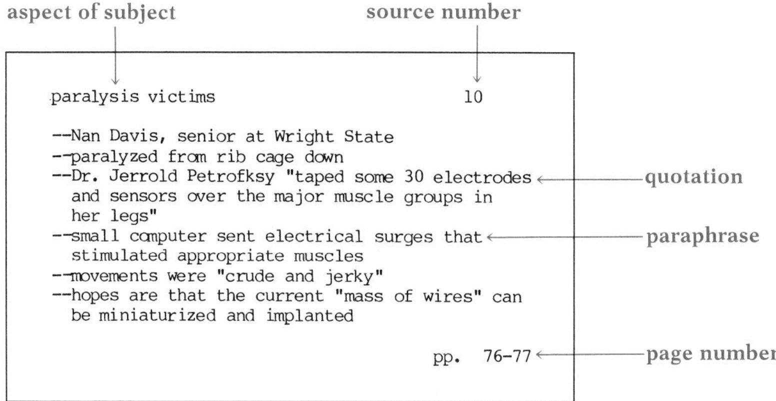

Include only those notes on one card that relate closely to the aspect of your subject identified at the top. Later you will need to sort your notes according to the various aspects, and, if you have notes on more than one aspect on a card, sorting will be difficult.

When you have finished taking notes from one source, clip together all your note cards from that source with a paper clip. Check to make sure that each separate card carries the identifying number in the upper right-hand corner and the page number of the information.

EXERCISE 8 Taking Notes and Summarizing

The following excerpt is about Stonehenge, the ancient structure in England built of huge gray stones through which the rising and setting of the sun, along with other celestial activities, can be observed. It is from pages 117–118 of a source titled *Stonehenge Decoded,* by Gerald S. Hawkins in collaboration with John B. White. Assume it has been given the identifying number 3 and make a note card for it. Summarize the main points in your own words, record any good quotations, and identify the aspect of the subject being discussed. Use the sample note card on page 582 as a model.

> The Stonehenge sun-moon alignments were created and elaborated for two, possibly three, reasons: they made a calendar, particularly useful to tell the time for planting crops; they helped to create and maintain priestly power, by enabling the priest to call out the multitude to see the spectacular risings and settings of the sun and moon, most especially the midsummer sunrise over the heel stone[1] and the midwinter sunset through the great trilithon,[2] and possibly they served as an intellectual game.
>
> To amplify a little on those three supposed reasons, let me state that it is well known that methods for determining the times of planting were of most vital concern to primitive peoples. Those times are hard to detect. One can't count backwards from the fine, warm days; one must use some other means. What better means could there be for following the seasons than observation of those most regular and predictable recurring objects, the heavenly bodies? Even in classic times there were still elaborate sets of instructions to help

[1] A large stone standing alone outside the circular structure and marked with a heel-shaped nick at the bottom.

[2] A trilithon is a grouping of three rocks in which two tall pillar rocks are connected at the top by a third that spans the distance between them.

farmers to time their planting by celestial phenomena. Discussing the "deep question" of the "fit time and season of sowing corn," Pliny[3] declared, "this would be handled and considered upon with exceeding great care and regard; as depending for the most part on Astronomy . . ." Doubtless there are today farmers who time their planting by the sky.

As for the value of Stonehenge as a priestly power enhancer, it seems quite possible that the person who could call the people to see the god of day or night appear or disappear between those mighty arches and over that distant horizon would attract some of the aura of deity. Indeed, the whole people who possessed such a monument and temple must have felt lifted up.

The other possible reason for the astronomical ingenuity . . . of Stonehenge is, I must admit, my own invention. I think that those Stonehengers were true ancestors of ours. I think that the people who designed its various parts, and perhaps even some of the people who helped to build those parts, enjoyed the mental exercise above and beyond the call of duty. I think that when they had solved the problem of the alignments efficiently but unspectacularly, they couldn't let the matter rest. They had to set themselves more challenges, and try for more difficult, rewarding, and spectacular solutions, partly for the greater glory of their pre-Christian gods, but partly for the joy of humans, the thinking animals. I wonder if some day some authority will establish a connection between the spirit which animated the Stonehenge builders and that which inspired the creators of the Parthenon, and the Gothic cathedrals, and the first space craft to go to Mars.

Organizing Your Notes

When your research and note-taking are complete, you can use your guide questions once again to help you sort your note cards into categories of information. Notice how the following categories on the subject of computers and the handicapped are related to the questions that guided the research.

Category 1 Computers helping people with certain language disabilities

Category 2 Computers helping people with vision-related problems

[3] An ancient Roman writer.

Category 3	Computers helping people with motion lost by paralysis or loss of limb
Category 4	Costs vs. benefits of equipment
Category 5	Other ways computers are helping handicapped

24h Group your notes into three or more main categories of information, using your guide questions as a basis.

Once you have determined the categories, you can re-sort your note cards so that each group relates to one of your main categories. Clip the cards in each group together. If any notes do not fit into a category, clip them separately. You may be able to work them into the introduction or conclusion of your report.

Writing a Working Thesis Statement. When you have finished gathering information, you are ready to begin synthesizing it. *(See page 573.)* The first step is to read over your note cards, reviewing what you have learned from your research. The next step is to formulate a draft of a thesis statement. *(See pages 481–482.)* This *working thesis statement* will help keep your mind directed to the purpose and main idea of your research paper. Notice how the following working thesis statement on computers and the handicapped is drawn from the categories of information on pages 584–585.

WORKING THESIS STATEMENT Computers are able to help people with language disabilities, vision problems, and problems of motion related to paralysis and loss of limb.

You can revise and polish your thesis statement later when you are preparing the first draft of your research paper.

EXERCISE 9 Creating Categories

The following pieces of information are on the subject of robot sensors, or devices that allow robots to sense objects around them. Number your paper 1 to 3, skipping three lines after each number. Next to the numbers, write three main categories into which the pieces of information can be grouped. Underneath, write the letter of each item that belongs in the category. Save your work for Exercises 10 and 12.

Robot Sensors

a. Some robots are programmed to hear and respond to only one human voice giving commands.
b. The sense of touch in some robots is controlled by the machine's receiving an electrical charge when it comes in contact with an object.
c. Some robots can be programmed to hear and respond to any human voice by being instructed to "edit out" the differences in voice quality.
d. The simplest form of robot sight is the ability to detect the presence or absence of light.
e. In some hearing robots, a double entry system is used. The first step is a voice command from its programmer; the second step requires an additional command from the programmer before the robot will begin to follow the command given.
f. Some robots can control the amount of pressure they exert on an object they are touching through what is called force feedback.
g. Some robots can "see" gradations of light and dark, not merely its presence or absence.
h. TV cameras are used in some robots as a vision device.
i. Some robots do not have to touch things to know they are nearby; proximity sensors tell them when they are near metal objects or certain levels of air pressure.

EXERCISE 10 Writing a Working Thesis Statement
Look over the notes that you grouped into categories in Exercise 9. Using the categories as a guide, write a working thesis statement for a research paper on robot sensors. Save your work for Exercise 12.

Outlining

The last step in the prewriting stage is organizing your notes into an outline that will guide your writing. The categories into which you grouped your notes will serve as the basis for the outline. Look over your notes and working thesis statement to determine the type of organization that suits your information best. *(See page 428.)* If your subject is an historical event or a process that proceeds step by step, chronological order would probably be most appropriate. If you intend to describe or analyze your subject, spatial order may be most logical. Order of importance and developmental order are probably the most common ways to organize materials in a research paper. This is because research papers are largely factual, and order of importance and developmental order are the best means of showing the relative importance and logical relationship of facts. These methods of organization can be used with a wide variety of research subjects.

24i Begin the **outline** of your research paper by deciding on a method of organization and assigning your categories Roman numerals accordingly.

The categories on computers helping the handicapped were arranged in developmental order. In the following beginning of an outline, notice that each category is phrased in a form parallel to all the others. *(See pages 390–391 on revising for parallelism.)*

I. Computers helping language-disabled people
II. Computers helping vision-disabled people
III. Computers helping motion-disabled people

As you can see, this outline does not include the categories of costs of equipment and other ways computers are helping the handicapped. The outline above represents the body of the paper only. The missing categories have been saved for the introduction and conclusion.

Once your main topics are outlined, the next step is to add subtopics (capital letters) and supporting points (Arabic numerals) to finish the plan for your paper. Your note cards will help you supply these levels of detail.

24j Use your note cards to add **subtopics** and **supporting points** to the skeleton of your outline.

The following outline on computers helping the handicapped can be used as a model for your own outline. Notice that at each level of detail, the items are listed in parallel phrasing. Notice also that the working thesis statement is written at the top of the outline.

WORKING THESIS STATEMENT — Computers are able to help people with language disabilities, vision problems, and problems of motion related to paralysis and loss of limb.

MAIN TOPIC — I. Computers helping language-disabled people

SUBTOPIC — A. Children who are slow at developing speech

SUPPORTING POINTS — 1. Computers that name objects chosen by pressing a key with a picture on it

2. Computers that synthesize speech

B. Adults suffering from a stroke or cerebral palsy who cannot speak

II. Computers helping vision-disabled people

A. Guide computers

1. Equipment involved

2. Messages blind person receives

B. Vision simulators

III. Computers helping motion-disabled people

A. Artificial limbs

B. Paralyzed limbs

When you have finished your outline, check its form by using the checklist on page 479.

EXERCISE 11 Completing an Outline

Use the following list of unsorted items to complete the outline that follows it.

List of unsorted items

- How timber operations can help
- Warbler's need for young jack pines, which can grow only when forest fires clear space for sunlight to spawn new trees
- Wildlife helped by human takeover
- Efforts to save Kirkland's warbler
- Creation of edge effect when farmers cleared land for tilling
- Adaptation of chimney swifts
- Growth of young jack pines
- Efficient fire fighting prevents growth of new jack pines
- Learned how to make nests in chimneys

Humans and Wildlife Habitats

I. Wildlife hurt by human takeover of habitat
  A. Effects of fire fighting on Kirkland's warbler
    1.
    2.
  B.
    1. Planned "forest fire" managed by humans
    2. Positive effect of heat from fire on scattering new seeds
    3.
II. Wildlife able to adapt to human takeover
  A.
    1. Used to live in hollow trees
    2.
  B. Bluebirds' adaptation to birdhouses provided by humans
III.
  A. Benefit to wildlife of the "edge effect"
    1. Difficulty of new growth in dense old forest because sunlight cannot penetrate
    2.
  B. How farmers can help
  C.

EXERCISE 12 Outlining
Using your work from Exercises 9 and 10, write a simple outline showing three main topics (Roman numerals) with at least three subtopics (capital letters) under each. Copy your working thesis statement above the outline. Check to be sure that your outline follows the correct form. Save your work for Exercise 15.

EXERCISE 13 On Your Own
Review what you have learned about prewriting on pages 573–588. Then find and limit a subject for a research paper. Use the library to gather information from at least three sources and take notes on cards from each source. Organize your information into categories. Write a working thesis statement. Then use your categories to write an outline for the body of your paper. Save your work for Exercise 20.

WRITING

After synthesizing what you have researched, you next need to present the information so that it will be clear to readers. Your main goals in writing the first draft are to flesh out your outline, adding an introduction and conclusion, and to work the information from your sources into the flow of your paper.

Writing the Thesis Statement

A clear, well-worded thesis statement will serve as a guiding beacon as you write the first draft, keeping your thoughts directed to your main idea. For this reason you should be satisfied with your thesis statement before writing the rest of your paper. Use the following guidelines to revise your working thesis statement.

24k

Guidelines for a Thesis Statement

1. A thesis statement should make the main point of your research paper clear to a reader.
2. A thesis statement should be broad enough to cover all the main topics listed in your outline.

Suppose you were researching the subject of animal camouflages and you created the following main topics.

I. Creatures with spots resembling eyes that appear threatening to would-be predators
II. Creatures with coloration that matches the environment
III. Creatures whose coloration changes with the seasons

You might have written the following working thesis statement to cover the main topics of your paper.

WORKING THESIS STATEMENT — Many creatures are colored in such a way that they blend in with the environment.

One problem with this thesis statement is that it is too narrow. It fails to include the category of creatures with eyespots, whose camouflage does not blend into the environment but instead makes the creature appear to be more threatening than it really is. A simple revision improves the thesis statement and broadens it to include all the topics.

REVISED THESIS STATEMENT — Many creatures adopt a disguise that helps protect them from predators.

EXERCISE 14 Revising Thesis Statements

Each of the following thesis statements fails to include all the main topics listed in the outline accompanying it. Rewrite each statement so that it is broad enough to cover all the main topics.

South of the Border

1. Many of Mexico's most important exports are foodstuffs.
    I. Sugar
    II. Cotton
    III. Coffee
    IV. Forestry products
2. The three climate zones of Mexico are determined by the various altitudes of the lands.
    I. Tierra fría (cold lands), above 1830 m (6,000 ft)
    II. Tierra templada (temperate lands), plateau region at 1830 m
    III. Tierra caliente (hot lands), coastal areas below 900 m (3,000 ft)
    IV. Shortage of rainfall in all climate zones except in some coastal areas
3. The Social Security System in Mexico is similar to that of the United States.
    I. Benefits for accidents and disability
    II. Retirement pensions
    III. Differences
4. The Spanish influence of Mexico was overpowering.
    I. Changes in language
    II. Changes in customs
    III. Survival of ancient Indian languages and customs in some parts of Mexico
5. The site of Mexico City is plagued with water and drainage problems.
    I. Situated on former lake; land under buildings is sinking
    II. Valley location makes waste disposal a problem
    III. High altitude makes air pollution from cars a problem

EXERCISE 15 Revising a Working Thesis Statement
Using your work from Exercise 12, revise your thesis statement if it does not cover all the main topics in your outline.

Structuring the Research Paper

With your thesis statement revised, you can move on to building the entire structure of your paper. The following shows the parts and special features of research papers.

241

The Structure of a Research Paper

PARTS	PURPOSE
TITLE	• suggests the subject of the report
INTRODUCTION	• captures attention • provides necessary background information • contains the thesis statement
BODY	• supports the thesis statement with information drawn from research • contains well-developed paragraphs
CONCLUSION	• brings report to a close by restating thesis or referring to earlier ideas with fresh emphasis
SPECIAL FEATURES	
FOOTNOTES	• give credit to other authors for words and ideas • appear at bottom of pages
BIBLIOGRAPHY	• lists sources used in preparing the report • appears at end of paper

As you work on the first draft of your paper, place a number above each line in which you have borrowed a word, idea, or fact from your sources. On a separate sheet of paper, keep track of the source and page number from which each borrowed detail is taken. In a later draft you can prepare the footnotes or endnotes and bibliography in their proper form.

Read the following sample research paper, noticing how each element fits into the whole structure and how borrowed details are worked in and cited.

TITLE

New Help for the Handicapped

INTRODUCTION: GIVES BACKGROUND INFORMATION AND LEADS UP TO THESIS STATEMENT

Time after time, computers have proved their usefulness and efficiency in business, learning, and play. For most of the population, they make ordinary tasks easier or more fun to accomplish. In the business world, the computer's ability to link up electronically with other terminals miles away has given workers a new flexibility, including the option to work at home in some cases. This option is especially important to some disabled workers, for whom commuting to an office may be difficult. At least one program, Disabled Individuals Studying Computers (DISC) in New Jersey, is training wheelchair-bound workers for careers in computers. [1] Computers, however, can do more than make the already possible task easier. For many handicapped people, computers are making the impossible possible by providing language for the speechless, vision for the sightless, and movement for victims of paralysis or loss of limb.

THESIS STATEMENT

MAIN TOPIC I FROM OUTLINE

At the Los Angeles-based Exceptional Children's Foundation, computers are being used to give youngsters who are slow at developing speech a way to communicate. For some, progress comes after using a computer that names, "in a low-pitched electronic voice," the object pictured

BORROWED WORDS IN QUOTATION MARKS

FOOTNOTES

[1] "Teaching Disabled Individuals Computer Skills," New York Times, 27 March 1983, Sec. xi, p. 3, col. 1.

on a key they press.[2] Dr. Laura Meyers, a specialist in language, theorizes that "the computer is giving [the children] control over their own meaning."[3] Once the computer has spoken for them, they find it easier to speak for themselves. Other pupils with physical disabilities that prevent them from speaking can use a speech synthesizer, a device that uses pre-programmed sound to form words chosen by the user. One child with Downs Syndrome learned 25 words in his first session with the speech synthesizer, while in the previous year he had learned only five words.[4] Adults unable to speak, especially because of a stroke or cerebral palsy, are also using speech synthesizers to recapture their previously lost ability to communicate. Most of the compact, portable speech synthesizers have only a few dozen stock words and phrases available.[5] However, more sophisticated devices that would greatly expand the communication potential of disabled persons are already being tested.

BORROWED FACT CITED WITH A NOTE

Computers are also opening new doors to

MAIN TOPIC II FROM OUTLINE

FOOTNOTES

[2] Paul Trachtman, "Putting Computers into the Hands of Children Without Language," <u>Smithsonian</u>, Feb. 1984, p. 43.

[3] As quoted in Trachtman, p. 43.

[4] Trachtman, p. 43.

[5] Doug Carr, "Computereyes," <u>Science Digest</u>, Jan. 1983, p. 68.

independence for the blind. "Seeing eye" computers are being developed that can alert a sightless person to objects in his or her path. A camera worn on the person's shoulder takes in images of objects ahead. A computer then processes these images and, with a speech generator, "talks" to the blind person. "The blind person is told what direction to take and how far away an obstacle is. The computer provides an update on landscape every 1 or 2 feet."[6] Even more sophisticated vision enhancers may also be available soon. These require the implanting of 64 electrodes into the visual center of the brain. Wires between the skull and scalp lead from these electrodes to a computer "activated by a television camera."[7] The images picked up by the camera are converted into signals for the electrodes, which act as replacement parts for the blind person's damaged visual nerves. The new electrodes send a signal to the part of the brain that interprets visual messages and re-forms images. Dr. William H. Dobelle of the Institute for Artificial Organs in New York hopes that, with even more implanted electrodes, "a blind person may be

FOOTNOTES

[6] Sandy Hintz and Martin Hintz, Computers in Our World, Today and Tomorrow (New York: Franklin Watts, 1983), p. 23.

[7] Lynne Lamburg, "Amazing Advances in Medical Technology," Better Homes and Gardens, Jan. 1984, p. 17.

able to 'see' a picture in tones of black and white."[8]

MAIN TOPIC III FROM OUTLINE

Computer-aided motion for people who have lost a limb or been paralyzed does not require the implanting of electrodes. Some advanced artificial arms are able, with a microcomputer, to pick up electrical signals from the remaining healthy nerves and transmit them into motion. A user of such a limb would simply think "pick up that book," for example, and the command, in the form of electrical signals, would reach the receiver in an artificial limb. There it would be re-processed into a command to turn on a battery powered motor that would move the appropriate joints in the limb.[9] Using a similar technique, Dr. Jerrold Petrofsky at Wright State University in Dayton, Ohio has been developing a technique to remobilize the legs of paralyzed people.[10] After the healthy nerves and muscles send their signals for movement, a computer takes over the crippled muscles and sends electrical bursts at the right time and place to get them moving. The device is clumsy and massive now and the resulting movements are jerky. The future, however, holds promise for a much smaller system

FOOTNOTES

[8] Lamburg, pp. 18-19.

[9] Lamburg, p. 15.

[10] Philip Faflick, "Power to the Disabled," <u>Time</u>, 13 December 1983, p. 77.

that can be implanted like a pacemaker and that would provide a greater variety of motions.

CONCLUSION: RESTATES THESIS

Although the costs--in time and money--of developing these technological aids for the handicapped are staggering, the rewards are difficult to dispute. As the devices become more widely available, their cost is likely to decrease. The money previously spent on long-term care and hospitalization or lost wages due to disability can be turned to further research in improving the lives of the handicapped.

Bibliography

Carr, Doug. "Computereyes." Science Digest, January 1983, p. 68.

Faflick, Philip. "Power to the Disabled." Time, 13 December 1983, pp. 76-77.

Hintz, Sandy and Martin Hintz. Computers in Our World, Today and Tomorrow. New York: Franklin Watts, 1983.

Lamburg, Lynne. "Amazing Advances in Medical Technology." Better Homes and Gardens, January 1984, pp. 15-21.

"Teaching Disabled Individuals Computer Skills". New York Times, 27 March 1983, Sec. xi, p. 3, col. 1.

Trachtman, Paul. "Putting Computers into the Hands of Children Without Language." Smithsonian, February 1984, pp. 42-51.

Transitions. Transitions will help you link sentences and paragraphs within your paper and achieve a smooth flow. They will also help your readers follow the logical progression of your thoughts.

24m

Ways to Connect Ideas

1. Use transitional words and phrases such as *first, second, most important,* and *finally. (See pages 431 and 511 for lists of transitions.)*
2. Repeat key words or phrases from earlier sentences or paragraphs.
3. Use pronouns in place of nouns used earlier.

EXERCISE 16 Recognizing Transitions
Answer the following questions about the research paper on computers and the handicapped on pages 593–597.

1. What transitional word showing contrast prepares readers for the thesis statement?
2. What key word from the thesis statement is repeated in the first sentence of the second paragraph?
3. What transitional word leads into the third paragraph?
4. What transitional phrase in the third paragraph shows the relative sophistication of the vision aid that requires the implantation of electrodes?
5. What key words used in the last sentence of the third paragraph are repeated in the first sentence of the fourth paragraph?

Using and Citing Sources

Just as products are protected by patents, the words and ideas of authors are protected by copyrights. Failure to give proper credit for borrowed words, ideas, and facts is called plagiarism, a serious and unlawful offense. All borrowings must be cited in your paper with a footnote or endnote that gives credit to the original author. In addition, a bibliography —a complete list of the sources you consulted—must appear at the end of the paper.

Using Sources. Giving due credit to sources is only one aspect of using them well. The other is working borrowed words and ideas smoothly into your own writing. Study the following five ways to work in borrowed material.

24n

Tips for Using Sources

1. Use a quotation to finish a sentence you have started.

   EXAMPLE Dr. Laura Meyers, a specialist in language, theorizes that "the computer is giving [the children] control over their own meaning."[1] (The words inside the brackets do not appear in the original. In the original, the word is *them,* which refers to *the children* mentioned earlier. To help readers understand the exact meaning, you may change the quotation slightly, putting the new word(s) in brackets.)

2. Quote a whole sentence.

   EXAMPLE "The blind person is told what direction to take and how far away an obstacle is."[2]

3. Quote just a few words.

   EXAMPLE The computer names, "in a low-pitched electronic voice," the object pictured on the key the child has pressed.[4]

4. Paraphrase and summarize information from a source. *(See Chapter 23.)*
5. Quote five or more lines from your source. (Start the quotation on a new line after skipping two lines and indenting ten spaces. Single space the quoted lines. Do not use quotation marks for such an extended quotation. Use a colon in the sentence that introduces the quotation.)

   EXAMPLE The first walk Nan Davis took since her 1978 car crash was a breakthrough in medical technology:

   > Throughout her programmed "walk" at the Wright State biomedical engineering lab, Davis was bolstered by props. She was strapped to a parachute that supported a third of her 130 pounds and she gripped a pair of parallel bars as her legs stepped ahead . . .[3]

EXERCISE 17 Using Sources
Read the following article about continental drift. Use it as a source to complete the assignment that follows it.

Catching the Drift

The longer you wait to take that trip to Europe, the farther you'll have to go. Researchers at the National Aeronautics and Space Administration say that the continents of Europe and North America may be drifting apart at the rate of as much as two-thirds of an inch a year.

"Not only that," says Goddard Space Flight Center geophysicist David Smith, "but Peru moved two inches away from Hawaii in 1983, while Australia drifted two inches toward it." Smith and his colleagues have been collecting data from laser tracking stations located all over the world. The stations shoot a beam of laser light at a satellite as it flies overhead. The satellite is studded with hundreds of mirrors that are constructed in such a way that they reflect a light beam back at its source. By accurately calculating the orbit of the satellite and timing the laser beam's trip to the satellite and back, Smith and other geophysicists can map the positions of the tracking stations on the Earth to within nearly an inch. The scientists get similar results by clocking radio waves from space as they arrive at various points on Earth.

The research is the first direct measurement of the rate of continental drift. According to the theory of plate tectonics, already widely accepted among geologists on the basis of other geological evidence, the continents and ocean floors are not firmly rooted on the Earth but rather are part of large plates that "float" on the Earth's mantle. As the plates drift and slide into each other they are deformed, creating mountain ranges and deep sea trenches and causing earthquakes along the fault lines where the two plates meet. At one potential earthquake zone, California's San Andreas fault, tracking stations on either side of the fault moved nearly three inches in one year. —*Science '84*

1. Write a sentence about the drifts of Europe and North America. End your sentence with a quotation.
2. Write three sentences describing how the laser measurements are taken. One sentence should be a direct quotation.
3. Write a paragraph about continental drift and the theory of plate tectonics. Include an extended quotation of at least

five lines. Be sure to indent and space the quoted lines correctly. Remember that quotation marks are not necessary.

4. Write a sentence about land drifting toward and away from Hawaii that quotes just a few words from the source.
5. Write a paraphrase of the last sentence.

Citing Sources. The notes that show the original sources of borrowed words or ideas are called citations. There are three different types of citations.

Types of Citation

FOOTNOTES	apear at bottom of page.
ENDNOTES	appear on a separate sheet at end of paper, after the conclusion but before the bibliography.
PARENTHETICAL CITATIONS	appear within parentheses directly following the borrowed material in the paper itself.

24o Cite the sources of information you include in your research paper by using **footnotes, endnotes,** or **parenthetical citations.** Use only one type consistently in the paper.

When in doubt about which information requires a citation, use the following guidelines.

24p **Citing Sources**

1. Cite the source of a direct quotation. Use direct quotations only when the author's original wording makes the point more clearly than you could by using your own words.
2. Cite the sources of ideas you gained from research, even though you express the ideas in your own words.
3. Cite the sources of figures and statistics you use.
4. Do not cite facts or ideas that are common knowledge.

The correct form for footnotes and endnotes is essentially the same. Both use a *superscript,* a number above the line in the text, to refer readers to the footnote or endnote with the same number. The superscript comes immediately after the borrowed material. Parenthetical citations do not require a superscript, but they do require the same three pieces of information used in all citations. Provided to help readers locate the original source, the three essential pieces of information are the author and title, publication information, and page number.

The examples below show the correct form for footnotes and endnotes. The only difference in the form of footnotes and endnotes is that footnotes are single-spaced (with a double-space between each footnote), while endnotes are double-spaced.

Correct Form for Footnotes and Endnotes

GENERAL REFERENCE WORKS
[1] George Epstein, "Computer," World Book Encyclopedia, 1983 ed.

BOOKS WITH A SINGLE AUTHOR
[2] Patrick Henry Winston, Artificial Intelligence, 2nd ed. (Menlo Park: Addison-Wesley, 1984), p. 3.

BOOKS WITH MORE THAN ONE AUTHOR
[3] Sandy Hintz and Martin Hintz, Computers in Our World, Today and Tomorrow (New York: Franklin Watts, 1983), p. 23.

ARTICLES IN MAGAZINES
[4] Doug Carr, "Computereyes," Science Digest, Jan. 1983, p. 68.

ARTICLES IN NEWSPAPERS
[5] "Teaching Disabled Individuals Computer Skills," New York Times, 27 March 1983, Sec. 11, p. 3, col. 1.

INTERVIEWS
[6] Personal interview [*or* Telephone interview] with Dr. Michelle Harper, ophthamologist, Roseville Hospital, Milwaukee, Wisconsin, 31 August 1984.

Notice that if the author of an article is not given, the footnote begins with the title of the article. (See number 5 above.) For repeated references to a work already cited, you can use a shortened form of footnote. The author's last name and the page number are enough to refer to a work already cited in full. If you have cited more than one work by the author, include the title in the shortened footnote.

REPEATED REFERENCES	[1] Lamburg, p. 15 [2] Winston, "The MIT Robot," p. 53.

Sources cited in notes or mentioned in the research paper must also be listed in a bibliography.

24q A **bibliography** is an alphabetical listing of sources used in a research paper. It appears at the end of the paper.

Bibliography entries differ from footnotes in four main ways: (1) The first line is not indented, but the other lines are. (2) The author's last name is listed first. (3) Periods are used in place of commas, and parentheses are deleted. (4) No specific page reference is necessary.

The following examples show the correct form for bibliography entries. They would be listed in alphabetical order (according to the first word of the entry) on a separate page at the end of your research paper. There is a double-space within and between each entry in a bibliography for a research paper.

Correct Form for a Bibliography

GENERAL REFERENCE WORKS	Epstein, George. "Computer." World Book Encyclopedia. 1983 ed.
BOOKS WITH A SINGLE AUTHOR	Winston, Patrick Henry. Artificial Intelligence. 2nd ed. Menlo Park: Addison-Wesley, 1984.
BOOKS WITH MORE THAN ONE AUTHOR	Hintz, Sandy and Martin Hintz. Computers in Our World, Today and Tomorrow. New York: Franklin Watts, 1983.
ARTICLES IN MAGAZINES	Carr, Doug. "Computereyes." Science Digest, Jan. 1983, p. 68.
ARTICLES IN NEWSPAPERS	"Teaching Disabled Individuals Computer Skills." New York Times, 27 March 1983, Sec. 11, p. 3, col. 1.
INTERVIEWS	Harper, Michelle. Telephone interview. 31 August, 1984.

Additional examples of footnotes and other guidelines for citing sources when writing a research paper are included in the Appendix on pages 663–665.

EXERCISE 18 Preparing Footnotes
Use the information in each item to write a footnote for the source. Use the model footnotes on page 602 as a guide.

1. Title of newspaper article: Engineers Fight the Mississippi's Sense of Direction
   Date of newspaper: August 30, 1984
   Location of article: Section 1A, p. 36, col. 1
   Name of newspaper: Chicago Tribune
2. Title of book: Mighty Mississippi: Biography of a River
   Publishing Company: Ticknor and Fields
   Author: Marquis W. Childs
   Place of Publication: New Haven
   Page number: 72
   Date of publication: 1982
3. Title of article in encyclopedia: Mississippi River
   Edition of encyclopedia: 1980
   Author of article: Johnson E. Fairchild
   Name of encyclopedia: Collier's Encyclopedia
4. Name of magazine: National Geographic
   Page number: 227
   Author of magazine article: Douglas Lee
   Title of article: Mississippi Delta: The Land of the River
   Date of magazine: August 1983
5. Author of magazine article: Susan Tiftt
   Date of magazine: January 23, 1984
   Page number: 19
   Name of magazine: Time
   Title of article: Going with the Floe

EXERCISE 19 Preparing a Bibliography
Use the information from Exercise 18 to prepare a bibliography for a research paper on the Mississippi River. Remember to alphabetize the entries and follow the format shown in the examples on page 603.

EXERCISE 20 On Your Own
Review what you have learned about writing the first draft of a report on pages 590–603. Use your outline from Exercise 13 to revise your working thesis statement as needed. Then write the first draft of a research paper, being sure to use and cite sources accurately. Save your work for Exercise 21.

REVISING

The following checklist will help you revise your report.

24r

Revision Checklist

Checking Your Research Paper

1. Does your introduction contain a well-worded thesis statement? *(See pages 590–591.)*
2. Does the body of your research paper support the thesis statement?
3. Did you use and cite sources correctly? *(See page 598.)*
4. Did you use transitional devices? *(See page 598.)*
5. Does your report have unity, coherence, and emphasis? *(See page 490.)*
6. Does your conclusion add a strong ending?
7. Does your report have a title?

Checking Your Paragraphs

8. Does each paragraph have a topic sentence? *(See page 451.)*
9. Is each paragraph unified and coherent? *(See pages 425–431.)*
10. Does one paragraph lead smoothly into the next?

Checking Your Sentences and Words

11. Are your sentences varied? *(See pages 377–383.)*
12. Are your sentences concise? *(See pages 373–376.)*
13. Did you avoid faulty sentences? *(See pages 385–392.)*
14. Did you use specific words with appropriate connotations? *(See pages 367–369.)*

EXERCISE 21 On Your Own
Using the Revision Checklist, revise the research paper you wrote for Exercise 20. Save your paper for Exercise 22.

EDITING

Using sources requires special care in the editing process. The following checklist will help you polish your research paper. You may wish to use the proofreading symbols on page 662 when you edit.

24s

Editing Checklist

1. Are your sentences free of errors in grammar and usage?
2. Did you spell each word correctly?
3. Did you capitalize and punctuate correctly?
4. If you quoted a source, did you use the exact words, just as the author wrote them? Did you put them in quotation marks? *(See pages 281–282.)*
5. Does your footnote or endnote form match the models on page 602?
6. Does your bibliography form match the model bibliography on page 603?
7. Did you use manuscript form? *(See pages 659–660.)*
8. Is your handwriting or typing neat and clear?

EXERCISE 22 On Your Own
Using the Editing Checklist, edit your research paper from Exercise 21.

CHAPTER REVIEW

Using what you have learned about prewriting, writing, revising, and editing, write a report on one of the following subjects or on one of your own choosing. Use the Steps for Writing Research Papers on page 607 as a guide.

1. underwater photography
2. acupuncture
3. the history of humane societies
4. the Everglades
5. the importance of the Dred Scott Supreme Court case
6. training for a career in military service
7. King Arthur: legend or fact?
8. electric cars
9. early Norse explorers in North America
10. the Prairie School of architecture
11. the personality of Abraham Lincoln
12. coastal ecology
13. the Concorde, a supersonic passenger jet
14. guide dogs for the blind
15. the cause of the northern lights

Steps for Writing

Research Papers

✓ **Prewriting**

1. After listing possible subjects, choose one and limit it. *(See pages 574–576.)*
2. Make a list of questions to guide your research. *(See pages 576–577.)*
3. Gather information from books, magazines, newspapers, and interviews with experts. *(See page 577.)*
4. Use note cards for taking notes and summarizing your sources. *(See pages 581–583.)*
5. Organize your notes by finding categories. *(See pages 584–585.)*
6. Write a working thesis statement. *(See page 585.)*
7. Use your working thesis statement and note categories to outline the body of your research paper. *(See pages 586–589.)*

✓ **Writing**

8. Revise your working thesis statement as needed. *(See page 590.)*
9. Write your first draft, including an introduction, body, and conclusion. *(See pages 592–598.)*
10. Avoid plagiarism by using and citing sources carefully. *(See pages 598–603.)*
11. Add a title.

✓ **Revising**

12. Using the Revision Checklist, check your report for structure, well-developed paragraphs, unity, coherence, emphasis, and varied and lively sentences and words. *(See page 605.)*

✓ **Editing**

13. Using the Editing Checklist, check your grammar, spelling, mechanics, manuscript form, and footnote and bibliography form. *(See page 606.)*

25

Business Letters

The ability to write clear, direct business letters is a useful skill to have no matter what your future plans include. As a consumer, you may need to write a letter ordering merchandise or registering a complaint about a product or service. If you plan to attend college, you can use the business-letter form to request catalogs from various schools and to apply for admission. If you plan to enter the business world, you will need to write letters of application as well as regular business correspondence once you begin working. In this chapter you will learn the correct form for business letters and some tips for writing them effectively.

USING THE CORRECT FORM

Since a business letter represents you, it should present a neat appearance. A neat letter, free from errors, assures that your message will be understood.

Tips for Neatness in Business Letters

1. Use white paper, preferably $8\frac{1}{2}$ by 11 inches in size.
2. Leave margins at least one-inch wide.
3. Type whenever possible.
4. If you type your letter, type your envelope.
5. Fold your letter neatly to fit into the envelope.

Modified block and block are two styles considered to be correct form for writing business letters. Notice that each one has the same six parts.

Modified Block Style

heading — 222 Jackson Street
Glendon, NC 27251
August 13, 1986

inside address — Consumer Response
Hecht's Camping Goods
3114 Radcliffe Road
Worthington, KY 41183

salutation — Dear Sir or Madam:

body — ____________________

closing — Yours truly,

signature — Carol Brien
Carol Brien

Block Style

heading	222 Jackson Street Glendon, NC 27251 August 13, 1986
inside address	Consumer Response Hecht's Camping Goods 3114 Radcliffe Road Worthington, KY 41183
salutation	Dear Sir or Madam:
body	______________________
closing	Yours truly,
signature	Carol Brien Carol Brien

Sample Envelope

Carol Brien
222 Jackson Street
Glendon, NC 27251

Consumer Response
Hecht's Camping Goods
3114 Radcliffe Road
Worthington, KY 41183

25a The parts of a business letter are the **heading, inside address, salutation, body, closing,** and **signature.**

Use the following checklist to make sure each part of the letter is correct.

HEADING Write your full address, including the ZIP code. Write the name of your state in full or use the two-letter postal code. *(See page 612 for a full listing.)* Write the date.

INSIDE ADDRESS Write the receiver's address two to four lines below the heading. Include the name of the person if you know it, using *Mr., Ms., Mrs., Dr.,* or other title. If the person has a business title, such as *Manager,* write it on the next line. Use the same way of identifying the state as you used in the heading.

SALUTATION Start two lines below the inside address. Use *Dear Sir or Madam* if you do not know the name. Otherwise, use the person's last name preceded by *Mr., Ms., Mrs.,* or other title. Use a colon after the salutation.

BODY Start two lines below the salutation. Double-space a single paragraph. For longer letters single-space each paragraph, skipping a line between paragraphs.

CLOSING Start two or three lines below the body. Use a formal closing such as *Sincerely, Sincerely yours,* or *Yours truly,* followed by a comma.

SIGNATURE Type (or print, if your letter is handwritten) your name four or five lines below the closing. Then sign your name in the space between the closing and your typed or printed name.

Your teacher or employer will tell you which style of business letter to use. Although business letters differ slightly in form, they all contain the six basic parts. As long as one style is used throughout, the letter will look neat and professional. (All sample letters in this chapter use the modified block style.)

Keep a copy of each business letter you send. You can make a copy with carbon paper or use a copying machine.

Postal Codes. Use the following state abbreviations in your business letters.

Postal Codes

State	Code	State	Code
Alabama	AL	Montana	MT
Alaska	AK	Nebraska	NE
Arizona	AZ	Nevada	NV
Arkansas	AR	New Hampshire	NH
California	CA	New Jersey	NJ
Colorado	CO	New Mexico	NM
Connecticut	CT	New York	NY
Delaware	DE	North Carolina	NC
District of Columbia	DC	North Dakota	ND
Florida	FL	Ohio	OH
Georgia	GA	Oklahoma	OK
Hawaii	HI	Oregon	OR
Idaho	ID	Pennsylvania	PA
Illinois	IL	Puerto Rico	PR
Indiana	IN	Rhode Island	RI
Iowa	IA	South Carolina	SC
Kansas	KS	South Dakota	SD
Kentucky	KY	Tennessee	TN
Louisiana	LA	Texas	TX
Maine	ME	Utah	UT
Maryland	MD	Vermont	VT
Massachusetts	MA	Virginia	VA
Michigan	MI	Washington	WA
Minnesota	MN	West Virginia	WV
Mississippi	MS	Wisconsin	WI
Missouri	MO	Wyoming	WY

TYPES OF BUSINESS LETTERS

Business letters are written for many purposes. Four common purposes are to request information, to order merchandise, to register a complaint, and to apply for a job.

25b Use business-letter form for letters of request, order letters, letters of complaint, and application letters.

Letters of Request

When you write a letter of request, be as direct and clear as possible and keep your message brief. Always remember to proofread your letter before mailing it. The following example shows how to request information in a business letter.

Letter of Request

2119 Hillside Street
New Tazewell, TN 37825
October 14, 1986

Executive Director
Guide Dogs for the Blind, Inc.
P.O. Box 1200
San Rafael, CA 94902

Dear Sir or Madam:

I am eighteen years old and have been blind since the age of 11. I will be going to college next year, and I would like to obtain a guide dog.

Please send me information about how to get a dog and how much time it is likely to take to obtain one. I would also like to know about the training the dog received and the training I must have to work successfully with it. If there is a cost involved, please inform me about that also.

Thank you very much.

Sincerely,

Thomas Daniels

Thomas Daniels

EXERCISE 1 Writing a Letter of Request
Write a letter of request to your local public broadcasting station. Request information about how the station chooses the programs it televises. Use the modified block style.

Order Letters

If the catalog or advertisement from which you are ordering merchandise does not include an order blank, use the business letter to place your order. To make sure that you receive exactly what you want, be sure to include the order number, price, quantity, size, and color of the item. If you are sending a check or money order (never send cash), state the amount you have enclosed. Be sure to include any shipping and handling charges in the total.

Order Letter

1711 Maplewood
Evanston, Illinois 60201
March 17, 1986

Dan's Fishing Supplies
R.R. 135
Trout Creek, Montana 59874

Dear Sir or Madam:

Please send me the following items from your Spring 1986 catalog.

1 pair wading boots, # 32-A	$16.00
1 fly-tying kit, # 47-B	$ 8.50
shipping and handling	$ 2.00
	$26.50

A check for $26.50 is enclosed.

Sincerely,

Don Caldwell

Don Caldwell

Letters of Complaint

If a product or service fails to measure up to its promise, you can write a letter of complaint to try to remedy the problem. Most companies stand behind their goods and services and are willing to make suitable adjustments if there is a problem. If you write your letter as soon as you become aware of the problem and if your letter is reasonable and polite, chances are it will bring the desired results. Notice how the following letter of complaint offers a reasonable solution.

Letter of Complaint

4544 Canyon Drive
Reno, Nevada 89543
June 11, 1986

Adjustments
Keynote Stationers
435 Pine Street
Salt Lake City, Utah 84137

Dear Sir or Madam:

In a letter dated May 15, I ordered several items from your catalog, including a Norman Rockwell poster. On June 9 I received the other merchandise in the mail, but the poster was not in the package. Since I have paid in full for the poster, I request an explanation of the missing merchandise as soon as possible. I am enclosing a copy of the packing slip which shows that the poster was not included. If for some reason the poster is no longer available, please return my money. Thank you very much.

Sincerely,

Susan Lee

Susan Lee

EXERCISE 2 Writing an Order Letter
Use the following information to order merchandise from a catalog. Unscramble the information in the inside address and write it in the proper order. Use your own name and address and today's date. Add $2.00 for shipping and handling. Use the modified block style.

INSIDE ADDRESS	Rutger's Music Store, Order Department, Ramsey, New Jersey, 07446, 465 Washington Street.
MERCHANDISE	sheet music for piano and voice for *Folk Songs* by Luciano Berio ($2.50)
	2 spiral-bound music notebooks, #357-33 ($1.95 each)
	1 Patriot harmonica (in the key of G), #471-12, red ($5.95)

EXERCISE 3 Writing a Letter of Complaint
Using the information from Exercise 2, write a letter of complaint to Rutger's Music Store because you did not receive the Patriot harmonica with the rest of your order. Be sure that the tone of your letter is polite and that the solution you offer is reasonable. Use your own name and address and today's date.

Writing Extra

You can use the business letter to express an opinion in a newspaper or magazine. Most periodicals have a "Letters to the Editor" page in which they print letters sent in by readers. The majority of the letters published comment on a recent article in the periodical. Readers can also, however, offer suggestions about future articles the magazine should include.

EXERCISE 4 Writing a Letter to a Newspaper or Magazine
Choose a recent issue of a newspaper or magazine and read it carefully. Write a letter to the editor that either expresses your opinion on an article or that recommends a topic to be covered in future issues. Find the address of the periodical on the first page or inside cover.

Application Letters

When you send a letter of application, you are asking the receiver to judge you favorably for a position in a school or place of employment. A letter of application should be neat and carefully worded. It will be the first impression the director of admissions or an employer will have of you.

If you are applying for a job, be sure to enclose a résumé. *(See pages 682–683.)* Attach a cover letter that introduces you to your prospective employer by highlighting those parts of your background, interests, and hobbies that relate to the job.

Letter of Application for Employment

362 Raintree Drive
Madison, WI 53713
June 4, 1986

Janet Redsky
Personnel Director
Lake of the Woods Camp
Manitowish Waters, WI 54545

Dear Ms. Redsky:

I am writing to apply for the position of Counselor advertised in The Gazette on May 30. The enclosed résumé summarizes my background and experience in working with children and in teaching water safety. My previous work at Camp Pinewood and my lifesaving certification show I am well qualified for the position you seek to fill.

I intend to enter the field of physical education in college, and the job as counselor would provide me a good opportunity to broaden my experience. Since school does not begin until late September, I am available all summer for the position at Lake of the Woods Camp.

I look forward to meeting you in person soon.

Sincerely,

Jesse Long

Jesse Long

A letter of application to a college, university, or trade school resembles a letter of request. In addition to requesting specific information about the courses of study, also request an application form.

Letter of Application to a School

5324 S. Harper
Indianapolis, IN 46231
September 7, 1986

Director of Admissions
Bowman Technical School
3657 Prairie Drive
Indianapolis, IN 46219

Dear Sir or Madam:

I wish to apply for admission to your school in the fall of 1987. I would like to pursue training in electrical engineering.

Please send me a catalog and schedule of classes, information on financial aid, and any special materials or brochures yuou have on your program in electronics. Also, please send me an application form if one is required.

Thank you very much.

Sincerely,

Cary Silver

Cary Silver

EXERCISE 5 Writing a Letter of Application for a Job
Write a letter answering the following job notice from your school bulletin board. Use the letter on page 617 as a model.

WANTED: Sales Clerk for Museum Gift Shop
The Museum of Natural History seeks a full-time sales clerk to work in the gift shop selling and pricing merchandise. Hours include one evening a week and Saturdays. No experience necessary, but pleasant outgoing personality desired. Send résumé and cover letter to Carl Heinz, Gift Shop, Museum of Natural History, Los Angeles, California 90003.

EXERCISE 6 Writing a Letter of Application to a School
Write a letter to a school, college, or university. Request a catalog, information about tuition and financial aid, and an application form. Address the letter to Undergraduate Admissions.

EXERCISE 7 On Your Own
Write a letter to one of the following television networks expressing your views about one of their shows.

American Broadcasting Company (ABC)
1330 Avenue of the Americas
New York, NY 10019

Columbia Broadcasting System (CBS)
51 W. 52nd Street
New York, NY 10019

National Broadcasting Company (NBC)
30 Rockefeller Plaza
New York, NY 10020

CHAPTER REVIEW

Use the address below to write each letter described. Use the Steps for Writing Business Letters on page 620.

Landmark Book Store
227 Live Oak Street
New Orleans, LA 70144

1. Write a letter requesting information about the historical significance of the building in which the store operates.
2. Write a letter ordering the following items from the Landmark catalog: 4 Landmark Bookmarks, #32, $ .75 each
   1 copy of Herman Melville's *Typee* #98702, paperback, $3.50
   Include $1.00 for shipping and handling.
3. Write a letter of complaint when the bookmarks do not arrive with the copy of *Typee.*
4. Write a letter applying for a job as a clerk at the bookstore.

Steps for Writing

Business Letters

1. Gather the information you need to explain your request, order, complaint, or application accurately.
2. Follow the Tips for Neatness on page 609.
3. Use the proper form for the heading, inside address, and salutation. *(See pages 609–611.)*
4. Express your message briefly and courteously, following the correct form for the body of the letter. *(See pages 609–611.)*
5. Use the correct form for the closing and signature. *(See pages 609–611.)*
6. Check your letter for errors in grammar, usage, spelling, and mechanics.
7. Keep a copy of your letter.
8. Address the envelope correctly. *(See page 610.)*

STANDARDIZED TEST

COMPOSITION

Directions: Decide which description below best fits each sentence. Fill in the circle containing the letter

A if the sentence contains a word with the wrong connotation
B if the sentence contains a cliché
C if the sentence is not concise
D if the sentence contains faulty coordination, faulty subordination, or faulty parallelism
E if the sentence contains none of the above

SAMPLE It seems as if the sky is clearing at last.

ANSWER Ⓐ Ⓑ ● Ⓓ Ⓔ

1. Our power went off, for we sat in the dark.
2. The fact is that Morocco is approximately the size of California.
3. Beneath Morgan's rough exterior beats a heart of gold.
4. Doreen, usually as meek as a lamb, astonished the others with her fiery words.
5. An acre was originally the area a yoke of oxen could plow in one day.
6. German, French, and Italian are all spoken in Switzerland; furthermore, German is used by 65 percent of the people.
7. The islands of Trinidad and Tobago, which lie off the northeast coast of Venezuela, formed a republic in 1976.
8. Ms. Holden grinned politely as each guest was introduced.
9. The layer of atmosphere that envelops the earth all around stretches several hundred miles into space.
10. The earth's atmosphere is far denser at sea level than when one is in space.
11. Working like a dog for two straight weeks, Mr. Kim was able to repair the roof before the first snowfall.
12. The striking originality, wit, and logic in Barbara's report on the election once again demonstrated her slyness.
13. As far as the senator is concerned, he is of the opinion that the current talk of a tax cut is premature.
14. Oriental rug experts can usually identify the source of a rug from its weave and design.
15. Because the porcelain figure was weak as well as valuable, it was kept inside a locked glass cabinet.

Directions: Reword each sentence as directed and make any other changes required by the revision. Then choose the phrase that must be included in the revised sentence. Fill in the circle containing the letter of your answer.

SAMPLE It was a time for acting, not deliberating. Change *acting* to *to act*

A not deliberation **C** not for deliberating
B not to deliberate **D** not for deliberation

ANSWER Ⓐ ● Ⓒ Ⓓ

16. Fish have vertical tails. Whales have horizontal tails. Begin with *While*

    A tails, whales **C** tails, but whales
    B tails; whales **D** tails; however, whales

17. We saw the town from above. It looked small and vulnerable. Change *We saw the town* to *Seen*

    A from above. It **C** from above. We
    B from above, we **D** from above, the town

18. Slowly it was realized by Ken that he had found the answer. Change *it was realized* to *realized*

    A Slowly there was **C** Slowly Ken
    B It was Ken who slowly **D** Ken realized that slowly

19. Wishing for success is childish; working for it is mature. Change *Wishing* to *Ramona asserted that to wish*

    A childish, but working **C** childish, but to work
    B childish; however working **D** childish, to work

20. It was the sudden rise in temperature inside the spacecraft that convinced the scientists of the need for further tests. Begin with *The sudden rise*

    A spacecraft; it **C** spacecraft, and it
    B spacecraft convinced **D** spacecraft, convincing

Unit 7

Test Taking

26

Standardized Tests

Whatever your plans for the future—education, career, or military service—you are likely to have to take a standardized test. Standardized tests are designed to measure your abilities, skills, progress, and achievement.

The best way to prepare for a standardized test, as for any other test, is to work conscientiously on all classwork, to read widely, and to become familiar with standard testing formats. This chapter provides practice in taking such tests and advice on answering the kinds of questions you will encounter.

Strategies for Taking Standardized Tests

1. Read the test directions carefully. Answer sample questions to be sure you understand what the test requires.
2. Relax. Although you can expect to be a little nervous, concentrate on doing the best you can.
3. Preview the whole test by quickly skimming. This will give you an overview of the kinds of questions on the test.
4. Plan your time carefully, allotting a certain amount of time to each part of the test.
5. Answer first the questions you find easiest. Skip those you find too hard, coming back to them later if you have time.
6. Read all choices before you choose the best answer. If you are not sure of the answer, eliminate any choices that are obviously wrong. Making an educated guess is generally wise.
7. If you have time, check your answers. Look for omissions and careless errors on your answer sheet.

VOCABULARY TESTS

A standardized vocabulary test measures your knowledge of words and how they are used in sentences. Vocabulary questions come in many forms. A synonym question asks you to find a word similar in meaning to another word. An antonym question asks you to locate a word opposite in meaning to another word. An analogy question requires that you figure out a relationship between two sets of paired words. A sentence-completion question asks you to fill in a blank with a word that makes the best sense in the context of the sentence.

Synonyms and Antonyms

Two of the most common kinds of vocabulary questions are the synonym and antonym questions. Sometimes synonym questions are mixed with antonym questions on the same test, requiring you to decide whether a synonym or an antonym is the appropriate answer.

Synonym questions require you to recognize words that are nearly the same in meaning, such as *renown* and *fame*. Antonym questions require you to recognize words that are most nearly opposite in meaning, such as *harmony* and *discord*. On both synonym and antonym questions, you must find a word or a group of words that is most nearly the same or most nearly the opposite in meaning to a word in capital letters.

Try to find a synonym for *surmise* among the list of choices in the following synonym question.

SURMISE (A) guess (B) demand (C) relieve
(D) astonish (E) prove

The answer is *guess*. No other choice is acceptable. Neither *demand* nor *relieve* is a synonym for *guess*. *Astonish* might mislead you into mistaking the word *surmise* for *surprise*. *Prove* is nearly the opposite, not the same, in meaning to *surmise*.

Now try to find an antonym for *preceding* among the list of choices in the following antonym question.

PRECEDING (A) postponing (B) arriving
(C) previous (D) following (E) denying

If you chose *following,* you are correct. With antonym and synonym questions, you must pay close attention to the directions and then check your answers. It is all too easy to choose a synonym—*previous,* in this case—when you are working on an antonym test, or an antonym on a synonym test.

Some questions ask you to find *either* a synonym *or* an antonym among the list of choices. Keep in mind that there is only *one* correct answer. Before you make your final selection, skim the list of choices for a synonym, then for an antonym, for the word in capital letters.

In the following question, look for a word that is *either* a synonym *or* an antonym for *impede.* Use the same strategies you would use to answer a synonym or an antonym question.

IMPEDE (A) cover (B) excavate (C) suggest
(D) find (E) hinder

If you chose *hinder,* a synonym for *impede,* you are correct.

Always consider every choice carefully. Eliminate the choices that are clearly incorrect. If you do not know the exact meaning of a particular word, look for clues to its meaning in a prefix, a root, or a suffix.

EXERCISE 1 Recognizing Antonyms

Write the letter of the word most nearly opposite in meaning to the word in capital letters.

1. ORNATE (A) attractive (B) fancy (C) colorful
(D) plain (E) delicious
2. COMPASSION (A) cruelty (B) foolishness
(C) mischief (D) grief (E) generosity
3. SKEPTIC (A) truant (B) believer (C) victim
(D) adventurer (E) nonconformist
4. PLACID (A) icy (B) turbulent (C) waterlogged
(D) gullible (E) undecided
5. NOVICE (A) doubter (B) traveler (C) performer
(D) coward (E) expert
6. SOCIABLE (A) antagonistic (B) coordinated
(C) charming (D) forgetful (E) sympathetic
7. DORMANT (A) romantic (B) prejudiced
(C) literal (D) active (E) painful

8. PARDON (A) annoy (B) discuss (C) accuse (D) refuse (E) release
9. MOROSE (A) dull (B) cheerful (C) innocent (D) active (E) gloomy
10. PUTRID (A) grim (B) unobtainable (C) fresh (D) positive (E) snowy
11. BOLDNESS (A) loudness (B) bravery (C) familiarity (D) strength (E) timidity
12. CAREFUL (A) honorable (B) indifferent (C) untrue (D) humble (E) cautious
13. CREDIBLE (A) brutal (B) unbelievable (C) desirable (D) invisible (E) trustworthy
14. INCESSANT (A) intermittent (B) immoral (C) serious (D) delightful (E) grating
15. PRUDENT (A) unyielding (B) discreet (C) foolish (D) forgotten (E) specific
16. BENIGN (A) famous (B) happy (C) precise (D) counterfeit (E) malignant
17. INACTIVE (A) passive (B) disorganized (C) animated (D) traditional (E) negative
18. AMBIGUOUS (A) white (B) sneaking (C) brave (D) obvious (E) disinterested
19. TRANSITORY (A) lighthearted (B) lost (C) enduring (D) emotional (E) productive
20. IMPROMPTU (A) rehearsed (B) delayed (C) forgotten (D) rational (E) frightening

EXERCISE 2 Recognizing Synonyms and Antonyms
Write the letter of the word most nearly the same *or* most nearly the opposite in meaning to the word in capital letters.

1. SHORTEN (A) demand (B) listen (C) prolong (D) ensure (E) understand
2. WAN (A) pale (B) triumphant (C) spectacular (D) cool (E) disillusioned
3. ERRONEOUS (A) offensive (B) correct (C) wealthy (D) patient (E) temporary
4. COMPONENT (A) number (B) machine (C) formula (D) element (E) supporter
5. VOUCH (A) verify (B) disregard (C) argue (D) exasperate (E) measure

6. AVID (A) angry (B) handsome (C) honest (D) indifferent (E) dutiful
7. AFFINITY (A) crookedness (B) deterioration (C) attraction (D) truthfulness (E) purity
8. MORTIFY (A) stumble (B) puzzle (C) encounter (D) bury (E) humiliate
9. IMPROVISE (A) exaggerate (B) improve (C) admit (D) invent (E) debate
10. PAUCITY (A) abundance (B) courage (C) dryness (D) villainy (E) perfection
11. CONTEMPTUOUS (A) clever (B) precious (C) modern (D) gleeful (E) respectful
12. OPPORTUNE (A) insignificant (B) wealthy (C) inappropriate (D) swift (E) brief
13. VELOCITY (A) dignity (B) speed (C) accuracy (D) eccentricity (E) power
14. AVERSION (A) poetry (B) loss (C) dislike (D) retreat (E) confession
15. FEIGN (A) swoon (B) pretend (C) defeat (D) inspire (E) lessen
16. EXASPERATED (A) regretful (B) annoyed (C) dull (D) deadly (E) legitimate
17. VALID (A) elected (B) comfortable (C) brilliant (D) rational (E) unsound
18. SUCCUMB (A) arrive (B) swell (C) ratify (D) explain (E) yield
19. COVERT (A) friendly (B) forewarned (C) stolen (D) secret (E) revived
20. UNCERTAINTY (A) equality (B) division (C) hesitancy (D) security (E) agreement

Analogies

Analogy questions test your skill at figuring out word relationships. Your first step is to decide how the first two words are related. In the analogy *spine:vertebra,* for example, the relationship is whole-to-part. Your next step is to find the pair among the choices that shows the same kind of relationship as that of the first pair. Find the answer below.

SPINE:VERTEBRA:: (A) author:story (B) top:bottom (C) state:city (D) joke:laughter (E) handle:mug

The answer is *state : city* because it contains the only whole-to-part relationship among the choices. The other choices are incorrect. The relationship of *author : story* is worker-to-product, not whole-to-part. *Top : bottom* is a word-to-antonym relationship, and *handle : mug* is a part-to-whole relationship. *Joke : laughter* is a cause-to-effect relationship.

Sometimes analogies are written in sentence form and require you to select the word that best completes the analogy. Following is an example of such an analogy.

Decipher is to *decode* as *proclaim* is to ____.
(A) influence (B) acknowledge (C) announce
(D) annoy (E) encode

The first two italicized words, *decipher* and *decode,* are synonyms. Therefore, the correct answer must be a synonym for *proclaim*—that is, *announce. Encode* may seem closer in meaning to *decipher* and *decode* than *announce* does, but that is not the point. In an analogy question, only the relationship of words—the word-to-synonym aspect, in this case—is important.

The word order must be the same in the answer as it is in the main pair. If the word order is reversed, as in *(E) handle : mug* in the *spine : vertebra* analogy, the analogy is wrong.

Remember that many words have more than one meaning. Carefully consider the various meanings. In addition, knowing some common types of analogies, such as those in the chart below, will help you figure out word relationships.

Common Types of Analogies

Analogy	Example
word : synonym	evade : escape
word : antonym	feasible : impossible
part : whole	caboose : train
cause : effect	exercise : fitness
worker : tool	mason : trowel
worker : product	publisher : magazine
item : purpose	bus : transport
item : category	architecture : profession

EXERCISE 3 Verbal Analogies

Write the letter of the word that is related to the *third* italicized word in the same way that the second word is related to the first.

EXAMPLE *Plumber* is to *wrench* as *architect* is to ____.
(A) symmetry (B) builder (C) blueprint
(D) office (E) easel

ANSWER (C)

1. *Purpose* is to *intention* as *surplus* is to ____.
(A) excess (B) equipment (C) storage
(D) discussion (E) determination
2. *Heat* is to *expansion* as *wind* is to ____.
(A) erosion (B) donation (C) dismissal (D) breeze
(E) temperature
3. *Talent* is to *achievement* as *genius* is to ____.
(A) innovation (B) prodigy (C) underachievement
(D) shrewdness (E) failure
4. *House* is to *frame* as *body* is to ____.
(A) skin (B) torso (C) muscle (D) skeleton
(E) brain
5. *Merge* is to *separate* as *flippant* is to ____.
(A) swimming (B) unbalanced (C) talkative
(D) thrown (E) respectful
6. *Corrode* is to *metal* as *decay* is to ____.
(A) organism (B) erosion (C) statement (D) rust
(E) plastic
7. *Zealous* is to *eager* as *specific* is to ____.
(A) ambiguous (B) lengthy (C) morose (D) gaudy
(E) precise
8. *Buyer* is to *merchandise* as *accountant* is to ____.
(A) formality (B) success (C) calendar
(D) precision (E) ledgers
9. *Splendid* is to *elegant* as *dubious* is to ____.
(A) authentic (B) sincere (C) doubtful (D) similar
(E) strong
10. *Penal* is to *punishment* as *regal* is to ____.
(A) lecture (B) laughter (C) royalty (D) exercise
(E) truth

EXERCISE 4 Recognizing Analogies

Write the letter of the word pair that has the same relationship as the word pair in capital letters.

1. PATERNAL : MATERNAL :: (A) precise : accurate (B) numerous : many (C) frequent : seldom (D) brave : fearless (E) descended : related
2. VERTEBRATE : MAMMAL :: (A) crustacean : snake (B) money : bank (C) fog : precipitation (D) element : copper (E) silver : ore
3. TIRED : EXHAUSTED :: (A) alike : dissimilar (B) won : lost (C) confirmed : denied (D) constructed : built (E) feared : disliked
4. WRISTWATCH : DIGITAL :: (A) sneakers : shoes (B) camera : tripod (C) academic : textbook (D) tree : cypress (E) steel : iron
5. INSPECT : EXAMINE :: (A) condemn : encourage (B) cease : begin (C) attempt : try (D) lead : inspire (E) inform : confuse
6. TRIVIAL : IMPORTANT :: (A) windy : wet (B) insignificant : worthless (C) fashionable : stylish (D) complete : finished (E) stale : fresh
7. CONVENE : DELEGATES :: (A) students : dismiss (B) repeat : answers (C) round up : horses (D) voters : register (E) lower : reduction
8. PETITE : HUGE :: (A) calm : peaceful (B) gazing : staring (C) miniscule : tiny (D) curious : inquisitive (E) meager : abundant
9. CURE : REMEDY :: (A) agree : decide (B) ask : answer (C) protect : shield (D) dampen : lighten (E) seek : solve
10. BRUSH : PAINTER :: (A) sports : competitor (B) jeweler : gem (C) stonecutter : chisel (D) salesperson : price (E) bowl : chef
11. EPITAPH : TOMBSTONE :: (A) poem : verse (B) prose : speech (C) radio : music (D) inscription : monument (E) story : narrative
12. CARDINAL : BIRD :: (A) wren : hawk (B) burlap : cloth (C) fish : mackerel (D) flag : country (E) duck : drake

13. FOYER : HOTEL :: (A) room : closet
(B) house : apartment (C) lobby : theater
(D) tent : barracks (E) door : window
14. IRRELEVANT : UNIMPORTANT :: (A) honest : deceitful
(B) prior : former (C) arrogant : humble
(D) pointless : active (E) humorous : serious
15. MAST : SHIP :: (A) rowboat : oar (B) dentist : drill
(C) sedan : automobile (D) string : violin
(E) igloo : house
16. EXERTION : EFFORT :: (A) construction : plans
(B) allegiance : fidelity (C) election : votes
(D) latch : key (E) flight : kite
17. DISAGREEMENT : ACCORD :: (A) software : computer
(B) preference : choice (C) expansion : contraction
(D) grievance : complaint (E) precision : exactness
18. FAWN : DEER :: (A) cow : bull (B) mutton : sheep
(C) leather : suede (D) hog : pig (E) gosling : goose
19. SPOUSE : WIFE :: (A) husband : in-law
(B) cousin : uncle (C) nephew : aunt
(D) partner : marriage (E) sibling : sister
20. DAWN : SUNSET :: (A) stamp : letter (B) star : light
(C) preface : conclusion (D) treatment : injury
(E) planet : earth

Sentence Completion

Sentence-completion questions test your ability to choose the best word or words to use in a given context. *(See page 301.)* These questions demand skill in figuring out what word or words make the most sense in the blanks in the sentences. Although the sentences in these tests cover a variety of subjects, they do not require that you have a prior knowledge of those subjects. By noticing key words that appear in the sentences, you can figure out answers from context alone.

Complete the following sentence by choosing the most appropriate word from the list of choices.

Because you failed to meet the April 30 deadline and have since refused to say when or whether you will complete the work, we are forced to ____ our contract with you.
(A) honor (B) discuss (C) terminate (D) negotiate
(E) extend

The answer is *terminate*. The rest of the sentence, including its tone, clearly suggests that the contract has not been honored and that the time for discussing, negotiating, or granting an extension of time has passed. The other choices—*honor, discuss, negotiate,* and *extend*—do not make sense in the context of the sentence.

Sentence-completion questions sometimes have two blanks in the same sentence. See if you can find the correct answer in the following example.

Despite ____ to the contrary, the detective was ____ that Mrs. Arnold had mislaid her jewels.
(A) suspicions . . . pleased
(B) evidence . . . convinced
(C) decisions . . . certain
(D) confessions . . . depressed
(E) excitement . . . surprised

The answer is *evidence . . . convinced. Decisions . . . certain* contains a contradiction, while the other choices simply do not make good sense in the context of the sentence.

EXERCISE 5 Sentence Completion
Write the letter of the word or group of words that best completes each of the following sentences.

1. Since we had to meet at the Lincoln Memorial at exactly 2:35 P.M., we decided to ____ our watches.
(A) synchronize (B) ignore (C) wind (D) consider (E) conceal
2. His use of short sentences and contractions made his speech seem ____ rather than formal.
(A) unacceptable (B) hilarious (C) slurred (D) colloquial (E) pompous
3. Jill came so close to winning many of the track events, without actually winning any of them, that she was awarded a special ____ prize.
(A) academic (B) financial (C) unsuitable (D) patronizing (E) consolation
4. The crowd at the international convention heard a number of ____ speakers demanding that war be outlawed.
(A) bored (B) pacifist (C) natural (D) inactive (E) war-mongering

5. An economist stated that the ____ of foreign currency could stimulate the small country's economy.
   (A) influx (B) suppression (C) study
   (D) suitability (E) lack
6. After auditioning unsuccessfully for more than a dozen roles, the actor remarked that ____ is as important as talent.
   (A) unselfishness (B) perseverance (C) timidity
   (D) brutality (E) underhandedness
7. Our guide pointed out that the giraffe is ____, feeding only on plants.
   (A) quadruped (B) hoofed (C) herbivorous
   (D) huge (E) endangered
8. King Edward VIII said he would ____ the throne of England in order "to marry the woman I love."
   (A) destroy (B) climb (C) decorate (D) abdicate
   (E) reevaluate
9. Her acceptance speech was so long that we can print only an ____ of it in the newspaper.
   (A) extension (B) array (C) excerpt (D) overture
   (E) understatement
10. As a young man, the actor was slim and lithe; but as the years passed, he became a ____ character actor.
    (A) loose-limbed (B) portly (C) well-paid
    (D) forgotten (E) lackluster
11. The humor in the comedy was so absurd that it bordered on ____.
    (A) concern (B) smiles (C) tragedy
    (D) significance (E) farce
12. Frogs are ____ creatures, for they can live both on land and in water.
    (A) unique (B) live (C) amphibious (D) aquatic
    (E) inflexible
13. The Confederate $100 bill looked genuine, but my father assured me it was only a ____.
    (A) photograph (B) mistake (C) reality
    (D) figment (E) counterfeit
14. Under the jury system, it is important that both the judge and the jury be ____.
    (A) elected (B) professional (C) impartial
    (D) liberal (E) gruff

15. The most ____ person in the group was chosen to explain the complicated science project to the judges.
(A) articulate (B) ironic (C) tongue-tied
(D) hostile (E) witty
16. When more than half the voters failed to register, both candidates complained about the ____ of the electorate.
(A) candor (B) enthusiasm (C) choice (D) apathy
(E) mania
17. He had little mathematical ability, but he suffered from the ____ that he was Albert Einstein.
(A) rumor (B) declaration (C) delusion
(D) resemblance (E) actuality
18. When the police chief arrived at the scene of the demonstration, he ordered the crowd to ____.
(A) cheer (B) disperse (C) congregate (D) dinner
(E) emigrate
19. Linda had no belief in the ____, but she could not explain the eerie yellow lights on the horizon.
(A) fashionable (B) inexplicable (C) supernatural
(D) predictable (E) rational
20. The river ____ sediment at its mouth until it had built up a sizable delta.
(A) dissolved (B) floated (C) suspended
(D) deposited (E) withdrew

EXERCISE 6 Sentence Completion with Two Blanks

Write the letter of the pair of words that best completes each of the following sentences.

1. It was quite a moment when he ____ into the room and casually ____ he had been signed by the Celtics.
(A) stormed . . . growled (B) strode . . . snapped
(C) walked . . . shouted
(D) sauntered . . . announced
(E) rushed . . . trumpeted
2. The detective claimed that the suspect, in his ____ to leave the scene, ____ left a laundry ticket behind.
(A) reluctance . . . surprisingly
(B) frenzy . . . inadvertently
(C) plot . . . absentmindedly
(D) decision . . . foolishly (E) anger . . . purposely

3. Great Britain, with its long coastline and ____ ports, is one of the leading ____ nations in the world.
   (A) many . . . agricultural
   (B) outstanding . . . industrial
   (C) excellent . . . nautical
   (D) crowded . . . financial
   (E) overabundant . . . debtor
4. Ted was far ahead in the game and was ____ to win, but his opponent refused to ____.
   (A) likely . . . play (B) demanding . . . agree
   (C) playing . . . reason (D) doubtful . . . lose
   (E) certain . . . yield
5. The ____ dictionary is about a foot thick; the ____ edition is only about one quarter as large.
   (A) unabridged . . . concise (B) enormous . . . other
   (C) modern . . . recent
   (D) paperback . . . recognized
   (E) children's . . . old-fashioned
6. When the ____ was cut to 18 players, Phil was retained despite his ____ playing.
   (A) team . . . superb
   (B) management . . . unsatisfactory
   (C) staff . . . improved (D) roster . . . inconsistent
   (E) choice . . . exuberant
7. By the terms of the will, Marie's ____ was to be invested, and she was to receive ____ payments.
   (A) future . . . limited (B) inheritance . . . periodic
   (C) account . . . spectacular (D) income . . . no
   (E) property . . . worthwhile
8. The good news made Freddie's ____ brighter, and he smiled ____.
   (A) expression . . . enthusiastically
   (B) outlook . . . solemnly (C) aspect . . . grimly
   (D) afternoon . . . thoughtlessly
   (E) well-being . . . happily
9. After a lengthy discussion, the ____ of the group was that our ____ affairs should be handled by an experienced accountant.
   (A) disagreement . . . legal (B) intent . . . basic
   (C) equality . . . fund-raising (D) vote . . . important
   (E) consensus . . . budgetary

10. We agreed that any ____ who could play both Juliet and Lady Macbeth had to be very ____.
    (A) woman . . . elderly (B) performer . . . tricky
    (C) actress . . . versatile (D) stagehand . . . flexible
    (E) amateur . . . professional

READING-COMPREHENSION TESTS

Reading-comprehension questions, based on passages of one or more paragraphs, test your ability to understand and analyze written information. Sometimes the information you need to answer the questions is directly stated in the passage; at other times the information is only implied. In either case, you must study, analyze, and interpret each passage carefully in order to answer the questions that follow it. The following strategies will help you prepare your answers to reading-comprehension questions.

Strategies for Answering Reading-Comprehension Questions

1. Begin by quickly skimming the questions that follow the passage. If there is a question on tone, for example, you should pay close attention to the tone of the passage as you read.
2. Read the passage carefully and closely. Notice the main ideas, organization, style, and key words.
3. Study all possible answers. Avoid choosing one answer the moment you think it is a reasonable choice. There may be a better choice.
4. Use only the information in the passage when you answer the questions. Do not rely on your own knowledge or ideas on this kind of test. Even though a particular answer may not be obvious at first, remember that the answer *is* in the passage. Search for the answer and draw conclusions if you have to.

Most reading-comprehension questions will ask you to interpret or evaluate one or more of the following characteristics of a written passage.

• *Main idea.* At least one question will focus on the central idea of the passage. Remember that the main idea of a passage covers all sections of that passage—not just one section or paragraph.

• *Supporting details.* Questions about supporting details test your ability to identify the statements in the passage that back up the main idea.

• *Implied meanings.* In some passages not all information is directly stated. Some questions ask you to draw inferences, or interpret information that the author has merely implied.

• *Tone.* Questions on tone require that you interpret or analyze the author's attitude toward his or her subject.

The following passage is an example of the kind you will find on reading-comprehension tests. Study it, use the strategies recommended in this chapter, and then answer the questions that follow the passage.

One of the more fascinating institutions in American history was the short-lived pony express, established in 1860. The plan seemed brilliant at the time. The pony express, a relay system of horseback riders, would carry mail between Missouri and California in the breathtaking time of ten days. The feat required the building of 190 way stations at ten-mile intervals between St. Joseph, Missouri, and San Francisco. As work on the way stations progressed, five hundred horses were chosen; and a group of experienced, rough-and-ready riders were hired.

April 3, 1860, was the day this new, lightning-fast mail service began operations. Cheering crowds in St. Joseph and San Francisco sped the first two riders on their way. Each rider raced at full gallop for ten miles, then came flashing into a way station where another mount was saddled and waiting. The rider would leap on the fresh horse, flinging the *mochila*, or mail pouch, onto the new saddle, and dash off again. Each rider put in 70 miles of this grueling work at breakneck speed before turning his mail over to the next rider.

The pony express made Americans proud. It cut a full ten days off the usual stagecoach schedule, and it was the stuff of romance. Eighty riders were always traveling, day and night, winter and summer, rain or shine, forty of them racing east, forty flying west. They braved open prairies, twisting mountain trails, and ever-present threats of Indian attacks.

Alas, the glory of the pony express exceeded its profits, and technology soon made it obsolete. Despite rates of four to ten dollars per ounce, and despite the steady increase in letters carried, each piece of mail cost the company thirty-eight dollars to transport. The venture was already losing money when, on October 24, 1861, an unbeatable competitor entered the field. On that date the wires of a new transcontinental telegraph company were joined, and communication time between the coasts dropped from ten days to a fraction of a second. Then, if not earlier, the pony express was doomed.

1. The best title for this passage is
   (A) A Dangerous Experiment
   (B) How the Pony Express Operated
   (C) Transcontinental Communication
   (D) The Ill-Fated Pony Express
   (E) Technology and the Pony Express
2. The pony express failed because
   (A) it set its rates too high
   (B) Samuel F. B. Morse invented the telegraph
   (C) the trip was too dangerous to be practical
   (D) the service was slower than predicted
   (E) operating costs and competition made it unprofitable
3. It seems to be true that the pony express
   (A) made money at first but not later on
   (B) experienced many disasters on the trail
   (C) appealed to the Americans of that time
   (D) might have succeeded with better management
   (E) was an unworkable scheme because of its organization
4. This passage would most likely appear in
   (A) a Western novel
   (B) a textbook on the American westward movement
   (C) a local history of St. Joseph, Missouri
   (D) a concise history of nineteenth-century economics
   (E) a book on the telegraph in America

These four questions are similar to the kinds described on pages 637–638. The correct answers are as follows.

1. *(D) The Ill-Fated Pony Express*. Choices *(A)* and *(C)* are too broad. Choice *(B)* is too narrow. Choice *(E)* does not reflect the main idea of the passage.

2. *(E) operating costs and competition made it unprofitable.* These two reasons for the failure of the pony express are directly stated in the passage. Choice *(A)* is untrue; if anything, the company set its rates too low. Choice *(B)* suggests, in a remote way, one of the two causes of failure; but it is not the best answer. Choices *(C)* and *(D)* are not accurate statements about the content of the passage.

3. *(C) appealed to the Americans of that time.* Although this is an inference, it is a very clear one. The third paragraph of the passage begins, "The pony express made Americans proud." There is nothing in the passage to support the inferences in choices *(A)*, *(B)*, or *(D)*. Choice *(D)* begins accurately—the pony express "was an unworkable scheme"—but, as the passage makes clear, it was unworkable because of cost and competition, not because of poor organization.

4. *(B) a textbook on the American westward movement.* This question involves both tone and content. The fact-filled passage might appear in a novel (choice *A*), but probably not. Choices *(C)*, *(D)*, and *(E)* are either too specific or unrelated to the topic.

EXERCISE 7 Reading Comprehension

Read the following passage and write the letter of each correct answer.

Although Edgar Allan Poe was a demon-haunted man who made many enemies in his brief lifetime, he is also the honored father of the detective story, a genre that has been continuously popular ever since "The Murders in the Rue Morgue" first appeared in print in 1841. In that one story, Poe introduced a number of features that have since become traditional, such as the eccentric private detective, the relatively dull-witted but admiring narrator, the locked room, the unjustly suspected person, and the presentation of clues to the reader. Had Poe stopped with "The Murders in the Rue Morgue," his place in the long history of the mystery genre would already have been secure. But he did not stop there. With his second story, "The Mystery of Marie Rogêt," he added to his achievement. By bringing back his imaginative and keenly observant C. Auguste Dupin as the detective, he created the first series fictional detective, as well as the first armchair detective, since in this case Dupin never leaves his quarters. The last Dupin case, "The Purloined Letter," introduces psychological detection, the clue in plain sight, the staged diversion, and the long and condescending explanation at the end—all elements familiar to readers of detective stories. Even though some critics argue otherwise, with these three short stories, Poe furnished future generations of mystery writers, from Baroness Orczy to Agatha Christie, from Arthur Conan Doyle to Ellery Queen, with the essential features of their tales.

1. The main idea of this passage is
   (A) that Edgar Allan Poe deserves to be remembered as a great writer
   (B) that Poe introduced many features of the traditional detective story
   (C) that Poe was not a well-liked man, despite his remarkable achievements
   (D) that Poe wrote formula stories for later, and lesser, writers to copy
   (E) that only three of Poe's famous short stories deserve to be remembered today
2. Whenever a modern detective story uses an obvious clue, the writer owes a debt of gratitude to
   (A) "The Purloined Letter"
   (B) "The Mystery of Marie Rogêt"
   (C) Arthur Conan Doyle
   (D) "The Murders in the Rue Morgue"
   (E) Agatha Christie
3. Poe is the father of the detective story but not of the mystery story because
   (A) "The Murders in the Rue Morgue" is not a mystery
   (B) mystery stories do not have detectives
   (C) Sherlock Holmes appeared earlier than Dupin
   (D) mystery stories existed before Poe
   (E) detective stories and mystery stories are the same
4. This passage contains many facts, and its intent seems to be both to inform and to
   (A) amuse
   (B) disprove
   (C) argue
   (D) irritate
   (E) persuade

TESTS OF WRITING ABILITY

Standardized tests measure writing ability in two ways. One is by means of an objective test of standard written English. This multiple-choice test asks you to identify sentence errors or to choose the best wording from a number of choices. The second way of measuring writing ability is through a writing sample. This essay test requires you to write one or more original paragraphs on an assigned topic.

Tests of Standard Written English

An objective test of standard written English contains sentences with underlined words, phrases, or punctuation. The underlined parts may contain errors in grammar, usage, mechanics, vocabulary, and spelling. You must find the error in each sentence or, on some tests, identify the best way to correct the faulty sentence.

Error Recognition. This kind of question tests grammar, usage, capitalization, punctuation, word-choice, and spelling. As a rule, each item consists of a sentence with five underlined parts. Four of these underlinings suggest possible errors in the sentence. The fifth indicates that there is no error. No sentence has more than one error. Try to find the error—if there is one—in the following example.

The Pacific Ocean (A) is 36,198 feet deep in the Mariana Trench, (B) even deeper then (C) Mount Everest or the mountain K2 is (D) high. No error (E)

The correct answer is *C*. Standard usage requires *than* rather than *then* in this sentence. Sometimes you will find a sentence that contains no error. Be careful, however, before you choose *E* as the answer. The errors included in this kind of test are very often ones that are so common they are hard to identify.

A useful hint is to remember that everything *not* underlined in a sentence is correct. You can use this knowledge to help you search for errors in the underlined parts.

EXERCISE 8 Recognizing Errors in Writing
Write the letter of the underlined word or punctuation mark that is incorrect. If the sentence contains no error, write *E*.

In a Manner of Speaking

1. The Reverend (A) William Spooner, who's (B) last name became a common noun, had (C) an (D) unusual quirk of speech. No error (E)
2. Spooners' (A) quirk was to (B) transpose the initial sounds of two (C) or more (D) words. No error (E)
3. There (A) are (B) a great many examples of his (C) odd, (D) humorous mistakes. No error (E)
4. When Spooner spoke (A), "a well-oiled bicycle," (B) for example, would come out as (C) "a well-boiled icicle". (D) No error (E)
5. Spooner was an experienced, knowledgeable (A) teacher who (B) his (C) students liked and respected. (D) No error (E)
6. If you was (A) to ask most of his students, (B) they would say (C) he was (D) unforgettable. No error (E)
7. After all, (A) how could anyone (B) forget a man who said, "Let me sew you to your sheet," when he intends (C) to show you to your seat? (D) No error (E)
8. Everyone who (A) knew Reverend Spooner had (B) their (C) own story to tell about him (D). No error (E)
9. Still, as time went by, the old man's (A) long service at New College (B), Oxford, (C) was all but forgotten (D). No error (E)
10. The "spoonerisms," however, are remembered to this day, (A) and are (B) the classic examples used (C) in all dictionary definitions of the word based on his (D) name. No error (E)

Sentence Correction. Sentence-correction questions test your ability to recognize appropriate phrasing. Instead of locating an error in a sentence, you select the most appropriate and effective way to write the sentence.

In this kind of sentence-correction question, a part of the sentence is underlined. The sentence is followed by five different ways of writing the underlined part. The first way shown, *A*, is the same as the underlined part. The other four ways, *B* through *E*, present alternative ways of writing the underlined part. The choices may involve questions of grammar, usage, capitalization, punctuation, or diction. Be sure the answer you choose does not change the meaning of the original sentence. If more than one answer seems correct, choose the one that is most effective in the context. Study the following example of a sentence-correction test item and choose the best way of stating the underlined portion.

We all agreed that the guest lecturer was well informed, articulate, and <u>he had a nice personality.</u>
(A) he had a nice personality.
(B) he had a pleasant personality.
(C) a nice personality.
(D) likable.
(E) nice personalitywise.

The answer is *(D)*. The problem in the original sentence, as well as with choices *(B)* and *(C)*, is lack of parallelism. *(See pages 390–391.)* Choice *(E)* is parallel, but the awkward verbal construction makes *(E)* a poor answer. Notice that *(D)* introduces a new adjective, *likable,* although *personable* would have been equally satisfactory.

EXERCISE 9 Correcting Sentences

Write the letter of the correct way, or the best way, of phrasing the underlined part of each sentence.

1. Walking through the unfamiliar park at noon, <u>a statue of Thoreau was visible to me.</u>
(A) a statue of Thoreau was visible to me.
(B) a statue of Thoreau caught my eye.
(C) I saw a statue of Thoreau.
(D) Thoreau's statue became visible.
(E) my eyes caught a glimpse of a statue of Thoreau.

2. Each of us in the audience hopes to learn your views on the bond issue.
   (A) of us in the audience hopes
   (B) of we in the audience hopes
   (C) of us in the audience hope
   (D) of we in the audience hope
   (E) member of the audience hope
3. The prince, along with all his supporters, were observed coming toward the village.
   (A) his supporters, were observed coming toward
   (B) his supporters were observed, coming toward
   (C) his supporters, was observed coming toward
   (D) his supporters, was observed, coming toward
   (E) his' supporters, was observed coming toward
4. Was it he who said, Its not too late to get a collar for your puppy?
   (A) Its not too late to get a collar for your puppy?
   (B) "Its not to late to get a collar for your puppy"?
   (C) "It's not too late to get a collar for you're puppy?"
   (D) It's not to late to get a collar for your puppy.
   (E) "It's not too late to get a collar for your puppy"?
5. The alarm should of begun ringing by now.
   (A) alarm should of begun
   (B) alarm, it should of begun
   (C) alarm should have begun
   (D) alarm should have began
   (E) alarm should of began
6. Begin by stating what your occupation is, where you come from, and your reason for deciding to enter the contest.
   (A) your reason for deciding to enter the contest.
   (B) you're reason for deciding to enter the contest.
   (C) your reason for deciding too enter the contest.
   (D) why you decided to enter the contest.
   (E) your reason to decide to enter the contest.
7. "It seems," Joanne said, "As if they're pleased with the results."
   (A) "As if they're pleased with the results."
   (B) "as if they're pleased with the results."
   (C) "as if they're pleased with the results".
   (D) "like there pleased with the results."
   (E) "like they're pleased with the results".

8. Mr. Ferris spoke very angry about losing the women's tickets.
   (A) angry about losing the women's tickets.
   (B) angry about loosing the women's tickets.
   (C) angrily about losing the women's tickets.
   (D) angrily about losing the womens' tickets.
   (E) angrily about loosing the women's tickets.
9. Her popular books on European history made the Middle Ages come alive.
   (A) history made the Middle Ages
   (B) History made the Middle Ages
   (C) history made the middle ages
   (D) History made the Middle ages
   (E) History made the middle ages
10. The editor hadn't hardly given him the assignment when a new story broke.
   (A) hadn't hardly given him
   (B) hadn't hardly gave him
   (C) had hardly give him
   (D) had hardly given him
   (E) had hardly gave him

Sentence Rephrasing. A sentence-rephrasing question tests your ability to reword a sentence but also to retain its original meaning. First you are given a correct sentence. Then you are asked to revise the sentence, placing a given phrase in a certain position. Making the changes that are requested will often require that you change other parts of the sentence as well. Once you have revised the sentence, you must choose from a list of choices the word or phrase that appears in your rephrased sentence. Note the following: an example sentence, instructions for rephrasing the sentence, and five choices of rephrasing that could appear in the revised sentence. Read the instructions below and choose the correct rephrasing of the sample sentence.

ORIGINAL SENTENCE	Very few actors or actresses have accomplished the feat of winning an Academy Award more than once.
REPHRASING INSTRUCTIONS	Begin your rephrased sentence with *Winning an Academy Award.*

Before you select one of the five phrases, think of a way to rephrase the original sentence. Following is the most likely rephrasing.

Winning an Academy Award more than once is a feat accomplished by very few actors or actresses.

Now look at the choice of phrases that might appear in the rephrased sentence.

(A) Award is accomplished
(B) accomplished by very few actors
(C) actors or actresses accomplish it
(D) more than a very few
(E) feat of very few actors

The correct choice—the one that appears in the rephrased sentence—is *accomplished by very few actors.* The other choices would make the rephrased sentence awkward, if not ungrammatical. In working with questions of this kind, be sure to do your own rephrasing first, either in your head or on paper, before looking for an appropriate choice. Otherwise, you may find sentence-rephrasing questions more confusing than they actually are.

Now try to work out the following example.

The famous general Abner Doubleday probably did not invent the game of baseball in quite the way he was originally credited.

Rephrase the sentence, changing the words *the famous general* to an appositive phrase.

(A) general, Abner Doubleday
(B) Doubleday invented baseball
(C) Doubleday, the famous general,
(D) the famous Abner Doubleday
(E) Doubleday was the famous

The answer is *Doubleday, the famous general,*. The logical way to rephrase the sentence is to put *Abner Doubleday* first, followed by *the famous general* as an appositive enclosed by commas. *(See pages 258–259 for the definition and an example of an appositive.)*

EXERCISE 10 Rephrasing Sentences

Write the letter of the word or phrase that would most likely be included in the rephrased sentence.

1. Some people regard computers as mechanical geniuses, but the truth is that computers cannot think at all.
   Begin with *Although.*
   (A) geniuses, the truth is
   (B) Although the truth is
   (C) think at all, but
   (D) the truth is, some people
   (E) computers are mechanical geniuses
2. The Grand Canyon is so awesome that visitors are often struck speechless when they first see it.
   Begin with *When visitors first see.*
   (A) they are often struck speechless.
   (B) Grand Canyon, is so awesome
   (C) that visitors are
   (D) so awesome as to be speechless.
   (E) that it is so awesome
3. Tasmania is the island state of Australia; it is a favorite place for vacationers.
   Insert *which* after Tasmania.
   (A) Australia, it is a favorite place
   (B) Australia, but it is a favorite place
   (C) Australia, is a favorite place
   (D) Australia; is a favorite place
   (E) Australia is a favorite place
4. "Charles Dickens wrote *A Tale of Two Cities.*"
   Insert *I pointed out* after *Dickens.*
   (A) Dickens" I pointed out, "wrote
   (B) Dickens," I pointed out, "Wrote
   (C) Dickens", I pointed out, "wrote
   (D) Dickens, I pointed out, wrote
   (E) Dickens," I pointed out, "wrote
5. Engineers take the theories that scientists have developed and apply them to the needs of the marketplace.
   Change *Engineers take* to *An engineer takes.*
   (A) and apply it
   (B) developed, applying it
   (C) and applies them

(D) to apply them
(E) and apply theories

6. Stephen Crane wrote feverishly and finished the first draft of *The Red Badge of Courage* in only ten days.
Begin with *Writing.*
(A) and feverishly finished
(B) feverishly, Stephen Crane finished
(C) feverishly, he finished
(D) feverishly and finishing
(E) and feverishly finishing

7. Cats have been domesticated for several thousand years, but they have not lost their air of fierce independence.
Begin with *Domesticated.*
(A) years, they have not
(B) years have not
(C) years, but cats have not
(D) years, cats have not
(E) years and have not

8. The earliest American presidents were not photographed; portrait photography has been widespread since 1850.
Insert *only.*
(A) only since 1850
(B) portrait photography only
(C) has only been widespread
(D) only portrait photography
(E) not only were photographed

9. A book that appeals to all ages is *Gulliver's Travels.*
Begin with *One of.*
(A) books that appeals
(B) books that appeal
(C) *Gulliver's Travels* appeals
(D) *Gulliver's Travels* appeal
(E) all ages appeal

10. Theodore Dreiser's novels prove that a passionate sincerity can sometimes overcome an ungainly style.
Begin with *That a passionate sincerity.*
(A) is proved by
(B) proves the novels of
(C) is Theodore Dreiser's proof
(D) is by way of proof
(E) is proof of

The 20-Minute Essay

The 20-minute essay measures your ability to write quickly, clearly, and logically on an assigned topic. You will be given guidelines to follow when you write the essay of approximately 175 to 200 words.

If you can write a short composition, you should be able to write the 20-minute essay. There may be some differences, however, between your usual classroom assignments and this kind of test. For example, essays on most standardized tests call for general responses, rather than for answers containing specific subject matter. The following guidelines will help you when you write an essay on a standardized test.

Writing the 20-Minute Essay

1. Go over the test carefully before beginning to write. Plan the amount of time you should spend on each part of the test. The time you spend should be in proportion to the number of points allotted to each part. If you are given a choice, select the question or questions you can answer best.
2. Read the directions carefully, making certain you understand what you are expected to do. Notice everything that is required in your answer. Find key words, such as those that follow, that tell what task is required and how you should construct your answer.

Analyze	Separate into parts and examine each part.
Compare	Point out similarities and differences.
Contrast	Point out differences.
Define	Clarify meaning.
Discuss	Examine in detail.
Evaluate	Give your opinion.
Explain	Tell how, what, or why.
Illustrate	Give examples.
Summarize	Briefly review main points.
Trace	Show development or progress.

3. List the main points you need to cover, numbering them in the order in which you intend to cover them. This simple but useful outline will give structure to your essay and will help you avoid leaving out important parts of the answer.

4. As you write your essay, follow these guidelines:
    - State the main idea and the purpose of your essay in the opening paragraph.
    - Follow the order of your outline. Write one paragraph for each main point and include a topic sentence in each paragraph.
    - Supply adequate, specific support for your main points, using facts, examples, and other details.
    - Write a concise concluding paragraph.
    - Proofread your essay, correcting any errors you find in grammar, usage, spelling, and punctuation.
5. Keep in mind the special requirements of the essay test.
    - Some tests do not allow you to erase mistakes. In that case, draw a line through any material you wish to omit.
    - If you are allowed only one answer sheet, check carefully to see where you can jot down notes or an outline. You may be able to do this preparation in the examination book itself.
    - Pay close attention to the time limit. Make sure you apportion your time properly between planning and writing. Spend only the amount of time you have allotted to each part of the answer.

EXERCISE 11 Writing a 20-Minute Essay

Choose one of the following essay topics. Allow yourself exactly 20 minutes to outline and write the essay.

1. The high school curriculum has evolved over many years and represents a consensus of what should be taught. Nevertheless, it can always be changed. Suggest *one* course not now taught in your high school that you think ought to be taught and explain how that course would improve the curriculum.
2. A persistent criticism of television news is that the newscasters have become entertainers rather than reporters. Evaluate this criticism, giving specific examples from your own experience.
3. Carl Sandburg wrote, "There are poets of the cloister and the quiet corner . . . and . . . [t]here are poets of streets and struggles, of dust and combat. . . ." Choose one poet of each kind and contrast the two.

CHAPTER REVIEW

A. Write the letter of the word or group of words most nearly the same *or* most nearly the opposite in meaning to the word in capital letters.

1. APPROPRIATE (A) handsome (B) unsuitable (C) forgotten (D) exceptional (E) disturbing
2. PROFOUND (A) likable (B) impartial (C) sensible (D) shallow (E) courageous
3. KINSHIP (A) echo (B) relationship (C) alteration (D) grain (E) leafiness
4. PERSUADE (A) praise (B) convince (C) emerge (D) explain (E) rival
5. PRETENSE (A) cosmetic (B) refusal (C) sham (D) parade (E) fortune
6. AGREEABLE (A) unpleasant (B) disconnected (C) lazy (D) foolish (E) arctic
7. SAVORY (A) careful (B) respectful (C) upsetting (D) solid (E) flavorful
8. SCORN (A) honesty (B) fortune (C) brilliance (D) travel (E) admiration
9. SEVER (A) scold (B) improve (C) cut (D) laugh (E) worsen
10. VULNERABLE (A) factual (B) ancient (C) edible (D) protected (E) interested

B. Write the letter of the word pair that has the same relationship as the word pair in capital letters.

1. PLACARD : SLOGAN :: (A) acceptance : rejection (B) fish : haddock (C) microscope : scientist (D) keyboard : computer (E) postcard : message
2. DISPUTE : ARGUE :: (A) organize : divide (B) sing : dance (C) propose : demand (D) originate : initiate (E) replenish : empty
3. NAUTICAL : SHIP :: (A) maneuvers : military (B) quarterback : athletic (C) theatrical : stage (D) secretary : executive (E) book : binding
4. LOATHE : ADMIRE :: (A) accuse : decide (B) love : adore (C) experiment : research (D) confirm : deny (E) retreat : fail

5. MOLLUSK : CLAM :: (A) bird : bluejay
(B) extinction : dinosaur (C) camera : shutter
(D) horse : mammal (E) mammal : reptile
6. STETHOSCOPE : DOCTOR :: (A) wrench : mechanic
(B) technician : surgeon (C) employee : employer
(D) baseball : bat (E) entertainer : microphone
7. RESOLUTE : WAVERING :: (A) patient : calm
(B) honest : straightforward (C) protecting : sheltering
(D) vivid : dull (E) springlike : rainy
8. GRANITE : ROCK :: (A) rain : hail (B) beach : ocean
(C) limestone : sandstone (D) typewriter : paper
(E) fir : evergreen
9. CABOOSE : TRAIN :: (A) steamship : paddle wheel
(B) finale : opera (C) igloo : ice (D) currency : coins
(E) bicycle : tricycle
10. ENTERTAINING : DRAMA :: (A) effort : rewarding
(B) travel : broadening (C) milk : healthful
(D) clever : comedian (E) painting : artistic

C. Write the letter that is below the underlined word, group of words, or punctuation mark that is incorrect. If the sentence contains no error, write *E*.

A Novel Approach

1. Charles Dickens was (A) one of those (B) writers who seems (C) born to create memorable stories (D), settings, and characters. No error (E)
2. Born on February 7, 1812, (A) he had (B) to go to (C) work at the age of 12 to help support his (D) family. No error (E)
3. Dickens then goes (A) to school again briefly, (B) quitting (C) at the age of 15 to become an office boy in a firm of attorneys (D). No error (E)
4. As a young parliamentary (A) reporter, he began writing (B) fiction, (C) and soon the *Monthly Magazine* published one of his Stories (D). No error (E)

5. His first great triumph came with the publication of
A
Pickwick Papers, which acheived bestsellerdom. No error
B C D E

6. Dickens, a writer of enormous energy, continued to
A B C
produce novels, short stories, sketches, and essays.
D
No error
E

7. Most of the novels, including "A Tale of Two Cities,"
A
received their first printing in serial form. No error
B C D E

8. Dickens toured the United States twice, reading from
A
his works and acting out dramatic scenes. No error
B C D E

9. His last novel, a mystery, was unfinished at his death,
A B
but it is a popular book irregardless. No error
C D E

10. One critic, Walter Allen, has called Dickens "the greatest
A B C
entertainer, probably, in the history of fiction. No error
D E

Appendix

Study Skills
- Taking Notes
- Studying for a Test
- Using Standard Manuscript Form
- Using Proofreading Symbols
- Using Correct Footnote Form

Communication Skills
- Speaking to an Audience
- Participating in Group Discussions
- Listening for Information
- Evaluating What You Hear

Career Skills
- Writing Letters to Schools and Colleges
- Completing College Applications
- Completing an Essay on an Application
- Interviewing for College Admissions
- Writing a Résumé
- Writing Letters about Employment
- Interviewing for a Job

TAKING NOTES

Note-taking is an important skill for helping you remember what you have read in a textbook or heard during a lecture. Notes are also a valuable study aid in preparing for a test.

Two methods for taking notes are the modified outline and the summary. In a *modified outline,* words and phrases are used to record main ideas and important details. A modified outline is especially useful in studying for a multiple-choice test, because it allows you to see the most important details and facts.

In a *summary,* sentences are used to express important ideas in your own words. A summary is especially useful in preparing for an essay test. Writing a summary requires you to think about the information, to see relationships between ideas, and to draw conclusions. It is also good practice in stating information briefly and clearly.

In the following passage from a textbook on English literature, the essential information is underlined. Following the passage are examples of notes in both modified-outline form and summary form.

> Thomas Hardy had two distinct literary careers, the first as a novelist, and the second as a poet. His deepening pessimism in *Jude the Obscure,* coupled with the public burning of the book by an Anglican bishop, turned him away from novel-writing and toward poetry.
>
> Until the age of 58, Hardy was known only as a novelist. His novels, based on his own classification, are of three types. Only those he classified as novels of character and environment are familiar to modern readers. Among them are *The Return of the Native* and *The Mayor of Casterbridge.* These novels show Hardy's pervasive gloominess, yet his rustic characters also reveal an underlying sense of humor. Hardy considered himself a meliorist, one who believes that things tend to improve.
>
> For the last 30 years of his life, Hardy wrote nothing but poetry. His great epic drama, *The Dynasts,* is less well known than his shorter poems, such as "The Man He Killed," "Channel Firing," and "In Time of 'The Breaking of Nations.'" These poems tend to be sad and pessimistic, like his novels, but they also suggest the heroic dignity of humanity's struggle.

MODIFIED OUTLINE

Thomas Hardy

1. Two writing careers—novelist and poet
2. Novels of character and environment (his classification) best known
   a. Show gloominess but also humor
   b. Reflect Hardy's belief that things tend to improve
3. Short poems most familiar
   a. Display sadness and pessimism
   b. Reveal heroic dignity of human beings

SUMMARY

Thomas Hardy

Hardy had two different writing careers: he was a novelist until age 58 and a poet thereafter. The novels he classified as novels of character and environment are gloomy but show an underlying sense of humor. Hardy believed that things tend to improve.

Hardy's short poems, for which he is best known, display sadness and pessimism but also reveal the heroic dignity of human beings.

These guidelines will help you take well-organized notes.

Taking Notes

- Record only the main ideas and important details.
- Use the titles, subtitles, and words in special type or color to help you select the most important information.
- Use your own words; do not copy word for word.

Modified Outline
- Use words and phrases.
- Use main ideas for headings.
- List any supporting details under each heading.

Summary
- Write complete sentences, using your own words.
- Show the relationship between ideas, being careful to use only the facts stated in the textbook or lecture.

STUDYING FOR A TEST

You should begin to study for a test long before test day. To do well on a test, you must keep up with your daily reading assignments, take clear and complete notes, and review the material in each subject regularly.

Developing Effective Study Habits. If you develop good study habits, you will find them useful for test taking as well as for daily classroom assignments. Use the following procedures to help you study more effectively and improve your test grades.

How to Study Effectively

- Choose an area that is well lighted and free from noise and other distractions.
- Equip your study area with everything you need for reading and writing, including a dictionary, a thesaurus, and other reference books.
- Keep an assignment book for recording assignments and due dates.
- Allow plenty of time for studying. Begin your reading and writing assignments early.

Preparing for a Test. If you keep up with your assignments and take good notes, you should have no difficulty preparing for tests. The following guidelines will help you do your best.

How to Prepare for a Test

1. Study the notes you took in class and those you took on assigned reading.
2. Focus on topics that were discussed in class or stressed by the teacher.
3. Review the questions at the end of main sections in your textbook. Write the answer to each question to help you organize your thoughts and recall important details.
4. Review any prior tests or quizzes you have taken that cover the material on which you will be tested.

USING STANDARD MANUSCRIPT FORM

The appearance of your composition can be almost as important as its content. A paper with jagged margins and words crossed out or crowded together is difficult to read. A neat, legible paper, however, makes a positive impression on your reader. Use the following guidelines for standard manuscript form to help you prepare the final copy of a composition or report.

Standard Manuscript Form

1. Use standard-size 8½- by 11-inch white paper. Use one side of the paper only.
2. If handwriting, use black or blue ink. If typing, use a black typewriter ribbon and double-space the lines.
3. Leave a 1¼-inch margin at the left and a 1-inch margin at the right. The left margin must be even. The right margin should be as even as possible, without too many hyphenated words.
4. Put your name, the course title, the name of your teacher, and the date in the upper right-hand corner of the first page.
5. Center the title about 2 inches from the top of the first page. Do not underline or put quotation marks around your title.
6. If handwriting, skip 2 lines between the title and the first paragraph. If typing, skip 4 lines.
7. If handwriting, indent the first line of each paragraph 1 inch. If typing, indent 5 spaces.
8. Leave a 1-inch margin at the bottom of all pages.
9. Starting on page 2, number each page in the upper right-hand corner. Begin the first line 1 inch from the top of the page.

The following sample illustrates the first page of a typewritten composition. Notice the placement of the name, class, teacher, date, and composition title. Also notice that the margins are consistent. When writing or typing your compositions, be sure your paper is double-spaced, clear, and easy to read.

Sample of Standard Manuscript Form

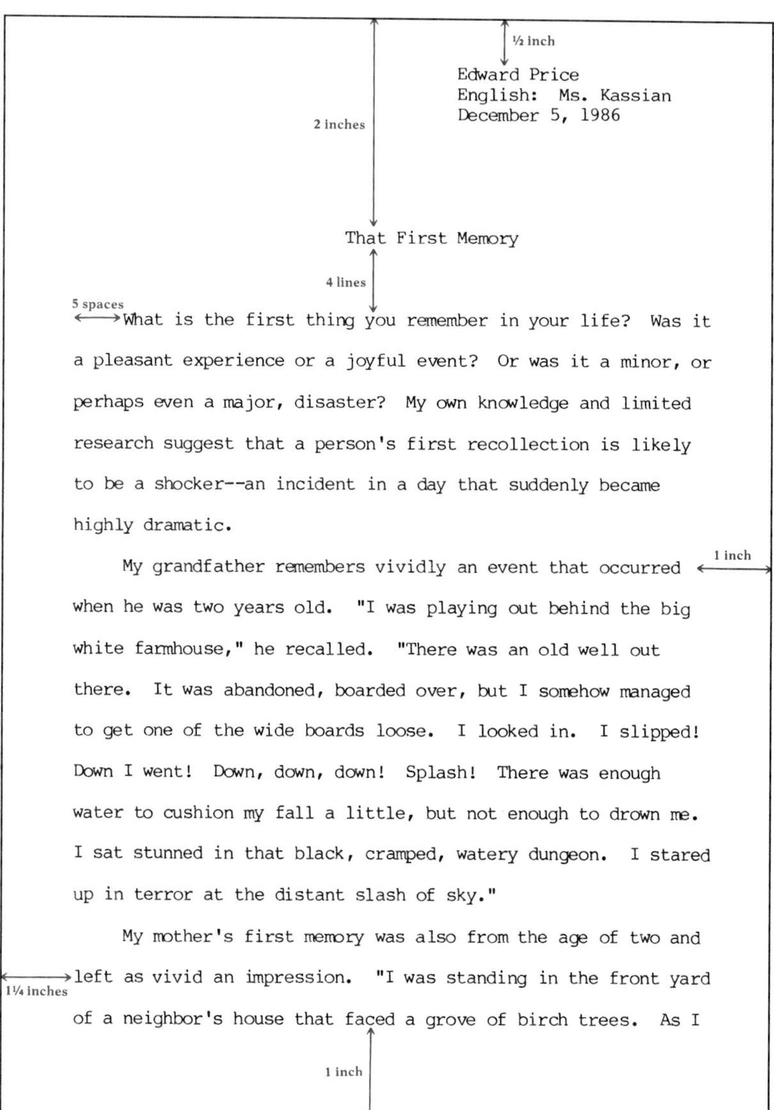
Edward Price
English: Ms. Kassian
December 5, 1986

That First Memory

What is the first thing you remember in your life? Was it a pleasant experience or a joyful event? Or was it a minor, or perhaps even a major, disaster? My own knowledge and limited research suggest that a person's first recollection is likely to be a shocker--an incident in a day that suddenly became highly dramatic.

My grandfather remembers vividly an event that occurred when he was two years old. "I was playing out behind the big white farmhouse," he recalled. "There was an old well out there. It was abandoned, boarded over, but I somehow managed to get one of the wide boards loose. I looked in. I slipped! Down I went! Down, down, down! Splash! There was enough water to cushion my fall a little, but not enough to drown me. I sat stunned in that black, cramped, watery dungeon. I stared up in terror at the distant slash of sky."

My mother's first memory was also from the age of two and left as vivid an impression. "I was standing in the front yard of a neighbor's house that faced a grove of birch trees. As I

In addition to using standard form, you should always proofread your completed work carefully. Also, keep in mind the following guidelines as well as the usage, mechanics, and spelling chapters in this book.

Dividing Words. Although you should avoid dividing words whenever possible, sometimes doing so is necessary to keep the right-hand margin of your paper fairly even. For dividing words, follow the rules on pages 289–290.

Writing Numbers. In general, spell out the numbers one through ten. Use numerals for numbers above ten.

two ten 11 57 289 1,554 6,328,730

To avoid six or more zeros, use a combination of numerals and words.

five million 94 million 216 billion 3.5 billion

Always spell out a number at the beginning of a sentence, or revise the sentence.

Three hundred twenty-seven votes were cast for Myer.
The voters cast 327 votes for Myer.

Use numerals for dates, street and room numbers, page numbers, percents, decimals, and times with A.M. or P.M.

July 14, 1789 room 8 page 5 2 percent 5:40 P.M.
125 Spring Street 7.2

Using Abbreviations. Most abbreviations should be avoided in formal writing. Do not abbreviate names of states, countries, days of the week, months, weights, or measurements. See page 247 for examples of abbreviations that are acceptable in formal writing.

Quoting Long Passages. When you write a research paper and want to quote a passage of five or more lines from a source, skip two lines and indent ten spaces along the left margin. Quotation marks are not necessary for a quotation of this length. A colon is usually used in the sentence that introduces the quotation. *(See pages 275–276.)* Remember to give credit to the author for the quoted material. *(See pages 598–603.)*

USING PROOFREADING SYMBOLS

Proofreading symbols make revising and editing easier. The most commonly used symbols are shown below. Use these symbols when you revise and edit your writing.

Proofreading Symbols

Symbol	Meaning	Example
∧	insert	Ms. Tey spoke∧gardening. (about)
	delete	The fair is a big colossal success.
....	let it stand	Pago Pago is in American Samoa.
#	add space	We are allready to leave.
⌢	close up	Every set of finger prints varies.
∼	transpose	They only arrived yetserday.
no ¶	no paragraph	no ¶ Sara decided to attend.
¶	new paragraph	¶ Dunn Field resounded with cheers.
≡	capital letter	Is Ohio in the east or Midwest?
/	lowercase	To the East was barren desert.

Sample Student Paper with Proofreading Symbols

¶ For a time in the 1970s, it seemed as if the metric system would become the standard of measurement ∧(in) the United States. A specific date was set. The date came and went. Nothing much happened. The United States continues to use roughly 80 different standards of measurement to day.

As long ago as 1790, Thomas Jefferson proposed that the United States adopt the metric system. Conrgess passed a law in 1866, giving the metric system specific legislative approval. The United States signed a treaty that was su∧(p)osed to bring the country into line with most of the other nations of the World. Tradition, however∧ has been too strong so far.

Customary measurement still prevails, although the metric system deos continue to make real inroads. perhaps some day

USING CORRECT FOOTNOTE FORM

The main goal in presenting a neat and polished report is to help make it easy to read. The following are guidelines for setting off footnotes or endnotes neatly from the main text of your report.

Placement of Footnotes

1. Skip four spaces after the last line of your main text before typing the first footnote.
2. Indent the first line of the footnote five spaces.
3. Type the number of the note slightly above the line and leave one space between the number and the first word of the note.
4. Single space each footnote, but leave a double space between footnotes.
5. Make sure to leave a one-inch margin at the bottom of all pages.
6. Number your footnotes in consecutive order. If the last footnote on a page is [7], the first footnote on the next page is [8].

Placement of Endnotes

1. Endnotes appear on a separate sheet of paper at the end of the research paper before the bibliography.
2. Write the title *Notes* two inches from the top of the page. Center it.
3. Skip three lines below the title, indent five spaces, and write the first note (in the same manner as for footnotes).
4. Double space within and between notes.
5. Number the notes consecutively.

All footnotes and endnotes present information in the same order. Not all of the information, however, will apply to each source you use. Omit whatever information does not apply, but present the remaining information in the following order: (1) author's name (in normal order) (2) title of article (in quotation marks) (3) title of book or magazine (underlined)

(4) translator's name (5) editor's name (6) edition (7) place and name of book publisher (separated by colon) (8) date of publication (in parentheses with book publisher's place and name) (9) volume number (10) issue number (11) page number.

Use the following sample footnotes as models when you write a research paper.

Books

1. A book with a single author

   [1] Richard Attenborough, In Search of Gandhi (Piscataway: New Century, 1982), p. 14.

2. A book with two authors (Give the names in the order they appear on the title page.)

   [1] Sandy Hintz and Martin Hintz, Computers in Our World, Today and Tomorrow (New York: Franklin Watts, 1983), p. 23.

3. A book with four or more authors

   [1] Helen C. White and others, Seventeenth-Century Verse and Prose, 4th ed. (New York: Macmillan, 1971), p. 17.

4. A work in a book that contains a collection of works by different authors

   [1] Dorothy B. Vitaliano, "Atlantis from a Geological Point of View," in Atlantis: Fact or Fiction?, ed. Edwin S. Ramage (Bloomington: Indiana University Press, 1978), p. 139.

5. A book that has been translated

   [1] Otto Muck, The Secret of Atlantis, trans. Fred Bradley (New York: Times Books, 1978), p. 131.

6. An edition other than the first

   [1] Randolph Lee Clark and Russel W. Cumley, eds., The Book of Health, 3rd ed. (New York: Van Nostrand Reinhold, 1973), p. 201.

7. A book that is part of a series

   [1] Clarence L. Ver Steeg, The Formative Years: 1607–1763, The Making of America, Vol. 1 (London: Macmillan, 1965), p. 125.

8. A work in several volumes, each with a separate title

   [1] Dumas Malone, The Sage of Monticello, Vol. VI of Jefferson and His Time (Boston: Little, Brown, 1981), pp. 20–28.

9. A work in several volumes without individual titles

   [1] David Daiches, A Critical History of English Literature, 2nd ed. (New York: Ronald, 1970), II, pp. 690–93.

Articles and Other Sources

10. A magazine article with author's name given

    [1] Sharon Bealey, "Giving Sharks a Good Name," Newsweek, 2 Aug. 1982, p. 64.

11. A magazine article with no author's name given

[1] "Mysterious Island," National Geographic World, Oct. 1983, p. 8.

12. A newspaper article

[1] "Teaching Disabled Individuals Computer Skills," New York Times, 27 March 1983, Sec. xi, p. 3, col. 1.

13. An article in an encyclopedia

[1] Earl F. Cheit, "Aging," International Encyclopedia of the Social Sciences, 1968 ed., p. 178.

14. An editorial

[1] "Framed—in Poland," Editorial, New York Times, 31 May 1984, Sec. A, p. 22, cols. 1–2.

15. An article from a journal with volume and issue numbers

[1] Kenneth G. Johnson, "Hemingway and Cézanne: Doing the Country," American Literature, 56, No. 1 (1984), 31–32.

16. An interview

[1] Personal interview with Dr. Michelle Harper, Roseville Hospital, Milwaukee, Wisconsin, 31 August 1984.

17. A letter to the editor of a newspaper or magazine

[1] John Marsh, Letter, Concord Journal, 11 Oct. 1984, p. 5.

18. A review

[1] Mark Stevens, "Paying Tribute to the 'Primitive,'" rev. of "'Primitivism' in 20th Century Art," exhibit at Museum of Modern Art, New York, Newsweek, 1 Oct. 1984, p. 93.

Abbreviations Used in Citing Sources

Abbreviations are used in notes in order to keep the notes as short as possible. Following are some abbreviations commonly used in citing sources.

Abbreviations Used in Citing Sources

Abbreviation	Meaning
ed.	editor, edited, edition
rev. ed.	revised edition
trans.	translator, translated
p., pp.	page, pages
col.	column
sec.	section
vol.	volume
rpt.	reprint

SPEAKING TO AN AUDIENCE

You speak to an audience every time you speak in class or to a group of friends. Whether your audience is large or small, strangers or friends, you want the speech to convey a message.

A speech may be formal or informal, long or short, prepared or impromptu. A prepared speech is planned carefully before it is delivered. An impromptu speech is one given without preparation. Whatever its nature, you will find the following guidelines helpful.

Choosing and Limiting a Subject

The first step in preparing a speech is to choose the subject of your speech carefully.

How to Choose and Limit a Subject

1. Choose a subject that interests you and is likely to interest your audience.
2. Choose a subject you know well or can research very thoroughly.
3. Limit the subject to one that can be covered in the time allowed.
4. Determine the purpose of your speech—to explain or inform, to persuade, or to entertain.

Gathering Information

After you have chosen and limited your topic, begin to gather information. One source of information is your own experience. You may know more about your subject than you realize. Start by brainstorming. *(See page 474.)* Jot down your ideas freely without stopping to evaluate each one.

You may want to interview people who are knowledgeable about your subject. Make a list of the questions you want to ask during the interview. The usefulness of the information you gather will depend in large on how well you have prepared your questions.

Another excellent source of information is the library. Look for useful encyclopedia articles, books, and magazines. *(See pages 356–363.)*

Taking Notes

Be sure to take notes throughout your research. If you take notes based on personal experience, group your ideas into categories. *(See page 584.)* If you interview someone, take notes in modified outline form or use a tape recorder. If you plan to use quotations, write down accurately the words you intend to quote and use quotation marks.

Note cards are the best way to record information from encyclopedias, magazines, and books. Note cards make it easy to organize the information later. The following sample note card was written by a student preparing for a speech on the early history of Nantucket.

Sample Note Card

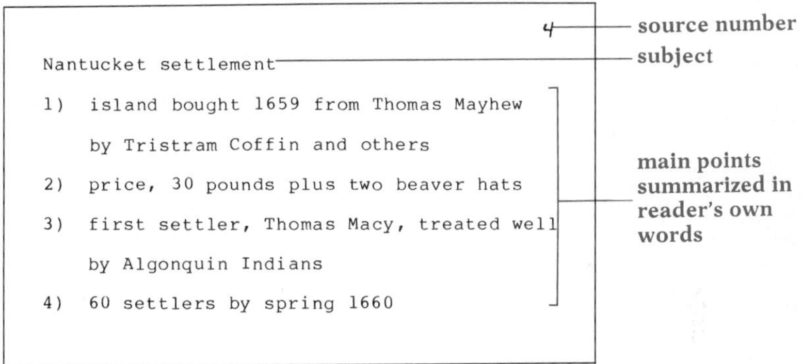

Organizing Information

Begin to organize your information by writing a working thesis statement. *(See pages 590–591.)* Your working thesis statement should indicate the main idea and the purpose of your speech. Next prepare an outline for the body of your speech. *(See pages 586–588.)* The body of the speech should support your thesis statement and should logically develop the main points of your outline with facts, details, examples, and illustrations. Use a Roman numeral for each main topic and a capital letter for each subtopic. Use Arabic numerals for supporting details. Remember to write headings in the same grammatical form (either phrases or sentences). Also, if you subdivide a topic, always have at least two subdivisions. Use the following form for outlining the body of your speech.

Form for Outlining a Speech

Limited Subject: ____
Thesis Statement: ____
Body: I. (Main Topic)
  A. (Subtopic 1)
    1. (Supporting Detail)
    2. (Supporting Detail)
    3. (Supporting Detail)
  B. (Subtopic 2)
    1. (Supporting Detail)
    2. (Supporting Detail)
  C. (Subtopic 3)
II. (Main Topic)
  A. (Subtopic 1)
  B. (Subtopic 2)
  C. (Subtopic 3)

When you have completed the outline, you will be ready to write your introduction and conclusion. To catch the interest of your audience, begin the introduction with an anecdote, an unusual fact, a question, or an attention-getting quotation. Include your thesis statement at the end of the introduction, revising it as necessary. *(See pages 483–484.)*

The conclusion of the speech is your final opportunity to reinforce the ideas you want your listeners to remember. Restate your thesis statement in your conclusion. The last few sentences of your speech should signal the audience that you have finished.

Preparing to Deliver the Speech

Rehearse your speech but do not memorize it. Instead, use either your outline or your cue cards to remind you of the important points of your speech. Cue cards contain key words and phrases or key topics listed in the order you want to follow in your speech. The kind of cue card you make will depend on the type of information in your speech and on your style of presentation. Following is an example of a cue card for a speech entitled "Elizabethan Public Theaters."

Sample Cue Card

```
                                                  3
Building
    --held more than 2,000 people
    --built around courtyard with no roof
    --contained three levels of galleries
Stage
    --projected into audience
    --allowed close contact between actors and
      audience
```

Number your cue cards to simplify keeping them in order. A good set of cue cards will help you speak with confidence.

Rehearsing the Speech

Practice your speech until you know it well. If possible, record your speech on a tape recorder. Listen to your delivery. Note where you should use more emphasis, show greater enthusiasm, or speak more slowly or distinctly.

Delivering the Speech

If you have researched your subject well, planned the content carefully, and rehearsed, you will deliver a good speech. Be confident! You are now an expert on your subject. Following are five tips for delivering a speech.

Tips for Delivering a Speech

1. Relax and breathe deeply before you speak.
2. Glance at your outline or cue cards to refresh your memory. Avoid reading your speech.
3. Look at your audience. Either make eye contact or focus on points just behind the audience.
4. Speak slowly, clearly, and loudly enough to be heard.
5. Use gestures and facial expressions to help you emphasize your main points.

PARTICIPATING IN GROUP DISCUSSIONS

Group discussion is a method of communicating ideas, exchanging opinions, solving problems, and reaching conclusions. Group discussions may be as informal as a small-group discussion or as formal as a symposium or forum. Learning group-discussion skills will help you to present your own ideas effectively and to listen thoughtfully to the ideas of others.

Types of Group Discussions

There are five common kinds of group discussions, each with its own format and rules.

Classroom Discussion. All members of the class participate in the discussion. First, students prepare information for the topic of discussion, which is often based on a homework or classroom assignment. Then they exchange information or discuss the problem or topic. The teacher or a student leads the discussion.

Small Group Discussion. Sometimes the leader of a large group breaks it up into small groups to discuss a specific question or topic. After the discussion one member of each small group reports its results to the large group.

Panel Discussion. The panel consists of four to eight members. Each panelist is knowledgeable about a particular aspect of the topic. Panelists express opinions and may disagree with and challenge each other. A leader directs the discussion and summarizes it at the end. Members of the audience may ask questions of the panelists.

Symposium. Speakers in a symposium present prepared talks on the subject being discussed. After these talks the speakers question one another. Finally the discussion leader invites the audience to question or challenge the speakers.

Forum. A forum differs from a symposium in that it has only one speaker. Following the talk or lecture, the discussion leader asks for questions and comments from the audience.

Duties of Discussion Leaders

When you act as a group-discussion leader—also called a moderator or a chairperson—you have responsibility for guiding and directing the discussion.

Responsibilities of Discussion Leaders

1. Introduce the topic, question, or problem.
2. Control the discussion so that everyone has a chance to contribute.
3. Act as timekeeper, allowing an appropriate amount of time to each speaker and each subtopic.
4. Make sure the discussion stays on target.
5. Keep the discussion well paced, asking questions or shifting the direction of the discussion if necessary.
6. Help participants settle differences and arrive at a general agreement.
7. Summarize the main points of the discussion and note any conclusions or decisions the group has reached.

Duties of Discussion Participants

No matter how effective a discussion leader is, the ultimate success of any group discussion depends on the participants. When you act as a participant in a group discussion, you will have an important role to play in making it work.

Responsibilities of Discussion Participants

1. Prepare for the discussion by reading about the topic.
2. Take part in the discussion by expressing ideas and asking questions.
3. Listen carefully to the ideas expressed by others.
4. When recognized by the chairperson, speak clearly and distinctly, supporting main points with reasons, facts, examples, and other evidence.
5. Be objective and tactful when responding to other participants, making an effort to understand other peoples' opposing points of view.

LISTENING FOR INFORMATION

Listening to a speech or lecture requires that you pay close attention in order to gain information as well as to evaluate what you hear.

Concentrate on the Speaker's Words. Sit comfortably but stay alert. Focus on what the speaker is saying, without being distracted by noise or by the speaker's appearance, gestures, or mannerisms.

Determine the Speaker's Purpose. As the speaker begins, determine the purpose of the speech—to inform, to explain, or to persuade.

Listen for Verbal Clues. Identify the speaker's main ideas. A speaker may use key words or phrases to show you connections between ideas, to alert you to important information, or to signal that the speech is about to end. Often a speaker will use verbal signals such as the following to emphasize important points.

Let me begin	Also consider	Most important
Remember that	Finally	In summation

Notice Nonverbal Clues. A speaker may use gestures that will help you understand a key point. The movement of an arm or a change in pace of speaking, for example, can signal that the speaker is saying something important.

Evaluate the Information. Listen critically and evaluate what you hear. Try to separate fact from opinion. Watch out for propaganda devices that try to persuade you to believe as the speaker does. One such device is the slogan. A slogan is a simple word or phrase that oversimplifies a complex issue by reducing it to a word or a phrase.

Take Notes. Writing notes can help you organize your thoughts and remember details. Use a modified outline when you take notes on a speech. You may also find it helpful to write a summary of the speech. *(See pages 656–657.)*

EVALUATING WHAT YOU HEAR

Always listen critically and evaluate what you hear. Try to separate fact from opinion. Watch out for the following propaganda devices that try to persuade you to believe just as the speaker does.

Slogans. A slogan is a word or phrase that oversimplifies a complex issue. Slogans are popular in advertising and politics because they are brief and catchy. However, they are sometimes used by speakers as substitutes for thoughtful analysis.

Name-Calling. Name-calling is a device that some speakers use to try to injure the reputation of an opponent. The words they use to describe their opponents often substitute opinion for fact and contain generalities rather than specific information.

Testimonials. A testimonial is a statement, usually by a well-known person, that indicates support for an idea or a product. The technique is legitimate, but it is often abused. The person giving the testimonial, however, may know little more about the idea or product than the listeners do.

Bandwagon Appeals. People like to be assured that their actions are both wise and socially acceptable. The bandwagon appeal is an invitation to "Get on board!" and do the same thing, hold the same opinions, and make the same choices as everyone else. Like the testimonial, the bandwagon appeal is effective with those who dislike doing their own thinking.

Unproved Generalizations. A generalization, or a conclusion based on particular facts or examples, must have no exceptions. Generalizations that contain words such as *always, never, all,* and *none* can be limited with words such as *sometimes, many,* and *most.* *(See pages 400–402.)*

False Analogies. An analogy is a comparison that a speaker may use to explain or clarify a point. If the analogy compares two items but includes no adequate points of comparison between the two, the analogy is false. *(See pages 412–413.)*

WRITING LETTERS TO SCHOOLS AND COLLEGES

If you plan to continue your education after high school, there are two kinds of letters you will probably write. The first kind is a request for information from a professional school or college. This should be a short letter, usually asking for a catalog. If you want specific material—such as information on costs or on particular courses—be sure to ask for it. The following letter is a brief, general request for information.

339 Wayland Street
Apt. 14-A
Lubbock, Texas 79400
November 6, 1986

Director of Admissions
Grand Canyon College
Phoenix, Arizona 85061

Dear Sir or Madam:

I am a senior at Lubbock High School in Lubbock, Texas. In the fall I plan to attend college with the intention of majoring in early childhood education. I would like to know if Grand Canyon College offers a degree in early childhood education.

Please send me your current catalog, an application for admission, and any information on scholarships.

Thank you very much.

Sincerely yours,

Joyce Inman

Joyce Inman

The second kind of letter you will write is one requesting an interview. Like the request for information, it should be as brief and specific as possible. From the response to your first letter, you may know the name of the director of admissions. If not, you can obtain it from a book such as *Barron's Profiles of American Colleges.* Also, if you want to visit the campus, be sure you include this request in your letter. It can be very helpful to talk with students during your visit, since students give you a direct impression of the college or university. The following letter is one requesting an interview.

945 Olaf Road
Dorney, Minnesota 56500
February 2, 1986

Mr. Daniel J. Murray
Director of Admissions
Hamline University
St. Paul, Minnesota 55104

Dear Mr. Murray:

Thank you for sending me the Hamline University catalog and the applications that I requested. I would like to learn more about the university before I submit my application. Would it be possible to visit classes for one day during the week of April 7 through 11? I will be on vacation from school that week and can arrive any day that you suggest. If possible, I would like to visit music theory and computer science classes, since I hope to major in one of these disciplines. I would also like to stay overnight on campus during my visit so that I can talk with students.

In addition, I would like to arrange an interview with someone from your office. Please let me know a convenient time for my visit. I look forward to seeing Hamline University and learning more about it.

Sincerely yours,

George Chen

George Chen

COMPLETING COLLEGE APPLICATIONS

Once you decide that you would like to attend a particular college or university, you will fill out an application form. Since you may apply to more than one college, you may fill out more than one application form. Even though college applications are somewhat different from one another, they all have similarities. For example, all college applications ask for your full name, address, telephone number, and date of birth. In addition, most application forms ask for your educational background, your work experience, and references.

When filling out a college application form, keep the following points in mind.

How to Fill Out a College Application

1. Be careful. You will receive only one copy of the form. Read the application thoroughly before filling it in.
2. Follow all directions carefully. If you are asked to print the information, do so. If your last name is to appear first, make sure it does.
3. Be neat. Try to avoid mistakes. If you do have to change something, erase it. Do not cross out.
4. Abbreviate when necessary. Most forms have too little space in which to fit some of the required information. You may have to write 3/14/68 rather than March 14, 1968.
5. Do not leave blank spaces. If the question does not apply to you, write N/A (for "not applicable"). By doing so, you will show that you have not skipped any questions by accident.
6. Ask permission to use the names of the references you provide. Some application forms will specify the kinds of references the college prefers—teachers, employers, family friends. Be sure you include the kinds of references requested.

Like many other students, you may want to apply to several colleges. If you do so, it might be helpful to include the following in your choice of schools.

- a college with entrance standards slightly higher than those you seem able to meet
- a college with entrance standards that appear to be right on target for your qualifications
- a college with entrance standards that you easily exceed

This system gives you a chance to apply to the college that you consider most desirable, even if its standards are higher than your record appears to justify. If the standards of the college are *too* high, however, you may decide that an application there would be unrealistic.

There is a good reason for applying to a college whose requirements you easily exceed. You want to try to ensure your acceptance at a college even if your first two choices do not accept you. In choosing this "safety" college, be sure it is one you will be satisfied to attend.

During the process of selecting and applying to colleges or universities, you should consult with your guidance counselor or faculty advisor. Ask questions about the schools that would be suitable for you and about the application process. Use any printed material about higher education—catalogs from the individual schools or general guides to colleges and universities—that are available to you in the guidance office. Talking with people who are knowledgeable about your qualifications as well as about the standards and offerings of the colleges or universities you are interested in will help you select a school that is appropriate to your interests, talents, and abilities.

COMPLETING AN ESSAY ON AN APPLICATION

College admissions officers usually want to see a sample of your writing. Effective writing is important to success in college, and a good writer is likely to be a good student. In addition, a sample of your writing illustrates how well you organize your thoughts, how clearly you express yourself, and how effectively you use the English language.

Ordinarily you will be asked to write an essay on a specific topic. You may be told how long your essay should be and whether it should be typed or handwritten. While the possible topics for essays are almost limitless, they tend to fall into three categories.

Ideas. This kind of writing assignment assesses your understanding of a problem or an issue. It may be a topic of local, national, or international interest. Your response will show your breadth of knowledge, your ability to analyze an issue, and your maturity. The following example is a typical question of this kind: "Choose one issue that is a subject of debate in your city, county, or state. Briefly describe the nature of the debate. Then take a stand on the issue."

Goals. Some essays on college applications ask you to discuss your future plans or goals. You may be asked to explain your plans for college, your plans for a career, or both. The following is a typical question of this kind: "Discuss the reasons why you think this college will provide you with the kind of education you will need for the career you hope to pursue."

Background. Autobiographical questions are among the ones most frequently asked on college applications. You may be asked to focus on one of your particular skills or interests. This kind of question is less speculative than the other two kinds, yet your answer often reveals much more about your personality. Writing about yourself in a way that is engaging, modest, and at the same time enhances your strengths and potentials can be a real challenge. The following is a typical question: "Choose one accomplishment in your life of which you are particularly proud. Describe it, and explain why it gives you satisfaction."

Whatever questions you are called upon to answer, your essay should be neat, well organized, and clearly written. Following are some useful tips for writing an essay that will make a good impression.

Writing an Essay on a College Application

- Plan your essay carefully. List your ideas and organize them into an outline. Then prepare a first draft.
- Stick to the topic.
- Begin each paragraph with a topic sentence.
- Provide specific support for each point you make; avoid vagueness and unproven generalizations.
- Supply clear transitions between sentences and between paragraphs.
- Restate your main point or points.
- Check and double-check grammar, usage, spelling, capitalization, and punctuation.
- Have someone else—a family member or a teacher—read your essay before you write it on the application form.

INTERVIEWING FOR COLLEGE ADMISSIONS

Some colleges require an interview. Even if an interview is not necessary, however, you may find it helpful.

An interview gives you the chance to ask questions that have not been answered fully in the literature you received. An interview is an ideal opportunity to get firsthand information about the college. Also, if the interview takes place at the college, you can visit the campus and talk to faculty members and students.

A good time to visit a college is when classes are in session. This may mean going during spring break in your senior year of high school. But an interview can be scheduled for any time of year. Arrangements for an interview should be made well in advance of your visit.

Sometimes interviews can be arranged closer to your home, if the college or university is located far away. In this case, representatives from the college travel to specific locations at certain times of the year. In addition, graduates of the college who act as representatives often conduct interviews in their geographical areas.

If you do arrange an interview, it would be worth your while to plan your answers to the interviewer's questions in advance. Some typical questions follow.

Questions an Interviewer May Ask

1. What has been your best subject in high school?
2. Which subject has given you the greatest difficulty?
3. What are the extracurricular activities in which you have participated?
4. To what extent has high school been a worthwhile educational experience? How might it have been improved?
5. How do you spend your time outside of school?
6. What hobbies or sports do you especially enjoy?
7. What is the last book you read that was not required reading for school?
8. Have you decided on a college major yet? If so, what is it?
9. What specific courses would you like to take in college?
10. How do you expect to benefit from your college years?

Just as the college interviewer will have questions for you, you should have questions to ask about the college. You might jot down your questions before the interview. Following is a list of questions that you might want to ask. Certainly this list is not complete, but it might help you formulate questions on your own.

Questions for College Interviews

1. What is the average class size?
2. What is the ratio of students to professors?
3. How frequently can students expect to consult on an individual basis with faculty members?
4. At what point must a student decide on a major? Can a student choose a major as well as a minor?
5. Are there specific course requirements for freshmen? What are those requirements?
6. Are there any foreign exchange or intercollegiate exchange programs offered at the college?
7. Do students take part in decisions made at the college?
8. Does a good relationship exist between the college and the local community?
9. What is the average total cost of the first year of college?
10. How does a freshman go about getting an on-campus or off-campus job to help pay expenses?
11. Are there special rules and regulations that apply to first-year students? If so, what are they?
12. What kinds of medical services are available on campus?
13. Does the college sponsor intercollegiate and intramural sports programs? If so, what are they?
14. What importance is placed on fraternities and sororities? What percentage of students belong?

Once your interview is arranged, be sure to arrive on time. Dress neatly and appropriately. Ask the questions that you have come prepared to ask. Answer all the interviewer's questions in an honest and open way. You will make the best possible impression if you simply act naturally. It is a good idea to follow up your visit with a brief note of thanks to the interviewer or interviewers.

WRITING A RÉSUMÉ

A résumé is a summary of your work experience, education, and interests. The purpose of a résumé is to give a potential employer a brief but positive overview of your qualifications for a job. The following guidelines will help you write your own résumé.

How to Write a Résumé

Form

1. Use one sheet of white 8½- by 11-inch paper.
2. Use even margins and leave space between sections.
3. Center your name, address, and telephone number at the top of the page.

Work Experience

1. List your most recent job first.
2. Include part-time, summer, and volunteer jobs.
3. For each job, list the dates you worked, your employer's name, your title, and your primary responsibilities.

Education

1. List the name and address of each school and the years you attended.
2. List any special courses you have taken that would help make you a valuable employee.

Skills, Activities, Awards, Interests

1. List skills, such as typing, computer programming, or fluency in a foreign language, that relate to the position for which you are applying.
2. List school or community activities in which you have participated, such as music lessons or volunteer work.
3. List awards or certificates of merit you have earned.
4. Include your hobbies and special interests.

References

1. Give the names and addresses of people who have agreed to give you a recommendation, or state that references are available on request.
2. As references, list one previous employer, one teacher or school administrator, and one family friend. Be sure you obtain permission in advance from the people you list as references.

Sample of a Résumé

Use the following sample as a model when you prepare your own résumé.

Cynthia Klein
21 Bluebonnet Lane
Rayburn, Texas 75296
Telephone: (214) 426-7135

WORK EXPERIENCE	
1984 - present	Alvis Dance Studio, 945 Main Street, Rayburn, Texas 75291 Position: Part-time dance instructor Responsibilities: Teach ballet to children ages 5 to 12
1982 - 1984	CRM Store, Ravenswood Mall, Rayburn, Texas 75295 Position: Cashier Responsibilities: Ring up and bag purchases at variety store
EDUCATION	
1983 - present	Lone Star High School, Fassett Highway, Rayburn, Texas 75295 Special courses: Fundamentals of business machines, history of dance, modern dance
1981 - 1983	Nimitz Junior High School, 350 Route 17, Rayburn, Texas 75295
SPECIAL SKILLS	On-line and batch computer processing, type 70 words per minute, speak Spanish
ACTIVITIES	Tenth-grade class president, Computer Club and Drama Club member
AWARDS	National Merit Scholarship semi-finalist, Rayburn Fine Arts Achievement Award, 1985
SPECIAL INTERESTS	Electronic data processing, dance, drama
REFERENCES	Available on request

WRITING LETTERS ABOUT EMPLOYMENT

When you apply for a job, you may write a letter to your potential employer. First and foremost, your letter must be specific. State whether you are looking for part-time employment (a few hours a week), temporary employment (a vacation or summer job), or full-time employment (35 or more hours a week for the whole year).

In addition, your job application should make a strong, favorable impression. Remember that the purpose of an employment letter is to get you an interview. If there are many applicants for a particular job, some of them will be rejected on the basis of the letter. Your letter should be grammatically correct, informative, and neat. Make sure it contains the following information.

Position Sought. The first paragraph should state the job you are seeking and tell how you learned about the opening.

Education. Include both your age and your grade in school. Emphasize courses you have taken that apply directly to the job you are seeking. Mention any other studies that may have a bearing on your qualifications.

Experience. As a student, you may not have had much work experience that relates to the position open. Nevertheless, state the kinds of work you have done and emphasize your belief that you can meet the requirements of the job if it is offered to you.

References. Include at least two references, with either an address or a telephone number for each. You will need to obtain permission in advance from the people you name as references. These people should be able to testify to your character and abilities. A teacher, a member of the clergy, a community leader, and a former employer are all good choices.

Request for Interview. The last paragraph should ask for an interview. Indicate where and when you can be reached to make an appointment.

Sample of an Employment Letter

The following sample illustrates an employment letter written by a student who is seeking employment as a management trainee at a place of business. Note that the letter is typed neatly and that it includes all the important information listed on the previous page.

72 Halsey Avenue
Kilmer, New Jersey 07800
June 11, 1986

Mr. William Coles
Optima Office Supplies, Inc.
South Suburban Mall
Kilmer, New Jersey 07800

Dear Mr. Coles:

I would like to apply for the management trainee position advertised in this morning's Daily Express. Next week I will graduate with honors from Boles High School, where I have taken courses in retailing and business procedures.

For the past three years, I have worked as a part-time sales clerk for the Monroe Computer Center in West Kilmer. Last summer I was a lifeguard at Lenape State Park.

Ms. Toni Armand, owner of the Monroe Computer Center, and Mr. Lance Dooley, staff coordinator at Lenape State Park, have agreed to supply references. Ms. Armand's business phone number is 663-3886. Mr. Dooley's is 947-2431.

I believe that my background and interests qualify me for the position you have advertised. I would be pleased to come in for a personal interview at your convenience. My home telephone number is 884-3887.

Very truly yours,

Michael Paci

Michael Paci

INTERVIEWING FOR A JOB

When you apply for a job, the employer may ask you to come in for an interview. The more preparation you do prior to your interview, the more confident you will be during your appointment. The way you present yourself during the interview may also determine whether or not you get the job.

An excellent way to prepare for an interview is to learn as much as possible about the employer's business. The more you know about what the employer does and how the business operates, the better you will be able to discuss the job for which you are interviewing. The following suggestions will help you increase your chances of success at an interview.

Hints on Interviewing for a Job

1. Before your interview, try to get printed information about the company or consult with people you know who are employed there.
2. Prepare a list of questions about the job that you would like to ask the person who interviews you.
3. Be on time for the interview.
4. Present a neat, clean appearance.
5. Be polite to the interviewer.
6. Look at the interviewer when you speak.
7. Speak clearly and distinctly.
8. Answer all questions carefully and honestly.
9. Ask questions about the job that show your interest in the work and in the place of employment.
10. Thank the interviewer when the interview is over.
11. Follow up the interview with a letter thanking the interviewer and expressing your interest in the position. Give reasons why you think you are a good candidate for the job.

Index

D

E

P

T

Tab Index

Grammar

Chapter 1 The Parts of Speech

Chapter 2 The Sentence Base

Chapter 3 Phrases

Chapter 4 Clauses

Chapter 5 Sound Sentences

Usage

Chapter 6 Using Verbs

Chapter 7 Using Pronouns

Chapter 8 Subject and Verb Agreement

Chapter 9 Using Adjectives and Adverbs

Mechanics

Chapter 10 Capital Letters

Chapter 11 End Marks and Commas

Chapter 12 Other Punctuation

Composition

Chapter 17 Words and Sentences

Chapter 18 Clear Thinking

Chapter 19 Paragraphs

Chapter 20 Expository Essays

Chapter 21 Other Kinds of Essays

Chapter 22 Writing about Literature

Chapter 23 The Summary

Chapter 24 Research Papers

Chapter 25 Business Letters